HANDBOOK OF RESEARCH ON INTERNATIONAL STRATEGIC MANAGEMENT

T0329880

Handbook of Research on International Strategic Management

Edited by

Alain Verbeke

McCaig Chaired Professor in Management, Haskayne School of Business, University of Calgary, Canada, Associate Fellow, Centre for International Business and Management, Judge Business School, University of Cambridge, UK and Solvay Business School, University of Brussels (VUB), Belgium

Hemant Merchant

Professor of Management, University of South Florida – St. Petersburg, USA

Edward Elgar
Cheltenham, UK • Northampton, MA, USA

Published by
Edward Elgar Publishing Limited
The Lypiatts
15 Lansdown Road
Cheltenham
Glos GL50 2JA
UK

Edward Elgar Publishing, Inc.
William Pratt House
9 Dewey Court
Northampton
Massachusetts 01060
USA

A catalogue record for this book
is available from the British Library

Library of Congress Control Number: 2012935254

ISBN 978 1 84720 193 5 (cased)

Typeset by Servis Filmsetting Ltd, Stockport, Cheshire
Printed and bound by MPG Books Group, UK

Contents

Contributors

Lori Allen-Ford, Doctoral student, College of Business, Florida Atlantic University, USA

Christian Geisler Asmussen, Associate Professor, Department of Strategic Management and Globalization, Copenhagen Business School, Denmark

Gabriel R.G. Benito, Professor, BI Norwegian Business School, Norway

Julian Birkinshaw, Professor of Strategy and Entrepreneurship, London Business School, UK

Paul Brugman, Research Associate, Department of Business Economics and Strategic Management, Vrije Universiteit Brussel

Peter Buckley, OBE, Professor of International Business, University of Leeds, UK

Jonathan P. Doh, Professor, Department of Management, Villanova School of Business, Villanova University, USA

Alex Eapen, Lecturer, The University of Sydney Business School, Australia

William G. Egelhoff, Professor, Graduate School of Business, Fordham University, New York, USA

Tiffany Galvin, Assistant Professor, University of Massachusetts Amherst, USA

Ajai S. Gaur, Assistant Professor, Department of Management and Global Business, Rutgers Business School, USA

Nathan Greidanus, Assistant Professor, Asper School of Business, University of Manitoba, Canada

Birgitte Grøgaard, Assistant Professor, Haskayne School of Business, University of Calgary, Canada

Ben L. Kedia, Professor, Director of Wang Center for International Business Education and Research, The University of Memphis, USA

Ans Kolk, Professor of Sustainable Management, University of Amsterdam Business School, The Netherlands

Rekha Krishnan, Assistant Professor of International Business, Simon Fraser University, Canada

Jing Li, Associate Professor, Faculty of Business Administration, Simon Fraser University, Canada

Yong Li, Assistant Professor, School of Management, State University of New York at Buffalo, USA

Sarianna M. Lundan, Chair in International Management and Governance, University of Bremen, Germany

Hemant Merchant, Professor of Management, University of South Florida – St. Petersburg, USA

Debmalya Mukherjee, Assistant Professor, Department of Management, College of Business Administration, The University of Akron, USA

Rajneesh Narula, Professor of International Business Regulation, Henley Business School, University of Reading, UK

Niels G. Noorderhaven, Professor of International Management, Faculty of Economics, Tilburg University, The Netherlands

Jennifer Oetzel, Associate Professor, Department of International Business, Kogod School of Business, American University, Washington, DC, USA

Lars Oxelheim, Professor, Lund Institute of Economic Research, Lund University, Sweden

Bent Petersen, Professor, Copenhagen Business School, Denmark

Jonatan Pinkse, Associate Professor of Strategy, Grenoble Ecole de Management, France

Shameen Prashantham, Associate Professor in International Business and Strategy, Nottingham University Business School, China

Trond Randøy, Professor, Department of Economics and Business Administration, University of Agder, Norway

Miguel Rivera-Santos, Associate Professor of Strategy and International Business, Babson College, USA

Carlos Rufín Associate Professor of Strategy and International Business, Suffolk University, USA

Alan M. Rugman, Professor of International Business, Henley Business School, University of Reading, UK

Grazia D. Santangelo, Professor, Facoltà di Scienze Politiche, University of Catania, Italy

Deeksha Singh, Assistant Professor, Department of Strategic Management, Fox School of Business, Temple University, Philadelphia, USA

Arthur Stonehill, Professor of Finance and International Business, University of Hawaii at Manoa, USA

Dara Szyliowicz, Assistant Professor of Management, Eberhardt School of Business, University of the Pacific, USA

Rosalie L. Tung, Professor of International Business, Simon Fraser University, Canada

Alain Verbeke, Professor of International Business Strategy, McCaig Chair in Management, Haskayne School of Business, University of Calgary, Canada, Associate Fellow of the Centre for International Business and Management, Judge Business School, University of Cambridge, UK and Solvay Business School, University of Brussels (VUB), Belgium

Lawrence S. Welch, Professorial Fellow – International Marketing and International Business, Melbourne Business School, Australia

Joachim Wolf, Professor, Chair of Organization Theory and Design, University of Kiel, Germany

H. Emre Yildiz, PhD candidate, Stockholm School of Economics, Sweden

Lena Zander, Professor, Department of Business Studies, Uppsala University, Sweden

Udo Zander, Professor, Department of Marketing and Strategy, Stockholm School of Economics, Sweden

Introduction

Alain Verbeke and Hemant Merchant

International strategic management research is a relatively new field of scholarly enquiry, but it has nevertheless contributed uncommonly high value added to the practice of strategy. There are three reasons for this high value added.

First, the field systematically studies the most complex firms that can be subjected to empirical analysis. The largest non-state-owned firms in the world, with size measured in terms of sales, assets or number of employees, are almost invariably multinational enterprises (MNEs) with substantial product and geographic diversification.

Second, irrespective of the size of the firms involved, the field addresses the most complex problems facing these internationally diversified firms, namely the challenges of resource recombination in high-distance markets, whereby this distance can be measured in cultural, economic, institutional or merely geographic terms.

Third, the field is one where theory and practice are closely intertwined. This is in sharp contrast with many other subareas of management, where scholars can get away with elegant modelling at the expense of managerial relevance, and with mathematical or statistical sophistication as a substitute for true insight. One seldom observes such dysfunction in published studies on large, multiproduct and multimarket MNEs. This does not mean that only high-quality research is published. Chapter 6 in this volume, on testing the quality of multinationality–performance research, provides a fairly devastating account of one area of extraordinarily poor scholarship within the international strategy field.

Fortunately the guardians of the field, such as the successive editors-in-chief of key journals, including the *Journal of International Business Studies*, *Management International Review* and *International Business Review*, have often exercised superior judgement when assessing manuscripts, and have shown courage that has led to the publication of critical analyses of mainstream models in international strategy research. As a result, ill-conceived notions that lack true managerial or policy relevance have typically not been allowed to dominate the field for prolonged periods of time, in sharp contrast to what has often been observed in areas such as mainstream economics and sociology.

The present volume includes 24 chapters, subdivided into four main parts, each with six chapters. Part I discusses conceptual foundations, whereas Part II delves into a variety of structural complexities affecting international strategy. Part III focuses on the implications for strategy of the various distance dimensions facing MNEs. Finally, Part IV provides analysis of important new topics in international strategy. 'New' does not imply the absence of past scholarship on these topics, but rather that these are critical subject matters being addressed in a rapidly growing literature, closely linked with international strategy practice, the last chapter, on MNE climate change strategies, being a case in point.

Apart from including chapters written by the volume editors themselves, we selected authors who in our view have developed creative and significant ideas in the international strategy field that will also remain important in the decades to come. We are grateful to these scholars for writing clear and concise pieces, addressing the topics assigned by this volume's editors.

Chapter 1 describes 20 key hypotheses that make internalization theory the general theory of international strategic management. Internalization theory is undoubtedly the dominant paradigm in international strategy research, but it was surprising to observe that no single source could be found in the scholarly literature with the key hypotheses made explicit and with the use of coherent language throughout the analysis. In fact, the authors were somewhat surprised that even Professor Jean-François Hennart's *oeuvre*, which contains several influential empirical pieces testing internalization theory, did not systematically use common language and concepts in the main studies he performed with various co-authors throughout his illustrious career. This chapter convincingly demonstrates that internalization theory is still the key to understanding the existence of the MNE, as well as its main strategy choices.

Chapter 2 was published as a paper in 2009 in the *Journal of International Business Studies*, and in spite of its low citation count at the time of putting together the present book, the first volume editor views it as one of the most important papers in his academic career. This paper provides a credible alternative to the conventional behavioural assumptions of opportunism and trust adopted in the mainstream management literature. Behavioural assumptions are critical, especially in the context of strategy design. The opportunism assumption is dismissed, as is the opposite assumption of trust. A sole focus on opportunism leads to an exaggerated importance attached to worst-case scenarios of intentional deceit, whereas a sole focus on creating trust neglects the dark side of trust. Unfettered trust equals total vulnerability because no credible safeguards were introduced to address failure: this is the worst situation imaginable for a transacting party in the context of ongoing business relationships. Instead, bounded reliability, reflecting scarcity of making good on open-ended promises, is a more credible and managerially relevant behavioural assumption (Verbeke and Greidanus, 2009).

Chapter 3 describes the latest version of John Dunning's 'eclectic paradigm' and its relevance to international business strategy. The late John Dunning, OBE, was the world's premier international business scholar. Sarianna Lundan, the co-author of the second edition of his *magnum opus*, *Multinational Enterprises and the Global Economy*, with approximately 5000 Google Scholar citations at the time of editing this volume, wrote the third chapter, and suggests that the eclectic paradigm can be useful especially for linking micro- and macro-levels of analysis as inputs for international strategy research (Dunning and Lundan, 2008). Chapters 4 and 5 introduce novel conceptual perspectives on the MNE. Chapter 4 views the MNE as a 'global factory', a term popularized by Peter Buckley, OBE, whereas Chapter 5 looks at foreign operating modes as idiosyncratic bundles of international expansion vehicles subject to a variety of sophisticated change processes over time. Chapter 6 provides a new, integrated approach to assessing the quality of research on the linkages between multinationality and performance (Verbeke and Brugman, 2009). The chapter concludes with a rather pessimistic account of past and present research, but also suggests a way forward for this type of scholarship, to be both more rigorous and more managerially relevant in the future.

Part II analyses various structural complexities in international strategic management. Chapter 7 introduces a number of powerful ideas about the organizational design of contemporary MNEs. Chapter 8 includes a useful synthesis of the literature on entrepreneurial initiatives in MNE subsidiaries, where much of the entrepreneurial action in large firms appears to be concentrated in the twenty-first century, irrespective of the organizational structure chosen. The following two chapters address structural complexities related to strategic alliance formation, with a focus on emerging economies. More specifically, Chapter 9 assesses the benefits of alliance formation in emerging economies, whereas Chapter 10 focuses more on how to configure such alliances in the context of large emerging markets (Merchant, 2008). Substantial structural complexities arise in the context of international acquisitions, and Chapter 11 provides a particularly useful analysis from a managerial perspective, given its focus on parameters that do not lend themselves easily to formal modelling, including elements such as culture, status and meritocracy. Finally, Chapter 12 convincingly makes the point that international finance can add value to international strategy.

Part III focuses on what constitutes perhaps the core difference between domestic and international business, namely the impact of distance. Chapter 13 is a rather hard-hitting piece on services firms' international expansion patterns, published earlier in a special issue of *Management International Review* (Rugman and Verbeke, 2008). It dismisses much of the past literature on the alleged specificities of services firms' internationalization, and shows why this literature is largely ill conceived. It demonstrates on the basis of comprehensive sales and asset data of the world's largest companies that multinational services firms are even less global, and more regionally oriented than manufacturing MNEs. The various distance dimensions often prevent profitable international expansion beyond the home region. Chapter 14 is a truly insightful follow-up on the previous chapter and addresses in an impressive fashion both the conceptual underpinnings and empirical evidence of regional versus global MNE strategies. Chapter 15 is a particularly useful piece on the role of location advantages in international innovation. It provides a substantive extension of the eclectic paradigm discussed in Chapter 3, and clarifies the linkages between location and firm-specific (or ownership) advantages. Here the benefits of co-location of activities must be carefully weighed against the benefits of value chain dispersion or activity fine-slicing across borders. Chapter 16 addresses one specific dimension of distance, namely cultural distance, and its complex linkages with international strategy. After reading this chapter, no serious international strategy scholar will (or should) ever again simply use a readily available index of cultural distance in empirical work, without at least mentioning the limits of using such an index. Chapter 17 explores the institutional distance concept in international strategy as a complement or even substitute for cultural distance, and compellingly argues in favour of using institutional distance proxies in empirical work. Chapter 18 is a fine paper on the potential of using real options theory in international business. It also explores the more general implications of adopting real options thinking in the field of international strategic management. Real options theory predictions are consistent with those of the more conventional internationalization theory framework of sequential, incremental expansion in foreign markets, and have the benefit of solid conceptual foundations.

Finally, Part IV explores new topics in international strategic management. Chapter 19 includes a particularly relevant overview of strategic management research challenges and opportunities in emerging markets. It also provides key directions for future research in this area. Chapter 20 usefully explores the linkages between institutions and international entrepreneurship. It credibly argues in favour of using insights from main-stream institutional theory when analysing phenomena in the realm of international entrepreneurship. Chapters 21 and 22 address hotly debated topics in international strategy, namely offshoring and bottom-of-the-pyramid (BOP) strategies respectively. The great strengths of the offshoring chapter are its classification of various types of offshoring, as well as its thoughtful analysis of the practice's potential benefits. The importance of the BOP paper lies in its recognition that a BOP strategy does not arise in an institutional vacuum, but actually requires institutional embeddeness in a localized network: more than in conventional business dealings, thoughtful crafting of partnerships is crucial to success in BOP markets. Chapter 23 is a follow-up to the previous chapter and addresses the broader issue of linkages between MNE strategy and macro-level economic development, with a focus on the role of complementary resources. The authors make a compelling case for MNEs supporting development goals in order to gain and maintain a social licence to operate, and also credibly advocate MNE–NGO collaboration in order to build combinative capabilities, which should serve all stakeholders involved. The last contribution in this volume, namely Chapter 24, provides a reflection on MNEs and climate change strategies. It carefully explains the trade-offs involved in centralizing MNE climate change strategy at the head office versus delegating to the foreign subsidiary level. Importantly, it describes how climate change strategy could become a source of competitive advantage for some MNEs.

The 24 chapters in this book form a powerful bundle of scholarly analyses. The research volume provides an impressive state-of-the-art overview of the international strategic management field as an area of scholarly enquiry. The great strength of this set of chapters is the thoughtfulness of the messages conveyed by the expert authors. There are no simple but fallacious how-to-do-it prescriptions here, nor long-winded and useless theoretical musings.

This collection is truly a complete *Handbook of Research on International Strategic Management*, and should serve international strategy scholars and reflective MNE managers alike. The implications for future international strategy research and for international management are profound. As editors of this volume, we hope that the core messages found in this handbook will influence the next generation of scholars in international strategy as well as practising managers, who will continue to be faced with a world that is far from flat.

REFERENCES

Dunning, J.H. and S.M. Lundan (2008), *Multinational Enterprises and the Global Economy, Second Edition*, Cheltenham, UK and Northampton, MA, USA: Edward Elgar Publishing.
Merchant, H. (2008), 'International joint venture configurations in big emerging markets', *Multinational Business Review*, **16**(3), 93–119.
Rugman, A.M. and A. Verbeke (2008), 'A new perspective on the regional and global strategies of multinational services firms', *Management International Review (MIR)*, **48**(4), 397–411.
Verbeke, A. and P. Brugman (2009), 'Triple-testing the quality of multinationality–performance research: an internalization theory perspective', *International Business Review*, **18**(3), 265–75.
Verbeke, A. and N.S. Greidanus (2009), 'The end of the opportunism vs trust debate: bounded reliability as a new envelope concept in research on MNE governance', *Journal of International Business Studies*, **40**(9), 1471–95.

PART I

CONCEPTUAL FOUNDATIONS OF INTERNATIONAL STRATEGIC MANAGEMENT

1 Twenty key hypotheses that make internalization theory the general theory of international strategic management

Birgitte Grøgaard and Alain Verbeke

INTRODUCTION

Internalization theory has over the past 35 years become central to our understanding of multinational enterprise (MNE) functioning. In this chapter, we discuss 20 key hypotheses that make internalization theory the general theory of international strategic management. These hypotheses synthesize the main insights we have gained from a large number of conceptual and empirical studies related to MNE strategic decision-making.

Early contributions to internalization theory challenged the dominant neoclassical trade theories of international exchange by questioning the underlying assumption of efficient cross-border markets and the lack of attention devoted to firms. Seminal works by internalization theory scholars thus explored how market imperfections create differences in costs between activities conducted inside firms versus through external markets (Buckley and Casson, 1976; Hennart, 1982; Rugman, 1981). The early contributions improved our understanding of the nature of firms (Coase, 1937) and further extended Hymer's (1970) work on why MNEs exist. These studies focused especially on the growth of large MNEs, exploring how external market imperfections create both opportunities and challenges when transferring technology and other knowledge-intensive assets or capabilities across borders (Buckley and Casson, 1976; Hennart, 1982; Rugman, 1981). Here, MNEs internalize intermediate markets (the range of activities needed to bring goods and services to the final output market) when internal organization (i.e. hierarchy) enables the more efficient creation, transfer, deployment and exploitation of proprietary assets and capabilities. Firms do not in practice 'avoid markets' through internalization but eliminate external uncertainties and potentially unreliable behavior of external parties by introducing alternative governance mechanisms such as employment contracts and management directives, which obviously also have their own costs (Buckley and Strange, 2011). For example, the equivalent of 'cheating' in external market contracts is 'shirking' in the context of employment contracts. Internalization is thus only attractive when the costs of organizing interdependencies inside the MNE are lower than in the marketplace (Hennart and Park, 1993).

Despite internalization theory's influence in the scholarly international business (IB) community and the large number of related conceptual and empirical studies, it has also faced much criticism. For instance, its focus on governance costs generated by market inefficiencies has been criticized for isolating strategic management decisions as distinct rational choices that overemphasize opportunistic behavior (Kogut and Zander, 1993), and for insufficiently recognizing the heterogeneity of – and limited accessibility to – resources that underpin growth (Cantwell, 2000). The discussion of the hypotheses below will demonstrate, however, that contemporary internalization theory actually addresses these concerns, and that the criticism voiced against it may result from an imperfect understanding of the theory.

We shall argue through these hypotheses that internalization theory prevails, and appropriately so, as the dominant theory in international strategic management despite its limitations. Recent internalization theory-based studies have further strengthened the theory's foundations by recognizing the importance of two elements. First, the governance costs associated with utilizing the external market should always be compared with internal organizational costs for multiple transactions in multiple markets simultaneously, which is approximately the equivalent of farsighted contracting encompassing the entire value added chain, i.e. from knowledge creation to final output delivery (and even beyond, e.g. including after sales service and product retakes). Second, the analysis of governance choices should not occur in an MNE-centric fashion, but always recognize the strategy of the 'other party' (or parties) involved in addition to the MNE's strategy (Chen, 2010; Hennart, 2009). Here, the continued emphasis of critics on strategic and managerial issues beyond economizing on governance costs in a narrow contextual setting has paradoxically – through many extensions of the theory over time – strengthened further the status of internalization theory as the most insightful lens to understand cross-border activities (Buckley and Casson, 2009; Dunning, 2009; Hennart, 2010; Rugman et al., 2011a).

The essence of internalization theory in the international context can be synthesized as follows: institutions of capitalism such as MNEs will choose (and retain) comparatively more efficient governance mechanisms over less efficient ones to conduct economic activities whose main purpose is to develop, deploy, exploit and further augment firm-specific advantages (FSAs) across borders. FSAs are company strengths relative to those held by relevant rivals that allow survival, profitability and growth. FSAs are the raison d'être for the presence of firms and determine the scope (levels of product diversification, vertical integration and geographic diversification) of the economic activities the firm will involve itself in. The most critical selection and retention decisions on governance mechanisms are related to: (1) choosing to use the external market or internal organization (buy or make) for each economic activity, resulting in the boundaries of the firm; (2) organizing the interface with the external environment for activities not performed internally (e.g., choice of short term contracts versus long term ones versus cooperative alliances); (3) organizing the economic activities performed internally, inside the firm (e.g., choice of organizational structure and internal incentive systems). More efficient governance mechanisms are those that on balance allow: (1) superior economizing on bounded rationality; (2) superior economizing on bounded reliability; and (3) creating an organizational context conducive to managing the innovation process in its entirety, i.e., from FSA creation to customer delivery of the products and services that embody these FSAs (Verbeke and Kenworthy, 2008).

The hypotheses formulated in this chapter highlight the key insights we have gained from examining MNEs through an internalization theory lens. We did not seek to include an exhaustive list covering all applications that can be found in the extant literature, and only refer to some key references in this context. Each hypothesis we included will be followed by a brief explanation of the underlying theoretical rationale and – where relevant – by a reflection on its potential to predict internationalization patterns and to provide diagnostic guidance for strategic decision-making in MNEs. As the discussion will show, its broad range of applicability explains why internalization theory prevails as the dominant conceptual lens in IB that provides insights into when, where and how MNEs will expand across borders. Our main focus will be on MNE operating mode choices in foreign markets. These operating mode choices determine the boundaries of the firm in international markets, and set the stage for subsequent management of both the economic activities conducted internally and the economic activities involving other economic actors (e.g. contracting partners).

A DISCUSSION OF THE 20 KEY HYPOTHESES OF INTERNALIZATION THEORY

Hypothesis 1   A firm with stronger upstream technological competencies and down-stream marketing competencies (as proxied by its R&D and advertising intensities) is more likely to engage in foreign expansion.

International expansion enables firms to capitalize on existing FSAs by transferring these to new host environments, whether these firms seek merely to expand their customer base or to tap into value-adding location advantages. While a company's FSAs have generated competitive advantage in the home country, and are at the heart of why the firm actually exists, their value may diminish in cross-border activities due to an inherent liability of outsidership (Hennart et al., 2002; Zaheer, 1995 for a related institutional theory perspective). The liability of outsidership suggests that foreign firms entering new host countries face additional costs due to their lack of 'insider' knowledge, experience and local visibility. The liability of outsidership creates difficulties exploiting existing FSAs as well as gaining access to local complementary resources (Zaheer, 1995). The additional costs are often generated from factors such as existing customer preferences, established local networks, formal institutional barriers, or the general perception that foreign firms lack legitimacy. Higher distances between home and host countries, whether geographic, cultural, administrative or economic, further increase a firm's liability of outsidership (Ghemawat, 2001), although such distances may sometimes also be associated with risk reduction benefits, as well as potential access to resources unavailable in any low-distance environment. The main feature of the additional costs of doing business abroad, at least according to internalization theory thinking, is that these do not primarily relate to production, but to governance, although there may be a significant impact on production costs too, especially if an inefficient governance system was selected to exploit and further augment extant FSAs. The strength of a company's FSAs relative to rivals operating in a particular host country thus becomes particularly important in the sense that the value that can be derived from these FSAs should be high enough to warrant the governance costs, especially contracting frailties associated with international FSA transfer, as well as with actual FSA deployment, exploitation and augmenting over time in the host environment.

Hypothesis 1 illustrates internalization theory's emphasis on value creation from unique resources. Some critics have been concerned that this theory focuses more on costs than on value creation (Kogut and Zander, 1993). However, internalization theory suggests merely that the challenge of cross-border activity governance must be purpose-fully addressed in order to enable value creation and reduce the probability of value destruction. Indeed, the presence of strong FSAs has been a key pillar of internalization theory (Dunning, 2003), with a longstanding recognition of the importance of creating value in host countries by combining FSAs with country-specific (location) advantages, but doing so in an economizing fashion (Rugman and Verbeke, 1992, 2003). Early inter-nalization theory studies specifically emphasized the transfer of technology (R&D FSAs) and brand names to host countries. Such FSAs typically reflect complex knowledge bundles and high asset specificity, and are therefore typically better governed through internal markets than through imperfect external ones. If the above governance prob-lems can be solved and firms internalize with a market-seeking motive, then bring-ing strong technology or brand name type FSAs to a broader (international) customer base should reduce total costs per unit by spreading R&D or advertising investments; i.e. scale or scope economies in production will be captured as a result of proprietary knowledge not freely available in external markets or imitable/accessible by other economic actors.

Firms with stronger FSAs are therefore better positioned to succeed internationally. Hypothesis 1 implicitly suggests that firms lacking strong FSAs should think carefully about internationalizing, as their ability to overcome the liability of outsidership through proprietary knowledge will be weaker. However, as the next hypothesis specifies, strong FSAs in today's business environments are not limited to technology or brand names.

Hypothesis 2   A firm with stronger organizational capabilities is more likely to engage in foreign expansion.

While much of the early focus in internalization theory was on technology and estab-lished brand names, overcoming the liability of outsidership is not limited to those FSA types only. Some firms operate in industries where brand name differentiation and tech-nology transfer are challenging. Competitive advantage can also be generated by the ability to coordinate – and leverage linkages within – a geographically dispersed organi-zation (Rugman et al., 2011a; Rugman et al., 2011b). Deploying unique internal organi-zational capabilities developed in the home country or in the extant MNE network, including capabilities that enable the firm to successfully tap into or copy local resources in a new host country, can therefore be more important than R&D or advertising to succeed internationally. In fact, in some cases, such as emerging economy MNEs, as well as in MNEs in resource-based sectors, it can be organizational capabilities that allow international firm growth rather than the more conventional technology and brand names.

Strong organizational capabilities enable firms to tap into attractive location advan-tages as firms increasingly internationalize their value chains. Firms thus do not neces-sarily need to have direct ownership of technology or downstream assets/capabilities, but may compete on the ability to access and effectively recombine externally available assets/capabilities with other organizational strengths. This is particularly relevant for firms internationalizing with efficiency- or asset-seeking motives that seek to create value by drawing upon specific location advantages other than the presence of local buyers/cus-tomers for their products. We can therefore also expect that firms with strong organizational capabilities are more likely to internationalize as they are better equipped to create value and profits that outweigh any liability of outsidership.

As Hypothesis 2 illustrates, the types of FSAs that increase firms' propensity to internationalize vary greatly. Understanding which internal strengths trigger and enable successful internationalization is therefore important, and these strengths may be partly dependent on industry and country contexts. The presence of strong FSAs, however, does not answer the question as to where or how to internationalize.

Hypothesis 3　An MNE is more likely to select foreign entry into a host country characterized by comparatively lower cost access to complementary assets and capabilities for effective FSA exploitation.

As discussed above, value creation in host countries is achieved through recombining transferable FSAs with local complementary assets and capabilities. The MNE's strengths and internationalization motives will largely determine which local complementary assets and capabilities will be required when expanding internationally, but the costs of accessing such assets or capabilities may vary substantially across host countries. Here, it is not so much the production costs that are critical (although these can obviously lead to eliminating possible locations from an initial choice set), but rather the difficulties of contracting with external economic actors who own or otherwise control the requisite assets and capabilities. As noted above, such difficulties can be boiled down to challenges of economizing on bounded rationality and bounded reliability, and creating a context conducive to managing the innovation process in its entirety.

Early contributions to internalization theory have been criticized for being too MNE-centric (Hennart, 2009). More specifically, there have been implicit and explicit assumptions that local complementary assets and capabilities are easily accessible to MNEs without addressing how MNEs actually gain such access (Chen, 2010). In reality, complementary assets and capabilities are often owned and controlled by local firms, which can limit MNE access (Chen, 2005). The accessibility and related cost of local complementary assets and capabilities will therefore directly affect the choice of where to internationalize.

Firms should not contemplate only the absolute efficiency of a single input or (intermediate) output market, but should select a host country based on the overall relative efficiency of multiple relevant markets, with Khanna et al. (2005) distinguishing among labor markets, financial markets and output markets. While conventional internalization theory applications have focused on country A being preferable over country B if the governance-related costs of contracting (such as licensing) for manufacturing capabilities are lower in country A, a fuller range of transactions, spanning various types of requisite assets and capabilities in the same host country (or rather candidate host countries), should be entered into the equation, and not only the costs of a contract manufacturer. This fuller range on the input market side might include transactions with financial institutions, external logistics services providers, distributors, information technology providers, government agencies etc. Chen (2010) argues that, even when focusing on only a single transaction, three different core markets must be considered where contracting is sought for an asset/capability: (1) the market for outputs, as with contract manufacturing, whereby the contract manufacturer will make the desired product for the MNE based upon the latter's FSAs; (2) the market for assets/capabilities, whereby the MNE subsidiary will purchase the required assets/capabilities on the open market and will subsequently engage in in-house manufacturing; and (3) the market for 'equity', whereby the MNE will acquire another firm that controls the coveted assets/capabilities.

Cross-border transactions are therefore associated with multiple external markets, even when considering only a single asset or capability. The MNE in the example above is not limited to comparing contracting manufacturing options (output market) in various potential host countries, but may in this case also consider acquiring local firms (equity market), or alternatively acquiring human assets and even teams with capabilities embedded in them, through giving them employee contracts within a wholly owned subsidiary context.

Hypothesis 3 thus emphasizes that localization decisions are affected by the possibilities to access locally owned/controlled complementary assets and capabilities. As locally owned complementary assets and capabilities can be both costly and difficult to obtain (Hennart, 2009), MNEs should examine the relative efficiency of transacting such assets and capabilities in multiple markets, within each potential host country. Recognizing which geographical locations are best equipped in terms of providing easy access to needed complementary assets and capabilities can significantly affect the probability of success of the international expansion move.

Hypothesis 4   An MNE is more likely to select foreign entry into a host country characterized by comparatively lower FSA adaptation requirements for effective FSA exploitation.

Expanding into host countries where the value of existing FSAs can be retained, and where less adaptation is required, reduces the need to tap into local complementary assets and capabilities, and to incur the related linking investments. MNEs with strong, transferable FSAs that require minimal linking investments for successful FSA deployment and exploitation in particular host countries have traditionally been assumed to prefer exporting to localizing activities in such host countries, since the latter governance type may not add significant value, yet may be associated with much higher governance costs before products ultimately reach the buyer (Dunning, 1988).

When firms internationalize, building upon strong FSAs that are also associated with low-linking investments in a particular host country, we can expect the requisite host country complementary assets and capabilities to be more generic in nature, and not needing extensive tailoring in order to augment the FSAs transferred (i.e. standard plant machinery assets or basic manufacturing capacity). The more generic the requisite local complementary assets and capabilities in a particular host country, the more likely it is that these will be transacted efficiently in the host country environment, often through mere purchases in the external market (Hennart, 2009; Teece, 1986). The success of the foreign activity will then become less dependent on overcoming barriers to accessing local complementary assets and capabilities.

Pressures for FSA adaptation to suit host country needs through linking investments are particularly challenging for market-seeking firms. Such pressures typically increase the MNE's dependence on access to complementary local assets and capabilities. We can thus expect that market-seeking MNEs will be particularly attracted to those host countries where lower-linking investments must be made, i.e. where transferable FSAs retain comparatively more of their original value in the home country and where less uncertainty prevails regarding the challenges associated with accessing local complementary assets and capabilities.

Hypotheses 1–4 have emphasized when and where firms internationalize. As discussed above, strong FSAs are necessary to overcome liabilities of outsidership. However, these FSAs are not necessarily sufficient for foreign direct investment (FDI) to actually take place as compared to alternative entry modes (Rugman et al., 2011a). The following hypotheses summarize some of the main insights from internalization theory on how firms internationalize.

Hypothesis 5   An MNE with FSAs more vulnerable to appropriation by third parties in a host country is more likely to select an equity-based entry mode than a contractual arrangement for its FSA exploitation.

When entering a host country, the MNE must make multiple decisions to secure the optimal governance of its future operations. The question of whether to 'make or buy' remains one of the most fundamental strategic challenges in this regard. Why would a firm engage in direct investment in a host country if it could efficiently sell or rent out its assets and capabilities though contractual agreements? Further, if a direct investment is preferred, should the firm seek full or joint ownership? The array of possible operating modes and ownership structures increases the complexity of these questions.

Operating modes are typically categorized into contractual versus equity modes. Much internalization research has focused on licensing technology (contractual mode) versus engaging in FDI (equity mode) in the foreign market. There is an inherent paradox in that the strongest FSAs may generate sustainable competitive advantage but are also typically much more difficult to transfer and transact with third parties in external markets for reasons such as their novelty or tacit elements, and most importantly because of their public-good nature, meaning a high probability of income dilution for the MNE in case the knowledge is shared with third parties (Verbeke, 2009). If the MNE reveals too much detail about FSA characteristics to third parties, in particular its tacit component, then host country actors could potentially act opportunistically (Slangen and Hennart, 2007). The high costs of negotiating and implementing contractual agreements thus push many MNEs that enter host countries and command strong knowledge assets and capabilities towards equity-based modes instead of using external market contracts. In such cases, it is viewed as more attractive to enter the host country through FDI to overcome market inefficiencies in the realm of transacting the MNE's FSAs (Hennart, 2009); see the right-hand side of Figure 1.1. In Figure 1.1, the horizontal axis describes whether or not efficient markets exist for transacting MNE FSAs in a particular host country. The vertical axis describes whether efficient markets are present in that same host country for the requisite complementary assets and capabilities to be accessed by the MNE.

In quadrant 3 of Figure 1.1, foreign subsidiaries can be established through internal growth (greenfield investments) or acquisitions. Greenfield investment is typically more efficient when transferring strong FSAs abroad in the market-seeking sphere due to greater control over how the knowledge is transferred and the greater ability to influence

		MNE FSAs	
		Efficient market	Inefficient market
Complementary assets/ capabilities held by third party	Efficient market	1. Contractual agreements (CA)	3. MNE wholly owned subsidiaries (WOS)
	Inefficient market	2. Wholly owned third-party subsidiaries (WOTPS)	4. Strategic partnerships (SP)

Source: Inspired by Hennart (2009).

Figure 1.1   Operating mode selection as a function of external market efficiency

the local receptiveness of these FSAs through hiring a carefully selected workforce (Slangen and Hennart, 2007). Acquisitions often require extensive integration efforts during which local resistance can hamper successful FSA transfer. Resistance to such integration may arise when an already established organizational culture and related set of routines in a host country firm need to be integrated with the MNE's culture and routines, to enable successful FSA transfer and improvement. By entering a host country through wholly owned greenfield operations, MNE senior management thus secures greater control over the FSA transfers as well as their usage and integration in the local operation (Hennart and Park, 1993).

Hypothesis 6   An MNE requiring complementary assets and capabilities that are easy to transact, as a complement to its vulnerable FSAs, is more likely to select an equity-based entry mode than external contracting for FSA exploitation in a host country.

The choice in favor of equity-based entry, on the right-hand side of Figure 1.1, is not solely dependent on the difficulties of transacting the MNE's FSAs in the host country as discussed under Hypothesis 5. The ability to access local complementary assets and capabilities without excessive linking investments and related governance costs and uncertainties also affects the decision. As a general rule, the firm with the assets and capabilities that are hardest to transact in the host country should seek full ownership of the local, equity-based entity. This is typically the MNE, as suggested by quadrant 3 in Figure 1.1. If both the MNE's assets and capabilities, and the host country complementary ones, are difficult to transact, joint ownership should be considered; see quadrant 4 in Figure 1.1 (Hennart, 2009).

As discussed under Hypothesis 4, strong (non-location-bound) FSAs often require only generic local complementary assets and capabilities that are easily transacted in external markets in the host country. When the MNE enters a host country with strong, difficult-to-transact FSAs and seeks to recombine these with easily transacted local complementary assets and capabilities available in external markets, a wholly owned greenfield investment will typically be preferred, as shown in quadrant 3 of Figure 1.1. Here, the MNE retains full control over the assets and capabilities that would be subject to the frailties of external contracting, while it can contract efficiently for complementary assets and capabilities. This entry mode and ownership structure enable the firm to achieve an economizing outcome by circumventing external market inefficiencies.

The preference for an equity-based entry mode is therefore influenced by the characteristics of the MNE FSAs as well as the characteristics of the locally owned complementary assets and capabilities. In this context it should be remembered that easily replicable, stand-alone FSAs held by the MNE may in theory make external markets more efficient for transacting these FSAs, but the MNE often faces a new challenge related to unwanted knowledge dissemination; see also Hypothesis 5. This suggests that even when a firm's FSAs would be easy to transact in a host country from a technical perspective, the presence of bounded rationality and bounded reliability challenges originating from (potential) contracting parties implies risks of knowledge appropriation when entering contractual agreements and therefore *de facto* vitiates the suggestion of easy external contracting. Problematic external contracting should not come as a surprise: FSAs are to an 'innovation process in its entirety' what Williamsonian asset specificity (Williamson, 1996) is to a simpler, farsighted contracting process.

Aligning interests in the host country thus becomes critical to avoid bounded reliability problems created by contractual partners. Equity-based entry modes, whether achieved through a wholly owned subsidiary or joint ownership with a local partner, provide the possibility to align MNE and local interests. As later hypotheses will address, the institutional quality of locations can also influence MNEs' ability to safeguard themselves against various forms of bounded reliability, including opportunistic behavior.

Hypothesis 7   An MNE entering a host country with FSAs that represent 'old technology' is more likely to select contracting with external parties than an equity-based entry mode.

The discussion under Hypothesis 6 may trigger the question as to when the MNE would actually prefer contractual operating modes, if even stand-alone (easily transacted) FSAs, vulnerable to appropriation, should remain under the firm's control via internalization. Contractual agreements (such as licensing) are commonly found in situations where firms enter host markets with older and better known technology (Hennart, 2010). The explanation for this observation is closely related to the rationale for Hypothesis 5. Proven and established technology facilitates market actors' correct assessment of the price and quality of an asset or capability. The MNE entering the market will also potentially have gained experience and improved the codifiability from prior experience with transferring this knowledge. This reduces the negotiation and implementation costs, making contractual relationships much more attractive in host countries, as illustrated by the left-hand side of Figure 1.1. Working with wholly owned, foreign subsidiaries for older, proven technology is often less efficient than utilizing contractual agreements in the host market, since governance through internal organization adds internal managerial costs without compensating benefits.

It may also be attractive to recombine FSAs representing 'old technology' with complementary assets and capabilities in host countries to achieve synergies and identify new avenues for competitive advantage. Here, it may be the linking investments made by an entrepreneurial, local contracting party that create value. Exposure to such new opportunities is greater outside the firm boundaries where internalization could potentially reduce such opportunities for innovative recombination (Verbeke, 2003). MNEs seeking to internationalize with 'old technology' will thus benefit from entering host markets through contractual agreements, as shown in quadrant 1 of Figure 1.1. The advantages include: (1) minimizing governance costs through efficient market transactions and (2) enabling synergies to develop through recombination opportunities with external partners. Evaluating opportunities for such recombination should also be included in assessments of the optimal governance mode.

Hypothesis 8   An MNE requiring only easily accessible and absorbable complementary assets and capabilities as a complement to its vulnerable FSAs is more likely to select wholly owned, equity-based operations (greenfield entry or acquisition) than an operation with a local, strategic partner.

Early contributions within internalization theory have been criticized for treating local firms as partners of unequal status and not adequately recognizing the reciprocal nature of local complementary assets (Chen, 2010; Hennart, 2009). As discussed above, access to locally controlled, complementary assets and capabilities varies, and may be challenging.

When the MNE chooses to enter a market with equity-based operations, this is a choice co-determined by the characteristics of its FSAs, and the location characteristics of the host country involved *vis-à-vis* other countries. But the optimal ownership structure then still needs to be addressed. The MNE can choose full or partial ownership. MNEs typically prefer full ownership when their FSAs are strong but very vulnerable to appropriation by other parties (Chen and Hennart, 2002). While strategic partnerships with local firms (i.e. partial ownerships) can create new mutually beneficial opportunities, they also demand continuous realignment efforts and involve parent organizations that may have diverging interests and expectations. Strategic partnerships therefore lead to significant management costs that should be avoided if their value added does not outweigh the additional governance costs.

When complementary assets and capabilities are easy to access and absorb, strategic partnerships are unnecessary. The MNE can then establish a wholly owned subsidiary and contract for additional local complementary assets and capabilities, as illustrated by quadrant 3 in Figure 1.1. Wholly owned operations can be achieved through greenfield establishments. Greenfield investments enable the MNE to better control the transfer of FSAs and to influence all aspects of the local organization, but can take time to set up and may be associated with high, upfront managerial costs (Slangen and Hennart, 2007).

However, easy access may not always be achievable directly through the market for local assets and capabilities, but may require working via the equity market. Full acquisitions can then provide an opportunity to establish a local organization more efficiently. Studies show that MNEs choose to access local complementary assets and capabilities through the equity market (acquisitions) if these are easily absorbable (Hennart and Reddy, 1997). Acquiring any firm, even in the case of high absorbability of desired assets and capabilities, typically also involves ownership of at least some non-desirable assets. Wholly owned operations are therefore attractive when 'a' market, whether the market for assets/capabilities or the market for equity, is efficient, allowing the MNE to concentrate efforts on efficiently transfering FSAs internally. Quadrant 3 in Figure 1.1 does not distinguish between preferences for establishing the wholly owned operation as a greenfield entry versus an acquisition (the latter in case of an efficient equity market).

Hypothesis 8 suggests that the characteristics of local complementary assets and capabilities directly influence chosen operating modes and ownership structures. For the MNE entering a new host country, the ability to access and absorb complementary assets and capabilities will determine the desired degree of control over the local organization. Strategic partnerships should only be considered if the local complementary assets and capabilities are costly and difficult to access (e.g. exclusive distribution networks tightly controlled by local owners), and the MNE's FSAs are challenging to transact in external markets across the board, as illustrated by quadrant 4 in Figure 1.1.

Hypothesis 9   An MNE entering a host country characterized by comparatively more efficient direct markets for complementary assets and capabilities is more likely to select wholly owned, equity-based, greenfield entry than operating with a local, strategic partner.

MNEs have little incentive to engage in strategic partnerships or access requisite complementary assets and capabilities through the equity market (acquisitions) if the external markets for direct purchasing of complementary assets and capabilities are efficient in the host country. Strategic partnerships or integrating an acquired firm can be fraught with governance costs, since such operating modes require the integration of two pre-existing organizations, each with established cultures and routines. The MNE should thus only consider committing to such costs if there are market inefficiencies affecting the negotiation and implementation of contractual agreements (e.g. difficulties in assessing price or quality).

As discussed under Hypothesis 8, when the market for purchasing local complementary assets and capabilities directly is efficient, the choice of entering the foreign market through a wholly owned, equity-based greenfield operation is largely driven by the characteristics of the MNE's transferable FSAs. If the MNE's FSAs are technically difficult to transact externally in the local market or at risk of knowledge appropriation, greenfield wholly owned subsidiaries are preferred, and complementary assets and capabilities will be contracted externally (Hennart, 2009).

Hypothesis 9 highlights the complexities of Figure 1.1 and the multiple decisions facing MNEs. Foreign entry and ownership decisions reflect a joint optimization challenge. Joint optimization means that the governance form selected depends on: (1) the MNE's FSAs; and (2) the complementary assets/capabilities provided by host country actors, rather than on the absolute efficiency of the market for either. The requisite complementary assets/capabilities may cover a wide variety of economic activities in the value chain, and thus various external markets. Further, for each identifiable, complementary asset/capability, only the assessment of multiple market levels (output, direct asset/capability purchasing and equity) can determine the relative efficiency of the external market *vis-à-vis* internal organization (Chen, 2010; Hennart, 2009). The main point is that foreign firms should avoid equity ownership or investment in local complementary assets and capabilities when those are easily and efficiently transacted in an external market.

Hypothesis 10   An MNE entering a host country characterized by a comparatively stronger appropriability regime (e.g. as measured by its patent protection system and effective court system to settle contracting disputes) is more likely to use contracting with external parties for its own FSA exploitation and access to complementary assets/capabilities.

Profits generated from strong FSAs are highly dependent on ownership rights (e.g. patents or copyrights). The existence of supporting institutions to enforce ownership rights and contractual safeguards is thus vital for external markets to function efficiently, particularly where proprietary knowledge is involved (Hennart, 1994, 2009; Teece, 1986; Williamson, 1996). Entering foreign markets through contractual agreements can expose MNEs to greater risk of knowledge appropriation. The potential risk of knowledge appropriation generates additional governance costs in the form of more complex contract negotiations and more extensive contractual safeguards as well as longer-term risks of knowledge dissipation. The quality of the host country's legal system is therefore critical as it determines the firm's ability to take legal action against opportunistic behavior and other forms of unreliability. The ability to protect and enforce contracts acts as a deterrent to unreliable behavior and reduces uncertainty for firms entering the host market.

Research shows that the strengthening of property rights improves external market efficiencies relative to those associated with internalizing markets (Buckley and Casson, 2009). MNEs entering a host country will therefore find contractual agreements more attractive if this host country has a stronger appropriability regime. Weaker host country institutions will push firms to internalize intermediate markets to avoid exposure to opportunistic and otherwise unreliable behavior, particularly where the ability to enforce contracts through the use of the legal system is weak. Obviously, the above does not imply that internalization solves all problems of a weak appropriability regime: employees may steal knowledge from the firm or sabotage its operations, and governments themselves may change the rules of the game, including nationalizing foreign-owned operations. However, the point is that at the margin, replacing external contracts by internal ones will be more attractive from an MNE perspective, since MNE senior management can act as its own court of appeal for many types of conflicts and contractual frictions. One caveat of this perspective could be that in some countries external formal contracting, however imperfect, may be complemented with relational contracting features, thereby making internalization the most desirable option only in extreme cases of weak formal appropriability regimes (Zhou and Poppo, 2010).

Hypothesis 10 emphasizes the need to include several dimensions when assessing market efficiencies. With the increased attraction of tapping into host countries that are emerging economies, such as the BRICs (Brazil, Russia, India and China), characterized by local advantages such as low labor costs and high domestic growth, these immediate cost-related advantages should be assessed within a broader institutional context, with the appropriability regime affecting the relative efficiency of contractual agreements.

Hypothesis 11   A firm entering a host country associated with higher institutional uncertainty is more likely to select a local, strategic partner than to engage in wholly owned, equity-based, greenfield entry.

The discussion above highlights some of the inherent challenges of assessing external market efficiencies in host countries. If there is perceived institutional uncertainty in the host country, then MNEs entering this country will typically seek a local strategic partner with 'insider' experience and knowledge of the host country institutions that cannot be purchased freely on external markets. Since the relationship with the owners of local complementary assets and capabilities is reciprocal, however, local firms will only be interested in strategic partnerships if the external markets for the MNE's assets and capabilities are also inefficient. As quadrant 4 in Figure 1.1 suggests, such situations lead to a higher propensity to engage in strategic partnerships such as equity-based joint ventures that ensure alignment of goals and interests of both organizations. MNEs and local partners will be particularly attracted to strategic partnerships when institutional uncertainties affect multiple markets, i.e. the market for outputs; the market for purchasing assets/capabilities; and the equity market. For example, if the market for equity were efficient, one party might select the acquisition alternative as the more optimal governance option. In other words, strategic partnerships are only deemed attractive when neither party can more efficiently acquire the assets and capabilities of the other party (Hennart, 2009). By entering into a strategic partnership, the two parties can align their interests and address frictions, especially in the distributive sphere, though internal, mutual adjustment.

Hypothesis 11 highlights the possible effects of institutional uncertainty on MNE entry into a host country. Such institutional uncertainty increases the attractiveness of enlisting the support of a local strategic partner, since the capabilities required to reduce or otherwise address local institutional uncertainties can typically not be bought in full in external markets on an ongoing basis, although some types of uncertainties might be reduced through purchasing legal services, specialized consulting services, support from lobbyists etc. However, there is only so much an external consultant can do, and the absence of a dedicated local partner may ultimately expose the firm to comparatively greater, unwanted uncertainties.

Hypothesis 12   A firm facing higher entry barriers in a host country, in the form of trade barriers to imports, is more likely to select production/servicing in that country than exporting to that country.

One of the fundamental assumptions of localizing activities in a host country, regardless of the 'make-or-buy' decision, is that locating activities abroad must be more efficient than exporting products or activities to the host country. MNEs must thus continuously assess the decision of whether to locate activities in the host country or export to this market, particularly in light of uncertain or weak institutions, as discussed above. By exporting products or services, MNEs can reduce their exposure to knowledge appropriation challenges in host country environments. The MNE thereby avoids the costs of having to use inefficient intermediate product markets by achieving FSA transfers in the form of exporting goods and services that embody the FSAs, and selling these in the final output markets.

Despite its benefits, exporting to host countries can also generate significant costs related to transportation and to trade barriers, which have a direct bearing on governance. Host country governments may impose trade barriers for several reasons, such as protecting domestic firms or merely to generate revenues. Similar to institutional uncertainty, trade barriers also represent a form of administrative distance, but intentionally created, in this case usually to promote domestic producers' interests over foreign MNE interests (Ghemawat, 2007). From a host country perspective, importing final end products creates less value in the local market in the short run as compared to attracting intermediate products used for creating local economic activities and related capabilities. Trade barriers may therefore be imposed. Since trade barriers immediately increase costs of exporting to a host country, MNEs are more likely to assess the feasibility and efficiency of localizing activities in that host country. While trade barriers increase firms' impetus to locate production/servicing in a host country, the assessment of relative benefits must also include the ability to achieve an efficient scale of operations and access to the requisite local complementary assets and capabilities (whether available through the output, asset/capability purchase or equity markets), as well as protection against unwanted MNE FSA dissipation, sometimes inappropriately referred to as 'technology transfer', although 'attempt at technology theft' may be a more accurate representation of reality, in which case no foreign investment may materialize (Hennart, 1989).

Hypothesis 12 suggests that trade barriers motivate firms to localize activities, but it does not further guide decisions related to operating methods or ownership structures.

Hypothesis 13   An MNE facing higher 'distance' (geographic, cultural, institutional and economic) between its home country and a host country is more likely to select a local, strategic partner than wholly owned, equity-based, greenfield entry, especially if the needed complementary assets and capabilities for effective FSA exploitation are controlled by host country resource owners and cannot be accessed easily in external markets.

A number of studies have found that perceived distances to host markets affect MNE internationalization patterns, operating modes and ownership decisions (Hennart and Larimo, 1998; Slangen and Hennart, 2007). Distance has many dimensions, the most obvious one being physical, geographic distance, which generates transportation costs and added managerial complexity. Physical distance also pushes MNEs to localize activities in foreign markets if products are perishable or transportation costs overshadow potential profits. But physical distance reflects only part of the picture, as Hypotheses 10–12 suggest. The perceptions of distance are also influenced by differences in national cultures, institutions, and economic characteristics of the home and host countries. All of these distance dimensions generate additional costs, including governance costs, which affect firm-level internationalization patterns and propensities to internalize intermediate markets.

Assessing distance through an internalization theory lens suggests that higher distances between the home and host country generate more governance costs associated with all operating modes in the host country, but the related uncertainties may especially visibly reduce the efficiency of external markets. MNEs experience more difficulties when transfering assets and capabilities to higher-distance countries, and lack valuable local market knowledge (Slangen and Hennart, 2008). Higher distances create difficulties in transacting products or services for both the MNE and the local owners of complementary assets and capabilities. Sharing equity can bridge the distance for both parties: shared equity aligns the organizations' goals and reduces risk of unreliable behavior by creating interdependencies through shared profits and costs. It also enables reciprocal learning opportunities. However, it should be remembered that, at least in a first stage, external distance is simply replaced by internal distance, and external market costs are therefore replaced by internal management costs.

Acquisitions are not expected to be equally efficient as shared equity for a number of reasons. First, because of high distance, the MNE faces major challenges in assessing the value of complementary assets and capabilities, and in contrast to shared equity it is usually much more difficult (if not impossible) to revisit transaction terms after the acquisition has taken place. Second, the local organization will be used to different ways of doing things in terms of dominant logic and routines, and these differences will be exacerbated by high distance, which can create major governance challenges (even potential resistance) when trying to meld MNE FSAs with the assets and capabilities held by the acquired company.

Shared equity will also be more efficient than attempting to develop in-house complementary assets and capabilities through greenfield investments in the high-distance setting, as the local partner already has the necessary local know-how that will immediately be available through shared equity agreements (Hennart and Larimo, 1998). Although the costs of managing greenfield investments are not expected to increase with higher distances as far as simply adopting the MNE's extant routines in the new subsidiary is concerned (Slangen and Hennart, 2008), attempting to replicate local assets or capabilities currently owned/controlled by other economic actors may not only be costly and time-consuming, but also nearly impossible due to the additional difficulties of codifying tacit knowledge developed by local economic actors in a high-distance environment.

Hypothesis 13 focuses on the reciprocal value added through local strategic partnerships, benefiting both the MNE and third-party owners of local complementary assets and capabilities. It also highlights the need to assess the relative efficiencies of governance modes in multiple markets rather than only the efficiency of alternative governance modes for existing MNE FSAs transferred to the host country. MNEs entering a host country with perceived higher distances should therefore carefully assess whether strategic partnerships can provide comparatively superior governance for managing interdependencies between the MNE and local asset/capability owners.

Hypothesis 14   An MNE with prior international experience in a high-distance country is more likely to enter this country through wholly owned, equity-based, greenfield investment than through operating with a local strategic partner.

One of the main reasons for choosing a strategic partnership versus a wholly owned venture is to lower the costs of intermediate inputs by reducing unreliable behavior through joint ownership (Hennart, 1991). As Hypothesis 13 suggests, this is particularly desirable in high-distance markets. Perceived distances are not static, however, and will probably change with increased international experience. In other words, the uncertainties MNEs face as well as the related expected governance costs and their dependence on local know-how to be accessed from other economic actors will be lower with increased experience in high-distance countries. Locally owned complementary assets and capabilities will also be more readily identified, and thus will often be perceived as easier to transact.

Assuming that longer experience does not reduce the difficulty of transacting the MNE's FSAs in external markets in the host country, there will be a continued preference for equity-based operations when transferring FSAs to the host country and exploiting these. As a result, the MNE may seek to enter the host country through a greenfield investment rather than a local partnership. In general, higher distance implies more benefits to be gained from a local partnership. However, as the MNE gains experience in the high-distance market, the benefits of local partnerships decrease (Slangen and Hennart, 2008).

As discussed under Hypothesis 8, wholly owned operations can be established through both greenfield investments and the acquisition of a local firm. Greenfield investments are attractive as internal transfers of FSAs in the MNE are typically conducted more efficiently due to full managerial control over the transfer process. The MNE can then set up its own routines, as well as hire and train carefully selected employees who are supposedly receptive to FSA transfer. While acquisitions secure a speedier access to local complementary assets and capabilities, they generate substantial management costs related to the integration of the target firm with already established routines (Hennart and Reddy, 1997). As the MNE accumulates local knowledge and is increasingly capable of developing or accessing location-bound assets and capabilities independently of a local partner, post-acquisition integration challenges and uncertainties may eventually outweigh the perceived initial benefits *vis-à-vis* greenfield investments.

We can expect firms with more international experience in high-distance countries to prefer wholly owned greenfield investments when entering these markets rather than strategic local partnerships. However, this argument is contingent on the assumption that the MNE FSAs remain vulnerable to contracting in external markets.

Hypothesis 15   An MNE already producing in – or locally servicing – a host country is more likely to select production/servicing in that host country as entry mode for a new product/service offering.

The long-term implication of experience in a host country is also reflected in the MNE's propensity for producing in – or locally servicing – this host country. The decision to locate activities in a host environment is typically determined both by the attractiveness of the location and the identification and establishment of an optimal local governance structure that can generate sufficient profits in that host environment. For already established MNEs, both the attractiveness of the location and the efficiency of the chosen governance approach will have been validated through existing activities. The established local organization and its accumulated experience will thus reduce the governance costs of additional investments (Hennart and Park, 1994).

MNEs that are already established in a host country should therefore consider potential synergies when introducing new products or services in this country. Hypothesis 15 illustrates key dynamic aspects of internalization theory, which has frequently been criticized as static and focused on distinct rational choices (see Buckley and Strange, 2011, for a summary of criticism voiced against the theory). Hypothesis 15 implies that decisions are not only influenced by previous experience. Managers also need to approach each decision holistically by assessing the market entry decisions in light of interlinkages with existing operations.

Hypothesis 16   An MNE entering a host country for purposes of diversification into less-related sectors rather than mere FSA exploitation purposes is more likely to select a strategic partner than a wholly owned, equity-based, greenfield entry.

As previously discussed, when entering a host country with strong FSAs that are difficult to transact in that country, internalization can reduce governance costs arising from various uncertainties (e.g. in the realm of pricing the MNE's FSAs) and the potential unreliability of economic actors in external markets. The benefits of internal organization thus often outweigh the costs of internal growth through greenfield investments. When diversifying into less-related sectors, however, the motives behind entry mode and ownership decisions change drastically. Specifically, in a governance context, the main threats no longer originate from the fear of knowledge appropriation by external economic actors, nor from difficulties in pricing and measuring the value of the MNE's FSAs.

Should internationalization even be considered if the MNE is diversifying into less related sectors rather than expanding for the purpose of exploiting existing FSAs? Diversification into less related sectors does not equate to internationalizing without strong FSAs. As the first two hypotheses in this chapter suggest, strong FSAs are critical when internationalizing to be attractive in a foreign host environment. However, strong FSAs are not limited to technology or capabilities that can be transferred as stand-alone items. Strong FSAs can also include less tangible strengths such as deeply embedded organizational capabilities and entrepreneurial capacity, which may add value when diversifying into less related sectors. While such strengths are important to gain competitive advantage, they require the MNE to connect with a strategic partner with industry-specific knowledge, whether upstream or downstream knowledge or both.

Accessing industry-specific knowledge through a strategic partner is particularly important when such knowledge is costly or impossible to acquire in external markets, and difficult to create/imitate internally within a reasonable time frame. Another option is to engage in a full acquisition of an existing firm with the relevant industry-specific knowledge. If the industry-specific knowledge is considered a competitive asset by the firm controlling it, however, such acquisitions will be costly. Furthermore, the MNE runs the risk of losing part of the knowledge's value if intangible dimensions of the acquired assets do not change hands with shifts in ownership (Chen and Hennart, 2002), for example if lead scientists or marketing experts leave the acquired company. Hence the necessary industry-specific knowledge when diversifying into less related sectors may be difficult to efficiently purchase on the external market, replicate or acquire (Hennart and Park, 1993; Slangen and Hennart, 2007).

Hypothesis 17   An MNE entering a host country with a larger-scale operation as compared to the extant size of the firm is more likely to select a strategic partner than a wholly owned, equity-based, greenfield entry.

The recognition that MNE resources are scarce and heterogeneous has many implications for international expansion. Managerial constraints, limited funding opportunities and limitations on the ability to recruit and train local employees affect the feasibility of operating methods and ownership structures in foreign markets. If the scale of the operations is large in the foreign market, as compared with the extant size of the MNE, managerial and resource constraints often deter firms from selecting governance of the foreign operations through wholly owned greenfield investments (Hennart and Park, 1993).

The foreign MNE must thus consider the benefits and costs of fully acquiring the local operation or entering into a strategic partnership. Studies have shown that foreign subsidiaries that are large compared to the rest of the organization are more commonly acquired than established as greenfield ventures to overcome internal resource constraints (Slangen and Hennart, 2007). However, managerial constraints may be equally challenging when the foreign entry is pursued through a full acquisition. Although the foreign MNE would not need to recruit and train new employees, full acquisitions require extensive integration of an existing organization. Post-acquisition integration is inherently challenging due to established routines and social interactions. If, in addition, the foreign subsidiary is relatively larger than the extant organization, the governance challenges may escalate, driven by parent organization managerial constraints and stronger resistance from the large host country unit to adopt the MNE's main routines and social practices.

Strategic partnerships can therefore be particularly attractive when the host country operations are relatively large. The two organizations can effectively work together by aligning interests and complement each other in terms of assets and capabilities. The strategic partnership effectively functions as a 'joint hierarchy', limiting, *inter alia*, the incentives to act opportunistically thanks to internal governance mechanisms (Hennart, 2010).

The arguments underlying Hypothesis 17 highlight the resource-based component of internalization theory, much in line with Penrose (1959). Entry mode and ownership decisions are directly affected by the MNE's resource base. Firms in the process of internationalizing should ensure that careful attention is not only given to the potential value creation from existing resources but also to potential resource constraints that lower the feasibility of success when selecting particular foreign entry modes and ownership structures.

Hypothesis 18   An MNE entering a host country is more likely to select a joint venture than a full acquisition if the needed complementary assets and capabilities are difficult to transact in external markets, even though they may be easily unbundled from the strategic partner's remaining assets and capabilities.

When local, complementary assets and capabilities can be easily unbundled from a host country firm's overall asset and capability base, we might assume that a foreign MNE will prefer full acquisitions over joint ventures (Hennart and Reddy, 1997). Yet we see many MNEs entering into joint ventures in such situations. A number of factors influence this choice. First, the unbundling of assets and capabilities is often more complex than anticipated, as tacit elements are frequently embedded in the local organization. That actual value of unbundled assets or capabilities (as opposed to expected market price) may thus depreciate when isolated from the rest of the organization. Engaging in joint ventures allows the foreign MNE to capitalize on these assets and capabilities without the risk of reducing their value. Second, acquiring a firm inevitably also involves the acquisition of non-value-adding resources that will require managerial attention either to divest or integrate into the organization. Joint ventures enable the MNE to tap into the complementary assets and capabilities of a partner firm without these additional managerial constraints. Finally, acquiring a firm always generates costly and time-consuming integration efforts that may or may not be successful. If the requisite, local complementary assets and capabilities are easily unbundled, the joint venture can effectively be built around these. Limiting the joint venture activities to the easily unbundled assets and capabilities enables the foreign MNE to effectively tap into them without experiencing extensive integration costs.

Joint ventures are of course not without challenges. Typically, joint ventures are recommended when markets are inefficient for the assets and capabilities brought to the table by both parties (Hennart, 2010), as shown in quadrant 4 of Figure 1.1. Here, entering the foreign market through a wholly owned greenfield investment will be inefficient as the linking investments in terms of cost and time of imitating and developing the requisite assets or capabilities internally may be prohibitively high. MNEs seeking to obtain the assets or capabilities through full acquisitions would face the uncertainties and potential costs discussed above, leaving joint ventures as a more attractive and efficient governance option.

Hypothesis 19   An MNE operating a joint venture with a partner from a lower-distance host country is more likely to experience higher joint venture longevity.

A key challenge of succeeding with joint ventures is the ability to work toward common goals despite inherent organizational differences. Such differences will be challenging in any situation as each organization develops its unique routines and organizational culture. Communication between the joint venture partners is thus a critical governance feature to bridge organizational differences by identifying and agreeing on common goals, resolve any conflicts in the ongoing relationship, and respond to external dynamics.

Research suggests that distance between the home and host countries directly influences firms' abilities to communicate effectively (Hennart and Zeng, 2002). Language differences, even subtle ones, can create misunderstandings and conflicts. National culture also affects how organizational values and cultures develop, so that firms from culturally similar countries are also expected to have more similar organizational values and cultures that can facilitate communication. Administrative and economic differences between countries can also affect how firms address conflicts or interpret external changes, leading to divergence in goals and managerial styles. Distance between the home and host countries can thus create significantly different managerial mindsets as well as organizational values and cultures that may challenge the joint venture partners' abilities to find common ground through communication.

MNEs should therefore assess the likely impact of distance between their home country and a potential host country on the ability of the joint venture partners to communicate effectively. Higher distances will demand more investment in the communication and alignment of goals and management practices. Joint ventures with local partners in low-distance host markets are therefore more attractive in terms of the likelihood of higher joint venture longevity.

The arguments behind Hypothesis 19 further highlight some of the dynamic aspects of internalization theory, which is an area where the theoretical perspective has received criticism (Buckley and Strange, 2011). It reinforces the need to assess the long-term implications of a chosen governance mode. Hence, while Hypothesis 13 recommends joint ventures in higher-distance markets, MNEs should also assess the location choice in terms of probability for long-term retention (as optimal operating mode) of such foreign ventures.[1]

Hypothesis 20   An MNE operating a joint venture in a host country is likely to transform this joint venture into a wholly owned operation over time.

As discussed above, the longevity of joint ventures requires effective communication as ongoing dynamics push joint venture partners to realign their goals, ways of working together and how to respond to external changes. Statistics show that most joint ventures are dissolved over time, although the actual rates vary greatly across studies (Hennart and Zeng, 2002). The dissolution of a joint venture, however, does not translate into failed operations. Many MNEs actively seek to transform their foreign joint ventures into wholly owned operations.

There are many reasons for this. Wholly owned operations eliminate the communication challenges discussed above. Once sufficient experience or knowledge is accumulated, the MNE may feel more confident to take full control over the local organization through an acquisition or to be capable of accessing necessary complementary assets and capabilities through external market contracts. Further, the MNE might have successfully learned to develop the necessary complementary local assets and capabilities through the joint ownership. The incentive to remain in the joint venture thus depends on the perceived interdependence of the firms and the expected ability to develop, manage or access complementary assets and capabilities independently.

Hypothesis 20 suggests that MNEs operating in host markets through joint ventures should continuously assess the relative efficiency of this ownership structure, as compared with a wholly owned operation. With accumulated experience, many MNEs feel more confident and competitively positioned to transform the current joint venture into a wholly owned operation. As discussed in previous hypotheses, although there are many benefits to joint ventures, the benefits of full control may at some point outweigh potential costs. Joint ventures should primarily be chosen when the markets for assets and capabilities of both parties are inefficient. With increased experience, many foreign firms have either managed to develop the complementary assets and capabilities internally or may find it easier to transact through contracts in the host country environment.

Hypothesis 20 also highlights the dynamics of internalization theory: strategic decisions subsequent to foreign market entry must continuously reassess what constitutes the most efficient governance mode. Internal dynamics such as accumulated experience with complementary assets and capabilities in the host country environment will also affect internal resources and managerial capabilities of the MNE, and these will in turn affect future expansion patterns and their governance.

CONCLUSION

In this chapter, we have discussed 20 key hypotheses derived directly from internalization theory. We have shown how this conceptual lens provides insight into when, where and how firms internationalize. The hypotheses capture key contributions from conceptual and empirical studies over the past decades. By presenting all 20 hypotheses in a single chapter, and reformulating these into (we hope) a coherent set, one of internalization theory's key strengths becomes apparent: its complementary relationship with other theoretical perspectives such as the resource-based view of the firm (Rugman et al., 2011a; Verbeke, 2003).

Summarizing internalization theory's implications through the use of key hypotheses also clarifies its broad diagnostic potential to support managerial decision-making in the international strategy sphere. Internalization theory is supposedly a positive theory with predictive capacity, but 'efficient' outcomes in the long run and across firms/industries result from numerous senior management decisions at the micro-level, whereby wrong decisions are sanctioned, and firms characterized by a cumulative sequence of misguided decisions weeded out. Internalization theory recognizes the immense importance of resource heterogeneity among firms. Here, internalizing decisions may be driven as much by FSAs in the form of tacit organizational capabilities as by technological innovation and brand names. From both an empirical perspective, when testing internalization theory's predictive power in industry, and in terms of normative guidance provided to managers in a specific company, it is imperative for the IB researcher to have a solid grasp of the relevant FSAs of the enterprise(s) studied.

Further, internalization decisions affect firms that internationalize with various motives, and these motives will determine the FSAs most critical to foreign entry and operation, as well as the complementary assets and capabilities required from third parties in the host countries selected. A number of hypotheses described above are more applicable to particular motives than to others. For example, market-seeking firms are more likely to choose locations where FSA exploitation requires less adaptation (e.g. Hypothesis 4). Other hypotheses apply to a range of motives such as the importance of the cost of accessing local complementary assets and capabilities (e.g. Hypothesis 3), although the specificity of those assets and capabilities will precisely depend on the MNE's strategic motive for international expansion. For example, market-seeking firms will need to access local distribution channels; natural-resource-seekers expand abroad with the prime purpose to utilize particular host country resources; strategic-asset-seeking firms will need to access knowledge, including know-how embedded in particular institutions; efficiency-seeking firms may require the capabilities of low-cost suppliers in host countries to support a lean supply chain.

The emphasis placed in internalization theory on distance and differences in institutions is particularly relevant to the ongoing debate of emerging markets. As the above hypotheses suggest, the ability to assess the relative efficiency of multiple markets relies mainly on the stability of institutions. Further, the value of FSAs when transferred to foreign markets differs as a function of distance. The potential impact of distance increases the need to evaluate what types of FSAs generate competitive advantage and how this advantage can be affected by distance. A related point is that higher distance may simultaneously create stronger needs for linking investments to access assets and capabilities from host country partners. The location characteristics and available complementary assets and capabilities in emerging markets may force developed economy MNEs to revisit their conventional business model in terms of which value-adding FSAs should be transferred and deployed there.

Finally, the 20 key hypotheses, when considered as a set rather than individually, remind us that firms face multiple, interrelated decisions when entering and operating in a foreign market. Foreign entry and operation are thus not necessarily based on a simple choice between the absolute efficiency of contract (e.g. licensing) versus FDI in one 'isolated' market. Benito et al.'s (2009) observation of MNEs using several entry modes simultaneously when entering a host country is fully consistent with our analysis. Even when contemplating only a single expansion move into a host country, strategic decision-making must take into account markets for multiple inputs and (intermediate) outputs, with each of these markets characterized by a specific ownership structure and accessibility of complementary assets and capabilities. Internalization theory is well positioned as a superior conceptual lens for the requisite analysis of these complexities that impose critical challenges of bounded rationality and bounded reliability, and make it more difficult to create a favorable context for innovation in its entirety.

While the key hypotheses presented in this chapter show internalization theory's impressive breadth and applicability, the main emphasis has so far been placed on external markets' impact on governance costs. We propose that internal governance issues warrant further attention in future research to enhance the MNE's ability to make sound strategic decisions. As discussed in this chapter, governance costs associated with utilizing external markets should always be compared with governance costs of internalizing markets. Yet internal governance costs have so far received less research attention when examined from an internalization perspective. Internalization theory is a particularly suitable lens for further studies on internal governance costs due to its complementarity with other theoretical perspectives (Verbeke and Kano, forthcoming). Unfortunately, the power of internalization theory has so far been underutilized for the study of MNE internal strategic management challenges (Rugman and Verbeke, 2003; Verbeke, 2003; Verbeke and Greidanus, 2009).

NOTE

1. We recognize that long-term success will be defined differently across firms and industries.

REFERENCES

Benito, G., B. Petersen and L. Welch (2009), 'Towards more realistic conceptualisations of foreign operation modes', *Journal of International Business Studies*, **40**(9), 1455–70.

Buckley, P.J. and M.C. Casson (1976), *The Future of the Multinational Enterprise*, London: Macmillan.

Buckley, P.J. and M.C. Casson (2009), 'The internalisation theory of the multinational enterprise: a review of the progress of a research agenda after 30 years', *Journal of International Business Studies*, **40**(9), 1563–80.

Buckley, P.J. and R. Strange (2011), 'The governance of the multinational enterprise: Insights from internalization theory', *Journal of Management Studies*, **48**(2), 460–70.

Cantwell, J. (2000), 'A survey of theories of international production', in C.N. Pitelis and R. Sugden (eds), *The Nature of the Transnational Firm*, 2nd edn, London: Routledge, pp. 10–56.

Chen, S.-F.S. (2005), 'Extending internalization theory: a new perspective on international technology transfer and its generalization', *Journal of International Business Studies*, **36**(2), 231–45.

Chen, S.-F.S. (2010), 'A general TCE model of international business institutions: market failure and reciprocity', *Journal of International Business Studies*, **41**(6), 935–59.

Chen, S.-F.S. and J.F. Hennart (2002), 'Japanese investors' choice of joint ventures versus wholly-owned subsidiaries in the US: the role of market barriers and firm capabilities', *Journal of International Business Studies*, **33**(1), 1–18.

Coase, R.H. (1937), 'The nature of the firm', in J.B. Barney and W.G. Ouchi (eds), *Organizational Economics*, San Francisco, CA: Jossey Bass, pp. 80–98.

Dunning, J.H. (1988), 'The eclectic paradigm of international production: a restatement and some possible extensions', *Journal of International Business Studies*, **19**(1), 1–31.

Dunning, J.H. (2003), 'Some antecedents of internalization theory', *Journal of International Business Studies*, **34**(2), 108–15.

Dunning, J.H. (2009), 'The key literature on IB activities: 1960–2006', in A. Rugman (ed.), *The Oxford Handbook of International Business*, 2nd edn, Oxford: Oxford University Press, pp. 39–71.

Ghemawat, P. (2001), 'Distance still matters', *Harvard Business Review*, **79**(8), 137–47.

Ghemawat, P. (2007), *Redefining Global Strategy*, Boston, MA: Harvard Business School Publishing.

Hennart, J.-F. (1982), *A Theory of Multinational Enterprise*, Ann Arbor, MI: University of Michigan Press.

Hennart, J.-F. (1989), 'Can the '*new forms*' of investment substitute for the '*old forms*'? A transaction cost perspective', *Journal of International Business Studies*, **20**(2), 211–33.

Hennart, J.-F. (1991), 'The transaction costs theory of joint ventures: an empirical study of Japanese subsidiaries in the United States', *Management Science*, **37**(4), 483–97.

Hennart, J.-F. (1994), 'The "comparative institutional" theory of the firm: some implications for corporate strategy', *Journal of Management Studies*, **31**(2), 193–207.

Hennart, J.-F. (2009), 'Down with MNE-centric theories! Market entry and expansion as the bundling of MNE and local assets', *Journal of International Business Studies*, **40**(9), 1432–54.

Hennart, J.-F. (2010), 'Transaction cost theory and international business', *Journal of Retailing*, **86**(3), 257–69.

Hennart, J.-F. and J. Larimo (1998), 'The impact of culture on the strategy of multinational enterprises: does national origin affect ownership decisions?', *Journal of International Business Studies*, **29**(3), 515–38.

Hennart, J.-F. and Y.R. Park (1993), 'Greenfield vs. acquisition: the strategy of Japanese investors in the United States', *Management Science*, **39**(9), 1054–70.

Hennart, J.-F. and Y.R. Park (1994), 'Location, governance, and strategic determinants of Japanese manufacturing investment in the United States', *Strategic Management Journal*, **15**(6), 419–36.

Hennart, J.-F. and S. Reddy (1997), 'The choice between mergers/acquisitions and joint ventures: the case of Japanese investors in the United States', *Strategic Management Journal*, **18**(1), 1–12.

Hennart, J.-F., T. Roehl and M. Zeng (2002), 'Do exits proxy a liability of foreignness? The case of Japanese exits from the US', *Journal of International Management*, **8**(3), 241–64.

Hennart, J.-F. and M. Zeng (2002), 'Cross-cultural differences and joint venture longevity', *Journal of International Business Studies*, **33**(4), 699–716.

Hymer, S. (1970), 'The efficiency (contradictions) of multinational corporations', *American Economic Review*, **60**(2), 441–8.

Khanna, T., K.G. Palepu and J. Sinha (2005), 'Strategies that fit emerging markets', *Harvard Business Review*, **83**(6), 63–76.

Kogut, B. and U. Zander (1993), 'Knowledge of the firm and the evolutionary theory of the multinational corporation', *Journal of International Business Studies*, **24**(4), 625–46.

Penrose, E. (1959), *The Theory of the Growth of the Firm*, 3rd edn, Oxford: Oxford University Press.

Rugman, A. (1981), *Inside the Multinationals: The Economics of Internal Markets*, London: Croom Helm.

Rugman, A.M. and A. Verbeke (1992), 'A note on the transnational solution and the transaction cost theory of multinational strategic management', *Journal of International Business Studies*, **23**(4), 761–71.

Rugman, A.M. and A. Verbeke (2003), 'Extending the theory of the multinational enterprise: internalization and strategic management perspectives', *Journal of International Business Studies*, **34**(2), 125–37.

Rugman, A.M. A. Verbeke and Q.T.K. Nguyen (2011a), 'Fifty years of international business theory and beyond', *Management International Review*, **51**(6), 755–86.

Rugman, A., A. Verbeke and W. Yuan (2011b), 'Re-conceptualizing Bartlett and Ghoshal's classification of national subsidiary roles in the multinational enterprise', *Journal of Management Studies*, **48**(2), 253–77.

Slangen, A.H.L. and J.-F. Hennart (2007), 'Greenfield or acquisition entry: a review of the empirical foreign establishment mode literature', *Journal of International Management*, **13**(4), 403–29.

Slangen, A.H.L. and J.-F. Hennart (2008), 'Do multinationals really prefer to enter culturally distant countries through greenfields rather than through acquisitions? The role of parent experience and subsidiary autonomy', *Journal of International Business Studies*, **39**(3), 472–90.

Teece, D.J. (1986), 'Transaction cost economics and multinational enterprise', *Journal of Economic Behavior and Organization*, **7**(1), 21–45.

Verbeke, A. (2003), 'The evolutionary view of the MNE and the future of internalization theory', *Journal of International Business Studies*, **34**(6), 498–505.

Verbeke, A. (2009), *International Business Strategy: Rethinking the Foundations of Global Corporate Success*, Cambridge: Cambridge University Press.

Verbeke, A. and N.S. Greidanus (2009), 'The end of the opportunism vs trust debate: bounded reliability as a new envelope concept in research on MNE governance', *Journal of International Business Studies*, **40**(9), 1471–95.

Verbeke, A. and L. Kano (forthcoming), 'A transaction cost economics (TCE) perspective on trading favours', *Asia Pacific Journal of Management*.

Verbeke, A. and T. Kenworthy (2008), 'Multidivisional vs metanational governance of the multinational enterprise', *Journal of International Business Studies*, **39**(6), 940–56.

Williamson, O.E. (1996), *The Mechanisms of Governance*, Oxford: Oxford University Press.

Zaheer, S. (1995), 'Overcoming the liability of foreignness', *Academy of Management Journal*, **38**(2), 341–63.

Zhou, K. and L. Poppo (2010), 'Exchange hazards, relational reliability, and contracts in China: the contingent role of legal enforceability', *Journal of International Business Studies*, **41**(5), 861–81.

2 The end of the opportunism versus trust debate: bounded reliability as a new envelope concept in research on MNE governance
Alain Verbeke and Nathan Greidanus

INTRODUCTION

Transaction cost economics (TCE) has fast become one of the most influential theories within the social sciences (Carroll and Teece, 1999; Carter and Hodgson, 2006). Its applications in the international business (IB) context have shown its relevance to explaining and predicting a wide variety of IB phenomena, including, *inter alia*, the existence of MNEs (Buckley and Casson, 1976; Rugman, 1980; Teece, 1981; Hennart, 1982), MNE foreign entry mode decisions and interactions with external parties (Beamish and Banks, 1987; Hennart, 1988; Buckley and Casson, 1998a; Chen, 2005; Hennart, 2009), but also MNE internal governance choices (Hennart, 1993; Verbeke and Kenworthy, 2008).

TCE thinking as applied in the IB context (usually referred to as internalization theory or transaction cost internalization – TCI theory) relies heavily on Coase's (1937) original analysis of the relative costs of external versus internal markets, and parallels to a large extent Williamson's (1975, 1985, 1996a) development of TCE as a general theory of the firm (Safarian, 2003). However, Williamson's TCE approach relies heavily on the behavioral assumptions of bounded rationality and opportunism, whereas other TCE-related theories do not appear to require the latter concept (North, 1990). In the IB field, a number of scholars have developed MNE theories that allow for opportunism, but do not assume it is necessarily the decisive factor in governance choices; see, *inter alia*, Casson's (2000) information cost perspective and Rugman and Verbeke's (2003) joint transaction cost and strategic management explanation of internal MNE functioning. Despite these efforts, concerns surrounding the behavioral assumption of opportunism, a cornerstone of Williamsonian thinking (Williamson, 1993a), continue to reduce the legitimacy of TCE as a general theory of the firm, and as the core of IB theory (Conner and Prahalad, 1996; Ghoshal and Moran, 1996; Ghoshal, 2005). The present chapter's purpose is to advance IB theory through proposing a more valid concept, substituting for simple Williamsonian opportunism.

Simon (1985, p. 303) has clearly acknowledged the importance of specific behavioral assumptions: 'Nothing is more fundamental in setting our research agenda and informing our research methods than our view of the nature of the human beings whose behavior we are studying. It makes a difference, a very large difference.' A number of recent decade award-winning articles in the *Journal of International Business Studies* (*JIBS*) also reveal the continued relevance of exploring the models of man upon which much of IB theory rests. For example, the opportunism assumption has been addressed (utilized, extended or discounted) in papers as varied as Gomes-Casseres's (1990) integration of the ownership and bargaining perspectives in MNE decision-making, Kogut and Zander's (1993) knowledge view of the MNE, Oviatt and McDougall's (1994) perspective on international new ventures, and Madhok's (1995) emphasis on trust in international joint ventures. More generally, a search of the *JIBS* archive of the past 20 years (1988–October 2008) yields an impressive number of 116 separate, substantive entries referring to the opportunism concept.

Assessing the validity of critical behavioral assumptions, and refining these assumptions when describing variety, selection and retention of governance mechanisms, is fundamental to advancing management theory, including IB theory. Unfortunately, the empirical efforts to date to address the validity of the opportunism assumption, whether through testing it directly or through testing alternative behavioral assumptions with proposed higher relevance, have remained unsatisfactory (Tsang, 2006). The present chapter performs such an assessment within IB research, with a specific focus on identifying the mechanisms explaining failed human commitments in internal MNE functioning. The importance of assessing the opportunism assumption cannot be overstated, but approaching the topic has proven difficult in practice. Deciphering the nature of man, and assessing the various forms of self-interest (from weak to strong), has plagued philosophers (e.g. Plato, 375 BC; Hobbes, 1651), economists (e.g. Smith, 1776; Mill, 1867), and more recently social scientists (Axelrod, 1984; Ridley, 1998). Despite the broad treatment of the subject throughout the history of science, scholars in management and IB have rarely attempted to assess in a non-ideological fashion whether an assumption of opportunism is warranted. Management and IB scholars have mostly chosen to reject (Ghoshal and Moran, 1996), incrementally extend (Heiman and Nickerson, 2002), ignore (Conner and Prahalad, 1996), or view as relevant only in well-defined circumstances (Casson, 2000; Madhok, 2006a; Verbeke, 2003), Williamson's strong-form view of self-interest, without attempting to analyze more broadly the mechanisms underlying failed human commitments and critical to governance choices.

In an effort to advance TCE-based thinking, we propose the concept of 'bounded reliability'[1] as a more appropriate behavioral assumption. We develop the bounded reliability concept by analyzing case studies of the nine truly global MNEs in the *Fortune* Global 500 (Rugman and Verbeke, 2004). These nine MNEs are firms with proven, successful global strategies, as measured by the balanced dispersion of their sales across the triad of North America, Europe and Asia. Our analysis suggests that while Williamsonian opportunism may sometimes be at play, there are more common reasons for the non-fulfillment of commitments inside the MNE. Bounded reliability, much like bounded rationality, suggests that economic actors may be reliable but only boundedly so (Simon, 1955).

The remainder of this chapter takes the following form: in the next section we outline some key elements in the debate surrounding opportunism. The section following focuses on opportunism in the IB context, where we contrast the Williamsonian view on opportunism with the contemporary perspective of three IB scholars – Alain Verbeke, Mark Casson and Anoop Madhok – who have been particularly outspoken on this issue. We highlight the common conceptual weakness present in each of these three perspectives, and introduce bounded reliability as an envelope concept describing the limits of human reliability inside the MNE. We then attempt to define more precisely bounded reliability's substance, building upon case studies of nine global MNE and suggest a number of implications of bounded reliability for MNE research and management.

OPPORTUNISM AND TCE

TCE proposes that economic organization aims to align transactions, which differ in their attributes (such as frequency, uncertainty and asset specificity) from governance mechanisms (such as market contracts, various forms of organization inside a single firm and hybrids) in a discriminating, and mainly transaction-cost-economizing, way (Williamson, 1991). In managerial terms, TCE addresses three broad questions. First, what activities/ transactions should be conducted within the firm's boundaries? Second, how should the linkages be governed with external actors that are relevant to the activities/transactions performed within the firm? Third, how should the activities/transactions conducted within the firm be governed? The general answer to each of these questions is that business firms – given a particular macro-level institutional context – will be driven mainly by joint efficiency/effectiveness considerations, meaning the goal of achieving the best attainable output–input relation given the available governance alternatives, each of which is associated with costs and benefits and is subject to risks. Here, TCE relies heavily on the behavioral assumptions of bounded rationality (Simon, 1955) and opportunism, the latter being defined as self-interest-seeking with guile (Williamson, 1985). Opportunism is considered core to TCE: absent opportunism, markets alone, through autonomous contracting, would be sufficient for handling most economic activities/transactions (Williamson and Ouchi, 1981; Williamson, 1985). For Williamson, managing the looming problem of opportunism is the key to understanding the micro-level institutions of capitalism (Williamson, 1996b). While opportunism is not assumed to be present all the time, bounded rationality constrains the ability both to write complete contracts and to identify *ex ante* possible occurrences of opportunism. In combination, these assumptions create hazards that need to be guarded against. Adopting appropriate safeguards in contracting reduces the occurrence of opportunism and mitigates its impacts when it occurs.

Opportunism manifestations, according to Williamson (1985, p. 47), include 'calculated efforts to mislead, distort, disguise, obfuscate or otherwise confuse'. Inside the firm, shirking is a common expression of opportunism, whereas in the context of hybrid governance, opportunism often expresses itself as the deceitful appropriation of the partner firm's knowledge (Parkhe, 1993). However, various scholars have criticized the opportunism assumption, *inter alia* because of its limited conceptual grounding and the absence of analysis of its complexity (Wathne and Heide, 2000). Moreover, research that actually attempts to measure opportunism directly is scarce (Boerner and Macher, 2001).

From a conceptual perspective, at least four credible points of criticism have been voiced against the opportunism concept. First, Williamsonian opportunism reflects a dispositional (non-contextual) view of human nature, with a lack of detail provided on how opportunism develops or how it can be reduced. For example, Moran and Ghoshal (1996) have referred to a TCE schizophrenia, whereby opportunism is static and dispositional, yet safeguards against opportunism are dynamic and situational. Following the dispositional critique, these authors have criticized Williamson for not differentiating between opportunism as an attitude and opportunism as a behavior.

Second, opportunism has also been criticized for its potential influence on enacted societal and individual behavior: propagating the belief that opportunism reflects 'standard behavior' (i.e. 'this is to be expected') is likely to reinforce any initial intentions to cheat, shirk etc., and such intentions in turn will express themselves as actual opportunistic behavior. In other words, focusing on guarding against opportunism actually gives license to – and may even increase the levels of – the behavior one wants to safeguard against.

Third, the capabilities school (including the resource-based, knowledge-based and learning views of the firm) has argued that firms may exist for many reasons even absent opportunism in external markets (e.g. for the efficient and effective development, transfer and exploitation of knowledge, i.e. for its superiority in managing the innovation process in its entirety). The capabilities view has also suggested that interfirm relationships offer value creation and knowledge-sharing opportunities that cannot develop if a prime focus is maintained on guarding against opportunism (Ouchi and Price, 1993; Noorderhaven, 1994; Madhok, 1995; Dyer, 1997; Dyer and Singh, 1998; Gulati and Singh, 1998). Conner and Prahalad (1996), in providing one of the first links between the knowledge-based view of the firm and TCE, have argued that even in the absence of opportunism, transaction costs will still exist in knowledge-based transactions. These costs arise because knowledge is often tacit, embedded in organizational routines, and learning may need to occur through direct observation (Afuah, 2001; Conner and Prahalad, 1996).

Fourth, Ghoshal and Moran (1996) have suggested that purpose plays the role in organizations that price plays in markets: the advantage of firms over markets may not lie in overcoming human pathologies through hierarchy substituting for price, but instead in the firm's purpose of leveraging the human ability to take initiative, to cooperate and to learn.

Trust, as a substitute for or complement to opportunism, has probably generated the most interest. Trust centers on the truster's vulnerability, and the trustee's reliability and perceived benevolence. Zaheer et al. (1998) have argued that trust reflects the expectation an actor can be relied upon to fulfill obligations and to behave in a predictable manner. Implicit in reliability is the notion of ability or competence (Nooteboom et al., 1997), and this is viewed as an essential condition for trust (Mayer et al., 1995). Benevolence is the extent to which a trustee is believed to want to do good or to cooperate with the truster, due to moral obligation or internalized norms (Delerue-Vidot, 2006; Mayer et al., 1995). The inclusion of benevolence in trust definitions highlights the difficulties in combining both trust and opportunism (strong-form self-interest) within a single theory. In choosing between the two constructs, many scholars find trust a more satisfying behavioral assumption than opportunism (Gambetta, 1988). From the trust perspective, the solution to the incentive loss problem associated with hierarchical coordination (meaning that incentives are arguably lower-powered in firms than in markets) lies not in firms emulating markets, but in firms creating a context of identification, commitment and benevolence that clearly differentiates them from markets (Ghoshal and Moran, 1996).

Trust has sometimes been interpreted as a complement to conventional restraints on opportunism, and therefore as a component of an interrelated bundle of governance mechanisms (Nooteboom et al., 1997; Alvarez et al., 2003). It has even been argued that beyond Williamson's contractual coercion (legal ordering) and self-interested incentives (private ordering), trust constitutes a significant addition to governance (Madhok, 1995; Nooteboom et al., 1997). Trust's ability to reduce opportunism operates through reducing the likelihood of negative interpretations of a partner's actions, allowing for the benefit of the doubt. Such allowance facilitates openness in sharing knowledge and reduces unwarranted fear of opportunistic behavior by partners (Krishnan et al., 2006).

However, viewing trust as a governance mechanism to curb opportunism remains ultimately unsatisfactory, since trust may reduce the alertness needed when economic actors such as alliance partners or even loyal employees respond to environmental change. Krishnan et al. (2006) have suggested that reduced alertness may stem from trust's encouragement of economic actors to minimize redundancies in the search process as they rely on the partner's purported expertise to engage in specialized search. From a cognitive–heuristic perspective, trust may also be dangerous, since it may produce systematic biases, and even strategic blindness, resulting in significant errors (Ferrin and Dirks, 2003; McEvily et al., 2003). Jap and Anderson's (2003) findings illustrate this point: when all is well, the confidence that two individuals place in each other may allow their relationship to perform better in every respect, but these positive performance effects may diminish, even evaporate, as *ex post* opportunism mounts. In this situation, it is actually the prior trust that allows opportunism to come to fruition.

Williamson (1993b) has argued that most, if not all, economic trust can be reduced to calculative trust. Williamson further contends that calculative trust is a contradiction in terms, and therefore the study of economic organization should refrain from adopting trust as an analytical construct (Williamson, 1993a). Williamson's focus on farsightedness also conflicts with the trust perspective. Farsightedness suggests that when looking forward and identifying the danger of opportunism materializing, economic actors should give and receive credible commitments (in a cost-effective manner) (Williamson, 1996b). In contrast, myopic parties must rely on altruism when a bad state of affairs materializes, and then suffer from having neglected to introduce *ex ante* proper safeguards in the exchange and to contemplate the contracting process in its entirety. Williamson has suggested that the concept of 'credible commitments' provides an effective response to the substantive challenge of effective contracting, and eliminates the need for references to trust (Williamson, 1993a, p. 100).

Another key to the opportunism concept is found in Williamson's statement that to accept the opportunism is not to celebrate it (Williamson, 1996a). The main purposes of recognizing the possibility of opportunism are that it avoids contractual naïveté when a contract as a mere promise (unsupported by credible commitments) is put forward, and invites identifying, making explicit and mitigating hazards that have their origins in opportunism. This view does not imply that all economic actors are mean spirited or immoral, nor should it promote opportunism (Williamson, 1996b).

The above offers a brief outline of various key elements in the debate surrounding opportunism within the TCE context. In the following section we turn our attention to modern IB theory, which – while similar to the general TCE perspective – offers a departure from conventional TCE regarding the opportunism assumption.

TRANSACTION-COST-BASED REASONING IN INTERNATIONAL BUSINESS THEORY

Infusion of Williamsonian Behavioral Assumptions in IB

Modern IB theory (especially internalization theory or TCI) shares with Williamsonian TCE a Coasian foundation (Safarian, 2003).[2] IB theory essentially describes the MNE as an internal market that operates across national boundaries. For example, as with conventional TCE, IB theory suggests MNE foreign entry mode choices will vary depending upon the nature of the transactions at hand, e.g. as a function of the risk of proprietary knowledge dissipation, the risk of negative effects on brand name reputation, the probability that the required complementary knowledge of economic actors can (or cannot) be accessed etc. Here, the focus is more on the complex and dynamic process of efficiently transferring, deploying, augmenting and exploiting firm-specific advantages (FSAs), linking these with complementary assets of local partners and coordinating the resulting internal and external networks, rather than on merely assessing the potential redeployment without loss of economic value of narrowly defined assets involved in a particular transaction. To put it differently: the MNE as an entity is itself a governance mechanism specialized in resource recombination, meaning that a joint capability perspective and TCE perspective, as provided by internalization theory, is required to analyze properly decisions such as entry mode choices and subsequent network governance. Consistent with TCE logic, when penetrating foreign markets MNE managers must align efficiently and effectively entry mode characteristics (such as the characteristics of a subsidiary or a licensing agreement with a foreign partner) with the attributes of the cross-border transaction, but taking into account the MNE's extant resource basis (Verbeke, 2009). Given this resource base, the ultimate choice is guided by the relative efficiency and effectiveness of internalization versus the use of external markets.

As regards the use of the opportunism concept in the empirical IB literature, we revisited comprehensively all 38 empirical studies included in the meta-analysis performed by Zhao et al. (2004), which addressed the TCE determinants of ownership-based entry mode choice, and complemented this analysis with a further study of five more recent empirical articles, which in our view satisfied the requirements for inclusion in the meta-analysis (Yiu and Makino, 2002; Brouthers et al., 2003; Chen, 2007; Chen and Mujtaba, 2007; Quer et al., 2007). Importantly, many of the papers briefly mention the opportunism concept or expressions thereof (such as shirking), but only one of these papers, namely Brouthers et al. (2003), came close to actual measurement of the concept. These authors used a 'behavioral uncertainty' measure, reflecting the dangers of free-riding, information dissipation and shirking. Behavioral uncertainty was assessed on the basis of answers to five Likert-type questions, including three items about monitoring performance related to product/service quality, one item about monitoring/safeguarding proprietary knowledge, and one item about the costs of search, contracting and enforcement. Many of the other papers (26 of the 43) propose asset specificity or a special form thereof, namely R&D intensity, as a variable expected to influence entry mode choice, and the rationale for this is regularly couched in traditional TCE terms, including references to opportunism, but no effort was undertaken to assess directly whether safeguarding against opportunism was actually instrumental to governance choices. The general assumption is that high asset specificity in terms of difficult asset redeployment and high-value losses associated with such redeployment, or perhaps more to the point, the easy dissipation of FSAs in the form of the proprietary (knowledge) resources' value-creating features, will lead MNEs to favor internalization, so as to avoid the possibility of cheating (reneging on contractual terms or not abiding by the spirit of these terms) by external contracting parties.

On the issue of internal MNE governance choices there is an even greater paucity of empirical research in terms of directly measuring the potential for opportunism. However, three well-known IB scholars have recently put forward new conceptual approaches, which are all similar in terms of underlying behavioral assumptions, but ultimately fall short in providing an acceptable 'behavioral envelope' for capturing fully failed human commitments inside the MNE.

Alain Verbeke's (2003) Perspective on Opportunism

The best-known scholarly IB piece discussing opportunism in the intra-MNE context is Kogut and Zander's (1993) knowledge-based view of the MNE, which dismisses the opportunism concept in terms of relevance to the internal functioning of MNEs. This article offers no alternative behavioral assumption beyond the bounded rationality concept. Verbeke (2003), discussing Kogut and Zander's work, indeed notes a problem with the Williamsonian TCE logic wherein bounded rationality is viewed primarily as a constraint facing any economic actor, and actively managing opportunism becomes the key challenge that arises in this constrained universe. However, in contrast to Kogut and Zander (1993), who reject the opportunism concept altogether and focus on the MNE's alleged, superior knowledge combination capabilities *vis-à-vis* markets, Verbeke (2003) suggests that the key governance challenge for the MNE appears to be the creation of value by economizing on bounded rationality, and the problem of opportunism, though important, is merely a constraint. Here, the bounded rationality concept may need to be somewhat extended so as to address the specificities of internal MNE management. Verbeke and Yuan (2005) extend the bounded rationality concept in the context of MNEs with widely dispersed, specialized knowledge, and argue that bounded rationality in such MNEs has four main sources, with the first two being the conventional ones: (1) incomplete information; (2) limited managerial information-processing capacity; (3) multifacetedness of information, with different economic actors inside the MNE selecting different information facets as the basis of their biased decision-making, thereby typically triggering head office–subsidiary conflicts (this is an issue of selectively picking items from the same overall information sets); (4) divergence in judgment when contemplating identical information, as an outcome of a differential functional/educational background and experience in the MNE. As regards the latter two points, common manifestations of bounded rationality within the MNE appear to be the head office managers' choice of different information facets than those selected by foreign subsidiary managers, and the more negative assessment of autonomous projects arising in foreign subsidiaries as compared to the choices and assessments made by the foreign subsidiary managers themselves. Various best practices, such as giving seed money to subsidiaries, formally requesting subsidiary proposals, allowing some subsidiaries to act as incubators for new ideas and developing intra-MNE subsidiary networks, have been shown to alleviate bounded rationality challenges, but obviously subject to the constraint that implementing these best practices comes with a cost attached (Birkinshaw and Hood, 2000; Verbeke, 2009).

Verbeke (2003) argues that the closest link between opportunism and value creation may be the intrinsic value arising from a reputation for not acting opportunistically, whether in the context of internal or external contracts (compare with Hill, 1990). A reduced role for opportunism in MNE internal governance is also suggested by the fact that opportunistic managers in the Williamsonian sense seldom continue to work in large, modern MNEs over prolonged periods of time (Rugman and Verbeke, 2003). The problem with Verbeke's view, however, is that proposing a hierarchy among behavioral assumptions in terms of relevance to managers (bounded rationality being the primary managerial challenge, and opportunism only a secondary one), while perhaps useful for managerial purposes, hardly constitutes a proper foundation for general IB theory, unless it could be convincingly demonstrated that failed human commitments beyond those triggered by bounded rationality systematically disappear after internalization has taken place.

Mark Casson's (2000) Perspective on Opportunism

Casson (2000) has suggested an ambitious new agenda for research on the MNE, focused on information cost economizing, in line with Egelhoff's (1988) classic work, thereby moving away from conventional TCE and resource-based theories: 'Transaction cost analysis . . . explains the boundaries of the firm extremely well . . . What lies inside the boundaries of the firm is not explained so well, however, because this is not the focus of the theory' (Casson, 2000, p. 118). He further argues that the main challenge for companies is the efficient integration of activities ranging from procurement to marketing 'through the structuring of information flow', thereby 'dictating the internal organization of the firm' (ibid.). Casson's perspective is one that allows for opportunism, particularly as regards transactions for intermediate product flows, which have been the traditional focus of internalization theory (although even there, some transaction costs, such as determining intermediate product specifications, may be incurred without opportunism being present). However, MNE theorizing needs to refocus on the role of information costs, especially the information costs that are 'independent of any specific transaction . . . [and] . . . can only be attributed to large sets of transactions' (ibid., p. 122). Casson's perspective implies, *inter alia*, that some types of information are more costly to communicate than others. Communication costs are incurred even when information is truthful, again if no party to a transaction would benefit from providing false information (i.e. absent opportunism).

The problem with Casson's perspective is similar to Verbeke's (2003): opportunism is presented as a critical behavioral assumption in the realm of determining firm boundaries (e.g. entry mode choice in the MNE context), but then largely disappears from the analytical picture when studying internal MNE governance: 'lying would normally be self-defeating in activities [related to the information-processing demands of procurement and marketing]. The key to success is to process information efficiently, and not to invest at great expense in checking that every item of information supplied by other people is true' (Casson, 2000, p. 125). Casson then proposes a number of useful principles of efficient information processing inside the firm, especially the principle of sequential information collection, meaning that 'a sequential investigation strategy confers option value. The option value arises from the costs that are saved from avoiding the collection of unnecessary information' (ibid., p. 135). In addition, Casson (ibid., p. 145) argues that over time the more established firm (with a focus on market-making companies) may need skill sets different from those that led to its original, entrepreneurial success: the diagnostic skills required (e.g. processing information on unexpected cost increases or slumps in demand) are different from the initial prospecting skills (e.g. processing information on new market opportunities). Here, the information-processing challenges faced by MNEs are typically more severe than those found in domestic contexts, given the presence of, e.g., cultural differences and the higher number of sources of environmental volatility.

Casson's analysis is largely based on the behavioral assumption of meta-rationality, meaning that decision-makers take into account information costs when deciding how to come to a decision (e.g. they adopt standard procedures in a succession of similar situations characterized by uncertainty) (Casson and Wadeson, 2000). In this context of information cost economizing, Casson implicitly rejects the importance of failed commitments and the need for preventive or mitigating action against such failure. The key types of costs relevant to internal MNE decision-making are 'the costs of handling information which is believed to be honest. The information may not be entirely accurate because of measurement error, and errors may be aggravated by the incompetence of those who are responsible for making observations. Nevertheless, the quality of the information will not be improved significantly by altering incentives, because those involved have no particular reason to lie.' This last statement is particularly important because it assumes that, save simple human error/functional incompetence, failed commitments will normally occur only when there are reasons to lie, i.e. when substantial benefits would accrue to the individual(s) providing false information. In practice, however, it is our view that there may not only be good reasons to lie, but also other reasons than opportunism explaining (beyond functional incompetence) why failed commitments may occur, thereby negatively affecting firm-level performance.

Anoop Madhok's (2006a) Perspective on Opportunism

Madhok (2006a), while not focused on the issue of information costs *per se*, provides an original storyline with a starting point and conclusion similar to those of Verbeke and Casson above. The common starting point is that TCE-based analysis may be particularly useful when the firm emerges (following a Coasian logic), but much less so when studying management inside the firm that is concerned with improving value creation (Madhok, 2006a, p. 116). Madhok accepts the presence of Williamsonian opportunism inside the firm, but views it as '*relatively* less important' as compared to the need for knowledge management: 'In spite of the (occasional) acts of opportunism, building trust relations may have a greater general payoff' (ibid., p. 119). Here, individuals are viewed as having 'at their core' the potential for both opportunistic and trusting behavior, with managerial action capable of influencing which side will prevail inside the firm. Firms incur both Type A costs to manage opportunism and Type B costs required to manage knowledge flows. Type B costs are essentially the same as Casson's information-processing costs that cannot be attributed to individual transactions or Verbeke and Yuan's (2005) suggested investments in bounded rationality economizing, but with an emphasis on intra-MNE, relationship-building elements such as the fostering of 'greater cognitive alignment . . . so as to "lubricate" the coordinating interface and increase actors' receptivity toward one another' (Madhok, 2006a, p. 112). Madhok's useful contribution to the scholarly literature is that a relatively greater focus on Type B costs *vis-à-vis* Type A ones, especially in knowledge-intensive firms facing strong pressure to innovate, will lead to increased value creation over time, and may, through the infusion of trust elements, actually reduce the propensity for opportunistic behavior.

The above perspective is similar to Madhok's (1995) celebrated exposition on trust in international joint ventures. In reflecting on his *JIBS* decade award-winning 1995 article, Madhok (2006b) proposed that if opportunism is assumed to be rare, then non-opportunism (trustworthiness) is the more likely condition. He suggested that the value creation from assuming trust can outweigh the costs associated with the occasional cases of partner opportunism. Madhok (2006b, p. 9) specifically argued that 'a more holistic approach towards trust and opportunism, and perhaps a re-examination of deep-seated and implicit assumptions may change firms' attitudes and behavior towards their international partnerships'.

Importantly, the same conceptual problem arises as observed in Verbeke's (2003) and Casson's (2000) approaches described above. Opportunism inside the firm is viewed largely as a constraint, and is perceived as having been given too much attention in mainstream TCE theory. Managers should therefore focus more on bounded rationality economizing/value creation, with the substance of bounded rationality being somewhat extended so that it can address the specific knowledge management challenges in large organizations, thereby also reducing opportunism problems. No alternative behavioral assumption is introduced, and the outcome is one whereby only an extended (and improved) version of bounded rationality is assumed. This outcome is thus similar to the ones proposed by Casson, who built upon the meta-rationality concept and focused on information-processing cost optimizing, and Verbeke, who attempted to extend the bounded rationality concept to cover more adequately the information-processing challenges specific to MNEs (see especially Verbeke and Yuan, 2005). Madhok (2006a, p. 114) argues in this context: 'what if the failure to perform may be not for self-interested reasons but, rather, due to cognitive limitations of a genuine nature to do with bounded rationality, which results in different understandings, different interpretations of internal and external developments and the like?' He then concludes: 'management plays a dual function in guarding against dissipation of the rent stream, both checking opportunistic behavior and coordinating knowledge flows'. Here, investments in trust play an important role as a moderating variable between managerial costs and firm-level performance. Investments in trust do not merely allow reducing Type A costs in the firm, but also provide the seeds for future value creation through better knowledge management; i.e. they improve the return on Type B expenditures, with the manager being 'an orchestrator of knowledge flows . . . in order to generate surplus value through the cooperative efforts of individuals and teams' (ibid., p. 117).

The Unsolved Verbeke–Casson–Madhok Puzzle

Verbeke, Casson and Madhok, though criticizing the opportunism concept in terms of the alleged excessive weight given to it in TCE-based work, actually endorse the concept, but mainly in the context of setting the firm-level boundaries and selecting entry mode choices, rather than in the context of management inside the MNE. What occurs inside the MNE is then largely driven by sophisticated information-processing and knowledge management considerations. Such considerations allow economizing on (extended and contextually relevant forms of) bounded rationality. Madhok contends that this approach inside the firm may have further value-creating properties. In Casson's case, meta-rationality may not be consistent with Simon's definition of bounded rationality (see also Casson, 1999), but if one moves away from Simon's notion of mere satisficing, and bounded rationality is viewed as an envelope concept describing the various challenges of managing information faced by decision-makers given their limited information-processing capacity, and the complexity, uncertainty and geographic dispersion characterizing relevant information, meta-rationality (which reflects calculative/optimizing behavior rather than satisficing) can probably be subsumed within a bounded rationality envelope as Casson's (1999, p. 115) interpretation of imitation in business strategy illustrates.

The puzzling outcome of the Verbeke–Casson–Madhok approaches is that the presence of Williamsonian opportunism (whether in its dispositional or situational form) is accepted as an accurate behavioral foundation for scholarly work explaining – or militating against – failed human commitments in the context of establishing firms or redrawing firm-level boundaries. However, at the same time, economizing on opportunism is viewed as a rather minor challenge inside the firm, in spite of substantial empirical evidence suggesting otherwise, especially in the contemporary accounting and finance literatures that focus on agency and economic entrenchment challenges, but also in the rich scholarly work on the historical growth patterns and functioning of the world's largest enterprises; see, e.g., Chandler et al. (1997) on the rise of large firms and MNEs worldwide, and Chandler (1994) on the restructuring of American industry between 1960 and 1990. The governance challenges identified cannot be reasonably reduced to bounded rationality problems only, even if bounded rationality's substance is extended in the ways contemplated by Verbeke–Casson–Madhok, thereby making it an envelope concept to which new components can be added, as the situational context changes over time and space. In our view, the systematic occurrence of failed human commitments makes it essential to study MNE internal governance (as a general case for developing a theory of the firm, in line with Casson, 1987) using an appropriate behavioral assumption addressing the sources of failed commitments, in addition to the bounded rationality envelope concept accepted by most scholars. Casual observation of real-world problems in IB allows making three points regarding failed commitments inside the firm beyond bounded rationality.

First, Chandler (1994, pp. 17–18) powerfully describes the excessive commitment of senior management in large American firms towards unrelated diversification in the 1960s, fuelled by fast historical growth and an overrating of the 'potential of their enterprises' product-specific organizational capabilities. The information revolution reinforced a belief in the new view of management as a set of skills unrelated to specific products or industries.' In a number of cases, the outcome of this lack of importance attached to domain knowledge was a failure to achieve the expected growth rates and profitability promised to shareholders. In part this undoubtedly reflected a bounded rationality problem, since 'the top managers often had little specific knowledge of, or experience with, the technological processes and the markets of many of the businesses they had acquired' (p. 18) and these new businesses 'created an extraordinary demand for decision making that overloaded the corporate office' (ibid.). Here, Chandler observes that most large, diversified US MNEs managed a maximum of ten divisions before World War II and only a few firms had 25 divisions, whereas in 1969 several US MNEs managed between 40 and 70 divisions. However, there is more going on here than imperfect information availability or imperfect information processing, as the mere presence of such information problems should have led to the rapid shedding of difficult-to-manage, unrelated activities, once the performance effects proved unsatisfactory. The real source of the failure to make good on promises to shareholders was the perhaps good-faith – but certainly exaggerated – self-confidence in the senior management teams' organizational capabilities, a belief that was reinforced rather than moderated by the possibilities offered by modern information and communications technology. This exaggerated self-confidence led to organizational overcommitment, which then had to be scaled back at a later stage. The scaling back sometimes came in the form of hostile takeovers by short-term-oriented raiders and financial intermediaries, who prevented the required investments in R&D and capital equipment to sustain growth. As a result, many extant stakeholders, sometimes including the original shareholders, suffered the consequences of the broken promises by the senior management teams involved.

Second, senior management in large MNEs nowadays often publicly voices commitment towards decentralized entrepreneurship, but then fails to make good on such commitment. This common phenomenon has been demonstrated in a large body of literature on the challenges faced by enterprising subsidiaries that identify new market opportunities downstream or develop innovative solutions upstream in the value chain, but must then confront a corporate immune system that appears at odds with head office management's promises towards decentralized entrepreneurial initiatives; see Birkinshaw (2000) for an overview. The point is not only that head office managers face bounded rationality problems when trying to distinguish between valuable subsidiary initiatives and initiatives that can best be pursued outside of the company boundaries, especially when head office managers face information problems resulting from high cultural, economic and administrative distance. In addition, corporate managers' support expressed toward decentralized entrepreneurship may actually not be implemented when (especially peripheral) subsidiaries attempt to gain head office attention and resources for their initiatives. The 'let a thousand flowers bloom' philosophy is a powerful driver of variety generation in MNEs, but one that appears difficult to implement in practice when one arrives at the stage when head office management must actually select 'winners' and weed out 'losers'. Bouquet and Birkinshaw (2008) provide an overview of various governance design elements to facilitate peripheral units escaping from head office management's tendency towards *de facto* subsidiary initiative neglect, such as fostering successful representatives from the periphery being promoted to the head office or creating formal and informal opportunities for subsidiaries to showcase their capabilities etc. Unfortunately, it is clear from their analysis that the promise of decentralized entrepreneurship as a tool to serve long-term corporate objectives is often replaced by the pursuit of 'local' goals, paradoxically established at the head office level rather than the foreign affiliate level, since the MNE 'involves a cacophony of competing initiative attempts, with actors at all levels pushing for issues of particular importance to their own strategic agendas' (Bouquet and Birkinshaw, 2008, p. 490). Here, actual resource allocation then typically favors established businesses and managers with a long track record of success, which implies a reversal of the promised focus on decentralized entrepreneurship.

Third, although the two above points demonstrate that broken promises are common, even in the absence of opportunism, this concept remains of some relevance. A large literature describes the negative effects of managerial discretion in large firms, whether domestic firms or MNEs, with alleged managers' motivations ranging from Marris's (1964) growth maximization goals to Bertrand and Mullainathan's (2003) preference for a 'quiet life'. Here, information asymmetries might allow deviations from effort to increase shareholder profits, and introducing new governance mechanisms, such as better financial disclosure and oversight, may curb such discretionary behavior. In addition, information-processing requirements may be particularly severe in the MNE context (Tihanyi and Thomas, 2005). Managers supposedly committed to serving shareholders' interests are often observed failing on their commitments and pursuing other objectives. Luo (2005) enumerates several distinct components of MNE corporate governance design that should be considered as MNEs become more internationally diversified, in order to avoid collapses resulting from various forms of intentional deceit (Luo, 2005, p. 37). Useful governance design measures include, *inter alia*, larger and more culturally diverse board structures, more outside directors on corporate boards, more specialized committees within the corporate boards etc. In other words, opportunism in the sense of intentional deceit, resulting in failure to make good on commitments, actually is a common phenomenon, even at the highest levels in the MNE.

The three above elements suggest the importance of various sources of broken promises inside firms, *inter alia*, promises made to shareholders, top–down promises made to affiliates, bottom–up promises made by affiliates etc. The observation of broken promises resulting from what is ultimately imperfect effort towards actually fulfilling commitments is obviously not new, and has been studied in great depth by many scholars, e.g. in the context of managerial incentive problems and discretionary behavior. Particularly notable is the work of the late Harvey Leibenstein (1966, 1976), a Harvard economist. The problem with Leibenstein's *oeuvre*, however, is that his conceptualization of X-inefficiency requires assessment/measurement of observed performance *vis-à-vis* a theoretical optimum suggested by perfect competition in neoclassical economics. A more actionable approach is to compare the performance of real-world alternatives, i.e. discrete governance choices, each with particular bounded-reliability-economizing properties. In addition, Leibenstein viewed the 'personality' of economic actors as the ultimate source of X-inefficiency, with little analysis of the linkages between personality traits and observed inefficiency. In contrast, we view the occurrence of imperfect effort (whether by head office managers, subsidiary managers, non-managerial employees etc.) as a behavioral phenomenon that can inform comparative institutional analysis in well-defined situational contexts. Specific promises, whether in the context of individual transactions or large sets of transactions, may not be kept, and such failures may arise to a greater or lesser extent with different, discrete governance alternatives in place. In the next section, we present the results of an analysis of 30 MNE case studies, leading to the development of a new envelope concept complementing bounded rationality, namely bounded reliability, against which economizing action can be undertaken so as to avoid failed commitment or mitigate the effects of such failure.

CASE STUDY ANALYSIS

We draw on existing case studies to describe tentatively the potential mechanisms underlying failed human commitments, and the managerial actions undertaken to avoid or mitigate such failures, within the MNE context. We explore why managers fail on commitments, asking whether such failure results solely or partly from a strong-form self-interest, i.e. intentional deceit, or whether other mechanisms can trigger failure. To put it differently: what are managers actually safeguarding against when making governance choices affecting the MNE's internal functioning?

To answer the above questions we adopted a largely inductive design (though building upon the insights presented above) that utilized purposive or theoretical sampling (Yin, 1994; Eisenhardt, 1989), thereby selecting 30 case studies for our analysis. We selected case studies that focused on the nine global MNEs identified in Rugman and Verbeke (2004). These nine global MNEs, namely Canon, Coca-Cola, Flextronics, IBM, Intel, LVMH, Nokia, Royal Philips Electronics and Sony, are the only MNEs in the *Fortune Global 500* with over 20 percent of total sales revenues coming from each of the triad regions (North America, Europe and Asia). These MNEs, though having varying administrative heritages, all operate as differentiated networks, and are appropriate subjects for our analysis due to the size and scope of their operations as well as their observed success in addressing the complexities of major operations in all three triad regions, as demonstrated by the balanced geographic distribution of their sales.

The 30 cases describing various aspects of the internal functioning of the nine MNEs were also selected through purposive sampling to ensure the quality of the description of managerial decision-making and intentions. The cases were drawn exclusively from four recognized case producers and distributors, namely the Harvard Business School, Stanford University, the Ivey School of Business and the International Institute for Management Development (a list of the cases is provided in the Appendix). These case studies were typically crafted to offer insight into managerial responses to business opportunities and to the potential of failure associated with these opportunities, including the potential for failed human commitments. The objectivity of such cases can be debated as they may stretch information to make a particular point or to appease company management, who often must sign off on the final product (thereby making it less likely that intentional deceit is discussed). While this limitation poses a challenge to theory testing, the cases do offer a rich source of real-world examples useful to theory development regarding the mechanism(s) underlying failed commitments.

Our analysis of the cases focused on the underlying intentions involved in managerial decision-making and commitments. We started from our casual observations described in the previous section that MNE managers often fail to make good on their commitments, and that other mechanisms appear to be in play than opportunism as intentional deceit. Within this context, we searched for emerging themes within the aggregate of all the cases (Glaser and Strauss, 1967). Upon identifying themes from the aggregate, we looked across the cases on the nine MNEs for within-group similarities and inter-group differences (Eisenhardt, 1989). This process followed the four iterative stages of the constant comparative method, which begins with comparing incidents applicable to each category, integrating categories and their properties, focusing the theory and writing the theory (Shah and Corley, 2006).

Finally, we note that qualitative research often lacks robust reporting techniques, which leaves readers wondering how the conclusions were drawn from the data (Eisenhardt, 1989). Thus we utilized a summary theme support table and summary vignettes to illustrate the linkages between our propositions and the data (a theme quote support table, consistent with Sharma and Vredenburg, 1998, is available from the authors upon request).

RESULTS AND DISCUSSION

A number of themes emerged from our analysis of the global MNE cases, much in line with our prior casual observations. These themes suggest a plurality of mechanisms, including but not limited to opportunism as intentional deceit, that underlie both realized failed commitments and the adoption of safeguards against the potential for failed commitments. We suggest these individual mechanisms can be conceptualized under the broad envelope concept of bounded reliability. Bounded reliability reflects the fact that expressed (or reasonably expected) commitments to achieve a particular outcome do not always result in the promised outcome due to a variety of factors (but excluding elements such as technical error, functional incompetence or exogenous circumstances, e.g. unpredictable environmental change). Thus, whereas bounded rationality reflects the scarcity of mind, bounded reliability reflects the scarcity of making good on open-ended promises.

Our analysis identified three main themes or bounds on a manager's reliability to fulfill commitments.[3] We categorized these bounds on reliability as follows: opportunism as intentional deceit; benevolent preference reversal associated with reprioritization; and benevolent preference reversal associated with scaling back on overcommitment. In the following paragraphs we provide examples of each of these three types of bounds on reliability for illustrative purposes only. Table 2.1 provides a summary of the extent of support for these three themes in terms of literal representations (L), wherein the theme was a clear and explicit element in the cases (Christensen and Bower, 1996; Yin, 1994).[4] Thus, as regards bounded reliability, literal representation captures examples of: (1) observable commitments; (2) that are not fulfilled; (3) due to identifiable mechanisms;

Table 2.1   Prevalence of bounded reliability examples in MNE cases

	Opportunism	Benevolent preference reversal – reprioritization	Benevolent preference reversal – overcommitment
IBM	L	L/E	L/E
Sony	L	L	L
Royal Philips		E	
Nokia		L/E	L
Intel	L	L	
Canon	E	E	L
Coca-Cola	L	L	L
Flextronics			L
LVMH		E	E

Notes:
L = Literal replication of theme found in cases studied.
E = Possible economizing mechanisms found in cases studied.

(4) attributable to specific economic actors; (5) resulting in a dysfunctional consequence for the MNE (loss of efficiency/effectiveness).

Opportunistic Bounds on Reliability

In line with traditional TCE-based thinking, opportunism as intentional deceit or the threat of opportunistic behavior was an emergent theme in a number of the cases. One example of opportunism as a bound on reliability is found in the case discussing IBM's emerging business opportunity (EBO) program. While this was an important program, the then newly appointed CEO Lou Gerstner was concerned that managers might attempt to 'game the system' by reclassifying horizon 1 businesses as horizon 2 or 3 (horizon 1 businesses being traditional, established operations subject to standard performance targets, and horizons 2 and 3 being new and emerging businesses), thereby avoiding the requirement to meet specific targets. Here, the scenario was contemplated that employees/managers might act opportunistically by advancing their private interests by obfuscating the true nature of their operations.

Benevolent Preference Reversal – Reprioritization

A second emerging theme revolved around failed commitments stemming from benevolent preference reversal associated with good-faith reprioritization. This bound on reliability captures instances whereby managers make *ex ante* commitments in good faith (with benevolent intent), but the importance of that commitment diminishes over time (preferences are reordered). This theme is consistent with a substantial body of literature in psychology that has identified two main reasons for the occurrence of good-faith reprioritization. First is the psychological phenomenon of preference reversal over time (Tversky et al., 1990). The relevance to the bounded reliability concept is that a manager may make *ex ante* commitments to a particular course of action, e.g. based on a high probability of at least some payoff. In carrying out the commitment, however, other opportunities may arise with a higher payoff, at least in terms of net benefit categories perceived relevant by this manager, and therefore be valued more positively, causing a reversal in the original commitment. The relevant point here is not uncertainty reduction as time goes by (making the second course of action comparatively more attractive), which would make it a mere bounded rationality issue, but the fact that an original commitment was made to a contracting party to implement the first course of action (e.g. by a subsidiary manager to the MNE's head office), and that this contracting party, with a continued preference for the original course of action, might now suffer from the managerial reprioritization towards pursuing the second course of action. Obviously, a dysfunctionality negatively affecting the firm only results if the new course of action focuses too much on 'local' goals rather than 'global', firm-level goals, in spite of the manager believing the new course to be in the best interest of the firm.

The second major cause of reprioritization is the cognitive bias known as the time discounting bias. This bias suggests that individuals place a lower value on future events than on more proximate ones. Time discounting broadly encompasses any reason for caring less about a future consequence, and the associated preference for immediate utility over delayed utility (Frederick et al., 2002). Within the bounded reliability context, such discounting can cause managers to postpone fulfilling commitments (i.e. to procrastinate) to the point where such commitments can no longer be fulfilled. Again, this is not a bounded rationality problem in terms of incomplete information about the future or limited information-processing capacity, but rather a systemic source of individuals being unreliable, and engaging in procrastination over and over again, though knowing full well, based on past experience, that such behavior endangers making good on commitments (Steel, 2010).

Within the internal MNE context, this type of benevolent preference reversal in the case studies typically took the form of refocusing on local priorities at the expense of head office priorities or global priorities, which ultimately was detrimental to the firm. Refocusing on local priorities is particularly salient within MNEs as distance in time between a promise and its expected fulfillment can be further exacerbated by various other dimensions of distance (cultural, economic, institutional, geographic etc.). For subsidiary managers, *bona fide* local economic opportunities not condoned by the corporate head office may arise with rewards perceived as more immediate, while managers may also be insulated from some of the head office's monitoring apparatus by cultural and geographic distance. The cultural and spatial separation between head office and subsidiaries may also contribute to the cognitive distance between head office and subsidiary managers, thereby increasing the likelihood of a reordering of preferences after an original commitment is made.

However, local reprioritization does not imply that the problem of failed commitment always arises at the subsidiary level; it may also have its source at the head office. As one example, prior to IBM's emerging business opportunities (EBO) program noted above, commitments made to fund new business projects would dry up if the division overseeing the project came under financial pressure. IBM typically made an initial commitment to new business ventures in terms of large-scale funding. Over time, the priority of this commitment would change due to a reordering of priorities, whereby typically a focus on success in traditional business activities would replace the initial priority to developing the new business. This preference reversal resulted in the whittling away of the new venture's resource allocation and possibly the complete abandonment of the commitment to the new venture. The dysfunctional consequence of such failed commitments was that IBM senior management appeared unable to capitalize on emerging business opportunities.

Several successful cases illustrated the potential governance mechanisms for economizing on bounded reliability, in terms of reducing good-faith local reprioritization. We acknowledge the difficulty in making causal inferences based on the absence of a failed commitment. Nonetheless, the following three examples illustrate this point. First, the eventual implementation of IBM's EBO program suggests a useful mechanism for economizing on this expression of benevolent preference reversal. The EBO program utilized both milestones and frequent project reviews to ensure fulfilled commitments. These reviews did not have to be extensive or formal, as suggested by one IBM executive's comment that just a 30-minute conference call would typically help keep the discipline. Such frequent reviews, though coming with a cost, imply an increase in fulfilled commitments through keeping these commitments cognitively proximate. In general terms, the use of milestones allows decomposing large temporally distant commitments (e.g. profitability of business operations) into smaller, more temporally proximate components (e.g. market feasibility, prototype development, production, monthly sales growth). Temporally proximate commitments are less prone to preference reordering as the commitments remain 'top of mind' (cognitively proximate), in this case with IBM's business unit managers.

Second, Canon's new product development guidelines provided a mechanism for the regular and ongoing review of each innovation project's progress (e.g. new fax scanning technology). These guidelines broke long-term commitments into smaller, more temporally proximate commitments (milestones), and this undoubtedly helped reduce the occurrence of local reprioritization. The case of Canon also usefully illustrates the role of expectation alignments with and within development teams as a bounded-reliability-economizing mechanism. The *ex ante* alignment of expectations (as opposed to the simple alignment of incentives to curb opportunism) increased goal clarity and buy-in from the parties involved. The Canon example suggests that there were few failed commitments from the head office to development teams and vice versa.

Third, still in the realm of expectation alignment, it is worth noting that many of the MNE cases (e.g. Philips, Nokia, Canon and Sony) suggest the use of expatriates in foreign subsidiaries as a mechanism to develop and sustain a unified MNE vision. Expatriates' understanding of – and informal connections with – the head office offer the ability better to align the subsidiaries' and headquarters' expectations. Thus expatriates can serve as a bounded-reliability-economizing mechanism by bridging the cognitive distance between the head office and geographically distant affiliates. In doing so, subsidiary commitments to the head office are less likely to suffer from benevolent preference reversal, and thus are more likely to be fulfilled.

Benevolent Preference Reversal – Scaling Back on Overcommitment

A third major theme that emerged was the tendency for managers to fail due to benevolent preference reversal, in the form of *ex ante* overcommitments that had to be scaled back *ex post*. Overcommitment reduces reliability, and stems from the behavioral phenomena of impulsivity and an unrealistic belief in one's own abilities. There is a vast psychology literature on the personality, cognitive and behavioral aspects of impulsivity. The two types of impulsivity usually distinguished include dysfunctional impulsivity, i.e. the tendency to act with less forethought than most people of equal ability, with this tendency acting as a source of subsequent difficulties, and functional impulsivity, i.e. the tendency to act with relatively little forethought when such a style is optimal (Dickman, 1990). Dysfunctional impulsivity as a bound on reliability suggests that economic actors may commit themselves *ex ante* with little forethought, thus bringing into question their ability to fulfill the commitment made. From a more dynamic perspective, impulsivity as a bound on reliability can also occur when subsequent commitments are made with little reflection on their impact on current commitments.

The planning fallacy also contributes to overcommitment and has been studied in the planning fallacy biases literature (Buehler et al., 1994; Tversky and Kahneman, 1974). The planning fallacy means that planners rely on their best-case plans for a project (transaction) even though similar tasks in the past have typically run late. The planning fallacy leads managers to pursue initiatives that are unlikely to come in on budget, on time, or to ever deliver the expected returns (Lovallo and Kahneman, 2003). The planning fallacy was observed in Durand's (2003) study, which found that a high illusion of control increases positive forecast bias. This bound on reliability is also evidenced by economic actors' propensity to overlook failures because organizational learning produces a biased history: 'As learners settle into those domains in which they have competence and accumulate experience in them, they experience fewer and fewer failures. Insofar as they generalize that experience to other domains, they are likely to exaggerate considerably the likelihood of success' (Levinthal and March, 1993, p. 104). Here, an *ex ante* misconception of one's own abilities to fulfill a commitment results in an increased likelihood of failing to meet that commitment and to scale back.

Similar to what was noted in the context of good-faith reprioritization, the above sources of overcommitment cannot be simply reduced to bounded rationality problems, because sufficient objective information is usually available to assess correctly *ex ante* which commitments can be fulfilled and which ones reflect overcommitment. In addition, there is no conventional problem of limited human information-processing capacity, because past experience actually allows identifying with a high probability (and again *ex ante*) when an overcommitment is being made. Here, psychological biases lead to a neglect of both the objective information and the outcome of the rational processing of this information, in terms of what can actually be achieved and what cannot.

As one example, Flextronics made a commitment to Microsoft to manufacture the X-box game console with aggressive requirements such as a DVD port, Ethernet port, 733 MHz processor, high-end graphic chips, with a size no larger than a standard video cassette, that could be sold for under $400 and be on the shelves by October 2001 for the holiday season. Flextronics further committed to provide all this in conjunction with a simultaneous launch in Europe and North America using two separate manufacturing facilities. This already aggressive target was further complicated by Flextronics' lack of computer and coordinated global production experience. While Flextronics was able to produce the X-box, early shipments of the console did not meet expectations and Flextronics' inability to adopt a unified shop floor system for both the North American and European manufacturing plants became a stumbling block for the successful fulfillment of the firm's original commitment. For Microsoft this delay had the dysfunctional consequence of lost revenue due to insufficient product availability. While one could argue that Flextronics was merely acting opportunistically by knowingly overcommitting to Microsoft (i.e. engaging in intentional deceit), evidence from the case suggests that good-faith overcommitment represents the more likely bound on reliability. For example, the description of the Flextronics' entrepreneurial culture and the firm's history of success probably increased benevolent overcommitment by allowing impulsivity and self-evaluation bias to influence the scope of top management commitment made to Microsoft. Flextronics' CEO (at that stage Michael Marks) disliked both formal processes and large teams requiring several weeks before making decisions. He preferred a culture whereby individuals were allowed to make strong commitments, a culture he himself viewed as somewhat chaotic. While there are advantages to such an entrepreneurial culture, the combination of employee empowerment and lack of formal process within the firm allowed for individual impulsivity, and in its dysfunctional form this triggers overcommitment, to be scaled back at a later date. Flextronics was also subject to a self-evaluation bias stemming from the firm's rapid global expansion and growth in developing manufacturing competencies (including building keyboards and joysticks for

Microsoft). These past successes reduced Flextronics' senior management desire properly to assess the extent of the commitment that was being made.

As a second example, Coca-Cola provides another illustration of good-faith overcommitment. As CEO, the late Roberto Goizueta consistently set bold targets, e.g. a commitment to the board and shareholders to increase earnings by 18 percent and volume by 7 percent annually. As with the example above, this could simply be interpreted as a case of opportunism on the part of Goizueta so as to increase his power and personal financial rewards. The case, however, suggests that Goizueta truly believed Coke's global market potential was enormous, and he correctly stated that the firm had yet to overpromise. It is likely that in this case, self-evaluation bias and a high illusion of control were creating a positive forecast bias. Goizueta's reliance on Coke's past successes influenced his desire to assess properly the extent of the commitment he was making. This benevolent overcommitment set him and Coke's entire senior management up for subsequent failure. It later became apparent that Coke's senior management reverted to balance-sheet maneuvers to hit many of these targets, and by the time Douglas Daft took over as CEO, these commitments had to be scaled back considerably. In the end, Goizueta's overcommitment to the board and shareholders, and resulting failure, damaged Coke's reputation and had a negative impact on overall shareholder value.

IMPLICATIONS OF BOUNDED RELIABILITY

Illustrations from our case analysis combined with findings from the extant psychological and economics literature suggest that bounded reliability as an envelope concept includes the following three main components, within the context of global MNE internal governance: opportunism as intentional deceit, benevolent preference reversal as local reprioritization and benevolent preference reversal as scaling back on overcommitment, with both expressions of benevolent preference reversal resulting from decisions made in good faith, but ultimately with negative (dysfunctional) consequences for the firm.

Assessing Bounded Reliability

The adoption of behavioral envelope assumptions such as bounded rationality and bounded reliability, while managerially relevant, comes with the threat of reducing the parsimony of a theory. However, bounded reliability replacing the opportunism assumption does not detract from the parsimony of TCE/internalization theory, or more generally comparative institutional analysis. The multifacetedness of the bounded reliability envelope concept is also consistent with other TCE constructs. For example, in the MNE context we argued earlier that four dimensions of bounded rationality are critical, rather than merely the two conventional dimensions. We should also remember that Williamson distinguishes among six forms of asset specificity: site, physical, human, dedicated, brand name capital and temporal (see, e.g., Williamson, 1996a), and acknowledges various forms of uncertainty: behavioral, technological and demand related (Williamson, 1985).

In assessing bounded reliability, it is of course critical to demonstrate that each identified facet of bounded reliability is distinct and cannot simply be collapsed into the single facet of opportunism. As our case analyses suggest, each of the three bounded reliability

Table 2.2   Sources of bounded reliability and economizing mechanisms

Bounded reliability facet	Sources of bounded reliability (leading to failed commitments)	Economizing mechanisms	Specific examples of economizing
Opportunistic bounds	*Ex ante*, intentional false commitments and *ex post*, malevolent reneging on commitments (strong-form self-interest)	Interest alignment	• Contractual safeguards • Institutionalizing the importance of reputation
Benevolent preference reversal as reprioritization	Good-faith reordering of commitments over time (time discounting bias and changes in preference ordering)	• Expectation alignment • Continued cognitive proximity	• Joint goal development • Goal segmentation/ milestones • Frequent communication
Benevolent preference reversal as scaling back on overcommitment	Good-faith overcommitment (overconfidence bias and impulsivity)	Organizational routines for reducing individual evaluation bias and impulsivity	Multilevel decision processes

facets derives from different sources. Opportunism as intentional deceit is driven by strong-form self-interest; benevolent preference reversal as local reprioritization is driven by changes in preference ordering as new information becomes available and time discounting bias; benevolent preference reversal as scaling back on overcommitment is driven by impulsivity and self-assessment biases. Beyond the idiosyncratic sources of each bounded reliability facet, a distinction that is even more managerially relevant is that each of the three facets is associated with specific economizing mechanisms. For example, economizing on opportunism as intentional deceit can be achieved, *inter alia*, through interest alignment (e.g. by adopting similar parameters to determine performance bonuses of subsidiary managers and head office managers). Economizing on benevolent preference reversal as dysfunctional local reprioritization can occur, *inter alia*, through expectation alignment and increasing cognitive proximity. Economizing on benevolent preference reversal as scaling back on dysfunctional overcommitment may require, *inter alia*, organizational routines that limit individual impulsivity and biased assessments of actual capabilities. A summary of each distinct source of bounded reliability and related economizing mechanisms is provided in Table 2.2.

A conceptual focus on the firm's ability to economize on both bounded rationality and bounded reliability offers a number of advantages. First, it allows TCE (and more generally comparative institutional analysis) to operate as a dynamic theory, one that invites analysis on how bounded reliability develops in particular situational contexts. This is in sharp contrast with blindly accepting Williamson's (1993a) limited view of man, which pushes the case for systematic (and costly) safeguarding against worst-case scenarios, and basically shuts down any appetite for further in-depth analysis of the phenomenon, as shown above by the Verbeke–Casson–Madhok perspectives on the concept. Our approach also invites serious study of the reasons why opportunism as intentional deceit may be stronger in some situational contexts, whether at the firm level or societal level, than in others. For all the emphasis on the need for adapting to changed environmental circumstances, Williamson's approach remains largely timeless (Slater and Spencer, 2000). Introducing elements that capture dynamics into the theory is a matter of urgency (Buckley and Casson, 1988b). While Buckley and Casson suggest that looking at costs over time or at the direction taken by the entrepreneur might be the appropriate way forward, we suggest a focus on economizing on bounded reliability and bounded rationality, which is a dynamic process in and of itself.

Second, Holt (2004) has argued that managers act from a complex set of motives, and rather than adopting standard modes of judgment or selection, remain responsive to the dynamics of an evolving set of cognitive and social influences. Bounded reliability captures the dynamic nature of managerial decision-making through the inclusion of benevolent preference reversal. As a result, we eliminate the danger voiced by Ghoshal (2005) that a wrong message is being sent to students, scholars, managers and society at large when governance mechanisms in organizations are described as serving merely to protect against strong-form self-interest.

Third, through introducing governance mechanisms economizing on bounded reliability, the net benefits of internal organization *vis-à-vis* markets, e.g. in terms of the former's ability to see through innovation processes in their entirety, may be increased further, whether opportunism mitigation is a prevailing consideration or quasi-absent. Some of the bounded-reliability-economizing mechanisms might, with effort, also be replicated in hybrids. Most TCE hybrid governance research has focused on equity versus non-equity joint ventures, with equity ventures approximating what occurs inside the single firm (Beamish and Banks, 1987; Hennart, 1988; Poppo and Zenger, 1995; Geyskens et al., 2006). TCE runs into problems, however, when attempting to explain cooperative behavior in the absence of credible commitments. Thus much of the literature in these areas has identified inter-organizational trust as a key factor in contributing to hybrids' success, the general view being that trust has a positive effect on hybrids' performance (Krishnan et al., 2006). Bounded reliability provides an alternative explanation for the attractiveness of hybrid governance. For example, the trust literature suggests that frequent interaction of contracting parties increases trust and therefore levels of cooperation. An alternative interpretation, however, is that frequent interactions allow economizing on bounded reliability by increasing cognitive proximity (commitments are kept 'top of mind'), thus reducing the likelihood of preference reordering and time discounting bias.

Fourth, within both single firms and hybrids, economizing on benevolent preference reversal as reprioritization can also be activated through the *ex ante* alignment of the transacting parties' expectations. By crafting a shared vision of the future, parties will become less likely to reorder their preferences over time. To assist in this process, milestones or frequent contact also ensure that parties' preference orderings remain consistent with the original commitment. In this regard, the role of the 'contract' extends beyond enforcing transactions towards ensuring that all parties understand future expectations. Economizing on bounded reliability through, *inter alia*, *ex ante* expectation alignment, frequent communication, subgoals and milestone specification etc. also allows for hybrid governance forms to be applied in transactions involving highly specific assets. In line with Ghoshal's (2005) perspective, the main outcome of bounded reliability economizing may be to articulate better – and to reinforce – the common purpose of the transacting parties.

Bounded Reliability and MNE Research

We now very briefly explore the implications of bounded reliability for MNE research. For clarity of exposition, we distinguish among three key areas of research, namely location, internalization and management of proprietary knowledge (see Dunning's 1988 eclectic paradigm).

First, on the issue of location advantages, bounds on reliability are likely to be influenced by the distance (e.g. cultural, economic, institutional, geographic) between the MNE's home and host countries. Opportunism as intentional deceit can be expected to increase when crossing borders, due to the divergence in national institutional structures that make enforcement of open-ended commitments more difficult, especially if intentional deceit can take advantage of latent societal xenophobia *vis-à-vis* foreign business interests in a host country environment, leading macro-level institutional safeguards (including the application of the rule of law by the judiciary) to break down. Informal safeguards such as reputation effects may also be diminished as the MNE becomes more geographically diversified, and moves towards higher-distance host country environments where the firm's reputation is largely unknown. Benevolent preference reversal as local reprioritization can increase due to cross-border economic and institutional differences that make *ex ante* expectation alignment more difficult. Cultural and geographic distance can also increase the cognitive distance between actors inside the MNE. As described earlier, greater cognitive distance suggests that original commitments are no longer 'top of mind', thus allowing for preference reversals. Finally, overcommitment may also increase, e.g. as head office managers make commitments based on previous successes of operations in low-distance countries that do not necessarily transfer to new, higher-distance target countries. The scale of potential opportunities in the international context may also offer more 'temptations', thus magnifying impulsivity's influence on overcommitment (e.g. large commitments to new opportunities jeopardizing the ability to fulfill current commitments). The general implication of bounded reliability for location advantages is thus that expansion into higher-distance countries is likely to amplify reliability problems, both inside the MNE and in transactions with third parties, thereby increasing the vulnerability of the MNE when it attempts to access and exploit host country location advantages, whether in the sphere of input markets or output markets. From an MNE network perspective, the prediction is that bounded reliability will become more of a problem in cases of unrelated as compared to related geographic diversification.

Bounded reliability can also inform research on the regionalization phenomenon. The majority of the world's largest companies are home region oriented (Rugman and Verbeke, 2004). The various distance components with host regions are likely to increase at the micro-level the cognitive distance between home region head office and host region subsidiaries, thereby increasing benevolent preference reversal challenges. If bounded reliability levels are systematically higher when expanding to host triad regions, the question arises whether this higher propensity towards unfulfilled commitments of subsidiaries to the head office, and vice versa, should trigger limits on FSA transfers and on the allocation of subsidiary charters in host regions. The question also arises whether the strong likelihood of higher bounded reliability across regions implies that the nine global MNEs covered in our case studies have developed superior bounded reliability economizing routines as compared to their single-region counterparts.

Still in the realm of location, countries that facilitate bounded reliability economizing are likely to be more attractive to MNE entry and expansion. Bounded-reliability-economizing country-specific advantages (CSAs) include institutions that promote fulfilling commitments and punish reneging on them. While legal institutions such as stringent property rights protection rules obviously allow to economize on opportunism as intentional deceit, other institutions, such as industry groups and associations open to foreign investors, may serve to align expectations of members (e.g. through the development of industry standards), thereby reducing preference reversals (e.g. in the realm of local subsidiary management being expected to enforce stringent product health and safety controls). Public institutions can also be instrumental to bounded-reliability-economizing CSAs if they introduce policy routines that limit the possibilities for single actors (such as a country's head of state) or small groups in the executive branch of government to overturn prior government commitments towards foreign investors. For example, a layer of civil servants and bureaucracy just below government-level decision-makers limits the impulsivity and overconfidence bias found in individuals and small groups (as in 'let's nationalize the oil industry and redistribute the wealth it creates to our citizens'), and thus increases the likelihood of a fulfilled commitment. From a normative perspective the question arises, in the context of government–MNE relations: what governance mechanisms provide the best bounded-reliability-economizing outcomes? For example, beyond legal institutions, what other steps can emerging market countries take to facilitate bounded reliability economizing in their country?

Second, as we indicated at the outset of this chapter, the intellectual stimulus for developing the bounded reliability concept was born out of internalization theory (TCI) thinking, in part due to the theory's reduced emphasis on opportunism. The internalization perspective has provided great insight on MNE entry mode choice (see, *inter alia*, Buckley and Casson, 1998a), and adopting the bounded reliability concept should influence this area of research. For example, if benevolent preference reversal challenges are greater in more distant host country contexts, the question arises as to the impact on internalization levels, with unified governance probably better at economizing on this form of bounded reliability than alternative entry modes. As regards international joint ventures with culturally, economically, institutionally and geographically distant partners, we should see success being more dependent upon explicit *ex ante* communication to encourage expectation alignment and alignment of preference ordering, and increased use of subgoals and milestones to reduce the time discounting bias.

In terms of internal MNE governance, a specific area of IB research to be influenced by the adoption of bounded reliability is the analysis of head office–subsidiary relationships. As our analysis has indicated, the use of expatriates in subsidiaries may facilitate expectation alignment between subsidiary and head office. Expatriates also offer informal network linkages with the head office that guarantee frequent communication and keep commitments more cognitively proximate. The prediction is therefore that subsidiaries with expatriates are more likely to fulfill commitments to the head office. If so, the question arises whether this effect will be magnified in more cognitively distant environments.

Bounded reliability and the subsidiary context also suggest a number of interesting questions surrounding subsidiary initiatives (Birkinshaw, 1997). In most cases, economizing on bounded reliability would be desired in order to ensure fulfilled commitments from head office to subsidiaries, and vice versa. Reducing overcommitment (e.g. keeping in check impulsivity and overconfidence bias), however, may actually imply setting limits on autonomous subsidiary initiatives, resulting in missed opportunities for the MNE. Interesting questions in this area include: Do higher levels of autonomous subsidiary initiatives correspond with more severe challenges of bounded reliability in subsidiaries? Do MNEs differentiate bounded-reliability-economizing mechanisms imposed on their subsidiaries depending upon these subsidiaries' role or charter in the internal network?

Third, as regards ownership advantages (or FSAs), or more broadly the management of proprietary knowledge, the main point to be remembered from the above analysis is that continuous attention devoted to mechanisms to economize on bounded reliability, such as knowledge management routines, may itself become one of the MNE's core FSAs. The key question then arises which types of MNEs with which types of knowledge assets are most likely to specialize in developing FSAs in bounded reliability reduction. Given that investment in bounded reliability reduction is costly, the additional question is how much investment might be optimal, and how this optimal level of investment might affect both the scale and scope of the MNE's international diversification efforts, and the management of the resulting internal network.

CONCLUSION

Bounded reliability as an envelope concept captures the mechanisms underlying and linking failed human commitments. Bounded reliability is dispositional, as is the case with bounded rationality: in any managerial context, one can always assume some level of intrinsic scarcity of effort to making good on open-ended promises, just as one can always assume some intrinsic scarcity of mind. However, the observed types of bounded reliability and the losses in efficiency and effectiveness these engender, as well as the remediating governance mechanisms, are largely situational, as is also the case with bounded rationality. In other words, an *ex ante* comparative institutional assessment is always required to assess whether economizing on bounded rationality and bounded reliability can reasonably be achieved, given the presence of real-world, discrete governance alternatives.

We identified two broad sources of bounded reliability inside the MNE, namely opportunism as intentional deceit, and benevolent preference reversal in the form of local reprioritization and overcommitment requiring subsequent scaling back of promises. The bounded reliability concept offers a more complete behavioral understanding – as compared with Williamson's view – of the reasons why economic actors inside the MNE fail to fulfill commitments. Bounded reliability as a behavioral phenomenon can affect performance at various levels inside the MNE: it can therefore influence the relative efficiency and effectiveness of alternative governance mechanisms, assuming these alternatives have idiosyncratic bounded-reliability-economizing properties.

Williamson's behavioral assumptions suggest a view of human nature whereby failed commitments need not occur all the time, but due to bounds on rationality it is difficult to assess *ex ante* who might act opportunistically. As a result, all transacting parties should be treated assuming that the worst-case scenario could transpire. Importantly, if such a worst-case scenario did materialize, the probability of amicably resolving the conflict at hand and sustaining the extant relationship would appear remote: few people would choose to work again with a party that has knowingly and willingly put a knife in their back. In other words, contracting parties are asked to focus on safeguarding against actions whose occurrence would *de facto* terminate their relationship, and the risks associated with such actions largely determine governance choices. But in the context of MNEs (and for that matter in many other governance contexts), most failures to expend sufficient effort to fulfill a commitment do not lead to automatic relationship termination. Rather, such failures lead to feedback/attribution of why they occurred, to a dialogue on how to improve performance, to corrective action so as to avoid similar failures in the future etc. In other words, save the case of intentional deceit, which might lead the guilty party to be expelled from the firm (or more generally the relationship to be terminated), the first assumption is that wrong courses of action were probably pursued in good faith, and the question then becomes whether governance redesign can prevent this problem from occurring again with the same parties being involved. In this context, the joint adoption of bounded rationality and bounded reliability as behavioral assumptions in management research suggests that all individuals have the propensity to fail on commitments, without the need to focus exclusively on the probability that self-interest-seeking with guile might materialize. Here, the optimal mix of governance elements to reduce bounded reliability problems is fully situational, meaning that one need not necessarily prepare for the worst-case scenario (i.e. to invest heavily in *ex ante* opportunism avoidance and *ex post* opportunism mitigating measures).

The concept of bounded reliability offers a non-ideological view of human nature: human beings do not need to be assumed intrinsically trustworthy versus non-trustworthy, or having a strong inclination to do good or bad. They just have a propensity towards imperfect effort to make good on commitments. Optimal governance as well as governance redesign precisely result from past experience with such imperfect effort, and are achieved through a combination of trial-and-error and emulating best practices observed inside and outside the organization ('rights from wrongs').

Our new perspective should benefit future MNE research, but the current chapter is not without limitations. Most notably, our inductive approach with case studies, though informed by some prior, casual observation of various forms of bounded reliability, is merely a first attempt to identify broad classes of sources of failed commitments inside MNEs. Future research is needed to further delineate the core facets of bounded reliability and the corresponding economizing governance mechanisms. While the current chapter is but a first step, the rationale for developing the bounded reliability concept is to capture, in a comprehensive and testable fashion, the critical mechanisms underlying failed human commitments. As research into bounded reliability progresses, the potential for objective measures and scale development of the construct will be realized. As we noted in our review of the opportunism papers in IB, the direct measurement of opportunism is currently missing in most empirical work that assumes opportunism. The development of clear bounded reliability measures will not only refine the concept, but will also allow for empirical testing of the interaction levels with more established TCE measures such as asset specificity, uncertainty and frequency. The adoption of more accurate behavioral assumptions should improve MNE theory, in terms of predicting the selection and retention of specific governance mechanisms in particular contexts, and in terms of normative implications, and by doing so should make theory more relevant to MNE managers. In many cases, the core TCE predictions might remain valid, such as the predicted positive impact of asset specificity (or R&D and advertising expenditures) on internalization levels, but the underlying explanation of this phenomenon should be more accurate than the Williamsonian one, thereby also improving TCE's legitimacy in the social sciences.

Finally, the development of bounded reliability in the IB context should spill over to the more general management literature. It is fitting that the study of the MNE as the general case – i.e. the case whereby distance always does matter – in this instance grappling with the foundational assumptions of human nature, may inform the broader theory of the firm, and may result in a new dialogue between TCE scholars and researchers in other management and organization sub-disciplines. Ultimately, the key point for managers – especially for those faced with high-distance situational contexts – is simple: Do not attribute to malevolence what can more reasonably be explained as good-faith reversal of preference.

NOTES

1. The authors presented a first version of this chapter at the Academy of Management 2004 Meetings in New Orleans, and have been refining the ideas presented there since that date. Verbeke and Kenworthy (2008) and Verbeke (2009) also refer to the bounded reliability concept, but build on earlier drafts of the present chapter, which appeared in *Journal of International Business Studies*, **40**(9), 1471–95.
2. Dunning (2003) notes that from the citations in Buckley and Casson's (1976) classic book, *The Future of the Multinational Enterprise*, it would appear that the authors did not draw (or did not think they needed to draw) upon the writings of organizational theorists such as Williamson to expound or justify their own particular theoretical model of the MNE.
3. Another recurring theme associated with failed commitments was the influence of changes in the external environment on managers' ability to fulfill commitments. Such factors, however, are already largely captured within TCE through the concepts of uncertainty and bounded rationality, and thus do not contribute directly to the development of the bounded reliability concept, though it can be argued that environmental changes can act as the trigger for a variety of preference reversals, whether benevolent or not.
4. Ideally, we would also like our analysis to provide examples in the form of theoretical replication, wherein contrasting results are found for predictable reasons (Yin, 1994). While some examples from the cases provide evidence of bounded-reliability-reducing processes and associated fulfilled commitments, the nature of the cases studied did not allow us to conclude definitively whether the absence of processes to reduce bounded reliability would in fact lead to more unfulfilled commitments. We thank an anonymous reviewer for pointing out this limitation.

REFERENCES

Afuah, A. (2001), 'Dynamic boundaries of the firm: are firms better off being vertically integrated in the face of a technological change?', *Academy of Management Journal*, **44**(6): 1211–28.

Alvarez, S., Barney, J. and Bosse, D. (2003), 'Trust and its alternatives', *Human Resource Management*, **42**(4): 393–404.

Axelrod, R. (1984), *The Evolution of Cooperation*, New York: Basic Books.

Beamish, P. and Banks, J. (1987), 'Equity joint ventures and the theory of the multinational enterprise', *Journal of International Business Studies*, **18**(2): 1–16.

Bertrand, M. and Mullainathan, S. (2003), 'Enjoying the quiet life? Corporate governance and managerial preferences', *Journal of Political Economy*, **111**: 1043–75.

Birkinshaw, J. (1997), 'Entrepreneurship in multinational corporations: the characteristics of subsidiary initiatives', *Strategic Management Journal*, **18**(3): 207–29.

Birkinshaw, J. (2000), *Entrepreneurship in the Global Firm*, London: Sage.

Birkinshaw, J. and Hood, N. (2000), 'Unleash innovation in foreign subsidiaries', *Harvard Business Review*, **79**(3): 131–7.

Boerner, C. and Macher, J. (2001), 'Transaction cost economics: an assessment of empirical research in the social sciences', unpublished manuscript, Georgetown University.

Bouquet, C. and Birkinshaw, J. (2008), 'Managing power in the multinational corporation: how low-power actors gain influence', *Journal of Management*, **34**(3): 539–62.

Brouthers, K.D., Brouthers, L.E. and Werner, S. (2003), 'Transaction cost-enhanced entry mode choices and firm performance', *Strategic Management Journal*, **24**(12): 1239–48.

Buckley, P. and Casson, M. (1976), *The Future of the Multinational Enterprise*, London: Macmillan.

Buckley, P. and Casson, M. (1998a), 'Analyzing foreign market entry strategies: extending the internalization approach', *Journal of International Business Studies*, **29**(3): 539–62.

Buckley, P. and Casson, M. (1998b), 'Models of the multinational enterprise', *Journal of International Business Studies*, **29**(1): 21–45.

Buehler, R., Griffin, D. and Ross, M. (1994), 'Exploring the "planning fallacy": why people underestimate their task completion times', *Journal of Personality and Social Psychology*, **67**: 366–81.

Carroll, G. and Teece, D. (1999), *Firms, Markets, and Hierarchies: The Transaction Cost Economics Perspective*, Oxford: Oxford University Press.

Carter, R. and Hodgson, G. (2006), 'The impact of empirical tests of transaction cost economics on the debate of the nature of the firm', *Strategic Management Journal*, **27**: 461–76.

Casson, M. (1987), *The Firm and the Market*, Cambridge, MA: MIT Press.

Casson, M. (1999), 'The organisation and evolution of the multinational enterprise: an information cost approach', *Management International Review*, Special Issue 1999/1: 77–121.

Casson, M. (2000), *The Economics of International Business*, Cheltenham, UK and Northampton, MA, USA: Edward Elgar.

Casson, M. and Wadeson, N. (2000), 'Bounded rationality, meta-rationality and the theory of international business', in M. Casson (ed.), *The Economics of International Business*, Cheltenham, UK and Northampton, MA, USA: Edward Elgar, pp. 94–116.

Chandler, A.D. Jr (1994), 'The competitive performance of U.S. industrial enterprises since the Second World War', *Business History Review*, **68**(1), 1–72.

Chandler, A.D. Jr, Amatori, F. and Hikino, T. (eds) (1997), *Big Business and the Wealth of Nations*, Cambridge: Cambridge University Press.

Chen, L.Y. (2007), 'TCE mode selection criteria and performance', *Journal of American Academy of Business*, **11**(1): 244–52.

Chen, L.Y. and Mujtaba, B. (2007), 'The choice of entry mode strategies and decisions for international market expansion', *Journal of American Academy of Business*, **10**(2): 322–37.

Chen, S. (2005), 'Extending internalization theory: a new perspective on international technology transfer and its generalization', *Journal of International Business Studies*, **36**: 231–45.

Christensen, C. and Bower, J. (1996), 'Customer power, strategic investment, and the failure of leading firms', *Strategic Management Journal*, **17**: 197–218.

Coase, R. (1937), 'The nature of the firm', *Economica*, **4**(3): 386–405.

Conner, K. and Prahalad, C. (1996), 'A resource-based theory of the firm: knowledge versus opportunism', *Organization Science*, **7**(5): 477–501.

Delerue-Vidot, H. (2006), 'Opportunism and unilateral commitment: the moderating effect of relational capital', *Management Decision*, **6**(44): 737–51.

Dickman, S. (1990), 'Functional and dysfunctional impulsivity: personality and cognitive correlates', *Journal of Personality and Social Psychology*, **58**(1): 95–102.

Dunning, J. (1988), 'The eclectic paradigm of international production: a restatement and some possible extensions', *Journal of International Business Studies*, **19**(1): 1–31.

Dunning, J. (2003), 'Some antecedents of internalization theory', *Journal of International Business Studies*, **34**(2): 108–15.

Durand, R. (2003), 'Predicting a firm's forecasting ability: the roles of organizational illusion of control and organizational attention', *Strategic Management Journal*, **24**(9): 821–38.

Dyer, J.H. (1997), 'Effective interfirm collaboration: how firms minimize transaction costs and maximize transaction value', *Strategic Management Journal*, **18**(7): 535–56.

Dyer, J.H. and Singh, H. (1998), 'The relational view: cooperative strategy and sources of interorganizational competitive advantage', *The Academy of Management Review*, **23**(4): 660–79.

Egelhoff, W. (1988), *Organizing the Multinational Enterprise: An Information-Processing Perspective*, Cambridge, MA: Ballinger.

Eisenhardt, K.M. (1989), 'Building theories from case study research', *The Academy of Management Review*, **14**(4): 532–50.

Ferrin, D. and Dirks, K. (2003), 'The use of rewards to increase and decrease trust: mediating processes and differential effects', *Organization Science*, **14**(1): 18–31.

Frederick, S., Loewenstein, G. and O'Donoghue, T. (2002), 'Time discounting and time preference: a critical review', *Journal of Economic Literature*, **40**(2): 351–401.

Gambetta, D.G. (1988), 'Can we trust trust?', in D.G. Gambetta (ed.), *Trust*, New York: Basil Blackwell, pp. 213–37.

Geyskens, I., Steenkamp, J. and Kumar, N. (2006), 'Make, ally, or buy? A meta-analysis of transaction cost theory', *Academy of Management Journal*, **49**(3): 519–43.

Ghoshal, S. (2005), 'Bad management theories are destroying good management practices', *The Academy of Management Learning and Education*, **4**(1): 75–91.

Ghoshal, S. and Moran, P. (1996), 'Bad for practice: a critique of the transaction cost theory', *The Academy of Management Review*, **21**(1): 13–47.

Glaser, B.G. and Strauss, A.L. (1967), *The Discovery of Grounded Theory: Strategies For Qualitative Research*, Chicago, IL: Aldine.

Gomes-Casseres, B. (1990), 'Firm ownership preferences and host government restrictions: an integrated approach', *Journal of International Business*, **1**: 1–22.

Gulati, R. and Singh, H. (1998), 'The architecture of cooperation: managing coordination costs and appropriation concerns in strategic alliances', *Administrative Science Quarterly*, **43**(4): 781–814.

Heiman, B. and Nickerson, J. (2002), 'Towards reconciling transaction cost economics and the knowledge-based view of the firm: the context of interfirm collaborations', *Journal of the Economics of Business*, **9**(1): 97–116.

Hennart, J.F. (1982), *A Theory of Multinational Enterprise*, Ann Arbor, MI: University of Michigan Press.

Hennart, J.F. (1988), 'A transaction costs theory of equity joint ventures', *Strategic Management Journal*, **9**(4): 361–74.

Hennart, J.F. (1993), 'Explaining the swollen middle: why most transactions are a mix of "market" and "hierarchy"', *Organization Science*, **4**(4): 529–47.

Hennart, J.F. (2009), 'Down with MNE-centric theories. Market entry and expansion as the bundling of MNE and local assets', *Journal of International Business Studies*, **40**(9): 1432–54.

Hill, C.W. (1990), 'Cooperation, opportunism, and the invisible hand: implications for transaction cost theory', *The Academy of Management Review*, **15**(3): 500–513.

Hobbes, T. (1651), *Leviathan*, accessed March 2008 at http://studymore.org.uk/xhobint.htm.

Holt, R. (2004), 'Fear prudence: Hobbes and Williamson on the morality of contracting', *Journal of Economic Issues*, **38**(4): 1021–37.

Jap, S. and Anderson, E. (2003), 'Safeguarding interorganizational performance and continuity under ex post opportunism', *Management Science*, **49**(12): 1684–701.

Kogut, B. and Zander, U. (1993), 'Knowledge of the firm and the evolutionary theory of the multinational corporation', *Journal of International Business Studies*, **4**: 625–45.

Krishnan, R., Martin, X. and Noorderhaven, N. (2006), 'When does trust matter to alliance performance?', *Academy of Management Journal*, **49**(5): 894–917.

Leibenstein, H. (1966), 'Allocative efficiency versus X-efficiency', *American Economic Review*, **56**: 392–415.

Leibenstein, H. (1976), *Beyond Economic Man: A New Foundation for Microeconomics*, Cambridge, MA: Harvard University Press.

Levinthal, D. and March, J. (1993), 'The myopia of learning', *Strategic Management Journal*, **14**: 95–112.

Lovallo, D. and Kahneman, D. (2003), 'Delusions of success: how optimism undermines executives' decisions', *Harvard Business Review*, **81**(7): 56–63, 117.

Luo, Y. (2005), 'Corporate governance and accountability in multinational enterprises: concepts and agenda', *Journal of International Management*, **11**(1): 1–18.

Madhok, A. (1995), 'Revisiting multinational firms' tolerance for joint ventures: a trust-based approach', *Journal of International Business Studies*, **26**(1): 117–37.

Madhok, A. (2006a), 'Opportunism, trust and knowledge: the management of firm value and the value of firm management', in R. Bachmann and A. Zaheer (eds), *Handbook on Trust*, Cheltenham, UK and Northampton, MA, USA: Edward Elgar, pp. 107–23.

Madhok, A. (2006b), 'How much does ownership really matter? Equity and trust relations in joint venture relationships', *Journal of International Business Studies*, **37**: 4–11.

Marris, R. (1964), *The Economic Theory of Managerial Capitalism*, Glencoe, IL: Free Press.

Mayer, R., Davis, J. and Schoorman, F. (1995), 'An integrative model of organizational trust', *The Academy of Management Review*, **20**(3): 709–34.

McEvily, B., Perrone, V. and Zaheer, A. (2003), 'Trust as an organizing principle', *Organization Science*, **14**(1): 91–103.

Mill, J.S. (1867), *The Collected Works of John Stuart Mill*, ed. J.M. Robson, Toronto: University of Toronto Press, 1991.

Moran, P. and Ghoshal, S. (1996), 'Theories of economic organization: the case for realism and balance', *The Academy of Management Review*, **21** (1): 58–72.

Noorderhaven, N. (1994), 'Transaction cost analysis and the explanation of hybrid vertical interfirm relations', *Review of Political Economy*, **6**(1): 19–36.

Nooteboom, B., Berger, H. and Noorderhaven, N. (1997), 'Effects of trust and governance on relational risk', *The Academy of Management Journal*, **40**(2): 308–38.

North, D.C. (1990), *Institutions, Institutional Change and Economic Performance*, New York: Cambridge University Press.

Ouchi, W.G. and Price, R.L. (1993), 'Hierarchies, clans, and theory Z: a new perspective on organization development', *Organizational Dynamics*, **78**(7): 24–44.

Oviatt, B. and McDougall, P. (1994), 'Toward a theory of international new ventures', *Journal of International Business Studies*, **25**(1): 45–64.

Parkhe, A. (1993), 'Strategic alliance structuring: a game theoretic and transaction cost examination of interfirm cooperation', *Academy of Management Journal*, **36**(4): 794–829.

Plato (approx. 375 BC; 1987), *The Republic*, 2nd edn, trans. Desmond Lee, New York: Penguin Books.

Poppo, L. and Zenger, T. (1995), 'Opportunism, routines and boundary choices: a comparative test of transaction cost and resource-based explanations for make-or-buy decisions', *Academy of Management, Best Papers Proceedings*: 42–6.

Quer, D., Claver, E. and Rienda, L. (2007), 'The impact of country risk and cultural distance on entry mode choice: an integrated approach', *Cross Cultural Management: An International Journal*, **14**(1): 74–87.

Ridley, M. (1998), *The Origins of Virtue: Human Instincts and the Evolution of Cooperation*, New York: Penguin Books.

Rugman, A.M. (1980), 'Internalization as a general theory of foreign direct investment: a re-appraisal of the literature', *Weltwirtschaftliches Archiv*, **116**: 365–79.

Rugman, A. and Verbeke, A. (2003), 'Extending the theory of the multinational enterprise: internalization and strategic management perspectives', *Journal of International Business Studies*, **34**(2): 125–37.

Rugman, A. and Verbeke, A. (2004), 'A perspective on regional and global strategies of multinational enterprises', *Journal of International Business Studies*, **35**(1): 3–18.

Safarian, E.A. (2003), 'Internalization and the MNE: a note on the spread of ideas', *Journal of International Business Studies*, **34**(2): 116–24.

Shah, S. and Corley, K. (2006), 'Building better theory by bridging the quantitative–qualitative divide', *Journal of Management Studies*, **43**(8): 1821–35.

Sharma, S. and Vredenburg, H. (1998), 'Proactive corporate environmental strategy and the development of competitively valuable organizational capabilities', *Strategic Management Journal*, **19**(8): 729–53.

Simon, H. (1955), 'A behavioral model of rational choice', *The Quarterly Journal of Economics*, **69**(1): 99–118.

Simon, H. (1985), 'Human nature in politics: the dialogue of psychology with political science', *The American Political Science Review*, **79**(2): 293–304.

Slater, G. and Spencer, D. (2000), 'The uncertain foundations of transaction cost economics', *Journal of Economic Issues*, **34**(1): 61–87.

Smith, A. (1776), *Wealth of Nations*, ed. C.J. Bullock. Vol. X. The Harvard Classics. New York: P.F. Collier and Son, 1909–14.

Steel, P. (2010), *The Procrastination Equation: The Science of Getting Things Done*, Toronto: Random House.

Teece, D.J. (1981), 'The market for know-how and the efficient international transfer of technology', *The ANNALS of the American Academy of Political and Social Science*, **458**(1): 81–96.

Tihanyi, L. and Thomas, W. (2005), 'Information-processing demands and the multinational enterprise: a comparison of foreign and domestic earnings estimates', *Journal of Business Research*, **58**(3): 285–92.

Tsang, E. (2006), 'Behavioral assumptions and theory development: the case of transaction cost economics', *Strategic Management Journal*, **27**(11): 999–1011.

Tversky, A. and Kahneman, D. (1974), 'Judgment under uncertainty: heuristics and biases', *Science*, **185**(4157): 1124–31.

Tversky, A., Slovic, P. and Kahneman, D. (1990), 'The causes of preference reversal', *The American Economic Review*, **80**(1): 204–17.

Verbeke, A. (2003), 'The evolutionary view of the MNE and the future of internalization theory', *Journal of International Business Studies*, **34**(6): 498–504.

Verbeke, A. (2009), *International Business Strategy: Rethinking the Foundations of Global Corporate Success*, Cambridge: Cambridge University Press.

Verbeke, A. and Kenworthy, T. (2008), 'Multidivisional versus metanational governance of the multinational enterprise', *Journal of International Business Studies*, **39**(2): 940–56.

Verbeke, A. and Yuan, W. (2005), 'Subsidiary autonomous activities in multinational enterprises: a transaction cost perspective', *Management International Review*, **2**: 31–49.

Wathne, K.H. and Heide, J.B. (2000), 'Opportunism in interfirm relationships: forms, outcomes, and solutions', *Journal of Marketing*, **64**(4): 36–51.

Williamson, O.E. (1975), *Markets and Hierarchies*, New York: Free Press.

Williamson, O.E. (1985), *The Economic Institutions of Capitalism: Firms. Markets, Relational Contracting*, New York: Free Press.

Williamson, O.E. (1991), 'Comparative economic organization: the analysis of discrete structural alternatives', *Administrative Science Quarterly*, **36**(2): 269–96.

Williamson, O.E. (1993a), 'Opportunism and its critics', *Managerial and Decision Economics*, **14**(2): 97–107.

Williamson, O.E. (1993b), 'Calculativeness, trust, and economic organization', *Journal of Law and Economics*, **36**(1): 453–86.

Williamson, O.E. (1996a), *The Mechanisms of Governance*, Oxford: Oxford University Press.

Williamson, O.E. (1996b), 'Economic organization: the case for candor', *The Academy of Management Review*, **21**(1): 48–57.

Williamson, O.E. and Ouchi, W. (1981), 'The markets and hierarchies and visible hand perspectives', in A.H. Van de Ven and W.H. Joyce (eds), *Perspectives on Organization Design and Behavior*, New York: Wiley, pp. 347–70.

Yin, R. (1994), *Case Study Research Design and Methods*, Applied Social Research Methods Series, Thousand Oaks, CA: Sage.

Yiu, D. and Makino, S. (2002), 'The choice between joint venture and wholly owned subsidiary: an institutional perspective', *Organization Science*, **13**(6): 667–83.

Zaheer, A., McEvily, B. and Perrone, V. (1998), 'Does trust matter? exploring the effects of interorganizational and interpersonal trust on performance', *Organization Science*, **9**(2): 141–59.

Zhao, H., Luo, Y. and Suh, T. (2004), 'Transaction cost determinants and entry mode choice: a meta-analytical review', *Journal of International Business Studies*, **35**(6): 524–44.

APPENDIX

Table 2A.1   Cases analyzed for the nine global MNEs

Company	Cases analyzed
IBM	'Emerging Business Opportunities at IBM (A)' (Garvin and Levesque, 2004, Harvard Business School Publishing, Boston, MA)
	'Emerging Business Opportunities at IBM (B)' (Garvin and Levesque, 2004, Harvard Business School Publishing, Boston, MA)
	'Emerging Business Opportunities at IBM (C): Pervasive Computing' (Garvin and Levesque, 2004, Harvard Business School Publishing, Boston, MA)
	'Waking Up IBM: How a Gang of Unlikely Rebels Transformed Big Blue' (Hamel, 2001, Harvard Business School Publishing, Boston, MA)
Sony	'Sony Europa (A)' (Kashani and Kassarjian, 2002, International Institute for Management Development, Lausanne, Switzerland)
	'Sony Europa (B)' (Kashani and Kassarjian, 2002, International Institute for Management Development, Lausanne, Switzerland)
	'Sony Europa (C)' (Kashani and Kassarjian, 2002, International Institute for Management Development, Lausanne, Switzerland)
Royal Philips	'Philips versus Matsushita: A New Century, a New Round' (Bartlett, 2003, Business School Publishing, Boston, MA)
	'Philips Electronic NV' (Lorsch and Chernak, 2006, Harvard Business School)
	'Revitalizing Philips (A)' (Ghemawat and Nueno, 2003, Harvard Business School)
Nokia	'Nokia Beyond 2003: A Mobile Gatekeeper?' (Burgelman and Meza, 2003, Stanford Graduate School of Business, Stanford, CA)
	'Nokia Corporation Innovation and Efficiency in a High-Growth Global Firm' (Doornik and Roberts, 2002, Stanford Graduate School of Business, Stanford, CA)
	'Nokia Telecommunications: Redesign of International Logistics' (Jarvenpaa, 1995, Harvard Business School Publishing, Boston, MA)
Intel	'Intel Corporation: 1968–2003' (Casadesus-Mansanell, Yoffie and Mattu, 2004, Harvard Business School Publishing, Boston, MA)
	'Intel Beyond 2003: Looking for its Third Act' (Burgelman and Meza, 2003, Stanford Graduate School of Business, Stanford, CA)
	'Inside Intel Inside' (Moon and Darwall, 2002, Harvard Business School Publishing, Boston, MA)
	'Intel in China' (Everatt, Slaughter and Xiaojun, 2002, Ivey Publishing, London, ON).
	'The Intel Pentium Chip Controversy (A)' (Evans and Narayanan, 2002, Harvard Business School Publishing, Boston, MA)
	'The Intel Pentium Chip Controversy (B)' (Evans and Narayanan, 2002, Harvard Business School Publishing, Boston, MA)
	'Intel Corporation's Internal Ecology of Strategy Making' (Burgelman and Christensen, 2001, Stanford Graduate School of Business, Stanford, CA)
	'Intel Corporation – Leveraging Capabilities for Strategic Renewal' (Nanda and Bartlett, 1994, Harvard Business School Publishing, Boston, MA)
	'Intel Corporation: Strategy for the 1990s' (Cogan and Burgelman, 1991, Stanford Graduate School of Business, Stanford, CA)

Table 2A.1 (continued)

Company	Cases analyzed
Canon	'New Product Development at Canon' (Partington and Bower, 1996, Harvard Business School Publishing, Boston, MA)
	'Canon Inc.: Worldwide Copier Strategy' (Ishikura and Porter, 1988, Harvard Business School Publishing, Boston, MA)
Coca-Cola	'The Coca-Cola Company (A): The Rise and Fall of M. Douglas Ivester' (Reavis, Watkings and Knoop, 2001, Harvard Business School Publishing, Boston, MA)
	'The Coca-Cola Company (B): Douglas Daft Takes Charge' (Reavis, Watkings and Knoop, 2001, Harvard Business School Publishing, Boston, MA)
Flextronics	'Flextronics: Deciding on a Shop-Floor System for Producing the Microsoft Xbox' (Polzer and Berkley, 2004, Harvard Business School Publishing, Boston, MA)
	'Flextronics International Ltd.' (Huckman, Pisano and Strick, 2003, Harvard Business School Publishing, Boston, MA)
LVMH	'The Perfect Paradox of Star Brands: An Interview with Bernard Arnault of LVMH' (Wetlaufer, 2001, Harvard Business School Publishing, Boston, MA)
	'LVMH in 2004: The Challenges of Strategic Integration' (Burgelman, Antoni and Meza, 2004, Stanford Graduate School of Business, Stanford, CA)

3 The new eclectic paradigm and international business strategy
Sarianna M. Lundan

INTRODUCTION

Combining the influence of ownership-specific (O) advantages, location-specific (L) advantages and internalization (I) advantages, the eclectic or OLI paradigm has become the pre-eminent framework used to explain the form and pattern of the cross-border activities of multinational enterprises (MNEs). This chapter will examine what the paradigm has to offer for scholars of strategic management, focusing particularly on the role of ownership advantages in allowing one firm to outcompete another, and in shaping the structure of markets in the global economy.

The chapter is organized as follows. We begin by briefly describing the evolution of the OLI paradigm from an eclectic theory to a paradigm, outlining how the increasing complexity of the cross-border activities of firms has changed the constituent parts of the paradigm. We then present the most recent version of the paradigm, and examine the influence of new theoretical perspectives as well as new empirical realities on our understanding of the cross-border activities of MNEs. We then demonstrate how the paradigm allows one to move between the micro- and macro-levels of analysis by exploring the interaction of the accumulation and evolution of firm capabilities, and the way in which these interact with locationally immobile (dis)advantages. We conclude by highlighting new areas of research, particularly in connection with emerging markets, where a deeper exploration of the interaction and co-evolution between firms, institutions and markets is likely to yield important insights for management and policy.

FROM A THEORY TO AN EVOLVING PARADIGM

The eclectic theory (as it was first called) was introduced in 1977, and subsequently amended on several occasions to account for new developments in the global economy and in the activities of MNEs (Dunning, 1977, 1979, 1980, 1988, 1995, 2000a). As Dunning himself readily acknowledged (Dunning, 2000b, 2001), the OLI paradigm is not a theory in the strict sense, but rather a synthesizing framework that brings together different strands of the economic and business literature to answer three basic questions. These are, first, what enables foreign firms to overcome their 'liability of foreignness' and to outcompete domestic firms in the host country? Second, why do firms in general, and multinational firms in particular, choose specific locations for their activities? Third, why would a firm choose to engage in equity investment across borders rather than to exploit its ownership advantages through licensing, exports or some cooperative entry mode such as joint ventures or contractual alliances?

These questions correspond to the three elements that comprise the OLI paradigm, namely ownership advantages (O), locational advantages (L) and internalization advantages (I). Although initially the OLI paradigm was mainly directed to explaining the aggregate pattern and distribution of foreign direct investment (FDI) across countries, over time it began to be increasingly applied also at the level of the firm, in order to explain, for example, why a particular kind of firm would choose a particular modality to enter a specific market (Brouthers et al., 1996; Oxelheim et al., 2001; Singh and Kundu, 2002). In the context of the internationalization process of firms, the basic strategy question of why and how one firm is able to outcompete another was restated in the form: what enables foreign firms to outcompete domestic firms in the host country? A related question is: what allows firms of one nationality to outcompete those of another nationality in different host countries?

In terms of its theoretical underpinnings, the understanding of ownership-specific advantages was mainly based on industrial organization economics, with a particular emphasis on intangible asset advantages. Later on, this came to be followed by the resource-based theory of the firm, and specifically the work of Penrose, as well as the concept of dynamic capabilities (Dunning, 2003; Dunning and Lundan, 2010). At the same time, drawing on the work of some early scholars like Hymer, Dunning was quite conscious of the coexistence of explanations of ownership advantage that relied on market power on one hand, and the internalization of the development and exploitation firm-specific knowledge on the other (Dunning and Pitelis, 2008).

The locational component relied initially on the scholarship in regional economics and geography to explain the location choices of MNEs and the geographical clustering often associated with foreign investment. In a *JIBS* decade award-winning article, Dunning (1998) emphasized the increasing importance of location-specific factors, as the O-specific advantages of firms were becoming more mobile and able to be relocated freely. Later on, the analysis of the L factors relevant for MNE activity was expanded to include differences in the quality of political governance institutions and the institutions supporting the functioning of markets (Dunning and Lundan, 2008a).

The theory behind the internalization component was the theory of internalization put forward by Buckley and Casson (1976) and others, derived from the seminal work of Coase (1937). It refers to the conditions under which firms would commit resources to cross-border equity investment instead of relying on less burdensome means such as licensing and exports. According to the theory, internalization of the market for intermediate inputs was most likely for transactions that involved proprietary knowledge, transaction-specific investments and that were recurrent.

However, over time, as the composition of competitiveness-enhancing assets became more knowledge-intensive and relationally-based (Dunning, 2004), the economic value created by the firm came to be more closely related to the way in which the O advantages are created and deployed, rather than a return to investment in the sense of a return to the owners of capital equipment and property. The ownership boundaries of firms have been reconfigured as a result of the downsizing of their physical assets, including productive assets and real estate, and the corresponding increase in contractual outsourcing (Contractor et al., 2010). Only those activities in which the firm possesses unique skills and capabilities are likely to be internalized. For other activities, the increasing modularization of design, and the commoditization of the modular components, have led to a dramatic increase in the number of firms capable of providing such intermediate inputs at low cost, and according to high specifications.

As a result, in later versions of the eclectic paradigm (Dunning, 1995, 2000a; Dunning and Lundan, 2008a, 2008b), the MNE is increasingly viewed as a system of interrelated activities, both internal and external to the ownership boundary of the firm, and internalization is seen as a matter of degree, involving the governance of both the assets owned by the MNE, as well as those that are accessed by it. Furthermore, it is not only the failures in the market for knowledge, but also in other markets along the value chain, that are seen to determine the governance options available to the MNE.[1]

The initial conception of asset-based ownership advantages is also reflected in the definition of the asset-based ownership advantages (Oa) and the economies of common governance (Ot) as the two main types of O advantages (Dunning, 1988). The Oa advantages refer to advantages the firm owns, whether this is intellectual property rights in the form of patents and trademarks, or stocks of tacit knowledge, tangible property and equipment. The Ot advantages, by contrast, are derived from the economies achieved by a multiplant firm over a single-plant firm, and they also incorporate any advantages derived from multinationality *per se*. This formulation of ownership advantages thus separates the advantages based on the possession of superior competitive assets, whether intellectual or real assets, from those that are based on the cross-border coordination of these assets.

Defined this way, the Oa advantages are in line with the resource-based view, which argues that a firm can sustain its competitive position if the assets it possesses are valuable, rare, and difficult to imitate or substitute (Barney, 1991; Peng, 2001; Peteraf, 1993). Furthermore, while new competitive assets can be procured from the market, these resources must represent a bargain in the sense that the firm can derive more value from them in combination with its other assets than it paid to acquire them.

On the other hand, the Ot advantages derived from the economies of common governance can be related directly to the ideas of Penrose (1959) on the managerial limits to growth. While expanding the scale and scope of the firm provides it with many advantages, as firms grow, the ability of management to oversee an increasingly diverse set of operations declines, and sets the limits to further growth, since top management cannot be expanded *ad infinitum*. Similar ideas were also expressed by Chandler (1990) in his analysis of the emergence of the multidivisional structure. He argued that as functionally organized firms were diversifying both in terms of their product range as well as in terms of their geographical reach, the M form became the preferred structural solution to reduce the complexity confronting top management.

However, while the existence of such managerial limits has some resonance, from a contemporary perspective this analysis ignores the increasing ability of firms to expand their value-adding activities through contractual means. This neither requires the resource commitment nor carries the problems of hierarchical coordination envisaged by Penrose and Chandler. As a result, to the extent that the ability to contract for output simplifies the coordination task, managers should find it possible to control a firm of greater complexity than would be possible through only hierarchical means.

THE NEW OLI PARADIGM

The strengths of the OLI paradigm lie in its apparent simplicity, its robustness in the face of changing circumstances, and the ability to simultaneously consider the impact of three interrelated groups of explanatory variables. As we have outlined, the eclectic paradigm has also been amended several times. Not surprisingly, this eclecticism has also been a source of criticism from scholars who think that the paradigm has become unwieldy and burdened with too many variables (e.g. Narula, 2010).[2]

The latest and only co-authored version of the paradigm reflects a changing understanding of the role of institutions, as both the source of some ownership advantages and in shaping the locational advantages or disadvantages of different host countries or regions. Specifically, Dunning and Lundan (2008a, 2008b) set out to amend the eclectic paradigm in order to be able to simultaneously consider the institutional influences inside the firm as well as those between the firm and the external environment in which it operates. This view of MNEs is focused on the active agency of firms rather than on institutional embeddedness, and as such it is part of a wider shift in the study of institutions in the social sciences that sees firms as change agents (Kogut et al., 2002; Kostova et al., 2008; Morgan, 2005; Morgan and Quack, 2005). To achieve a unified framework within which to accommodate both firm- and country-specific considerations, Dunning and Lundan (2008a, 2008b) chose to use and to extend the analysis of North (1990, 2005).

There are three principal reasons to emphasize the importance of institutions. First, economic growth can be understood as a process of development of more complex institutions to deal with the uncertainties that arise from more complex forms of exchange, involving both market and non-market actors (North, 1990, 2005). Different institutional systems have become increasingly interconnected over geographical space, and MNEs both contribute to, and are affected by, the institutions in their home and host countries.

Second, increasing social and technological complexity and interconnectedness lead to high levels of uncertainty, which MNEs attempt to counter through experimentation with new operational approaches and institutional entrepreneurship, manifested in a greater variety of organizational forms and practices (Cantwell et al., 2010). This experimental character of business is an essential feature of the evolutionary perspective (Day, 1998; Eliasson, 1991). Third, the more profound nature of uncertainty has led to the emergence of open business network structures (Chesbrough, 2006) that provide greater flexibility in adapting to changes in the institutional environment.

While the Oa and Ot advantages as outlined earlier can be used to explain the growth and boundaries of MNEs, they relate primarily to a firm that coordinates its activities within the auspices of the firm, and faces essentially a dichotomous choice between market and hierarchy. However, in order to account for the growth and boundaries of the contemporary MNE that uses a variety of different forms of governance, and employs a decentralized governance structure, we should consider what additional governance challenges this implies, and whether it might be useful to distinguish another category of ownership advantages to account for the ways in which firms overcome these challenges.

Two governance challenges in particular confront contemporary MNEs. In the first category are the problems that are caused by decentralized structures within the firm. These are essentially caused by the presence of innovative activity at the subsidiary level, which contributes to the overall innovativeness of the firm, but also introduces agency problems and motivational conflict with the headquarters and other subsidiary units (Mudambi, 1999; Verbeke and Kenworthy, 2008). Thus subsidiaries that gain mandates and prominence within the MNE network become more powerful players in their own right, and may try to extract rents or otherwise influence the strategic direction of the firm.

The second challenge is posed by the number of transactions that extend beyond hierarchical control, but that are not simple transactions over the market. Such transactions, whether they involve original equipment manufacturer (OEM) production or design contracts, or various types of nonmarket arrangements, incorporate a variety of ways to balance the interests on both sides (Chen, 2010). These might include sequential equity purchases, and various other means to align the incentives of the contracting parties, or they might include some types of social capital. It is likely that some firms are able to develop superior skills at managing such relationships that may provide them with a competitive advantage, but such advantages are not the traditional multiplant economies envisaged by the Ot advantages.

Both types of governance challenges require considerable organizational Oa advantages for value creation to take place. However, it is particularly the latter kind of governance challenge, extending beyond the boundaries of the firm, and possibly including different kinds of nonmarket activities, that we felt required a third type of ownership advantage. The nonmarket relationships may extend from the simple philanthropic activities undertaken by MNEs to multi-stakeholder partnerships involving governments and NGOs (Teegen et al., 2004). As a result of their engagement in the nonmarket domain, MNEs shape the institutional environment in their home and host countries, and contribute to the mixing of the boundaries between what has traditionally been the role of the state (the public domain) and what has belonged to the private domain (Cantwell et al., 2010; Scherer and Palazzo, 2011).

The basic governance structures firms employ in such relationships are similar to the ones they employ when dealing with the market interface, ranging from joint ventures or public–private partnerships to contractual development and marketing alliances. However, the uncertainties related to incentive alignment, which arise mainly out of the diffuse expectations and different competence levels of the different stakeholder groups in the nonmarket context, make these relationships different from supplier relationships, and may therefore require different kinds of ownership advantages to govern effectively.

To address the capabilities required to manage such relationships, Dunning and Lundan (2008a, 2008b) introduced a third category of ownership advantages, namely institutional advantages (Oi). They argued that the ability of the MNE to grow requires effective management of both the market and nonmarket domains, and necessitates the simultaneous deployment of asset-based advantages, advantages of common governance and institutional advantages.

The Oi advantages include the formal and informal institutions that govern the value-added processes within the firm, and between the firm and its stakeholders. This might include instruments such as codes of conduct, norms and corporate culture, and such advantages might also be incorporated into the incentive system of the firm. In this sense some of the Oi advantages resemble intangible Oa advantages, but they relate specifically to the expectations and limits set by the institutional framework in the home and host countries.[3] Because of this, the cases where Oi advantages are most visible arise in connection with the exploitation and augmentation of the firm's ownership advantages using the nonmarket interface.

Any one of three kinds of ownership advantages can become the limiting factor in the cross-border expansion of the value-added activities of MNEs. Traditional asset-based ownership advantages (Oa) might become obsolete, or they might otherwise not be able to be regenerated within the firm. A 'born global' firm (Gabrielsson and Kirpalani, 2004; Yli-Renko et al., 2001) may not possess many traditional asset-based ownership advantages, but it may possess above average organizational or network-related capabilities. It may also possess institutional advantages that allow it to take advantage of opportunities on the public–private boundary. In other cases, it may be that the primary limitations to further cross-border expansion lie in the inability of management to learn at a sufficient rate to cope with the coordinating challenges posed by the increasing size and complexity of the firm (Ot). Since increasing the geographical scope of the firm also increases the institutional complexity it is confronted with, insufficient Oi advantages might be responsible for the limited ability of many MNEs to expand beyond their regional market, as described by Rugman and Verbeke (2004).

Finally, substantial Oi advantages may be required for the firm to be able to exploit its existing Oa and Ot advantages. In some emerging markets, the inability of the firm to manage the nonmarket relationships in a way that allows it to carry out its primary value-adding activities may curtail expansion. This is the case, for example, when there are 'institutional voids' that need to be overcome in order for value-adding activity to take place (Rodriguez et al., 2005). The MNEs might also be faced with competition from firms whose organizational capabilities are not higher than average, but whose Oa advantages are superior (and possibly monopolistic), and who may enjoy preferential political access (Oi). This could be the case, for example, for protected incumbent firms in emerging markets that have faced relatively low levels of competition (Guillén, 2000).

FROM FIRM ADVANTAGES TO MARKET STRUCTURE

The combination of increasing interconnections between geographically dispersed markets and the greater use of market-based transactions has intensified the incentives for MNEs to invest in the creation of transferable routines. We have argued that the structural and managerial solutions MNEs have developed for dealing with the problems and uncertainties related to exchange over multiple markets (Oi advantages), and the acquisition and recombination of dispersed knowledge, are primary among such innovations. By continuously searching for new solutions, and developing them into transferable routines and best practices, MNEs give rise to new forms of embryonic institutions, which are disseminated to internal and external network parties, and gradually become diffused more widely in the local economy.

To understand this process of diffusion, Dunning and Lundan (2010) drew on the literature on dynamic capabilities, which has examined how firms identify and develop new opportunities, how they coordinate the assets required to exploit such opportunities, and how, in the course of doing so, they develop new business models and governance forms (Teece and Pisano, 1994; Teece et al., 1997). The dynamic capabilities framework itself has drawn from several different schools of thought, including transaction cost economics, the behavioral theory of the firm and evolutionary economics, with the aim of offering an integrative and managerially relevant paradigm that recognizes the challenges related to value appropriation as well as dynamic value creation (Teece, 2007).

Following Augier and Teece (2007, p. 179), 'Dynamic capabilities refer to the (inimitable) capacity firms have to shape, reshape, configure and reconfigure the firm's asset base so as to respond to changing technologies and markets.' They include 'the organization's (non-inimitable) ability to sense changing customer needs, technological opportunities, and competitive developments; but also its ability to adapt to – and possibly even to shape – the business environment in a timely and efficient manner'.

In the context of multinational enterprises, Dunning and Lundan (2010) made two related points. First, that neither the dynamic capabilities literature, nor the international business literature, has fully acknowledged the influence of the institutional context of the firm on the development of new routines. Second, that there has not been sufficient attention to the process of diffusion of new governance forms across borders.

In their seminal contribution, Buckley and Casson (1976) argued that technological resources that are difficult to trade over the market owing to information asymmetry and asset specificity could be traded by internalizing the transaction. Thus, at the very core of the explanation of why MNEs exist lies the superior ability of hierarchies to organize transactions involving knowledge-intensive assets. In light of this, the recent shift by MNEs towards increased flexibility, whether in terms of increased outsourcing, particularly of services, or in terms of contractual R&D (Chesbrough and Teece, 2002), presents something of a paradox.

Why have the costs of using market-based transactions fallen? Part of the explanation must lie in lower information and transportation costs. But Dunning and Lundan (2010) argued that, in part, this is also due to the activities of the MNEs themselves. Entrepreneurs within MNEs help create new markets, as de-internalization requires the ability to find or create suitable counterparties to a particular transaction. Contract research is a case in point. Traditionally, MNEs carried out R&D within the auspices of the firm, and such activity was geographically concentrated in the home country (Dunning and Lundan, 2009). However, in recent years we have seen MNEs extending the range of the R&D activities that are conducted abroad, and also engaging in market-based exchanges for contract research. Such markets do not come into existence automatically, but instead require a process whereby potential market participants create the standards and interfaces that allow for successful transactions to take place. In line with Augier and Teece (2007), we think that the growth of outsourcing is in part attributable to proactive entrepreneurial behavior by MNEs, and the Oi advantages they have accumulated.

At the same time, as MNEs strive to become more locally responsive and globally integrated in order to fully utilize the knowledge and capabilities of locally embedded subsidiaries, they face the problems stemming from delegated authority. On one hand, such problems include motivation and commitment issues that are caused by the inability of the headquarters to make a credible commitment not to interfere in the management of subsidiaries that have gained a mandate (Foss, 2003). On the other hand, the rent-seeking behavior of subsidiaries that develop strategically important competencies is likely to militate against the broad adoption of flat or so-called 'metanational' organizational structures involving an extensive delegation of authority (Kristensen and Zeitlin, 2005; Mudambi and Navarra, 2004; Verbeke and Kenworthy, 2008).[4]

To overcome these control and coordination problems, MNEs have experimented with both external and internal governance hybrids by combining intrafirm transactions with external contractual parties, and by adopting market-based incentives inside the firm. However, since innovative subsidiaries are also likely to be disruptive, an MNE might prefer to see its subsidiaries behave as 'boy scouts' that are more amenable to managerial direction by the headquarters than as 'subversive strategists' (Andersson et al., 2007; Morgan and Kristensen, 2006). This implies that the creation and transfer of new routines is likely to be problematic, even as the very essence of the coordinating function of the MNE is to disseminate technology, including organizational innovations, within the firm.

One important reason why the transfer of new routines is likely to be problematic is that such routines are 'sticky' (Szulanski, 1996), and incorporate tacit knowledge that cannot be fully articulated. Another reason is that the development of new routines is likely to be highly contextual, and dependent on the existing institutions. Indeed, there are many examples in the management literature of large organizations that have found it difficult to develop new routines in response to changed conditions (Henderson and Clark, 1990). This is because new routines do not simply outline what should be done, but also incorporate information on what should be rewarded, and in doing so, they rewrite the relational contracts that are in force (Kaplan and Henderson, 2005).

Put slightly differently, routines represent a 'truce' within the organization that solves a particular set of coordination problems (Coriat and Dosi, 1998). Since routines incorporate elements of both cognition and incentives, they are difficult, but not impossible, to adjust to new circumstances and to transfer across borders. This has been seen, for example, in the case of the transfer of the M-form organization to Europe in the 1950s and 1960s, or the transfer of Japanese-style manufacturing to the USA in the 1980s (Kipping and Bjarnar, 1998; Kogut and Parkinson, 1998; Westney, 2001).

The structural features of the MNE bring an additional layer of complexity to the question of the development of dynamic capabilities and the transfer of new routines across borders. An MNE subsidiary is likely to present an amalgam of at least four different kinds of institutional contexts. In terms of the informal institutions, these comprise the firm-specific norms and values that can be characterized as corporate culture, the norms and values that are specific to the home country of the MNE, but that are institutionalized inside the MNE, the norms and values that arise from the host country environment, and some norms and values that transcend national boundaries, such as the influence of the capital markets. All of these are likely to influence the development of dynamic capabilities, and to imprint the creation of any new routines.

The development and diffusion of new routines also contributes to the changing structure of markets. By internalizing transactions in cases where markets are thin or nonexistent due to co-specialized assets or information asymmetries, the MNE makes it possible for certain forms of economic activity to take place (Teece, 2006). However, in other cases, through its own activities the MNE may make the markets thicker, by transferring knowledge and providing training to its contractual partners (Pitelis and Teece, 2010). Indeed, there is a long history of such training being provided by MNEs to their suppliers, the impact of which has at times been quite significant, particularly in developing countries, as new technologies and organizational methods have become diffused into the local economy (Dunning and Lundan, 2008b).

In some cases the process of codification and subsequent training may help contribute to the emergence of modularity in the market for intermediate goods, which in turn allows for new entrants to enter the marketplace (Teece, 2006). Here we can think of technological modularity, as seen for instance in the emergence of standards such as GSM (global system for mobile communications) that allowed for the explosive growth of mobile phone services (Leiponen, 2006). However, we might also think in terms of organizational modularity, i.e. the development of routines for organizing transactions that become sufficiently clear and codified so that they too can become diffused in the marketplace, and influence the prevailing standards of how transactions are conducted.

Thus, in some cases, the external market comes into existence only because of the desire by the MNE to externalize rather than internalize particular transactions, and its willingness to incur the costs involved in training the counterparties to the transaction. This implies that the ability of the firm to choose a contractual governance form that provides it with, for example, more flexibility may depend on its ability to support the emergence of such markets in the first place, which we see as being influenced by its Oi advantages.

NEW RESEARCH DIRECTIONS

We believe that the OLI paradigm can continue to offer important insights for strategic management by emphasizing the interdependence of the micro- and macro-levels of analysis. This is particularly in connection with the increasing activities of established MNEs in emerging markets, and the way in which they are able to encounter the influence of incumbent business groups and different kinds of governance deficits in the host country. It is equally relevant for emerging multinationals investing in mature markets, particularly by means of mergers and acquisitions. These investors also have to overcome the power of entrenched incumbents, and to find their way into the national business systems and innovation systems of the host countries.

In terms of the kinds of responses MNEs are likely to exhibit, we argue in line with Cantwell et al. (2010) that avoidance, adaptation and co-evolution are likely to be employed in different home and host countries, in different industrial sectors and at different points in time. We would expect, however, that adaptation would be more likely to occur in relatively stable environments and in less innovative sectors, while more dynamic environments are likely to both allow and require innovation and a continuous co-evolution for the firm to sustain a competitive advantage. In a comparatively settled local environment, it is likely that subsidiaries would mainly adapt to their local surroundings. By contrast, in a faster-moving environment, perhaps associated with a process of political and institutional reform, the co-evolution of MNE subsidiaries and the institutional environment is more likely, and the variety they introduce to the local environment is more likely to influence (as well as be influenced by) the behavior of other agents.

In particular, an institutional system that is in flux is likely to exhibit 'institutional voids' that offer opportunities for institutional entrepreneurship and co-evolution. Consequently, in emerging markets, MNEs might be welcomed in part because they introduce institutional elements that are missing in the local environment (Hoskisson et al., 2000; Meyer, 2004; Peng et al., 2008). By the same token, in such dynamic environments MNEs are more likely to be seen as legitimate if they contribute to a transformational process that is already ongoing. New practices introduced by MNEs can become a part of the wider process of changing values and institutional structures in the host country, but even in such cases, institutional entrepreneurship by MNEs, supported by their Oi advantages, is likely to contribute only one element of the broader restructuring under way.

Even as we acknowledge that MNEs are likely to play only a partial role in reshaping the institutional environments in which they operate, their contribution extends far beyond technological knowledge transfer, or traditional political influence activities. The heterogeneity of both market demands (influenced by technological change) and societal expectations results in an extraordinary diversity of strategic options that require new kinds of capabilities to manage effectively. The development of such capabilities by MNEs, their transferability, and the impact on the home and host countries in terms of both effectiveness and legitimacy are likely provide fruitful avenues of research in the G-20/G-77 world.

NOTES

1. See, e.g., Chen (2005), who analyzed not just failures in the market for technology (the original licensing vs FDI decision), but also those in the market for manufacturing (the original equipment manufacturer (OEM) vs FDI decision).
2. Since the number of basic variables comprising the eclectic paradigm has always been three, the issue is really of the kind of interpretation and emphasis that is given to these three factors.
3. There is no fundamental reason why the Oi advantages could not be considered simply a sub-category of Oa advantages. However, the range of contexts in which it is useful from an analytical standpoint to separate the governance forms from the other assets developed by the firm led us to separate them from Oa advantages.
4. See also Pitelis (2007) for a discussion illuminating why, following Penrose (1959), the resource-based view and the dynamic capabilities literature have tended to ignore questions of intrafirm conflict.

REFERENCES

Andersson, U., Forsgren, M. and Holm, U. (2007), 'Balancing subsidiary influence in the federative MNC: a business network view', *Journal of International Business Studies*, **38**(5): 802–18.
Augier, M. and Teece, D.J. (2007), 'Dynamic capabilities and multinational enterprise: Penrosean insights and omissions', *Management International Review*, **47**(2): 175–92.
Barney, J.B. (1991), 'Firm resources and sustained competitive advantage', *Journal of Management*, **17**(1): 99–120.
Brouthers, K.D., Brouthers, L.E. and Werner, S. (1996), 'Dunning's eclectic theory and the smaller firm: the impact of ownership and locational advantages on the choice of entry-modes in the computer software industry', *International Business Review*, **5**(4): 377–95.
Buckley, P.J. and Casson, M.C. (1976), *The Future of the Multinational Enterprise*, London: Macmillan.
Cantwell, J., Dunning, J.H. and Lundan, S.M. (2010), 'An evolutionary approach to understanding international business activity: the co-evolution of MNEs and the institutional environment', *Journal of International Business Studies*, **41**(4): 567–86.
Chandler, A.D. (1990), *Scale and Scope: The Dynamics of Industrial Capitalism*, Cambridge, MA: Harvard/ Belknap.
Chen, S.-F.S. (2005), 'Extending internalization theory: a new perspective on international technology transfer and its generalization', *Journal of International Business Studies*, **36**(2): 231–45.
Chen, S.-F.S. (2010), 'A general TCE model of international business institutions: market failure and reciprocity', *Journal of International Business Studies*, **41**(6): 935–59.
Chesbrough, H. (2006), *Open Business Models: How to Thrive in the New Innovation Landscape*, Cambridge, MA: Harvard Business School Press.

Chesbrough, H.W. and Teece, D.J. (2002), 'Organizing for innovation: when is virtual virtuous?', *Harvard Business Review*, **80**(8): 127–35.

Coase, R.H. (1937), 'The nature of the firm', *Economica*, **1**(Nov.): 386–405.

Contractor, F.J., Kumar, V., Kundu, S.K. and Pedersen, T. (2010), 'Reconceptualizing the firm in a world of outsourcing and offshoring: the organizational and geographical relocation of high-value company functions', *Journal of Management Studies*, **47**(8): 1417–33.

Coriat, B. and Dosi, G. (1998), 'Learning how to govern and learning how to solve problems: on the co-evolution of competences, conflicts, and organizational routines', in A.D. Chandler, Jr, P. Hagström and Ö. Sölvell (eds), *The Dynamic Firm: The Role of Technology, Strategy, Organization, and Regions*, Oxford: Oxford University Press, pp. 103–33.

Day, R.H. (1998), 'Bounded rationality and firm performance in the experimental economy', in G. Eliasson, C. Green and C. McCann (eds), *Microfoundations of Economic Growth: A Schumpeterian Perspective*, Ann Arbor, MI: University of Michigan Press, pp. 119–30.

Dunning, J.H. (1977), 'Trade, location of economic activity and the MNE: a search for an eclectic approach', in B. Ohlin, P.O. Hesselborn and P.M. Wijkman (eds), *The International Allocation of Economic Activity: Proceedings of a Nobel Symposium Held at Stockholm*, London: Macmillan, pp. 395–418.

Dunning, J.H. (1979), 'Explaining changing patterns of international production: in defense of the eclectic theory', *Oxford Bulletin of Economics & Statistics*, **41**(4): 269–95.

Dunning, J.H. (1980), 'Toward an eclectic theory of international production: some empirical tests', *Journal of International Business Studies*, **11**(1): 9–31.

Dunning, J.H. (1988), 'The eclectic paradigm of international production: a restatement and some possible extensions', *Journal of International Business Studies*, **19**(1): 1–31.

Dunning, J.H. (1995), 'Reappraising the eclectic paradigm in the age of alliance capitalism', *Journal of International Business Studies*, **26**(3): 461–91.

Dunning, J.H. (1998), 'Location and the multinational enterprise: a neglected factor?', *Journal of International Business Studies*, **29**(1): 45–66.

Dunning, J.H. (2000a), 'The eclectic paradigm as an envelope for economic and business theories of MNE activity', *International Business Review*, **9**: 163–90.

Dunning, J.H. (2000b), 'The eclectic paradigm of international production: a personal perspective', in Christos N. Pitelis and Roger Sugden (eds), *The Nature of the Transnational Firm*, 2nd edn, London and New York: Routledge, pp. 119–39.

Dunning, J.H. (2001), 'The eclectic (OLI) paradigm of international production: past, present and future', *International Journal of the Economics of Business*, **8**(2): 173–90.

Dunning, J.H. (2003), 'The contribution of Edith Penrose to international business scholarship', *Management International Review*, **43**(1): 3–19.

Dunning, J.H. (2004), 'An evolving paradigm of the economic determinants of international business activity', in Joseph L.C. Cheng and Michael A. Hitt (eds), *Managing Multinationals in a Knowledge Economy: Economics, Culture, and Human Resources*, Amsterdam: Elsevier, pp. 3–27.

Dunning, J.H. and Lundan, S.M. (2008a), 'Institutions and the OLI paradigm of the multinational enterprise', *Asia Pacific Journal of Management*, **25**(4): 573–93.

Dunning, J.H. and Lundan, S.M. (2008b), *Multinational Enterprises and the Global Economy*, 2nd edn, Cheltenham, UK and Northampton, MA, USA: Edward Elgar.

Dunning, J.H. and Lundan, S.M. (2009), 'The internationalization of corporate R&D: a review of the evidence and some policy implications', *Review of Policy Research*, **26**(1–2): 13–33.

Dunning, J.H. and Lundan, S.M. (2010), 'The institutional origins of dynamic capabilities in multinational enterprises', *Industrial and Corporate Change*, **19**(4): 1225–46.

Dunning, J.H. and Pitelis, C. (2008), 'Stephen Hymer's contribution to international business scholarship: an assessment and extension', *Journal of International Business Studies*, **39**(1): 167–76.

Eliasson, G. (1991), 'Modeling the experimentally organized economy', *Journal of Economic Behavior and Organization*, **16**(1–2): 153–82.

Foss, N.J. (2003), 'Selective intervention and internal hybrids: interpreting and learning from the rise and decline of the Oticon Spaghetti Organization', *Organization Science*, **14**(3): 331–49.

Gabrielsson, M. and Kirpalani, V.H.M. (2004), 'Born globals: how to reach new business space rapidly', *International Business Review*, **13**(5): 555–71.

Guillén, M.F. (2000), 'Business groups in emerging economies: a resource-based view', *Academy of Management Journal*, **43**(3): 362–80.

Henderson, R.M. and Clark, K.B. (1990), 'Architectural innovation: the reconfiguration of existing product technologies and the failure of established firms', *Administrative Science Quarterly*, **35**(1): 9–30.

Hoskisson, R.E., Eden, L., Lau, C.M. and Wright, M. (2000), 'Strategy in emerging economies', *Academy of Management Journal*, **43**(3): 249–67.

Kaplan, S. and Henderson, R. (2005), 'Inertia and incentives: bridging organizational economics and organizational theory', *Organization Science*, **16**(5): 509–21.

Kipping, M. and Bjarnar, O. (eds) (1998), *The Americanisation of European Business: The Marshall Plan and the Transfer of US Management Models*, London: Routledge.

Kogut, B. and Parkinson, D. (1998), 'Adoption of the multidivisional structure: analyzing history from the start', *Industrial and Corporate Change*, **7**(2): 249–73.

Kogut, B., Walker, G. and Anand, J. (2002), 'Agency and institutions: national divergences in diversification behavior', *Organization Science*, **13**(2): 162–78.

Kostova, T., Roth, K. and Dacin, M.T. (2008), 'Institutional theory in the study of MNCs: a critique and new directions', *Academy of Management Review*, **33**(4): 994–1006.

Kristensen, P.H. and Zeitlin, J. (2005), *Local Players in Global Games: The Strategic Constitution of a Multinational Corporation*, New York: Oxford University Press.

Leiponen, A. (2006), 'National styles in the setting of global standards: the relationship between firms' standardization strategies and national origin', in John Zysman and Abraham Newman (eds), *How Revolutionary was the Digital Revolution? National Responses, Market Transitions, and Global Technology*, Stanford, CA: Stanford University Press, pp. 338–58.

Meyer, K.E. (2004), 'Perspectives on multinational enterprises in emerging economies', *Journal of International Business Studies*, **35**(4): 259–76.

Morgan, G. (2005), 'Introduction: changing capitalisms? Internationalization, institutional change, and systems of economic organization', in Glenn Morgan, Richard Whitley and Eli Moen (eds), *Changing Capitalisms? Internationalization, Institutional Change, and Systems of Economic Organization*, Oxford and New York: Oxford University Press, pp. 1–18.

Morgan, G. and Kristensen, P.H. (2006), 'The contested space of multinationals: varieties of institutionalism, varieties of capitalism', *Human Relations*, **59**(11): 1467–90.

Morgan, G. and Quack, S. (2005), 'Institutional legacies and firm dynamics: the growth and internationalization of UK and German law firms', *Organization Studies*, **26**(12): 1765–85.

Mudambi, R. (1999), 'MNE internal capital markets and subsidiary strategic independence', *International Business Review*, **8**(2): 197–212.

Mudambi, R. and Navarra, P. (2004), 'Is knowledge power? Knowledge flows, subsidiary power and rent-seeking within MNCs', *Journal of International Business Studies*, **35**(5): 385–406.

Narula, R. (2010), 'Keeping the eclectic paradigm simple', *Multinational Business Review*, **18**(2): 35–49.

North, D.C. (1990), *Institutions, Institutional Change and Economic Performance*, Cambridge: Cambridge University Press.

North, D.C. (2005), *Understanding the Process of Economic Change*, Princeton, NJ: Princeton University Press.

Oxelheim, L., Randøy, T. and Stonehill, A. (2001), 'On the treatment of finance-specific factors within the OLI paradigm', *International Business Review*, **10**(4): 381–98.

Peng, M.W. (2001), 'The resource-based view and international business', *Journal of Management*, **27**(6): 803–29.

Peng, M.W., Wang, D.Y.L. and Jiang, Y. (2008), 'An institution-based view of international business strategy: a focus on emerging economies', *Journal of International Business Studies*, **39**(5): 920–36.

Penrose, E.T. (1959), *The Theory of the Growth of the Firm*, Oxford: Basil Blackwell.

Peteraf, M.A. (1993), 'The cornerstones of competitive advantage: a resource based view', *Strategic Management Journal*, **14**(3): 179–91.

Pitelis, C.N. (2007), 'A behavioral resource-based view of the firm: the synergy of Cyert and March (1963) and Penrose (1959)', *Organization Science*, **18**(3): 478–90.

Pitelis, C.N. and Teece, D.J. (2010), 'Cross-border market co-creation, dynamic capabilities and the entrepreneurial theory of the multinational enterprise', *Industrial & Corporate Change*, **19**(4): 1247–70.

Rodriguez, P., Uhlenbruck, K. and Eden, L. (2005), 'Government corruption and the entry strategies of multinationals', *Academy of Management Review*, **30**(2): 383–96.

Rugman, A.M. and Verbeke, A. (2004), 'A perspective on regional and global strategies of multinational enterprises', *Journal of International Business Studies*, **35**(1): 3–18.

Scherer, A.G. and Palazzo, G. (2011), 'The new political role of business in a globalized world: a review of a new perspective on CSR and its implications for the firm, governance, and democracy', *Journal of Management Studies*, **48**(4): 899–931.

Singh, N. and Kundu, S. (2002), 'Explaining the growth of e-commerce corporations (ECCs): an extension and application of the eclectic paradigm', *Journal of International Business Studies*, **33**(4): 679–97.

Szulanski, G. (1996), 'Exploring internal stickiness: impediments to the transfer of best practice within the firm', *Strategic Management Journal*, **17**: 27–43.

Teece, D.J. (2006), 'Reflections on the Hymer thesis and the multinational enterprise', *International Business Review*, **15**(2): 124–39.

Teece, D.J. (2007), 'Explicating dynamic capabilities: the nature and microfoundations of (sustainable) enterprise performance', *Strategic Management Journal*, **28**(13): 1319–50.

Teece, D.J. and Pisano, G. (1994), 'The dynamic capabilities of firms: an introduction', *Industrial and Corporate Change*, **3**(3): 537–56.

Teece, D.J., Pisano, G. and Shuen, A. (1997), 'Dynamic capabilities and strategic management', *Strategic Management Journal*, **18**(7): 509–33.

Teegen, H., Doh, J.P. and Vachani, S. (2004), 'The importance of nongovernmental organizations (NGOs) in global governance and value creation: an international business research agenda', *Journal of International Business Studies*, **35**(6): 463–83.

Verbeke, A. and Kenworthy, T.P. (2008), 'Multidivisional vs metanational governance of the multinational enterprise', *Journal of International Business Studies*, **39**(6): 940–56.

Westney, D.E. (2001), 'Japan', in Alan M. Rugman and Tom Brewer (eds), *The Oxford Handbook of International Business*, Oxford: Oxford University Press, pp. 623–51.

Yli-Renko, H., Autio, E. and Sapienza, H.J. (2001), 'Social capital, knowledge acquisition, and knowledge exploitation in young technology-based firms', *Strategic Management Journal*, **22**(6–7): 587–613.

4 The multinational enterprise as a global factory
Peter Buckley

THE GLOBAL FACTORY

There have been significant changes in the organization and configuration of MNEs. The balance between internalization and externalization has shifted partly because of reactions to increased volatility and opposition to monopoly (Buckley and Casson, 1998b), and partly because of management learning and improved techniques of managing through contracts.

Managers compare external (transactions) costs – the costs of using the market – with internal (agency) costs – the costs of carrying out operations under their own managerial control. The balance of these two sets of costs determines the scope of the firm at any given point of time. Managers endeavour to reduce agency costs. It is only when agency costs are falling relative to transaction costs that the scope of managerial control and therefore the size of the firm will increase (Buckley, 1997). Transaction costs exist in assembling the business processes of the firm (collections of activities that are technologically or managerially linked) so that they jointly contribute to value added. The overall costs of organization are determined by losses due to the imperfect motivation of process members, imperfect information and coordination losses resulting from the architecture of the firm (the allocation of responsibilities among individuals and groups and the communication between them), and the resource costs associated with incentives and organization. Identifying transactional links within 'the black box' of the firm enables us to trace the costs and benefits of combining activities within the firm. Further, it is possible to specify losses from imperfections in motivation, information and coordination and to balance these against the costs of correcting them (Buckley and Carter, 1996). Action within the firm on improving business processes and agency costs may entail expansion or contraction of the firm as individual elements of each business process are compared against external provision of the same sub-process. This 'fine-slicing' of activities (Buckley, 2004a) means that every element of the firm can be evaluated by comparison with the market alternative and can be externalized if it is profitable to do so (outsourcing) or can be relocated if this reduces overall costs (offshoring). These two decisions – the first on internalization/externalization control choice and the second a location decision – have led to the creation of the 'global factory' (Buckley, 2004a, 2004b, 2007; Buckley and Ghauri, 2004).

The opening up of the global factory has provided new opportunities for new locations to enter international business. Emerging countries such as India and China are subcontracting production and service activities from the brand-owning MNEs. The use of the market by MNEs enables new firms to compete for business against the internalized activities of the MNE. This not only subjects every internalized activity to 'the market test'; it also results in a differentiated network (as presented in Figure 4.1) that we term 'the global factory'.

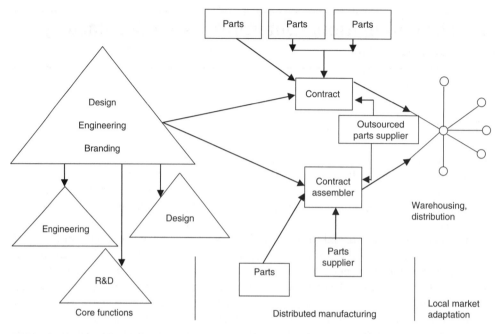

Figure 4.1   The global factory

COMPONENTS OF THE GLOBAL FACTORY

The global supply chain is divided into three parts. The original equipment manufacturers (OEMs) control the brand and undertake design, engineering and R&D for the product (although these may be outsourced). They are customers for contract manufacturers (CMs) who perform manufacturing (and perhaps logistics) services for OEMs. In this so-called modular production network, CMs need to possess capabilities such as mix, product and new product flexibilities while at the same time carrying out manufacturing activities at low cost with mass production processes. Flexibility is necessary to fulfil consumers' product differentiation needs (local requirements) and low cost for global efficiency imperatives (see Wilson and Guzman, 2005). The third part of the chain is warehousing, distribution and adaptation carried out on a 'hub-and-spoke' principle in order to achieve local market adaptation through a mix of ownership and location policies. As Figure 4.2 shows, ownership strategies are used to involve local firms with marketing skills and local market intelligence in international joint ventures (IJVs), whilst location strategies are used to differentiate the wholly owned 'hub' (centrally located) from the jointly owned 'spokes'.

Two simple illustrations can be given of the power of the global factory to use location and ownership decisions to create a complex, but efficient, response to global economic conditions – and to respond to changes in those conditions. First, a complex offshoring and outsourcing strategy can reduce location and transaction costs. A simple offshoring decision involves relocating the early stages of processing to a lower-cost foreign country.

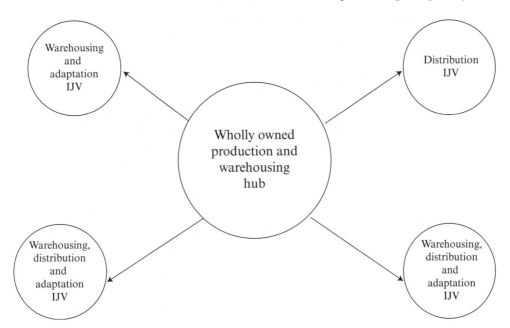

Figure 4.2   Hub and spoke

Intermediate inputs are exported to this foreign-located facility and finished goods are transported from it. Local inputs are supplied to the offshore unit (thus providing linkage and spillover effects to the local economy) (Buckley et al., 2002, 2004, 2006, 2007a, 2007b). This location decision can be combined with an ownership/internalization decision because the offshore plant can be 'captive' (owned, internalized) or non-captive-controlled through the market by contract. If we envisage the full panoply of such decisions in a global factory, we can see the complexity, sophistication and difficulty of these ever-changing strategies in a volatile world economy.

Multinational firms have to reconcile pressures to be globally efficient with the need to be locally responsive. The efficiency imperative dictates standardization, economies of scale and uniformity of product and process. The localization motive mandates adaptation, differentiation and close liaison with customers. Those pressures have to be accommodated and the global factory is the ideal structure with which to do so. Figure 4.3 shows how a mixed 'glocal' strategy can steer an optimal path between rigid standardization versus differentiation strategies for the example of marketing. The 'glocal' strategy seeks the best compromise for each element of the marketing strategy as the balance of global and local pressures dictates across different national markets. This glocalized strategy is well suited to being combined with the 'fine-slicing' of activities across the complex set of processes in the whole network of the global factory.

The global factory is, of course, a network (Buckley, 2004b). It is a network held together by control of key assets and flows of knowledge and intermediate products (Buckley, 2007). Networks, like any other form of organization, have both benefits and costs (the latter are often ignored). Global factories are both horizontal and vertical

GLOBAL	LOCAL
Cost	Revenue
Efficiency	Responsiveness
Centralization	Decentralization
Standardization	Adaptation
GLOCAL?	

Figure 4.3   Global/local

	Benefit of open and transparent	Cost of closed and opaque
Horizontal	Learning/Diffusion	Collusion on price
Vertical	Coordination of intermediate product markets and upstream/downstream investments	Vertical integration as barrier to entry

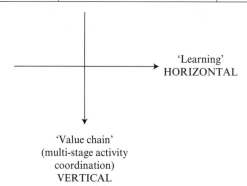

'Learning'
HORIZONTAL

'Value chain'
(multi-stage activity
coordination)
VERTICAL

Figure 4.4   Networks

networks (Figure 4.4). The benefits of the horizontal network arise from learning and the diffusion of knowledge. The benefits of the vertical network arise from the coordination of activities. However, the horizontal network runs the risk of collusion on price, while vertical integration can be used as a barrier to entry. The degree to which benefits outweigh costs depends on the extent to which the global factory's networks are open and transparent versus closed and opaque.

THE INFORMATION STRUCTURE OF THE GLOBAL FACTORY

Casson (1997) highlights the importance of information costs in the structure of business organization. He sees the brand owner as essentially a specialist in the search and specification functions (for customers and products respectively). 'The brand owner, by intermediating between the producer and the retailer, coordinates the entire distribution channel linking the worker to the final customer' (Casson, 1997, p. 159). This intermediation by the brand owner/market maker is intermediation of information, not production. This shows that the brand owner is the information hub of the global factory. The brand owner organizes the market process itself. The organization of production is conventionally within firms but the organization of the whole production and trade sequence is intermediated by the market-making global factory. In many industries, particularly service industries, such as banking and insurance, the essence of competitiveness is the processing of information.

KEY ELEMENTS OF THE GLOBAL FACTORY

A key attribute of a successful global factory is flexibility. Flexibility is the ability to reallocate resources quickly and smoothly in response to change. This will never be costless and the costs of flexibility need to be borne in mind (Buckley and Casson, 1998b). Flexibility is a response to increasing volatility arising from globalization and from opposition to monopoly, including internal monopoly. The idea that global factories avoid internal monopoly, in order to escape 'hold-up' problems from crucial single activities underperforming, is borne out by the extent of internal (and quasi-internal) competition throughout the system, leading to dualities and multiplicities of supply sources and to the use of the market to put competitive pressure on internal activities.

A key purpose of flexible structures is to provide resilience. Systems are resilient if they can absorb shocks. Resilient firms can thus survive downturns, crises and panics (like the 'credit crunch' of 2009). In a globalized world, shocks from any part of the global economy are rapidly transmitted around the world (the 'sub-prime' crises of 2008–09). Competition with the global factory, multiple alternative sources of supply of key inputs, access to many national markets and supply sources, intelligent use of forecasting and internal transfer of knowledge are all sources of built-in resilience of the global factory.

TRANSACTION-COSTS-MINIMIZING CONFIGURATIONS IN THE FIRM

Transaction costs exist in assembling the business processes of firms – collections of activities that are technologically or managerially linked so that they jointly affect value added. The overall costs of organization are determined by losses due to the imperfect motivation of process members (which result, in part at least, from the incentive structure) and imperfect information and coordination that flow from the architecture of the

Table 4.1   Inflow and coordination costs

	Tangible	Intangible
Stock	(Fixed)	Brand
	Capital	Intellectual capital
Flow	Product	Information on market, production
	Distribution	

firm (the allocation of responsibilities among individuals and groups and communication between them), together with the resource costs associated with incentives and architecture (Buckley and Carter, 1996). Thus transactional links within the firm enable us to split up the 'black box' and trace costs and benefits of combining activities within intrafirm processes. Further, it is possible to specify losses from imperfections in motivation, information and coordination, and to balance these against the costs necessary to correct these imperfections, as in Table 4.1.

Views about the nature of human behaviour and actions will influence how an outsider might feel about the likelihood of these costs being significant; for example, motivation loss (and the cost of correcting it) will be greater, the greater is the degree of opportunism ('self-seeking with guile'). However, if we believe that individuals naturally seek and appreciate teamworking, then motivation costs will be low.

Buckley and Casson (1988) applied internalization theory to international joint ventures (IJVs). IJVs are conceptualized as arising from three key factors: internalization economies in one or more intermediate goods markets, indivisibilities and barriers to merger. Under certain environmental conditions, IJVs can be an optimal organizational solution (Buckley and Casson, 1996). In joint ventures, mutual trust can be a substitute for expensive legalism. Joint ventures provide an ideal institution for the exercise of mutual forbearance, leading to a commitment to cooperation and to the creation of reputation effects where a reputation for cooperative behaviour can lead to further coordination benefits. These effects can be good substitutes for ownership. Skills in joint venturing and the learning effects that arise can lead to widespread non-ownership forms of cooperation, as in many global factories.

NEW MANAGEMENT SKILLS

The rise of the global factory has been paralleled by the growth of new management skills. These include the ability of managers to 'fine-slice' activities – to cut the constituent elements of processes into finer and finer slivers. The virtue of this strategy is that it allows each element to be optimally located and controlled. The advantages of the choice of location and the choice of mode of governance can then be forensically applied to each component of the global factory by management.

Together with fine-slicing goes control of information. The information structure of the global factory is a major source of its strength, allowing information to be obtained and to be disseminated to those decision-takers best placed to use it. It is the control of this complex flow of information on external conditions and internal competences that is far more important than control of physical assets, the use of which can be increasingly outsourced. The general adage that 'you don't have to own something to control it' applies increasingly to physical assets but emphatically not to intangible assets such as brands and to knowledge.

The use of increasingly complex structures involving both internalized and external-ized activities requires that externalized activities be carefully monitored (for quality control reasons, for example) and integrated with those activities under the ownership of the global factory. 'Interface competence' – the ability to coordinate external organ-izations into the strategy of the focal firm, to liaise with external bodies and govern-ments and to cohere these activities into a grand strategy – are at the heart of the skills necessary to organize a successful global factory. This has implications for the style of management that is needed. A new, more subtle cooperative mode of operation is increasingly necessary. Management needs to be 'hard nosed' in requiring adherence to targets (on quality and reliability), but in managing outside the boundaries of the firm, with subcontractors and alliance partners, skills beyond 'command and control' are vital.

ROLE OF HEADQUARTERS

It is something of an irony that the spatial distribution strategies – ownership and location – make the role of headquarters more important in global factories than in conventional vertically and horizontally integrated firms. The authority and choice of headquarters has expanded. The development of 'fine-slicing' means that the determina-tion of ownership and control of each specialized sliver of activity expands headquar-ters' area of choice. Evidence of the increased power of headquarters might be the level of salaries there compared to elsewhere (even in other units in the home country). Remuneration in headquarters is also likely to increase over time relative to other loca-tions. The control of information in global factories is crucial and the mechanisms determining strategy are more subtle. The doctrine that 'you don't have to own an activity to control it' requires new skills of headquarters functions in global factories. There are important dynamics in this process as headquarters learns how to manage spatially dispersed and organizationally diffuse units within the global factory. This is not a one-way process. Units within the global factory also learn how to manage head-quarters (Buckley et al., 2002). The management style that new configurations require is vastly different from conventional 'command-and-control' methods and the full implications of this are yet to be explored. Headquarters as a 'controlling intelligence' or orchestrator of activities emerges as the best metaphors for its role in the global factory.

In emphasizing extra degrees of autonomy given to subsidiaries and other units within the global factory, we should not forget the big picture. The key issue is competition to be the marketing and distribution platform of the big products of the future. That is the key question for headquarters. Other units must operate within this framework set by headquarters; while they may well have crucial areas of decision-making and discretion given to them, it is within this overall paradigm that they operate.

UNRESOLVED ISSUES

Two issues of great importance may be considered unresolved. The first is the spatial element in internalization. The advantages and disadvantages of internalization are assumed to be invariant to distance. This issue is resolved by the addition of the location factor, which is then combined with internalization to give a satisfactory explanation of the growth and development of MNEs. The investigation of spatial elements in the internalization decision itself may be a fruitful avenue for further research.

Second, there is an unresolved (unresolvable?) conflict in modelling MNEs between the role of human agency and the result of impersonal forces. How far is human agency (management decision-making) the determinant of outcomes? Much of economics assumes that impersonal forces determine the configuration of the world economy. The strategy literature sometimes reads as if all managers have to do to change the world is to exercise will and decide. Work around entrepreneurship (Casson, 2000) decision-making under uncertainty (Buckley and Casson, 2001) and investigations of 'how managers decide' (from Aharoni, 1966, onwards, including Buckley et al., 2007a, 2007b) are attempting to clarify this issue in the international business area but the philosophical problems run deep (and long – back to Adam Smith, 1759, 1776).

GLOBALIZATION AND CORPORATE GOVERNANCE

Two key issues interact to provide governance issues arising from the globalization of business. The first is the existence of unpriced externalities. These impose costs (e.g. pollution) on the local economy and environment. The second is the remoteness of production and service activities from their ultimate owners or controllers (e.g. the shareholders). These two factors interact because the mechanism for correcting negative externalities becomes difficult to implement because of remoteness and lack of immediate responsibility.

Perceived difficulties of global governance in multinational firms are exacerbated by the current crises in governance of firms in the West. The shareholder-return-driven environment that prevails today is very much the creature of the merger wave of the 1980s (Buckley and Ghauri, 2002). The feeling that corporations are outside social controls and that current forms of governance benefit only executives (and owners) rather than other stakeholders contributes to the concerns outlined in the previous section.

MNE – host country relations in middle-income countries have fully emerged onto the world stage, leaving behind a group of largely inert less developed countries that have so far been bypassed by globalization. Large, emerging countries, which contain significant middle-class markets, cheaper and well-educated labour and stabilizing political regimes (India, China, Brazil) are no longer seen just as new markets for old products (Prahalad and Lieberthal, 1998), but as significant locations requiring reconfigurations of the economic geography of MNEs' operations. Not only do MNEs adapt products to local markets; local markets also provide ideas for new global products (Murtha et al., 2001). Increasing location 'tournaments' to attract FDI may have reduced the benefits to the host countries, as has the increasing skill of the managers of MNEs in making their investments more 'footloose'. Corresponding skills on the part of host countries to make FDI 'sticky' are not developing at the same rate. Differences within developing countries may lead to divergence between those that can develop the velocity to catch up and those that will fall behind as the world economy becomes more interdependent.

EMERGING COUNTRIES

Three possible strategies suggest themselves to create a global factory under a single country (or region) governance. The first is to expand from the subordinate contractual manufacturing provider by adding activities. The second is to internationalize from an 'almost complete' local factory lacking, perhaps, branding or R&D. The third is to build a full range of activities in the host country or regions and then internationalize the whole range from a domestic base. We shall analyse the first strategy in detail. The second strategy, feasible only where global networks are patchy or intrinsically difficult to create, is at first sight more hopeful. However, 'gaps' in global factories are difficult to fill because they represent deficiencies in local conditions. They are most usually in branding, distribution or R&D, and are, as we shall see, the most difficult and complex part of the network of the global factory to enter. Alliances are a potential means of filling gaps but are open to potential power inequalities and to the threat of takeover. Finally, building a local network and then internationalizing the whole of it is a formidable task. Such a strategy only arises when the local economy is large (China, India, Brazil, Russia) or is protected by artificial barriers (such as tariffs) or cultural barriers. Korean chaebols might be an example and their extremely patchy success rate is testament to the difficulties of internationalizing even from a strong, artificially protected and culturally distorted base. It could also be argued that Korean firms lacked the basic R&D strength to anchor a true global factory, being dependent on second-generation Japanese technology.

In emerging countries (*par excellence* China) the first step is to produce components or complete products to the specifications of foreign firms that market the final product. Such original equipment manufacturers (OEMs) are a subservient part of the global factory's network and are often in a weak bargaining position *vis-à-vis* the principal. There are many OEMs to play off against one another, and OEMs are often forced to be price takers. A crucial and neglected (Casson, 1999) aspect of breaking into the global factory is the ability of indigenous firms to assume the role of market-making intermediaries. A market-making intermediary establishes trading links that would not otherwise exist. In so doing, such a firm creates a network of buyers and sellers that could not easily trade with each other. This requires negotiating skills, a reputation for honesty and, crucially, the firm must recognize systematic changes in demand and supply conditions that create opportunities to profit from the creation of new markets. Therefore information costs are vital. The entrepreneur's task is to collect the relevant information and to identify opportunities to satisfy latent demand. The creation of a new market involves set-up costs. These are non-recoverable sunk costs analogous to those involved in innovation. In order to recover these costs, a degree of monopoly is essential. The first-mover advantages that confer such a monopoly can be protected by secrecy or some form of legal entry prevention – a patent or licence. An effective form of protection is to reach customers quickly and defend a reputation for quality by branding.

The status of the OEM allows benefits to the emerging country firm (Shenkar, 2005).

The firm can achieve incremental upgrading of quality and manufacture to customer requirements. It is plugged into the network of the global factory (albeit in a subservient position) and gains access, indirectly, to the global market. The OEM also receives technological support derived from the detailed specification of the customer. More enlightened principals also supply financial and managerial help, and may impose health and safety and environmental standards as well as upgrading the labour force.

Step 2 involves performing design and some development work and becoming an original design manufacturer (ODM). This strategic decision requires a significant upgrading of technological capability and the recruitment of engineers and designers capable of meeting world standards. It is significant that these categories of skills are priorities of the Chinese leadership (Shenkar, 2005, p. 89). A successful ODM can bypass middlemen and go direct to the buyer (usually the brand owner will control this process). The move from OEM to ODM is a profound one, requiring high levels of managerial and technological skill and political nous. An UNCTAD (2005) study identifies the need for host countries for textile MNEs to develop the ability to upgrade from simple assembly to 'full package production' (in textiles). It provides the following list of key policy areas to enable this to happen: identify specialist niches; skills and technological upgrading; investment in information technology; improvement of infrastructure; and utilizing tariff preferences. This is a formidable list for low- and even middle-income countries and firms to achieve, especially in view of their competitors also attempting to achieve the same goal.

The final step is to design, manufacture and sell the product under the firm's own name. This move to original brand manufacturer (OBM) involves control not only of production engineering and design, but also of branding and marketing. It requires marketing and research skills. Given the global market, it will also require exporting and foreign direct investment (FDI) and the establishment of the brand in foreign markets. Some Chinese firms (Haier, Huawi Technologies) have achieved modest success in creating their own global factories. Some outward FDI from China is designed to support such activities. Other outward FDI from emerging countries is intended to secure brands to be exploited worldwide. The main reasons why Shanghai Automotive Industry Corporation (SAIC), China's biggest car maker, was interested in buying Rover in 2005 were (1) to obtain the Rover brand and (2) to obtain the ability to design and manufacture cars (*Financial Times*, 2005).

ENTRY BY BUYING BRANDS

Brands, just like any other asset, can be acquired. Purchasing brands might seem to be a relatively easy way for outsiders to enter the global factory. This will usually mean the acquisition of the whole company because brands are embedded and are often unavailable except as part of the takeover of the brand owner. However, it is often ailing companies that are most likely to be takeover targets, and such companies may be owners of tired, dated or obsolescent brands. Moreover, because of the potential value as assets, brands are expensive to acquire and this may put good healthy brands with potential longevity beyond the purchasing power of emerging country firms.

THE DYNAMICS OF UPGRADING

The progress from contract OEM to ODM, to OBM and finally to full global factory, involving contracting out of activities, is a set of enormous leaps. The degree of skill and managerial resources can only be accumulated, financed and protected by an immense effort of will and concentration of resources. There is a requirement for entrepreneurial ability of a high order and, moreover, the type of entrepreneurial skill required varies over time. Initially, the entrepreneur has to secure and fulfil demanding and competitive contracts in order to achieve a position as OEM in the global factory. Reliability and quality of output must be achieved. Upgrading to ODM requires real vision, a global outlook, long-term planning and the ability to build a high-level multidisciplinary team. Designers and engineers have to be integrated into the firm and they require a different style of management from production workers. A shift from accepting design and engineering specifications to their creation is a profound step change. The final stage – the move to OBM – is even more difficult. The creation of an original brand is a huge undertaking. Quality, reliability, a good design and the maintenance of world-class standards are not easily achieved. This has to go together with the creation of global distribution and marketing. Thus a primarily national, dependent organization needs to become international and independent, central to a new global factory.

CONSOLIDATION

It is clear that OEMs have little bargaining power and this constrains their ability to amass the resources necessary to break out of their subservient role in the global factory. There is evidence that this is happening, and situations approaching bilateral monopoly (or at least oligopoly) are occurring in several sections where one or more powerful principals confront multiskilled 'factories for hire' that are approaching a scale, competence and self-confidence to break out of the role of mere contractors.

A clear example of this process occurs in the textile and clothing sector (UNCTAD, 2005). A small number of large retailing companies transmit demands from Western consumers and largely shape trade and production patterns. However, with the removal of tariff protection from manufacturing in selected lower-cost production locations, there is increasing pressure on producers to consolidate production into larger factories to gain economies of scale and reduce costs. This consolidation produces MNEs – mainly from East Asia (Hong Kong, Taiwan, Korea) with multiple production locations to supply the retailers.

AN EXAMPLE OF STRATEGIC CHANGE IN THE GLOBAL FACTORY: 'FRECKNALL'

This example concerns the transfer of commercial expertise to new affiliates in emerging markets. The company, which we shall refer to as Frecknall, is a US-owned research-based ethical pharmaceutical manufacturer. During the 1980s and 1990s, the company established new subsidiaries in developing markets throughout the world. By the late

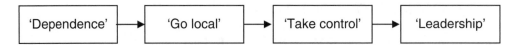

Figure 4.5   Frecknall's sequential affiliate business models

1990s, it had established a four-stage process that was in use in Eastern Europe and in Africa. The developments in these territories were administered through the UK/Europe subsidiary rather than directly from the US parent. The discussion here will examine both the knowledge transfer to the new subsidiaries and the organization of this process from the US parent and the UK/European regional headquarters.

Frecknall conceives the stages of establishing a new subsidiary in terms of a sequence of four 'affiliate business models' (Figure 4.5). The transfer of expertise takes place over an extended period, and each phase represents an increase in the degree and scope of local control and responsibility. These become possible as the number of individuals with appropriate expertise becomes larger over time, as the depth of knowledge grows and as local operations become more established and aligned both with local conditions and market requirements and with the strategic direction established by the corporation.

In the earliest stage, the subsidiary is directed and monitored in a directive hierarchical relationship by specialists in the regional headquarters. By the final stage, the subsidiary is integrated into Frecknall's matrix form of organization in which geographical reporting is combined with reporting in the product-based 'global business units'. The organizational and knowledge-process characteristics of each stage can be briefly summarized as follows.

Dependence

In the first stage that a local company is established, these activities are limited to the sales and distribution of Frecknall products. Management of this business is the responsibility of an experienced Frecknall manager, who is therefore almost always an expatriate from the USA or Europe. The subsidiary manager reports to the unit in regional headquarters, which is responsible for developing markets within its designated region. This unit is responsible for the marketing strategy for all products handled by the 'dependent' subsidiary and is accountable for its profit. Registration of medicines for sale in the new market is carried out by staff at the regional headquarters, with the subsidiary manager and staff in the developing markets unit acting as mediators with the regulatory authority and healthcare providers in the target country. The subsidiary manager recruits sales personnel and sets up a distribution network typically by contracting with an established local business. He or she, and the staff recruited for sales, are the main channel through which the developing market unit in headquarters acquires knowledge of local market conditions and requirements.

At this stage, the principal requirements for knowledge transfer into the target country are product knowledge, selling experience and good distribution practice concerning the control of medicines. This knowledge is provided through training courses, provided both locally by division staff visiting the subsidiary and centrally by subsidiary staff visiting regional headquarters and, where appropriate, through monitoring visit audits by staff from regional headquarters.

Go Local

This stage is structurally and operationally similar to the previous one, and characterized by the appointment of local managers to carry the day-to-day responsibility of the business rather than expatriate managers. Marketing decisions continue to be the responsibility of the development market unit in regional headquarters, which is also still the profit centre for the operation. During this phase, it is also possible that local managers may take over the direct responsibility for product registration and medical liaison with the country authorities and health providers. The individuals who take these senior positions in the developing market have usually benefited from 'switch programme' training, in which they are relocated to an established Frecknall subsidiary for a period to gain operating experience and improve their understanding of and alignment with Frecknall custom and practice. An important mechanism for raising local awareness of Frecknall's corporate perspectives and aims is linking the subsidiary into the company intranet. This provides ready access to technical information, information about market developments and perspectives on corporate priorities and strategy. It not only provides information but also enhances the degree to which local managers identify with the corporation and not simply their own subsidiary, for example through receiving directly regular statements from the chairman. At this stage, there continues to be close supervision from staff at regional headquarters, who are likely to visit the subsidiary frequently. Headquarters staff must still approve many aspects of local activity. For example, they may wish to ensure that low-price decisions are not inconsistent with global pricing policy across the corporation.

Take Control

This is the stage in which the subsidiary becomes a profit centre and local management takes over formal responsibility for product registration, marketing and sales. Operationally, there continue to be 'dotted line' links to functional managers for each activity in the regional headquarters. Headquarters staff continue to pay regular visits to audit both financial and medicinal good practice. They will also review major contracts.

Coherence with corporate aims is further developed through the subsidiary's participation in the corporate planning process. Two annual meetings consider three-year strategic business plans and one-year operating plans. These meetings bring together subsidiary and corporate managers from several levels of organization. The forum promotes alignment by the subsidiary with the corporation practice, and permits dialogue and exchange of understanding in both directions. The subsidiary continues to be accountable to the regional headquarters for its activities, and control of the subsidiary is centralized in unitary form through functional managers reporting to the subsidiary CEO.

Leadership

The final stage brings about a significant structural change. The organization switches from a functional basis in which the CEO provides central control of the subsidiary to a more decentralized product-based organization. Product strategies are determined by specialists who now communicate directly with product-based global business units in the

US parent. The subsidiary managers continue to oversee sales and distribution, and may now be permitted to establish local manufacturing if this is the most cost-effective means to supply the local market. This form of organization, with a network of communication channels between product and functional specializations globally and operational managers locally, is the normal structure adopted by Frecknall for operating in mature country markets.

The stages outlined briefly here indicate several ways in which the company overcomes knowledge combination barriers of the kind discussed earlier. For example, the responsibility for new market development is given to a specialist group. This group is located in Europe, a regional headquarters where there is plenty of mature experience, but from where travel to and communication with the new market is easier than it would be for the US parent. The development from 'dependence' to 'go local' to 'take control' illustrates the gradual transfer of expertise into the subsidiary – 'unsticking' the expertise. While the expertise is located mainly in the regional headquarters, profit responsibility lies there, but it is transferred as the knowledge is progressively transferred. In the final mature form of organization, corporate expertise and practices are sufficiently diffused within the subsidiary that it is possible to decentralize the combination of local and global knowledge from its focus in the subsidiary CEO and the development unit of the regional headquarters to separate product managers and global business units. In terms of the literature on the strategy-active subsidiary, we can see a temporal sequence of transferring to the subsidiary the rights and abilities to set its own strategic parameters. In examining issues of the spatial location of decision-making, we should not neglect temporal factors. Examining the subsidiary in its 'leadership' phase gives a very different picture from that of 'dependence'. Analysts who have identified the strategy-active subsidiary may be focusing on a particular phase in the development of global knowledge management practices as they evolve over time.

A complementary study is that of Delany (2000), who examines the strategic development of subsidiaries of MNEs in Ireland. He produces an eight-stage composite development model of subsidiaries but, it should be emphasized, this is not within a single firm and the cases are compiled into a linear model that is not followed throughout by a single firm. Delany further suggests that the headquarters may be hostile to initiatives taken by subsidiaries or at best 'compliant' with them. In Delany's model, the headquarters management is relatively passive and accepts (or hinders) initiatives at subsidiary level. This is not the case with Frecknall, where subsidiary initiatives are encouraged and indeed anticipated (planned for) by headquarters.

Views of entrepreneurial activity in subsidiaries differ greatly in the literature. Studies such as Delany's are often conducted solely at the level of the subsidiary. When interviewed, subsidiary managers are likely to attribute wide decision-making powers and initiatives to themselves, and for this reason it is good practice to conduct dyadic interviews at both parent and subsidiary. Much of the real entrepreneurship is conducted at headquarters, where judgement is exercised as to when and where to allow subsidiary autonomy and over what areas of decision-making subsidiary autonomy is best fostered (Casson, 1982).

REFERENCES

Aharoni, Yair (1966), *The Foreign Investment Decision Process*, Cambridge, MA: Harvard Business School Press.

Buckley, P.J. (1997), 'Trends in international business research: the next 25 years', in I. Islam and W. Shepherd (eds), *Current Issues in International Business*, Cheltenham, UK and Lyme, NH, USA: Edward Elgar, pp. 218–28.

Buckley, Peter J. (2004a), 'The role of China in the global strategy of multinational enterprises', *Journal of Chinese Economic and Business Studies*, **2**(1): 1–25.

Buckley, P.J. (2004b), 'Cartography and international business', *International Business Review*, **13**(2): 239–55.

Buckley, Peter J. (2007), 'The strategy of multinational enterprises in the light of the rise of China', *Scandinavian Journal of Management*, **23**(2): 107–26.

Buckley, Peter J. and Martin J. Carter (1996), 'The economics of business process design: motivation, information and coordination within the firm', *International Journal of the Economics of Business*, **3**: 5–25.

Buckley, P. and M. Casson (1988), 'A theory of co-operation in international business', in F.J. Contractor and P. Lorange (eds), *Co-operative Strategies in International Business*, Lexington, MA: D.C. Heath & Co., pp. 31–53.

Buckley, Peter J. and Mark Casson (1996), 'An economic model of international joint ventures', *Journal of International Business Studies*, **27**(5): 849–76.

Buckley, Peter J. and Mark Casson (1998a), 'Models of the multinational enterprise', *Journal of International Business Studies*, **29**(1): 21–44.

Buckley, Peter J. and Mark Casson (1998b), 'Analysing foreign market entry strategies: extending the internalisation approach', *Journal of International Business Studies*, **29**(3): 539–61.

Buckley, Peter J. and Mark Casson (2001), 'The moral basis of global capitalism: beyond the eclectic theory', *International Journal of the Economics of Business*, **8**(2): 303–27.

Buckley, P.J. and P.N. Ghauri (eds) (2002), *International Mergers and Acquisitions: A Reader*, London: International Thomson Press.

Buckley, Peter J. and Pervez N. Ghauri (2004), 'Globalisation, economic geography and the strategy of multinational enterprises', *Journal of International Business Studies*, **35**(2): 81–98.

Buckley, Peter J., Jeremy Clegg and Chengqi Wang (2002), 'The impact of inward FDI on the performance of Chinese manufacturing firms', *Journal of International Business Studies*, **33**(4): 637–55.

Buckley, P.J., J. Clegg and C. Wang (2004), 'The relationship between inward foreign direct investment and the performance of domestically-owned Chinese manufacturing industry', *Multinational Business Review*, **12**(3): 23–40.

Buckley, P.J., J. Clegg and C. Wang (2006), 'Inward foreign direct investment and host country productivity: evidence from China's electronics industry', *Transnational Corporations*, **15**(1): 13–37.

Buckley, P.J., J. Clegg and C. Wang (2007a), 'Is the relationship between inward FDI and spillover effects linear? An empirical examination of the case of China', *Journal of International Business Studies*, **38**(3): 447–59.

Buckley, P.J., J. Clegg and C. Wang (2007b), 'The impact of foreign ownership, local ownership and industry characteristics on spillover benefits from foreign direct investment in China', *International Business Review*, **16**(2): 142–58.

Buckley, Peter J., Keith W. Glaister and Rumy Husan (2002), 'International joint ventures: partnering skills and cross-cultural issues', *Long Range Planning*, **35**: 113–34.

Casson, M.C. (1982), 'Transaction costs and the theory of the multinational enterprise', in A.M. Rugman (ed.), *New Theories of the Multinational Enterprise*, New York: St Martin's Press, pp. 24–43.

Casson, M.C. (1997), *Information and Organization*, Oxford: Oxford University Press.

Casson, Mark (1999), 'The organisation and evolution of the multinational enterprise', *Management International Review*, **39**, Special Issue 1: 77–121.

Casson, M.C. (2000), *Enterprise and Leadership: Studies on Firms, Networks and Institutions*, Cheltenham, UK and Northampton, MA, USA: Edward Elgar.

Delany, E. (2000), 'Strategic development of the multinational subsidiary through subsidiary initiative-taking', *Long Range Planning*, **33**(2): 220–44.

Financial Times (2005), 'What Shanghai sought from Longbridge', 1 June, p. 15.

Murtha, T.P., S.A. Lenway and J.A. Hart (2001), *Managing New Industry Creation*, Stanford, CA: Stanford University Press.

Prahalad, C.K. and K. Lieberthal (1998), 'The end of corporate imperialism', *Harvard Business Review*, July–August: 69–79.

Shenkar, O. (2005), *The Chinese Century: The Rising Chinese Economy and its Impact on the Global Economy, the Balance of Power, and your Job*, Upper Saddle River, NJ: Wharton School.

Smith, A. (1759), *The Theory of Moral Sentiments*.
Smith, A. (1776), *The Wealth of Nations*.
UNCTAD (2005), *TNCs and the Removal of Textiles and Clothing Quotas*, Geneva: UNCTAD.
Wilson, J. and G.A.C. Guzman (2005), 'Organisational knowledge transfer in modular production networks: the case of Brazil', paper presented to AIB World conference, Quebec, July.

5   Dynamics of foreign operation modes and their combinations: insights for international strategic management
Gabriel R. G. Benito, Bent Petersen and Lawrence S. Welch

1.   INTRODUCTION

Companies' choice of foreign operation modes (FOMs) has been a core subject of international business studies basically from its beginning (Hymer, 1960 [1976]; Root, 1964). A half-century of research has brought us a set of established perspectives on companies' FOM choices, the most important being the economics-based approaches of internalization and transaction cost theories (Anderson and Gatignon, 1986; Buckley and Casson, 1976; Hennart, 1982), evolutionary and resource-based approaches (Andersen, 1997; Kogut and Zander, 1993; Madhok, 1997), institutional approaches (Kostova and Zaheer, 1999; Meyer and Peng, 2005), and process models based on learning and decision behaviour theories (Johanson and Vahlne, 1977, 2009).

The various approaches have been usefully summarized in comprehensive frameworks such as Dunning's well-known OLI framework (ownership–location–internalization) and the eclectic framework proposed by Hill et al. (1990).

Alongside conceptual developments there has also been a surge of empirical studies, especially from the mid-1980s when research templates emerged through the groundbreaking studies by Davidson and McFetridge (1985), Caves and Mehra (1986), Anderson and Coughlan (1987), Gatignon and Anderson (1988), Hennart (1988) and Kogut and Singh (1988); see also Kogut (2001). Several overview articles (Brouthers and Hennart, 2007; Canabal and White, 2008) and meta-analyses (Morschett et al., 2010; Tihanyi et al., 2005; Zhao et al., 2004) have been published recently, indicating that this has become a mature field of research. Well-established research templates and a dearth of innovative contributions indicate that the field has developed paradigm-like characteristics. Recent research has above all expanded the empirical domains of entry mode studies.[1]

It is uncontroversial to state that this research has been successful in improving our understanding of companies' foreign operation mode choices and their implications, but it has also became increasingly apparent – as is typical of paradigmatic evolution – that potentially important issues remain rather overlooked by international business scholars. First, there has been a focus on the point of entry into specific foreign markets, with a corresponding disregard for what happens after entry.[2] Of course, if firms make few changes and adjustments to their entry modes as time passes, one could consider this a trivial oversight. However, some studies have shown that mode changes occur with sufficient frequency to merit much closer investigation (Benito et al., 2005; Calof, 1993; Clark et al., 1997; Fryges, 2007; Swoboda et al., 2011).

Second, the literature envisages operation mode decision-making as a static rather than dynamic process (Petersen et al., 2010). The issue is not just whether decisions (i.e. the outcomes of a decision-making process) are durable (i.e. are seldom reconsidered; see above), but also how the decision-making process itself proceeds. In theory, operation mode choices are made based on considerations regarding how a range of internal and external contingencies are best matched with the particular characteristics (e.g. control, flexibility, costs etc.) of given modes of operation. However, do decision-makers act according to beliefs based on 'perfect' foresight (*a priori* optimization), do they live with their mistakes should match-disparities arise, or do they proceed in gradual, incremental ways to pragmatically adjust to changing circumstances? In other words, are operation modes decided or managed, and, if the latter, in what ways?

Third, as pointed out by Petersen et al. (2008), the bulk of research has examined the possible effects of a large range of explanatory factors (independent variables) on FOM choice. An enduring and somewhat surprising characteristic of that research is that the dependent variable itself – FOMs – has barely been discussed. Studies have tended to treat FOMs as choices among a restricted set of well-specified discrete alternatives – the choice between contractual and equity-based types of operation modes (e.g. Anderson and Coughlan, 1987; Davidson and McFetridge, 1985), or that between partly owned and fully owned operations (e.g. Benito, 1996; Gatignon and Anderson, 1988; Hennart, 1991). There is some evidence for a 'messier' reality (Benito et al., 2009; Clark et al., 1997; Kedron and Bagchi-Chen, 2011; Petersen and Welch, 2002; Welch et al., 2007), with companies using many different modes at the same time, and even concurrently for the same type of activity in a given location, but the systematic mapping of mode diversity and mode combinations has only just begun (Asmussen et al., 2009; Benito et al., 2011; Hashai et al., 2010). Within the broad categories of modes – contractual, exporting and equity – there are many different sub-categories, each important in its own right. For example, contractual modes include licensing, franchising, management contracts, outsourcing and some forms of alliances. Exporting might be handled indirectly, such as via a trading company, or through different types of foreign intermediary arrangements. Equity-based modes range from minority equity alliances to majority or fully owned foreign subsidiary forms. The combination possibilities are immense, and are used extensively: for example, licensing and equity-based modes are common partners, as are franchising and equity-based modes (Welch et al., 2007).

In this chapter we take a critical view of the established operation mode literature, with a focus on the themes outlined above. We apply a strategic management approach to FOMs. The strategic management approach to FOMs is far from new. Almost 50 years ago, when Franklin Root introduced FOMs as a key IB theme (Root, 1964), he basically applied a strategic management approach inasmuch as he provided prescriptions as to how firms could achieve competitive advantage in foreign markets through formulation and implementation of FOM strategies. Since then, however, FOM scholars have mostly subscribed to descriptive and – in particular – predictive approaches.

Descriptive approaches have been applied when a new FOM emerged in the international marketplace and researchers addressed the *how* and *why* questions through in-depth case studies. As an example, international management contracts were described through case studies in a range of industries in the 1980s (Brooke, 1985). Most FOM researchers, however, have focused on the question of *when* firms would prefer one FOM over another. Introduction of new theories – transaction cost theory in the 1980s, the resource-based perspective in the 1990s, and new institutional theory in the 2000s – has driven this penchant for predictive approaches. Since the prime aim has been to test the explanatory power of these theories on FOM choices, the predictive approach could rightly be labelled a theory-testing approach. The theory-testing approach enquires about variety in terms of theory-specific factors that may explain simple – often binary – and standardized FOM choices (outcomes). A strategic management approach, in contrast, looks for variety and uniqueness of FOM outcomes since standardized outcomes require a minimum of management discretion and no inimitable capabilities. As such, standardized FOM outcomes can hardly explain sustainable competitive advantage – the very aim of strategic management research.

Our strategic management approach addresses a fundamental FOM management dilemma: the pursuit of operational efficiency through FOM variety that, in turn (and as will be elaborated on later), threatens to trigger excessively high transaction costs. Our discussion of this dilemma will be organized along 'the three Cs' of FOM *choice, change* and *combination*. We start by questioning the enduring myth of static decisions between durable discrete entry modes, and then proceed to look into how the puzzle of mode packages or combinations can be explained once certain commonly held preconceived ideas are discarded. We close with some reflections about the managerial and research implications of broader conceptualization of FOMs.

2.   SKETCH OF A MANAGEMENT DILEMMA

FOM variety potentially leads to higher operational efficiency than FOM simplicity, but variety also implies higher transaction costs – i.e. costs of drafting, (re-)negotiating, enforcing and coordinating multiple FOM contracts. As an example, the operational efficiency (e.g. in terms of scale and scope economies) of licensing succeeded by a production subsidiary is higher in an initially small, but growing, foreign market than is the efficiency of the two modes individually and persistently; but the switch between the two modes is likely to incur take-down and set-up costs (Benito et al., 1999).[3] However, negotiating an exit option in the licensing contract may curb the 'switching costs'. Conversely, an aloof, forced and sudden cancellation of the licensing contract may incur very high transaction costs in the form of high take-down costs as well as set-up costs associated with the move to an alternative mode or mode combination. Hence FOM variety in the form of mode switches and mode combinations may differ substantially in terms of transaction costs depending on whether they are well prepared and well orchestrated – or exercised in an improvised and awkward manner.

The logic is illustrated in Figure 5.1. The figure depicts the marginal cost (*MC*) and benefit (*MB*) of FOM variety, i.e. the number of modes employed after entry of a given foreign market. The *MB* curve (*MB* = marginal benefit of one additional FOM) reflects diminishing returns to scale: the *MB* curve has a strong downward slope and moves asymptotically towards zero (the *x*-axis). The marginal cost (*MC*) of adding one more FOM after entry is assumed constant. However, the cost level across the added FOMs is

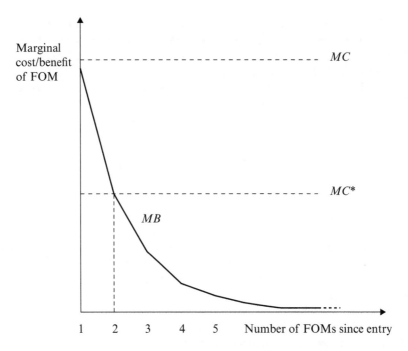

Figure 5.1   The management choice between FOM simplicity and diversity

assumed to be strongly influenced by MNE managers. Managers' potential influence on *MC* levels is indicated by including two different horizontal cost lines in the figure: *MC* > *MC**. The upper cost line, *MC*, does not intersect with the *MB* curve at any point simply because the potential marginal cost (switching costs, coordination costs etc.) exceeds the marginal benefit of any additional FOM – even the first, most beneficial. The lower cost line, *MC**, intersects the *MB* curve at two additional FOMs. Hence the MNE will be better off by adding one FOM beyond its entry mode and will neither be better nor worse off by adding one more FOM (that is, a total of three FOMs). The level of transaction costs in the *MC** case is significantly lower than in the *MC* case – indicating that the MNE managers in the former case are much better at preparing switches (e.g. by putting in exit options at market entry) and curbing costs of coordinating multiple FOMs. Consequently, a manager in the *MC** case is closer to achieving the 'best of both worlds' in the foreign market: maximum operational efficiency with a minimum of transaction and governance costs.

3.   TO CHANGE OR NOT TO CHANGE? CHARACTERISTICS, IMPETUS AND BARRIERS

Received theories of FOM choices (or entry mode choices, as these decisions are usually, but often inaccurately, referred to) typically view such decisions as discrete as well as discriminate: at a given decision point (which could be at entry or later) companies choose one among several alternative ways of organizing their operations in a foreign market – the mode of operation – and the use of that mode is normally assumed to exclude the concurrent use of other modes.

Some conceptualizations tend to be static, thereby emphasizing the initial point of entry and, if at all, projecting a persistence of the selected mode over the relevant time horizon. Others take a more dynamic approach and accentuate (or at least recognize) the conditions under which changes of FOMs might be expected. Transaction cost theory and the resource-based and institutional approaches have tended to be on the static end of a static–dynamic continuum, whereas internationalization process theory has been on the other end. Although their key explanatory variables and mechanisms differ,[4] the former approaches have in common a focus on static – but typically long-term – discrete choices, and which consequently may seem to provide limited opportunities for mixing different FOMs.[5]

The dynamic approach offered by internationalization process theory could perhaps be seen as more 'fluid' and hence as more open to mode combinations, and the case study approach favoured by many internationalization process scholars often produces rich narratives that include descriptions of mode combinations, mixes and packages, but most studies have actually focused on the transition from one (main) mode to another; for example how an entrant firm's gradual acquisition of foreign market knowledge and/or development of local networks reduces perceived market risk and uncertainty, which in turn could induce a switch from a low-risk and commitment mode (e.g. a sales agent) to a high commitment mode (e.g. a wholly owned sales and marketing subsidiary). Hence the internationalization process approach explains why (but not how) mode changes take place, whereas it is more silent as regards mode combinations.

Even though the dynamics of FOMs have been relatively neglected, that is not to say that received theories cannot deal with changes. Benito et al. (2005) combine transaction costs and resource-based theories with internationalization process theory in their study of changes in international sales and distribution channels.[6] They model changes in the way exporters organize such activities in foreign markets as driven by factors that motivate switches as well as factors that work against making switches. The former are called switch motivators while the latter are labelled switch deterrents.

The two types of factors work in opposite directions. Motivators are factors that to some extent reduce the perceived utility of continuing with the current set-up, and which should therefore increase the probability of making changes to the current FOM. Key factors include market growth, company growth, accumulation of market knowledge, disappointing performance and increasing asset specificity. In contrast, switch deterrents are the set of factors that make it difficult or costly to carry out such changes; these factors have hence also been labelled 'switching costs' (Benito et al., 1999).

In their study of Danish exporters, which largely corroborated their model, Benito et al. (2005) found evidence of both within-mode changes (e.g. substituting an intermediary with another) and between-mode changes (e.g. moving from a contractual arrangement with a distributor to in-house operations), but only a limited extent of mode combinations.[7] However, Clark et al. (1997) uncovered a substantial amount of mode combinations, which they called mixed approaches; in a sample of 25 UK firms (that had made a total of 679 foreign operations) they detected 203 mode changes, of which 36 (18 per cent) entailed mode combinations.

4.   HOW LARGE A STEP AND HOW MANY? MANAGING THE INTERNALIZATION PROCESS

The concept of internalization lies at the core of influential theories in international business, with their focus on choice of FOMs (Buckley and Casson, 1976; Hennart, 1982; McManus, 1972; Rugman, 1981); the aim is to use theory to explain the circumstances under which a firm replaces imperfect (or non-existent) external markets by internal coordination (Buckley, 1993). Together with market power explanations (Hymer, 1960/1976) and knowledge-based explanations (Grant, 1996; Kogut and Zander, 1993), internalization theory offers a paradigm which explains – with a high degree of accuracy under certain assumed conditions – why MNEs choose to exercise tight managerial control over foreign operations rather than work through other firms under contractual or other arrangements. Hence, on a general level internalization theory can explain the existence of MNEs (Rugman and Verbeke, 2003). By including time-responsive factors that pull in the direction of internalization, the theory can also predict patterns and directions of the growth of MNEs. However, the theory downplays any meaningful role for management, particularly in the real-world dynamic context of constantly evolving foreign market conditions and operations of an MNE (Buckley, 1993).

We argue, however, that internalization theory could be taken a step further by including managerial judgement considerations in the context of dynamic influences on the development of foreign operations. The market transaction costs of using outside agents (local operators) are frequently negligible at market entry, but usually increase over time. A key question pertaining to such situations is: what management instruments may ensure persistent concurrence between a changing pressure for internalization in a foreign market and the effectuated internalization of an MNE in that market?

Internalization theory basically assigns three roles to MNE management. First, managers need to decide whether the MNE should produce at home and export to the foreign market in question or produce in the foreign market (see e.g. Horst, 1974). Second, the managers face a make-or-buy choice whenever localization advantages favour production in the foreign market (Dunning, 1980). Third, managers have to decide the timing of internalization (Buckley and Casson, 1981) in cases where the 'buy' choice precedes internalization.[8]

Seeing market exchange as the 'default option', internalization theorists have first of all focused on the identification and analysis of various market imperfections that may result in internalization. Since theorists have focused on a market efficiency rather than market power explanation (see e.g. Calvet, 1981), MNE managers have been assigned a 'neoclassical' role as omniscient administrators of market imperfections – and not creators of market imperfections.[9] In this perspective the managerial task in internalization theory is first of all to observe the various relevant – mostly exogenous – choice factors, and only to a limited extent to involve oneself in complex managerial discretion. Exact observation of internalization-relevant factors (such as market size and degree of asset specificity) unequivocally directs the right choice. Furthermore, the choices are relatively simple ones: produce at home or in the foreign market; make or buy; when to internalize? Ideally, as depicted in Figure 5.2, there should be a perfect concurrence between the particular need for internalization at a certain point in time – which would be determined by the underlying internalization drivers – and the actual internalization:

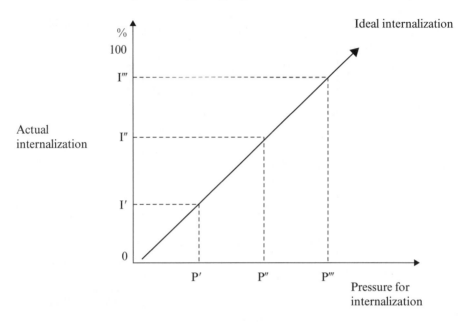

Figure 5.2   The ideal degree of internalization

that is, firms should respond to a pressure P' for internalization by choosing a I' degree of internalization, and correspondingly choose I'' for P'', and I''' for P'''.

In the real world, the chosen levels of internalization may of course differ from the optimal ones, e.g. due to incomplete information, changes in internal and external contingencies, and various impediments (e.g. switching costs) to carrying out changes. Hence, as shown in Figure 5.3, a company might have chosen a level of internalization, e.g. point A, which is considerably lower than the ideal; or, conversely, chosen a much higher level of internalization, e.g. point B, than really needed. In case A, the company should further internalize until point A*, whereas in case B, it should de-internalize until reaching B*. In Figure 5.3, points C, A* and B* indicate optimal choices.

In an ever-changing and complex world it seems unlikely that companies as a rule will have reached the ideal level of internalization, so there is obviously plenty of scope for management to fine-tune operations in order to try to get as close as possible to the optimal line. Buckley (1993) and Rugman and Verbeke (2003) argue that there is considerable room for developing internalization theory in a more management-oriented direction.[10] In particular, Buckley stresses the need for theory development incorporating a more important role for management in the following two, closely interrelated, issues:

- The theory maintains a rather static view of internalization – being considered a state rather than a process. Hence, 'to incorporate a theory of management, it is essential to move away from a comparison of states to a comparison of processes ... Progress can be made by comparisons of the changing balance of the boundary between "firm" and "market" and intermediate states over given time periods' (Buckley, 1993, p. 201).

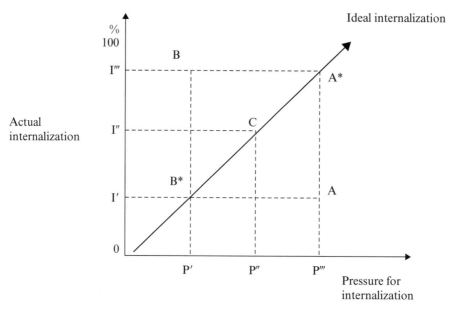

Figure 5.3   Internalization decisions

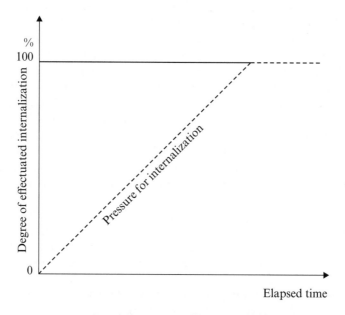

Figure 5.4   Pressure for internalization as a function of time

- There is an oversimplified choice for managers between markets and hierarchies. Hence, 'the narrow view that managers simply make "buy or build" decisions . . . needs to be extended' (ibid., p. 206).

The two issues point in the same direction, namely that internalization may be a long-term manageable process rather than a time-compressed, binary choice.[11] A pertinent circumstance is when non-hierarchical entry modes enjoy a temporal superiority over hierarchical modes. For example, licensing or joint ventures may be used before wholly owned production subsidiaries, or independent distributors may precede sales subsidiaries.

When the transition from non-hierarchical to hierarchical FOMs unfolds as a managed and stepwise process, this could suitably be termed 'staged internalization'. The potential pay-off to MNEs of undertaking staged internalization may be considerable: at any point in time, the ideal outcome for the firm would be when the degree to which a firm has internalized its foreign activities is in perfect balance with the underlying drivers of internalization. For example, an MNE typically undertakes several different value activities in a given foreign market. Some of the activities in that country may be characterized by a high degree of asset specificity whereas other activities could have low specificity. Due to the considerable scale and scope economies and local market knowledge typically enjoyed by a local, outside agent (e.g. a licensee of the MNE), the entrant MNE may initially choose only to internalize local activities for which a high degree of control is considered to be of utmost importance, such as R&D (Buckley and Hashai, 2005). However, the MNE may internalize more and more value activities in the foreign country as the degree of asset specificity of these activities increases, which typically occurs in small, consecutive steps.

The logic is illustrated in Figure 5.4. It is assumed that the underlying pressure for internalization (or internalization advantage) increases monotonically with elapsed time of operations in the foreign market through, *inter alia*, learning and an increased concern for control. Thus the x-axis indicates elapsed time of operations in the market and the y-axis shows the degree to which the foreign market operations are internalized (measured as a continuum from 0 to 100 per cent). Exactly where on the y-axis does a company choose to operate, given the evolving pressure for internalization as time passes? Figures 5.5, 5.6 and 5.7 illustrate three different scenarios in terms of the fit between underlying internalization drivers (indicated by the dotted line), such as increasing asset specificity, and effectuated (i.e. actual) internalization of operations in a given foreign market.[12]

Figure 5.5 depicts a scenario of immediate internalization that, for example, may be justified by excessively high anticipated/potential switching costs (Benito et al., 1999). Such a scenario is typically assumed in the entry mode literature, especially that based on transaction cost economics, as illustrated by the following statement in the much-cited study of foreign distribution by Anderson and Coughlan (1987, p. 71): 'Channel choices, once made, are often difficult to change. Hence, the question of whether to integrate foreign distribution can have a large and lasting impact on the success of a firm's international operations.'

The situation depicted in Figure 5.5 is one in which internalization, although economically justified by potential switching costs, actually is 'premature' inasmuch as the hierarchical operation mode – the wholly owned subsidiary (WOS) – in contrast to, for example, a local, independent licensee – operates below minimum efficient scale during the first years after market entry. Hence the governance structure is suboptimal in terms of operational/production costs, although perhaps not with regard to transaction costs (including switching costs). The sub-optimization in terms of production costs

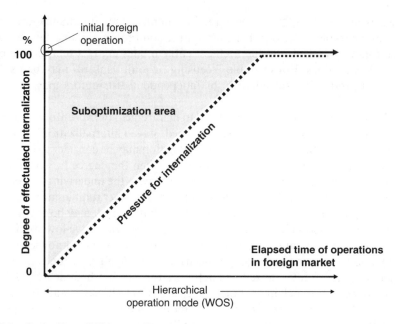

Figure 5.5   Immediate full internalization

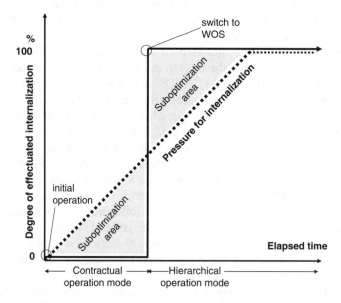

Figure 5.6   Internalization – one step

(i.e. sacrificed scale economies) is indicated by the shaded area. Figure 5.6 illustrates a scenario with one shift of governance structure – from a contractual mode (e.g. licensing) to the hierarchical mode (WOS). The shift halves the sub-optimization (shaded) area.[13]

The sub-optimization area is further reduced when the MNE makes two

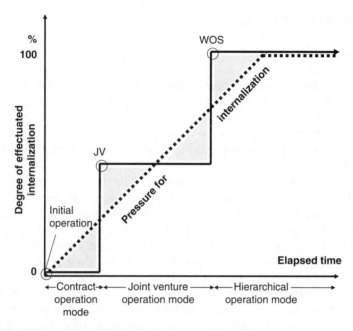

Figure 5.7   Internalization – two steps

shifts of governance structures/operation modes (see Figure 5.7). The first shift is from a contractual arrangement to a 50:50 equity joint venture, and later from a joint venture to a sole venture (WOS) – i.e. a hierarchical organization.

Altogether, the three scenarios show that the sub-optimization area diminishes as the number of shifts – or internalization steps – increases. Of course, a perfect concurrence between the particular need for internalization at a certain point in time – which would be determined by the underlying internalization drivers – and the actual internalization at that point in time would eliminate the sub-optimization area completely.

It is also clear that there is a trade-off between – on the one side – production cost savings due to perfect concurrence obtained through frequent internalization steps, and – on the other side – the additional transaction costs in the form of renegotiation costs. A basic premise of our line of reasoning is that while achieving a perfect fit between the underlying internalization drivers and the effectuated internalization may have a high payoff in terms of production efficiency, it also constitutes a major managerial challenge of curbing the transaction costs associated with exercising numerous internalization steps. Hence, determining the number of internalization steps is a managerial challenge that is part of the simplicity–diversity trade-off we outlined earlier (Section 2).

5.   COMBINING MODES

5.1   Why are Modes Combined?

As noted above, it has become increasingly clear that many companies are engaged in the use of various forms of mode combinations (Benito et al., 2011; Clark et al., 1997), and that they appear to be prepared to institute mode combination additions or deletions if conditions warrant such changes. On the other hand, academic researchers seem to be far more reticent about recognizing this reality and its implications for international business theory and strategy.

It is not surprising that companies are attracted to the use of mode combinations: they may deliver a range of strategic benefits that managers can readily relate to – such as operational efficiency, flexibility, control, income generation, strengthening of intellectual property protection and as stepping stones to a major change in FOM.

At a basic level, mode combinations provide a significantly wider array of options to companies in how they might go about entering or extending penetration of a given foreign market. Mode combination options go beyond, sometimes well beyond, the mainstream or primary mode that a company might employ in a particular foreign market situation. The universe of mode combination options is immense, especially when added to market location options.[14] Of necessity, managers tend to consider a far more restricted range of options, often driven by very specific market and/or foreign partner pressures (Larimo, 1987). The availability of mode combination options, assuming managerial recognition, provides greater flexibility to companies in the development of foreign market operations at the outset and beyond – providing an enhanced and broadened ability to adapt as circumstances change. Mode adjustments can be made without necessarily resorting to a potentially disruptive primary mode change. This could vary from fine-tuning of existing mode use to important adjustments that flow from the inevitable market and mode learning processes that unfold over time. The JV literature points to the different ways that JV arrangements evolve as the parties build up experience with each other (Becerra et al., 2008; Yan and Gray, 1994; Yan and Zeng, 1999).

Mode additions to the primary JV mode, at any stage, are often made in order to strengthen control over the joint venture – such as by the addition of a licensing or management contract. Control was an important concern for the multinational express delivery company, FedEx, in revising and upgrading its operation in China in 1999. At that stage it was not prepared to commit to a fully owned operation. It felt that having a Chinese partner was crucial in delivering political and other benefits to its service business, but a 50:50 JV fell short of delivering the control it regarded as also critical. Thus a management contract was negotiated alongside its 50:50 JV with a Chinese partner: the management contract was seen by FedEx as effectively delivering control of day-to-day operations of the venture (Welch et al., 2007). Licensing arrangements have long been used as a way of seeking to control the use of the licensor's technology, technical and commercial, by foreign partner firms (for example foreign outsourcing contractees), as well as trying to prevent unwanted dissemination. In general, mode combinations can be constructed in such a way as to strengthen intellectual property protection outside formal protection systems (patents, copyright etc.). Sales subsidiaries are sometimes used alongside a foreign intermediary in the foreign market as a way of extending control over the foreign sales activity and the intermediary (Petersen et al., 2001). In some instances an additional mode in a package delivers additional returns from a foreign operation, for example in the form of royalty payments under a licensing arrangement that operates alongside FDI (Welch et al., 2007).

Such mode combination steps may be useful in timing terms as well: rather than seeking to take over the JV partner when not prepared to do so, extended control could be achieved while building towards a move to full subsidiary status. At the same time, adding a mode could be a way of easing the process of ultimate primary mode change – additions to the original mode/s acting as stepping stones (Petersen et al., 2001; see also Petersen et al., 2010). Of course, flexibility would be significantly enhanced when the desired mode option is built into the starting mode arrangement (Petersen et al., 2000). In an overall sense, the availability of mode combination options provides a company with greater strategic control over when and how it develops foreign operations.

Such flexibility is further augmented by the additional possibilities for role variation and adjustment across a mode package: the starting roles performed by modes are not necessarily fixed over time. Companies can and do make mode role changes in response to developments in their external environment or because of modifications in company strategy. Such mode role variation may accompany mode combination changes, but could occur without them. For example, the starting mode arrangement for a company in a foreign market might be a joint venture with exporting from the home market. The starting roles for the two modes could be: the JV acts as a marketing and service base within the foreign market, basically to support the exporting activity; exports assist with home plant utilization, ensuring economies of scale at the production level. Over time, though, the operation within the foreign market may develop in various ways: successful market penetration to the point where production in the foreign market becomes feasible; the relationship with the JV partner advances to a stage characterized by a high level of trust; and management decides that an enhanced facility would be an effective base to service other markets within the same region. Thus the role of the JV is extended to production and its marketing role expanded. While exports from the home market diminish, they do not disappear as some intermediary products and raw materials are likely to be needed by the JV for some time. Even though the outer shell of the mode package remains unchanged, substantial change occurs within because of the shift in mode roles. In this respect, mode role changes are not dissimilar to within-mode changes in effecting changes without overall mode adjustment (Benito et al., 2009). Taken together, the potential to change mode combinations, mode roles and make within-mode adjustments delivers many mode options short of substantial mode change, enhanced flexibility and the ability to organically stage increased mode commitment within a foreign market.

As the various examples noted illustrate, the path adopted may be in response to circumstances that arise in the foreign market: a mode combination may not be the outcome of a distinct decision at a given point in time. Learning is likely to be a significant component of mode combination adoption or change – reflecting both market learning and mode learning (Barnett and Burgelman, 1996). Rather than being a fixed, carefully structured entity, a mode combination should be viewed as a fluid and adaptable instrument of foreign market penetration.

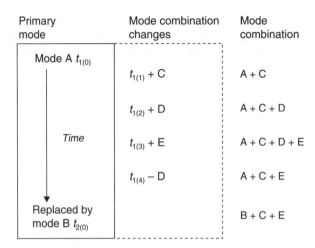

Figure 5.8   Mode combination evolution

From an evolutionary perspective, mode combinations reflect various process influences – externally and within a company. Figure 5.8 shows how a hypothetical company's mode combination might evolve in a foreign market, showing additions and a deletion over time, between the use of primary mode A at t_1 and the switch to primary mode B at t_2.

5.2   Barriers to Mode Combination

Clearly, there are substantial benefits for companies in developing mode packages as a way of penetrating foreign markets. The benefits are seemingly so obvious that it begs the question as to why such arrangements are not the almost automatic default position for companies in devising foreign operation strategies – i.e. instead of what mode, what mode combination should be employed? However, Norwegian data (Benito et al., 2011) indicate that mode combinations fall well short of being the automatic choice in mode strategy. It could be argued that this is because of ignorance: the possibilities are simply not recognized. Other explanations are that managers perceive various barriers to mode combinations, and that the range of possibilities is seen as somewhat overwhelming.

One important form of mode combination barrier or constraint might simply be mode myopia or mode ignorance (Welch et al., 2007). Research indicates that companies tend to consider a limited range of mode options in devising foreign operation strategies, let alone the plethora of combination options (Larimo, 1987; Calof, 1993; Petersen et al., 2008). This is understandable given the limited exposure to, or experience that managers have in utilizing, all modes and their combination potential.

Faced with so many mode and mode combination options, depending on the extent to which they are perceived, it is not surprising that many managers fall back on those modes they are familiar and comfortable with, and feel confident about using. This may be reinforced by the learning experiences that unfold through mode use. As companies and managers become experienced and adept at using a given set of modes, there is an automatic tendency to maintain and re-use this strength over time – so-called exploitation learning (March, 1991). It becomes harder to introduce a previously unused mode into an existing mode package: there is comfort and assurance in the known. There are examples of companies using a preferred operation mode over extended periods of internationalization. The UK firm Pilkington internationalized its float glass business over a very long period pre-eminently via the licensing of foreign manufacturers (Taylor, 1994). This is despite the fact that the starting mode(s) may have been used without careful analysis in response to an approach by a potential foreign customer, distributor, franchisee or licensee – a common starting point (Welch et al., 2007).

Because of inexperience initially, companies may engage in mode experimentation, but over time, following feedback, they engage in a more constrained approach to mode use. In extreme cases, involving what managers regard as highly negative outcomes, the experience can lead to the excision of a particular mode or modes from any consideration. For example, the private US multinational DDI, a provider of human resource services (talent management), entered foreign markets in the 1970s and expanded to 29 countries by 2010 (Warren-Smith, 2010). In its earlier international forays it used a range of operation modes, including wholly owned subsidiaries, licensing, joint ventures and project operations. By 2010, this range had been substantially reduced: before 1990 licensing and JVs constituted 82 per cent of mode use, but this had declined to 23 per cent by 2010, with JVs dropped altogether because of perceived problems with this form. In contrast, over the same period, wholly owned subsidiaries had become the dominant form – rising from 12 per cent to 77 per cent of total mode use. The ability to provide consistent services to multinational clients was an important driver of the shift to wholly owned subsidiaries, along with control of intellectual property. Thus a company might arrive at a position of considerable mode inertia over time (Benito et al., 2009), thereby not seriously canvassing other mode, including combination, options. Of course, companies could undertake exploratory learning (March, 1991), deliberately researching and expanding mode knowledge, even sending staff to training programmes, perhaps sparked by emerging pressures for change in different foreign markets, as most long-term internationalizers tend to experience. But overall there seems to be less evidence of exploratory activities.

Switching costs have been noted as a further constraining factor in the preparedness of companies to adopt new mode constructions (Benito et al., 1999). Existing modes are not always readily able to be deleted because of a range of factors – including host government and trade union pressure, and the contractual conditions surrounding a particular mode, for example limiting the ability to exit the arrangement within a stipulated time frame (Petersen et al., 2000). Beyond these constraints there are the set-up costs of adding new modes – not least learning costs. Fixed costs are typically incurred when adding a new mode – even for a relatively straightforward addition such as a licensing arrangement: i.e. covering the costs of negotiating, writing and implementing the licence contract. There may also be relationship costs in situations where companies are seeking to add a mode to an existing foreign set-up. Companies sometimes try to add altered arrangements on top of existing foreign distributor connections to advance foreign market penetration – effectively moving to a mode combination basis, sometimes as a deliberate prelude to subsidiary establishment (Petersen et al., 2001). Not surprisingly, foreign intermediaries are prone to resist such moves, and can ensure that their accomplishment is difficult and costly. Mode combination choices, like mode choices in general, are constrained, or compromised, by the realities of the situation and context they are used in, as well as companies' own limitations – of resources and of managerial vision.

Last, but not least, the cost of coordinating multiple FOMs may constitute an effective barrier to mode combination. A clear-cut division of responsibilities and roles among a number of local operators (including the entrant firm) is, in practice, easier said than done. Duplication of tasks and blurred market segmentation may result in inconsistent foreign market servicing, and – in turn – confused customers and dissatisfied operators. Poor coordination and communication may foster scepticism and competition – rather than collaboration – among third-party local operators. From this perspective the entrant firm managers may prefer one FOM at a time.

6.   COMBINING MODES INTO PACKAGES

Our analysis so far has shown that the array of mode combination options is substantial: there are many different ways in which FOMs can be assembled or packaged in servicing a given foreign market. While a company could be using various modes in a foreign market, they may not necessarily be 'combined', i.e. there may be little connection between them in terms of how they are used. The use of multiple modes could be because of geographical or other forms of market segmentation or because they are used in different parts of the value chain (Petersen and Welch, 2002). The Norwegian multinational Norsk Hydro had different divisions active in India in the 1990s, using a range of modes, but there was little coordination of these activities (Tomassen et al., 1998). Similarly, the Australian beer company Foster's kept their beer and wine operations separate in the USA, in part because their wine operations resulted from the acquisition of Beringer, a major US wine company (Speedy, 2007). The organization of its beer operations in the USA illustrates the type of mode arrangement along the value chain that a company may assemble.

Foster's licensed Molson in Canada to brew its beer for the US market, while marketing and distribution were undertaken through a JV with the US company Miller Brewing. When Molson merged with the US brewer Coors, Foster's cancelled its licensing agreement with Molson and signed one with Miller, thus generating a tighter overall mode package. At the same time, all the parts of the value chain in Canada – production, marketing and distribution – continued to be handled through a licensing agreement with the

Production	Marketing and distribution
Pre-2007: via licensing agreement (with Molson)	JV (with Miller)
2007: licensee change from Molson (Canada) to Miller (USA)	2007 – Foster's + Miller JV: no change

Figure 5.9   Foster's beer in the USA

Primary mode: joint venture • market penetration • revenue generation		
Associate Mode 1: **Licensing** • technology control	Associate Mode 2: **Management contract** • management control	Associate Mode 3: **Exporting** • domestic plant utilization

Source: Adapted from Petersen and Welch (2002), p. 161.

Figure 5.10   Modes packages: an example

newly formed Molson Coors (Speedy, 2007). Sometimes different modes are used simultaneously in a foreign market for the same type of activity. For example, the Israeli software firm Fundtech performed R&D in the USA through a joint venture, a greenfield subsidiary and an acquired subsidiary, while its marketing and customer support services there were conducted through distributors, a joint venture, a greenfield sales office and an acquired subsidiary (Welch et al., 2007). Thus the fact that multiple modes are used by a company may tell us little about the degree to which they are packaged together or how they are connected in order to achieve foreign market penetration goals. On one end of a connectedness scale we might have two divisions of a company (like Norsk Hydro) that use different modes but their operations (and thereby modes) are not at all integrated or coordinated. At the other extreme is the type of example shown in Figure 5.10, where modes are tightly connected in a supportive manner around the achievement of a set of goals: in general to ensure success of a company's foreign market involvement. The primary mode is a JV, the main vehicle for achieving foreign market penetration and revenue generation, with associate modes 1–3 in supportive positions, particularly in terms of control.

Competing modes are sometimes used by companies in the same foreign market, even targeting the same segment and market area. This often occurs when a company is seeking to have an alternative marketing channel to its independent foreign intermediary. In a Danish study, 27 per cent of companies retained their independent foreign intermediaries after establishing a subsidiary (Pedersen and Petersen, 1998).

7.   PROACTIVE MODE COMBINATION STRATEGY

Mode combinations have been shown to potentially play an important role in achieving a range of companies' foreign market penetration objectives, and therefore should be considered more seriously in the design of international strategy. However, developing a coherent and more deliberative mode combination strategy as part of general international strategy is not a straightforward exercise, as we have alluded to in previous sections. Companies do not have full control over the way that their foreign operations evolve. Managers are unlikely to be aware of the full extent of mode combination options, and changes may occur on the ground in the foreign market without full strategic assessment by a company. Mode strategy is therefore bound to include elements of emergent strategy (Mintzberg and Waters, 1985), for example as opportunities and approaches arise in the foreign market or in the nearby region. Sales to other markets could develop because of general networks maintained by a foreign JV partner. In various ways foreign, not just JV, partners (e.g. including intermediaries, licensees and the like) inevitably influence the way a company's foreign operation strategy evolves – often in subtle ways that are not obvious in the first place. Mode choices may be emergent initially but can become intended (deliberate) over time, even locked in, as part of a more consistent international mode strategy. Mode inertia is a factor (Benito et al., 2009). There is comfort in continuing to employ those modes, and mode packages, that a company's managers have become knowledgeable about and adept at using in different foreign markets.

Limited evidence indicates that companies make little if any attempt to include mode combinations in the development of international strategies, despite the potential benefits for international operations noted above, and the reality of their sometimes extensive use (Benito et al., 2011). Nevertheless, it is appropriate to ask: in what ways might a more proactive mode combination strategy be developed? Of course, any strategic posture regarding mode combinations cannot be disconnected from general FOM strategy – covering aspects such as mode choices, mode commitment (resources etc.), and mode switching over time – in existing and new foreign markets. A first step in strategic development is to simply recognize the role that mode combinations can potentially play in a company's internationalization. Beyond recognition there may be an issue of adequate knowledge of mode and combination options within a company, or more particularly those designing international strategies. There is likely to be the need for learning about different modes that have not been employed by the company previously, and building competence in a wider range of modes. As Sanchez and Heene (1997) note, competence development is a basic way of widening the range of strategic options available to a firm – of enhancing strategic flexibility. It is difficult for managers to contemplate employing modes they have not used before, have little knowledge of, and lack understanding of as to their potential role: the strategic flexibility provided by mode combinations in the evolution of international operations will only arise if managers are equipped and prepared to use them – in response, at times, to situations where rapid reaction is required. However, the number and complexity of mode combination options, particularly when examined at a disaggregated value chain level, mean that any consideration of feasible combination strategies has to be necessarily limited in scope (Petersen et al., 2008).

Within the context of a company's overall FOM strategy, key steps in building in a more proactive strategic approach to mode combinations include:

- establishing the current state of mode combination use in different markets;
- considering the potential for, and benefit of, expanding combinations, as well as potential barriers and how they might be overcome;
- developing a plan for mode combination use – including how to deal with possible emergent pressures and opportunities; and considering the scope for contractual arrangements with built-in switching options;

- implementation, which may require negotiation with foreign partners and expanded mode training for local and foreign staff – as a forerunner to any mode combination actions.

8. CONCLUSION

Thinking strategically about FOMs requires moving beyond making a choice for the initial entry into a country. The rethinking about FOMs and how they are used in international business activity has ushered in consideration of the reality of mode combinations as part of mode strategy. We advance theoretical justification for the use of mode combinations. In general, there are strong arguments as to why companies can gain significant benefits from building mode combinations, but mode combinations are as such no panacea. We have also stressed that there are potential barriers to their adoption, and costs in implementing them. Changing modes or mode combinations is not a frictionless exercise. Some companies use mode combinations extensively, while others shy away from them (Benito et al., 2011). It is not surprising that many companies baulk at the change process. Mode learning may be part of the solution, but it should be recognized that learning-by-doing with respect to already adopted modes may entrench the position of these modes or mode combinations, which is supported by growing confidence in their use. Mode learning may therefore evolve into mode inertia, transferred into new markets (Benito et al., 2009).

Despite such limitations, there are examples of mode combinations being employed successfully, and in creative ways. We suspect that, for many companies, mode combinations are assembled almost unconsciously – that they are not seen as anything unique or unusual, just part of the response to foreign market pressures and opportunities. This certainly seemed to be the case for the Finnish multinational Kone as it penetrated the Japanese market with a more complex mode package over time (Benito et al., 2009). But we know little about how mode combinations are regarded by companies and how they fit into international strategy: our impression is that the strategies we see tend to be emergent strategies.

Clearly, there is need for a substantial effort on empirical research – both in terms of detailed case studies and broad, cross-sectional studies to better understand this phenomenon. We also encourage conceptual development based on a modelling approach, of which Asmussen et al. (2009) is an example. There is also considerable scope for companies to become more knowledgeable about the potential role of mode combinations, and more proactive, and strategic, in their use.

NOTES

1. Initial work tended to focus on entry mode choices made by internationalizing manufacturing firms from the USA, the UK and Northern Europe. Research then spread to service firms (e.g. Erramili and Rao, 1993), middle-income countries (e.g. Campa and Guillén, 1999; Pla-Barber, 2001), and emerging markets (e.g. Filatotchev et al., 2007).
2. Following the established research template, studies have typically used cross-sectional designs. Longitudinal studies are relatively rare, partly because of the difficulties and costs of obtaining reliable

data over extended periods of time. Although some (cross-sectional) studies look exclusively at 'real' entry modes (i.e. the mode used to enter a country in which a firm has never had operations), *in praxis* many studies take the modes of operations actually used when the studies were conducted, thus lumping entry modes and subsequent modes into the same category.

3. These comprise the costs of taking down existing mode of operation (e.g. severance payments and other outlays involved in the termination or modification of existing contracts) and the costs of setting up a new mode (such as business registration fees, recruitment and training of employees etc.).

4. Transaction cost theory focuses on the need to safeguard specific assets against opportunistic actions; resource-based theory emphasizes the appropriation of rents generated by the possession of valuable and unique resources and capabilities; institutional theory emphasizes the (structural and behavioural) adaptation to external demands, regulations and norms.

5. However, a distinct contribution is that of Hennart (1993), who argues that mixed methods of organization are commonplace (i.e. the simultaneous use of rules as well as prices), and that activities (transactions) are seldom carried out in the extreme (caricatures) of either bureaucracies or spot markets. Nevertheless, it must be noted that Hennart's thesis is that real-life solutions to the organization problem – say, the choice of an FOM – typically involve combinations ('mixes') of different organization methods, not that different FOMs are used simultaneously. Hence his approach is also rooted in a discrete-choice perspective.

6. Other studies of mode changes include Calof (1993), Casillas et al. (2011), Clark et al. (1997), Fryges (2007) and Swoboda et al. (2011).

7. In their sample of 260 foreign operations, only six involved mixed or dual arrangements. It should be noted, however, that their study was not specifically designed to detect mode combinations. Instead, it aimed at examining the main modes of operation in a key foreign market.

8. Internalization theory may include two additional management roles although one may consider these to be at the periphery of the theory, namely (a) the timing of initial export replacement with local production ('offshoring'), and (b) the specific choice of mode of operation in the case of a 'buy' decision (Contractor, 1990; Datta et al., 2002).

9. In some models based on internalization theory, MNE managers are assumed 'bounded' and not fully rational (see e.g. Buckley et al., 2002).

10. This was not to say that the role of management has been totally ignored inasmuch as 'strategic behaviour can be identified within the internalisation framework by firms securing exclusive access to key inputs and tieing in customers' (Buckley, 1993, p. 206).

11. Of course, in those situations where no markets – not even contractual ones – exist, internalization from the outset is the sole foreign entry mode, and it is meaningless to talk about internalization processes (other than post-internalization processes such as post-acquisition integration processes). Most often, however, non-hierarchical entries (i.e. arm's-length, contractual modes, and shared ownership operations in foreign markets) are feasible alternatives to establishing wholly owned subsidiaries.

12. This material (including the figures) is based on Petersen et al. (2010).

13. This can be viewed as somewhat simplistic as it is clear that many companies using, for example, licensing employ a range of techniques within licensing arrangements to ensure that a degree of control or internalization of the licensee is generated (Welch et al., 2007).

14. Following Petersen et al. (2008) and Hashai et al. (2010), the FOM matrix (i.e. the configuration) of an international firm that operates in I host markets and has J identifiable activities in its value chain can at a given point in time be denoted $\mathbf{M} = (m_{ij})$, where $i = 1 \ldots I$ indexes host markets and $j = 1 \ldots J$ indexes value chain activities. Each cell in the matrix (m_{ij}) may then contain one or multiple operation modes (k) under which the given activity is performed in the given host market. Since the number of relevant alternatives in a country is k^J, even seemingly simple country configurations quickly result in a rather large number of alternatives. For example, the extremely simple case of a country $m_i = \{$production, R&D, sales$\}$, i.e. three activities, which can be done either in-house or outsourced, i.e. $k = 2$, gives $2^3 = 8$ combinations. Adding another mode (e.g. an alliance) results in $3^3 = 27$ combinations. The number of potential combinations rises exponentially by adding further countries (and/or additional activities) to its portfolio, so a company would quickly face immense combination opportunities: e.g. for two countries, $27^2 = 729$; for three countries, $27^3 = 19\,683$; for four countries, $27^4 = 531\,441$; and for five countries $27^5 = 14\,348\,907$, i.e. more than 14 million combinations.

REFERENCES

Andersen, O. (1997), 'Internationalization and entry mode choice: a review of theories and conceptual frameworks', *Management International Review*, **37** (Special Issue 2), 27–42.

Anderson, E. and A.T. Coughlan (1987), 'International market entry and expansion via independent or integrated channels of distribution', *Journal of Marketing*, **51**(1), 71–82.

Anderson, E. and H.A. Gatignon (1986), 'Modes of foreign entry: a transaction cost analysis and propositions', *Journal of International Business Studies*, **17**(3), 1–26.

Asmussen, C.G., G.R.G. Benito and B. Petersen (2009), 'Organizing foreign market activities: from entry mode choice to configuration decisions', *International Business Review*, **18**(2), 145–55.

Barnett, W.P. and R.A. Burgelman (1996), 'Evolutionary perspectives on strategy', *Strategic Management Journal*, **17** (special issue, summer), 5–19.

Becerra, M., R. Lunnan and L. Huemer (2008), 'Trustworthiness, risk, and the transfer of tacit and explicit knowledge between alliance partners', *Journal of Management Studies*, **45**(4), 691–713.

Benito, G.R.G. (1996), 'Ownership structures of Norwegian foreign subsidiaries in manufacturing', *International Trade Journal*, **10**(2), 157–98.

Benito, G.R.G., T. Pedersen and B. Petersen (1999), 'Foreign operation methods and switching costs: conceptual issues and possible effects', *Scandinavian Journal of Management*, **15**(2), 213–29.

Benito, G.R.G., T. Pedersen and B. Petersen (2005), 'Export channel dynamics: an empirical investigation', *Managerial and Decision Economics*, **26**(3), 159–73.

Benito, G.R.G., B. Petersen and L.S. Welch (2009), 'Towards more realistic conceptualisations of foreign operation modes', *Journal of International Business Studies*, **40**(9), 1455–70.

Benito, G.R.G., B. Petersen and L.S. Welch (2011), 'Mode combinations and international operations: theoretical issues and an empirical investigation', *Management International Review*, **51**(6), 803–20.

Brooke, M.Z. (1985), *Selling Management Services Contracts in International Business*, London: Holt, Rinehart and Winston.

Brouthers, K.D. and J.-F. Hennart (2007), 'Boundaries of the firm: Insights from international entry mode research', *Journal of Management*, **33**(3), 395–425.

Buckley, P.J. (1993), 'The role of management in internalisation theory', *Management International Review*, **33**(3), 197–207.

Buckley, P.J. and M.C. Casson (1976), *The Future of the Multinational Enterprise*, London: Macmillan.

Buckley, P.J. and M.C. Casson (1981), 'The optimal timing of a foreign direct investment', *Economic Journal*, **91**(361), 75–87.

Buckley, P.J. and N. Hashai (2005), 'Firm configuration and internationalisation: a model', *International Business Review*, **14**(6), 655–75.

Buckley, P.J., M.C. Casson and M.A. Gulamhussen (2002), 'Internationalisation – real options, knowledge management and the Uppsala approach', in V. Havila, M. Forsgren and H. Håkansson (eds.), *Critical Perspectives on Internationalisation*, Oxford: Elsevier, pp. 229–62.

Calof, J.L. (1993), 'The mode choice and change decision process and its impact on international performance', *International Business Review*, **2**(1), 97–120.

Calvet, A.L. (1981), 'A synthesis of foreign direct investment theories and theories of the multinational firm', *Journal of International Business Studies*, **12**(1), 43–59.

Campa, J.M. and M.F. Guillén (1999), 'The internalization of exports: firm- and location-specific factors in a middle-income country', *Management Science*, **45**(11), 1463–78.

Canabal, A. and G.O. White III (2008), 'Entry mode research: past and future', *International Business Review*, **17**(3), 267–84.

Casillas, J.C., A.M. Moreno and F.J. Acedo (2012), 'Path dependence view of export behaviour: a relationship between static patterns and dynamic configurations', *International Business Review*, **21**(3), 465–79.

Caves, R.E. and S.K. Mehra (1986), 'Entry of foreign multinationals into U.S. manufacturing industries', in M.E. Porter (ed.), *Competition in Global Industries*, Boston, MA: Harvard Business School Press, pp. 449–81.

Clark, T., D.S. Pugh and G. Mallory (1997), 'The process of internationalisation in the operating firm', *International Business Review*, **6**(6), 605–23.

Contractor, F.J. (1990), 'Contractual and cooperative forms of international business: towards a unified theory of modal choice', *Management International Review*, **30**(1), 31–54.

Datta, D.K., P. Herrmann and A.A. Rasheed (2002), 'Choice of foreign market entry modes: critical review and future directions', *Advances in International Management*, **14**, 85–153.

Davidson, W.H. and D.G. McFetridge (1985), 'Key characteristics in the choice of international transfer mode', *Journal of International Business Studies*, **16**(2), 5–22.

Dunning J. (1980), 'Towards an eclectic theory of international production', *Journal of International Business Studies*, **11**(1), 9–31.

Erramilli, M.K. and C.P. Rao (1993), 'Service firms' international entry-mode choice', *Journal of Marketing*, **57**(3), 19–38.

Filatotchev, I., R. Strange, J. Piesse and Y.-C. Lien (2007), 'FDI by firms from newly industrialised economies in emerging markets: corporate governance, entry mode and location', *Journal of International Business Studies*, **38**(4), 556–72.

Fryges, H. (2007), 'The change of sales modes in international markets: empirical results for German and British high-tech firms', *Progress in International Business Research*, **1**, 139–85.

Gatignon, H. and E. Anderson (1988), 'The multinational corporation's degree of control over foreign subsidiaries: an empirical test of a transaction cost explanation', *Journal of Law, Economics and Organization*, **4**(2), 305–36.

Grant, R.M. (1996), 'Toward a knowledge-based theory of the firm', *Strategic Management Journal*, **17** (special issue), 109–22.

Hashai, N., C.G. Asmussen, G.R.G. Benito and B. Petersen (2010), 'Technological knowledge intensity and entry mode diversity', *Management International Review*, **50**(6), 659–81.

Hennart, J.-F. (1982), *A Theory of Multinational Enterprise*, Ann Arbor, MI: University of Michigan Press.

Hennart, J.-F. (1988), 'A transaction cost theory of equity joint ventures', *Strategic Management Journal*, **9**(4), 361–74.

Hennart, J.-F. (1991), 'The transaction costs theory of joint ventures: an empirical study of Japanese subsidiaries in the United States', *Management Science*, **37**(4), 483–97.

Hennart, J.-F. (1993), 'Explaining the swollen middle: why most transactions are a mix of "market" and "hierarchy"', *Organization Science*, **4**(4), 529–47.

Hill, C.W.L., P. Hwang and W.C. Kim (1990), 'An eclectic theory of the choice of international entry mode', *Strategic Management Journal*, **11**(2), 117–28.

Horst, T. (1974), 'The theory of the firm', in J. Dunning (ed.), *Economic Analysis and the Multinational Enterprise*, London: George Allen & Unwin, pp. 31–46.

Hymer, S.H. (1976/1960), *The International Operations of National Firms: A Study of Direct Foreign Investment*, Cambridge, MA: MIT Press (originally presented as the author's thesis, Massachusetts Institute of Technology, 1960).

Johanson, J. and J.-E. Vahlne (1977), 'The internationalization process of the firm – a model of knowledge development and increasing foreign market commitments', *Journal of International Business Studies*, **8**(1), 23–32.

Johanson, J. and J.-E. Vahlne (2009), 'The Uppsala internationalization process model revisited: from liability of foreignness to liability of outsidership', *Journal of International Business Studies*, **40**(9), 1411–31.

Kedron, P. and S. Bagchi-Chen (2011), 'US market entry processes of emerging multinationals: a case of Indian multinationals', *Applied Geography*, **31**(2), 721–30.

Kogut, B. (2001), 'Methodological contributions in international business and the direction of academic research', in A. Rugman and T. Brewer (eds), *The Oxford Handbook of International Business*, Oxford: Oxford University Press, pp. 785–817.

Kogut, B. and H. Singh (1988), 'The effect of national culture on the choice of entry mode', *Journal of International Business Studies*, **23**(3), 411–32.

Kogut, B. and U. Zander (1993), 'Knowledge of the firm and the evolutionary theory of the multinational corporation', *Journal of International Business Studies*, **24**(4), 625–45.

Kostova, T. and S. Zaheer (1999), 'Organizational legitimacy under conditions of complexity: the case of the multinational enterprise', *Academy of Management Review*, **24**(1), 64–81.

Larimo, J. (1987), 'The foreign direct investment decision process', Research Paper No. 124, Proceedings of the University of Vaasa, Finland.

Madhok, A. (1997), 'Cost, value and foreign market entry mode: the transaction and the firm', *Strategic Management Journal*, **18**(1), 39–61.

March, J.G. (1991), 'Exploration and exploitation in organizational learning', *Organization Science*, **2**(1), 71–87.

McManus, J. (1972), 'The theory of the international firm', in G. Paquet (ed.), *The International Firm and the Nation State*, Don Mills, Ontario: Collier Macmillan Canada, pp. 66–93.

Meyer, K.E. and M.W. Peng (2005), 'Probing theoretically into Central and Eastern Europe: transactions, resources and institutions', *Journal of International Business Studies*, **35**(6), 600–621.

Mintzberg, H. and J.A. Waters (1985), 'Of strategies, deliberate and emergent', *Strategic Management Journal*, **6**(3), 257–72.

Morschett, D., H. Schramm-Klein and B. Swoboda (2010), 'Decades of research on market entry modes: what do we really know about external antecedents of entry mode choice?', *Journal of International Management*, **16**(1), 60–77.

Pedersen, T. and Petersen, B. (1998), 'Explaining gradually increasing resource commitment to a foreign market', *International Business Review*, **7**(5), 483–501.

Petersen, B. and L.S. Welch (2002), 'Foreign operation mode combinations and internationalization', *Journal of Business Research*, **55**(2), 157–62.

Petersen, B., G.R.G. Benito, L.S. Welch and C.G. Asmussen (2008), 'Mode configuration diversity: a new perspective on foreign operation mode choice', in A.Y. Lewin, S.T. Cavusgil, G.T.M. Hult and D. Griffith (eds), *Thought Leadership in Advancing International Business Research*, Basingstoke: Palgrave Macmillan, pp. 57–78.

Petersen, B., D.E. Welch and L.S. Welch (2000), 'Creating meaningful switching options in international operations', *Long Range Planning*, **33**(5), 688–705.

Petersen, B., L.S. Welch and G.R.G. Benito (2010): 'Managing the internalisation process', *Management International Review*, **50**(2), 137–54.

Petersen, B., L.S. Welch and K.V. Nielsen (2001), 'Resource commitment to foreign markets: the establishment patterns of Danish firms in South-East Asian markets', in S. Gray, S.L. McGaughey and W.R. Purcell (eds), *Asia-Pacific Issues in International Business*, Cheltenham, UK and Northampton, MA, USA: Edward Elgar, pp. 7–27.

Pla-Barber, J. (2001), 'The internalisation of foreign distribution and production activities: new empirical evidence from Spain', *International Business Review*, **10**(4), 455–74.

Root, F.R. (1964), *Strategic Planning for Export Marketing*, Copenhagen: Department of International Economics and Management.

Rugman, A.M. (1981), *Inside the Multinationals: The Economics of Internal Markets*, New York: Columbia University Press.

Rugman, A. and A. Verbeke (2003), 'Extending the theory of the multinational enterprise: internalization and strategic management perspectives', *Journal of International Business Studies*, **34**(2), 125–37.

Sanchez, R. and A. Heene (1997), 'Reinventing strategic management: new theory and practice for competence-based competition', *European Management Journal*, **15**(3), 303–17.

Speedy, B. (2007), 'Foster's licenses new brewer', *Australian*, 27 June, 25.

Swoboda, B., E. Olejnik and D. Morschett (2011), 'Changes in foreign operation modes: stimuli for increases versus reductions', *International Business Review*, **20**(5), 578–90.

Taylor, A. (1994), 'Pilkington emerges with advantages', *Financial Times*, 27 May, 6.

Tihanyi, L., D.A. Griffith and C.J. Russell (2005), 'The effect of cultural distance on entry mode choice, international diversification, and MNE performance: a meta-analysis', *Journal of International Business Studies*, **36**(3), 270–83.

Tomassen, S., G.R.G. Benito and L.S. Welch (1998), 'Norwegian companies in India: operation mode choice', *Asian Journal of Business & Information Systems*, **3**(1), 1–20.

Warren-Smith, A. (2010), 'Internationalisation in a private services firm – how should DDI continue its international expansion?', Applied Management Research Project, Executive MBA, Melbourne: Melbourne Business School.

Welch, L.S., G.R.G. Benito and B. Petersen (2007), *Foreign Operation Methods: Theory, Analysis, Strategy*, Cheltenham, UK and Northampton, MA, USA: Edward Elgar.

Yan, A. and B. Gray (1994), 'Bargaining power, management control and performance in United States–China joint ventures: a comparative case study', *Academy of Management Journal*, **37**(6), 1478–517.

Yan, A. and M. Zeng (1999), 'International joint venture instability: a critique of previous research, a reconceptualization, and directions for future research', *Journal of International Business Studies*, **30**(2), 397–414.

Zhao, H., Y. Luo and T. Suh (2004), 'Transaction cost determinants and ownership-based entry mode choice: a meta-analytical review', *Journal of International Business Studies*, **35**(6), 524–44.

6 Triple testing the quality of multinationality–performance research
Alain Verbeke and Paul Brugman

The international business literature has suggested various linkages between multinationality (M) and performance (P). A number of authors have recently put forward an S-shaped curve, allegedly describing a generalized MP relationship. However, internalization theory, in line with Buckley and Casson (1976), Hennart (1982) and Hennart (2007), challenges the concept itself of such a generalized relationship between these two parameters. This chapter adopts an internalization theory perspective, meant to improve the design of MP studies, and cautions against assuming too quickly a generalized MP relationship. In line with internalization theory, we argue that firm-level performance depends primarily on the characteristics of the companies' firm-specific advantages (FSAs) rather than on their degree of multinationality. We propose triple testing the quality of MP studies by assessing how well they address the various challenges related to conceptualizing and measuring M, P and the MP relationship itself.

> 'Fortune,' said Don Quixote to Sancho Panza, 'is arranging matters for us better than we could have hoped. Look there, friend Sancho Panza, where thirty or more monstrous giants rise up, all of whom I mean to engage in battle and slay, and with whose spoils we shall begin to make our fortunes.'
>
> Miguel de Cervantes, *Don Quixote* (1605)

INTRODUCTION

Studies on the linkages between multinationality (M) and performance (P) have been flooding publication outlets in international business (IB) for half a century. Hitt et al. (2006) suggest that the literature on the linkages between M and P is indeed vast, but represents only a fraction of the broader research stream on international diversification. We focus our attention in this chapter on MP linkages only. More specifically, we assess the contribution of this research to our understanding of multinational expansion patterns. Here we should note that most of the MP research uses (increasingly sophisticated) quantitative techniques applied to large data sets, but the conceptual foundations of these studies appear at odds with mainstream IB theory, i.e. internalization theory.

We find many attempts in the IB literature to determine MP linkages. Hymer (1960, Table 2.2, pp. 56–9) was among the first to try to establish a linkage between M (which then implied 'being present in more than one nation') and P. In his 1960 thesis, he tried to uncover why multinational enterprises (MNEs) existed and whether – at that time – they were more profitable than domestic firms. He observed that US firms engaged in foreign expansion, building upon asset-based advantages, the exploitation of which yielded significant benefits to them (Hymer, 1960, p. 56). After Hymer, a large number of papers addressing the MP relationship have been published in well-respected journals and other credible publication outlets. However, the results of this impressive body of research have been particularly inconsistent, with almost any conceivable outcome showing up in at least some of the studies. Interestingly, rather than continuing to explore whether MNEs are more (or less) profitable than domestic firms, the research focus has shifted to the issue of how performance (allegedly) evolves with increasing multinationality. For illustrative purposes, Appendix Table 6A.1 lists the most influential empirical papers and books on the topic. We selected these studies (the 20 most cited articles and four books), based on their citation count (SSCI) and cross-checked the results with Google Scholar citation counts.

Recent MP research has identified an S-shaped curve, allegedly describing a commonly occurring MP relationship (for an overview of the empirical studies, see Table 6A.1 in the Appendix).[1] S-curve reasoning suggests that firms go through three distinct stages during their internationalization process. In the first stage, firms expanding abroad must confront liabilities of newness and foreignness. These firms must therefore learn how to operate in foreign markets. As a result, an increase in M induces a decline in P. However, thanks to learning, the firm then enters into a second stage: P starts to increase as M increases, at least up to a threshold beyond which the firm finds itself in a third, more unfortunate, stage, whereby foreign operations become too difficult to manage and P declines as M increases. The intuitively plausible, central message of S-curve reasoning is therefore that firms should expect a drop in performance as they begin to internationalize, but should then pursue their efforts towards higher multinationality, while avoiding over-extension. The threshold determining over-extension is critically important to large, mature MNEs that have become accustomed to improved performance accompanying international expansion: the normative implication is that these firms should refrain from 'excessive' internationalization or geographic diversification in order to avoid negative effects on performance.

S-curve reasoning assumes learning. Learning allows firms to improve performance as multinationality increases. However, the presence of learning and subsequent adaptation, embodied in routines and resource recombination capabilities, i.e. higher-order firm-specific advantages (FSAs), is also an argument against the concept of a generalizable S-curved MP relationship. Indeed, if learning and therefore adaptation occur continuously, thereby generating higher-order FSAs that allow economizing on bounded rationality and the hazards of doing business internationally, no empirical study should observe a systemic overstretching associated with weakened performance at the tail end of the S-curve. In this context, internalization theory thinking would readily accept that suboptimal (meaning 'too low' or 'too high') levels of multinationality at the firm level may exist in the short run. Temporary suboptimality would not necessarily occur at either low or high levels of M, but whenever projects are undertaken whereby MNE management faces new bounded rationality problems and international expansion hazards facing decision-makers, i.e. whenever the firm expands into 'high-distance' locations (see below). However, in the longer run, proper governance mechanisms should eliminate systemic underachievement associated with specific levels of internationalization or international diversification. Suboptimality is also consistent with Nelson and Winter's (1982) perspective, which suggests that firms have a (limited) capability to adapt their routines in response to environmental changes. However, such adaptation may take time and some firms may not be able to change sufficiently rapidly and effectively, implying that the 'survival of the fittest' principle will hold in the longer run.

Internalization theory, as exemplified by the classic work of Buckley and Casson (1976), casts doubts on the concept itself of a generalized MP relationship.[2] First, economic activities will only be performed inside the firm if this is more cost efficient and effective than arm's-length transactions, and this holds for both domestic and foreign expansion projects. At the margin, a comparative institutional assessment will guide the investment decisions that determine the boundaries of the firm, irrespective of the domestic or foreign nature of these investments.

Second, a firm will only engage in investment projects abroad if the expected performance outcome is higher than that of domestic investment projects, though acknowledging that new bounded rationality problems and hazards of international expansion into high-distance environments may affect short-term performance levels. The point is, however, that at the margin one would not expect any difference between the expected performances of domestic projects versus foreign projects.

Extending the above line of thought: new investment projects will only be undertaken if specific performance targets can be achieved. Thus, whenever a firm decides to undertake foreign activities in-house, expected performance should, at the very least, remain at current levels. Expected performance should also compare favorably with expansion through contracting modes. This in turn implies that multinationality is a design variable: the MNE will select the entry modes and geographic configuration of its activities that best match its FSAs, and therefore a particular level of multinationality *per se* should not systematically (e.g. across firms in an industry, and over a long time period) affect performance outcomes upward or downward. Although firms with strong FSAs are more likely to be internationally oriented, i.e. have a higher M than firms with weaker FSAs because, *inter alia*, of scope economies gained through deploying proprietary upstream or downstream knowledge (e.g. patents and brand names) across borders, there should not be a fixed or dominant relationship between M and P. In this context we should also mention that a truly correct assessment of M on P should isolate the effect of international activities on P from those of the MNE's home country activities, but this may be difficult to achieve in any scholarly analysis that lacks inside knowledge (including detailed accounting data) of MNE operations.

The apparent contradiction between S-curve reasoning and the internalization perspective invites further reflection on the matter. In the remainder of this chapter we identify a set of nine conceptual and measurement challenges associated with attempts to establish a generalized MP linkage such as the S-curve. These nine challenges are classified into three main categories, namely those related to properly conceptualizing and measuring M, P and the MP relationship itself. Formally assessing the extent to which MP studies have been able to address appropriately these three categories of challenges amounts to triple testing the quality of empirical research on the MP relationship.

TRIPLE TESTING THE QUALITY OF MP STUDIES

Below we discuss nine conceptual and measurement challenges arising in MP studies. We subdivided these nine challenges into three categories. Evaluating the extent to which these three categories have been addressed implies triple testing the quality of the MP studies considered. We pay special attention to the papers that have established an S-curve in MP research, as this is the latest and most 'advanced' curve found in the empirical literature. However, this analysis is done for illustrative purposes only, as the triple testing proposed can be applied to any past or ongoing MP study. Table 6.1 provides an overview of these S-curve papers, and lists the nine challenges to be addressed, subdivided into three categories, namely challenges related to conceptualizing and measuring M, P and the MP linkage itself. The three challenges related to the multinationality construct are: (1) a reductionist perspective on the value chain activities considered relevant; (2) the absence of distinguishing between the firm's degree of internationalization and its degree of international diversification; and (3) the absence of distinguishing between related and unrelated diversification. Three additional challenges are related to the performance construct: (1) the neglect of the expected impact of strategic investment motives on performance; (2) the non-recognition of the differential meaning of alternative performance measures; and (3) the non-recognition of the dynamic aspects (especially the impact of external shocks) to be considered in performance assessments. Finally, there are three potential problems related to the MP interaction itself: (1) the use of cross-sectional data instead of longitudinal data, and even in the case of longitudinal data, the absence of tracking MNEs during their relevant international expansion trajectories, meaning from their first footsteps in international markets; (2) the problem of reverse causality; and (3) the problem of endogeneity. In Table 6.1, 'Yes' implies that the problem has been addressed in the study, whereas 'No' means that the problem has not been dealt with. It should be kept in mind, however, that even if all the above issues were taken into account, and a particular MP linkage is established for a specific sample of firms, the key internalization theory point made in this chapter remains valid: there is no convincing theoretical rationale to support a specific relationship between M and P that would be generally applicable across situational contexts (i.e. across industries, countries, time periods etc.)

TEST 1: MULTINATIONALITY

Many authors have commented on the conceptual and measurement challenges regarding multinationality. Fifteen years ago, Sullivan (1994a) not only provided an extensive overview of shortcomings in prior studies, but also introduced a multidimensional construct as an alternative. Despite the critical comments by Ramaswamy et al. (1996) regarding the conceptual and empirical validity of using a single construct to measure multinationality, many issues raised by Sullivan remain valid today. However, Sullivan believed that a 'good' measure of multinationality could be constructed, although it remains unclear whether this is actually the case.

As shown in Appendix Table 6A.1, early research measured multinationality on a binary scale; that is, firms were either present in more than one country or not. In most past studies, however, multinationality has been measured as the ratio of size of foreign operations to total operations, and this has become known as the 'degree of internationalization' (DI). DI has been operationalized in many different ways, such as foreign sales over total sales (FSTS), foreign assets over total assets (FATA), count measures such as

Table 6.1   Triple testing S-curve papers in MP research. Were key conceptual and measurement challenges addressed?

Quality test	Test 1: Multinationality			Test 2: Performance			Test 3: MP Linkage		
	Value chain	Degree of internation-alization vs diversification	Related vs unrelated diversification	Investment motives	Measurement issues	Dynamic aspects	Time period	PM relationship	Endogeneity
Sullivan (1994)	Yes	Yes	Yes	No	Yes	No	No	No	No
Riahi-Belkaoui (1998)	No	No	No	No	No	No	No	No	No
Contractor et al. (2003)	Partly	Partly	No	No	No	No	No	No	No
Lu and Beamish (2004)	No	Partly	No	No	Partly	No	No	Yes	No
Thomas and Eden (2004)	Yes	Yes	No	No	No	Partly	No	No	No
Li (2005)	No	No	Partly	No	No	No	No	No	No
Chang and Wang (2007)	No	Yes	Partly	No	No	No	No	No	No
Ruigrok et al. (2007)	No	No	No	No	No	No	No	No	No

the number of countries in which the firm is present, or the international orientation of the management team (see Appendix Table 6A.1 for details). In a number of cases, composite measures have been used.

Quality Test 1A: Value Chain Activities Considered

Although a choice can be made among various measures for M (see Table 6A.1 in the Appendix), various problems remain in adequately measuring multinationality. For example, if one wishes to determine the degree of multinationality of 'operations', these could be defined in terms of any part of the value chain, including R&D, procurement, logistics, administration, production, marketing or sales. Here, it should be kept in mind that the use of a single-item measure builds upon the assumption that all firms considered are either equally present in foreign markets with respect to all other value chain activities, or that differences in DI for those other activities have no impact on performance. This assumption is problematic. For example, firms that source 90 percent of their inputs abroad will probably experience vastly different performance effects, in both substance and outcome, from this particular (very high) DI as compared to firms that realize 90 percent of their sales abroad. Unfortunately, this complexity is seldom recognized, one exception being Katrishen and Scordis (1998). With respect to the S-curve papers in Table 6.1, we find that three of these address the issue. Not surprisingly, Sullivan (1994b) is among them. Thomas and Eden (2004) measure multinationality through a construct using FSTS, a country count and FATA, thus trying to account for both upstream and downstream activities. Contractor et al. (2003) make use of a composite measure of FSTS, the number of subsidiaries and foreign employment over total employment (FETE).

Irrespective of how M has been measured in extant studies, we should mention that from an internalization theory perspective, researchers should actually also take into account market-based entry modes such as licensing. For example, in cases of host government regulations impeding the establishment of subsidiaries or imports (so-called unnatural market imperfections) by foreign MNEs, these firms may revert to granting licenses for production to host country actors, assuming a number of transaction-cost-economizing conditions (related to natural market imperfections) can be fulfilled (e.g. is it possible to find qualified licensees to negotiate mutually beneficial licensing contracts with them, and to safeguard against *ex post* hazards of contracting?).

Quality Test 1B: Degree of Internationalization versus Diversification

An additional complexity must be noted: there is an important difference between DI and the degree of international diversification (DID). That is, the performance effects of international expansion can be expected to be different depending upon the level of geographic diversification across foreign countries. If FSTS is used as a proxy for DI, a firm that sells 50 percent of its production in a neighboring country would have the same DI as a firm with 50 percent foreign sales, but spread over ten countries. However, the DID of the two firms would obviously be very different, since activities in different host countries face idiosyncratic challenges, in terms of both external opportunities and threats, and the firm-level capability to profitably transfer, deploy and exploit the MNE's FSAs.

In the case of diversification across ten host countries, there may well have been ten distinct decision-making processes on internalization, *inter alia*, as a function of country-specific transaction costs, arising from idiosyncratic natural and government-imposed market imperfections. In addition, several operations-related parameters will probably be vastly different. For example, substantially lower scale economies will be achieved if activities need to be adapted to each host country's economic, institutional and cultural characteristics, and the activities' business risk profile may also be different in each country. Not making the distinction between DI and DID thus leads to quantitative and qualitative aspects (in this case related to environmental diversity) of multinationality being lumped together, thereby possibly generating spurious results when studying MP linkages. Sundaram and Black (1992) also argued in favor of distinguishing between internationalization and international diversification in empirical studies, and some empirical papers have indeed incorporated this distinction between DI and DID; see Qian and Li (2002) and Goerzen and Beamish (2003).

Five of the S-curve papers in Table 6.1 address this problem, but two of these only partially. Sullivan's (1994b) piece and Thomas and Eden's (2004) paper explicitly account for the number of countries. Contractor et al. (2003) count the number of subsidiaries but do not determine how this measure is related to the number of countries, while Lu and Beamish (2004) do recognize the issue but do not present a diversification measure. Finally, Chang and Wang (2007) include both an entropy measure of international sales and a separate count of the number of countries where a firm is present.

Quality Test 1C: Related versus Unrelated Diversification

Finally, the nature of the above diversification, in terms of related versus unrelated geographical diversification, as distinguished by Vachani (1991), is also likely to affect performance. For example, does it make sense to suggest that a Swiss firm, selling 30 percent of its products in neighboring Germany and Austria, is likely to experience performance effects from its international diversification similar to those experienced by a Swiss firm selling the same percentage of output abroad but in the USA and Japan? Although this complexity has been recognized in several studies (see especially Goerzen and Beamish, 2003; Zahra et al., 2000), the question remains how to determine appropriately the 'degree of relatedness'. Although Hofstede (1980) is one of the most cited references, the debate is ongoing as to what constitutes culture, whether and how it can be measured, what is related and what is relevant; see, *inter alia*, McSweeney (2002). Indeed, why not make use of the completely different model by Schwartz (1992), or focus solely on attitudinal dimensions as in Ronen and Shenkar (1985)? In other words, not only the degree of cultural relatedness is important; the model used to determine this degree will fundamentally affect the final result. Indeed, although Gómez-Mejia and Palich (1997) explicitly tested for cultural diversity and found no significant differences, even they state that more research into cultural differences and its impact on performance is much needed. In this context, recent research by Hutzschenreuter and Voll (2008) suggests that the measurement of macro-level distance, for example in the cultural sphere, between home and host countries may sometimes be completely irrelevant. In the case of established MNEs, it is the additional distance that counts, e.g. the cultural distance between a newly entered host country and the country where the MNE is already established that exhibits the smallest distance with that new home country. The point is – from an internalization theory perspective – that the transaction-cost-economizing challenges associated with coordinating economic activities across borders depend crucially on the distance between the MNE's extant network and the newly entered foreign environment. This distance can have economic, institutional and cultural components (Verbeke, 2009).

It is important to understand the above differences between DI and DID on the one hand, and related versus unrelated diversification on the other. As regards the first case, when diversification is contemplated, the number of countries entered should be viewed as relevant to the performance impact question. In the second case, the similarity between the home country and the host countries, or perhaps more correctly between the MNE's extant network and the new host environment, in terms of economic, institutional and cultural differences, determines the relatedness/unrelatedness of the diversification, and this may be critical to performance. Unfortunately, Sullivan (1994b) stands alone among the S-curve papers in addressing this issue, although Chang and Wang (2007) make a distinction among four different geographic regions in the world, and Li (2005) also addresses regional diversification issues.

TEST 2: PERFORMANCE

Venkatraman and Ramanujam (1986, p. 801) stated that 'the treatment of performance in research settings is perhaps one of the thorniest issues confronting the academic researcher today'. More than 20 years later, the measurement of performance in IB studies is still far from standardized. Appendix Table 6A.1 shows that performance has been measured in many different ways. In spite of the fact that MP studies have been conducted for a long time, no consensus has yet been reached in the literature on the adoption of a specific proxy for P. Although some form of profitability (return on assets (ROA), return on investment (ROI), return on equity (ROE)) is generally accepted as the key performance measure, focusing on this single measure can be misleading, since the investment paths of different firms may be guided by profitability objectives that take into account diverging time lines (short, medium and long term), each associated with a particular level of risk. The risk issue itself, critical to any investment decision, is usually completely neglected, even though any introductory finance textbook focuses extensively on the risk/return trade-off of investment projects. This neglect of the risk issue in the more recent MP literature is somewhat bizarre, since many earlier MP studies explicitly focused on risk, as it was believed that higher geographic diversification could lead to risk reduction (see, e.g., Kim et al., 1993). That belief was obviously rather naïve itself, since many of the risk reduction benefits from international diversification can be achieved through market contracting (supply contracts, licenses etc.) without the need for the firm itself to engage in international operations. In addition, the MNE faces many diversification barriers, especially at the institutional level, that make proximate, home region expansion less risky and more likely than broader diversification, especially in output markets (Rugman, 2005). In any case, by adopting an overly simplified view of what constitutes firm-level performance, and neglecting the firm's motives for internationalization, the effects on performance may remain ill understood.

Quality Test 2A: Strategic Investment Motives

Compare a firm engaged in strategic-asset-seeking FDI in a promising country with another firm engaged in simple market-seeking FDI in that same country. The investment projects of both companies will probably have very different profitability trajectories over time, with some strategic assets even acting as options and thus not intended to contribute to short-term profitability.

Not a single study has yet addressed investment motives (e.g. differentiating between market seeking, natural resource seeking, efficiency seeking and strategic asset seeking), as empirical analyses on the basis of large data sets make this task almost impossible to perform. Nevertheless, the study of investment motives, and the unbundling of empirical samples into groups of firms with similar, principal investment motives, has been heralded as critically important; see Verbeke et al. (2009) for an in-depth analysis of this specific issue. The *ex ante* theoretical prediction as to why international expansion might have an effect on performance is also critically dependent upon the strategic motives involved: market-seeking investment might benefit from economies of scope in sharing technological and marketing knowledge across borders at low cost. Resource-seeking investment might lead to improved performance through accessing inputs unavailable in the domestic input market. Strategic-asset-seeking investment might lead to improved performance by absorbing complementary knowledge into the firm that leads to synergies with extant knowledge. Finally, efficiency-seeking investment might lead to improved performance by supporting specialized affiliates with distinct resource bundles in the MNE's internal network.

Part of the response to the above challenges should be to study samples characterized by a single strategic investment motive, or – when large, established firms are involved – by a dominant investment motive, meaning that the main transaction-cost-economizing challenges related to bounded rationality problems and hazards of international expansion, as well as the main rationale for a possible effect of M on P, would be similar across firms.

Quality Test 2B: Appropriateness of P Measures

In spite of the problems relating to the timing of performance effects as noted above, it could be argued that the performance variable itself can be more easily measured than the level of multinationality, but is this really the case? Performance has been operationalized in past studies using accounting-based, market-based and operational measures. Accounting-based measures reflect historical performance (e.g. ROA), while market-based measures are forward looking (e.g. Tobin's q). Operational variables, such as market share, product quality etc., are assumed to reflect more accurately the firm's 'fundamentals' (Venkatraman and Ramanujam, 1986).

Each of the above measurement approaches is associated with specific problems. For example, accounting measures can be manipulated and accounting systems differ among nations and are subject to change. In addition, reporting periods and statement dates need not coincide. For example, in Japan, the fiscal year ends in March, whereas for US-based firms it ends in December. Alternative accounting measures do matter, as does the impact of foreign exchange exposure and the effects of changes in accounting systems. All these issues combined imply that comparing firms across nations or through time is exceptionally difficult. However, in the past few years, the International Accounting Standards Board (IASB), the Financial Accounting Standards Board (FASB) of the USA and the Accounting Standards Board of Japan (ASBJ) have begun discussions to allow for a convergence between the various accounting systems. These discussions have culminated in a memorandum of understanding between the IASB and the FASB, while the elimination of major differences between the Japanese GAAP (generally accepted accounting principles) and IFRS was targeted for the end of 2008.

However, the above challenges can be considered minor as compared to the conceptual problems involved. For example, one of the main problems with accounting-based measures is that they do not take account of intangible assets. That is, investments in R&D and marketing are recorded as expenditures rather than as assets, thereby making comparisons difficult between firms that invest substantially in R&D and marketing, and those that do not. Ignoring these differences creates a major problem: firms that invest a great deal in R&D and marketing are likely to have built up a large stock of intangible assets. If the market for intangible assets is prone to market failure, which is a cornerstone of internalization theory, a firm's optimal entry mode choice might be to expand geographically through internalization to reap the benefits of these assets in the form of scope economies (in the case of market-seeking investment) or access to complementary resources and strategic assets (in the cases of resource-seeking investment and strategic-asset-seeking investment respectively) that can be integrated in the firm's value chain thanks to its higher-order recombination FSAs. This implies that a firm may experience a strong, positive performance effect when investing abroad thanks to its extant (unmeasured) intangible assets, not because of its DI *per se*, a point already made by Severn and Laurence in 1974. Conversely, firms without strong intangible assets should be cautious when contemplating international expansion. The problem of intangibles' valuation is a well-known challenge, and most of the recent studies therefore include a measure of R&D and/or marketing expenditures as a proxy for the importance of intangibles in the analysis when making use of an accounting-based measure.

However, firms suffering from a technological or marketing knowledge gap may want to invest abroad to overcome that gap, or to enter a new market segment (Miller, 2004). Here, asset-seeking FDI is supposed to increase performance. However, this approach, if it is to be successful, still requires at least some complementary intangible knowledge, typically reflected in the entrepreneurial skills of the company's founder(s) or top management. This type of intangible knowledge cannot be assessed directly in large samples. In the absence of such internationally deployable intangible knowledge, the performance impact of multinationality is likely to be weak or negative, especially if stronger rivals can benefit more immediately from economies of scope when deploying their existing intangible assets across borders. Increasing the level of multinationality can thus positively or negatively affect the firm's overall performance as a function of the MNE's and its rivals' FSA bundles derived from intangible assets. Here, the strength of the MNE's FSAs relative to rivals causes performance differences, not the firm's DI *per se*. As argued by Shaver (1998, p. 571), 'firms choose strategies based on their attributes and industry conditions; therefore, strategy choice is endogenous and self-selected'. Indeed, even with an identical DI, performance differences will arise among companies because of different FSAs; see also below for a separate analysis of this point.

Market-based measures (Tobin's q) are also inadequate as they assume that markets are efficient, meaning that they are supposed to reflect accurately the firm's value. In reality, other parameters than fundamentals often appear to determine market valuation (Schiller, 2000), as demonstrated by the collapse of stock markets globally in late 2008. This issue is not addressed in the current MP literature, although market performance may be a poor proxy for 'true' performance, and the difference between both may be idiosyncratic for each firm.

In a number of cases, researchers have acknowledged the inherent differences between market-based and accounting-based measures and have therefore used both. Such an approach, however, does not necessarily alleviate the problems reported above. For example, many papers use ROA and Tobin's q. Crucially, both measures rely on the firm's assets. Conceptually, four situations can arise: (1) low ROA, low Tobin's q; (2) high ROA, high Tobin's q; (3) low ROA, high Tobin's q; and (4) high ROA, low Tobin's q. Cases 1 and 2 do not constitute a problem since in both cases the market valuation is consistent with accounting results; that is, the company is valued given a high (low) valuation and is presently making a high (low/negative) accounting profit. Cases 3 and 4, however, are more problematic, since the market values the firm differently from what would be suggested by accounting data. More specifically, the market can give a firm a high (low) valuation due to market expectations, even if present accounting profits are low (high). Reporting both performance measures would result in confusion since multinationality would then simultaneously seem to lead to diverging effects on performance. Reporting only a single performance measure, however, would not suffice either, since it is unclear which performance measure is superior. Dubofsky and Varadarajan (1987) speculated that a discrepancy between accounting-based measures and market-based measures may occur because of time lags reflecting performance results from a particular course of action. A strong divergence between accounting-based and market-based performance typically also arises in volatile environments or after an internal or external shock. Precisely because of the unexpectedness of such shocks and the multitude of differences among firms with respect to their idiosyncratic bundles of FSAs, location advantages etc., each firm will be affected uniquely, and will respond in its own way. Averaging data in an econometric analysis may smooth out these differences and mask real-world developments. The issue of external shocks, and their potential impact on performance, is discussed below.

As noted above, making use of a single measure does not 'solve' the problem, as shown by Geringer et al. (2000) and Siddharthan and Lall (1982), who attribute their inconclusive findings to a volatile environment. Only two S-curve papers address this issue: Sullivan (1994b) and Lu and Beamish (2004). The latter only deal with the issue partially; they adopt two performance measures (ROA and Tobin's q), but only discuss potential problems related to Tobin's q.

Quality Test 2C: Dynamic Aspects

Horst (1972, p. 265) stated more than 30 years ago: 'if we are ever to unravel the complexity of the foreign investment process, a systematic study of the dynamic behavior of firms must be undertaken'. Unfortunately, despite the importance of dynamic aspects, most MP studies fail even to acknowledge the issue. Those that do, include Geringer et al.

(2000), Gomes and Ramaswamy (1999), Grant et al. (1988), Kumar (1984), and Severn and Laurence (1974). In this context, Grant and Cibin (1996), among others, observed that the firms in their sample adjusted to a new reality, and engaged in corporate refocusing and changes in the geographic scope of their activities after industry-wide shocks. In other words, to the extent that these firms had an optimal geographic scope before the industry-wide shock, this scope needed adjustment after the shock had occurred. Unfortunately, we are not aware of a single MP study that has actually incorporated in its *ex ante* research design the impact of shocks of any kind, macroeconomic, technological or other. All past MP studies have thus assumed either that no such shocks occurred during the period under investigation, or that these shocks did not fundamentally affect firm performance in the samples considered, or that these shocks' impact was identical for all firms.

In reality, large shocks have occurred regularly in the past decades, e.g. the first oil crisis in 1973, the collapse of communism, the rise of the Asian dragons, China's entry into the World Trade Organization (WTO), the 9/11 terrorist attack etc. In each of those cases, both the bounded rationality challenges facing MNE managers and the hazards of doing business internationally changed dramatically, thereby affecting international expansion commitments in terms of size, geographic scope, governance and expected performance.

Thomas and Eden's piece (2004) represents the only S-curve paper that to some extent addresses dynamic aspects. That is, the paper does take into account short-term and long-term effects, but stops short of introducing shocks and measuring the impact of refocusing efforts on performance.

TEST 3: MULTINATIONALITY–PERFORMANCE LINKAGES

Here, the key problem is to include data in empirical samples in such a way that any statistically observed MP linkage reflects an actual substantive relationship. A substantive relationship means going beyond alleged, convenient MP linkages such as U-curves, inverted U-curves and S-curves, neatly fitted to the data, and accompanied by intuitively plausible storylines, which unfortunately do not bear any relationship with managerial reality.

Quality Test 3A: Use of Cross-sectional versus Longitudinal Data

Many MP studies have used cross-sectional data rather than longitudinal data, so that they are not actually measuring at all any 'real' linkage between M and P in individual firms, but only observe that firms with a specific level of M in the empirical sample have a higher or lower level of P than other firms with a different level of M. In some cases, panel data have been used, spanning time periods that cover several years. The time periods 'chosen' by the researchers are usually dependent solely on data availability; i.e. they represent 'convenience time periods', not time periods a serious IB history scholar would ever consider. The point is that properly performed MP studies, especially those searching for S-curves, should cover the entire period relevant to testing the underlying S-curve paradigm. These studies should start from either the moment of the firms' first international activity, or from the point in time when a significant increase occurred in international activity, e.g. driven by a large-scale reduction in trade and investment barriers, a technological or governance innovation etc. The studies should then follow the international expansion trajectories and associated performance over time of the firms involved. Perhaps unsurprisingly, no paper has addressed or even discussed this issue.

Quality Test 3B: Testing the PM Relationship

Several authors have noted that any observed linkage between M and P may actually reflect causality moving from performance to multinationality. In other words, prior investments (e.g. in R&D, brand names and proprietary routines) and performance at home make feasible a firm's international expansion. Hence, even if a relevant and statistically significant linkage can be established between M and P, the possibility of a PM linkage rather than an MP linkage should be carefully assessed; see also Grant et al. (1988), Kim and Lyn (1986), Kumar (1984), Morck and Yeung (1991), Severn and Laurence (1974), Siddharthan and Lall (1982). Lu and Beamish (2004) explicitly tested for this problem of reverse causality, but it is the only S-curve paper where this occurred.

Quality Test 3C: Endogeneity

Hamilton and Nickerson (2003) and Shaver (1998) have argued, in line with internalization theory predictions, that most empirical strategic management research does not adequately address endogeneity. That is, 'managers make strategic organizational decisions not randomly, but based upon expectations of how their choices affect future performance' (Hamilton and Nickerson, 2003, p. 51). By not taking into account endogeneity, results from statistical analyses may be biased, and significant results may have limited managerial relevance. Applied to the context of MP studies, and especially S-curve reasoning, this means that firms choose a specific geographic scope of their activities to maximize performance, based on internal strengths and weaknesses, and external opportunities and threats. Plotting MP combinations for large samples of firms, and then formulating recommendations on optimizing the level of M, may be of little use to individual companies. Trying to achieve an 'optimal' geographic configuration, as a function of the MP results obtained for a large sample, might actually reduce performance for the individual firm attempting this, unless the internal and external circumstances facing this firm also change!

CONCLUSION

Our internalization theory perspective on the MP relationship in IB research suggests that it is doubtful if any particular *a priori* linkage should be assumed between these two parameters. Focusing especially on recent S-curve reasoning, we have argued that the past empirical work on the MP relationship has not addressed fully the nine conceptual and methodological challenges outlined in this chapter, and which allow so-called triple testing the quality of past and ongoing MP studies.

  The issues of reverse causality and endogeneity are probably the most critical challenges facing researchers studying MP linkages. Internalization theory, built upon the intellectual foundations established by Coase and first applied to the MNE by Buckley and Casson (1976) and Hennart (1982), suggests that it is FSAs that determine the firm's domestic and international success, with the environment acting as a constraining or facilitating force. If the environment becomes a constraint, the adaptive and learning capabilities of management must be deployed so that the environment can become facilitating again (Hitt et al., 1994) Firm-level performance, whether domestic or international, depends critically on the strengths of the MNE's FSAs and on its related higher-order capabilities to adapt to environmental changes. It is therefore doubtful that any generalizable recommendations can be formulated on an optimal degree of multinationality without in-depth knowledge of individual firms' strengths and their FSA development capabilities over time. Importantly, this suggests a promising future for case-based MP research, focused on truly longitudinal analyses of individual firms' international expansion trajectories. Here, it would be wise to include in empirical samples firms that face similar strategic drivers/motivations for international expansion, a common and well-understood environmental context such as a mature home market, and taking into account the firms' critical FSA bundles.

When conducting large-scale statistical studies, based on, e.g., panel data, IB researchers should be able to improve their research design by carefully subjecting their proposed conceptual and measurement approaches regarding M, P and the MP linkage to the triple testing outlined in this chapter. In addition, formulating well-grounded propositions, richly informed by business history cases and by credible theory, such as internalization theory, may be more effective than providing long, speculative shopping lists of possible costs and benefits of international expansion that are not tested directly, but are merely enumerated to support allegedly observed statistical curves. U-curves, inverted U-curves and S-curves are more often than not the equivalent of the monstrous giants observed by Don Quixote.

NOTES

1. Sullivan (1994b) and Hitt et al. (1994) were the first to propose an S-shaped relationship. However, as the latter paper is a conceptual piece rather than an empirical study, we did not include it in our list of the 20 most influential MP publications. As noted, all S-curve papers that the authors are aware of were included in Table 6.1; none of these studies has yet made it into the top 20 of MP papers.
2. In this chapter, we argue against the existence of a single, generalized MP relationship, in accordance with Hennart's (2007) superb conceptual analysis, but we focus on triple testing the quality of past and ongoing MP studies; see below. This chapter should thus be viewed as a complement to the Hennart (2007) piece.

REFERENCES

Bergsten, C.F., Horst, T. and Moran, T.H. (1978), *American Multinationals and American Interests*, Washington, DC: The Brookings Institution.
Buckley, P.J. and Casson, M. (1976), *The Future of the Multinational Enterprise*, London: Macmillan.
Chang, S.-C. and Wang, C.-F. (2007), 'The effect of product diversification strategies on the relationship between international diversification and firm performance', *Journal of World Business*, **42**(1), 61–79.
Contractor, F.J., Kundu, S. and Hsu, C. (2003), 'A three-stage theory of international expansion: the link between multinationality and performance in the service sector', *Journal of International Business Studies*, **34**(1), 5–18.

Delios, A. and Beamish, P.W. (1999), 'Geographic scope, product diversification, and the corporate perform-ance of Japanese firms', *Strategic Management Journal*, **20**(8), 711–27.

Doukas, J. and Travlos, N.G. (1988), 'The effect of corporate multinationalism on shareholders' wealth: evi-dence from international acquisitions', *The Journal of Finance*, **43**(5), 1161–75.

Dowell, G., Hart, S. and Yeung, B. (2000), 'Do corporate global environmental standards create or destroy market value?', *Management Science*, **46**(8), 1059–74.

Dubofsky, P. and Varadarajan, P. (1987), 'Diversification and measures of performance: additional empirical evidence', *Academy of Management Journal*, **30**(3), 597–608.

Errunza, V.R. and Senbet, L.W. (1981), 'The effects of international operations on the market value of the firm: theory and evidence', *The Journal of Finance*, **34**(2), 401–17.

Gedajlovic, E.R. and Shapiro, D.M. (1998), 'Management and ownership effects: evidence from five countries', *Strategic Management Journal*, **19**(6), 533–53.

Geringer, J.M., Beamish, P.W. and daCosta, R.C. (1989), 'Diversification strategy and internationalization: implications for MNE performance', *Strategic Management Journal*, **10**(2), 109–99.

Geringer, J.M., Tallman, S. and Olsen, D.M. (2000), 'Product and international diversification among Japanese multinational firms', *Strategic Management Journal*, **21**(1), 51–80.

Goerzen, A. and Beamish, P.W. (2003), 'Geographic scope and multinational enterprise performance', *Strategic Management Journal*, **24**(13), 1289–306.

Gomes, L. and Ramaswamy, K. (1999), 'An empirical examination of the form of the relationship between multinationality and performance', *Journal of International Business Studies*, **30**(1), 173–88.

Gómez-Mejia, L.R. and Palich, L.E. (1997), 'Cultural diversity and the performance of multinational firms', *Journal of International Business Studies*, **28**(2), 309–34.

Grant, R.M. (1987), 'Multinationality and performance among British manufacturing companies', *Journal of International Business Studies*, **18**(3), 79–89.

Grant, R.M. and Cibin, R. (1996), 'Strategy, structure and market turbulence: the international oil majors, 1970–1991', *Scandinavian Journal of Management*, **12**(2), 165–88.

Grant, R.M., Jammine, A.P. and Thomas, H. (1988), 'Diversity, diversification, and profitability among British manufacturing companies, 1972–1984', *Academy of Management Journal*, **31**(4), 771–801.

Hamilton, B.H. and Nickerson, J.A. (2003), 'Correcting for endogeneity in strategic management research', *Strategic Organization*, **1**(1), 51–78.

Hennart, J.-F. (1982), *A Theory of Multinational Enterprise*, Ann Arbor, MI: University of Michigan Press.

Hennart, J.-F. (2007), 'The theoretical rationale for a multinationality–performance relationship', *Management International Review*, **47**(3), 423–52.

Hitt, M.A., Hoskisson, R.E. and Ireland, R.D. (1994), 'A mid-range theory of interactive effects of international and product diversification on innovation and performance', *Journal of Management*, **20**(2), 297–326.

Hitt, M.A., Hoskisson, R.E. and Kim, H. (1997), 'International diversification: effects on innovation and firm performance in product-diversified firms', *Academy of Management Journal*, **40**(4), 767–98.

Hitt, M.A., Tihanyi, L., Miller, T. and Connely, B. (2006), 'International diversification: antecedents, outcomes and moderators', *Journal of Management*, **32**(6), 831–67.

Hofstede, G. (1980), *Culture's Consequences: International Differences in Work-related Values*, Beverly Hills, CA: Sage Publications.

Horst, T. (1972), 'Firm and industry determinants of the decision to invest abroad: an empirical study', *The Review of Economics and Statistics*, **54**(3), 258–66.

Hutzschenreuter, T. and Voll, J.C. (2008), 'Performance effects of "added cultural distance" in the path of international expansion: the case of German multinational enterprises', *Journal of International Business Studies*, **39**(1), 53–70.

Hymer, S.H. (1960), 'The international operations of national firms: a study of direct foreign investment', Ph.D. dissertation, MIT, USA.

Katrishen, F.A. and Scordis, N.A. (1998), 'Economies of scale in services: a study of multinational insurers', *Journal of International Business Studies*, **29**(2), 305–23.

Kim, W.C., Hwang, P. and Burgers, W.P. (1989), 'Global diversification strategy and corporate profit perform-ance', *Strategic Management Journal*, **10**(1), 45–57.

Kim, W.C., Hwang, P. and Burgers, W.P. (1993), 'Multinationals' diversification and the risk–return trade-off', *Strategic Management Journal*, **14**(4), 275–86.

Kim, W.S. and Lyn, E.O. (1986), 'Excess market value, the multinational corporation, and Tobin's q-ratio', *Journal of International Business Studies*, **17**(1), 119–25.

Kumar, M.S. (1984), 'Comparative analysis of UK domestic and international firms', *Journal of Economic Studies*, **11**(3), 26–42.

Li, L. (2005), 'Is regional strategy more effective than global strategy?', *Management International Review*, **45** (Special Issue 1), 37–57.

Lu, J.W. and Beamish, P.W. (2001), 'The internationalization and performance of SMEs', *Strategic Management Journal*, **22**(6–7), 565–86.

Lu, J.W. and Beamish, P.W. (2004), 'International diversification and firm performance: the S-curve hypothesis', *Academy of Management Journal*, **47**(4), 598–609.

McSweeney, B. (2002), 'Hofstede's model of national cultural differences and their consequences: a triumph of faith – a failure of analysis', *Human Relations*, **55**(1), 89–118.

Miller, D.J. (2004), 'Firms' technological resources and the performance effects of diversification: a longitudinal study', *Strategic Management Journal*, **25**(11), 1097–119.

Morck, R. and Yeung, B. (1991), 'Why investors value multinationality', *Journal of Business*, **64**(2), 165–87.

Nelson, R.R. and Winter, S.G. (1982), *An Evolutionary Theory of Economic Change*, Cambridge, MA: The Belknap Press of Harvard University Press.

Qian, G. and Li, J. (2002), 'Multinationality, global market diversification and profitability among the largest US firms', *Journal of Business Research*, **55**(4), 325–35.

Ramaswamy, K., Kroeck, K.G. and Renforth, W. (1996), 'Measuring the degree of internationalization of a firm: a comment', *Journal of International Business Studies*, **27**(1), 167–78.

Riahi-Belkaoui, A. (1998), 'The effects of the degree of internationalization on firm performance', *International Business Review*, **7**(3), 315–21.

Ronen, S. and Shenkar, O. (1985), 'Clustering countries on attitudinal dimensions: a review and a synthesis', *Academy of Management Review*, **10**(3), 434–54.

Rugman, A.M. (2005), 'Twenty-five years of "International diversification and the multinational enterprise"', in A. Verbeke (ed.), *Internalization, International Diversification and the Multinational Enterprise: Essays in Honour of Alan M. Rugman*, Oxford: Elsevier/JAI, pp. 203–17.

Ruigrok, W., Amann, W. and Wagner, H. (2007), 'The internationalization–performance relationship at Swiss firms: a test of the S-shape and extreme degrees of internationalisation', *Management International Review*, **47**(3), 349–68.

Schiller, R.J. (2000), *Irrational Exuberance*, Princeton, NJ: Princeton University Press.

Schwartz, S.H. (1992), 'Universals in the content and structure of values: theoretical advances and empirical tests in 20 countries', in M.P. Zanna (ed.), *Advances in Experimental Social Psychology*, Vol. 25, London: Academic Press, pp. 1–65.

Severn, A.K. and Laurence, M.M. (1974), 'Direct investment, research intensity, and profitability', *Journal of Financial and Quantitative Analysis*, March, 181–90.

Shaver, J.M. (1998), 'Accounting for endogeneity when assessing strategy performance: does entry mode choice affect FDI survival?', *Management Science*, **44**(4), 571–85.

Siddharthan, N.S. and Lall, S. (1982), 'The recent growth of the largest US multinationals', *Oxford Bulletin of Economics and Statistics*, **44**(1), 1–13.

Stopford, J.M. and Wells, L.T., Jr (1972), *Managing the Multinational Enterprise: Organization of the Firm and Ownership of the Subsidiaries*, London: Basic Books.

Sullivan, D. (1994a), 'Measuring the degree of internationalization of a firm', *Journal of International Business Studies*, **25**(2), 325–42.

Sullivan, D. (1994b), 'The threshold of internationalization: a replication', *Management International Review*, **34**(2), 165–86.

Sundaram, A.K. and Black, J.S. (1992), 'The environment and internal organization of the multinational enterprises', *Academy of Management Review*, **17**(4), 729–57.

Tallman, S. and Li, J. (1996), 'Effects of international diversity and product diversity on the performance of multinational firms', *Academy of Management Journal*, **39**(1), 179–96.

Thomas, D.E. and Eden, L. (2004), 'What is the shape of the multinationality–performance relationship?', *The Multinational Business Review*, **12**(1), 89–110.

Vachani, S. (1991), 'Distinguishing between related and unrelated international geographic diversification: a comprehensive measure of global diversification', *Journal of International Business Studies*, **22**(2), 307–22.

Venkatraman, N. and Ramanujam, V. (1986), 'Measurement of business performance in strategy research: a comparison of approaches', *Academy of Management Review*, **11**(4), 801–14.

Verbeke, A. (2009), *International Business Strategy: Rethinking the Foundations of Global Corporate Success*, Cambridge: Cambridge University Press.

Verbeke, A., Li, L. and Goerzen, A. (2009), 'Towards more effective research on the multinationality–performance relationship', *Management International Review*, **49**(2), 149–61.

Vernon, R. (1971), *Sovereignty at Bay: The Multinational Spread of U.S. Enterprises*, New York: Basic Books.

Zahra, S.A., Ireland, R.D. and Hitt, M.A. (2000), 'International expansion by new venture firms: international diversity, mode of market entry, technological learning and performance', *Academy of Management Journal*, **43**(5), 925–50.

APPENDIX

Table 6A.1   The most cited MP papers

Year	Author(s)	Multinationality	Performance	MP linkage
1960	Hymer	Binar	Net licence receipts	Linear positive
1971	Vernon	Binar	ROS, ROA	Linear positive
1972	Stopford, Wells	Binar	ROI, sales growth	ROI: insignificant, sales growth: linear positive
1972	Horst	Binar	Net profits	Insignificant
1978	Bergsten, Horst, Moran	Root of (foreign dividend + tax credits) over total assets	Domestic ROA	Linear positive
1981	Errunza, Senbet	FSTS, FATA, FITI[1]	Excess market value	FSTS: linear positive, FATA, FITI: insignificant
1987	Grant	FSTS	ROS, RONA, ROE, sales growth, profitability growth[1]	Linear positive
1988	Grant Jammine, Thomas	FSTS	ROA, sales growth	Linear positive
1988	Doukas, Travlos	International acquisition proposal, sample split in 3 groups: domestic, international first acquisition in target, international *n*th acquisition in target	Fama market model abnormal return (stock)	Total group: insignificant, Domestic = insignificant, International first = linear positive, International *n*th = insignificant
1989	Geringer, Beamish, daCosta	FSTS	ROS, ROA	Inverted U
1989	Kim, Hwang, Burgers	6-region, employee-based entropy measure	Operating profit margin, ROI[2]	Product unrelated global high-diversified firms outperform product unrelated global low-diversified firms, product related global high-diversified firms outperform product unrelated global low-diversified firms
1991	Morck, Yeung	Count subsidiaries, Count countries	Tobin's *q*	Linear positive if in possession of intangible assets
1993	Kim, Hwang, Burgers	6-region, employee-based entropy measure	Risk-adjusted 5-year average of the industry weighted ROA	Global market diversification has a favorable impact on risk-adjusted performance

Table 6A.1   (continued)

Year	Author(s)	Multinationality	Performance	MP linkage
1996	Tallman, Li	FSTS, count countries	ROS	FSTS: insignificant, count countries: linear positive
1997	Gómez-Meja, Palich	10 measures to distinguish between investments	ROA, market-to-book value[1]	Insignificant difference related and unrelated diversification
1997	Hitt, Hoskisson, Kim	Sales-based entropy measure	ROA	Inverted U-shaped
1998	Gedajlovic, Shapiro	FATA	ROA	Negative for US and German firms, positive for French firms, insignificant for UK and Canadian firms
1999	Delios, Beamish	Count FDI, count countries	Composite ROA, ROS ROE (5-year average)	Linear positive
1999	Gomes, Ramaswamy	Multi-item index of FSTS, FATA and count countries	ROA, OCTS[1]	ROA: inverted U, OCTS: U
2000	Geringer, Tallman, Olsen	FSR, ESR, IR	ROS, sales growth (1-year lagged)	ROS: FSR, IR linear negative, ESR linear positive; sales growth: FSR positive, ESR, IR: insignificant
2000	Zahra, Ireland, Hitt	Count countries, technological diversity, Hofstede's cultural diversity, geographic diversity, foreign segments	ROE, sales growth	Positive (count countries, Hofstede for ROE and sales growth), positive (technological diversity and geographic diversity for sales growth), negative (foreign segments for ROE)
2000	Dowell, Hart, Yeung	FATA	Tobin's q	Negative in group mean regression without industry dummy, insignificant if industry dummy is added or in random firm regressions with and without dummy
2001	Lu, Beamish	Count FDI, count countries	ROS, ROA	U
2003	Contractor, Kundu, Hsu	Composite of FSTS, FETE and FOTO	ROS, ROA	U for whole sample and capital-intensive industries, S for knowledge-based industries

Notes:
1. OCTS = Operating costs over total sales; Tobin's q = Market-to-book value; FITI = Foreign net income over total net income; RONA = Return on net assets; FSR = Foreign sales ratio (foreign subsidiary sales over total firm sales); ESR = Exports sales ratio (exports sales over total firm sales); IR = Internal ratio (foreign subsidiary sales over the sum of subsidiary and export sales).
2. Although Kim et al. (1989) state that they use ROA as a performance measure, their actual measure is closer to ROI ('after-tax earnings plus interest expressed as a percentage of stockholders' equity plus long-term debt').

PART II

STRUCTURAL COMPLEXITIES IN INTERNATIONAL STRATEGIC MANAGEMENT

7 New ideas about organizational design for modern MNEs
William G. Egelhoff and Joachim Wolf

1. INTRODUCTION

As international environments become more competitive, requiring ever more complex international strategies, organizing the multinational enterprise (MNE) becomes increasingly difficult. This chapter reviews how scholarly research and theory have addressed this problem in the past and then develops a kind of roadmap for where such theory needs to go in the future. We divide existing research and theory development into two broad literatures. The first we label the HQ–subsidiary relationship literature. This was important from the 1960s to the 1980s. The second we label the subsidiary-level, network perspective literature, and this has been important from the 1990s to the present. After reviewing and contrasting these two literatures, we argue that neither is sufficient for the future – neither by itself provides a suitable theory for organizing the modern MNE.

After presenting our assumptions about the environments and strategies that modern MNEs will have to cope with, we outline and illustrate a kind of contingency theory for organizing such firms. We argue that modern MNEs will require the combined coordination capabilities described by both the existing literatures, and that a contingency theory is the best conceptual framework for combining such sharply contrasting capabilities.

2. THE TWO EXISTING LITERATURES ON MNE ORGANIZATIONAL DESIGN

In this section we review each of the two literatures, with a view to identifying the strengths and weaknesses of each for implementing modern MNE strategies. These literatures are the existing context for future scholarly work, and to the extent they are relevant, it will be wise to build on them.

2.1 HQ–Subsidiary Relationship Literature

This broad stream of work was very important in international management research from the 1960s to the 1980s. It developed the first real models of what an MNE looks like and how it operates. This body of work contains the following important substreams.

Strategy–structure work
This substream began with the study of Stopford and Wells (1972), which sought to apply an earlier conceptual framework developed by Chandler (1962) to MNEs. This framework specified that there must be some kind of fit between a firm's formal organization

structure and its strategy for the firm to succeed. Stopford and Wells (1972) found that a high level of foreign product diversity encouraged the adoption of a product division structure, while a high level of foreign sales was associated with a geographical region structure. A low level of foreign sales was associated with an international division structure. Later studies tended to confirm these relationships and added additional contingency variables to the model (Franko, 1976; Egelhoff, 1982; Daniels et al., 1985; Habib and Victor, 1991). Type of MNE structure has been shown to have a conceptual and empirical fit with: foreign product diversity, product modification differences, rate of product change, size of foreign operations, size of foreign manufacturing, number of foreign subsidiaries, the extent of outside ownership, and the extent of acquisitions (Egelhoff, 1988). More recently a few studies have successfully linked different types of matrix structure to a similar set of strategic conditions or contingency variables (Wolf and Egelhoff, 2002; Donaldson, 2009).

In general, this work views formal organizational structure as the most important coordinating mechanism for successfully implementing a firm's strategy. This view is most explicit in the studies that use an information-processing perspective to conceptualize and explain the relationship between specific types of structure and specific elements of strategy (Egelhoff, 1982; Habib and Victor, 1991; Wolf and Egelhoff, 2002). This perspective sees strategy creating specific information-processing requirements, while the different types of structure provide different information-processing capacities. Successful strategy implementation requires fit between the information-processing requirements and capacities.

Centralization/decentralization work
This substream focused on the extent to which decision-making in an MNE was centralized at HQ or decentralized to foreign subsidiaries (Picard, 1977; Goehle, 1980; Hedlund, 1981; Garnier, 1982; Gates and Egelhoff, 1986). It sought to discover what environmental and strategic conditions influenced the degree of centralization in an MNE. Increasing company size and environmental complexity tend to encourage decentralization in an MNE, while interdependence between a specific subsidiary and the rest of the company encourages greater centralization of that specific subsidiary's decisions. Egelhoff (1988) examined the relative influence of these two pressures and found that company-level size and complexity tended to have more influence over the degree of centralization than subsidiary-level change and interdependence. Since he was sampling successful firms, he concluded that successful MNEs avoid information-processing overload at HQ by decentralizing, even if this means less than optimal centralization for specific subsidiaries. This literature tends to view centralization as an important coordinating mechanism, but one that is subject to limits.

Staffing work
This substream of work focused on the extent to which key subsidiary positions are staffed with local nationals or expatriates from the parent company (Daniels, 1974; Hulbert and Brandt, 1980; Toyne, 1980; Toyne and Kuhne, 1983; Baliga and Jaeger, 1984). It generally views expatriate staffing as an important way to influence and control subsidiary behavior and performance. Some studies also emphasize the role of staffing in transferring knowledge/skills and company culture to subsidiaries (Edstrom and

Galbraith, 1977) and in building effective communication bridges between subsidiary and parent (Harzing, 2001). The use of this mechanism seems to vary by parent country, with Japanese MNEs frequently using it (Negandhi and Welge, 1984; Tung, 1988), while US MNEs use it less frequently than Japanese or European MNEs (Hulbert and Brandt, 1980). At the subsidiary level, a subsidiary is more likely to have expatriate management if there are high interdependencies between the subsidiary and the rest of the company (Egelhoff, 1988), if there is a big cultural distance between the subsidiary and the parent country (Boyacigiller, 1990), and if the subsidiary is not very successful (Leksell, 1981). All three of these conditions would increase the requirement for coordination or information processing between a subsidiary and the parent HQ, and expatriate staffing is one way of attempting to meet this requirement.

In addition to the three substreams of work discussed above, additional research occurred around other organizational processes, including planning (Kono, 1976; Gotcher, 1977; Gouy, 1978; Hulbert and Brandt, 1980; Capon et al., 1984) and control (Youssef, 1975; Egelhoff, 1984). Space precludes a fuller discussion of such additional research, but the present discussion is adequate to identify the salient characteristics of the HQ–subsidiary relationship literature. First, this literature emphasizes the formal organization design and largely excludes the informal. Second, the organization is viewed as a hierarchy, where vertical as opposed to lateral relationships are the most important. Third, power and influence largely stem from hierarchical position, so legitimate power is most important. Fourth, firm-level coordination is largely achieved by formalization and the appropriate centralization of decision-making. And fifth, this literature assumes a top–down, firm-level perspective of the MNE.

2.2 Subsidiary-level, Network Perspective Literature

This broad stream of work has been important in international management research from the late 1980s until the present. From the 1990s on it has been the dominant approach assumed by most researchers of MNE organizational design. In this section we primarily discuss three important substreams of work.

The MNE as a heterarchy

This substream largely consists of the work of Hedlund (1986, 1993) and his co-authors (Hedlund and Nonaka, 1993; Hedlund and Ridderstrale, 1997). This perspective sees the MNE confronting numerous interdependencies that are constantly changing and cannot be prespecified. As a result, organization design needs to be less hierarchical and more heterarchical, with shifting positions and relationships, much more lateral sharing of knowledge, the development of shared vision across the organization, and more consensual forms of decision-making. Hedlund states that 'A heterarchy is by definition a more ambiguous creature than the hierarchy' (Hedlund, 1993, p. 229). As a result, its flexibility, lack of any fixed specification and self-organizing quality are key attributes of a heterarchy. 'Practical examples of heterarchical social systems are democratic political systems, employee share ownership, and many kinds of project councils and R&D boards in companies' (ibid., p. 231).

In a later article on the N form (where 'N' stands for novelty), Hedlund and Ridderstrale (1997) contrast knowledge exploitation and knowledge creation in MNEs. They argue that heterarchical models of the MNE are better able to represent it as a knowledge-creating organization, while traditional models largely represent it as a knowledge-exploiting organization. Thus this perspective was perhaps the first to suggest that existing models of the MNE lacked important capabilities that MNEs increasingly required and that successful MNEs undoubtedly already possessed. But this is where it stops. There is no attempt by this substream of work to integrate heterarchy and hierarchy, formal and informal organization design into a more complex and complete model of the MNE.

The transnational MNE

This substream is centered around the work of Bartlett and Ghoshal (Bartlett and Ghoshal, 1989, 1993; Ghoshal and Bartlett, 1990; Ghoshal et al., 1994; Nohria and Ghoshal, 1994; Ghoshal and Nohria, 1997; Tsai and Ghoshal, 1998). The basic definition of a transnational strategy is one that simultaneously attempts to realize global efficiency, local responsiveness and worldwide learning across a company's worldwide operations. Traditional notions of MNE strategy generally contained these same elements, but usually with more of a trade-off. This trade-off was based on the belief that available MNE organization designs could not implement strategies that called for high levels of all three elements. The most sophisticated organization design, a matrix design, could simultaneously implement some of these elements, but it too was limited and often regarded as too complex and costly for many MNEs to use.

The transnational model of organizational design got around the above problem by relying more on nonstructural and informal means of coordination in MNEs. The primary characteristics of a transnational organization design are that it is less symmetrical, more specialized and more flexibly coordinated than traditional designs. As a result, the transnational organization is much more willing than a traditional organization to change its strategy, organization design and behavior. In fact, it is through innovation and change that such an organization seeks to gain competitive advantage. There is a higher level of interdependence among subsidiaries and a greater exchange of knowledge. In addition to using more informal coordinating mechanisms, transnational designs also use socialization to build high levels of shared vision.

Subsidiary development work

This substream began with the work of Birkinshaw and his colleagues (Birkinshaw, 1996, 1997, 2000; Birkinshaw and Hood, 1998a, 1998b; Birkinshaw and Morrison, 1995). This work defines a much more important and active role for foreign subsidiaries than previously existed in the literature. It focused directly on the goals and decisions of subsidiary managers and described how these influenced the unique capabilities of a subsidiary, the specific initiatives it undertook, and its ultimate success in competing in external markets and expanding the subsidiary's charter or mandate within an MNE.

This substream of work tends to view the wider MNE as an inter-organizational network and internal market (Birkinshaw, 2000). Within this context, it is argued that subsidiary development has a direct and significant impact on corporate-level strategy and entrepreneurship. How such subsidiary entrepreneurship interacts with HQ and corporate-level actions, however, is not fully conceptualized or empirically studied by this substream of work.

Table 7.1   Two contrasting views of what is important for MNE organization design

HQ–subsidiary relationship literature	Subsidiary-level, network perspective literature
• Emphasizes formal organization design • Organization is viewed as a hierarchy (vertical relationships are most important) • Power and influence largely stem from hierarchical position (legitimate power is most important) • Firm-level coordination is largely achieved by formalization and the centralization of decision-making • Assumes a top–down, firm-level perspective of the MNE	• Emphasizes informal organization design • Organization is viewed as a non-hierarchical network (lateral relationships are most important) • Power and influence largely stem from task interdependence (expert power is most important) • Firm-level coordination is largely achieved by decentralized subsidiary-level networking • Assumes a bottom–up, subsidiary-level perspective of the MNE

The subsidiary-level, network perspective literature extends well beyond the three sub-streams discussed above. Indeed, most organizational studies of the MNE since 1990 have viewed it from a network perspective (Gupta and Govindarajan, 1991; Doz and Prahalad, 1993; Kogut and Zander, 1995; Malnight, 1996; Andersson et al., 2002; Forsgren et al., 2005). The reason we chose these three substreams to represent the broader perspective is that, in addition to occurring early and having a formative effect on subsequent work, they most sharply and explicitly challenge the logic and value of the HQ–subsidiary relationship literature. Since we are reviewing both literatures to create a context for what comes next, we are especially interested in making explicit the differences between the two literatures.

Based on the above review, we identify the salient characteristics of the subsidiary-level, network perspective literature. First, this literature emphasizes informal organizational design and largely excludes formal organizational design. Second, the organization is viewed as a non-hierarchical network, where lateral as opposed to vertical relationships are most important. Third, power and influence largely stem from task interdependence, so expert power is most important. Fourth, firm-level coordination is largely achieved by decentralized, subsidiary-level networking. And fifth, this literature assumes a bottom–up, subsidiary-level perspective of the MNE. Table 7.1 summarizes these characteristics and contrasts them with the earlier characteristics we associated with the HQ–subsidiary relationship literature.

The above review of the scholarly research and literature describes two very different views of how MNEs function and what is important. The earlier HQ–subsidiary relationship literature describes a hierarchically organized MNE, with HQ setting the goals, developing the strategy and making most of the important decisions. Subsidiaries operate within these higher-level constraints, and at times their behavior can be largely confined to directly implementing these higher-level decisions. The more recent subsidiary-level, network perspective literature, on the other hand, describes an MNE that is largely represented by networks of semi-autonomous subsidiaries. Subsidiaries tend to belong to two types of network (Forsgren et al., 2005). The first is an external network, which consists of a subsidiary and its local customers, suppliers and regulators. Subsidiaries often have high autonomy when it comes to developing and operating within this type of network. The second type of network is an internal network, which consists of a subsidiary and other subsidiaries and HQ subunits. While the concept of an HQ may seem to imply a hierarchy, the network perspective does not model a hierarchical relationship among the subunits of an internal network. It ignores legitimate or hierarchical power and generally focuses on task dependence as the basis for power. Because of task dependence (for knowledge, resources etc.), an HQ may have power over a subsidiary, but for the same reason the subsidiary may have power over the HQ. This is a very different view of power and influence from that associated with the HQ–subsidiary relationship literature.

A practitioner may wonder whether the researchers associated with the two perspectives of an MNE were looking at the same reality (a similar set of MNEs). It is true that the international environment underwent considerable change between 1970 and 2010. Since the HQ–subsidiary relationship literature was largely developed in the 1970s and 1980s, and the subsidiary-level, network perspective literature in the following two decades, there is undoubtedly some difference in the realities the two literatures are attempting to empirically understand and theoretically address. It is likely that changes in international environments and strategies did lead to a greater use of network coordination in MNEs during the later period, but it didn't lead to the complete elimination of hierarchical coordination in MNEs or the other pronounced changes in perspective reflected in Table 7.1. Instead, the new perspective and literature needs to be seen as a reaction to the perceived deficiencies of the older literature. In scholarly research, such reactions frequently attempt to cast themselves as totally new theory, as opposed to being an improvement on some existing theory. From the practitioner's perspective, however, this abrupt shift in theoretical perspective is problematic. If the older theory ever possessed merit (provided a useful understanding of reality), and reality has not completely changed, from the practitioner's perspective there is no logic for such an abrupt shift in thinking. Indeed, few practitioners in large MNEs today see their firm as solely or even primarily a non-hierarchical network, where HQ is struggling to remain relevant and prevent subsidiaries from taking over most strategic decision-making.

3.   WHAT FUTURE MNE ORGANIZATION DESIGNS WILL LOOK LIKE

Having reviewed the existing literature on organization designs for MNEs, we now look into the future and project what types of organization design are likely to be required over the next ten to 20 years. Since we believe that organization designs need to fit and implement a firm's strategy, we begin by discussing what international strategies will look like.

3.1   Assumptions about Future MNE Strategies

Most scholars and business forecasters seem to assume that recent dominant trends in the international business environment will continue into the foreseeable future. At least, there seems to be no predictable turning point or significant new trend apparent. Thus the following three trends are expected to continue, with:

- trade barriers, communication and transportation costs decreasing (facilitating more interdependence);
- speed and unpredictability of technology and environmental change increasing (more change and uncertainty); and
- intensity of international competition increasing (raising the performance bar).

While specific industry and firm environments can differ significantly from the above characteristics, we construct this chapter around this most challenging environment. Addressing the most challenging scenario moves the discussion to the forefront of international strategy formulation and implementation, where new insights and ideas are most required. To the extent that a firm faces less challenging conditions, the making and implementing of strategy should simply be easier.

While the globalization of technologies and products will continue, it is likely that many firms will still need to accommodate significant local variation at the level of countries and even customers. Pressures to achieve global economies of scale will frequently be accompanied by the opposing pressure to provide global customers with unique customer-specific products and services. To the extent this occurs, companies will need to formulate ever more complex transnational strategies, characterized by globally dispersed activities, high interdependence, and significant local variation and adaptation. Such strategies are difficult to implement, and the organizational and managerial problems they pose can easily exceed the capabilities of most companies and managers.

While the environmental conditions and strategies described above tend to be common knowledge among international scholars and practitioners, we now go a bit deeper and discuss a less obvious problem that seems to be rapidly emerging and complicating the strategies of many MNEs. As a result of the intensity of international competition, it is increasingly rare for a large MNE to have a business strategy that can be based on a few large firm-wide differential advantages (a dominant product technology, the best global brand, the absolute lowest cost). Instead, most firms are increasingly basing their business strategies on a growing number of smaller, more limited, differential advantages (in France we largely compete by having the dominant brand, in the UK we are attempting to compete by offering more competitive prices and better customer service to our distribution partners, while in China we are largely counting on our partnership with a government-owned company to achieve profitable growth). This example describes a strategy that is seeking different differential advantages in each country. But it is not the traditional multidomestic strategy, because at the same time it is seeking global economies of scale in R&D and regional economies of scale in sourcing the product in Europe and North America. These latter advantages involve high interdependencies among countries and differentiate this growing type of transnational strategy from the traditional and easier-to-manage multidomestic strategy. Thus a growing number of companies are now competing with this kind of complex, multi-level (global, regional, country-level) multi-advantage strategy, and strategy implementation must keep this in mind and explicitly address it.

3.2   The Need for a Contingency Model of MNE Organizational Design

Looking to the complex strategies of the future, the new need is for a theory of organization design that effectively integrates the wisdom and capabilities inherent in the two literatures we have already discussed. This is a tall requirement, since it calls for the knowledge contained in both literatures to be simultaneously present and available for application. This is not a call to resurrect the older literature and teach it to everyone alongside the newer literature. Such an approach would quickly overwhelm the information-processing capacities of most humans, and it wouldn't lead to the better application of existent knowledge. Instead, a largely new theory that abstracts, condenses and integrates the knowledge and insight of the two foundation theories (literatures) is required. Since the strengths and weaknesses of the two foundation theories are so different, we propose integrating them with a contingency theory – essentially tapping the strengths of one theory or the other, depending on the characteristics of the strategy and task that are to be implemented. In the remainder of this chapter, we discuss a specific way to conceptualize and develop such a theory.

To relate and fit organization design to strategy and environment, we propose using an information-processing perspective or model (Galbraith, 1973; Tushman and Nadler, 1978; Egelhoff, 1988, 1991). To date, such a model has primarily been used within the HQ–subsidiary relationship literature to relate formal mechanisms of organizational design (type of structure, degree of centralization) to elements of firm- and subsidiary-level strategy. But, since the information-processing requirements of strategy and the information-processing capacities of organizational design are abstract intervening concepts (Egelhoff, 1982), they can be as readily applied to informal as to formal characteristics of organizational design.[1] This facilitates modeling and understanding the coordinating capabilities of formal structures and informal networks (of hierarchical and non-hierarchical designs) with a common framework. This is necessary if we intend to build a more broadly integrated contingency theory of organizational design and strategy.

It is important to realize that the new integrated theory proposed here represents new knowledge and insight that is currently not contained in either of the two existing literatures. Yet developing the new integrated knowledge will require reading and using the knowledge of both literatures. The new conceptual framework or model will specify under what strategic conditions coordination can be better achieved with non-hierarchical, network information processing and under what conditions formal, hierarchical information processing should be superior for implementing an element of strategy and its associated tasks. Managers in MNEs today largely make these kinds of strategy implementation and organizational design decisions without the assistance of an explicit theory and established research. As a result, they are probably subject to considerable bias and a lack of rationality. In the modern and more complex MNEs that are emerging, managers will have to make such decisions more frequently and more rationally. The only way to accomplish this on a broad scale is with a more explicit, readily applicable theory. In the next section we provide some examples of what the new integrated theory might look like.

3.3   Examples of the Proposed Contingency Theory

To date, organizational contingency theory has primarily dealt with various types of formal organizational design: describing under what strategic conditions a product division structure is preferable to a functional division or geographical region structure (Stopford and Wells, 1972), or when decentralized decision-making is preferable to centralized decision-making (Gates and Egelhoff, 1986). To address the problems of the modern MNE, organizational contingency theory needs to distinguish between when to use formal, hierarchical information processing and when to use more informal, non-hierarchical information processing. This kind of theory is largely missing, and the logic for developing it is not clearly established. In this section we discuss two examples that attempt to develop such theory. Both are taken from a recent article by Egelhoff (2010), which develops a conceptual framework for understanding the different information-processing capacities of hierarchical structures and network structures or designs. This framework is summarized in Table 7.2. Egelhoff then applies this conceptual framework to two examples that illustrate how the different information-processing capacities of hierarchical structures and network structures tend to fit different task situations or different strategic conditions.

The tight coupling versus loose coupling example

Consider an MNE that supplies an important type of component to manufacturers of PCs and other electronics products. The component tends to be custom designed and manufactured for each customer. The firm has three regional subsidiaries: North America, Europe and Asia. Each subsidiary has its own value chain (sales, product design, manufacturing) and is responsible for conducting business in its region. Initially the firm pursues a multidomestic strategy, where each subsidiary largely develops its own unique strategy. Europe, for example, tries to avoid competing on price. It focuses on providing superior customer service and quick cycle times for relatively short production runs of a product. Asia, on the other hand, emphasizes low-cost production for large volumes of a product. While the three subsidiaries use similar technical knowledge, they otherwise operate independently of each other. The general manager of each subsidiary reports to the firm's CEO.

At some point the subsidiaries realize that there is substantial duplication going on in the product design area (largely circuit design). They establish an 'Engineering Council', which consists of the three product design heads, who begin to discuss how they can share and better leverage design knowledge. This leads first to some informal transfer of specific design information among the three subsidiaries and later evolves into a central electronic library of certain designs. A designer in any subsidiary can access these designs, select one that is similar to his needs, and modify or borrow ideas from the design to create a new design. The result of this coordination was a substantial reduction in design costs. In effect, a new differential advantage has been added to the firm's strategy. It now seeks to realize global economies of scale in the design area, by sharing design information and replacing three subsidiary-level experience curves with a single global experience curve. It is apparent that the firm used a network structure (the Engineering Council) and network information processing to achieve this increased coordination. The question we address is whether this coordination could have been better provided by a hierarchy or a network structure.

Table 7.2   Important differences between hierarchical structures and network structures that influence their information-processing capacities

Hierarchical structure	Network structure
Goal structure	
• Strategic firm-level goals held by HQ; diverse subunit goals held by subunits • Provides a reasonable level of goal congruence across levels and subunits, along the organizing dimension	• Diverse subunit goals held by subunits; unclear how firm-level goals will arise without some hierarchy • Primary mechanism for achieving congruence is shared vision and firm-level culture
Information flows	
• Formal information flows along the hierarchy are directed by fiat; augmenting informal flows develop from high position familiarity and trust. • Hierarchies centralize information as it moves up and becomes more strategic and disperse it as it moves down and becomes more tactical	• Information flows among subunits are voluntary, informal and flexible; they are influenced more by personal familiarity and trust than by position familiarity • Networks can take many shapes, so no single pattern to the shaping of information flows
Motivation and behavior	
• Provides a system of incentives that supports extrinsic motivation and the processing of explicit (as opposed to tacit) information	• Facilitates intrinsic motivation and the development and transfer of tacit knowledge
Decision-making	
• Tends to push decisions up the hierarchy when there is interdependence across subunits • Tends to standardize many decisions (often through centralization) to reduce complexity and achieve efficiency • Facilitates centralized, comprehensive decision-making by an HQ (where firm-level goals and knowledge are more important than subunit goals and knowledge)	• Tends to keep decisions at the subunit level and exchange the necessary information to take interdependence into account • Tends to tolerate diversity in decisions and decision-making • Facilitates decentralized, incremental decision-making by the local subunits (where subunit goals and knowledge are more important than firm-level goals and knowledge)

From an information-processing perspective, the network is the preferred mode of coordination for this type of problem. It decentralizes all of the decision-making to the subsidiary level, where local knowledge of the customer's needs and priorities and the manufacturing plant's capabilities and costs are best. This level of independence among subsidiaries is important, since customer characteristics and manufacturing characteristics vary widely across the three regions. At the same time, designers can informally and voluntarily share the technical knowledge that is accumulated in their past designs. They will be motivated to do this because they all expect to benefit from it (the norm of reciprocity applies). This level of interdependence among subsidiaries is also important, since it provides new, valuable information to the task of designing a new product. This information was previously lacking when decisions were decentralized and there was no network structure.

An alternative would be to address this task situation with a hierarchy. Here all designs executed by the three subsidiaries would be sent to a central design office in the firm's HQ. This office would organize them into a central library and make them available to all designers. If the role of the central design office stopped here, the end result might be similar to what it was with the network structure alternative (although the cost of maintaining the central design office would undoubtedly be greater). But with all of this centralized design information available, the central office will be tempted to play an additional role. It may attempt to evaluate the designs to determine preferred ones for given problems, and it may begin to press for more standardization in design approaches. We are not in a position to say whether this would be good or bad for the firm, but clearly it would be inconsistent with the current largely multidomestic strategy of the firm. It is important to realize that the projected difference in outcome arises from the different information-processing capabilities of the network structure and the hierarchy. The network-structure facilitates information-sharing and decentralized decision-making. It gives priority to subunit, not firm-level, goals. The hierarchy not only brings the interdependent information together; it encourages making some kind of centralized evaluation of the situation (a hierarchy that failed to do this would be considered remiss). It also develops firm-level goals for its areas of responsibility. If the intended strategy of the firm is a multidomestic strategy, coordinating interdependence in the design area with a hierarchy is problematic.

Now suppose we change the strategy and task situation. As a result of increased competition, our MNE decides it must move to a more global strategy in the design and manufacturing areas of the value chain. The plan is to concentrate certain types of products in certain plants and also to better balance the production across the plants. As part of the transition to a global strategy, the firm wants to develop and install an integrated CAD/CAM (computer-aided design/computer-aided manufacturing) system across all plants and design centers. This will reduce the time and cost associated with transferring design work and manufacturing among the various sites. Sales remains a regional or local activity to fit the customers.

This task situation involves a much higher level of interdependence and tighter coupling of subunit behaviors than the previous strategy. Local subsidiary information about the range of product designs that must be accommodated and the manufacturing capabilities of each site need to be accumulated during the design phase and explicitly built into the firm-level CAD/CAM software system, or they will subsequently be ignored by the standardized decision process. This accumulated local knowledge needs to be combined with leading-edge knowledge about CAD/CAM systems so that comprehensive evaluation and decision-making regarding the design of the system can occur. In this case, the manufacturing central office at HQ understands better than any of the local sites what kinds of coordination the new CAD/CAM system should provide. This knowledge comes largely from outside of the firm. A similar perspective, one that can take all of this interdependence into account, is required when it comes to maintaining and improving the CAD/CAM system. Based on the information in Table 7.2, a hierarchy as opposed to a network structure tends to provide the kind of centralized, comprehensive decision-making and firm-level perspective required by this task.

Following this logic, the firm should create central design and manufacturing offices at parent HQ, with the local subsidiary design centers and manufacturing plants reporting to the respective office. Sales activities remain decentralized and local, but instead of relating directly with the local design center and manufacturing plant, they must now turn their orders in to the central offices at HQ, since the order may now be designed and manufactured in a different region.

Now we compare the two strategies and their associated tasks and propose a logic that captures their difference. Coordinating the designing of new products so that the process benefits from a common or firm-level experience curve while remaining responsive to local conditions requires both firm-wide technical design knowledge (the central library of designs) and local subsidiary knowledge about customers and manufacturing capabilities. Since the technical design knowledge is codified and easy to transfer, and the local customer and manufacturing knowledge is difficult to transfer, it is best to keep decision-making at the local subsidiary level. Such coordination problems, which require both firm-level and subunit-level knowledge, where the latter is more difficult to transfer, are well suited to a network structure design. Such problems require independence among the subunits to respect the variation in local knowledge, and they require interdependence to construct and leverage a single experience curve for technical design knowledge. A network structure fits this situation precisely because it is a loosely coupled system.

Coordinating the development and implementation of a firm-wide CAD/CAM system within the context of a global strategy requires combining externally imported information about CAD/CAM systems with aggregated product design and manufacturing information from the subunits. Since developing the system requires comprehensive decision-making at the firm level, a hierarchy is the preferred design to coordinate this task. In this case, subunits do not autonomously seek to improve their decisions, as in the previous example. Instead, they act in a cooperative manner that contributes to the overall quality of firm-level decisions. They provide information requested by HQ and follow directives provided by HQ, ensuring that the high degree of firm-level optimization built into the comprehensive decisions and directives of HQ is accurate and fully realized. The CAD/CAM problem requires high interdependence (actually standardization) across the design and manufacturing sites with little or no local independence. A hierarchical structure fits this situation precisely because it is a tightly coupled system. This example yields the following proposition:

Proposition 1   Developing and implementing tight coupling of subunit behaviors across a firm is best coordinated with a hierarchical structure, while the loose coupling of subunit behaviors is best coordinated with a network structure.

The significant innovation example
Consider an MNE that must evaluate and act on a significant innovation, one that is big enough to alter or impact the firm's strategy. The innovation might be in technology, marketing or business practices. It can originate from HQ or foreign subsidiaries. The question we address is whether such an innovation can be better evaluated and implemented with a hierarchical structure or a network structure.

From an information-processing perspective, we see two reasons why a hierarchical structure should be superior to a network structure for addressing problems involving high levels of newness or innovation. First, it can readily pull together at a central point the relevant internal and external information. It will be more difficult for a network to accomplish this, and there may also be a tendency for subunits in a network to incrementally make decisions before a comprehensive evaluation has been done. The second reason for preferring a hierarchical structure is that it adds increased vertical specialization to the decision process. It will be easier for HQ managers in a hierarchy to assume a longer time horizon and view new innovation as discontinuous from the present, since they do not have to directly manage current operations. Subunit managers in a network organization, on the other hand, will have primary responsibility for current operations and performance. It would be natural for them to see the future as continuous with the present. In a mature industry with little prospect of significant change this may be acceptable, but it will be inappropriate if a firm faces significant new innovations. The advantage a hierarchical structure has over a network structure is that it can simultaneously support more radically different views of the present and future organization.

Proposition 2   Hierarchical structures are superior to network structures in identifying and incorporating significant new innovation into firm strategies.

This issue is especially important for MNEs, where newness in both markets and technologies often originates in different locations around the world. Making strategic sense out of such dispersed information, which potentially involves opportunities and threats, requires bringing it together at a point where there is a comprehensive and deep understanding of the firm's strategy. This is facilitated by a hierarchical structure.

The view expressed in Proposition 2 may appear to contradict some of the virtues currently attributed to network structures in MNEs. Many scholars believe that a great deal of innovation either enters or could potentially enter an MNE through its network of foreign subsidiaries (Birkinshaw, 2000; Forsgren et al., 2005). A critical part of this view is the embeddedness of subsidiaries in their local environments, whereby they pick up new innovative knowledge, which can be distributed and further developed through a network structure. Birkinshaw (2000), for example, explicitly argues that a good deal of new firm-level strategy should emerge from such subsidiary initiatives. Our view is that while subsidiary-level initiatives that seek to alter corporate-level strategy might initially be generated by a network structure, they should be further developed and adopted through a hierarchical structure rather than through a horizontal network structure. This exposes the new initiatives or innovations to a more comprehensive evaluation and a different perspective, as discussed in the logic supporting Proposition 2.

There is support for this argument elsewhere in the literature. In their analysis of the 'metanational' firm, Doz et al. (2001) found that vertical HQ–subunit links were more important for sensing and exploring, while lateral links between subunits were more important for mobilizing knowledge. Schulz (2001) found a similar pattern and believed that the reason for such a pattern of flows was the uncertain relevance of new knowledge generated by a subsidiary for other subunits. He concluded that it was more efficient to verify the relevance of such new knowledge by sending it up the hierarchy to HQ than sending it laterally to other subsidiaries. Using a somewhat different logic, Andersson et al. (2002) also found that the HQ has an important role to play in further developing external relationships that were initiated by subsidiaries (converting subsidiary-level relationships and opportunities into broader firm-level relationships and opportunities).

Thus a varied literature supports the need for hierarchical information processing when significant new innovation is to be incorporated into a firm's strategy.

In order to reconcile these seemingly opposing views – that networks and hierarchies both contribute to the level of new innovation in an MNE – it is necessary to further conceptualize the specific contributions of each. New innovations originating at the subsidiary level are often associated with a good deal of tacit knowledge (about customers, supply chains, production processes and product technologies). To further develop such knowledge to the point where it can be identified and evaluated as a new innovation, different kinds of network information processing are usually required. Cross-functional networks within subsidiaries allow an idea that might have originated within a single function to be tested from different functional perspectives (R&D, manufacturing, marketing). Functional networks between subsidiaries (an R&D network, manufacturing network, marketing network, each across subsidiaries) allows a higher level of functional specialization and experience effects to modify and enrich the original idea. External networks with customers, suppliers and competitors surround each subsidiary and also inform new innovations at the subsidiary level. This kind of flexible network information processing exposes new ideas to a potentially wide variety of inputs, increasing the chance that some valuable recombination of knowledge will occur. Since all transfers of knowledge encourage making it more explicit, the time innovations spend in subsidiary-level networks also helps to codify innovative knowledge so that it can be vertically transmitted by a hierarchy. This line of reasoning leads to the following proposition.

Proposition 3   The level of new innovations generated at the subsidiary level of an MNE will be positively influenced by: (1) the density of cross-functional (and cross-product) networks within subsidiaries; (2) the density of between-subsidiary networks within functions (or within products); and (3) the embeddedness of subsidiaries within local environments (external networks between subsidiaries and local environments).

The above discussion describes the creation or generation phase of bottom–up innovations in MNEs. For such innovations to be incorporated into firm-level strategy, the information-processing perspective would require that they subsequently undergo an evaluation and selection phase that involves hierarchical information processing. As already discussed, this subjects new ideas to a review that involves a firm-level strategic perspective, which tends to differ from the perspectives that were present during the generation phase. For example, imagine a new product innovation that has been generated by one or more subsidiaries of an MNE. As this innovation requires more resources (to develop, produce, market), it will typically be transmitted up some kind of hierarchy within the MNE. This hierarchical information processing will evaluate and probably modify the innovation before it is included in the MNE's firm-level strategy. If the innovation moves up the hierarchy of a worldwide product division structure, there will be a tendency to globally standardize the product, design the product for a few major markets, and realize global economies of scale in sourcing and production. These are the goals and perspectives that a product division hierarchy typically brings to the task. Subsidiary-level innovations that are not valued by this perspective are likely to be rejected and discouraged by such a hierarchy. On the other hand, if the same innovation moves up a geographical region hierarchy, there will be a tendency to regionally standardize the product (with tolerance for local variations varying by region), design the product for a wider range of markets, and forgo global economies of scale.

As illustrated above, changing the hierarchical structure changes the way information is aggregated and the kind of vertical specialization (in terms of goals, perspectives and knowledge) that managers bring to the task of evaluating and incorporating subsidiary-level innovations into higher levels of strategy. Subsidiary-level innovations that are rejected by one type of hierarchical structure may be embraced by another type, and the way different types of hierarchical structure further develop and incorporate such innovations into firm-level strategy differ significantly. Since one of these outcomes is likely to be superior to the other in terms of the firm-level advantages it provides, it is important for an MNE to have the most appropriate or suitable hierarchical structure in place. This line of reasoning leads to the following proposition:

Proposition 4   The level of subsidiary-generated new innovations selected for inclusion in an MNE's firm-level strategy will be positively influenced by: (1) the level of new innovations generated and codified as explicit knowledge; and (2) the existence of a suitable hierarchy (functional, product, geographic) for transmitting and evaluating new innovations above the subsidiary level.

Thus the proposed reconciling argument is that network structures facilitate the generation of subsidiary-level innovations, while suitable hierarchical structures are critical to the selection and incorporation of such innovations into MNE strategy.

The two examples described above illustrate how both hierarchical and non-hierarchical, network-like information processing are required to optimally address the varied problems that confront modern MNEs. Firms that cannot identify and deploy the proper organizational design and information-processing capacity will deal with such problems in a less than optimal manner.

4.   CONCLUSION

During the 1970s and 1980s MNE managers interested in strategy implementation were told that they generally needed to manage formal organization design and fit it to the international strategies of their firms. From the 1990s on they were told to pay less attention to formal design and instead facilitate socialization, the development of networks, and other aspects of a vibrant informal organization. The truth is that they always needed to do both, each at the appropriate time and place. The real MNE, as opposed to the measured MNE that scholars see, is always a combination of formal and informal organization design, of hierarchical and network coordination. To date, scholarly research and theory has not helped managers to choose between these two fundamentally different forms of coordination at the level of specific tasks and situations. Yet the foundations for building a more integrated theory of MNE organization design seem to be in place.

As strategies become more complex, more complex theories of MNE organization design will generally be required to implement them. In this context, more complex theory means theory that provides more alternatives and addresses a wider range of situations. When new theory replaces old theory without integrating it, a more complex theory is unlikely to emerge. The result is theory (knowledge) churn, as opposed to theory (knowledge) accumulation. In this chapter we have suggested a contingency theory that integrates the strengths of two different theories of MNE organization design. This brings widely varying capabilities into the same theory and increases the range of problems the theory can address. It is important to realize that such integration goes beyond the simple addition of two sets of capabilities (this is what one possesses today, if one is simply familiar with both underlying theories). Integrating with a contingency theory means that one must also know when one capability (hierarchical information processing) is preferable to an alternative capability (network information processing) at the level of specific tasks. This trade-off evaluation requires a deeper understanding of both capabilities than the two simpler existing theories provide. In the proposed theory, this deeper understanding comes from assessing the information-processing implications of both capabilities. Since the resultant contingency theory is more complex than the two theories it assimilates, it can better address the more complex international strategies that are associated with modern MNEs.

NOTE

1. Egelhoff (1982) argues that for macro-organizational design studies, information processing needs to be used as an abstract intervening concept (which cannot itself be directly measured) to relate two sets of variables that can be directly measured. In this case the two sets of measured variables are organization design (whether the firm has a product division structure or a geographical region structure) and strategy (the degree of product diversity in the firm's strategy). Since organization design and strategy are not directly comparable, they need to be translated respectively into their information-processing capacities and their information-processing requirements. The latter are comparable concepts, whereas the directly measured variables are not.

REFERENCES

Andersson, U., M. Forsgren and U. Holm (2002), 'The strategic impact of external networks: subsidiary performance and competence development in the multinational corporation', *Strategic Management Journal*, **23**(11), 979–96.
Baliga, B.R. and A.M. Jaeger (1984), 'Multinational corporations: control systems and delegation issues', *Journal of International Business Studies*, **15**(2), 25–40.
Bartlett, C.A. and S. Ghoshal (1989), *Managing Across Borders: The Transnational Solution*, Boston, MA: Harvard Business School Press.
Bartlett, C.A. and S. Ghoshal (1993), 'Beyond the M-form: toward a managerial theory of the firm', *Strategic Management Journal*, **14**(1), 23–46.
Birkinshaw, J.M. (1996), 'How subsidiary mandates are gained and lost', *Journal of International Business Studies*, **27**(3), 467–96.
Birkinshaw, J.M. (1997), 'Entrepreneurship in multinational corporations: the characteristics of subsidiary initiatives', *Strategic Management Journal*, **18**(2), 207–30.
Birkinshaw, J. (2000), *Entrepreneurship in the Global Firm*, Thousand Oaks, CA: Sage.
Birkinshaw, J. and N. Hood (1998a), *Multinational Corporate Evolution and Subsidiary Development*, London and New York: St Martin's Press.
Birkinshaw J. and N. Hood (1998b), 'Multinational subsidiary evolution: capability and charter change in foreign-owned subsidiary companies', *Academy of Management Review*, **23**(4), 773–5.

Birkinshaw, J.M. and A.J. Morrison (1995), 'Configurations of strategy and structure in multinational subsidiaries', *Journal of International Business Studies*, **26**(4), 729–54.

Boyacigiller, N. (1990), 'The role of expatriates in the management of interdependence, complexity and risk in multinational corporations', *Journal of International Business Studies*, **21**(3), 357–81.

Capon, N., C. Christodoulou, J.U. Farley and J. Hulbert (1984), 'A comparison of corporate planning practice in American and Australian manufacturing companies', *Journal of International Business Studies*, **15**(2), 41–54.

Chandler, A.D. (1962), *Strategy and Structure: Chapters in the History of Industrial Enterprise*, Cambridge, MA: MIT Press.

Daniels, J.D. (1974), 'The education and mobility of European executives in U.S. subsidiaries: a comparative study', *Journal of International Business Studies*, **5**, 9–24.

Daniels, J.D., R.A. Pitts and M.J. Tretter (1985), 'Organizing for dual strategies of product diversity and international expansion', *Strategic Management Journal*, **6**(3), 223–37.

Donaldson, L. (2009), 'In search of the matrix advantage: a re-examination of the fit of matrix structures to transnational strategy in MNCs', in J.L.C. Cheng, E. Maitland and S. Nicholas (eds), *Managing Subsidiary Dynamics: Headquarters Role, Capability Development, and China Strategy,* Advances in International Management Series, Bingley, UK: Emerald Publishing, pp. 3–26.

Doz, Y. and C.K. Prahalad (1993), 'Managing the DMNCs: a search for a new paradigm', in S. Ghoshal and E. Westney (eds), *Organization Theory and the Multinational Corporation*, New York: St Martin's Press, pp. 24–50.

Doz, Y., J. Santos and P. Williamson (2001), *From Global to Metanational: How Companies Win in the Knowledge Economy*, Boston, MA: Harvard Business School Press.

Edstrom, A. and J.R. Galbraith (1977), 'Transfer of managers as a coordination and control strategy in multinational organizations', *Administrative Science Quarterly*, **22**(2), 248–63.

Egelhoff, W.G. (1982), 'Strategy and structure in multinational corporations: an information-processing approach', *Administrative Science Quarterly*, **27**(3), 435–58.

Egelhoff, W.G. (1984), 'Patterns of control in U.S., UK, and European multinational corporations', *Journal of International Business Studies*, **15**(2), 73–83.

Egelhoff, W.G. (1988), *Organizing the Multinational Enterprise: An Information-Processing Perspective*, Cambridge, MA: Ballinger.

Egelhoff, W.G. (1991), 'Information-processing theory and the multinational enterprise', *Journal of International Business Studies*, **22**(3), 341–58.

Egelhoff, W.G. (2010), 'How the parent headquarters adds value to an MNC', *Management International Review*, **50**(4), 413–31.

Forsgren, M., U. Holm and J. Johanson (2005), *Managing the Embedded Multinational: A Business Network View*, Cheltenham, UK and Northampton, MA, USA: Edward Elgar.

Franko, L.G. (1976), *The European Multinationals: A Renewed Challenge to American and British Big Business*, Stamford, CT: Greylock.

Galbraith, J.R. (1973), *Designing Complex Organizations*, Reading, MA: Addison-Wesley.

Garnier, G.H. (1982), 'Context and decision making autonomy in the foreign affiliates of U.S. multinational corporations', *Academy of Management Journal*, **25**(4), 893–908.

Gates, S.R. and W.G. Egelhoff (1986), 'Centralization in headquarters–subsidiary relationships', *Journal of International Business Studies*, **17**(2), 71–92.

Ghoshal, S. and C.A. Bartlett (1990), 'The multinational corporation as an interorganizational network', *Academy of Management Review*, **15**(4), 603–25.

Ghoshal, S. and N. Nohria (1997), *The Differentiated MNC: Organizing the Multinational Corporation for Value Creation*, San Francisco, CA: Jossey-Bass.

Ghoshal, S., H. Korine and G. Szulanski (1994), 'Interunit communication in multinational corporations', *Management Science*, **40**(1), 96–110.

Goehle, D.G. (1980), *Decision Making in Multinational Corporations*, Ann Arbor, MI: University of Michigan Research Press.

Gotcher, J.W. (1977), 'Strategic planning in European multinationals', *Long Range Planning*, October, 7–13.

Gouy, M. (1978), 'Strategic decision-making in large European firms', *Long Range Planning*, **11**(3), 41–8.

Gupta, A.K. and V. Govindarajan (1991), 'Knowledge flows and the structure of control within multinational corporations', *Academy of Management Review*, **16**(4), 768–92.

Habib, M. and B. Victor (1991), 'Strategy, structure, and performance of U.S. manufacturing and service MNCs', *Strategic Management Journal*, **12**(8), 589–606.

Harzing, A. (2001), 'Of bears, bumble-bees and spiders: the role of expatriates in controlling foreign subsidiaries', *Journal of World Business*, **36**(4), 366–79.

Hedlund, G. (1981), 'Autonomy of subsidiaries and formalization of headquarters–subsidiary relationships in

Swedish MNCs', in L. Otterbeck (ed.), *The Management of Headquarters–Subsidiary Relationships in Multinational Corporations*, New York: St Martin's Press, pp. 25–78.

Hedlund, G. (1986), 'The hypermodern MNC: a heterarchy?', *Human Resource Management*, **23**(1), 9–35.

Hedlund, G. (1993), 'Assumptions of hierarchy and heterarchy, with applications to the management of the multinational corporation', in S. Ghoshal and E. Westney (eds), *Organization Theory and the Multinational Corporation*, London: Macmillan, pp. 211–36.

Hedlund, G. and I. Nonaka (1993), 'Models of knowledge management in the West and Japan', in P. Lorange, B.G. Chakravarthy, J. Roos and A. Van de Ven (eds), *Implementing Strategic Processes: Change, Learning, and Cooperation*, London: Basil Blackwell, pp. 117–44.

Hedlund, G. and J. Ridderstrale (1997), 'Toward a theory of the self-renewing MNC', in B. Toyne and D. Nigh (eds), *International Business: An Emerging Vision*, Columbia, SC: University of South Carolina Press, pp. 329–54.

Hulbert, J.M. and W.K. Brandt (1980), *Managing the Multinational Subsidiary*, New York: Holt, Rinehart and Winston.

Kogut, B. and U. Zander (1995), 'Knowledge of the firm and the evolutionary theory of the multinational corporation', *Journal of International Business Studies*, **25**(4), 625–46.

Kono, T. (1976), 'Long range planning – Japan – USA – a comparative study', *Long Range Planning*, October, 61–71.

Leksell, L. (1981), *Headquarters–Subsidiary-Relationships in Multinational Corporations*, Stockholm: Institute of International Business, Stockholm School of Economcis.

Malnight, T.W. (1996), 'The transition from decentralized to network-based MNC structures: an evolutionary perspective', *Journal of International Business Studies*, **27**(1), 43–65.

Negandhi, A.R. and M. Welge (1984), *Beyond Theory Z – Global Rationalization Strategies of American, German and Japanese Multinational Companies*, Greenwich, CT: JAI Press.

Nohria, N. and S. Ghoshal (1994), 'Differentiated fit and shared values: alternatives for managing headquarters–subsidiary relations', *Strategic Management Journal*, **15**, 491–502.

Picard, J. (1977), 'How European companies control marketing decisions abroad', *Columbia Journal of World Business*, **12**(2), 113–21.

Schulz, M. (2001), 'The uncertain relevance of newness: organizational learning and knowledge flows', *Academy of Management Journal*, **44**(4), 661–81.

Stopford, J.M. and L.T. Wells Jr (1972), *Managing the Multinational Enterprise*, New York: Basic Books.

Toyne, B. (1980), *Host Country Managers of Multinational Firms: An Evaluation of Variables Affecting Their Managerial Thinking Patterns*, New York: Arno Press.

Toyne, B. and R.J. Kuhne (1983), 'The management of the international executive compensation and benefits process', *Journal of International Business Studies*, **20**(3), 37–50.

Tsai, W. and S. Ghoshal (1998), 'Social capital and value creation: the role of intra-firm networks', *Academy of Management Journal*, **41**(4), 464–76.

Tung, R.L. (1988), 'Career issues in international assignments', *The Academy of Management Executive*, **2**(3), 241–4.

Tushman, M.L. and D.A. Nadler (1978), 'Information processing as an integrating concept in organizational design', *Academy of Management Review*, **3**(3), 613–24.

Wolf, J. and W.G. Egelhoff (2002), 'A reexamination and extension of international strategy–structure theory', *Strategic Management Journal*, **23**(2), 181–9.

Youssef, S.M. (1975), 'Contextual factors influencing control strategy of multinational corporations', *Academy of Management Journal*, **18**(1), 136–43.

8 Initiative in multinational subsidiaries
Julian Birkinshaw and Shameen Prashantham

Multinational corporations (MNCs) are complex, multifaceted entities. They can be studied through any number of conceptual lenses, and to some degree we, as researchers, are likely to see in them whatever we are looking for. MNCs have formal structures and control systems; they can be modeled as social networks; they are an arena for political and power games; they exhibit cultural disconnects. MNCs are also organic entities that evolve with the changing business environment, often with highly porous boundaries.

The view of the MNC we are interested in here is an entrepreneurial one; that is, we are concerned with how individuals (within the MNC) actively pursue new opportunities without regard to the resources they control (Stevenson and Jarillo, 1990). Moreover, we are particularly interested in entrepreneurship that comes from managers of foreign subsidiaries that are relatively limited in their resources and/or their degrees of freedom. By focusing on these somewhat unusual individuals, and the initiatives they pursue, we are able to open up important broader issues regarding the way that MNCs evolve over time, and their sources of competitive advantage.

This entrepreneurial perspective is one the first author mapped out almost 20 years ago in his doctoral thesis (Birkinshaw, 1995). This research was conducted in Canada in the aftermath of the Free Trade Agreement with the USA, and it documented issues and challenges that managers of foreign-owned subsidiary companies in Canada were preoccupied with. Subsequently, research on the phenomenon of subsidiary initiative was developed in a number of different empirical and theoretical directions (e.g. Birkinshaw, 2000; Bouquet and Birkinshaw, 2008; Rugman and Verbeke, 2001; Verbeke and Yuan, 2005).

This chapter serves two functions. First, it reiterates and reinforces the original ideas about the phenomenon of subsidiary initiative, drawing from and updating Birkinshaw (1995, 1997, 2000). Second, it puts these original ideas into perspective with a discussion of some of the subsequent research conducted in this area – both at the level of the subsidiary and at the level of the MNC as a whole.

THE CONCEPT OF SUBSDIARY INITIATIVE

Corporate entrepreneurship can be defined as the pursuit of opportunity without regard to the resources one controls, within the context of an existing organization (Stevenson and Jarillo, 1990). Corporate entrepreneurship can then be divided into two basic forms. 'Focused' corporate entrepreneurship, also called corporate venturing, works on the premise that entrepreneurship and management are fundamentally different processes that require different modes of organization to occur effectively, so it involves the establishment of a separate unit, often called a new venture division, whose mandate is to identify and nurture new business opportunities for the corporation (Burgelman, 1983;

Sathe, 1985; Sykes, 1986). 'Dispersed' corporate entrepreneurship, also called intrapreneurship, works on the premise that every individual in the company has the capacity for both managerial and entrepreneurial behavior more or less simultaneously. Rather than hiving off separate groups or divisions to be entrepreneurial, while the rest are left to pursue the ongoing managerial tasks (Galbraith, 1982), the dispersed approach sees the development of an entrepreneurial culture as the key antecedent to initiative (Covin and Slevin, 1991; Ghoshal and Bartlett, 1994; Stopford and Baden-Fuller, 1994), and it assumes a latent dual role for every employee, consisting of the management of ongoing activities and the identification and pursuit of new opportunities (Kirzner, 1973).

'Initiative', as used here, is the primary manifestation of dispersed corporate entrepreneurship, and it is defined as a discrete, proactive undertaking that advances a new way for the corporation to use or expand its resources. The initiative process, by which specific opportunities are pursued, is bounded by the identification of an opportunity at the front end and the commitment of resources to the undertaking at the back end. The long-term success, or not, of the resultant business activity is a secondary issue. The entrepreneurial challenge is to move from an idea to a commitment of resources; the managerial challenge is to make the resultant business activity profitable.

This distinction between focused and dispersed entrepreneurship is paralleled by the distinction that is often made between 'assigned' and 'assumed' roles in foreign subsidiary units in multinational firms. 'Assigned roles' are given to the subsidiary, in a top–down manner, by the parent company. Bartlett and Ghoshal (1986), for example, make the observation that national subsidiaries can take one of four generic roles, based on the strategic importance of the local environment and the competence of the subsidiary. These roles are enacted through the structural context of the multinational firm. Thus, as shown by Ghoshal and Bartlett (1988), autonomy, local resources, normative integration and inter-unit communication are associated with creation (of innovations) in subsidiaries, but negatively associated with adoption and diffusion. 'Assumed roles' are those that subsidiary managers take on, as a function of the opportunities they perceive within their sphere of influence (Birkinshaw, 1997; Burgelman, 1983; Hedlund, 1986). The idea that subsidiaries might assume roles suggests that the subsidiary's strategy is constrained (rather than defined) by the structural context, and the local subsidiary managers have considerable latitude within the imposed constraints to shape a strategy as they see fit.

Types of Subsidiary Initiative

As described by Birkinshaw (1995), a useful way of framing subsidiary initiative is to see it as a response to some sort of market opportunity. Traditionally, most observers saw the subsidiary as responding to opportunities in its local or national market. That is, the subsidiary's role was first to adapt the multinational firm's technology to local tastes, and then to act as a 'global scanner', sending signals about changing demands back to head office (Vernon, 1966, 1979). Subsequently, it was recognized that subsidiaries often have unique capabilities of their own, as well as critical links with local customers and suppliers. In such situations, the subsidiary's ability to pursue local opportunities itself, and subsequently to exploit them on a global scale, becomes an important capability (Bartlett and Ghoshal, 1986; Hedlund, 1986).

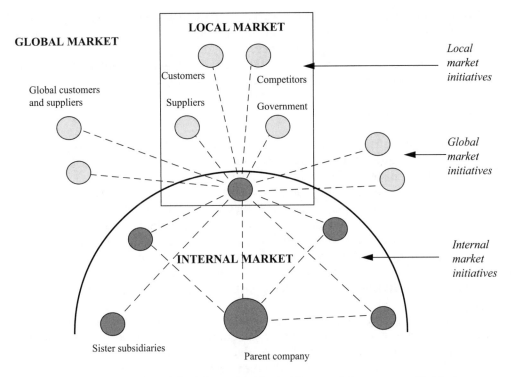

Figure 8.1   Conceptual model of the national subsidiary and three types of initiative

But to view market opportunity solely in terms of the subsidiary's local relationships is somewhat restricting. It is widely recognized that the multinational firm can usefully be modeled as an interorganizational network (Forsgren and Johanson, 1992; Ghoshal and Bartlett, 1990), in which the subsidiary has multiple linkages to other entities both inside and outside the formal boundaries of the multinational firm. Viewed in this way, the subsidiary sits at the interface of three 'markets': (1) the local market, consisting of competitors, suppliers, customers and regulatory bodies in the host country; (2) the internal market, comprising head office operations and all corporate-controlled affiliates worldwide; and (3) the global market, consisting of competitors, customers and suppliers that fall outside the local and internal markets. This conceptualization is depicted in Figure 8.1.

The novel insight from Figure 8.1 is that the internal market can be a source of opportunities for the subsidiary to respond to. The nature of these opportunities will be discussed shortly, but it is clear that they are rather different from the traditional idea of initiatives being directed towards new product or new market possibilities. It also becomes apparent, when one starts exploring internal market initiative in the field, that two important subtypes can be identified. These are called 'internal market initiatives' as in Figure 8.1, and 'internal–global hybrid initiatives' for reasons that will be explained. The other important insight from figure is that the 'external market' can be divided into a local and a global component.

Four categories of initiatives can therefore be identified. The important dimensions are the locus of opportunity, meaning the market (from Figure 8.1) in which the initiative opportunity emerged, and the locus of pursuit, meaning the market in which the process was realized. In the first three cases, the locus of opportunity and the locus of pursuit are coincident, and there is no ambiguity. For the internal–global hybrid initiative, however, the locus of opportunity is global but the locus of pursuit is internal.

Local Market Initiatives

A local market initiative is one that is identified and pursued in the subsidiary's national market, and subsequently developed on a global basis. For example, in 1985, Gerhard Schmid, Calgary district sales manager for Hewlett-Packard (Canada), identified an opportunity for a 'remote terminal unit' for monitoring oil wells in the Alberta oil fields. He outlined the opportunity, and how HP might address it, and he was given the go-ahead to pursue it by the Canadian country manager, Malcolm Gissing. He spoke with a number of the major oil companies in Calgary and Houston, and established that there was a clear need for a software system to integrate the various elements of the oil production process. Shell Oil, in particular, were very interested, and they essentially agreed to buy the entire supervisory control package once it was complete in 18–24 months' time, a deal worth about $40 million.

Without a business group to support the initiative, Gissing funded the development through a 1 percent 'uplift' on a portion of Canadian product sales, an established approach when there was no readily available business group sponsorship. In 1986 Schmid hired five experienced people, who then 'locked themselves in a back room for a year to come up with the first release'. By the middle of 1988, they started to release components of the product, now named RTAP (real-time application platform), to local beta customers.

But in 1989 Schmid's group discovered that an HP product division in California was working on a very similar product. While Schmid's 'skunkworks' group had been working on a shoestring budget up in Calgary, this Californian group had 60 people, five times the budget and – most importantly – the official 'blessing' of the corporation. Schmid and Gissing argued that their product was actually more advanced, and already had a guaranteed sale to Shell Oil. Their tenacity prevailed, and eventually HP Corporate agreed to support the Calgary operation. The rival product group was disbanded. By 1991/92 the Calgary operation was making an operating profit, and worldwide sales (with hardware) of around $15 million annually.

This case of Gerhard Schmid and the RTAP product is a typical local market initiative. It was identified through discussions with a local customer, and then pursued in the local marketplace, though obviously with certain links back to head office for funding and sanctioning. Alongside other examples reported in Birkinshaw (1995, 1997), local market initiatives have the following key features:

- They are facilitated most effectively through a moderate level of autonomy in the subsidiary coupled with a fairly strong relationship back to the parent company. In the early stages of the initiative the subsidiary needs sufficient autonomy to be able to apply resources to the opportunity without interference. At the more advanced stage of viability it is important for the subsidiary to have a much stronger relationship with the parent so that the higher levels of resource commitment and sponsorship can be achieved.

- They require a well-established set of capabilities, so that the subsidiary is able to respond effectively to the opportunity as it arises. However, unlike the internally focused types below, it may be less critical for the subsidiary to prove that these capabilities are in place at the outset. As Gerhard Schmid showed, it is possible to build up the missing capabilities as long as there is sufficient autonomy to be able to act quickly.

- The process is primarily externally focused. Most of the early efforts are directed towards building a viable product or service for the customer in the local market, either using local sources of funding or through partnership with local allies. In the latter stages, assuming the venture has been a success, the challenge is one of selling the proven concept back to managers in the parent firm, and building some legitimacy for it in the firm as a whole.

- In terms of outcomes, local market initiatives lead in the first instance to new products or services for local customers. However, they typically also develop into new business opportunities for the firm as a whole, as the local customer base becomes global.

Global Market Initiatives

These are driven by unmet product or market needs among non-local suppliers and customers. In theory, the subsidiary could interact with any customer or supplier in the world, but realistically such initiatives occur as extensions to existing relationships. Consider the case of Westinghouse Canada. During the 1980s this subsidiary had a world product mandate granted by its parent company for computer terminals for airline reservation systems. On the basis of its existing strengths in this area, Westinghouse Canada was approached by the Los Angeles International Airport to provide a product that became known as CUTE, common use terminal equipment. This product sought to alleviate the space constraints at the airport by making it possible for different airlines to access the same terminals, rather than having their own dedicated terminals. The point, from our perspective, is that Westinghouse Canada was no longer just the Canadian arm of Westinghouse; it was an international business in its own right, free to identify new opportunities wherever in the world they should occur. More broadly, global market initiatives have the following key features:

- They are facilitated through a high level of autonomy. Because the subsidiary is typically building on its own existing business areas, it needs to be able to act swiftly to develop them rather than wait for permission from head office. For example, one subsidiary manager observed, 'The basic dilemma [here] is lack of investment funding. If the subsidiary manager wants $100 000 to develop a product the customer is paying for, he [often] has to make a couple of visits to head office, which might take three months. By the time approval is granted, the opportunity has passed.'

- A proven level of capability in the relevant areas. This is obvious, but it bears underlining that the subsidiary will not be trusted to take responsibility for developing global lines of business if it does not have all the necessary capabilities in place. The combination of high levels of proven capability and high autonomy typically means that such subsidiaries typically do not have a very close relationship with their counterparts in head office.

- The process, as with local market initiatives, is externally oriented, with little or no contact with the parent company in the earlier stages, and actually very little even in the latter stages. For significant investments permission has to be granted, of course, but assuming the business is doing well that is typically not an issue.
- The immediate outcome of global market initiatives is that a specific business area, and the capabilities associated with it, are developed further. Thus each initiative seeks to build a new product or market around an existing business line using the distinctive capabilities of that subsidiary. The term 'center of excellence' (Frost et al., 2002) is often used in this regard, the implication being that the parent company and other subsidiaries also stand to benefit from those capabilities. In terms of the broader corporate objectives, this can be seen as another facet of worldwide learning.

Internal Market Initiatives

These arise through 'market' opportunities identified within the corporate system. A clear example of this is seen in Honeywell Corporation. Honeywell Canada was a traditional branch-plant manufacturer until the mid-1980s. The Toronto plant manufactured control valves, thermostats and related devices primarily for the Canadian market, in volumes approximately one-tenth as large as the main manufacturing operation in Minneapolis. In a couple of lines – notably the 'Zone Valve' and the 'Fan and Limits Device' – Honeywell Canada also undertook some exports.

The winds of change in Honeywell began to blow in the mid-1980s, when it became obvious that the Canadian plant could face closure if and when the high tariffs between the USA and Canada came down. As one Canadian manager noted, 'we knew there was no future in being a branch plant operation . . . we knew we had to dramatically improve ourselves to survive'. Proposals were therefore put forward to US management regarding the upgrading of the Toronto plant, and the rationalization of production whereby Toronto would manufacture Zone Valves and Fan and Limits Devices on a North American basis, while the Minnesota plant would manufacture all other lines.

The reaction to these proposals in the USA was mixed. Many manufacturing managers were averse to losing out on specific product lines, but the general manager was open-minded: his attitude was 'let's not be political about this, let's collaborate and do the right thing'. Negotiations followed, leading eventually to the decision to enact the Canadian proposal. Two lines were therefore closed down in Minneapolis and moved up to Toronto, and Toronto in turn shut down its branch-plant operations and focused on its two North American mandates.

The Honeywell Canada case shows how some market opportunities arise within the existing multinational system. In this case, it was the existing internal sourcing relationships between the USA and Canada that were inefficient, and that Canadian management picked up on as an opportunity. By reconfiguring the existing operations, they showed it would be possible for both Toronto and Minneapolis plants to operate more efficiently than they had before. Of course, they could have waited for head office managers to come to the same realization, but by taking the initiative Canadian managers were able to promote a change that was in the interests of both the Canadian operation and the corporation as a whole. Looking more broadly, internal market initiatives have the following typical features:

- The key facilitator is the credibility of the subsidiary in the eyes of the parent company. This is a function of the subsidiary's existing capabilities and strong personal relationships. As described by one subsidiary manager: 'It is awfully important that we have a close association [with the US management]. We are talking frequently about what are the issues in their business, what are their problems, what are the opportunities that we can offer to help them solve their problems. That is important to do.' The other facilitator is a global orientation (Perlmutter, 1969) among the senior management of the parent firm – that is, a mindset oriented towards what is best for the corporation as a whole, rather than narrow or parochial interests.
- The process is inherently inward-looking. The primary objective is to get formal corporate approval so that the necessary resources are made available. Such initiatives typically involve a high level of selling, first of all by middle-level managers to their superiors in the subsidiary, and subsequently by the top subsidiary managers to their superiors in head office. Here is a typical example: 'First, the [subsidiary CEO] had to get approval for the initiative from the operations committee, who report directly to the chairman. Then he went to the sector meetings, where you had the division VPs [vice presidents]. There were three of them. He then went to a couple of other corporate bodies, the marketing council, the technical council as well, which is a huge group of the laboratory managers. So having cascaded it down he tried to pick large bodies where he would get to the level below division VP.'
- Internal market initiatives are fundamentally geared towards reconfiguring and rationalizing the activity system in the multinational firm. Thus the Honeywell example mentioned above led to the rationalization of activities between Canada and the USA, and hence a more efficient corporate system. Equally, such initiatives can lead to certain plants being closed down or moved, or marketing operations being consolidated on a regional basis. Overall sales volumes are rarely impacted in the short term. Rather, these initiatives are about taking the internal resources of the firm and configuring them more efficiently, rather than about increasing the resource base of the firm.

Global–Internal Hybrid Initiatives

The fourth type of initiative combines elements of the global and the internal types. Like global initiatives, the locus of the market opportunity is outside the subsidiary's home market. But like internal initiatives, the locus of pursuit is internal, in that it involves convincing head office managers, not external customers.

For example, Monsanto Agricultural Company is a leading producer of herbicides. In June 1991, senior management in Canada identified an interesting opportunity in the corporation's long-range strategic plan, namely the intended introduction around 1996 of a dry version of their very successful glyphosate technology. Building on the stated openness of top management in the USA to further investment in Canada, these individuals began looking into the possibility of bringing forward this planned dry glyphosate investment and locating it in Canada. A strong case was put forward, so a team was assembled to assess the viability of various sites around the world. Three sites made the final selection list, one in Manitoba, the other two in the USA. The Canadian team put together a very creative proposal for a plant organized around self-directed work teams with high levels of outsourcing, and on that basis they were able to convince the decision-making team that they had the best proposal. The plant was built in 1993 and began operations in 1994.

In terms of the process, the Monsanto case transpired rather like the Honeywell case described earlier. Subsidiary managers gradually sought out support for their proposal in head office, and then spent a considerable amount of time showing that they had the capabilities and the cost structure to make the Canadian investment location attractive. However, there is one fundamental difference between the two. The Honeywell case was about reconfiguring existing operations – about dividing the pie in a different way; the Monsanto case was about building a new operation – about increasing the size of the pie. Obviously the implications of the two cases for the MNC as a whole are thus rather different.

Another example of a global–internal market hybrid is Electrolux's decision to develop a washing machine that could be used in both Europe and North America. While the initial decision to start this project was made in Sweden (head office), much of the initial development was undertaken in Italy. US involvement was actively sought in the early days of the project (to ensure buy-in in the US market), but it never transpired. Instead, the North American responsibility ended up being assumed by the Canadian subsidiary, which was proactive in getting involved in both development and manufacturing (Ridderstrale, 1996).

This example shows how global–internal hybrid initiatives play into the broader agendas of corporate management. This project had a top-driven global logic that was perceived to be addressing customer needs, but the way it eventually transpired was a function of the specific agendas of a number of different subsidiary units. Thus the involvement of the Canadian unit could be seen as a hybrid initiative on their part, but it could also be seen in terms of the overall parameters of the project. Interestingly, subsidiary initiative (in the case of the Canadian unit, for example) can be seen as both a good and a bad thing in such projects. It is good because the active involvement of subsidiaries is necessary for these sorts of project to succeed, but it is bad because the project can be side-tracked towards the specific needs of the subsidiary, and away from the global project requirements. More broadly, global–internal hybrids appear to have the following key features:

- They are facilitated by a high level of credibility of the subsidiary (with head-office decision-makers), along with high levels of proven resources, strong parent–subsidiary communication and relatively low autonomy. As one subsidiary president observed, 'You end up with a couple of sites that come pretty close and one that will have a minor advantage economically, but sitting in an operating committee in the States, what really swings you is the credibility of the organization that's asking for the order.' The fact that the opportunity in the hybrid initiative is typically global has little bearing on the facilitating conditions, because the entire process is internal to the multinational firm. Research suggests that hybrid initiatives require the highest level of 'selling' of all four types, which in turn necessitates a high level of ongoing parent–subsidiary communication.

- The process for these initiatives is similar to that seen in internal market initiatives, with one difference, namely, that hybrid initiatives have parent management support in principle from the start, whereas internal market initiatives have to build their own support. This creates a rather subtle difference in process: internal market initiatives are iterative, involving several rounds of credibility-building with parent management and refining of proposals; hybrid initiatives are 'take-it-or-leave-it' proposals in which parent management often has to choose between several directly competing courses of action.
- In terms of outcomes, hybrid initiatives offer a similar outcome to internal market initiatives, in that they are intended to influence corporate decision-makers about where internationally focused activities will be located. However, they are different in one important respect, because they are concerned with large-scale projects such as Electrolux's new global washing machine. Thus hybrid initiatives can be seen as the subsidiary unit claiming 'a piece of the action' within a broader-scope corporate initiative, whereas pure internal market initiatives are typically smaller-scale projects initiated by the subsidiary unit.

By identifying these four different types of subsidiary initiative, Birkinshaw (1997, 2000) offered a more dynamic perspective on the role of the subsidiary manager in the MNC. He also helped to develop a useful enhancement of our understanding of the MNC as a whole, because according to this view the subsidiary is itself a meaningful unit of analysis in shaping the long-term evolution of the MNC. A number of empirical and theoretical advancements have subsequently been put forward that build on this notion, and in the second part of this chapter we briefly review them.

SUBSIDIARY INITIATIVE: RECENT ADVANCES

Over the last decade, MNC research has developed in a wide variety of directions, one of the most fruitful of which has been the knowledge perspective, i.e. a concern with understanding how the MNC's knowledge and capabilities can be a source of competitive advantage. Rugman and Verbeke (2001, 2003) identified an important link between this knowledge perspective and the earlier work on subsidiary initiative. Specifically, they noted that while local initiatives can increase autonomy, non-location subsidiary-specific competencies (i.e. those that are potentially exploitable on a global basis) are the most valuable outcomes of subsidiary initiative. By emphasizing the significance of subsidiary-specific advantage in the context of more traditional IB perspectives these authors further legitimated the study of subsidiary initiative. Three aspects of the ensuing research are worth highlighting here.

Gaining Attention

A key challenge for the MNC lies in coming to terms with promising subsidiary initiatives that are not wholly aligned with corporate objectives. Verbeke and Yuan (2005) have highlighted the role of internal governance mechanisms for mitigating the cognitive limitations of corporate executives. Consistent with this, Bouquet and Birkinshaw (2008) show that subsidiary initiatives, in part, influence the extent to which a subsidiary gains headquarters attention; this is more so at greater geographical distance and when they pertain to downstream competence. Attracting attention can, in turn, result in increased autonomy and influence for the subsidiary – although this may attract further scrutiny and be kept in check by headquarters monitoring (Ambos et al., 2010). Thus recent research has highlighted the complex relationship between subsidiary and headquarters and that therefore the impact of subsidiary initiative is contingent on how adeptly key intraorganizational relationships are handled.

Building Relationships

In addition to contending with intra-MNC challenges, the external environment is a major locus of subsidiary initiative-related activity. Indeed, Birkinshaw et al. (2005) suggest that the external competitive environment has a stronger bearing on subsidiary entrepreneurship in comparison to the internal. Reflecting the importance of the external milieu of the subsidiary, Dimitratos et al. (2009) argue that more developed sub-national regions witness more productive subsidiary activity that underlines the utility of a munificent host environment (Asmussen et al., 2009). That said, Cantwell and Mudambi (2005) point out that leveraging location is largely about subsidiaries building and leveraging relationships. External embeddedness can generate new technological knowledge for a subsidiary (Andersson et al., 2007) by, for instance, engaging in network-building initiatives (Prashantham, 2011). It can thus be seen that recent thinking on subsidiary initiative emphasizes relational assets not only within but, importantly, outside of the MNC as an integral input as well as output.

Creating Knowledge

Knowledge creation, and thereby competence creation, resulting from initiatives is arguably the most significant outcome of subsidiary initiative. By creating knowledge, a subsidiary can trigger strategic renewal within itself. Indeed, Verbeke et al. (2007) point out that much of the literature on subsidiary initiative speaks most directly to strategic renewal as an outcome – rather than corporate venturing, i.e. the setting up of a new business. Related, other research shows that managerial initiative in subsidiaries is more potent when applied to competence-creating rather than competence-exploiting activity (Cantwell and Mudambi, 2005). This is particularly so if it results in subsidiaries controlling knowledge that is relevant to the wider MNC (Mudambi and Navarra, 2004). Thus recent research on subsidiary initiative remains attentive, as did the early work in the 1990s, to the vital importance of knowledge as an integral focus.

The brief and selective summary of recent thinking above indicates that subsidiary initiative is alive and well, not only as an empirical phenomenon but also as a focus of inquiry. If anything, its relevance is greater than ever, given that, as Rugman et al. (2011) note, subsidiary initiative and competence is growing in specialization at the level of the value chain activity, thus, potentially, placing the subset of subsidiaries that do take initiative seriously in an even better position to become (or continue to be) ever greater contributors to the well-being of the MNE.

FROM THE SUBSIDIARY TO THE MNC AS A WHOLE

Finally, we consider three non-mutually exclusive themes that link the phenomenon of subsidiary initiative to the broader challenges of managing the MNC as a whole.

Boundary-spanning

Virtually by definition, if subsidiary initiative is to translate into benefits for the wider MNC, then boundaries must be spanned. Boundary-spanning in MNCs involves individuals (Kostova and Roth, 2003), yet there has been limited work beyond Birkinshaw (1995) that explicitly opens up the black box of subsidiary initiative to focus on the people involved and their actions. One exception is Balogun et al. (2011). Building on the 'strategy as practice' movement, which focuses on the day-to-day actions of managers in context, Balogun et al. (2011) studied the micropolitics of subsidiary–headquarters interaction, and showed that initiatives resulting in modified subsidiary roles often entail multiple discourses – selling, resistance and reconciliation. Their work usefully points to the 'messiness' of human interactions that affect the efficacy of subsidiary initiative in the context of the wider MNC. Of course boundary-spanning might also entail forging relationships outside of the immediate confines of the MNC to encompass ties within the broader interfirm network or 'ecosystem' (Doz et al., 2001). Future research could fruitfully uncover more fine-grained aspects of how relationships are actually built between an MNC subsidiary and key local actors.

Organizational Dynamics

The effects of subsidiary initiative on the wider MNC typically take time to accrue. Researchers have recognized that subsidiary characteristics and charters evolve (Rugman and Verbeke, 2001). Yet much of the extant research adopts a cross-sectional approach that precludes the prospect of examining the temporality of subsidiary initiative processes and outcomes. Greater attention to longitudinal research could extend understanding of, for instance, the nature and effects of subsidiary autonomy. Autonomy is portrayed in the literature as being earned as well as assumed (Birkinshaw, 2000). Illustrations used earlier in this chapter suggest that initially assumed autonomy could beget subsequently earned autonomy if subsidiary initiative generates new competences, therefore growth and ultimately charter enhancement. But questions still arise as to how such processes and the interplay between various forms of autonomy unfold in time (Young and Tavares, 2004), especially given that an initiative's outcomes may be contingent upon its objectives (Verbeke et al., 2007). More systematic analyses of organizational dynamics could also shed further light on the bottom–up effect of subsidiary initiative in enhancing the competence base of the MNE as a whole (Doz et al., 2001).

Management Innovation

The utility of subsidiary initiative – which often, but not exclusively, entails technological innovation – to the wider MNC might be predicated on the effective innovation of its management practices, processes and structures. While radical management innovation is new to the state of the art (Birkinshaw et al., 2008) there is considerable virtue even in more incremental management innovation that is new to the firm (Foss et al., 2012; Mol and Birkinshaw, 2009). Hitherto overlooked as an explicit focus of inquiry in research on subsidiary initiative, management innovation could well be a prerequisite enabler of proactive efforts around technological innovation. For instance, Prashantham and Birkinshaw (2008) refer to a forum that brought together subsidiaries and innovative local start-ups, essentially a management innovation instigated by Sun Microsystems' Scottish subsidiary in order to facilitate a technology initiative of its own that was intended to benefit the MNC as a whole. In some cases, management innovation may itself be the primary focus of subsidiary initiative. Again, the realm of partnering with local start-ups offers illustration. Microsoft subsidiaries across the world, including in France, India and Israel, have at various points in time introduced new practices to increase the odds of engaging with high-potential start-ups that arguably have been carried forward into a worldwide partnering initiative called BizSpark One carried out by Microsoft's Silicon Valley campus (Prashantham, 2011). We envisage the role of management in subsidiary initiative to be a potentially fruitful area of inquiry in the years to come.

CONCLUDING REMARKS

This chapter has provided an overview and discussion of the concept of subsidiary initiative. In this concluding section, we offer a brief reflection on how this concept emerged, and how it came to play an important role in our theorizing about the MNC.

Birkinshaw's (1995) study of subsidiary initiative was essentially phenomenon-based, that is, it was a description and explanation of what he saw happening in the Canadian business environment in the years following the opening up of the trade border with the USA. In documenting how some subsidiaries were taking charge of their destiny, and assuming new roles within their corporate system, this research built on two pillars. One was the emerging view of the MNC as an 'interorganizational network' or 'heterarchy' (Ghoshal and Bartlett, 1990; Hedlund, 1986), in which subsidiary units played increasingly varied and important roles. The other was the literature on corporate entrepreneurship (Burgelman, 1983; Stevenson and Jarillo, 1990), which had already recognized the potential value of mid-level managers proactively developing and running with their ideas, in a way that helped the corporation to deliver on its broader goals.

Viewed in this way, Birkinshaw's (1995) contribution was fairly straightforward: he simply imported Burgelman's (1983) concept of autonomous strategic behavior into the MNC context. However, as it turned out, this contribution ended up having a significant impact on the IB field because it helped researchers to think in terms of the subsidiary as a meaningful unit of analysis in its own right. Progress has now been made on understanding how subsidiaries evolve in part through their own efforts, on how they can influence the broader strategic goals of their parent companies, and on how they can have an influence on the local context in which they are located. We anticipate that each of these strands of research will continue to be active in the coming years, and we welcome further contributions.

REFERENCES

Ambos, T., U. Andersson and J. Birkinshaw (2010), 'What are the consequences of initiative-taking in multinational subsidiaries?', *Journal of International Business Studies*, **41**: 1–20.

Andersson, U., M. Forsgren and U. Holm (2007), 'Balancing subsidiary influence in the federative MNC: a business network view', *Journal of International Business Studies*, **38**: 802–18.

Asmussen, C.G., T. Pedersen and C. Dhanaraj (2009), 'Host-country environment and subsidiary competence: extending the diamond network model', *Journal of International Business Studies*, **40**: 42–57.

Balogun, J., P. Jarzabkowski and E. Vaara (2011), 'Selling, resistance and reconciliation: a critical discursive approach to subsidiary role evolution in MNEs', *Journal of International Business Studies*, **42**: 765–86.

Bartlett, Christopher A. and Sumantra Ghoshal (1986), 'Tap your subsidiaries for global reach', *Harvard Business Review*, **64**(6): 87–94.

Birkinshaw, Julian M. (1995), 'Entrepreneurship in multinational corporations: the initiative process in foreign subsidiaries', unpublished doctoral disseration. Westen Business School, The University of Western Ontario.

Birkinshaw, J.M. (1997), 'Entrepreneurship in multinational corporations: the characteristics of subsidiary initiatives', *Strategic Management Journal*, **18**(2): 207–30.

Birkinshaw, J.M. (2000), *Entrepreneurship in the Global Firm*, London: Sage.

Birkinshaw, J., G. Hamel and M.J. Mol (2008), 'Management innovation', *Academy of Management Review*, **33**: 825–45.

Birkinshaw, J., N. Hood and S. Young (2005), 'Subsidiary entrepreneurship, internal and external competitive forces, and subsidiary performance', *International Business Review*, **14**: 247–8.

Bouquet, C. and J. Birkinshaw (2008), 'Weight versus voice: how foreign subsidiaries gain the attention of headquarters', *Academy of Management Journal*, **51**: 577–601.

Burgelman, Robert A. (1983), 'A process model of internal corporate venturing in the diversified major firm', *Administrative Science Quarterly*, **28**: 223–44.

Cantwell, J.A. and R. Mudambi (2005), 'MNE competence-creating subsidiary mandates', *Strategic Management Journal*, **26**: 1109–28.

Covin, J.G. and D.P. Slevin (1991), 'A conceptual model of entrepreneurship as firm behavior', *Entrepreneurship Theory and Practice*, Fall: 7–25.

Dimitratos, P., I. Liouka and S. Young (2009), 'Location, entrepreneurial output, networking and economic development of multinational corporation subsidiaries: empirical evidence from the UK', *Journal of World Business*, **44**: 180–91.

Doz, Y.L., J. Santos and P. Williamson (2001), *From Global to Metanational: How Companies Win in the Knowledge Economy*, Boston, MA: Harvard Business School Press.

Foss, N.J., T. Pedersen, J. Pyndt and M. Schultz (2012), *Innovating Organization and Management: New Sources of Competitive Advantage*, Cambridge: Cambridge University Press.

Forsgren, Mats and Jan Johanson (1992), *Managing Networks in International Business*, Philadelphia, PA: Gordon & Breach.

Frost, T.S., J.M. Birkinshaw and P.C. Ensign (2002), 'Centers of excellence in multinational corporations', *Strategic Management Journal*, **23**(11): 997–1018.

Galbraith, Jay (1982), 'Designing the innovating organization', *Organizational Dynamics*, Winter: 5–25.

Ghoshal, Sumantra and Christopher A. Bartlett (1988), 'Creation, adoption and diffusion of innovations by subsidiaries of multinational corporations', *Journal of International Business Studies*, **19**(3): 365–88.

Ghoshal, Sumantra and Christopher A. Bartlett (1990), 'The multinational corporation as an interorganizational network', *Academy of Management Review*, **15**(4): 603–25.

Ghoshal, Sumantra and Christopher A. Bartlett (1994), 'Linking organizational context and managerial action: the dimensions of quality of management', *Strategic Management Journal*, **15**: 91–112.

Hedlund, Gunnar (1986), 'The hypermodern MNC: a heterarchy?', *Human Resource Management*, **25**: 9–36.

Kirzner, Israel M. (1973), *Competition and Entrepreneurship*, Chicago, IL: The University of Chicago Press.

Kostova, T. and K. Roth (2003), 'Social capital in multinational corporations and a micro–macro model of its formation', *Academy of Management Review*, **28**: 297–317.

Mol, M.J. and J. Birkinshaw (2009), 'The sources of management innovation: when firms introduce new management practices', *Journal of Business Research*, **62**: 1269–80.

Mudambi, R. and P. Navarra (2004), 'Is knowledge power? Knowledge flows, subsidiary power and rent-seeking within MNCs', *Journal of International Business Studies*, **35**: 385–406.

Perlmutter, H. (1969), 'The tortuous evolution of the multinational corporation', *Columbia Journal of World Business*, **4**: 9–18.

Prashantham, S. (2011), 'Social capital and Indian micromultinationals', *British Journal of Management*, **22**(1): 4–20.

Prashantham, S. and J. Birkinshaw (2008), 'Dancing with gorillas: how small companies can partner effectively with MNCs', *California Management Review*, **51**(1): 6–23.

Ridderstrale, J. (1996), 'Global innovation – Managing international innovation projects at ABB and Electrolux', Institute of International Business, Stockholm School of Economics, Stockholm.

Rugman, A.M. and A. Verbeke (2001), 'Subsidiary-specific advantages in multinational enterprises', *Strategic Management Journal*, **22**: 237–50.

Rugman, A.M. and A. Verbeke (2003), 'Extending the theory of the multinational enterprise: internalization and strategic management perspectives', *Journal of International Business Studies*, **34**: 125–37.

Rugman, A., A. Verbeke and W. Yuan (2011), 'Re-conceptualizing Bartlett and Ghoshal's classification of national subsidiary roles in the multinational enterprise', *Journal of Management Studies*, **48**: 253–77.

Sathe, Vijay (1985), 'Managing an entrepreneurial dilemma: nurturing entrepreneurship and control in large corporations', in J.A. Hornaday, E.B. Shils, J.A. Timmons and K.H. Vesper (eds), *Frontiers of Entrepreneurship Research*, Wellesley, MA: Babson College, pp. 636–57.

Stevenson, Howard H. and Jose-Carlos Jarillo (1990), 'A paradigm of entrepreneurship: entrepreneurial management', *Strategic Management Journal*, **11**: 17–27.

Stopford, John M. and Charles W.F. Baden-Fuller (1994), 'Creating corporate entrepreneurship', *Strategic Management Journal*, **15**: 521–36.

Sykes, Hollister B. (1986), 'The anatomy of a corporate venturing program: factors influencing success', *Journal of Business Venturing*, **1**: 275–93.

Verbeke, A., J.J. Chrisman and W. Yuan (2007), 'A note on subsidiary renewal and subsidiary venturing in multinational enterprises', *Entrepreneurship Theory and Practice*, **31**: 585–600.

Verbeke, A. and W. Yuan (2005), 'Subsidiary autonomous activities in multinational enterprises: a transaction cost perspective', *Management International Review*, **45**: 31–52.

Vernon, Raymond (1966), 'International investment and international trade in the product cycle', *Quarterly Journal of Economics*, May: 191–207.

Vernon, Raymond (1979), 'The product cycle hypothesis in a new international environment', *Oxford Bulletin of Economics and Statistics*, **41**: 255–67.

Young, S. and A.T. Tavares (2004), 'Centralization and autonomy: back to the future', *International Business Review*, **13**: 215–37.

9 Collaboration across borders: benefits to firms in an emerging economy
Rekha Krishnan, Niels G. Noorderhaven and Alex Eapen

1. INTRODUCTION

Business firms increasingly engage in collaborative relationships with other firms in order to further their interests (Hergert and Morris, 1988; Hagedoorn, 1995). This phenomenon has attracted considerable academic interest (Contractor and Lorange, 1988; Harrigan, 1988; Kogut, 1988; Osborn and Hagedoorn, 1997). However, the academic attention has been lopsided in that it has been focused predominantly on Western firms. In general, previous research has tended to focus on the multinational corporation's (MNC's) perspective and to neglect that of the local partner (Yan and Zeng, 1999). In the case of collaborations between Western firms and their partners in developing or emerging countries this one-sidedness is particularly inappropriate, since in these collaborations differences between the partners' perspectives often are more pronounced than in collaborations between Western firms (Yan and Luo, 2001, p. 135). But we do not know much about the impact of international collaboration on the performance of partners from emerging economies.

However, business collaboration may also be of the utmost importance to these firms. More and more formerly protected markets are gradually opening up to foreign firms, with the effect that indigenous firms have to enhance their strengths to stand up to global competition or perish. This chapter aims to begin to redress the existing asymmetry in the alliance literature by focusing explicitly on the benefits of international collaboration to firms from an emerging economy. In particular, we aim to complement a recent study by Shrader (2001), in which the benefits of international collaboration to young American high-technology firms are analyzed. We look at approximately the same phenomenon, and study largely the same variables. But in this case, we look from the perspective of partners from an emerging economy. Moreover, we also focus on the disruptive impact of differences in national culture on performance of the local firms as it collaborates with the MNC. Overall, we examine the conditions under which international collaborations are expected to be more or less beneficial to the local firms.

The country we focus on is India. Before the start of liberalization in the mid-1980s, the Indian government pursued an import substitution industrialization policy. Under this policy most Indian corporations were effectively shielded from foreign competition. Even competition among Indian firms was restricted, as a result of the industrial licensing system that functioned as an entry barrier. Incumbent firms in many industries preempted competition by licensing capacity without actually implementing it (Siddharthan and Pandit, 1998). As a result Indian firms were often operating in an environment where strategic rivalry was attenuated or frozen (Kaplinsky, 1997).

In this situation there were very few incentives for innovation or satisfying customer needs. After the 1985 reforms, licensing was abolished in a large number of industries. However, overall the liberalization measures for the Indian economy were implemented half-heartedly, and only in July 1991, due to a balance of payments crisis, liberalization was implemented seriously. Even then, liberalization and opening of the Indian economy remained largely confined to the manufacturing and trade sectors, leaving out banking, insurance and the retail sector (Bhalla, 1998). Privatization has been limited, little has been done to resolve the problem of the ailing public sector enterprises, and the restrictive labour legislation remains intact (Kaplinsky, 1997).

Nevertheless, the size of the Indian market and the availability of highly educated workers has attracted a growing stream of foreign direct investment. Siddharthan and Pandit (1998) note that affiliates of MNCs invested more and grew faster than indigenous firms in the post-liberalization period. Under a more liberal regime, MNC affiliates had an advantage in terms of technology, brand names and other intangible assets. Hence Indian firms in many industries face an increasingly competitive environment, and have to upgrade their skills and performance in order to survive.

Technical collaboration with a foreign firm can be a way to improve performance and to stand up against rising competition. Technical collaboration is attractive, as in-house development of enhanced technological capabilities may simply be too slow. Moreover, given the stagnation in Indian industrial development in the past decennia, many of the technologies sought by Indian firms are likely to be already in existence in other countries, such as the USA, Japan and Western European countries. By striking a deal with a firm from these countries, an Indian firm can avoid the costly and cumbersome process of in-house development and upgrading of technology, and jump to a higher level of competitiveness.

However, we should look not only at the benefits of collaboration. The Indian firms have to pay a price for the knowledge they acquire, and it is not *a priori* clear that collaboration will have a positive impact on their performance, or is always superior to the alternative of in-house development. In this chapter we focus on the factors that make foreign collaboration more or less beneficial for Indian firms.

Whereas the developments in India are interesting in their own right, the Indian firms studied also stand as examples of the local partners often neglected in international business research. Drawing on knowledge-based theory and transaction cost economics, we formulate hypotheses pertaining to the conditions under which technical collaboration with foreign firms may be expected to be more or less beneficial to these local partners. These hypotheses are subsequently tested on a data set of 1367 Indian firms in 16 industries, 399 of which have entered into one or more collaborations with foreign firms. In Section 2 the theoretical background of the study is described and the hypotheses discussed. Section 3 describes the data set and variables and the analytical methods employed. In Section 4 we present our empirical results. Discussion and conclusions follow in Section 5.

2.   THEORETICAL BACKGROUND

The proliferation of the use of alliances, and the attention paid to collaborative business strategies in the popular press as well as in academic journals, almost obscure the fact that in the 'age of alliance capitalism' (Dunning, 1995) there is no such thing as a free lunch. There clearly are benefits to be derived from business collaboration. But there are also costs, and both benefits and costs have to be taken into consideration in an assessment of international collaborations. We draw on two theoretical frameworks for explaining the relationship between collaboration and performance, the knowledge-based theory of the firm and transaction cost economics.

Knowledge-based theory focuses on the heterogeneous knowledge bases of individual firms as an explanation for differences in performance (Spender and Grant, 1996; Zack, 1999). Whereas many differences between firms can be identified, only those characteristics and resources that are difficult to imitate, trade, transfer, buy, sell or substitute can yield sustainable competitive advantages (Wernerfelt, 1984; Barney, 1986, 1991; Peteraf, 1993). These characteristics are associated with implicit or tacit knowledge, residing in firm-specific routines, that cannot easily be articulated and transferred. However, from a dynamic perspective knowledge that is tacit at one point in time may at a later point in time have become more explicit and codified. New technologies gradually spread and become better understood and documented, and hence can be easily transferred from one firm to another.

Looking at the knowledge base of a firm, two factors are relevant: the stock of knowledge of the firm at a given moment, and the processes of knowledge development or acquisition that the firm engages in. Hence knowledge-based theory points our attention to differences in the existing knowledge bases of firms and to differences in the ways in which firms try to increase these knowledge stocks. The two factors are related: the existing knowledge stock partly determines a firm's capability to learn, the possible amount and speed of new knowledge accumulation (Dierickx and Cool, 1989). We shall below focus on two general types of knowledge: marketing knowledge and technological knowledge, and their importance for the benefits a local Indian firm can reap from collaboration with a foreign firm.

Transaction cost economics looks at the relative costs and benefits of alternative arrangements for governing transactions between two (or more) partners (Williamson, 1985). In general, transactions over a market interface are compared with some form of internalization. In our study, the alternatives considered are the transfer of technological knowledge within an international collaboration and in-house development. Many factors may influence the relative attractiveness of the two alternatives, such as the institutional framework within which the transactions take place, the characteristics of the good or service transacted, and the characteristics of the transaction partners. As all the firms we study are located in the same country, the institutional environment can be assumed constant.[1] The characteristics of the good transacted – technological knowledge – are less likely to be constant over the cases we study. However, given the present state of development of the Indian economy, and since we are looking at the transfer of relatively codified knowledge over market interfaces, this factor is not likely to be a main one in the explanation of the net benefits of collaboration. Hence we shall focus below on the third source of differences influencing the relative costs and benefits of transactional arrangements, the characteristics of the transaction partners. More specifically, we shall look at the cultural distance between the Indian and the foreign partners as a reflection of cognitive, social and cultural differences that make technical collaboration more difficult and hence relatively less attractive.

Given that there are costs and benefits of collaborations, there is no *a priori* reason to expect a direct effect of collaborations on business performance (Shrader, 2001). Only under the right set of circumstances can superior performance due to collaborations be expected (Buckley and Casson, 1996). In the technical collaborations and industrial licensing agreements we look at, a price has to be paid for the advantages sought. It may be assumed that the foreign partner asks the highest fee that the market can bear. In the kind of collaborations we are studying we can expect a reasonably efficient market, since the technologies traded are proven and reasonably codified; otherwise transfer within a loose, arm's-length form of collaboration would not be possible. Hence there is no *a priori* reason to expect substantial net benefits to the Indian partner from the average collaboration. If that were the case, the technology offered by the foreign collaborators would be systematically underpriced. On the other hand, we do expect some Indian partners to profit more from their collaborations than others, and these differential benefits we aim to explain.

Marketing Skills

The many knowledge resources a firm needs to be competitive can be divided roughly into upstream and downstream skills. Upstream skills pertain to the activities in the value chain that are connected with development, design, sourcing and production processes (Porter, 1985). These upstream skills will be discussed in the next section. Here we concentrate on the downstream skills, which have to do with marketing, sales and distribution. These skills improve the competitive position of the firm because it is better able than competitors to differentiate its products, target market segments, and deliver its products to the customers.

In this study, advertising intensity (the ratio of advertising expenses to sales) is used as an indicator of marketing skills. Through advertising, brand names are established and customer loyalty is increased. Hence a positive effect of advertising intensity on firm performance could be expected. However, advertising has its costs, and it does not always automatically pay off. If we look at the Indian situation, most firms have operated for decades in heavily protected markets. Imports were kept at bay by quota systems and high tariff walls, and domestic rivalry was attenuated by the industrial licensing system described in the introduction. As a result, Indian producers could display an 'almost complete disregard for any form of consumer preference' (Mohan and Aggarwal, 1990, p. 690), and supply the market with poor-quality standardized products (Kaplinsky, 1997). Given the recent history, the value of past marketing efforts may be doubtful. Consequently, we do not expect a positive main effect of advertising intensity on firm performance.

On the other hand, there are reasons to assume that downstream skills accumulated over time may have a positive effect once an Indian producer has the capability to provide superior products. A firm lacking these skills may have trouble convincing its customers that it has something of value to offer. A firm that has over time invested in marketing efforts knows better how to reach its customers, even if past marketing efforts have resulted in little brand loyalty. Technical collaborations bring to the Indian firms the know-how to produce differentiated and superior products. Hence a technical collaboration with a foreign firm enables an advertising-intensive Indian firm to leverage its accumulated marketing skills and promote the superior product produced using the technology transferred. Shrader (2001), in his study of US firms entering foreign markets, also found a positive effect of the interaction between advertising intensity (of the American partner) and collaboration. Analogously, we expect a positive interaction effect of advertising intensity and foreign collaboration on firm performance:

Hypothesis 1 Foreign collaboration, coupled with advertising intensity, will be positively related to firm performance.

Technical Skills

Investments in downstream skills will enable a firm to develop and produce better products, or to produce more efficiently by the use of more advanced production technologies. Consequently, well-placed investments in R&D may be assumed to have a positive effect on firm performance, at least in the long run. However, looking at the Indian situation, there are serious doubts regarding the effectiveness of R&D investments in the past. The particularities of the Indian situation had a distorting effect on the incentives to do R&D. Given the restrictions to competition described above, there was little incentive for Indian producers to invest in new or improved products. On the other hand, one of the perennial problems under the old system was the difficulty of getting import licenses for necessary inputs in the production process. Reflecting the distorted management priorities that were the result of these pressures, much Indian R&D focused on technology to minimize materials imports, rather than improve products or production processes (Sinha, 1994). This would make us expect no positive main effect of R&D intensity on firm performance.

However, we have to take the present situation in Indian industry into account. The liberalization of the Indian economy from the mid-1980s onwards has substantially increased the uncertainty Indian firms have to cope with. In response, Indian firms have been very hesitant in their commitment to R&D (Jacobsson and Ghayur, 1994). Given this general picture, and on the basis of the fact that in the new situation incentives for the direction of industrial R&D reflect forces of market competition much better than in the past, those firms that do engage in R&D may be expected to fare better than those that do not. This expectation is also consonant with Shrader's (2001) results, which showed a moderate to strong positive main effect of R&D intensity on firm performance (for American firms). This is reflected in Hypothesis 2:

Hypothesis 2 R&D intensity will be positively related to firm performance.

When it comes to the interaction between R&D intensity and collaboration, our reasoning can go two ways. Based on transaction cost reasoning, Shrader (2001) hypothesized a negative effect on firm performance of the interaction of R&D intensity and the use of collaborations. The reason for this expectation was that the complex and often ill-codified knowledge developed in R&D is difficult (and hence costly) to transfer over a market interface. Internalization within the firm was therefore expected to lead to better performance, an expectation that was borne out by the empirical findings. For our study, analogous reasoning could be employed. Indeed, the cost of transferring technological knowledge over a market interface in the form of a technical collaboration could be so high that in-house development, avoiding these transaction costs, becomes more advantageous. Moreover, for R&D-intensive firms that do engage in technical collaboration with foreign corporations, it may be expected that the technology transferred is closer to the cutting edge, hence less well known and codified and more difficult to apply. The contractual (non-equity) collaborations we focus on may be expected to be relatively inefficient vehicles for the transfer of these technologies. The corresponding hypothesis is that there is a negative effect on firm performance of R&D intensity and the use of technical collaborations.

However, from a more dynamic perspective there are also plausible arguments pointing at a positive interaction effect of R&D intensity and collaboration. Experiences with technology transfer to developing countries have taught that the transfer of hard, embodied or codified technology alone is often not sufficient. This technology has to be accompanied by 'soft' or 'tacit' technology, i.e. the know-how necessary to use the embodied technology (Prahalad and Lieberthal, 1998). Whereas hard technology can easily be transferred over a market interface (e.g. through licensing), this is not the case with soft or tacit technology. Performing at least some in-house R&D may raise the absorptive capacities of local firms, enabling them to assimilate transferred technology more effectively (De Mello, 1997; Kumar and Nti, 1998; Niosi et al., 1995). A large technology gap has a negative impact on the absorptive capacity of the recipient firm (Cohen and Levinthal, 1990; Szulanski, 1996; Lyles and Salk, 1996), while smaller technology gaps are associated with more technology transfer (Liu et al., 2000).

We see no *a priori* reason to follow either of the two arguments discussed above. Since they lead to opposite conclusions, we formulate two alternative hypotheses concerning the effect of the interaction of R&D intensity and collaboration on firm performance:

Hypothesis 3a   Foreign collaboration, coupled with R&D intensity, will be positively related to firm performance.

Hypothesis 3b   Foreign collaboration, coupled with R&D intensity, will be negatively related to firm performance.

Cultural Distance

According to transaction cost economics, the relationship between collaboration and performance is moderated by factors that raise the transaction costs of the use of one type of institutional arrangements relative to alternative arrangements. Shrader (2001) looked at the R&D intensity of the supplier of technology, and found that higher R&D intensity made collaboration relatively unattractive, compared with internalization. Since we focus on the Indian partner as a technology-taker, rather than supplier, our reasoning is different. This is reflected in the preceding section, leading to Hypotheses 3a and 3b. Shrader's (2001) reasoning in principle also applies to our study, and differences in the complexity and codification of the technical knowledge transferred can be expected to influence the efficiency of interfirm collaboration. However, we lack data on the nature of the technology transferred in each collaboration, and hence we cannot replicate Shrader's analysis in this respect.

However, Shrader's argument can be generalized. Transfer over a market interface of complex knowledge is difficult because of the bounded rationality and opportunism of economic actors. With unbounded rationality this transfer would be costless. And without opportunism, it would be possible to trade knowledge on the basis of mutual trust, without complex and costly contractual safeguards. In general it can be said that all factors that increase the demands made on bounded rationality and that make the formation of trust more difficult can be assumed to increase the transaction costs involved in the technical collaboration, and hence this route to technological development becomes less attractive relative to in-house development.

We focus on one particular factor influencing the relative attractiveness of collaborations, i.e. the cultural distance between the Indian and the foreign partner. Communication and trust-building are difficult when large psychic distances have to be bridged, as in the cooperation between an Indian firm and a technology provider from a country with a very different national culture (Woodcock and Geringer, 1991; Olk, 1997; Park and Ungson, 1997; Simonin, 1999). Hence, for firms that engage in collaborations, we expect a negative effect of cultural distance on the performance of the firm.

Hypothesis 4 For firms that engage in collaborations, the cultural distance between the Indian partner and the foreign collaborator will be negatively related to firm performance.

Moreover, of the four cultural dimensions distinguished by Hofstede (2001) – power distance, uncertainty avoidance, individualism and masculinity – we expect uncertainty avoidance to be most detrimental to performance. Firms in countries where uncertainty avoidance is high tend to respond to uncertainties through formalized structures, while firms in countries where uncertainty avoidance is low tend to rely on flexible systems when faced with uncertainty (Hofstede, 2001). This difference in the way in which firms from countries with high uncertainty avoidance and low uncertainty avoidance respond to uncertainties in their environment leads to conflict and contention among collaborators. Since power distance and individualism relate to distribution of power within the organization and to the relationship among employees in the firm (Hofstede, 2001), these do not pose a serious threat to collaboration performance. This is particularly true with technical collaborations as the structuring of personnel within the organization largely rests with the local (Indian) firm. With regard to differences in masculinity, the combative approach of one partner and the sympathetic disposition of the other may balance each other rather than conflict (Barkema and Vermeulen, 1997). If this is the case, larger distances in this dimension would be expected to be associated with better, instead of worse outcomes. Hence, of the four dimensions in Hofstede (2001), we expect uncertainty avoidance to be most detrimental to firm performance.

Hypothesis 5 For firms that engage in collaborations, differences in uncertainty avoidance between the Indian partner and the foreign collaborator – rather than differences in power distance, individualism and masculinity – will be negatively related to firm performance.

Barkema and Vermeulen (1997) found support for the more detrimental effect of uncertainty avoidance compared to the other dimensions of Hofstede (2001) on the survival of international joint ventures of Dutch multinationals. Our study seeks to find support for the detrimental impact of uncertainty avoidance on the performance of local Indian firms having technical collaborations with foreign firms.

3.   METHODS

Sample and Data

We tested our hypotheses on a data set of 1367 Indian firms from the manufacturing sector. Data were obtained from annual reports published by Capitaline. Capitaline is widely used in business and academic circles in India – e.g. Institute for Economic Growth (IEG), New Delhi; PricewaterhouseCoopers India (PWC), to name a couple. The financial information from the annual reports of some randomly chosen firms in the sample was used to verify the figures obtained from Capitaline, and the information was found to be correct. The 1367 firms in our sample are distributed across different industries in the manufacturing sector, thereby making the sample representative of the organized sector of the Indian Industry. Data for all variables except performance were collected for the year 1999. Performance data were collected for the three-year period ending 1999–2000. This provided a sufficient time period for the independent variables to show their effect on performance.

Of the 1367 firms, almost 30 percent had at least one international technical collaboration. The highest number of collaborations of any firm was 14. In sum, the 1367 firms had 874 collaborations. The frequency of collaborations varies considerably between industries, as does the profitability, sales growth, advertising intensity and R&D intensity (see Table 9.1). The 16 broad industry categories in the sample included chemicals, auto and automotive components, rubber, plastics, metals and allied products, engineering, electronics, electrical equipment, paper and packaging, refineries, textiles, food and allied products, ceramics, cement, cables and telecommunication equipment, and aqua and marine products.

Measures

Dependent variables

Performance   We employed two financial measures of firm performance as our dependent variables: profitability and sales growth. Profitability may be seen as an immediate measure of firm performance, whereas sales growth is assumed to lead to higher profitability in the long run. It is important to take both measures into account, as firms may face a trade-off between profitability now and in the future. These were also the two performance indicators used in the study by Shrader (2001).

Profitability   Profitability was calculated as average return on sales (ROS) over the years 1998–2000 (Hagedoorn and Schakenraad, 1994). In all regressions the firm profit measure was corrected for systematic differences between industries by subtracting the mean profitability within the industry from the profit of the firm.

Table 9.1 Profit, sales growth, R&D intensity and advertising intensity

Industry	Number of firms	Proportion of firms with collaboration	Profit	Sales growth	R&D intensity	Advert. intensity
Chemical	305	0.230	−0.00258	0.04746	0.46844	0.74000
Automotive	64	0.641	0.02706	0.08920	0.61797	0.70693
Rubber	22	0.318	−0.08836	−0.10558	0.13773	0.29813
Plastics	40	0.375	−0.07618	−0.05845	0.08200	0.46708
Metals	130	0.269	−0.03840	−0.00006	0.07726	0.08880
Engineering	134	0.530	−0.04873	−0.00826	0.25299	0.33725
Electronics	38	0.500	−0.04084	0.10882	0.48500	0.99084
Electrical equip.	59	0.407	0.01882	0.02635	0.23051	0.81072
Paper & pack.	97	0.206	−0.04435	0.00884	0.04804	0.14000
Refineries	23	0.522	0.00870	0.03297	0.18739	0.23034
Textiles	253	0.134	−0.04139	0.00143	0.04518	0.28716
Food	87	0.161	0.03173	0.02967	0.36879	0.52027
Ceramics	48	0.271	−0.05500	0.08566	0.11063	0.89077
Cement	33	0.242	−0.05333	−0.04301	0.50939	0.71729
Cables & telec.	25	0.520	0.00680	0.09322	0.07240	0.24543
Aqua & marine	9	0.333	0.00197	0.05689	0.00000	0.05751
Sum/average	1367	0.292	−0.02343	0.02209	0.24954	0.47423

Sales growth   Sales growth was calculated on a yearly basis from 1998 to 2000. The sales growth for the individual time periods was averaged to get the final sales growth figure. In all regressions the sales growth measure was corrected for systematic differences between industries by subtracting the mean sales growth within the industry from that of the firm.

Independent variables

Collaboration   Collaboration is a dummy variable with the value 1 if the firm has at least one foreign technical collaboration, and 0 otherwise.

Advertising intensity   Advertising intensity was calculated as the ratio of advertising expenditures over sales in year 1999.

R&D intensity   R&D intensity was calculated as the ratio of R&D expenditures over sales in year 1999.

Cultural distance   Cultural distance was calculated on the basis of scores on Hofstede's (2001) indices. Following Kogut and Singh (1988), cultural distance was calculated as the average of squared deviations of each cultural block from the ranking of India. The countries in our sample were classified in eight cultural blocks – Anglo, Nordic, Germanic, Latin European, Latin American, Near East, Far East and Independent – following Ronen and Shenkar (1985). Since our sample contained firms with more than one collaboration, the final cultural distance score for each firm was obtained by multiplying the number of collaborations the firm has in each cultural block by the cultural distance score for that block. This procedure took into account the absence of collaborations in certain cultural blocks and also the cumulative cultural difference faced by that firm. Algebraically:

$$CD_{j1} = \Sigma_{i=1,2,3,4} \{(I_{ij} - I_{ii})^2 / V_i\} / 4$$

where
CD_{j1} = cultural distance of the *j*th cultural block from India
I_{ij} = index for the *i*th cultural dimension and the *j*th cultural block
i = India
V_i = the variance of the index of the *i*th dimension.

$$\text{Final } CD_j = \Sigma_{j=1\ldots8} \{CD_{j1} * n_j\}$$

where
CD_j = cumulative cultural distance of the Indian firm from all its collaborators
j = cultural block (e.g. Nordic, Germanic etc.)
n_j = number of collaborations in each cultural block.

Before calculating the interaction terms (advertising intensity × collaboration; R&D × collaboration, etc.), the advertising intensity and R&D intensity variables were standardized in order to avoid multicollinearity problems. To further reduce multicollinearity, we substituted dummy variables for advertising intensity and R&D intensity in regressions where advertising intensity and R&D intensity were included as main effects as well as interaction effects, with a value of 1 if the firm in question does engage in R&D or marketing, and 0 otherwise. To check for the severity of multicollinearity between the independent variables, we examined the conditioning index and variance proportions associated with each independent and control variable (Mehra et al., 2001). According to Tabachnik and Fidell (1996, pp. 86–7), a conditioning index greater than 30 and at least two variance proportions greater than 0.50 indicates serious multicollinearity. Since none of our independent variables violated this criterion, multicollinearity did not form a serious threat to the validity of our analyses.

Control variables
Firm size   There are several reasons for applying a control variable to the size of the Indian firms. During the times of market protection many firms operated at suboptimal levels of scale (Kaplinsky, 1997). This leads to the expectation that smaller firms will do relatively poorly, now that India is gradually opening up to global competition. On the other hand, suboptimal scale in production was often due to a lack of specialization (Kaplinsky, 1997). This would lead especially the bigger, too diversified firms into difficulties with rising competition. As we are not primarily interested in the issue of scale in this study, we control for these possible effects using a variable firm size, calculated as the log of sales for the year 1999 (Hagedoorn and Schakenraad, 1994), without specifying hypotheses regarding the direction of size effects. The interaction term of firm size and collaboration was also included in the analysis, to control for the possibility that larger firms systematically profit more or less from foreign collaborations.

Firm age   A second control variable that we employ is firm age, calculated as the number of years the firm has been in existence at the time of data collection. The reason for including this variable is that older firms may have relatively many problems adapting to the new competitive conditions. There are two reasons to expect this effect. First, the older firms have a tradition of coaxing the government bureaucracy into granting industrial licenses as one of the main competitive weapons. It will be difficult to shift from this preoccupation to a strategy geared to market competition. Second, older firms may have more sunk investment in older plants. Without scrapping these plants, technical collaboration may not be an option for these firms, as the newer technologies may be incompatible with those in use (Siddharthan and Pandit, 1998). For both reasons, older firms may underperform. Table 9.2 provides descriptive statistics and correlations between variables.

4.   RESULTS

Technical and Marketing Skills

We tested four regression equations for each performance variable. The first model included only control variables. As in Shrader (2001), we introduced the collaboration variable in the second model. To examine the main effects of R&D intensity and advertising intensity, we introduced them in the third. Interaction terms (advertising intensity × collaboration, R&D × collaboration, firm size × collaboration) were introduced in the fourth model.

Profitability

Four models came up with highly significant predictions for profitability ($p < 0.001$). The results are shown in Table 9.3. In all four models profitability is positively related to firm size ($p < 0.001$), showing that bigger firms perform better than smaller firms. Firm age is not significant in any of the models. Model 1 forms the base model with only control variables. The collaboration variable, introduced in the second model, is not significant, indicating that collaboration has no direct influence on performance. The main variables – R&D intensity and advertising intensity – are introduced in Model 3. Although the R^2 increases slightly, these variables do not have a significant direct effect on performance. Model 4, which is the final and full model, includes the interaction variables (advertising intensity × collaboration, R&D × collaboration, firm size × collaboration). The results of the model are significant ($F = 7.043$, $p < 0.001$), and show a significant improvement over the third model (R^2 changes from 0.040 to 0.045, $p < 0.1$). Controlling for the interaction effects, advertising intensity has a negative direct relationship with profitability ($p < 0.05$), but the interaction of advertising intensity with collaboration is positively related to profitability ($p < 0.1$). These results support Hypothesis 1. R&D intensity has positive direct relationship to profitability ($p < 0.05$), but the interaction of R&D intensity with collaboration is negatively related to profitability ($p < 0.05$). These results support Hypothesis 3b. The interaction between firm size and collaboration is not significant.

Table 9.2   Descriptive statistics and correlations[a]

	Mean	s.d.	1	2	3	4	5	6	7	8	9	10	11	12	13	14
1. Profit[b]	0.000	0.149														
2. Sales growth[b]	0.000	0.234	0.287													
3. Firm size	1.633	0.627	0.191	0.063												
4. Firm age	23.492	19.289	0.078	-0.118	0.323											
5. Advertising intensity	0.550	0.50	-0.040	0.039	0.018	0.055										
6. R&D intensity	0.250	0.44	0.024	-0.003	0.066	0.075	0.044									
7. Collaboration	0.292	0.455	0.019	0.010	0.251	0.098	0.039	0.105								
8. Cultural distance	0.999	2.243	0.009	-0.029	0.277	0.164	0.015	0.079	0.695							
9. Adv. intens. × Collaboration	0.002	0.008	0.019	0.043	0.075	0.060	0.544	0.013	0.302	0.189						
10. R&D intens. × Collaboration	0.133	1.087	-0.010	-0.034	0.055	0.067	-0.005	0.852	0.190	0.140	0.036					
11. Size × Collaboration	0.548	0.914	0.053	0.016	0.417	0.170	0.036	0.102	0.935	0.721	0.282	0.183				
12. Individualism–collectivism[c]	2.045	2.536	-0.002	-0.083	0.237	0.239	0.050	0.005	[d]	0.660	0.050	0.005	0.237			
13. Power distance[c]	5.252	5.543	-0.011	-0.101	0.280	0.249	-0.024	-0.028	[d]	0.851	-0.024	-0.028	0.280	0.717		
14. Masculinity–femininity[c]	2.858	3.770	0.030	-0.027	0.105	0.124	-0.049	0.045	[d]	0.702	-0.049	0.045	0.105	0.167	0.316	
15. Uncertainty avoidance[c]	3.554	3.861	-0.033	-0.072	0.206	0.085	-0.044	0.026	[d]	0.760	-0.044	0.026	0.206	0.197	0.421	0.635

Notes:

a   N = 1367 (398 for the correlations with culture-dimension distances).
b   Corrected for industry average.
c   Only for firms with a collaboration: cultural distance on this dimension.
d   Cannot be computed because one of the variables is a constant.

Table 9.3   Regression, dependent variable: profit corrected for industry average[a]

	Model 1	Model 2	Model 3	Model 4
Intercept	−0.075***	−0.075***	−0.073***	−0.073***
Firm size	0.185***	0.193***	0.192***	0.191***
Firm age	0.018	0.019	0.020	0.020
Collaboration		−0.032	−0.031	−0.032
Advertising intensity			−0.044	−0.082*
R&D intensity			0.015	0.112*
Adv int. × collaboration				0.059+
R&D int. × collaboration				−0.111*
Firm size × collaboration				−0.002
F	26.106***	17.852***	11.300***	7.043***
R^2	0.037	0.038	0.040	0.045
Change in R^2		0.001	0.002	0.005+

Notes:
a $N = 1367$. Values for independent variables are standardized estimates.
+ $p < 0.100$.
* $p < 0.050$.
** $p < 0.010$.
*** $p < 0.001$.

Sales growth

Four models came up with highly significant predictions for sales growth ($p < 0.001$). The results are shown in Table 9.4. In all four models sales growth is positively related to firm size ($p < 0.001$, $p < 0.001$, $p < 0.001$ and $p < 0.05$, respectively), showing that bigger firms perform better than smaller firms. Firm age is negatively related to sales growth in all four models ($p < 0.001$), showing that younger firms exhibit more growth. Model 1 forms the base model with only control variables. The collaboration variable, introduced in the second model, is not significant. This indicates that when considered alone, collaboration has no direct influence on performance. The main variables – R&D intensity and advertising intensity – are introduced in Model 3. Here, R^2 increases slightly, and advertising intensity shows a positive direct effect on performance ($p < 0.1$). In contrast, R&D intensity has no direct effect on sales growth. Model 4, which is the full model, again includes the interaction variables. The model is significant ($F = 5.493, p < 0.001$). In Model 4 advertising intensity has no direct relationship with sales growth, nor has the interaction of advertising intensity with collaboration. These results do not support Hypothesis 1. R&D intensity has positive direct relationship to sales growth ($p < 0.1$), but the interaction of R&D intensity with collaboration is negatively related to sales growth ($p < 0.05$). These results support Hypothesis 3b. The interaction between firm size and collaboration is not significant.

Cultural Distance

The relationship between cultural distance and performance (profitability and sales growth) was tested for the 399 firms that had collaborations with foreign partners. The model used Kogut and Singh's cultural distance formula, based on Hofstede's four

Table 9.4   Regression, dependent: sales growth corrected for industry average[a]

	Model 1	Model 2	Model 3	Model 4
Intercept	−0.025	−0.025	−0.027	−0.028
Firm size	0.113***	0.113***	0.114***	0.112**
Firm age	−0.154***	−0.154***	−0.157***	−0.156***
Collaboration		−0.004	−0.005	−0.005
Advertising intensity			0.046+	0.022
R&D intensity			0.000	0.069+
Adv int. × collaboration				0.034
R&D int. × collaboration				−0.111*
Firm size × collaboration				−0.002
F	17.671***	11.778***	7.667***	5.493***
R^2	0.025	0.025	0.027	0.031
Change in R^2		0.000	0.002	0.004

Notes:
  a $N = 1367$. Values for independent variables are standardized estimates.
  + $p < 0.100$.
  * $p < 0.050$.
  ** $p < 0.010$.
  *** $p < 0.001$.

dimensions. We tested four regression equations for each performance variable. The first model included only control variables. We introduced the cultural distance variable in the second model. To examine the main effects of R&D intensity and advertising intensity, we introduced them in the third. The four cultural dimensions of Hofstede (2001) – power distance, uncertainty avoidance, individualism and masculinity – were introduced in the fourth model, instead of the overall cultural distance measure.

Profitability
Four models came up with significant predictions for profitability ($p < 0.01$). The results are shown in Table 9.5. In all four models profitability is positively related to firm size ($p < 0.01$), showing again that bigger firms perform better than smaller firms. However, firm age is not significant in any of the models. Model 1 forms the base model with only control variables. The cultural distance variable is introduced in the second model. Although cultural distance is not significant, it shows the expected negative sign, and it does explain some additional variance (R^2 increases from 0.031 to 0.035). This result does not support Hypothesis 4. The main variables – R&D intensity and advertising intensity – are introduced in Model 3. The R^2 increases from 0.035 to 0.052 ($p < 0.05$), and these variables have a significant main effect on performance ($p < 0.1$). Model 4 introduces the four cultural dimensions instead of Kogut and Singh's (1988) index. The results of the model are significant ($F = 3.201, p < 0.01$). In Model 4 both advertising intensity and R&D intensity have a positive effect on profitability. Uncertainty avoidance is negatively related to profitability, although weakly ($p < 0.1$), while the other three dimensions are not significant. This result supports Hypothesis 5, indicating that differences in uncertainty avoidance are more detrimental to performance than differences in the other three dimensions.

Table 9.5   Regression, firms with collaborations, dependent: profit corrected for industry average[a]

	Model 1	Model 2	Model 3	Model 4
Intercept	−0.083**	−0.080**	−0.099***	−0.103***
Firm size	0.169**	0.184**	0.173**	0.188**
Firm age	0.017	0.026	0.003	−0.005
Cultural distance		−0.064	−0.072	–
Advertising intensity[b]			0.093+	0.097*
R&D intensity[b]			0.099+	0.100+
Individualism–collectivism				−0.034
Power distance				−0.033
Masculinity–femininity				0.098
Uncertainty avoidance				−0.122+
F	6.362**	4.758**	4.341**	3.201**
R^2	0.031	0.035	0.052	0.062
Change in R^2		0.004	0.017*	0.014[c]

Notes:
a $N = 398$. Values for independent variables are standardized estimates.
b   Dummy variable.
c   Compared with Model 3 without the cultural distance variable.
+ $p < 0.100$.
* $p < 0.050$.
** $p < 0.010$.
*** $p < 0.001$.

Sales growth

Four models came up with significant predictions for sales growth. The results are shown in Table 9.6. In all four models sales growth is positively related to firm size, showing that bigger firms again perform better than smaller firms. Unlike the case of profitability, firm age is negatively related to sales growth in all four models, showing that younger firms exhibit stronger growth. Model 1 again forms the base model with only control variables. The cultural distance variable is introduced in the second model. Cultural distance is negatively related to sales growth ($p < 0.1$) and Model 2 shows a significant improvement over the first model (R^2 changed from 0.020 to 0.029, $p < 0.1$).This result supports Hypothesis 4. The main variables – R&D intensity and advertising intensity – are introduced in Model 3. These variables are insignificant. Model 4 introduces the four cultural dimensions. None of the dimensions is significant; hence no clear support for Hypothesis 5 is found here. However, the coefficient of uncertainty avoidance is negative and larger than that of the other dimensions.

5.   DISCUSSION AND CONCLUSION

This study is a first step towards levelling out the existing asymmetry in the alliance literature by focusing explicitly on the benefits of international collaboration to firms from

Table 9.6   Regression, firms with collaborations, dependent: sales growth corrected for industry average[a]

	Model 1	Model 2	Model 3	Model 4
Intercept	−0.022	−0.016	−0.033	−0.039
Firm size	0.096+	0.118*	0.130*	0.142*
Firm age	−0.146**	−0.132*	−0.113*	−0.118*
Cultural distance		−0.098+	−0.092+	–
Advertising intensity[b]			0.063	0.066
R&D intensity[b]			−0.083	−0.083
Individualism–collectivism				−0.017
Power distance				−0.066
Masculinity–femininity				0.065
Uncertainty avoidance				−0.094
F	3.985*	3.856*	3.141**	2.240*
R^2	0.020	0.029	0.039	0.044
Change in R^2		0.009+	0.010	0.013[c]

Notes:
  a $N = 398$. Values for independent variables are standardized estimates.
  b   Dummy variable.
  c   Compared with Model 3 without the cultural distance variable.
  + $p < 0.100$.
  * $p < 0.050$.
  ** $p < 0.010$.
  *** $p < 0.001$.

an emerging economy. As the results point out, there are firm-specific differences in the ability to reap the benefits from foreign collaborations. Collaboration is beneficial to the firms only under the right conditions (Buckley and Casson, 1996; Shrader, 2001). As is evident from the results, international collaborations brought the expected benefits to the local Indian firms only under the following conditions.

The results support both the transaction cost and knowledge-based arguments. Indian firms that stood out from the crowd by sharpening their marketing skills were able to capitalize on the know-how that came from technical collaboration. Hence these advertising-intensive firms were able to improve performance by leveraging their accumulated marketing skills to promote the superior products produced using the transferred foreign know-how.

With the lack of support for Hypothesis 3a, the knowledge-based argument falls apart here, while the transaction cost argument comes to the forefront. As it turns out, the technical collaborations appear to be inefficient vehicles for the transfer of cutting-edge technologies brought in by the foreign partners. To enhance firm performance, it may be better for the R&D-intensive firms to adopt in-house development of technology or in the event of crucial need for superior technology engage in joint ventures with foreign firms to get hold of the hard-to-transact know-how (Hennart, 1988). This arrangement would bring the local firm closer to the foreign partner, thereby enabling it to assimilate tacit know-how in a better way.

The results support the premise that, for firms engaged in collaborations, large cultural distances between these firms and their foreign partners may hamper firm performance. Large cultural distances tend to disrupt interaction and trust building (Krishnan and Noorderhaven, 2001), thereby laying more emphasis on the need for complex and costly contractual safeguards. The increase in the transaction cost due to these safeguards has a negative impact on performance. Also the (partial) support for Hypothesis 5 shows that of the four cultural dimensions identified by Hofstede (2001), differences in uncertainty avoidance are more detrimental to performance than differences in power distance, individualism or masculinity. This presumably is because differences in uncertainty avoidance are difficult to resolve as they reflect on the way in which partners perceive the opportunities and threats in their environment (Barkema and Vermeulen, 1997). Since the other three dimensions deal with the management of personnel, they are more easily resolved (Barkema and Vermeulen, 1997), particularly if firms engage in technical collaborations, and the management of personnel remains the responsibility of the local (in our case Indian) firm.

All these results strongly suggest the importance of focusing on the benefits of international collaboration to firms from emerging economies. As the study reflects, explanations of the benefits to these kinds of firm can be based on the same theories used for explaining outcomes in Western economies, although some additional reasoning based on local circumstances may be necessary. Our findings suggest that, as for the American firms analyzed by Shrader (2001), collaborations bring benefits to Indian firms only under the right circumstances. The study also shows that firm performance is a multidimensional construct, and that various aspects of performance may be influenced by different factors. This is reflected in the many differences between our analyses with profit and with sales growth as dependent variable. This observation calls for the use of multiple measures when gauging the effect of collaboration on firm performance.

Our study has many limitations. What is evident from our research is that, apart from collaboration, there are many factors not included in the study that influence firm profitability. This is clearly reflected on the low R^2. This study also relies solely on structural conditions to explain the whole phenomenon of alliances. There could be interesting process aspects of collaborations that our model does not capture. These process aspects could also influence the costs and benefits of international collaborations to local firms. In future research, data rich in process aspects of collaborations in relation to firm performance could be collected. Future researchers also could focus on other emerging markets, to examine whether the same factors we found to be of influence in India are relevant there, too.

NOTE

1. There may be differences between the institutional and legal environments in different industries and states in India (Bhalla, 1998). In this study we do not take these differences into account, other than by controlling for differences between industry in average business performance. In a follow-up study, a more in-depth analysis of the possible influence of different industry regimes in India on the propensity to collaborate and the performance implications of international collaborations is envisaged.

REFERENCES

Barkema, H.G. and Freek Vermeulen (1997), 'What differences in cultural backgrounds of partners are detrimental for international joint ventures?', *Journal of International Business Studies*, **29**: 845–64.

Barney, J.B. (1986), 'Strategic factor markets: expectations, luck and business strategy', *Management Science*, **32**: 1231–41.

Barney, J.B. (1991), 'Firm resources and sustained competitive advantage', *Journal of Management*, **17**: 99–120.

Bhalla, A.S. (1998), 'Sino-Indian liberalization: the role of trade and foreign investment', *Economics of Planning*, **31**: 151–73

Buckley, P.J. and M.C. Casson (1996), 'An economic model of international joint venture strategy', *Journal of International Business Studies*, **27**: 849–76.

Cohen, W.M. and D.A. Levinthal (1990), 'Absorptive capacity: a new perspective on learning and innovation', *Administrative Science Quarterly*, **35**: 128–52.

Contractor, Farok and Peter Lorange (1988) (eds), *Co-operative Strategies in International Business*, Lexington, MA: Lexington Books.

De Mello, L.R. Jr (1997), 'Foreign direct investment in developing countries and growth: a selective survey', *Journal of Development Studies*, **34**: 1–34.

Dunning, J.H. (1995), 'Reappraising the eclectic paradigm in an age of alliance capitalism', *Journal of International Business Studies*, **26**(3): 461–91.

Dierickx, I. and K. Cool (1989), 'Asset stock accumulation and sustainability of competitive advantage', *Management Science*, **35**: 1504–13.

Hagedoorn, John (1995), 'A note on international market leaders and networks of strategic technology partnering', *Strategic Management Journal*, **16**: 241–50.

Hagedoorn, John and Jos Schakenraad (1994), 'The effect of strategic technology alliances on company performance', *Strategic Management Journal*, **15**: 291–309.

Harrigan, K.R. (1988), 'Strategic alliances and partner asymmetries', in F. Contractor and P. Lorange (eds), *Cooperative Strategies in International Business*, Lexington, MA: Lexington Books, pp. 205–26.

Hergert, M. and D. Morris (1988), 'Trends in international collaborative agreements', in F.J. Contractor and P. Lorange (eds), *Cooperative Strategies in International Business*, Lexington, MA: Lexington Books, pp. 99–110.

Hennart, J.F. (1988), 'A transaction costs theory of equity joint ventures', *Strategic Management Journal*, **9**: 361–74

Hofstede, G.H. (2001), *Culture's Consequences: Comparing Values, Behaviors, Institutions, and Organizations across Nations*, 2nd edn, London: Sage.

Jacobsson, S. and A. Ghayur (1994), *Liberalization and Industrial Development in the Third World: A Comparison of the Indian and South Korean Engineering Industries*, New Delhi: Sage.

Kaplinsky, R. (1997), 'India's industrial development: an interpretative survey', *World Development*, **25**: 681–94.

Kogut, B. (1988), 'Joint ventures: theoretical and empirical perspectives', *Strategic Management Journal*, **9**: 319–32.

Kogut, B. and H. Singh (1988), 'The effect of national culture on the choice of entry mode', *Journal of International Business Studies*, **19**: 411–31.

Krishnan, Rekha and N.G. Noorderhaven (2001), 'Alliance outcomes: the mediating effect of process', Academy of Management Conference, Washington, DC, August.

Kumar, R. and K.O. Nti (1998), 'Differential learning and interaction in alliance dynamics: a process and outcome discrepancy model', *Organization Science*, **9**: 356–67.

Liu, X., P. Siler, C. Wang and Y. Wei (2000), 'Productivity spillovers from foreign direct investment: evidence from UK industry level panel data', *Journal of International Business Studies*, **31**: 407–25.

Lyles, M.A. and J.E. Salk (1996), 'Knowledge acquisition from foreign parents in international joint ventures: an empirical examination in the Hungarian context', *Journal of International Business Studies*, **27**: 877–904.

Mehra, Ajay, Martin Kilduff and Daniel J. Brass (2001), 'The social networks of high and low self-monitors: implications for workplace performance', *Administrative Science Quarterly*, **46**: 121–46

Mohan, R. and V. Aggarwal (1990), 'Commands and controls: planning for Indian industrial development', *Journal of Comparative Economics*, **14**: 681–712.

Niosi, J., P. Hanel and L. Fiset (1995), 'Technology transfer to developing countries through engineering firms: the Canadian experience', *World Development*, **23**: 1815–24.

Olk, P. (1997), 'The effect of partner differences on the performance of R&D consortia', in P. Beamish and J. Killings (eds), *Cooperative Strategies, American Perspectives*, San Francisco, CA: New Lexington Press, pp. 133–59.

Osborn, R. and J. Hagedoorn (1997), 'The institutionalization and evolutionary dynamics of interorganizational alliances and networks', *Academy of Management Journal*, **40**: 261–78.

Park, S.H. and G.R. Ungson (1997), 'The effect of national culture, organizational complementarity, and economic motivation on joint venture dissolution', *Academy of Management Journal*, **40**: 279–307.

Peteraf, M.A. (1993), 'The cornerstones of competitive advantage: a resource based view', *Strategic Management Journal*, **14**: 179–88.

Porter, M.E. (1985), *Competitive Advantage: Creating and Sustaining Superior Performance*, New York: Free Press.

Prahalad, C.K. and K. Lieberthal (1998), 'The end of corporate imperialism', *Harvard Business Review*, **76** (July–August): 69–79.

Ronen, S. and O. Shenkar (1985), 'Clustering countries on attitudinal dimensions: a review and synthesis', *Academy of Management Review*, **10**(3): 435–54.

Shrader, R. (2001), 'Collaboration and performance in foreign markets: the case of young high-technology manufacturing firms', *Academy of Management Journal*, **44**: 45–60.

Siddharthan, N.S. and B.L. Pandit (1998), 'Liberalization and investment: behaviour of MNEs and large corporate firms in India', *International Business Review*, **7**: 535–48.

Simonin, B.L. (1999), 'Ambiguity and the process of knowledge transfer in strategic alliances', *Strategic Management Journal*, **20**: 595–624.

Sinha, R. (1994), 'Government procurement and technological capability: case of Indian electrical equipment industry', *Economic and Political Weekly*, **26**: 142–7.

Spender, J.C. and R.M. Grant (1996), 'Knowledge and the firm: overview', *Strategic Management Journal*, **17** (Special Issue, Winter): 5–9.

Szulanski, G. (1996), 'Exploring internal stickiness: impediments to the transfer of best practice within the firm', *Strategic Management Journal*, **17**: 27–44.

Tabachnik, B.G. and L.S. Fidell (1996), *Using Multivariate Statistics*, 3rd edn, New York: HarperCollins.

Wernerfelt, B. (1984), 'A resource-based view of the firm', *Strategic Management Journal*, **5**: 171–80.

Williamson, O. (1985), *The Economic Institutions of Capitalism*, New York: Free Press.

Woodcock, C.P. and M.J. Geringer (1991), 'An exploratory study of agency costs related to control structure of multi partner, international joint ventures', *Academy of Management Best Paper Proceedings*, Miami, FL, pp. 115–18.

Yan, A. and Y. Luo (2001), *International Joint Ventures; Theory and Practice*, Armonk, NY: M.E. Sharpe.

Yan, A. and M. Zeng (1999), 'International joint venture instability: a critique of previous research', *Journal of International Business Studies*, **30**: 397–414.

Zack, M.H. (ed.) (1999), *Knowledge and Strategy*, Boston, MA: Butterworth Heinemann.

10 Joint venture configurations in big emerging markets

Hemant Merchant

Empirical studies investigating capital markets' reactions to announcements of corporate participation in international joint ventures (IJVs) have usually focused on firm-specific factors – often without agreement about the impact of these factors on parents' shareholder value (Gulati, 1998). Rarely have studies included location-specific factors to explain shareholder value creation via IJVs. This is a crucial omission because the two sets of factors are interconnected and thus jointly influence firms' economic performance. One implication of this jointness is that while the efficacy of firm-specific advantages depends upon characteristics of the host country in which these advantages are deployed (Dunning, 1998), host country factors may offset certain firm-specific disadvantages (Makino and Delios, 1996). Although recent studies have investigated the contingency effects of home and host country locations on firm-specific advantages held by multinational firms (Erramilli et al., 1997), neither these nor previous joint venture studies have explicitly identified compensatory effects among firm- and location-specific factors. Moreover, no study has directly investigated the performance implications of such complementarities for firms. This study attempts to fill the noted gaps in the context of IJVs located in big emerging markets (BEMs).[1]

The issue of how firm-specific and location-specific factors interact empirically can be well scrutinized in the above-mentioned context. This is because every BEM portrays a distinct set of location-specific conditions (Garten, 1996). Moreover, most BEMs are developing countries, where more than 60 percent of managers seem dissatisfied with their firms' joint venture performance (Beamish, 1985). The focus on BEMs is also justified because these markets are strategically important to American firms (Garten, 1996) and have recently experienced an increase in IJV activity (UNCTAD, 1997). Given these motivations, this study asks: How do firm- and location-specific factors complement one another in the BEM context, and how do these complementarities impact shareholder value creation for parents whose IJVs are located in BEMs?

THEORY DEVELOPMENT: A TYPOLOGY OF IJVS

Numerous strategic management studies have recognized the interconnectedness of firms' internal and external contexts and their performance implications. Hence these contexts denote valid anchors for a conceptual scheme that attempts to identify configurations of firm- and location-specific conditions that result in shareholder value creation for parents. For discussion purposes, the relative economic appeal of both above-mentioned contexts can be considered in terms of degree and number of firm- and location-specific conditions.[2] This conceptualization yields three distinct IJV configurations: (i) firm-dominant configurations; (ii) location-dominant configurations; and (iii) mid-range configurations. Firm-dominant configurations are defined as those where, in the view of firms entering into IJVs, firm-specific factors are collectively more attractive than location-specific factors. In contrast, location-dominant configurations are defined as those where location-specific factors are collectively more attractive than firm-specific factors. Mid-range configurations are defined as those where firm-specific and location-specific factors are relatively equally attractive *vis-à-vis* each other, but relatively less attractive *vis-à-vis* their counterparts in the firm- and location-dominant configurations respectively.

Firm-dominant Configurations

Firm-dominant configurations denote IJVs typified by a portfolio of highly attractive firm-specific factors and comparatively moderate location-specific factors, the latter indicating riskiness of operating in less appealing host countries. The economic appeal of countries is often reduced in the presence of conditions such as: (i) high level of political risk; (ii) a weak property rights regime; (iii) limited supply of skilled labor; and so on. These conditions are probably offset by other location-specific traits such as: (i) high market growth rate; and (ii) small cultural distance. Thus a host country's attractiveness depends on the aggregation of locational factors. For firm-dominant configurations, this aggregation is expected to be skewed towards local conditions that generally retard FDI. Yet parents may be able to counter the aggregate downside effects of location-specific conditions with firm-specific advantages such as: (i) large firm size; and (ii) greater previous experience. Hence these parents could enhance their own firms' shareholder value. A focus on firm size can be justified, as researchers often consider largeness to be an indicator of resources held by individual firms (see Penrose, 1959). All else being equal, the possession of resources allows firms to expand geographically more than would otherwise be possible. Previous experience also aids such internationalization to the extent that greater experience augments a firm's own absorptive capacity to navigate hazards in the firm's institutional environment (Barkema et al., 1997).

The complementarity among firm- and location-specific conditions can be illustrated by focusing on an important firm-specific factor – firm size. Since large firms possess more (and often better-quality) resources than small firms, the stock of resources held by large firms indicates their tendency for greater risk-taking (Reuer and Miller, 1997) and higher risk-tolerance (Benito and Gripsrud, 1995, p. 49). Implicitly, large firms have a greater capacity to absorb 'spatial transaction costs' (Dunning, 1998). This view has indirect support: Merchant (2000b) reported a positive association between parents' firm size and their portfolio of IJV host countries. Thus parents in a firm-dominant configuration will be less reluctant to undertake IJVs in host countries with high transaction costs. As suggested earlier, these location-specific costs arise from conditions such as: (i) high levels of political risk; (ii) weak property rights regime; (iii) limited availability of skilled labor; and (iv) economies generally insulated from international trade. Such location-specific factors are expected to be associated with firm-dominant configurations.

Parents can reduce their spatial transaction costs by entering into partnerships with locally knowledgeable firms (Makino and Delios, 1996). However, parents are not immune from the risk of opportunistic exploitation by local partners. In principle, although all firms invoke this risk, large firms would be '*less* concerned' (Agarwal and Ramaswami, 1992, p. 4, emphasis added) with such a possibility. Stated differently, large parents can better withstand location-specific transaction costs because of advantages conferred by their (large) firm size.

Firm-specific conditions can complement unappealing host country characteristics in other ways. For example, firms can rely on their past experience to reduce the costs of undertaking IJVs in economically, geographically and culturally distant countries. Prior relationships offer parents 'a powerful *counterbalance* to cross-cultural differences' (Park and Ungson, 1997, p. 301, emphasis added). This is because experience-based learning reduces conflicts and misunderstandings caused by cultural distance between cross-border partners. Likewise, greater experience permits firms to undertake IJVs in more distant economic and/or geographical markets. Indeed, as Davidson (1980) found, the more experienced firms exhibited less affinity for near and similar markets. Experience allowed these firms to give higher investment priority to markets they initially perceived as being less attractive due to high uncertainty (Davidson, 1980). Fundamentally, greater experience offset location-specific uncertainty for these firms. Implicitly, greater experience mitigates transaction costs associated with firms' more distant economic undertakings (Benito and Gripsrud, 1995). Thus large and/or more experienced parents can be expected to undertake: (i) IJVs whose product-market scope minimally overlaps that of their respective parents' stand-alone operations; and (ii) IJVs that undertake multiple value chain activities concurrently. Such traits would be associated with firm-dominant configurations as well.

The above paragraphs illustrate how parents in firm-dominant configurations can engage their sizable firm-specific advantages in moderately attractive host countries and still undertake profitable IJVs. Contrary to the traditional view, location-based demerits need not limit shareholder value creation, provided there is a fit between parents' internal and external contexts. Firm-dominant configurations facilitate shareholder value creation by lowering parents' risks of operating in distant locations (via firm-specific advantages such as greater experience) while concurrently facilitating greater risk-tolerance and absorption of spatial transaction costs (via firm-specific advantages such as large size). These facilities allow parents with significant firm-level advantages to prospect the efficiency frontiers of their resources, and so to potentially gain from opportunities that might not accrue to other, less endowed firms. Consequently, shareholder value ought to be created for these parents – despite their ventures' location in host countries with moderate economic appeal. Firm-dominant configurations thus suggest a joint venture logic of 'push' or 'exploration' wherein shareholder value is created more from economic prospecting and relatively less from synergistic deployment of parents' resources.

Hypothesis 1   BEMs whose location-specific attractiveness is moderate will particularly appeal to large, more experienced parents. These parents will undertake multifunctional IJVs, and IJVs whose product-market scope minimally overlaps that of their respective stand-alone parent firms.

Hypothesis 2   Shareholder value will be created for parents whose IJVs indicate the firm-dominant configuration described above.

Location-dominant Configurations

Location-dominant configurations denote IJVs typified by a portfolio of highly attractive location-specific factors and comparatively moderate firm-specific factors. Attractive local factors include conditions such as: (i) low levels of political risk; (ii) a strong property rights regime; (iii) high market growth rates and so on. These conditions are probably offset by other location-specific traits. Clearly, a host country's appeal depends on the aggregation of location-specific conditions. For location-dominant configurations, this aggregation is expected to be skewed towards locational conditions that generally encourage FDI. This skewness should appeal even to parents who may encounter restrictive firm-specific conditions such as: (i) small size; and (ii) limited experience. Such firm-specific conditions are expected to be associated with location-dominant configurations.

Attractive locations represent opportunities for firms to leverage their own firm-specific advantages efficiently (Dunning, 1998, p. 51), thereby enabling even modestly endowed firms to concentrate more on achieving resource-based synergies and relatively less on navigating through locationally embedded hazards. Such focus can create shareholder value for parents, even those deficient in certain firm-specific advantages.

The complementarity among firm- and location-specific conditions in location-dominant configurations can be illustrated by focusing on an important location-specific condition – economic similarity between a parent's home country and its IJV's host country. Lesser economic distance can compensate for small firm size and limited international experience (Benito and Gripsrud, 1995). Although all parents can benefit from economic similarity, this condition would especially benefit small, usually resource-constrained, parents. This is because economic proximity facilitates scale economies and enhances firms' ability to serve foreign markets (Davidson, 1980). Moreover, economic proximity lowers managerial uncertainty and ignorance of local conditions, and permits information (say) about a new product to be disseminated 'more efficiently and effectively' (Davidson, 1980, p. 10). Thus it compensates for parents' limited international experience and reduces their cost of managing activity in foreign markets.

Location-specific conditions can complement restrictive firm-specific characteristics in other ways as well. For example, large and/or growing markets may permit firms without any clear dominant market position to avail themselves, at least in the short run, of scale economies embedded in host country market potential (Kravis and Lipsey, 1982). Clearly, attractive locations alleviate at least some constraints arising from moderate firm-specific advantages. Such trade-offs are 'of particular importance in early stages of internationalization when firms often are small and face severe resource constraints. Countries close to home country in geographical, economic, and/or cultural terms may be the preferred choices for first investments because the knowledge needed does not differ substantially from the knowledge already acquired' (Benito and Gripsrud, 1995, pp. 46–7). Thus small and/or less experienced parents can be expected to undertake: (i) IJVs whose product-market scope significantly overlaps that of their respective parents' stand-alone operations; and (ii) IJVs that undertake fewer value chain activities concurrently relative to those undertaken by large and/or more experienced parents.

The above paragraphs illustrate how parents in location-dominant configurations can deploy their modest firm-specific advantages in highly attractive locations and still pursue profitable IJVs. Contrary to the traditional view, lack of certain firm-specific advantages need not limit shareholder value creation, provided there is a fit between parents' internal and external contexts. Location-dominant configurations facilitate value creation by generating location-based incentive structures that not only attract focused resource deployments, but also safeguard the context in which these resources are deployed. These facilities allow parents – especially those with limited firm-specific resources – to pursue synergistic joint ventures, and so to potentially gain from undertakings that would not be economically feasible in less attractive locations. Consequently, shareholder value ought to be created for these parents – despite their modest firm-specific advantages. Location-dominant configurations thus suggest a joint venture logic of 'pull' or 'exploitation' wherein shareholder value is created more from locationally embedded incentives to increase synergies and relatively less from economic prospecting, as was the case with firm-dominant configurations.

Hypothesis 3   BEMs whose location-specific attractiveness is high will particularly appeal to small, less experienced parents. These parents will undertake less multifunctional IJVs, and IJVs whose product-market scope significantly overlaps that of their respective stand-alone parent firms.

Hypothesis 4   Shareholder value will be created for parents whose IJVs indicate the location-dominant configuration described above.

Mid-range Configurations

The preceding discussion can be extended to mid-range configurations that denote IJVs typified by a set of firm- and location-specific factors that are relatively equally attractive *vis-à-vis* each other. Moreover, as defined earlier, the collective economic appeal of firm-specific factors in this configuration is lower than that of their counterparts in firm-dominant configurations, and the collective appeal of location-specific factors is lower than that of their counterparts in location-dominant configurations. Thus this configuration lies on the continuum defined by firm- and location-dominant configurations; its discussion can therefore be omitted without significant loss of conceptual value.

Given their intermediate nature, mid-range configurations are expected to reflect firm-specific conditions that are less appealing than those in firm-dominant configurations (e.g. large firm size and greater previous experience). Likewise, mid-range configurations are expected to reflect locational traits that are less attractive than those associated with location-dominant configurations (e.g. low level of political risk, a strong property rights regime, host country openness to international trade and so on).

The above paragraphs suggest that parents in mid-range configurations can also undertake profitable IJVs. Contrary to the traditional view, a combination of modest firm-specific advantages and modest locational conditions need not limit shareholder value creation, provided there is a fit between parents' internal and external contexts. Logically, value-creating mechanisms associated with this configuration must denote some combination of the mechanisms associated with firm- and location-dominant configurations: (i) risk reduction; and (ii) synergistic resource deployment. Yet the existence of other value-creating mechanisms cannot be ruled out. Figure 10.1 depicts the principal

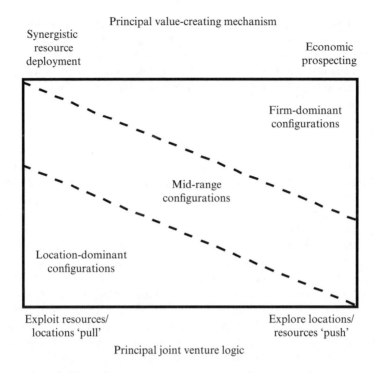

Figure 10.1 Shareholder value creation in international joint ventures

mechanism for creating shareholder value and the joint venture formation logic associated with each of the three configurations. Thus parents in mid-range configurations can be expected to undertake: (i) IJVs with intermediate levels of product-market scope; and (ii) IJVs that pursue a limited number of value chain activities concurrently. Such traits would also accompany mid-range configurations.

Hypothesis 5 BEMs with intermediate level of location-specific attractiveness will particularly appeal to medium-sized parents and/or parents with intermediate levels of previous IJV experience. These parents will undertake IJVs with intermediate levels of multifunctionality, and IJVs with intermediate levels of product-market scope overlap.

Hypothesis 6 Shareholder value will be created for parents whose IJVs indicate the mid-range configuration described above.

Although the preceding discussion has focused primarily on complementarities across firm- and location-specific factors, such complementarities also exist within each set of factors. For example, higher levels of partner–venture relatedness (Barkema et al., 1997, p. 437) and competitive positions (Merchant, 2000b) can favorably offset parents' lack of joint venture experience as well as their small firm size. Relatedly, large markets compensate for risky as well as slow-growth markets (Culem, 1988), whereas expanding domestic markets and economic infrastructures reduce the need for host country 'location tournaments' involving fiscal and other short-term incentives (Wheeler and Mody, 1992, p. 72). Likewise, for developing countries, economic policy variables can compensate for weak property rights regimes (Seyoum, 1996). The above exposition can be extended to other, less frequently studied, firm- and location-specific factors. Clearly, trade-offs between theoretical rigor and empirical completeness are inevitable.

METHODS

These trade-offs are particularly significant for studies that engage cluster analysis, given the methodology's sensitivity to input data. An important way of reducing this sensitivity is to include only those variables in analysis for which there is adequate theoretical grounding (e.g. Aldenderfer and Blashfield, 1984). This study attempted to balance the rigor–completeness trade-off in two stages, following considerable empirical precedent (Ketchen and Shook, 1996). In stage 1, the study identified salient theoretical influences on joint venture performance (see Appendix Table 10A.1); variables representing these constructs were used to determine joint venture configurations empirically. In stage 2, the study invoked other (descriptive) variables to highlight linkages between individual configurations and shareholder value creation associated with each. It must be emphasized that the study invoked these descriptive variables only after the configurations were empirically identified. None of the study's descriptive variables nor the variable representing shareholder value creation was used to generate clusters.

Data and Sample

The study searched Dow Jones News Retrieval Service for announcements of equity joint ventures formed over 1986 through 1993 between US firms and non-US partners. To be included in the sample, joint ventures had to be located in a BEM and their US parent traded on New York, American or NASDAQ stock exchanges. The study deleted announcements that did not meet these criteria. The 'publicly traded' requirement was needed to develop a measure of shareholder value creation – albeit only for US parents, due to concerns about reliability of non-US stock exchange data. The use of a capital-market-based measure is especially justified given the configurational approach's imperative for more accurate performance measures of the phenomenon under study (Ketchen et al., 1997, p. 235).

However, capital-market-based measures are sensitive to other firm-specific announcements of economically relevant events (e.g. dividend payout), which can distort findings – if these events are not controlled for. To eliminate their confounding effect, this study deleted announcements that also referred to non-IJV formation events during the two-day period of interest (see below). This protocol follows McWilliams and Siegel's (1997) guidelines for the use of a market-based measure of shareholder value creation, and is fully consistent with those adopted in earlier studies employing this measure. These requirements yielded a sample of 241 equity IJV formation announcements comprising manufacturing and non-manufacturing firms, 73 percent and 27 percent of the sample respectively. Approximately 90 percent of all non-US partners were firms and the remainder state-owned enterprises. About 95 percent of non-US partners were also domiciled in a BEM. South Africa was the only BEM not represented in the sample, either in terms of non-US partner domicile or as a joint venture location.

Variables and their Operationalization

Descriptive variables
This study used four descriptive variables: (i) host country of joint ventures (*JVLOC*); (ii) non-US partner's domicile (*CNTRY*); (iii) year in which an IJV was formed (*YEAR*), and (iv) industry sector (*SECTR*) in which US parents operated (manufacturing; non-manufacturing). The Dow Jones database provided information regarding the first three variables, whereas COMPUSTAT provided SIC data required to code the last variable. All variables were of a factual nature, and so could be coded unambiguously. Findings pertaining to these variables are integrated in the next section to enable the reader to better interpret the study's empirical results.

External variable
This study used the event-study technique to generate a measure of shareholder value creation, abnormal returns (*ABRET*). Abnormal return refers to the difference between actual market return associated with a particular firm-specific event (here IJV formation announcement) and the firm's historical return. Shareholder value is created when this difference is positive; shareholder value is destroyed when the difference is negative. Following convention, this study computed abnormal return on day t for each firm i as: $AR_{it} = R_{it} - (a_i + b_i*R_{mt})$, where R_{it} = actual rate of return for firm i on day t; a_i, b_i = estimated intercept and slope parameters (respectively) for firm i; and R_{mt} = rate of return on the value-weighted market portfolio on day t. The study estimated the above model over a 200-day period beginning 51 days before an IJV's announced formation. For each firm i, the study cumulated abnormal returns over a two-day 'event window' consisting of the day a firm's IJV participation was first announced and the following day. Event studies routinely undertake such aggregation to account for capital markets' reaction to announcements that may have been made after trading hours (McWilliams and Siegel, 1997). The two-day return for the sample was 0.54 percent ($p < 0.0948$); about 52 percent of all US parents obtained positive returns ($p < 0.0001$).

Cluster variates
This study employed 16 key theoretical variables to identify IJV configurations present in the data. As noted earlier, these variables emerged from a synthesis of empirical work on shareholder value creation via joint ventures (Merchant, 2000a) and a review of the FDI literature (see Appendix Table 10A.1).

Following Garcia-Canal (1996), this study defined task complexity (*TCPLX*) as the number of distinct types of value activities (upstream; midstream; downstream) simultaneously undertaken. Thus *TCPLX* assumed a minimum value of 1 and a maximum value of 3. Data for coding *TCPLX* were obtained from information reported in Dow Jones. The study subjectively coded rivalry between US parents and their non-US partners (*RIVAL*) on a five-point scale that measured the extent of product-market overlap between partners (Park and Russo, 1996); higher scores denoted greater overlap, and vice versa.[3] Principal International Businesses, and Value Line Investment Surveys provided the data for constructing *RIVAL*. The study also used this scale to measure the overlap in business scope (*SCOPE*) between US parents and their respective ventures (Koh and Venkatraman, 1991).[4] Value Line, Directory of Corporate Affiliations and Dow Jones provided data for constructing *SCOPE*.

This study measured previous joint venture experience (*JVEXP*) in terms of the frequency of US parents' participation in IJVs over a three-year period preceding the year in which a given IJV was announced. The period was selected based on data availability and resource constraints. The count measure is similar to those previously constructed (Park and Russo, 1996); higher counts denote greater experience, and vice versa. Following Das et al. (1998), this study measured firm size (*FSIZE*) as the logarithm of US parents' market value over the announcement period. The study measured firms' ownership (*OWNER*) of their IJVs in terms of percentage of equity held by a venture's US parent. Following Saxton (1997), the study measured ventures' decision-making structure (*DCMKG*) as a dichotomous variable so that *DCMKG* = 1 if decision-making was shared and *DCMKG* = 0 if it was not. Data required to code both variables were almost always reported in Dow Jones; the study discarded observations with missing or ambiguous data. Following Bleeke and Ernst (1991), this study subjectively coded firms' relative competitive position (*RLPOS*) on a three-point ordinal scale (1 = Strong to 3 = Weak). To operationalize this variable, the study undertook content analysis of the descriptive information contained in Value Line.[5]

Turning to location-specific variables, this study measured firms' accessibility to location-specific skilled labor (*SKILL*) in terms of host country literacy rate (Braunerhjelm and Svensson, 1996). It measured market size (*MSIZE*) and market growth rate (*MKTGR*) respectively in terms of host country total GDP (Kravis and Lipsey, 1982) and host country real GDP growth rate (Culem, 1988). Following Lummer and McConnell (1990), the study operationalized partner type (*PTYPE*) as a dichotomous variable, such that *PTYPE* = 1 if the non-US partner was a firm, and *PTYPE* = 0 if the partner was a state-owned enterprise.[6] Dow Jones yielded the data needed to code *PTYPE*. Following Seyoum (1996), this study measured strength of host country property rights regime in terms of the number of patents (*PATNT*) issued therein during the year in which an IJV was announced.

Following Cosset and Suret (1995), the study measured political risk (*PRISK*) in terms of annual scores reported by Political Risk Services, a prominent international agency providing political risk assessments. It measured openness of host country trading regime (*TRADE*) in terms of country-specific scores on trading openness, and cultural distance (*CDIST*) in terms of cumulated deviation between the variance-adjusted culture scores of partner countries (Kogut and Singh, 1988). Hofstede (1980) provided data for operationalizing *CDIST*, whereas data for operationalizing the remaining variables were obtained from Penn World Tables. A detailed description of how these tables are constructed can be found in Summers and Heston (1991).

Cluster Analysis Technique

Appropriateness of use
Cluster analysis refers to a wide array of multivariate techniques for reorganizing data into homogeneous groups. The methodology is appropriate for this study principally

because it better accommodates interconnectedness among a 'large' set of variables (e.g. Miller and Friesen, 1984). Cluster analysis can identify distinct groups of firm- and location-specific variables. Thus it enables a more meaningful evaluation of this study's research question about stickiness among firm- and location-specific factors. Stated differently, cluster analysis is suitable because this study emphasizes the collective impact, not individual impact, of firm- and location-specific variables on shareholder value creation. Thus this study's emphasis sharply differs from that of previous work that has investigated the role of individual variables on value creation in joint venture parents. Although regression analysis would be appropriate for these latter studies, it is inappropriate given this study's research question.[7]

The above position is valid even though regression analysis can specify the interaction effect of variables. However, modeling higher-order interactions raises the issue of how – even whether – the impact of three-way (and/or higher-order) interactions can be meaningfully interpreted (Miller and Friesen, 1984, p. 15n). Moreover, specification of interaction effects leads to multicollinearity and its derivative challenges. These issues justify the use of cluster analysis over regression for configuration studies such as the present one (Dess et al., 1993, p. 786; Miller and Friesen, 1984, pp. 56–7). Indeed, a key merit of cluster analysis is that it accounts for multiple interactions among variables concurrently (Dess et al., 1993, p. 789; Miller and Friesen, 1984, ch. 2).

Cluster analysis methodology

The cluster analysis technique is sensitive to differences in variables' measurement scales. These differences produce statistical distortions that jeopardize the meaningfulness of results. However, the distortions can be suppressed by standardizing the cluster variates – as numerous previous studies have done, and as is recommended in the literature (Ketchen and Shook, 1996). Essentially, standardization is required so that all variables contribute equally to cluster formation. Hence this study standardized all cluster variates to a mean of zero and standard deviation of 1 (Ketchen and Shook, 1996). Moreover, the study included as many firm-specific as location-specific variables to further ensure that neither set of variables dominated the empirical identification of clusters. Collectively, these efforts help better preserve structural integrity of the study's findings.[8]

This study submitted the standardized data to Ward's (hierarchical) algorithm to generate number of clusters and cluster centroids as subsequent input for K-means (non-hierarchical) algorithm.[9] This approach was necessary to ascertain the validity (Ketchen and Shook, 1996) and meaningfulness (Punj and Stewart, 1983) of clusters identified in the data. A visual inspection of dendograms generated via Ward's algorithm indicated between eight and ten clusters in the data, depending on the conducted sensitivity tests. Moreover, an examination of agglomeration coefficients also supported the cluster solution(s) identified above. Dendograms are graphs depicting the sequence in which observations join to form clusters and the similarity of joined observations. Agglomeration coefficients are the numerical value at which various observations merge to form a cluster.

Evaluating cluster validity

To ascertain the validity of cluster solutions generated via Ward's algorithm, this study performed cluster analysis for a second time – but using the K-means algorithm. This algorithm yielded results that were consistent with those obtained via the Ward's method. The *K*-means algorithm identified eight clusters, which represented almost 90 percent of the original data – after dropping 28 observations (based on density estimates) to reduce statistical distortions in the data (SAS, 1989, ch. 22). Moreover, the study conducted ANOVA (analysis of variance) on cluster variates to test the validity of eight identified clusters. As expected, ANOVA *F*-statistics were highly significant for 13 out of 16 variates (all $p < 0.0001$); the *F*-statistic for *OWNER* was significant at $p < 0.0337$, but it was not meaningful for *DCMKG* since all sampled firms shared decision-making with their joint venture partners. A more conservative MANOVA (multivariate analysis of variance) test reinforced the above findings. The MANOVA results rejected the null hypothesis of no overall cluster effect (Wilks's lambda $= 17.43$; $p < 0.0001$). These results empirically support the existence of distinct joint venture configurations in BEMs. More importantly, they corroborate an important conclusion of a meta-analytic study of configuration–performance relationships that 'the variables used to define configurations are probably *not deficient*' (Ketchen et al., 1997, p. 233, emphasis added).

To assess the predictive validity of cluster solutions, researchers have advocated conducting significance tests on variables not used to generate clusters (Ketchen and Shook, 1996). Hence this study conducted ANOVA analysis on *ABRET*, its external variable. The ANOVA results rejected the null hypothesis of no overall cluster effect ($p < 0.0717$); they reinforced validity of the identified eight-cluster solution. Having confirmed the robustness of this solution under two alternate algorithms and given non-hierarchical algorithms' relative merits, the following results are based on the *K*-means algorithm. Non-hierarchical algorithms, such as *K*-means, have two main advantages over hierarchical algorithms. One, they allow observations to switch cluster membership. Two, they make multiple passes though the data and so generate results that optimize within-cluster homogeneity and between-cluster heterogeneity (Ketchen and Shook, 1996).

RESULTS

Shareholder Value Creation via IJVs

The results in Table 10.1 indicate three clusters with significant mean abnormal returns. In absolute terms, these returns are highest for parents in cluster F (2.29 percent; $p < 0.0312$) and lower for those in cluster B (1.74 percent; $p < 0.0179$) and cluster C (1.09 percent; $p < 0.0841$). None of the three pairwise comparisons is significant below the 10 percent level. About 60 percent of parents in clusters F and C and 70 percent of parents in cluster B obtain positive returns (all $p < 0.0001$), which suggests that the findings are not driven by outliers (McWilliams and Siegel, 1997). The mean abnormal returns for the remaining five clusters lack significance below the 10 percent level. Further data analysis (not reported) suggests that this is probably due to the clusters' noticeable diversity *vis-à-vis* portfolio of BEM locations – all of which are characterized by high levels of institutional change and occasional macroeconomic instability (Garten, 1996; UNCTAD, 1997). These conditions jeopardize the 'value-in-use' of resources (Dunning and Rugman, 1985) and negate shareholder value creation. This view agrees with the empirical finding

Table 10.1 ANOVA results

External variable: abnormal returns (*ABRET*)
ANOVA *F*-statistic = 1.90 (*p* < 0.0717)

Cluster	A	B	C	D	E	F	G	H
Size	30	33	29	33	21	30	16	21
Mean (%)	−0.88	1.74	1.09	−0.68	−0.43	2.29	0.02	0.77
s.d.	0.06	0.04	0.03	0.02	0.02	0.05	0.02	0.07
p-value	n.s.	0.0179	0.0841	n.s.	n.s.	0.0312	n.s.	n.s.
% of cluster with positive returns	46	70	60	42	26	60	50	52

Significant pairwise contrasts[a]

B–A	*p* < 0.0250	C–A	*p* < 0.0996	F–A	*p* < 0.0084
B–D	*p* < 0.0338			F–D	*p* < 0.0115
B–E	*p* < 0.0959			F–E	*p* < 0.0413

Note: a. Contrasts are reported only for clusters with statistically significant abnormal returns.

that the multinationality–performance relationship has an optimal level beyond which the costs of managing multinationality outweigh the associated benefits (Gomez and Ramaswamy, 1999).

The following sections focus on results for clusters B, C and F, all with statistically significant mean abnormal returns. This emphasis is justified given the central role of 'performance' in the strategic management field. Moreover, the emphasis facilitates a parsimonious and more detailed discussion of results (Ketchen and Shook, 1996). The above focus should not be limiting because this study also discusses findings for the remaining five clusters, albeit in lesser detail *vis-à-vis* clusters B, C and F. A more detailed treatment of results for the five clusters is available upon request.

Configurations of IJVs

The results in Table 10.2 indicate substantial dissimilarity across clusters B, C and F *vis-à-vis* firm- and location-specific variables. Specifically, these clusters exhibit pairwise mean differences for five out of eight firm-specific variables (all *p* < 0.05 or lower). Contrasts are also significant for six out of eight location-specific variables (all *p* < 0.0001 usually). These differences are remarkable because they generally corroborate the typology developed earlier in this study. That is, clusters B and C differ on firm-specific as well as location-specific variables, whereas clusters B and F differ more on location-specific and relatively less on firm-specific variables. Relatedly, clusters C and F differ more strongly on firm-specific variables and relatively weakly (albeit unexpectedly) on location-specific variables. In general, all differences are in the expected direction.

Firm-dominant configurations
The results in Table 10.2 support Hypothesis 1, which predicted the characteristics of parents drawn to moderately attractive BEM locations. Cluster C denotes the predicted firm-dominant configuration. As expected, this cluster comprises very large firms and

Table 10.2 Standardized scores for cluster variates and ANOVA results

Cluster Size	A 30	B 33	C 29	D 33	E 21	F 30	G 16	H 21	ANOVA (p-value)	Pairwise contrasts (p-values) B-C	B-F	C-F
Firm-specific variables												
TCPLX	1.57	-0.48	0.13	-0.61	-0.09	-0.24	-0.74	0.22	0.0001	0.0009	n.s.	0.0393
SCOPE	0.00	0.32	0.14	-0.86	0.25	0.69	-0.52	0.00	0.0001	n.s.	n.s.	0.0272
RIVAL	0.07	0.12	-0.12	-0.33	0.34	0.17	0.09	-0.43	n.s.	n.s.	n.s.	n.s.
FSIZE	-0.13	-0.16	0.08	0.50	0.65	-0.74	0.13	-0.17	0.0001	n.s.	0.0175	0.0013
JVEXP	-0.17	-0.40	0.39	0.45	0.84	-0.55	-0.10	-0.17	0.0001	0.0162	n.s.	0.0024
OWNER	0.16	-0.14	-0.19	0.14	-0.45	-0.16	0.55	0.31	0.0337	n.s.	n.s.	n.s.
DCMKG	0.00	0.00	0.00	0.00	0.00	0.00	0.00	0.00	n.m.	–	–	–
RLPOS	0.26	-0.69	0.11	0.89	-0.72	0.20	-0.23	-0.29	0.0001	0.0004	0.0001	n.s.
Location-specific variables												
SKILL	0.05	0.48	-2.01	0.28	0.77	0.69	-0.03	-0.23	0.0001	0.0001	n.s.	0.0001
MSIZE	0.02	0.00	0.00	0.00	-0.02	0.00	-0.11	0.02	0.0001	n.s.	n.s.	n.s.
MKTGR	0.47	1.00	-0.23	0.19	-1.28	-1.16	0.28	0.49	0.0001	0.0001	0.0001	0.0001
PTYPE	0.35	0.35	0.35	0.35	0.19	0.35	0.16	-2.87	0.0001	n.s.	n.s.	n.s.
PATNT	0.03	0.05	-0.11	0.02	-0.02	-0.02	-0.09	0.02	0.0001	0.0001	0.0005	0.0429
PRISK	0.22	-0.01	0.82	-0.33	1.06	0.26	-2.22	0.21	0.0001	0.0014	n.s.	0.0314
TRADE	-0.28	0.01	-0.56	-0.02	-0.27	-0.38	3.22	-0.32	0.0001	0.0001	0.0002	0.0838
CDIST	0.40	0.78	-1.30	0.41	-1.62	0.33	0.20	0.37	0.0001	0.0001	0.0030	0.0001

those with the highest level of previous joint venture experience. Many firms in this cluster have moderate/strong competitive positions. These attributes suggest parents with considerable resources that tempt them to assume a high level of risk in their joint ventures (Reuer and Miller, 1997).

Specifically, parents in cluster C undertake most task-complex ventures whose business scope least overlaps those of their respective partners. The riskiness of undertaking implicitly less synergistic ventures is, moreover, compounded by a context that is characterized by the lowest levels of trading openness, the lowest levels of available skilled labor, the weakest property rights regime, and the highest level of political risk. These location-specific deficiencies are, however, mitigated by a modest level of market growth, the smallest cultural distance, and partnerships solely with local firms whose knowledge of domestic markets can lower firms' hazards of operating in international locations.

Despite locating their joint ventures in BEMs with moderate economic appeal, parents in cluster C obtain a mean abnormal return of 1.09 percent ($p < 0.0814$; see Table 10.1). This supports Hypothesis 2 about shareholder value creation for parents whose IJVs denote a firm-dominant configuration.[10] The gains in shareholder value appear to be supported by the fit between parents' internal and external contexts. An analysis of descriptive variables reveals that all ventures in cluster C are located in India. Perhaps therefore it is not surprising that all ventures involve partnerships with Indian firms nor that over 80 percent of these ventures are formed in the manufacturing sector – the focus of India's liberalization attempts.[11]

Clearly, the above findings suggest that firm-specific conditions (e.g. large size, high level of previous joint venture experience, and moderate/strong competitive position) not only can offset the limiting effects of moderately attractive joint venture host country locations, but also lead to increases in parents' shareholder value. This agrees with previous work:

> Countries that have a relatively lower market potential can be expected to have a lower likelihood of attracting foreign firms. However, firms that are *larger* and that have a regional or worldwide *presence* may be interested in entering these markets for achieving their growth and profit objectives. Note, for example, that developing countries such as Brazil and India, *even though not as attractive as the developed countries*, may still have *sufficient potential* and strategic importance to warrant consideration. An additional benefit offered by these target markets is the opportunity for *higher returns* (in excess of the risks taken) due to the presence of greater market imperfections. (Agarwal and Ramaswami, 1992, p. 7, emphasis added)

Location-dominant configurations

The results in Table 10.2 also support Hypothesis 3, which predicted the characteristics of parents drawn to highly attractive BEM locations. Cluster B denotes the predicted location-dominant configuration. As expected, this cluster comprises ventures located in BEMs with the highest level of trading openness, the strongest property rights regimes, the highest market growth rates, the lowest level of political risk, and a moderate level of available skilled labor. These traits suggest economically appealing locations that better facilitate synergistic exploitation of parents' resources.

Specifically, in relation to parents in cluster C, parents in cluster B deploy their resources to ventures whose business scope is more closely related to that of their own stand-alone firms. Moreover, defined in terms of task-complexity, these deployments are less risky than those by parents in cluster C ($p < 0.0009$). These patterns agree with the predicted level of firm-specific advantages in location-dominant configurations. Indeed, parents in cluster B are smaller as well as less experienced ($p < 0.0162$) than those in cluster C, albeit with more enviable competitive positions ($p < 0.0004$). All parents in cluster B have either a strong or moderate relative competitive position; unlike cluster C, none of the parents in cluster B is competitively weak.

Despite their moderately appealing firm-specific characteristics, parents in cluster B obtain a mean abnormal return of 1.74 percent ($p < 0.0179$; see Table 10.1). This supports Hypothesis 4 about shareholder value creation for parents whose IJVs denote a location-dominant configuration.[12] An analysis of descriptive variables points to the fit between internal and external contexts of parents in cluster B. Most joint ventures in this cluster are located either in China or South Korea (about 42 percent and 39 percent respectively, and the balance in rest of Asia), and invariably involve local partners.[13] Such partnerships enable parents to lower the costs of operating in unfamiliar and most culturally distant markets while permitting these parents to benefit from market growth. More than 80 percent of cluster B's ventures involve manufacturing activity – a trend generally consistent with the focus of economic activity in Asia, and one that is supported by the 'external' trading orientation of Asian economies.

These findings suggest that highly attractive host country locations can offset possible impositions of moderately attractive firm-specific traits, and increase parents' shareholder value. This agrees with previous work whose findings supported its hypothesis that

> [f]irms that are *smaller* and have *lower* multinational experience are not expected to have sufficient resources or skills to enter a large number of foreign markets. They therefore can be expected to use a selective strategy and *concentrate their efforts* in the more potential foreign markets. This is because their chances of obtaining *higher returns* are better in such markets. (Agarwal and Ramaswami, 1992, 7–8, emphasis added)

Mid-range configurations

The results in Table 10.2 support Hypothesis 5, which predicted the characteristics of parents drawn to BEMs with intermediate levels of locational appeal. Cluster F denotes the predicted mid-range configuration whose locational appeal is lesser than that for cluster B, a location-dominant configuration, and whose firm-specific appeal is lesser than that for cluster C, a firm-dominant configuration.

As expected, cluster F is characterized by: (i) weaker property rights regime relative to cluster B ($p < 0.0005$) but stronger relative to cluster C ($p < 0.0429$); (ii) higher level of political risk than in cluster B but lower than in cluster C ($p < 0.0314$); (iii) lower level of trading openness than in cluster B ($p < 0.0002$) but higher than in cluster C ($p < 0.0838$); and (iv) smaller cultural distance than that between partners in cluster B ($p < 0.0030$) but larger than that between partners in cluster C ($p < 0.0001$). Relatedly, parents in cluster F are smaller ($p < 0.0013$) as well as less experienced ($p < 0.0024$) than their counterparts in cluster C. Although these parents are smaller than those in cluster B ($p < 0.0175$), they are neither more nor less experienced than them. These findings suggest that cluster F is positioned between firm-dominant and location-dominant configuration(s) identified in the data.

Moreover, the findings imply existence of risk reduction as well as synergistic resource deployment forms of shareholder value creating mechanisms, which this study argued are associated with firm-dominant and location-dominant configurations respectively. Indeed, parents in cluster F undertake ventures that are: (i) less task-complex than those in cluster C ($p < 0.0393$) but not cluster B; and (ii) more related to their parents' business scope *vis-à-vis* cluster C ($p < 0.0272$) but not cluster B. These mechanisms create shareholder value for cluster F's parents, who obtain a mean abnormal return of 2.29 percent ($p < 0.0312$; see Table 10.1). This supports Hypothesis 6.[14]

An analysis of descriptive variables suggests a fit between internal and external contexts of parents in cluster F. Most joint ventures in this cluster are located in Mexico and most involve partnerships with Mexican firms (about 87 percent in each case).[15] Almost 90 percent of ventures in cluster F were formed during 1991–93. These findings indicate US parents' preference for Mexico during the early 1990s, and agree with NAFTA's (then) impending creation. Nearly 70 percent of parents in this cluster are non-manufacturing firms whose affinity for Mexico seems to be their response to increasing sectoral competitiveness in their home market (USA), which was rapidly becoming a 'service' economy. This view agrees with reports that '[d]uring the *first half of the 1990s*, FDI flows to Mexico were concentrated in *services*' (UNCTAD, 1997, p. 72, emphasis added). In an effort to leverage their competences, parents in cluster F appear to have formed joint ventures in another service economy – Mexico (*Economist*, 1997) – mostly with local firms with similar business interests.

In summary, the findings of this study uncovered three configurations of firm- and location-specific variables, and highlighted complementarities between these sets of variables. The findings agreed with theoretical predictions about systematic interrelationships between firm-specific and locational conditions and their implications for shareholder value creation. Moreover, the findings helped identify specific value-creating mechanism(s) associated with firm-dominant, location-dominant and mid-range configurations.

CONCLUSIONS

This study asserted that an important limitation of previous work was its inattention to IJVs' locational embeddedness (Merchant, 2000a). The neglect resulted in an inability to: (i) identify complementarities between firm- and location-specific factors; and (ii) ascertain their collective impact on shareholder value creation in parents. Addressing these gaps required theoretical and methodological upgrades – needs well served by adopting a configurational approach (Meyer et al., 1993; Miller and Friesen, 1984).

Contributions

This study tried to advance the theoretical literature by developing a typology of IJVs, predicting salient performance-augmenting mechanisms, and linking the typology to shareholder value creation. The study integrated (i) the FDI literature's emphasis on location-specific factors and their implications for firms' transactional efficiency and productivity in host countries (Dunning, 1998) with (ii) the strategic management literature's emphasis on extending these two notions into the domain of firm-specific factors and corporate economic performance. On the empirical front, this study conducted cluster analysis to expose certain complementarities between firm- and location-specific factors, and identified their collective impact on shareholder value creation. Thus this study demonstrated an alternative, more holistic (Dess et al., 1993; Miller and Friesen, 1984) way in which researchers can better evaluate the interconnectedness between, and trade-offs among, firm- and location-specific conditions.

Managerial Relevance

The study also has managerial relevance. Contrary to the conventional view, this study's findings suggest that firm-specific and location-specific conditions need not always be favorable for creating shareholder value via joint ventures. Even unfavorable and/or less favorable conditions can support significant value creation – provided they are skillfully combined with their more attractive complements. A combination of moderately attractive firm- and location-specific conditions can also support significant value creation. The finding that each of these combinations denotes an alternate – yet equally effective – path to shareholder value creation suggests that corporate managers need not feel constrained by individual firm- and location-specific conditions in their effort to create shareholder value via IJVs. These managers seem to have options regarding the manner in which such value is created in the context of BEMs.

However, mere participation in BEMs via joint ventures is not a 'sufficient' condition for creating shareholder value. The uncovered geographical patterns in joint venture formation activity in BEMs and widespread differences in the analyzed set of location-specific (and firm-specific) variables suggest that the 'emerging markets' label must both be applied as well as interpreted with caution.[16] In other words, although the collective economic potential of these markets is deemed to be greater than those that are not considered so (Garten, 1996), all BEMs are not the same nor even similar, at least in a locational sense. Hence managers must choose judiciously among these markets in ways that simultaneously accentuate strengths and attenuate weaknesses of firm- and location-specific conditions. Moreover, managers must devote particular attention to issues of 'fit' that apparently differentiate between configurations where significant shareholder value is created and where it is not. This study's findings illustrate some ways in which managers can make a beginning.

Limitations and Future Research

Despite its intended contributions, this study is not without limitations. First, the study does not include industry-specific variables in its set of cluster variates. However, their exclusion is not limiting because firm-specific differences – not industry-specific differences – are more fundamental determinants of firm profitability (e.g. Conner, 1994; Merchant, 2005). Second, this study's sample is biased towards two-party IJVs, and then only those located in BEMs. Third, the study's concept of performance (shareholder value) denotes only the expected – not realized – joint venture performance of parents. Nonetheless, this agrees with numerous studies that have used 'shareholder value' to investigate the performance implications of joint ventures for parents (Gulati, 1998). Finally, the study models a finite – yet still expansive – set of influences on shareholder value creation. However, as suggested throughout the study, none of these limitations jeopardizes the validity of this study's findings. In the interest of generalizability, future studies ought to address these limitations.

Future work can extend this study in at least two ways. It can generate a causal model of joint venture performance. Causal models would facilitate deeper understanding of the discussed interrelationships and furnish parametric information on their saliency. Such models represent an important area for study, especially in the joint venture context. Moreover, future work can utilize this study's findings to develop model(s) of IJV non-performance. The high failure rate of IJVs suggests that it may be worthwhile to compare and contrast joint venture configurations wherein significant shareholder value is created and where it is not. Although this study made a small start in that direction, much more needs to be done.

Researchers can identify configurations that retard shareholder value creation even when the combinations include 'favorable' performance influences. Strategic management studies have typically searched for influences on positive performance and identified many such influences with some consistency. Although these influences can prevail in the shadow case of non-performance, their interactions with attenuating forces may not be detected by traditional approaches. Perhaps only a configurational approach can expose such apparent anomalies.

NOTES

1. Big emerging markets are defined as markets holding enormous promise as 'engines of American growth' (Garten, 1996, p. 7). These markets include Argentina, Brazil, the Chinese economic area (China, Hong Kong and Taiwan), India, Indonesia, Mexico, Poland, South Africa, South Korea and Turkey.
2. It is pertinent to focus only on conditions that previous IJV and foreign direct investment (FDI) studies have recurrently theorized as influencing firm performance. Appendix Table 10A.1 identifies these conditions and highlights the rationale underlying their impact. The appendix table derives from: (i) synthesis of work on shareholder value creation via joint ventures (Merchant, 2000a), and (ii) review of the FDI literature.
3. To ascertain possible coding bias, this study devised an objective, SIC-based measure of rivalry. It defined the measure as the number of SIC industries common to both partners divided by the total number of SIC industries in which the two firms operated. The correlation between subjective and objective measure(s) varied between 0.49 and 0.65 (all $p < 0.001$ or lower), depending on the form of SIC data (2-digit; 4-digit). The associated Cronbach's coefficient was 0.84. These results should reduce concerns about quality of the subjective rivalry measure. Since the subjective measure had more data points than any objective measure, the study retained the former measure to enhance its own statistical power (Cook and Campbell, 1979).
4. Validity for the subjective coding of *SCOPE* can be assumed because: (i) *SCOPE* and *RIVAL* were coded similarly, and (ii) *RIVAL*'s coding was shown to be valid. An objective measure of *SCOPE* could not be constructed due to unavailable SIC data on joint ventures when these ventures were first announced.
5. To ascertain possible coding bias, this study correlated *RLPOS* with two Value Line indexes: (i) price growth persistence index, and (ii) earnings predictability index. Their choice was motivated by Strebel's thesis that 'financial market's assessment of [a firm's relative competitive position] is implicit in the proportion of the firm's value which it associates with *future growth*' (1983, p. 280, emphasis added; also see Gulati, 1998, p. 300). For each index, higher scores denoted more favorable positions. Cronbach's coefficient for the three proxies was 0.56, which provided some support for the approach used to code *RLPOS*. The low coefficient value was expected due to the limited range of values for *RLPOS*. Since the subjective measure had more data points than the two objective Value Line measures, the study retained the former measure to enhance its own statistical power (Cook and Campbell, 1979).
6. It is appropriate to classify 'partner type' (firm; state-owned enterprise) as a location-specific (not firm-specific) variable because governments – especially those of developing countries – often require multinational firms to enter into joint ventures with domestic state-owned enterprises.
7. A drawback of cluster analysis is that it obscures the role of individual variables. However, it must be

recalled that identifying the role of specific variables *vis-à-vis* shareholder value creation was never this study's objective.

8. Although not reported, the study's findings do not indicate high multicollinearity among cluster variates. The lack of multicollinearity is particularly desirable because it implies no unintentional weighting of cluster variates (e.g. Ketchen and Shook, 1996) – even after these have been standardized. Only five out of 120 correlations among the 16 cluster variates were greater than or equal to 0.40; the highest correlation, between *JVEXP* and *FSIZE*, was 0.56 ($p < 0.0001$).

9. Hierarchical algorithms begin by treating each observation as a separate cluster, and then join the two most similar observations into one cluster. Next, the observation most similar to this cluster is joined to the cluster, and the process is repeated until a single cluster comprising the entire sample is obtained (SAS, 1989, ch. 18). In contrast, non-hierarchical algorithms begin by assigning each observation to the nearest cluster centroid to form a temporary cluster. The cluster centroids are recomputed after each assignment, and a new observation is assigned to the nearest (recomputed) cluster centroid. Multiple passes are made through the data to allow observations to change cluster membership based on the recomputed centroid. The passes continue until no further changes occur in cluster membership (SAS, 1989, ch. 22).

10. Although cluster E also exhibits characteristics of a firm-dominant configuration, the mean abnormal return to parents in this cluster is not significant. Perhaps this is because parents in cluster E have the lowest equity stake in their ventures, which limits access to the ventures' future earnings. Moreover, cluster E is the most diverse among all clusters *vis-à-vis* partner domicile and joint venture location portfolios. As noted earlier, such diversity can compromise future earnings.

11. Approximately 5 percent of all joint ventures in clusters E and H also involve partnerships with Indian firms. Moreover, about 5 percent of all ventures in cluster H are located in India.

12. While cluster A also exhibits traits of a location-dominant configuration, the mean abnormal return to parents in this cluster is not significant below the 10 percent level. Analysis of results suggests that this may be because these parents undertake ventures not only with average potential synergies but also the highest level of task-complexity among all clusters. These parents, moreover, seem to increase (not decrease) their exposure to the implied risk of modest eventual performance through above-average equity ownership of their respective joint ventures.

13. Approximately 60 percent of ventures in cluster A, 20 percent of ventures in cluster D, and 75 percent of ventures in cluster H involve partners from China. About 10 percent of ventures in clusters A and D and 6 percent of ventures in cluster G involve partners from South Korea. These statistics remain unchanged *vis-à-vis* the locational preferences of parents in above-mentioned clusters.

14. While cluster D also exhibits traits of a mid-range configuration, the mean abnormal return to parents in this cluster is not significant below the 10 percent level. Analysis of results suggests that the (moderate) collective attractiveness of firm-specific and location-specific factors does not adequately compensate for the weak relative competitive positions of a majority of parents in the cluster – particularly in the presence of low potential synergies and a high cultural distance between partners' national cultures. Moreover, cluster D exhibits considerable diversity in terms of partner domicile and joint venture host country portfolios.

15. About 13 percent of ventures in clusters D and E involve Mexican partners; Mexico is also the preferred joint venture location for approximately 3 percent of ventures in cluster A and 13 percent of ventures in clusters D and E.

16. It is useful to reiterate that the uncovered geographical patterns are not a statistical artifact. This is because the set of cluster variates was: (i) standardized; (ii) evenly divided between firm- and location-specific variables; and (iii) did not exhibit significant multicollinearity.

REFERENCES

Agarwal, S. and Ramaswami, S.N. (1992), 'Choice of foreign market entry mode: impact of ownership, location, and internalization factors', *Journal of International Business Studies*, **23**(1): 1–27.

Aldenderfer, M.S. and Blashfield, R.K. (1984), *Cluster Analysis*, Beverly Hills, CA: Sage.

Barkema, H.G., Shenkar, O., Vermeulen, F. and Bell, J.H. (1997), 'Working abroad, working with others: how firms learn to operate international joint ventures', *Academy of Management Journal*, **40**(2): 426–42.

Beamish, P.W. (1985), 'The characteristics of joint ventures in developed and developing countries', *Columbia Journal of World Business*, Fall: 13–19.

Benito, G. and Gripsrud, G. (1995), 'The internationalization approach to the location of foreign direct investments: an empirical analysis', in M.B. Green and R.B. McNaughton (eds), *The Location of Foreign Direct Investment: Geographic and Business Approaches*, Brookfield, VT: Avebury Press, pp. 43–58.

Bleeke, J. and Ernst, D. (1991), 'The way to win in cross-border alliances', *Harvard Business Review*, **69**(6): 127–35.
Braunerhjelm, P. and Svensson, R. (1996), 'Host country characteristics and agglomeration in foreign direct investment', *Applied Economics*, **28**(7): 833–40.
Bresser, Rudi, Dunbar, Roger and Jitendranathan, T. (1994), 'Competitive and collective strategies: an empirical examination of strategic groups', in Paul Shrivastava and Anne Huff (eds), *Advances in Strategic Management*, vol. 106, Greenwich, CT: JAI Press, pp. 187–211.
Conner, K.R. (1994), 'The resource-based challenge to the industry-structure perspective', *Academy of Management Best Paper Proceedings*, 17–21.
Cook, Thomas D. and Campbell, Donald T. (1979), *'Quasi-experimentation: Design and Analysis Issues for Field Settings*, Boston, MA: Houghton-Mifflin.
Child, J. and Markoczy, L. (1993), 'Host-country managerial behavior and learning in Chinese and Hungarian joint ventures', *Journal of Management Studies*, **30**(4): 611–31.
Cosset, J.-C. and Suret, J.-M. (1995), 'Political risk and the benefits of international portfolio diversification', *Journal of International Business Studies*, **26**(2): 301–19.
Culem, C.G. (1988), 'The locational determinants of direct investments among industrialized countries', *European Economic Review*, **32**: 885–904.
Das, S., Sen, P.K. and Sengupta, S. (1998), 'Impact of strategic alliances on firm valuation', *Academy of Management Journal*, **41**(1): 27–41.
Davidson, W.H. (1980), 'The location of foreign direct investment activity: country characteristics and experience effects', *Journal of International Business Studies*, Fall: 9–22.
Demsetz, Harold (1988), 'The theory of the firm revisited', *Journal of Law, Economics and Organization*, **4**(1): 141–61.
Dess, G.G., Newport, S. and Rasheed, A.M.A. (1993), 'Configuration research in strategic management', *Journal of Management*, **19**(4): 775–95.
Dunning, J.H. (1998), 'Location and the multinational enterprise: a neglected factor?', *Journal of International Business Studies*, **29**(1): 45–66.
Dunning, J.H. and Rugman, A. (1985), 'The influence of Hymer's dissertation on the theory of foreign direct investment', *American Economic Association Papers and Proceedings*, 228–32.
Economist, (1997), *Pocket World in Figures*, London: Profile Books.
Erramilli, M.K., Agarwal, S. and Kim, S.-S. (1997), 'Are firm-specific advantages location-specific too?', *Journal of International Business Studies*, **28**(4): 735–57.
Fagre, N. and Wells Jr, L.T. (1982), 'Bargaining power of multinationals and host governments', *Journal of International Business Studies*, **13**(2): 9–23.
Garcia-Canal, E. (1996), 'Contractual form in domestic and international strategic alliances', *Organization Studies*, **17**(5): 773–94.
Garten, J.E. (1996), 'The big emerging markets', *Columbia Journal of World Business*, Summer: 7–31.
Gomez, L. and Ramaswamy, K. (1999), 'An empirical investigation of the form of the relationship between multinationality and performance', *Journal of International Business Studies*, **30**(1): 173–87.
Gulati, R. (1998), 'Alliances and networks', *Strategic Management Journal*, **19** (Special Issue): 293–317.
Harrigan, K.R. (1988), 'Strategic alliances and partner asymmetries', in F. Contractor and P. Lorange (eds), *Competitive Strategies in International Business*, Lexington, MA: Lexington Books, pp. 205–26.
Hofstede, G. (1980), *Culture's Consequences: International Differences in Work-related Values*, Newbury Park, CA: Sage.
Ketchen, D.J. and Shook, C.L. (1996), 'The application of cluster analysis in strategic management research: an analysis and critique', *Strategic Management Journal*, **17**: 441–58.
Ketchen, David J. et al. (1997), 'Organizational configurations and performance: a meta-analysis', *Academy of Management Journal*, **40**(1): 223–40.
Killing, P.J. (1988), 'Understanding alliances: understanding the role of task and organizational complexity', in F. Contractor and P. Lorange (eds), *Cooperative Strategies in International Business*, Lexington, MA: Lexington Books, pp. 55–67.
Kogut, B. and Singh, H. (1988), 'The effect of national culture on the choice of entry mode', *Journal of International Business Studies*, **19**(3): 411–32.
Koh, J. and Venkatraman, N. (1991), 'Joint venture formations and stock market reactions: an assessment in the information technology sector', *Academy of Management Journal*, **34**: 869–92.
Kravis, I.B. and Lipsey, R.E. (1982), 'The location of overseas production and production for export by U.S. multinational firms', *Journal of International Economics*, **12**: 201–23.
Loree, David W. and Guisinger, Stephen F. (1995), 'Policy and non-policy determinants of U.S. equity foreign direct investment', *Journal of International Business Studies*, **26**(2): 281–300.
Lummer, S.L. and McConnell, J.J. (1990), 'Stock valuation effects of international joint ventures', in S.G. Rhee and R.P. Chang (eds), *Pacific-basin Capital Markets Research*, Amsterdam: North-Holland, pp. 531–46.

Makino, S. and Delios, A. (1996), 'Local knowledge transfer and performance: implications for alliance formation in Asia', *Journal of International Business Studies*, **27**(5): 905–28.

McWilliams, A. and Siegel, D. (1997), 'Event studies in management research: theoretical and empirical issues', *Academy of Management Journal*, **40**(3): 626–57.

Merchant, H. (2000a), 'Event-studies of joint venture formation announcements: a synthesis and some possible extensions', in S.B. Dahiya (ed.), *The Current State of Business Disciplines*, Vol. 4 (Management I), Rohtak, India: Spellbound Publications, pp. 1837–61.

Merchant, H. (2000b), 'Configurations of international joint ventures', *Management International Review*, **40**(2): 107–40.

Merchant, H. (2005), 'Efficient resources, industry heterogeneity, and shareholder value creation: the case of international joint ventures', *Canadian Journal of Administrative Sciences*, **22**(3): 193–205.

Meyer, A.D., Tsui, A.S. and Hinings, C.R. (1993), 'Configurational approaches to organizational analysis', *Academy of Management Journal*, **36**: 1175–95.

Miller, D. and Friesen, P.H. (1984), *Organizations: A Quantum View*, Englewood Cliffs, NJ: Prentice-Hall.

North, D. (1991), *Institutions, Institutional Change, and Economic Performance*, Cambridge: Cambridge University Press.

Park, S.H. and Russo, M.V. (1996), 'When competition eclipses cooperation: an event history analysis of joint venture failure', *Management Science*, **42**(6): 875–90.

Park, S.H. and Ungson, G.R. (1997), 'The effect of national culture, organizational complementarity, and economic motivation on joint venture dissolution', *Academy of Management Journal*, **40**(2): 279–307.

Parkhe, Arvind (1993), 'Strategic alliance restructuring: a game-theoretic and transaction costs examination of interfirm cooperation', *Academy of Management Journal*, **36**(4): 794–829.

Penrose, E.T. (1959), *The Theory of the Growth of the Firm*, New York: Wiley.

Porter, M.E. and Fuller, M. (1986), 'Coalitions and global strategy', in M.E. Porter (ed.), *Competition in Global Industries*, Boston, MA: Harvard Business School Press, pp. 315–43.

Punj, G. and Stewart, D.W. (1983), 'Cluster analysis in marketing research: review and suggestions for application', *Journal of Marketing Research*, **20**: 134–48.

Reuer, J.J. and Miller, K.D. (1997), 'Agency costs and the performance implications of international joint venture internalization', *Strategic Management Journal*, **18**(6): 425–38.

SAS (1989), *SAS/STAT User's Guide*, Vol. 1, Cary, NC: SAS Institute Inc.

Saxton, T. (1997), 'The effects of partner and relationship characteristics on alliance outcomes', *Academy of Management Journal*, **40**(2): 443–61.

Seyoum, B. (1996), 'The impact of intellectual property rights on foreign direct investment', *Columbia Journal of World Business*, Spring: 51–9.

Strebel, P.J. (1983), 'The stock market and competitive analysis', *Strategic Management Journal*, **4**: 279–91.

Summers, R. and Heston, A. (1991), 'The Penn World Table (Mark 5): an expanded set of international comparisons', *Quarterly Journal of Economics*, **106**(2): 327–68.

UNCTAD (1997), *World Investment Report: Transnational Corporations, Market Structure, and Competition Policy*, New York: United Nations.

Wheeler, D. and Mody, A. (1992), 'International investment location decisions', *Journal of International Economics*, **33**: 57–76.

APPENDIX

Table 10A.1   Key theoretical influences on joint venture performance

Cluster variates	Theoretical rationale
Joint venture's task-complexity (*TCPLX*)	Complex tasks increase asset specificity (Garcia-Canal, 1996) as well as the need for inter-partner coordination (Killing, 1988), thus raising the risk of opportunistic exploitation by partners (Das et al., 1998)
Partner–venture business scope (*SCOPE*)	Greater product-market overlap facilitates scale and/or scope economies (Harrigan, 1988; Koh and Venkatraman, 1991) and lowers the costs of organizing resources (Demsetz, 1988) within the joint venture context
Inter-partner rivalry (*RIVAL*)	Greater overlap between partners' product-market scope facilitates scale and/or scope economies (Bleeke and Ernst, 1991; Koh and Venkatraman, 1991). However, it also increases the risk of opportunistic exploitation by partners (Park and Russo, 1996)
Firm size (*FSIZE*)	The largeness of firms indicates availability of (slack) resources with implications for their possible suboptimal deployment (Reuer and Miller, 1997). Size differentials hint at differentials in partners' administrative systems and procedures (Porter and Fuller, 1986), and so at differences in the cost of implementing a joint venture's plans
Previous joint venture experience (*JVEXP*)	Greater experience provides partners with the criteria for judging the efficacy of actions, such that experienced partners can better anticipate challenges related to their ventures' ultimate success (Harrigan, 1988). Moreover, greater experience lowers the cost of monitoring partners' conduct (Park and Russo, 1996)
Joint ventures' ownership structure (*OWNER*)	Ownership structure provides a rough indicator of partners' equity-based relative bargaining power (Fagre and Wells, 1982) and control (Bleeke and Ernst, 1991). Thus it hints at the complexity of managing joint ventures (Killing, 1988), and at the risk of opportunistic exploitation by partners (Park and Russo, 1996)
Joint ventures' decision-making structure (*DCMKG*)	Shared decision-making implies close interaction between partners, which facilitates inter-partner trust (Parkhe, 1993) and organizational learning (Saxton, 1997)
Partners' relative competitive position (*RLPOS*)	Relatively 'weak' resources limit a firm's potential for creating competitive advantage (Bresser et al., 1994) and raise the cost of joint venture management (Bleeke and Ernst, 1991)
Availability of location-specific skilled labor (*SKILL*)	Access to location-specific skilled labor yields a cost advantage to firms (Culem, 1988; Kravis and Lipsey, 1982). Moreover, the availability of skilled labor facilitates creation of knowledge-based externalitics (Braunerhjelm and Svensson, 1996)
Joint venture host country market size (*MSIZE*)	Large markets facilitate economies of scale (Braunerhjelm and Svensson, 1996; Davidson, 1980), and lower the breakeven level of international market entry (Kravis and Lipsey, 1982)
Growth rate of joint venture host country market (*MKTGR*)	Growing markets stimulate local demand (Culem, 1988) by increasing local income and purchasing power (Loree and Guisinger, 1995)

Table 10A.1   (continued)

Cluster variates	Theoretical rationale
Type of joint venture partner (*PTYPE*)	The dissimilar agendas of profit-seeking firms and state-owned enterprises require dissimilar approaches to joint venture management (Lummer and McConnell, 1990). This jeopardizes joint venture performance (Child and Markoczy, 1993). However, local partners (firms as well as state-owned enterprises) can also be important resource providers (Makino and Delios, 1996)
Property rights regime in joint venture host country (*PATNT*)	Strong property rights regimes offer protection against unfair competitive appropriation (Seyoum, 1996), and thus lower the business costs for economic actors (North, 1991)
Political risk in joint venture host country (*PRISK*)	Low levels of political risk render firms less vulnerable to the downside effects of unanticipated government-induced discontinuities. This preserves the value-in-use of firms' resource deployments (Dunning and Rugman, 1985)
Trading openness in joint venture host country (*TRADE*)	More 'open' trading regimes lower factor prices (Kravis and Lipsey, 1982) and thus reduce production costs. Moreover, such regimes lower firms' costs of obtaining local information (Benito and Gripsrud, 1995). However, open regimes also remove government-induced market failures (Kravis and Lipsey, 1982), and so eliminate economic rents (Agarwal and Ramaswami, 1992).
Cultural distance between partners' home and host countries (*CDIST*)	Greater cultural distance increases firms' perceived business uncertainty (Benito and Gripsrud, 1995) as well as the information costs of operating in international locations. Conversely, smaller cultural distance facilitates transfer of firms' home country management techniques (Bleeke and Ernst, 1991; Davidson, 1980), and reduces 'spatial transaction costs' (Dunning, 1998)

11 Building competitive advantage in international acquisitions: grey box conditions, culture, status and meritocracy

Udo Zander, Lena Zander and H. Emre Yildiz

PRELUDE

'It's living hell, dear!' was the gut response from the person at the helm of a British company when he was asked over the phone by one of the authors of this chapter about what it was like to be acquired.[1] The statement not only illustrates the tremendous turmoil that occurs when established identities and ways of doing things are questioned and 'crown jewels' are seen as 'stolen', but also the frustration of a group of people when they feel left at the mercy of 'the conquerors', and their work is being critically examined by 'the other'. When 'the other' is perceived as culturally strange and/or inferior, more than verbal negative gut responses can be expected to influence the post-acquisition process. When the acquiring firm is trying to extract, recombine and further develop knowledge that resides with individuals and the social community in the acquired company, post-acquisition integration is almost always a formidable task and notoriously fraught with problems.

Therefore much of the literature on the strategic management of international acquisitions has had a prime focus on handling post-acquisition integration processes – and rightly so. As both parties will always potentially be able to learn from the takeover – and as mutual learning and future knowledge development require some degree of motivation, identification and loyalty of knowledgeable employees from 'both sides' in the acquisition – the initial effects of 'guessing about the other' will loom large. This was the focus of ideas introduced in Zander and Zander (2010), and we shall draw on this when developing and extending the reasoning to value creation through the building of competitive advantage in international cross-border acquisitions.

INTRODUCTION

In this chapter, we highlight the importance of initial reference conditions, involving perceived differences in culture and status, for integration process dynamics. The fact that the acquiring side is always lacking knowledge about important aspects of what is bought, that is, is unpacking a 'grey box', leads to conclusions regarding the implications of *ex ante* perceptions of culture and status and their ensuing effects on the integration process. Due to grey box conditions experienced by both the acquirer and acquisition target, stereotypical perceptions of culture and status of 'the other' will initially dominate and set the stage for subsequent integration efforts. We argue that the shadows cast by sometimes rather haphazardly submitted pre-acquisition culture and status perceptions are indeed long, and that effects can be felt in terms of loss of key employees, organizational inertia and lack of mutual learning throughout post-acquisition integration processes. Permeability of group boundaries and intergroup contact conditions are introduced as variables moderating the effects of initial perceptions. The establishment of an informed, legitimate, negotiated and transparent meritocracy is suggested as an 'egg of Columbus' for improving the odds of inclusion and retention of key individuals into a new post-acquisition company that can harbor and develop capabilities leading to sustainable competitive advantage.

The structure of the chapter is the following: we shall start by introducing the importance and nature of international acquisitions, where we focus on the grey box perspective and knowledge before turning our discussion to the role of culture and status. In the subsequent sections we present a model of the influence of culture and status perceptions on post-acquisition acculturation and learning outcomes. We also introduce two moderating variables related to group boundaries and contact conditions. Before concluding, we propose and discuss how the establishment of a meritocracy can resolve some of the problematic and complex issues in international post-acquisition processes.

THE IMPORTANCE AND NATURE OF INTERNATIONAL ACQUISITIONS

International acquisitions account for nearly 70 percent of worldwide foreign direct investment (FDI) and therefore constitute the main vehicle through which multinational companies (MNCs) undertake investments in foreign-controlled assets (Peng, 2008; UN Conference on Trade and Development, 2000). The value of the over 300 deals closed in 2007 was over US\$ 1.6 billion, and in many OECD countries, cross-border mergers and acquisitions account for more than half of total FDI (OECD, 2007). It has been suggested that the majority of these cross-border transactions are unsuccessful or that the success rate is mediocre at best (see e.g. Kitching, 1967; Sirower, 1997; KPMG, 1999; Marks and Mirvis, 2001; King et al., 2004; Moeller et al., 2005; Cartwright and Schoenberg, 2006). However, rather ironically, this particular *modus operandi* of international expansion and growth continues relentlessly.

Acquisitions are not only a means of rapid growth, market entry, expansion and dominance – as in the case of the upsurge of acquisitions for instance in the European Union before its inception – but also a vehicle for acquiring critical technology, knowledge and capabilities, and strategically recombining and developing them (Hitt et al., 1991; Chaudhuri and Tabrizi, 1999; Coff, 1999; Ahuja and Katila, 2001; Ranft and Lord, 2002; Graebner, 2004; Al-Laham and Amburgey, 2005; Prabhu et al., 2005; Puranam and Srikanth, 2007). Great sums of money and future competitive advantage are at stake for individual firms involved, and post-acquisition process improvements on the fronts of learning and capability upgrading/improvements (even on the margin) are eagerly sought after.

In many cases, acquirers pursue 'predator and vulture strategies' (Verbeke, 2010), which entail accessing and securing resources by dominating, radically changing and/or eliminating the acquisition target. We see this kind of post-acquisition integration as neither particularly complex nor terribly interesting. When valuable resources have been captured and/or the acquirer's dominant logic has been introduced by force, the 'job is done' and the remnants of the acquired operations are left by the wayside. It has however been argued that heavy-handed hit-and-run behavior is not sustainable in the international acquisition sphere. As Hans Werthén, the long-time and legendary CEO of white-goods giant Electrolux, who was responsible for more than 200 acquisitions over 20 years that saw the company's sales grow by a factor eight and profitability rise, succinctly put it: 'The trick to doing business is being welcomed back.' If the reputation and legitimacy that an MNC and its management team attain over time as an acquirer do indeed affect the results of future attempts to integrate foreign units, unpacking an acquired grey box needs to be done with care to reap the full benefits of ensuing acquisitions. When often tacit valuable knowledge residing in key personnel, groups or organizing principles needs to be identified, studied and absorbed, careful integration of the acquired company and its personnel suddenly takes center stage. It could thus be argued that while the decisive brutality of predator and vulture strategies is rather straightforward, integration processes are often socially complex and intricate enough to deserve the full attention of managers and organization scholars alike.

When we think about mutual learning in acquisitions, the knowledge asymmetries both across and within firms should be the focus. In order to understand the situation of individuals acting on behalf of an acquiring company when trying to gain access to and utilize knowledge, we have earlier suggested that post-acquisition integration efforts should be seen as attempts to unpack a grey box (Zander and Zander, 2010).[2] The notion of an acquired company as a grey box is a simple reflection of the fact that people in the acquiring MNC will not know everything they would like to, before they start working with the target of acquisition. No due diligence in the world will for example ever be able to unravel the way a targeted company develops new technology through internal discovery, promotion, commercialization and international transfer. The fact that only certain things about an intended acquisition target are known before the post-acquisition integration process starts implies that an international acquisition should be seen as unpacking a grey box instead of the traditional 'black box' (or for that matter a 'white', 'glass', or 'clear' box).[3] When acquiring a company, the buyers are, to our mind, dealing with a system where the inner components or logic are only *partly* available for inspection at the outset. It is practically impossible to take stock of and communicate levels of technological competence, convey the workings of complex routines, map out employee skills and characteristics, explain higher-order organizing principles, and understand often implicit corporate values and culture before accessing an acquisition target. Even in cases when acquiring companies act as 'white knights' (and are contacted by the management of the would-be acquisition target) and where target companies clearly signal and (imperfectly) communicate their possession of valuable tacit capabilities and skills (Al-Laham and Amburgey, 2005), important content of the acquired grey box remains opaque. Before the unpacking of the grey box, managers and other employees in the acquiring company will often have a perception of the acquisition target's culture, performance in the marketplace, general level of technology, financial position and so on. Unfortunately, the fact is that even these rather general perceptions may prove to be wrong once the unpacking of an acquired company begins. The notion of post-acquisition processes as unpacking grey boxes thus implies a high probability of surprises and unexpected findings for people in both the acquiring and acquired companies. A certain openness of mind,

Fingerspitz-gefühl, willingness to communicate and learn, and process sensibility are required to handle negative surprises and to realize unexpected potential benefits.

In the next two sections, we shall revisit empirical findings regarding international acquisitions and try to develop ideas for contemporary scholars interested in complex integration processes involving mutual learning when integrating human resources, tasks and cultures. We shall discuss the consequences of the impossibility to know exactly what is acquired (the grey box) and the initial conditions in terms of perceived cultural and status differences for post-acquisition integration process dynamics. We also suggest possible ways to ensure that acquired knowledge and key personnel remain in the new entity to enhance sustainable competitive advantage.

A Grey Box Perspective on International Acquisitions

Viewing acquisition targets as grey boxes promotes a longitudinal approach to studying international acquisitions, focusing on informal systems and procedures, and exploration processes. The grey box view fundamentally reflects a research tradition born in close contact with large MNCs from small countries[4] (Zander and Glimstedt, 2006). In this research, the idea that MNC headquarters (or acquirers) can rarely know what goes on in the periphery (acquired firms) is a central point, as is the relative lack of parochialism on the part of managers in MNCs from small countries and their related willingness to learn from others. A related strong belief in the importance of foreign units and 'the periphery' for innovation and technological development (Regnér, 2003), combined with a belief in the impossibility of top–down control due to information and knowledge gaps, further fuels the logic. This approach also reflects ideas and visions of the knowledge-based view (see e.g. Kogut and Zander, 1992, 1993, 1996; Nonaka 1994; Zander and Kogut, 1995; Grant, 1996; Spender, 1996; Grandori, 2001; Grandori and Kogut, 2002; and Nickerson and Zenger, 2004.

This 'knowledge movement' (Eisenhardt and Santos, 2002) has emerged as an important part of the explanatory structure of management research, and has manifested itself in organization studies, strategic management, strategic human resource management (HRM), innovation studies, technology management and certain parts of economics[5] (Foss, 2009; Felin and Foss, 2005, 2009). The knowledge-based view has certainly in the past been criticized for its lack of emphasis on the use of organizational forms and governance arrangements to curb opportunism and gaming. The discourse, assumptions and theories on creating new enlarged social communities, as well as trusting and learning from 'others' in order to acquire capabilities used for example in Bresman et al. (1999), have thus also over the years been seen by some organizational economics scholars as part of an overly 'kind', 'virtuous' and possibly 'naïve' world-view. Recent developments, however, have led to leading organizational economics scholars arguing for establishing and strengthening the integrative links between organizational economics and the organizational capabilities view.

Based on an invocation of culture and status perceptions, we shall also point to some specific governance and organizational arrangements emerging from the knowledge-based view reasoning that could lead to value-creating post-acquisition processes in cases where knowledge and learning are seen as strategically important. The connection between knowledge and culture is made explicit in earlier work on the 'metanational'

(Doz et al., 2001) with its global reservoirs, knowledge brokerage and orchestration. Global inculcation of beliefs (often discussed as the creation of a 'global corporate culture') is also seen as a remedy for acquiring firms struggling to 'unite the forces'. The MNC is increasingly viewed as an umbrella under which cultural perspectives, experiences and insights can be leveraged. Doz et al. (2001), for instance, argue that the 'metanational' company will increase the knowledge stock by valuing cultural differences globally.

Regnér and Zander (2011) also focus on knowledge creation, the process by which MNCs combine and recombine knowledge. They suggest the social identity frame as a socio-cognitive deduction that invokes certain cognitive interpretations and normative evaluations in relation to knowledge. While a common corporate social identity frame in an MNC promotes knowledge transfer, the diversity within and between various subunits' social identity frames and the interchange among them are seen as advancing knowledge creation. Although this partly involves a serendipitous process, it promotes an MNC advantage compared to local firms in terms of both knowledge exploration and integration. Moreover, the advantage is firmly rooted in social complexity and may thus provide for sustainable competitive advantage.

Knowledge in International Acquisitions

Acquisitions are, as we have suggested, rarely just about securing the tangible assets of another firm. In many cases, tacit knowledge and human resources are the key elements that may affect the success of newly created organizations, which makes post-acquisition personnel turnover at all levels a critical issue (Sales and Mirvis, 1984; Walsh, 1989; Walsh and Ellwood, 1991; Cannella and Hambrick, 1993; Krug and Nigh, 1998; Lubatkin et al., 1999; Bergh, 2001; Krug and Hegarty, 2001; Ranft and Lord, 2002; Davis and Nair, 2003; Krug, 2003; Very, 2004; Kiessling and Harvey, 2006). Key individuals (or groups) may possess critical, organizational, technological as well as local institutional knowledge.

Research suggests that international acquisitions lead to higher than normal turnover among target company management and other employees compared to purely domestic acquisitions (Krug and Hegarty, 1997; Bergh, 2001), making commitment among key persons to the merged organization a priority in the post-acquisition process (Raukko, 2009). If learning from international acquisitions is to materialize, and the aim of the acquisition is to obtain technology, it is important to find out who knows what, and to motivate key personnel to 'stay on board' and make them committed to the success of the new organization. If the Hirschmanian (1970) 'exit' of important personnel is to be avoided at all cost, 'loyalty' seems to be something to strive for. However, we would also like to argue that in order to learn from international acquisitions, 'voice' on the part of key persons in the target company should not only be tolerated but also encouraged and cherished as a way to learn from the acquisition. If important people are 'seen and heard', taken seriously, and are rewarded for their efforts, and if they see an interesting future for themselves, they will most likely contribute to the benefit of the new joint organization.

A remaining problem in a situation of unpacking an acquired grey box is, of course, to get the right people to stay and to voice their opinions (see also Bergh, 2001). Who is 'right' inevitably depends on a variety of factors such as strategic intent behind the acquisition, capabilities, attitudes, as well as aspirations of employees. The prevention of post-acquisition turnover of acquired organization executives has been highlighted in the literature, emphasizing the problem of people in leading positions having to undergo the often difficult transition of becoming 'a small fish in a big pond' instead of 'a big fish in a small pond' (Walsh, 1988; Hambrick and Cannella, 1993). This problem is amplified when acquisitions are of cross-border nature (Krug and Hegarty, 1997; Krug and Nigh, 2001). Much of the process-oriented literature on acquisitions not surprisingly adheres to the central premise that the successful integration of acquisitions includes the retention of top managers in combination with effective communication and active HRM within the post-acquisition period (Jemison and Sitkin, 1986; Shrivastava, 1986; Haspeslagh and Jemison, 1991). As systematic differences in HRM practices exist over national cultures (see e.g. Brewster et al., 1992; Claus, 2003), it is plausible to assume that (modal) managers from different countries behave quite differently both when opening 'grey boxes' and when experiencing integration efforts.

Apart from able executives, key people highly desired by acquirers are often scientists and R&D workers. These 'prima-donnas' (Paruchuri et al., 2006) are conscious of their value to the company, but at the same time are quite sensitive to disturbances in their surrounding knowledge networks. As often witnessed in academia, managing a tight group of at the same time individualistic, highly self-reliant and authority-challenging researchers is a daunting task.[6] Similar patterns are discernible in other 'intellectual-property'-generating work settings. Identifying, retaining and managing key 'scientists whose work is deeply embedded in the acquired company' (Verbeke, 2010) is thus frequently as difficult as it is important for extracting value from an acquisition. To make matters worse, Zander (1991) and Zander and Kogut (1995) show that the loss of key personnel is a major factor increasing the risk of rapid imitation of unique technologies underlying sustainable competitive advantage.

During a post-acquisition process, identification of key personnel is a complex task that goes beyond mapping managers and scientists, and who is considered 'key' can also change over time and depending on strategic considerations. Importantly, in the context of unpacking a grey box, key personnel might be difficult to identify both from the acquiring and the acquired companies' viewpoint. On the part of the acquiring company, this is often simply a result of lacking knowledge about target company employees and their performance. On the part of the acquired firm, factors clouding the judgment as to who is part of the 'key personnel' group can be blindness to contributions by certain employees, historical interpersonal loyalties and a lack of understanding of the strategic objectives of the new organization.

One of the most striking and illustrative examples of both the importance and 'evasiveness' of key personnel comes from global construction- and mining-equipment manufacturer Atlas Copco.[7] Some 40 years ago, a number of producers of pneumatic rock drilling equipment had started developing the hydraulic technique demanded by customers interested in more efficient drilling machines. The first company to introduce the new type of equipment was the French company Montabert. Atlas Copco learned from the initial quality problems that the French experienced, and in 1973 introduced the first reliable hydraulic rock drill – the COP 1038 HD. Superior penetration rate, operational reliability and low drilling costs were fundamental reasons why the COP 1038 became the world's bestselling hydraulic rock drill.[8] The production and improvement of generations of hydraulic rock drills in Atlas Copco depended critically on one key employee (Mr

Hellman), who had acquired particular experiential knowledge about the hardening of the steel. His non-codified knowledge about how various drill designs would react to different types of hardening baths was instrumental in the introduction of new generations based on the initial innovation. Newly employed design engineers would look up Hellman for his advice (often resulting in a dirty fingerprint on a draft blueprint indicating where crucial holes should be placed) when he was tinkering in his hardening baths in the basement. Unfortunately, Mr Hellman left the company when a move of company facilities from one part of Stockholm to another was announced, and corporate management only much later understood the significance of the loss. It is also highly unlikely that a potential acquirer of Atlas Copco would have been able to identify Hellman's knowledge and importance *ex ante*. It is our contention that only heavy socialization efforts with resulting hands-on cooperation and exchange of knowledge could have alerted both companies' management to this evasive source of competitive advantage.

Thus a typical (but often neglected) grey-box problem is that not even management in the acquired company is aware of who the key people are that enable important work practices and drive the technological development. In general, there is empirical evidence that members of organizations do not know and agree on where in the company strategic capabilities reside. In an in-depth empirical study of capabilities central to knowledge management efforts in large leading MNCs, Denrell et al. (2004) show that the median inter-rater correlation for capabilities designated as strategic by top management is as low as 0.28. In other words, there is very little agreement on 'who knows what' in a multinational company. Analysis of the determinants of reliability show that the difference in evaluations is the largest for subsidiaries that managers know less about, for younger subsidiaries, and for subsidiaries in less important markets. Possibly, the 'fresh eyes' of an acquirer with novel strategic ideas can cut through the problems of identifying valuable knowledge, but the task is far from trivial.

In the literature, a rapid pulling in of mostly codified, patented knowledge from the acquired company to the acquiring company has often been interpreted as an attempt to learn more about the knowledge in order to build future possibilities for cooperation, recombination and innovation. It can however also be seen as a 'pre-emptive strike', emptying the acquired firm of valuable knowledge. Following this logic, the simplest explanation of what happens immediately after an acquisition is probably illustrated by the image of letting hordes of curious engineers into an until-recently closed technological 'toy store'. We believe that often the real value of accessing the 'toy store' is found in future close cooperation with store management, the designers, makers and sellers of 'the toys', which we believe requires a curious but also mutually decorous approach where knowledge is valued and identities are respected.

THE ROLE OF CULTURE AND STATUS

In order to pursue strategic objectives and secure value creation (Haspeslagh and Jemison, 1991), acquiring companies often impose considerable system changes on the target company, and initiate changes in administrative procedures, HRM procedures and leadership styles. International acquisitions involve unique challenges when changing ways of doing things (routines) in the acquired company due to their nature of bridging various economic, institutional, regulatory and cultural structures (Child et al., 2001; Very and Schweiger, 2001). This process is a chain of actions and reactions bounding between the acquiring and acquired companies where not only the former but also the latter 'acts', setting off or spiraling the chain (Zander and Lerpold, 2002).

Much of the literature concerning human resources in acquisitions deals with negative employee attitudes during the post-acquisition process, including lack of motivation, commitment, job satisfaction, productivity and performance in a stressful world characterized by power struggles and high employee turnover (Walsh, 1988; Buono and Bowditch, 1989; Cartwright and Cooper, 1990, 1993; Datta, 1991; Haspeslagh and Jemison, 1991; Schweiger and DeNisi, 1991; Gutknecht and Keys, 1993; Very et al., 1997; Hubbard, 1999; Marks and Mirvis, 2001; Risberg, 2001; Kusstatscher and Cooper, 2005; Klendauer and Deller, 2009; Raukko, 2009). To explain these negative attitudes, and their effects on knowledge transfer in acquisitions, scholars have persistently been concerned with issues of 'strategic' and 'cultural fit' or compatibility (see e.g. Jemison and Sitkin, 1986; Haspeslagh and Jemison, 1991; Cartwright and Cooper, 1993; Weber, 1996; Birkinshaw et al., 2000). The importance of cultural differences at the organizational and national level for the success of acquisition processes has repeatedly and consistently been invoked over time (Janson, 1994; Very et al., 1997; Morosini et al., 1998; Zaheer et al., 2003; Zander and Lerpold, 2002; Sarala and Vaara, 2010).

The reason for integration problems is indeed, as we see it, found in cultural dynamics that are fundamentally the result of identity clashes combined with fundamental underlying authority struggles. An acquiring company – with its own history, cultural background, values, organizational principles and view of the target company – is suddenly put in a position where it can dominate an acquired company (with its own background, practices and opinions). A long history of pre-acquisition interaction of the firms, sometimes in a competitive setting, might further complicate integration and cooperation (Zander and Lerpold, 2002). As the target company is a grey box, wherein it is not entirely clear what or who is valuable, a process of effective post-acquisition learning about the acquired company and its employees is of the essence. Often, the target company's knowledge about a potential acquirer is also quite limited, probably biased by reputation, possibly tainted by earlier interaction, or at least colored by common knowledge (Zander and Lerpold, 2002). Thus earlier superficial and superstitious learning, resulting in both cultural stereotyping and perceived status superiority (or anxiety), on both sides, may often complicate mutual learning, and poison attempts at integration and formation of a common identity. The acquired company's knowledge and capabilities may be destroyed through employee turnover and the disruption of organizational routines (Graebner, 2004) and the acquiring company may be reluctant to learn due to initial perceptions of culture and status. In this way, preconceived notions influence both the acquired and the acquiring firm, setting the stage for the integration process even before it has begun. In the next two sections we shall examine in more depth the importance of culture and status in turn, before discussing the acculturation process in international acquisitions.

The Importance of Culture

A large stream of management literature studying acquisitions, in particular the post-acquisition process takes a cultural perspective. Differences between the national cultures of acquirer and acquired companies have, after being largely ignored, become the most commonly examined factor to explain performance differences between domestic and international acquisitions (Arikan, 2004). When unpacking the grey box, cultural differences between the acquiring and the acquired firms surface and they are routinely reported to negatively influence post-integration efforts. Bresman et al. (1999) also argue that problems associated with knowledge transfer increase with geographic and cultural distance (Kogut and Singh, 1998). Overall, the negative view on cultural disparities has become more nuanced as empirical studies also displayed positive organizational outcomes associated with larger cultural distance (Morosini et al., 1998; Chakrabati et al., 2009). Dubbing cultural distance a 'two-edged sword' in international acquisitions, Reus and Lamont (2009) argue that integration capabilities are critical for whether positive organizational outcomes can be realized.

Cultural distance has been used, criticized and debated in the international management literature. Drogendijk and Zander (2010) take an inventory of the misleading assumptions that cultural distance rests on. Adding to those listed by others, and drawing on exciting new research, they propose alternative cultural conceptualizations useful for mapping companies and contrasting two cultural contexts. Björkman et al. (2007) build on dynamic interactions across cultural spheres (see also Shenkar, 2001; Shenkar et al., 2008), as they develop a model proposing a curvilinear relationship of the impact of cultural differences on capability complementarities.

Apart from any disagreements we may have with the measure as such, the view that large cultural distance will correspondingly involve large cultural differences, aligned with the 'cultural fit arguments' in the extant literature, is problematic. Despite its visual appeal, this view suffers from two serious flaws (Zander and Lerpold, 2002). First, to carry out cultural due diligence to evaluate cultural fit is not as clear-cut as perhaps envisioned by early advocates of such 'soft' evaluations in their ambition to achieve a 'fuller picture' of the acquisition 'target' by complementing the 'harder' financial side. Describing one culture in isolation from another often becomes misleading. Second, one of the main assumptions underlying a large body of the literature is that 'quantity' is key. The more cultural differences, the less fit, and correspondingly the more integration problems will follow. Without doubt quantity does matter, but a more critical part could be played by the nature of the cultural differences. For all practical purposes, only one cultural difference could exist, but it may be the one that not only sets the boat rocking but actually sinks it.

Subsequently, cultural differences in the grey box context of international acquisitions may vary in nature and quantity, but it is only during the integration process that the full effect of their impact on knowledge transfers becomes salient and decipherable. In addition, and most importantly, 'the other' almost always perceives cultures in value-laden terms. Respect and admiration are possible feelings towards 'the ways of the other', as well as disrespect and loathing. Even if cultural relativism is dominating the current discourse and many people would feel ill at ease with 'ranking' cultures, we assert that both national and corporate cultures[9] very often, rightly or wrongly, carry status connotations in the context of international acquisitions. An illustrative example featuring the case of DaimlerChrysler is provided by Pauleen et al. (2010). According to the authors, the German car maker, despite its meticulous preparatory work, found that unimaginable frictions and cantankerous behaviors led to mutual negative stereotyping (with each firm ranking themselves on top), the flight of their designers, and farcically petty wrangles over the size of business cards. Seemingly few *de facto* cultural differences took on a large proportion as they became the symptoms of a latent culture-status struggle. The authors conclude: 'it is clear that US–German spats were not inevitably the result of cultural differences. Rather, and at a more fundamental and manageable level, the issues of cultural differences were symptomatic of a situation in which various people at various levels in the organization considered themselves deceived, discredited or not treated as equals' (Pauleen et al., 2010, p. 386).

An exciting contemporary research agenda on the importance of individual-level integrative measures exists. Lyles and Salk, in their 1996 *Journal of International Business Studies* decade-award-winning article, highlight how high frequencies of interaction and communication in shared management international joint ventures led to the highest level of knowledge transfer. Frequent interaction, however, also made the parties involved more vulnerable to cultural conflicts and misunderstandings, increasing the need for managerial intervention. Björkman et al. (2007) model how individual integrative (social and informal) mechanisms (e.g. visits, personnel rotation, participation in joint training programmes and meetings and so on moderate the relationship between cultural differences and social integration. Negative effects of culture on integration are reduced, and integrative positive effects of social integration on capability transfer in cross-border acquisitions are found. The emphasis on individual action also comes to the fore in recent empirical work on international acquisitions. Brannen and Peterson (2009) draw our attention to how individual-level intervention promoted tacit learning and bonding in a Japanese–US merger. Successful interventions connecting employees to the acquirer's culture were found to minimize cross-cultural work alienation, avoiding the risk of failed integration and knowledge transfer. Even if these proposed integrative measures over time can refine and change perceptions initially held by 'outsiders', we believe that initial value-laden taken-for-granted assumptions taking the form of declarative knowledge can cast long shadows into the future. In particular, we are here thinking about perceived status differences between acquiring and acquired firms.

The Importance of Status

Incorporating status differences and their implications brings in an important dimension when thinking about the notion of grey box acquisitions. Status is one of the key parameters in social identity theory, which has been prominently used to understand the dynamics of sociocultural integration in acquisitions (Hogg and Terry, 2000). According to social identity theory, individuals are inherently motivated to enhance their self-concept and worth and, hence, are willing to be members of those groups that are positioned more favorably than others (Tajfel and Turner, 1979). In other words, whenever their existing group membership doesn't help attain positive social identity, members of low-status groups would exhibit the proclivity to gain membership in high-status groups. This point is supported by the corpus of empirical evidence reported in laboratory studies, in which it has been systematically shown that individuals belonging to high-status groups exhibit satisfaction with their group membership and exhibit patterns of ingroup favoritism (Ellemers et al., 1988). However, those who have membership in low-status groups tend to adopt an individual mobility strategy by seeking to gain membership in a high-status comparison group.

Applied to intergroup relations in the particular case of acquisitions, the preceding discussion shows that whenever members of an acquired company perceive their organization to occupy a lower position *vis-à-vis* an acquirer with higher status or image, they 'will attempt, as individuals, to de-identify and gain psychological entry to the other organization. This will increase their support for the merger and their commitment to and identification with the new merged organization' (Hogg and Terry, 2000, p. 133). As an alternative to this individualistic response, members of low-status groups may also utilize a social creativity strategy (Tajfel and Turner, 1979). This can be done by exhibiting outgroup favoritism on dimensions that are highly relevant to status differences, at the same time as displaying ingroup favoritism on new, and often irrelevant, dimensions as a way to make up for an otherwise unfavorable social identity (van Knippenberg, 1978). Social creativity strategy can also be manifested by altering the normative associations of the salient group attributes in order to render previously negative comparisons positive (e.g. 'Black is beautiful' or 'Less is more').

Earlier findings suggest that the choice between individual mobility and social creativity depends on the extent to which boundaries between groups are perceived to be permeable and transitory (Ellemers et al., 1988; Terry, 2001). For instance, the attrition of talent and capabilities could be the result of the unforeseeable or even unnoticed perceived changes in the status positions of groups of key personnel. Thus, analyzing the role of initial perceptions of culture and status in acquisitions is an alternative way of understanding the dynamics of exit (or selection) of acquired company employees, especially those who could better be identified as 'prima-donnas'. Similarly, roots of problematic post-acquisition issues such as loss of motivation, organizational commitment and identification at acquired firms can be traced in inherent perceived culture, status and power asymmetries among parties. The deleterious outcomes (e.g. syndromes of misidentification, schizo-identification and escalated job stress) of status and power differences in organizational contexts and feelings of being discriminated against and devalued are well documented in earlier status literature (see Elsbach, 1999; Jost and Elsbach, 2001).

We adopt the definition of status as 'a socially constructed, intersubjectively agreed-upon and accepted ordering or ranking of individuals, groups, organizations, or activities in a social system' (Washington and Zajac, 2005, p. 284). Accordingly, we contend that a fuller appreciation of status differences could also shed light on the oft-cited problem of alienation in acquisitions (see Brannen and Peterson, 2009). Perceived relative status characteristics, and expectations formed thereof, are also shown to affect the extent to which social actors are open and willing to accept new ideas, advice and practice coming from others (Kalkhoff and Barnum, 2000; Reid et al., 2009). Thus a systematic account of perceived status heterogeneities among the firms could also be informative concerning patterns (i.e. direction and effectiveness) of knowledge and capability transfer in acquisitions. As we emphasized earlier, opening the grey box in acquisitions entails, among other things, the challenge of identifying the key individuals in the acquired firms who for instance drive technological developments and innovations. Analyzing the incumbent status positions of individuals within the acquired firm, therefore, could help the acquirer to unpack the grey box by ascertaining who occupies high-status positions in the acquired firm thanks to their unique talent and capabilities. Also, at another level, systematic examination of pre-integration perceptions of 'the other's' culture and status may give important hints for what to expect from the integration process in terms of migration and cooperation patterns following an acquisition.

THE INFLUENCE OF PRE-ACQUISITION STATUS AND CULTURE PERCEPTIONS ON POST-ACQUISITION OUTCOMES

Acculturation theory was used early to provide a theoretical underpinning for immigration processes (see Berry, 1997 for an account of almost 30 years of his and others' work in this area). From theorizing about what happens when people with a different cultural background take up living in a foreign cultural environment, the step is not far to modeling post-acquisition and merger integration strategies and processes where acculturation theory is a given component (see e.g. Nahavandi and Malekzadeh, 1988; Haspeslagh and Jemison, 1991; Cartwright and Cooper, 1993; Marks and Mirvis, 2001; Zander and Lerpold, 2002). In the present chapter, we adopt the classic definition of acculturation as 'those phenomena which result when groups of individuals having different cultures come into continuous first-hand contact, with subsequent changes in the original culture patterns of either or both groups' (Redfield et al., 1936 as cited in Berry, 1997, p. 7). It is important to emphasize that this definition (a) implies potential cultural changes for both groups coming into contact with each other, and (b) entails the possibility of one or both parties' rejection of or resistance to the cultural elements imposed by the other.

The succinct models of acculturation in acquisitions provided by Nahavandi and Malekzadeh (1988) and Marks and Mirvis (2001) are particularly useful to examine different international post-acquisition integration end-states. These models specify acculturation outcome as a function of two key factors. The first is the degree of cultural change in the acquired firm during the post-acquisition phase. It is determined by the acquired company members' perception of the attractiveness of the acquirer, as well as the extent to which members of the acquired firm value and are willing to preserve their own pre-acquisition culture. The second factor of acculturation is the degree of cultural change in the acquiring firm, which is shaped by the extent to which the culture of the acquirer tolerates and promotes multiculturalism, as well as by the extent to which the newly acquired firm is related to the core business activities and models of the acquirer. Positioning the degrees of the cultural changes in both parties in a two-dimensional space, archetypical modes of acculturation in acquisitions have been identified in earlier studies. Acculturation may thus take the form of integration, assimilation, separation or deculturation, depending on the parties' satisfaction with the existing culture and the attractiveness of the other culture (Nahavandi and Malekzahdeh, 1988; Cartwright and Cooper, 1993). Marks and Mirvis (2001), synthesizing and developing the earlier work on acculturation modes and post-acquisition outcomes, list symbiosis/transformation (instead of integration), absorption/assimilation, preservation/separation, reverse takeover (instead of deculturation), and additionally 'best of both' as five probable 'end-states' of an acquisition integration process.

Based on our reasoning around the inevitability of gauging 'the other' in international acquisitions and its effects, we find it appropriate to frame the discussion in terms of how the acquiring firm and the acquired firm see each other with respect to not only culture but also to status at the beginning of an integration process. Below we shall address how perceptions of the 'other' predict acculturation outcomes, where entering status perceptions into the initial conditions will lead to a partially different set of post-acquisition integration end-states from those we are accustomed to in the extant literature.

Perceptions of 'the Other' as Predictors of Acculturation Outcomes

The perceived status of 'the other', based on culture, historical levels of profitability, technological achievements and so on, plays a major role in determining the dynamics of the integration process and possibilities for mutual learning. Our earlier discussion of the alternative mechanisms by which individuals cope with status differences provides a pertinent theoretical ground on which we can theorize which specific acculturation integration end-states and learning outcomes are more likely than others.

We claim that these outcomes depend heavily on initial culture and status perceptions conjointly with openness to cultural change. Thus we argue that it is plausible to estimate the likelihood of a specific outcome based on the perceptions of acquirer and acquired firm regarding each others' culture and status. Our claim is predicated upon the premise that individuals' willingness to learn largely depends on (1) the status of the source and (2) the direction of cultural change. In particular, a focal entity is more willing to accept cultural change as long as it entails the emulation of an entity with perceived high status and legitimate leadership position (Berger et al., 1977), which in our application could correspond to a positively perceived acquiring firm, and/or as long as the cultural change can help the focal entity enhance self-worth and self-concept by moving the membership from a lower status group to a higher one (see e.g. Tajfel and Turner, 1979). The target's perception of the acquiring firm's status also becomes essential for the retention of key people working for the acquired company. Based on these conjectured relationships and outcomes, we shall briefly touch upon the learning outcomes in each of the acculturation modes presented in Figure 11.1.

We believe that this model (see Figure 11.1) departs from earlier acculturation models and advances our thinking in novel ways. First, it features the perceptions and aspirations of two firms (the acquiring on the y axes, and the acquired on the x axes) at the point of acquisition. Second, it shows the interaction of the dimensions of perceived status and aspirations for cultural change in international acquisitions clearly and makes it explicit. This leads us to a somewhat different set of acculturation outcomes than what we have seen in the extant literature. While we are used to reading about 'absorption' (Cell A) and recently also about 'reverse takeovers' (Cell D), the addition of a status perspective leads to two indeterminate outcomes in two cells, namely open conflict versus reinvention (Cell B), and coexistence versus cold war (Cell C). The acculturation and learning outcomes in Figure 11.1 is discussed in more detail below:

- *Cell A: Absorption* involves high aspirations of change and learning in the acquired firm, which is seen as having low status, and little change and learning in the acquirer, which is perceived as having high status (see Figure 11.1). Due to desires of belonging to a high-status community, individuals in the acquired firm will not resist being assimilated into the buying firm's culture. They could even pursue such assimilation proactively by means of individual mobility in order to get a foothold

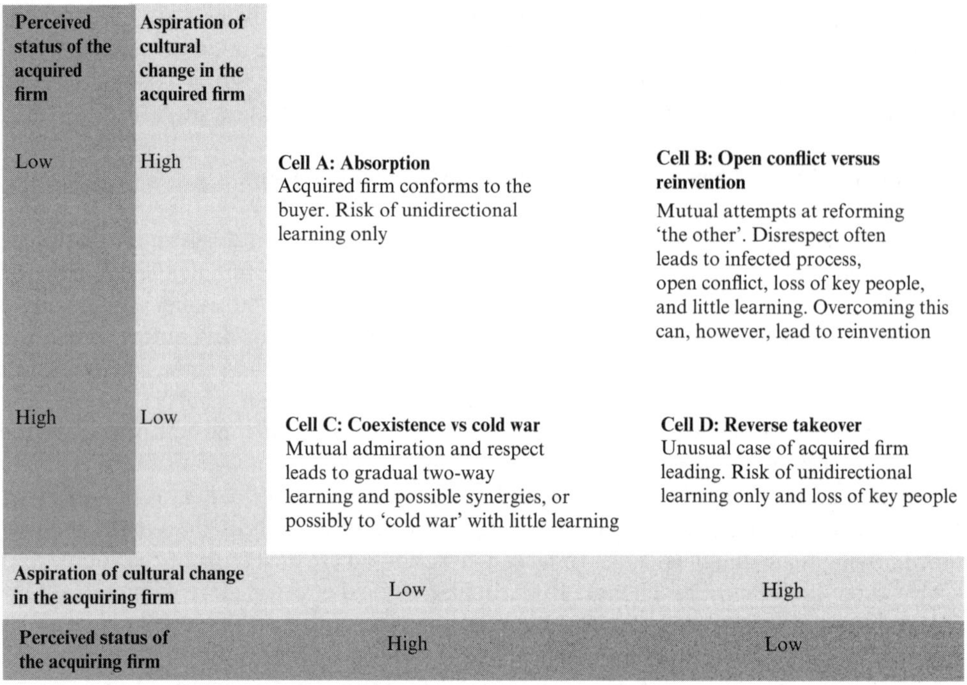

Perceived status of the acquired firm	Aspiration of cultural change in the acquired firm		
Low	High	**Cell A: Absorption** Acquired firm conforms to the buyer. Risk of unidirectional learning only	**Cell B: Open conflict versus reinvention** Mutual attempts at reforming 'the other'. Disrespect often leads to infected process, open conflict, loss of key people, and little learning. Overcoming this can, however, lead to reinvention
High	Low	**Cell C: Coexistence vs cold war** Mutual admiration and respect leads to gradual two-way learning and possible synergies, or possibly to 'cold war' with little learning	**Cell D: Reverse takeover** Unusual case of acquired firm leading. Risk of unidirectional learning only and loss of key people
Aspiration of cultural change in the acquiring firm		Low	High
Perceived status of the acquiring firm		High	Low

Source: Adapted from Marks and Mirvis (2001).

Figure 11.1 *Acculturation outcomes in acquisitions as predicted by perceived relative status positions and aspiration of cultural change*

in a company with a more desirable social image. The obvious risk is that there will be a unidirectional flow of knowledge; that is, relevant and potentially useful knowledge will not easily flow from the acquired firm to the acquirer.

- *Cell B: Open conflict versus reinvention* Open conflict is more likely when both the acquirer and acquired firm perceive each other as occupying low-status positions (see Figure 11.1). From a strategic vantage point, simultaneous changes at both ends of the deal could be attempted as a way of reinventing the organization and making a clean break with the perceived inefficiencies of the past (Evans et al., 2010). The initial condition of mutual disrespect is however not conducive to a process of parallel learning and change, and open conflict and loss of key people in both organizations remains an eminent risk. However, the acquirer and acquired companies' mutual desire to use the deal as a catalyst for a wholesale social and cultural change, for example by trying to attain a common brand new identity that is superior to any of the old ones, could possibly, but less probably, lead to reinvention.
- *Cell C: Coexistence versus cold war* is an integration end-state where both the acquirer and acquired firm go through a relatively gradual or low degree of post-acquisition cultural changes and learning. As we depict in Figure 11.1, this is the

acculturation outcome that *ex ante* entails two firms with mutual respect based on perceptions of high status. To be more specific, the acquirer respects the acquired firm's identity and therefore would tolerate its preservation and continuity in peaceful coexistence. A positive dynamic of gradual mutual learning is then a possibility, while a 'cold war' of attrition lurks in the background as both parties over time may want to prove their worth to the well-respected counterpart.

• *Cell D: Reverse takeover*, finally, represents the unusual case where the acquired company, in lieu of the acquirer, takes the lead. We expect this acculturation end-state to be more likely when an acquirer takes over a high-status target in order to, *inter alia*, get associated with the acquiring firm to improve its social standing and status in the eyes of both internal and external stakeholders. Examples of this are abundant in acculturation patterns observed in a recent wave of corporate takeovers by emerging country MNEs in developed markets (Kale et al., 2009). The flattering attention and willingness to change and learn on the part of the acquirer may counteract tendencies of 'keeping secrets' in the acquired firm. Similar to the case of absorption, an obvious risk in this case is however that relevant knowledge does not flow from the acquiring firm to the acquired. Employees in the acquired company may also begin to leave if changes in the acquiring company are slow.

In an ideal world, we could think of a desirable integration end-state where both organizations have learned from 'the other', undergone culture changes and re-evaluated negative and intimidating status perceptions in order to use best practices from both sides and achieve fruitful recombinations of capabilities. This is often the idea behind the 'symbiosis' and 'transformation' acquisition integration end-states, which we have not included in our model. Earlier studies claim that 'the best of both' is more common in deals that could be represented as 'mergers of equals' (Marks and Mirvis, 2001; Evans et al., 2010). However, the framework we propose wherein we include initial status perceptions in addition to the well-established cultural reasoning suggests that an acculturation outcome implying two-sided cultural change resulting in mutual learning is not easily achieved – albeit for different reasons in different cells of Figure 11.1. To this we shall in the next section add group boundary permeability and intergroup contact conditions as moderating the initial status and culture perceptions influence on the post-acquisition integration and acculturation outcomes.

Moderators of Pre-acquisition Status and Culture Influence on Post-acquisition Integration

Even if accounting for the perceived status of 'the other' firm involved in an acquisition process is useful to endogenize the mode of acculturation and connected degrees of change and learning, let us once again emphasize that the culture and status dimensions are helpful to estimate only the likelihood of a specific outcome. Our arguments concerning the culture- and status-driven acculturation processes presented above are built on the contention that members of cultures and high- and low-status groups would have certain 'default' responses to the changes they are exposed to throughout the post-acquisition process. To be more specific, there are reasons to expect that, in addition to a general tendency for most companies to secure their identity in an acquisition process, individuals in firms admiring their acquirers would be more open to changes initiated after the acquisition given that these changes would enable psychological entry into the other high-status group. In other words, individual mobility towards the core of the new entity would be an attractive option for employees on the 'admiring side'. On the other hand, individuals belonging to a group perceived as having relatively high perceived status would have fewer reasons to welcome challenges to the status quo. Hence we expect resistance to change and a low willingness to learn from 'the other' to be the default option for employees of a firm not admiring their acquisition counterpart.[10]

Even though these default responses are rather intuitive and follow straightforwardly from the basic principles of social identity theory, it is possible to pinpoint cases in which these acquisition outcomes become either impossible or less likely. We focus on two such circumstances under which one can observe such deviations. These are when (1) boundaries between the acquirer and the acquired are not permeable, and (2) the contact and acquaintance programs under which contact between the two firms takes place are not effective.[11]

Permeability of group boundaries
One of the main determinants of the way in which individuals cope with status hierarchies and more specifically their low/inferior position therein is the degree to which boundaries between their group and relevant comparison group(s) are seen as permeable (Tajfel and Turner, 1979). To the extent that objective and subjective barriers (or social and symbolic boundaries, to borrow the terminology of Lamont and Molnar, 2002) to leaving one's group are strong (intergroup boundaries are impermeable), individual mobility may be a less feasible or psychologically more costly way of dealing with status differences. Should this be the case, it would be more realistic to expect upwardly immobile members to adopt a social creativity strategy by transferring social comparison to new/irrelevant dimensions and/or alter the value connotations of status organizing characteristics. As a result, instead of being more open to change and eager to learn, initial 'admirers' of a culture under conditions of relative boundary impermeability become more resistant and hostile to changes initiated throughout the post-acquisition process. Therefore, whenever group boundaries are less permeable and transitory, unpacking of the grey box becomes more tedious and prone to risks such as attrition of talent, loss of commitment and motivation during the integration process influencing acculturation and learning outcomes.

Intergroup contact conditions
Individuals tend to use initial perceptions of the other's culture and status as a decision heuristic in order to be able to cope with the inherent uncertainties during the earlier stages of acquisitions. Subsequent stages of post-acquisition integration can, however, provide opportunities for obtaining additional information. Bresman et al. (1999) focus on successful attempts to create new enlarged social communities as well as trusting and learning from 'others' (including acquired or acquiring competitors). The results are especially interesting as they show that the attempts at socializing with what could well be perceived as 'the enemy' over time seem to facilitate a two-way transfer of technological know-how. Early studies of MNCs in general (Edström and Galbraith, 1977) and cross-border acquisitions in particular (Bresman et al., 1999) have revealed that increased

contact between subsidiaries/acquired units and headquarters/acquirers foster mutual understanding, shared objectives and reduced intergroup biases.

Explicating the fundamental notion of an intergroup contact hypothesis, Allport (1958, p. 454) states:

> To be maximally effective, contact and acquaintance programs should lead to a sense of equality in social status, should occur in ordinary purposeful pursuits, avoid artificiality, and if possible enjoy the sanction of the community in which they occur. The deeper and more genuine the association, the greater the effect. While it may help somewhat to place members of different ethnic groups side by side on a job, the gain's greater if these members regard themselves as part of a team.

The substantial body of empirical literature on the intergroup contact hypothesis reveals that to the extent that the conditions of effective contact are fulfilled, negative prejudices between groups are curtailed, common ingroup identity can be induced, intergroup cohesion is fostered, interactional anxiety is mitigated, and tolerance and trust among interacting parties are observed (see Pettigrew, 2008 for a review). In other words, the fulfillment of these conditions would engender the ideal situation under which intergroup contact can take place. While we concur with the intuition behind the idea that higher frequency of contact between firms would reduce intergroup biases and conflicts, an analysis of integration approaches in acquisitions would remain incomplete unless we acknowledged that 'theoretically, every superficial contact we make with an out-group member could by the "law of frequency" strengthen the adverse associations that we have' (Allport, 1954, p. 264). Hence intergroup contact can lead to the opposite of what is intended, fuelling negative initial perceptions of each other's status and cultural characteristics hampering the post-acquisition integration process, and ultimately lead to less than satisfactory acculturation outcomes.

Acculturation Outcomes: Culture, Status and Integration

Acculturation in acquisitions refers to the outcome of a cooperative process whereby the beliefs, assumptions and the values of two previously independent workforces form a jointly determined culture (Larsson and Lubatkin, 2001). In Figure 11.2 we present a dynamic model of acculturation in acquisitions building on and adapted from Zander and Lerpold (2002). In their post-acquisition integration model, as earlier mentioned in this chapter, a history of pre-acquisition interaction and knowledge about each other's reputation was explicitly introduced as determining the outset of a dynamic post-acquisition integration process characterized by a 'chain of action and reaction'.[12] In this chapter we theorize specifically on how status considerations of each other from both the acquiring and the acquired firm enter into what Zander and Lerpold (2002) label the pre-acquisition, acquisition integration, and adaptation phases. This is our attempt to specify and systematize the effects of salient initial heterogeneities including both perceptions of status and culture characteristics as well as the moderating effects of group permeability and intergroup contact conditions affecting the post-acquisition integration interaction and outcome (see Figure 11.2).

The starting condition of the model depicted in Figure 11.2 acknowledges the distinct culture and status characteristics of both acquirer and acquired firms and emphasizes, as

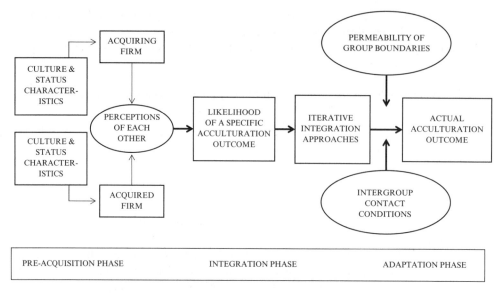

Source: Adapted from Zander and Lerpold (2002).

Figure 11.2   Model of the role of culture, status, boundary permeability and intergroup contact conditions in international acquisitions

we have discussed earlier in this chapter, the importance of initial perceptions of 'the other' for the dynamics of the integration phase.[13] A propelling assumption is that the acquisition process is inherently uncertain due to grey box properties of the companies involved. Therefore individuals involved in the process tend to use available perceptions and information about the 'others' in order to make sense of, adapt to and react to situations that occur and actions that take place.

By culture and status characteristics we mean implicitly or explicitly relativized attributes of focal social agents, which are associated with distinct moral, behavioral and performance expectations (Berger et al., 1980). Thus, by considering these characteristics, social actors form their view and expectations of each other. Culture and status not only generate certain expectations for the behavior but also make the individuals and organizations attain positive or negative degrees of respect in the eyes of others (Magee and Galinsky, 2008). The perceptions of both the acquirer and acquired firms related to their counterpart's culture and status, we argue, have direct implications for the ensuing process of acculturation and social integration. Even the iterative integration efforts that commonly involve 'integration managers', 'socialization activities' and meetings on a daily basis (Larsson and Lubatkin, 2001; Risberg, 2001), will be affected by a trajectory of action–reaction patterns with a history (Zander and Lerpold, 2002) reaching back at least to the pre-acquisition grey box conditions when stereotyping and rather uninformed ordering and ranking governs perceptions. Participation in corporate socialization mechanisms – which may include personnel rotation, short-term visits, joint training programs and meetings, and involvement in cross-unit teams, task forces and committees (see 'iterative integration approaches' in Figure 11.2), have been found to foster interpersonal network ties and informal relationships among personnel from the acquirer and acquired firms (Björkman et al., 2007) and lead to learning and knowledge transfer.

However, given what we have discussed and outlined above about the influence of acquiring and acquired firms' initial status and cultural perceptions of each other, and the moderating effects of group boundary permeability and intergroup contact conditions, a systematic transparent approach to retain key personnel and to choose leaders and managers becomes important.

THE MERITS OF MERITOCRACY

A central idea in building competitive advantage through international acquisitions is to, over time, create a joint social community to enable knowledge transfer and innovation through recombination (see Kogut and Zander, 1992; Regnér and Zander, 2011). The frequency of communications, visits, meetings, and the time elapsed after the date of acquisition facilitates a two-way transfer of technological know-how (Bresman et al., 1999). This illustrates well the knowledge-based theory of the firm's assertion that new knowledge is generated through continuous recombination in social communities with shared identity, and seems to resound well with the idea that the gradual building of a joint social community is beneficial if an acquired company is sought out for its technological treasures.

In some cases heavy involvement on the part of the acquiring company leads to mutual appreciation and agreement as to the long-term direction of the new company, in others to conflict. We have elaborated on the role of initial culture and status perceptions of each other as partial determinants of process outcomes, as well as on moderating variables related to group boundary permeability and intergroup contact. A number of activities and approaches have been proposed in the literature, all with the aim of creating a well-functioning new company where key personnel and capabilities are retained and recombined. It is our firm belief that the establishment of an informed, legitimate, negotiated and transparent meritocracy is an 'egg of Columbus' for improving the odds of inclusion and retention of key individuals into a new post-acquisition company that can harbor and develop capabilities leading to sustainable competitive advantage.

We thus believe that the literature on post-acquisition integration would benefit greatly from more of a study of microprocesses that key personnel are involved in, rather than trying to iron out differences and disagreements at the collective group and organizational levels. This resonates well with the current questioning of the 'black-boxing' of micro-level knowledge-related behaviors, such as knowledge sharing and integration behaviors. These ideas have led to consistent calls for the unpacking of microfoundations, that is, underlying individual-level microcomponents and actions, and interactional dynamics (see e.g. Felin and Foss, 2005; Gavetti, 2005; Felin and Hesterly, 2007). In the turmoil of an acquisition, when traditions are challenged and under threat, there is a possibility that previous ingroups are shattered and individuals start taking decisions more concerned with their own well-being rather than the former collective's. Sources of employee resistance to acquisitions may be individual or collective and may originate from different cultures but also from (often related) communication problems and negative effects of the acquisition at the personal level (Larsson et al., 2004). Depending on the individual, perceptions of identity, culture and status may or may not play a major role in his/her decisions about actions in future work-life. The decision to exit, remain loyal or raise one's voice is always personal, but definitely guided by perceptions of 'the other' in the context of international acquisitions.

Larsson et al. (2001) point to the importance of career concepts to better understand and manage sources and incentives for individual contributions and reactions to international acquisitions, in order to influence the resistance or support of people in the integration of two previously separate organizations. As 'merged' corporations integrate previously separate organizations, they can often disintegrate individual careers with lay-offs, reduced advancement opportunities, upset or changed career plans, and other resistance-generating changes. This is, according to the authors, the poorest means of mobilizing motivation, experience, commitment and competence, all of which are usually seen as critical justifications for international acquisitions in the first place. In *The Rise and Fall of Elites*, Pareto (1901/1991) argues that a dominant group survives only if it provides opportunities for the best persons of other origins to join in its privileges and rewards. This line of thought seems to us highly relevant for how to think about post-acquisition integration.

One way to increase inclusion and break deadlocks in post-acquisition processes would be to short-circuit conflicts based on stubborn conscious or subconscious adherence to pre-existing (or newly developed) views of 'the other'. This can be achieved, from the outset, by introducing a career system that gives all employees of the new company equal opportunity in the form of a transparent meritocracy. To increase the perception of equal opportunity in the new company, possibilities for training, professional and personal development across the board could be used to support the post-acquisition integration process. A meritocratic system gives opportunities and advantages to people on the basis of their contributions and abilities, rather than on the basis of their cultural or family background, job longevity, connections, status or other such attributes. We believe that people are more likely to contribute genuinely to the new company and maintain trust if there are clear promotion, advancement and recognition practices that are seen as fair and legitimate. In terms of our model in Figure 11.2, a functioning meritocracy can be seen as a tool to improve both inter-group permeability and contact.

A well-communicated post-acquisition meritocracy would ensure the possibility of upward mobility and inclusion in the new corporate 'elite' based on knowledge, skills and performance and irrespective of background and belonging. The key is to establish a career and reward system based on merit, and to rapidly effectuate a number of promotions in line with pronounced aims. We believe that bright individual prospects for employees in the new organization are necessary for people to downplay deep-seated loyalties with their old organizational unit in favor of the new company. Credible career opportunities in the new structure thus increase the possibility for individuals to improve status, job satisfaction, autonomy, professional development and personal growth – all factors that influence the decision to stay and be loyal (Krug and Nigh, 2001).

A definite possibility is, however, that initial culture or status differences strike back through selective perceptions of critical events and issues in the new company. Boussebaa and Morgan (2008) report a case where the concept of 'talent management', as understood by UK managers, could not simply be reproduced in the setting of an acquired French company being integrated. In the French unit, the idea of managing talent took on a different meaning and resulted in a complete failure of UK headquarters to develop a global talent management system. National cultures (manifested in institutional differences regarding management education) collided, status hierarchies were undermined, and the British acquirer gave up integration efforts and resorted to financial control to discipline the French unit (see also Faulkner et al., 2002).

Inevitably, the fairness and legitimacy of administrative systems in a new company formed through an international acquisition will be challenged by groups in both the acquiring and acquired companies feeling threatened by the changes. Both accusations of nepotism and rigging of systems are likely to be invoked. Therefore it is of great importance that human resource decisions are made jointly by knowledgeable, professionally respected representatives of both companies. Internally respected 'insiders' from the involved companies will be needed to help unpack the grey box and counter risks produced by initial culture and status perceptions. Discussions regarding the capabilities, knowledge and attitudes of employees in both the acquiring and acquired companies need to take place in the context of strategic intentions, and subsequent promotion decisions should be based on these. In order to identify key employees that are important for the success of the new organization, joint mapping-of-personnel exercises, heavy socialization and hands-on cooperation are beneficial. When key employees have been identified, ways in which individuals' contributions are recognized and valued must be decided upon. As each organization weights employees' contributions and abilities differently, it is important for managers to discuss the real reward systems that are in place in the merging companies and how these systems differ in the ways they are implemented and perceived by employees. The role of the corporate HRM function becomes strategically very important if a common meritocracy is to be established. This is in stark contrast to what often happens in international acquisitions (see e.g. Björkman and Söderberg, 2006).

Admittedly, the introduction of a 'negotiated' meritocracy requires personal integrity and professionalism from the managers involved. Discursive legitimation is also an essential part of the merger dynamics (Vaara and Monin, 2010). In whatever way managers communicate, behave and handle the situation, a certain attrition of employees is to be expected – some of them will unfortunately be 'key personnel'. Obviously the number of top managers competing for every position in the new post-acquisition company will normally increase. In order to ensure that not only managers from the acquiring company (who often negotiated the deal) initially occupy management positions in the new company, active involvement of the board or the owners may be required.[14] If this is carried out well, the increased competition from talented and capable employees in the acquired company can be used to weed out 'dead wood' in the acquiring company and to send signals of a working transparent meritocracy. Ideally, key personnel from both the acquiring and acquired company stay and are promoted while others from both camps leave. Inevitably, individuals will, after analyzing 'where the wind is blowing', self-select into categories of 'exit', 'loyalty' or 'voice'. Keeping close track on the profile of those choosing to exit is of utmost importance to evaluate if the acquisition aims will be achieved or not. These aims should be revised continuously with corresponding implications for acculturation, as more and more is known about the grey box as the culture and status perceptions change, and as new strategic opportunities may become apparent.

CONCLUSION

As scholars examining the multifaceted phenomenon of acquisitions across national and cultural borders, we need to use and further develop contemporary theories and models. This chapter is such an attempt. It is imperative to face the complexity of integrating international acquisitions today while retaining sight of crucial questions such as what the consequences of the grey box logic of international acquisition are. We have here begun to outline the effects of initial culture and status perceptions on integration processes, aiming at building competitive advantage in companies born through international acquisitions. We propose the introduction of a negotiated, transparent meritocracy as playing a key role in realizing learning objectives on the part of the involved actors.

NOTES

1. Reported in Zander and Lerpold (2002).
2. A thought experiment, presented in Zander and Zander (2010), inspired by Akerlof's 'lemon' metaphor and information asymmetries, might be enlightening at this point. Let us imagine a child involved in the 'lemonade business' wanting to acquire another's lemonade stand, with all its assets and personnel. Although our young acquirer has ample of time to observe the other business across the street in detail when sales are slow, there are most certainly aspects of the target business she or he will not know. One cannot, for instance, be sure about the recipe used in the secrecy of the kitchen lab, and there might be something the child across the street is saying or doing to prospective customers that makes them buy her lemonade instead of one's own. It is also hard to estimate the value of the acquisition target's external network (important, as it seems to affect sales), and the probability of the other child cooperating fully in the new 'lemonade-stand chain' to be formed in the neighborhood is unknown. Our simple point here is that if a lemonade stand is a grey box when it is an acquisition target, so is probably an infinitely more complex industrial firm, sometimes with its multiple functions distributed geographically. This fact should be reflected in our research on the integration of international acquisitions.
3. In software engineering the term 'white box' is used in the context that the program code can be seen, but the code is so complex that it might as well be a black box. Interestingly, in cybernetics Norbert Wiener (1961) saw the first step in self-organization as the ability to copy the output behavior of a black box.
4. Our interest in companies acquiring foreign units with the aim to access technology is no coincidence, but has emerged as a consequence of close contacts with CEOs, division heads and managers of Swedish MNCs. Influential executives and managers working for leading engineering-based Swedish MNCs have most often based their careers on the understanding of the development and acquisition of superior technology as well as the requirements for successful R&D processes. A successful career thus requires a technological perspective and deep understanding of how knowledge can be integrated into profitable technology-based innovations. In the context of doing research on these MNCs, a perceptive international business scholar involved in primary data collection will quickly, and at all levels of the corporate hierarchy, get involved in conversations regarding technology development (including acquisition) and transfer, competitive advantage, as well as power relationships based on knowledge.
5. A broad definition would include, for example, transaction cost economics, agency theory and information economics.
6. The process has appropriately been described as 'herding wild cats'
7. Earlier described in Zander (1991) and Zander and Zander (2010).
8. Atlas Copco realized early that the use of hydraulic technology gave an opportunity to use a better type of piston. Accordingly, a decision was taken to produce a drill with a so-called 'long and slender rock drill piston'. Using this design, the piston operated with higher impact energy than a thicker piston at the same maximum stress on the drill steel (until the late 1980s Atlas Copco had been the only producer using this solution). Atlas Copco also started producing a patented hydraulic shock absorber (1975), which until recently was unique in the industry. The shock absorber inside the drill protected the feed and boom of the rig from destructive forces. Installing a hydraulic shock absorber in the drill turned out to be very problematic, and Atlas Copco had some trouble with reliability of their initial products. These problems were eventually solved, and the new feature could be used to motivate a higher price of the drill since wear

was reduced and the life of drill-steel increased. The latter aspect was extremely important, since a large part of the costs in connection with rock drilling is the result of drill steel consumption.

9. We see national and corporate culture as closely related. Zander (2002) uses 'family' as a metaphor when arguing that national culture and national institutions are the 'parents' with organizational cultures as the 'children'. Just as siblings, organizational cultures, despite their differences, have similarities and share primary socialized values, beliefs and attitudes with their parents. Zander (2002) draws on a body of research demonstrating 'similarities' between companies with the same country of origin while differing from those 'born' in other countries

10. Throughout our reasoning we assume that admiration spills over and is picked up by the target of acquisition.

11. Perceived legitimacy and stability of the bases on which status distinctions are constructed are two additional factors that could determine individuals' choices of strategy to cope with status heterogeneities and achieve positive social identity (Haslam and Reicher, 2006). However, the definition of status we adopt in this chapter, which entails mutual agreement and consensus on status hierarchies (Washington and Zajac, 2005), makes these two factors less relevant to examine. Yet we encourage future conceptual and empirical research to encompass legitimacy and stability aspects while studying status and stratification processes in the context of acquisitions

12. Rottig (2011) has theorized on how internal and external social capital can mitigate negative effects of organizational and national cultural differences on post-acquisition integration over time.

13. It may be argued that the perception of self is as important, but we have focused on the primacy of attempts at understanding the relevant outside world and how it will affect us. Implicitly, notions of others' culture and status are of course rarely totally unrelated to (perceptions of) our own.

14. For simplicity we here assume that the acquiring company management occupies a dominant position in terms of decision-making and problem-solving.

REFERENCES

Ahuja, G. and R. Katila (2001), 'Technological acquisitions and the innovation performance of acquiring firms: a longitudinal study', *Strategic Management Journal*, **22**, 197–220.

Al-Laham, A. and T.L. Amburgey (2005), 'Knowledge sourcing in foreign direct investments: an empirical examination of target profiles', *Management International Review*, **45**(3), 247–75.

Allport, G.W. (1954), *The Nature of Prejudice*, Cambridge, MA: Addison-Wesley.

Allport, G.W. (1958), *The Nature of Prejudice* (abridged), Garden City, NY: Doubleday.

Arikan, A.M. (2004), 'Cross-border mergers and acquisitions: what have we learned?', in B.J. Punnett and O. Shenkar (eds), *Handbook for International Management Research*, Ann Arbor, MI: The University of Michigan Press, pp. 239–64.

Berger, J., M.H. Fisek, R.Z. Norman and M. Zelditch (1977), *Status Characteristics and Social Interaction: An Expectation-States Approach*, New York: Elsevier.

Berger, J., S.J. Rosenholtz and M. Zelditch (1980), 'Status organizing processes', *Annual Review of Sociology*, **6**, 479–508.

Bergh, D.D. (2001), 'Executive retention and acquisition outcomes: a test of opposing views on the influence of organizational tenure', *Journal of Management*, **27**(5), 603–22.

Berry, J.W. (1997), 'Immigration, acculturation, and adaptation', *Applied Psychology: An International Review*, **46**(1), 5–68.

Birkinshaw, J., H. Bresman and L. Håkanson (2000), 'Managing the post-acquisition integration process: how the human integration and task integration processes interact to foster value creation', *Journal of Management Studies*, **37**(3), 395–425.

Björkman, I. and A.-M. Söderberg (2006), 'The HR function in large-scale mergers and acquisitions: the case study of Nordea', *Personnel Review*, **35**(6), 654–70.

Björkman, I., G.K. Stahl and E. Vaara (2007), 'Cultural differences and capability transfer in cross-border acquisitions: the mediating roles of capability complementarity, absorptive capacity', *Journal of International Business Studies*, **38**, 658–72.

Boussebaa, M. and G. Morgan (2008), 'Managing talent across national borders: the challenges faced by an international retail group', *Critical Perspectives on International Business*, **4**(1), 25–41.

Brannen, M.Y. and M.F. Peterson (2009), 'Merging without alienating: interventions promoting cross-cultural organizational integration and their limitations', *Journal of International Business Studies*, **40**, 468–89.

Bresman, H., J. Birkinshaw and R. Nobel (1999), 'Knowledge transfer in international acquisitions', *Journal of International Business Studies*, **30**(3), 439–62.

Brewster, C., H. HoltLarsen and F. Trompenaars (1992), 'Human resource management in Europe: evidence from ten countries', *The International Journal of Human Resource Management*, **3**(3), 409–34.
Buono, A.F. and J.L. Bowditch (1989), *The Human Side of Mergers and Acquisitions*, San Francisco, CA: Jossey-Bass.
Cannella, A.A. and D.C. Hambrick (1993), 'Effects of executive departures on the performance of acquired firms', *Strategic Management Journal*, **14**(S1), 137–52.
Cartwright, S. and C.L. Cooper (1990), 'The impact of mergers and acquisitions on people at work: existing research and issues', *British Journal of Management*, **1**(2), 65–76.
Cartwright, S. and C.L. Cooper (1993), 'The psychological impact of merger and acquisition on the individual: a study of building society managers', *Human Relations*, **46**(3), 327–47.
Cartwright, S. and R. Schoenberg (2006), '30 years of mergers and acquisitions research: recent advances and future opportunities', *British Journal of Management*, **S1**, S1–S5.
Chakrabarti, R., S. Gupta-Mukherjee and N. Jayaraman (2009), 'Mars–Venus marriages: culture and cross-border M&A', *Journal of International Business Studies*, **40**, 216–36.
Chaudhuri, S. and B. Tabrizi (1999), 'Capturing the real value in high-tech acquisitions', *Harvard Business Review*, **77**(5), 123–30.
Child, J., D. Faulkner and R. Pitkethly (2001), *The Management of International Acquisitions*, Oxford: Oxford University Press.
Claus, L. (2003), 'Similarities and differences in human resource management in the European Union', *Thunderbird International Business Review*, **45**(6), 729–55.
Coff, R.W. (1999), 'How buyers cope with uncertainty when acquiring firms in knowledge-intensive industries: caveat emptor', *Organization Science*, **10**(2), 144–61.
Datta, D. (1991), 'Organizational fit and acquisition performance: effects of post-acquisition integration', *Strategic Management Journal*, **12**(4), 281–97.
Davis, R. and A. Nair (2003), 'A note on top management turnover in international acquisitions', *Management International Review*, **43**(2), 171–83.
Denrell, J., N. Arvidsson and U. Zander (2004), 'Managing knowledge in the dark: an empirical study of the reliability of capability evaluations', *Management Science*, **50**(11), 1491–503.
Doz, Y., J. Santos and P. Williamson (2001), *From Global to Metanational*, Boston, MA: Harvard Business School Press.
Drogendijk, R. and L. Zander (2010), 'Walking the cultural distance: in search of direction beyond friction', in T.M. Devinney, T. Pedersen and L. Tihanyi (eds), *Advances in International Management*, vol. 23, Bingley, UK: Emerald Publishing, pp. 189–212.
Edström, A. and J. Galbraith (1977), 'Transfer of managers as a coordination and control strategy in multinational organizations', *Administrative Science Quarterly*, **22**(2), 248–63.
Eisenhardt, K.M. and F.M. Santos (2002), 'Knowledge-based view: a new view of strategy', in A. Pettigrew, A. Thomas and R. Whittington (eds), *Handbook of Strategy and Management*, London: Sage, pp. 139–64.
Ellemers, N., A. van Knippenberg, N. De Vries and H. Wilke (1988), 'Social identification and permeability of group boundaries', *European Journal of Social Psychology*, **18**, 497–513.
Elsbach, K.D. (1999), 'An expanded model of organizational identification', *Research in Organizational Behavior*, **21**, 163–200.
Evans, P., V. Pucik and I. Björkman (2010), *The Global Challenge: International Human Resource Management*, New York: McGraw-Hill/Irwin.
Faulkner, D., R. Pitkethly and J. Child (2002), 'International mergers and acquisitions in the UK 1985–94: a comparison of national HRM practices', *The International Journal of Human Resource Management*, **13**(1), 106–22.
Felin, T. and N.J. Foss (2005), 'Strategic organization: a field in search of microfoundations', *Strategic Organization*, **3**, 441–55.
Felin, T. and N.J. Foss (2009), 'Organizational routines and capabilities: historical drift and a course-correction toward microfoundations', *Scandinavian Journal of Management*, **25**(2), 157–67.
Felin, T. and W.S. Hesterly (2007), 'The knowledge-based view, nested heterogeneity, and new value creation: philosophical considerations on the locus of knowledge', *Academy of Management Review*, **32**, 195–218.
Foss, N.J. (2009), 'Alternative research strategies in the knowledge movement: from macro bias to micro-foundations and multi-level explanation', *European Management Review*, **6**(1), 16–28.
Gavetti, G. (2005), 'Cognition and hierarchy: rethinking the microfoundations of capabilities' development', *Organization Science*, **16**, 599–617.
Graebner, M.E. (2004), 'Momentum and serendipity: how acquired leaders create value in the integration of technology firms', *Strategic Management Journal*, **25**(8–9), 751–77.
Grandori, A. (2001), 'Neither hierarchy nor identity: knowledge governance mechanisms and the theory of the firm', *Journal of Management and Governance*, **5**, 381–99.

Grandori, A. and B. Kogut (2002), 'Dialogue on organization and knowledge', *Organization Science*, **13**, 224–32.

Grant, R.M. (1996), 'Towards a knowledge-based theory of the firm', *Strategic Management Journal*, **17**, 109–22.

Gutknecht, J.E. and B. Keys (1993), 'Mergers, acquisitions and takeovers: maintaining morale of survivors and protecting employees', *Academy of Management Executive*, **7**(3), 26–36.

Hambrick, D.C. and B. Cannella (1993), 'Relative standing: a framework for understanding departures of acquired executives', *Academy of Management Journal*, **36**(4), 733–62.

Haslam, S.A. and S. Reicher (2006), 'Stressing the group: social identity and the unfolding dynamics of responses to stress', *Journal of Applied Psychology*, **91**(5), 1037–52.

Haspeslagh, P.C. and D.B. Jemison (1991), *Managing Acquisitions: Creating Value through Corporate Renewal*, New York: The Free Press.

Hirschman, A.O. (1970), *Exit, Voice, and Loyalty: Responses to Decline in Firms, Organizations, and States*, Boston, MA: Harvard University Press.

Hitt, M.A., R.E. Hoskisson, R.D. Ireland and J.S. Harrison (1991), 'Effects of acquisitions on R&D inputs and outputs', *The Academy of Management Journal*, **34**(3), 693–706.

Hogg, M.A. and D.J. Terry (2000), 'Social identity and self-categorization processes in organizational contexts', *Academy of Management Review*, **25**(1), 121–40.

Hubbard, N. (1999), *Acquisition: Strategy and Implementation*, London: Palgrave Macmillan.

Janson, L. (1994), 'Towards a dynamic model of post-acquisition cultural integration', in A. Sjögren and L. Janson (eds), *Culture and Management: In a Changing Europe*, Stockholm: The Swedish Immigration Institute and Museum, and Institute of International Business, pp. 127–52.

Jemison, D.B. and S.B. Sitkin (1986), 'Corporate acquisitions: a process perspective', *Academy of Management Review*, **11**, 145–63.

Jost, J.T. and K. Elsbach (2001), 'How status and power differences erode personal and social identities at work: a system justification critique of organizational applications of social identity theory', in M.A. Hogg and D.J. Terry (eds), *Social Identity Processes in Organizational Contexts*, Philadelphia, PA: Taylor and Francis, pp. 181–96.

Kale, P., H. Singh and A.P. Raman (2009), 'Don't integrate your acquisitions, partner with them', *Harvard Business Review*, **87**, 109–15.

Kalkhoff, W. and C. Barnum (2000), 'The effects of status-organizing and social identity processes on patterns of social influence', *Social Psychology Quarterly*, **63**(2), 95–115.

Kiessling, T. and M. Harvey (2006), 'The human resource management issues during an acquisition: the target firm's top management team and key managers', *The Journal of Human Resource Management*, **17**(7), 1307–20.

King, D.R., D.R. Dalton, C.M. Daily and J.G. Kovin (2004), 'Meta-analyses of postacquisition performance: indications of unidentified moderators', *Strategic Management Journal*, **25**, 187–200.

Kitching, J. (1967), 'Why do mergers miscarry?', *Harvard Business Review*, **45**(6), 84–101.

Klendauer, R. and J. Deller (2009), 'Organizational justice and managerial commitment in corporate mergers', *Journal of Managerial Psychology*, **24**(1), 29–45.

Kogut, B. and H. Singh (1988), 'The effect of national culture on the choice of entry mode', *Journal of International Business Studies*, **19**(3), 411–32.

Kogut, B. and U. Zander (1992), 'Knowledge of the firm, combinative capabilities, and the replication of technology', *Organization Science*, **3**(3), 383–96.

Kogut, B. and U. Zander (1993), 'Knowledge of the firm and the evolutionary theory of the multinational corporation', *Journal of International Business Studies*, **24**(4), 625–45.

Kogut, B. and U. Zander (1996), 'What firms do? Coordination, identity, and learning', *Organization Science*, **7**(5), 502–18.

KPMG (1999), *Mergers and Acquisitions*, Global Research Report, 1–21.

Krug, J.A. (2003), 'Why do they keep leaving?', *Harvard Business Review*, **81**(2), 14–15.

Krug, J.A. and W.H. Hegarty (1997), 'Postacquisition turnover among U.S. top management teams: an analysis of the effects of foreign vs. domestic acquisitions of U.S. targets', *Strategic Management Journal*, **18**(8), 667–75.

Krug, J.A. and W.H. Hegarty (2001), 'Predicting who stays and leaves after an acquisition: a study of top managers in multinational firms', *Strategic Management Journal*, **22**(2), 185–96.

Krug, J.A. and D. Nigh (1998), 'Top management departures in cross-border acquisitions: governance issues in an international context', *Journal of International Management*, **4**(4), 267–87.

Krug, J.A. and D. Nigh (2001), 'Executive perceptions in foreign and domestic acquisitions: an analysis of foreign ownership and its effects on executive fate', *Journal of World Business*, **36**(1), 85–105.

Kusstatscher, V. and C.L. Cooper (2005), *Managing Emotions in Mergers and Acquisitions*, Cheltenham, UK and Northampton, MA, USA: Edward Elgar.

Lamont, M. and V. Molnar (2002), 'The study of boundaries in the social sciences', *Annual Review of Sociology*, **28**, 167–95.

Larsson, R. and M. Lubatkin (2001), 'Achieving acculturation in mergers and acquisitions: an international case survey', *Human Relations*, **54**(12), 1573–608.

Larsson, R., M. Driver, M. Holmqvist and P. Sweet (2001), 'Career dis-integration and re-integration in mergers and acquisitions: managing competence and motivational intangibles', *European Management Journal*, **19**(6), 609–18.

Larsson, R., K.R. Brousseau, M.J. Driver and P.L. Sweet (2004), 'The secrets of merger and acquisition success: a co-competence and motivational approach to synergy realization', in A. Pablo and M. Javidan (eds), *Mergers and Acquisitions: Creating Integrative Knowledge*, Oxford: Blackwell, pp. 3–19.

Lubatkin, M., D. Schweiger and Y. Weber (1999), 'Top management turnover related to M&As: an additional test of the theory of relative standing', *Journal of Management*, **25**(1), 55–73.

Lyles, M. and J.E. Salk (1996), 'Knowledge acquisition from foreign parents in international joint ventures: an empirical examination in the Hungarian context', *Journal of International Business Studies*, **27**(5), 877–903.

Magee, J.C. and A.D. Galinsky (2008), 'Social hierarchy: the self-reinforcing nature of power and status', *Academy of Management Annals*, **2**, 351–98.

Marks, M.L. and P.H. Mirvis (2001), 'Making mergers and acquisitions work: strategic and psychological preparation', *Academy of Management Executive*, **15**(2), 80–92.

Moeller, S.B., F.P. Schlingemann and R.M. Stulz (2005), 'Wealth destruction on a massive scale? A study of acquiring-firm returns in the recent merger wave', *The Journal of Finance*, **LX**(2), 757–82.

Morosini, P., S. Shane and H. Singh (1998), 'National cultural distance and cross-border acquisition performance', *Journal of International Business Studies*, **29**(1), 137–56.

Nahavandi, A. and A.R. Malekzadeh (1988), 'Acculturation in mergers and acquisitions', *Academy of Management Review*, **13**(1), 79–90.

Nickerson, J. and T. Zenger (2004), 'A knowledge-based theory of the firm: the problem-solving perspective', *Organization Science*, **15**, 617–32.

Nonaka, I. (1994), 'A dynamic theory of organizational knowledge', *Organization Science*, **5**, 14–37.

OECD (2007), *International Investment Perspectives 2007: Freedom of Investment in a Changing World*, OECD: Directorate for Financial and Enterprise Affairs.

Pareto, V. (1901/1991), *The Rise and Fall of Elites: An Application of Theoretical Sociology*, New Brunswick, NJ: Transaction Publishers.

Paruchuri, S., A. Nerkar and D.C. Hambrick (2006), 'Acquisition integration and productivity losses in the technical core: disruption of inventors in acquired companies', *Organization Science*, **17**(5), 545–62.

Pauleen, D.J., D. Rooney and N.J. Holden (2010), 'Practical wisdom and the development of cross-cultural knowledge management: a global leadership perspective', *European Journal of International Management*, **4**(4), 382–95.

Peng, M.W. (2008), *Global Business*, Mason, OH: South Western.

Pettigrew, T.F. (2008), 'Future directions for intergroup contact theory and research', *International Journal of Intercultural Research*, **32**, 187–99.

Prabhu, J.C., R.K. Chandy and M.E. Ellis (2005), 'The impact of acquisitions on innovation: poison pill, placebo, or tonic?', *Journal of Marketing*, **69**, 114–30.

Puranam, P. and K. Srikanth (2007), 'What they know vs. what they do: how acquirers leverage technology acquisitions', *Strategic Management Journal*, **28**(8), 805–25.

Ranft, A.L. and M.D. Lord (2002), 'Acquiring new technologies and capabilities: a grounded model of acquisition implementation', *Organization Science*, **13**(4), 420–41.

Raukko, M. (2009), 'Organizational commitment during organizational changes: a longitudinal case study on acquired key employees', *Baltic Journal of Management*, **4**(3), 331–52.

Redfield, R., R. Linton and M.J. Herskovits (1936), 'Memorandum for the study of acculturation', *American Anthropologist*, **38**(1), 149–52.

Regnér, P. (2003), 'Strategy creation in the periphery: inductive versus deductive strategy making', *Journal of Management Studies*, **40**(1), 57–82.

Regnér, P. and U. Zander (2011), 'Knowledge and strategy creation in multinational companies: social-identity frames and temporary tension in knowledge creation', *Management International Review*, **51**(6), 821–50.

Reid, S.A., N.A. Palomares, G.L. Anderson and B. Bondad-Brown (2009), 'Gender, language, and social influence: a test of expectation states, role congruity, and self-categorization theories', *Human Communication Research*, **35**(4), 465–90.

Reus, T.H. and B.T. Lamont (2009), 'The double-edged sword of cultural distance in international business', *Journal of International Business Studies*, **40**, 1–19.

Risberg, A. (2001), 'Employee experiences of acquisition processes', *Journal of World Business*, **36**(1), 58–84.

Rottig, D. (2011), 'The role of social capital in cross-cultural M&As: a multinational corporation perspective', *European Journal of International Management*, **5**(4), 413–31.

Sales, A.L. and P.H. Mirvis (1984), 'When cultures collide: issues of acquisition', in J.R.R. Kimberley and R.E. Quinn (eds), *Managing Organizational Transitions*, Homewood, IL: Irwin, pp. 107–33.

Sarala, R.M. and E. Vaara (2010), 'Cultural differences, convergence, and crossvergence as explanations of knowledge transfer in international acquisitions', *Journal of International Business Studies*, **41**(8), 1365–90.

Schweiger, D.M. and A.S. DeNisi (1991), 'Communication with employees following a merger: a longitudinal field experiment', *Academy of Management Journal*, **34**(1), 110–35.

Shenkar, O. (2001), 'Cultural distance revisited: towards a more rigorous conceptualization and measurement of cultural differences', *Journal of International Business Studies*, **32**(3), 519–35.

Shenkar, O., Y. Luo and O. Yeheskel (2008), 'From "distance" to "friction" substituting metaphors and re-directing intercultural research', *Academy of Management Review*, **33**(4), 905–23.

Shrivastava, P. (1986), 'Postmerger integration', *Journal of Business Strategy*, **7**(1), 65–76.

Sirower, M.L. (1997), *The Synergy Trap: How Companies Lose the Acquisition Game*, New York: The Free Press.

Spender, J.C. (1996), 'Making knowledge the basis of a dynamic theory of the firm', *Strategic Management Journal*, **17**, 45–62.

Tajfel, H. and J.C. Turner (1979), 'An integrative theory of intergroup conflict', in W.G. Austin and S. Worchel (eds), *The Social Psychology of Intergroup Relations*, Monterey, CA: Brooks/Cole, pp. 33–47.

Terry, D.J. (2001), 'Intergroup relations and organizational mergers', in M.A. Hogg and D.J. Terry (eds), *Social Identity Processes in Organizational Contexts*, Philadelphia, PA: Psychology Press, pp. 229–48.

UN Conference on Trade and Development (2000), *World Investment Report: Cross-border Mergers and Acquisitions and Development*, New York: United Nations Publications.

Vaara, E. and P. Monin (2010), 'A recursive perspective on discursive legitimation and organizational action in mergers and acquisitions', *Organization Science*, **21**(1), 3–22.

Van Knippenberg, D. (1978), 'Status differences, comparative relevance and intergroup differentiation', in H. Tajfel (ed.), *Differentiation Between Social Groups*, London: Academic Press, pp. 171–99.

Verbeke, A. (2010), 'International acquisition success: social community and dominant logic dimensions', *Journal of international Business Studies*, **41**, 38–46.

Very, P. (2004), *The Management of Mergers and Acquisitions*, New York: John Wiley and Sons.

Very, P. and D.M. Schweiger (2001), 'The acquisition process as a learning process: evidence from a study of critical problems and solutions in domestic and cross-border deals', *Journal of World Business*, **36**(1), 11–31.

Very, P., M. Lubatkin, R. Calori and J. Veiga (1997), 'Recently acquired European firms', *Strategic Management Journal*, **18**, 593–614.

Walsh, J.P. (1988), 'Top management turnover following mergers and acquisitions', *Strategic Management Journal*, **10**, 307–22.

Walsh, J.P. (1989), 'Doing a deal: mergers and acquisition negotiations and their impact upon target company top management turnover', *Strategic Management Journal*, **10**(4), 307–22.

Walsh, J.P. and J.W. Ellwood (1991), 'Mergers, acquisitions, and the pruning of managerial deadwood', *Strategic Management Journal*, **12**(3), 201–17.

Washington, M. and E.J. Zajac (2005), 'Status evolution and competition: theory and evidence', *Academy of Management Journal*, **48**(2), 282–96.

Weber, Y. (1996), 'Corporate cultural fit and performance in mergers and acquisitions', *Human Relations*, **49**(9), 1181–203.

Wiener, N. (1961), *Cybernetics: Or the Control and Communication in the Animal and the Machine*, Cambridge, MA: MIT Press.

Zaheer, S., M. Schomaker and M. Genc (2003), 'Identity versus culture in mergers of equals', *European Management Journal*, **21**(2), 185–91.

Zander, L. (2002), 'Cultural families: reflections on the relationship between national culture and organisational culture', in N. Banno Gomes, A. Bigestans, L. Magnusson and I. Ramberg (eds), *Reflections on Diversity and Change in Modern Society: A Festschrift for Annick Sjögren*, Botkyrka: Multicultural Centre, pp. 159–80.

Zander, L. and L. Lerpold (2002), 'Managing international alliance and acquisition integration', in M. Tayeb (ed.), *International Management*, London: Pearson Education, pp. 132–55.

Zander, U. (1991), *Exploiting a Technological Edge: Voluntary and Involuntary Dissemination of Technology*, PhD Dissertation, Stockholm: IIB.

Zander, U. and H. Glimstedt (2006), 'Knowledge in international firms and networks: the Institute of International Business at the Stockholm School of Economics', *European Management Review*, **3**, 199–210.

Zander, U. and B. Kogut (1995), 'Knowledge and the speed of the transfer and imitation of organizational capabilities: an empirical test', *Organization Science*, **5**(1), 76–92.

Zander, U. and L. Zander (2010), 'Opening the grey box: social communities, knowledge and culture in acquisitions', *Journal of International Business Studies*, **41**(1), 27–37.

12 What can international finance add to international strategy?

Lars Oxelheim, Trond Randøy and Arthur Stonehill

INTRODUCTION

The 1980s and 1990s saw a remarkable increase in international financial integration of many OECD countries but left many small emerging and developing countries outside this 'global' financial market. In the integration process as described in Oxelheim (1996), the Nordic economies were able to foster a large number of high-growth capital-intensive companies, such as Nokia from Finland, Ericsson from Sweden, and Novo-Nordisk from Denmark. We argue that without the skillful global financial strategies that enabled these companies to access global savings, the limited domestic availability and high cost of capital would have hampered their growth. We suggest that these companies' historical accounts provide valuable insight for scholars as well as for executives today, in particular for smaller and medium-sized growth-oriented firms from emerging economies.

In order to succeed in a global financial market, firms' executives must be capable of delivering the strategy story to the stock analysts and, ultimately, share value to the money managers (Useem, 1998). We find that Useem's argument is equally true today. The ongoing globalization of equity markets provides the firm the opportunity to actively reduce information and agency costs, and hence to contribute to higher firm values by the means of lower cost of capital (Bekaert and Harvey, 2000; Doidge et al., 2004; Hearn et al., 2010; Mittoo and Zhang, 2008) and better corporate governance (Coffee, 2002; Oxelheim and Randøy, 2003). This is particularly true for emerging markets or thin capital markets (O'Connor, 2011). The rise of global portfolio investment has laid the ground for more emphasis on shareholder relations. The international portfolio managers judge the potential company to invest in against the best-performing firms in each industry and no longer against its domestic peers only. For small and medium-sized companies in particular, but also for large companies outside the Anglo-American world and major countries like Japan and Germany, the gain of access to highly liquid and competitively priced capital markets can effectively boost growth.

In the rest of this chapter we shall emphasize successful financial strategies for companies from small and/or emerging economies for gaining global investor recognition. The brief story of Nokia's rise to become the global leader in cell phone production may serve as an introduction.

When the fast-growing telecommunication company Nokia of Finland needed US$485 million in 1994, access to competitively priced funds was necessary in order to keep pace with competitors. In early 1994 the common stocks of Nokia's major competitors were priced at 22 (Motorola) and 25 (Ericsson) times earnings; however, Nokia was valued at only 14 times earnings. To become more attractive to global investors, the firm listed on the NYSE (New York Stock Exchange) and made a euro-equity offering. Within three months of NYSE trading, Nokia's stock had gained 45 percent versus a 2 percent gain for the NYSE composite index. Nokia had achieved global recognition among investors, and was now classified and priced as one of the peers in the telecommunication industry. Today the level of market segmentation in relation to a country like Finland is much smaller, and the costs of NYSE listing have increased significantly, so the net benefits of such listing are now less obvious. Hence it boils down to a cost–benefit analysis of investing in global recognition. Some of the investments coincide with investing in the build-up of a corporate brand name. Or to put it differently, the financial strategy to internationalize overlaps with the international marketing strategy.

The chapter is organized as follows. In the next section we address increased financial integration and a better access to global savings implying that a Swedish firm may borrow savings from households in Australia to invest in the USA. Thereafter we discuss why having a financial strategy matters. Then follows a review of barriers to an international cost of capital that have to be circumvented or overcome by the firm. We use longitudinal company cases to provide lessons to firms from thin or emerging capital markets of the early 2010s. Then follows a section in which we link the business strategy, financial strategy and corporate performance. The chapter ends with concluding remarks.

ON THE SEGMENTATION OF CAPITAL MARKETS

The benefits of having a corporate financial strategy are closely linked to the degree of capital market integration. Firms that are based in a country with a segmented and thin capital market have much to gain from breaking out of its domestic capital, thus being able to reap the benefit of a global cost of capital. Firms, facing a perfectly integrated financial market, should consequently not spend too much effort on cross-border financial issues. It can then be discussed how to measure the degree of international financial integration and how to act in accordance with this assessment. The overall financial integration encompasses all the financial market segments (money, bonds and equity), but the measurement process boils in all cases down to a 'law of one price' process (Oxelheim, 1990; Yeyati et al., 2009). Below we discuss the equity market integration.

Over the last decades a significant volume of research has focused on ways of measuring equity market integration from an econometric point of view. Various schools of thought have developed, but for most of them the point of departure has been much the same: the law of one price, which states that if two or more markets are integrated, then identical securities should be priced identically in all of them. The controversial issue dividing the different schools concerns what 'being priced identically' actually means.

One strand in the literature that highlights identical movements is based on the analysis of co-movements of equity-market returns. For the analysis of correlation of returns, prominent research has been done by: Ahn and Kudo (2011); Lau and Diltz (1994); Lin et al. (1994); for correlation of hourly returns, see Susmel and Engle (1994); for stability over longer periods, see Erb et al. (1994); Ibrahimi et al. (1995); Longin and Solnik (1995); and for stability around the Black Monday or Crash of 1987, see for example King et al. (1994). For the recent turmoil around the post-2008 financial crisis, see Mun and Brooks (2012). Furthermore, Solnik (1996) provides an overview of correlations between industrialized markets and concludes that whereas measuring co-movements in equity-market returns in isolation leads to conclusions in terms of weak integration, measures of strong integration also involve the analysis of return gaps between equity markets.

As the other major strand of literature, many schools of thought in the area of finance assume strong financial market integration – i.e. start from the law of one price, but only after risks have been taken into account. In studies adopting this more stringent definition of integration the thrust of the analysis can vary. For example, from the role of currency risk (see e.g. Jorion, 1985), long-term differences in risk-adjusted returns (see e.g. Ibbotson et al., 1985), optimal international asset allocation (see e.g. Glen and Jorion, 1993; Odier and Solnik, 1993), international asset pricing with extended CAPM (see e.g. Graham and Nikkinen, 2011; Hietala, 1989), home country preference bias (see e.g. French and Poterba, 1991; Cooper and Kaplanis, 1994; Tesar and Werner, 1995), the international pricing of risks (see e.g. Harvey, 1991; Dumas, 1994), international asset pricing with extended APT (see e.g. Bansal et al. 1993), and finally international asset pricing with consumption-based models (see e.g. Wheatley, 1988).

Taken together, all these studies point in the same direction: towards increasing equity market integration. But when it comes to the degree of integration, the results are often inconclusive, even in the case of comparable markets and periods. This claim is supported by Naranjo and Protopapadakis (1997), who provide an overview of integration test results. The authors argue that the conflicting results may be partly due to the lack of an economic benchmark of integration with which the statistical tests can be compared. Oxelheim (2001) argues that the inconclusive results as regards the degree of completeness of equity market integration reflects the composition of the stock market indices used and how they mirror a two-tier integration, i.e. the polarization of firms with global recognition and those without.

Fulfillment of the various prerequisites marks out different stages on the way towards perfect financial market integration (Oxelheim, 2001). The first prerequisite is the absence of capital controls that effectively prevent cross-border equity transactions issues and trade. The second prerequisite concerns the efficiency of internal regulations and the absence of tax wedges and prohibitive transaction costs. The third prerequisite concerns the exchange of information and the absence of cross-border information asymmetries, including differences between corporate governance systems and information costs.

The process of integration as comprised by the fulfillment of these three prerequisites reflects activities of three major stakeholder groups: politicians with their dual function of trying to retain control over capital flows on the one hand and achieving a sound and safe financial infrastructure on the other; investors searching for profit opportunities; and managers trying to internationalize the cost of capital while maintaining control.

Historically, there has been considerable theoretical and empirical research on the segmentation of international capital markets. However, few studies have addressed the specific managerial challenges that internationalization of capital implies. The research issue of this chapter is to focus on the way individual companies can undertake actions to improve their market valuations, and thus their cost of capital. The key ingredients are the linkages between business strategy, firm motivation and various financial strategies to reduce the corporate cost of capital.

WHY FINANCIAL STRATEGY MATTERS

There is a widespread misperception that financial strategy does not add value to the firm. This line of reasoning goes back to the research of two Nobel Prize economists, Modigliani and Miller. The implication of this view is basically that finance is irrelevant to corporate success. However, this argument ignores many facts, such as that all capital markets are not alike and information is not evenly distributed across nations. Even for highly liquid and well-functioning capital markets, such as the one in the USA, a study of 750 companies reveals that better disclosure boosts stock price (Lang and Lundholm, 1996). If there is no value creation in pursuing specific financial strategies, then companies ought to consider laying off their highly paid investor relations executives to enhance their stock price. On the contrary, we suggest that most markets are not fully financially integrated, providing companies from these countries a reason to invest more in financial strategies and investor relations than their peers in other markets in order to escape a mispriced and/or illiquid domestic stock market. The need for an active investor relations function is also shown by the fact that global investors strongly favor more visible (and larger) firms when investing in small equity markets (Dahlquist and Robertsson, 2001).

BARRIERS TO AN INTERNATIONAL COST OF CAPITAL

We argue that corporate competitiveness is enhanced when a firm's dependence on an illiquid or partially segmented capital market is reduced. Financial market segmentation implies that a firm from one country faces higher financial costs than an exactly similar company from another country. Research points to five major routes to achieve international cost of capital and increased competitiveness. The first route is to list the company's shares on one or more foreign stock exchanges and the second is to float equity issues to investors in one or more foreign countries. These two routes encompass many different levels of ambition, as highlighted in Figure 12.1. The safest alternative for the inexperienced firm is to follow all the steps of the staircase starting with listing bonds in a less prestigious market. The boldest firm, however, will go straight to the last step at once, even without a prior listing in its financial home market. This last-mentioned alternative has been adopted by many high-tech Israeli firms, finding the home market too small to digest the risks of the firm. The listing enhances liquidity of shares, and for the availability of new capital a float of an equity issue is necessary. A third route to internationalizing the cost of capital is via a strategic alliance. Foreign industrial investors can overcome a segmented capital market by infusing equity into a target partner. A fourth route is to import a harsher governance regime on the board of the firm by recruiting a board member from the country of that regime (Oxelheim and Randøy, 2003). Finally, the fifth avenue – for which the lasting impact can be debated – is to get a lower cost of capital by attracting support from central and local government agencies (Oxelheim and Ghauri, 2008).

In the 1980s and at the beginning of the 1990s one major venue for companies to escape a 'thin', inefficient and heavily regulated domestic market was to place an equity issue on a foreign 'prestigious' capital market. As previously stressed, the internationalization of the cost of capital was a process with three stakeholders: investors, regulators and

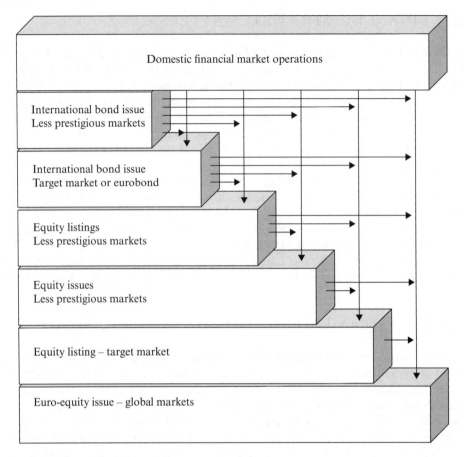

Source: Oxelheim (2001).

*Figure 12.1   Major corporate strategies for eliminating cross-border information
asymmetries in internationalizing the cost of capital*

managers. Investors are characterized by an endless search for new profit opportunities
and portfolio risk reduction. On the other hand, regulators pursue policies that are aimed
at insulating the domestic market from the global one, and managers strive to eliminate
disadvantages by trying to circumvent barriers and restrictions imposed by regulators. A
successful stock issue should render the company benefits from a higher price/earnings
ratio, or price to book ratio, abroad as compared to the one at home.

Corporate managers of firms resident in segmented equity markets will be rewarded
for financial strategies that overcome the causes of capital market segmentation. These
causes are as follows:

● Asymmetric information available to investors resident in different countries. This
includes not only financial data on corporations but also the analytic methods used
to evaluate the validity of a security's price.

- Different tax regulations, especially with regard to the treatment of capital gains and the double taxation of dividends.
- Regulation of securities markets.
- Alternative sets of optimal portfolios from the perspective of investors resident in one equity market compared to investors resident in other equity markets.
- Different agency costs for firms located in bank-dominated markets compared to firms located in the Anglo-American markets.
- Different levels of financial risk tolerance, such as debt ratios, in different countries.
- Differences in perceived foreign exchange risk, especially with respect to operating and transaction exposures.
- Takeover defenses that differ widely between the Anglo-American markets, characterized by one-share-one-vote norms, and other markets featuring dual classes of stock and other takeover barriers.
- The level of transaction costs involved in purchasing, selling and trading securities.
- Political risk such as unpredictable government interference in capital markets and arbitrary changes in rules.

The relative importance of each of these barriers changes over time and across countries, and produces the overall degree of international financial integration of a given country. Moreover, when it comes to the financial strategy of a given firm, it is also a question of firms' ability to benefit from market imperfections. However, it is hard to find consistent, i.e. across companies, evidence on how successful firms have been in exploiting these market imperfections. At the corporate level success is not only a matter of identification of misalignments in macro market prices but also a matter of the perceived ability of financial managers to exploit them (Oxelheim et al., 2012). In this chapter we use cases to illustrate the variety of corporate strategies employed to internationalize firms' cost of capital, as they evolved over time and across countries.

THE PATH TO INTERNATIONALIZATION OF CAPITAL

In this section we go deeper into the different financial strategies. Figure 12.1 shows how foreign equity markets are normally tapped using one or a combination of two financial strategies. The preparation and a first strategy consist of the cross-listing of the company's shares. The second strategy is then to make a directed issue of stocks, straight bonds, convertible bonds, or a hybrid instrument, sold in a specific foreign equity market. A directed private placement is also feasible. The broadening of the second strategy is to ensure a euro-equity issue is sold in several equity markets simultaneously. This usually includes the home market in addition to foreign markets. In addition to the two strategies highlighted in Figure 12.1, a third related strategy is to receive an equity injection from a foreign partner as part of a strategic alliance.

Because of transaction and information acquisition barriers in the international capital market, a firm typically starts to raise funds in the domestic financial market. The information barriers are commonly larger for equity issues than for bond issues. Ideally, firms would like to jump from the domestic capital market to a 'euro-equity issue'. This is usually impossible because the international investment community does not know the average firm.

The normal path of internationalizing a firm's capital is to start with an international bond issue in a less prestigious market. This provides the firm with added experience and enhanced visibility (and scrutiny) in the financial market. If possible, it is desirable to skip this first step and go directly to the next steps, international bond issue in a liquid target market or a eurobond issue sold in several markets. Raising equity requires more commitment to disclosure and investor relations. A firm could start by listing and selling equity in a less prestigious market, i.e. not the USA or the UK. This is even more costly in time and money than a bond issue, but still commonly less costly than a full-scale listing and equity issue in the USA or the UK.

The ultimate financial strategy – particularly for large firms – is to have a euro-equity issue sold simultaneously in both foreign equity markets and the domestic market. Within the Nordic area Electrolux (1986) was among the first to tap the euro-equity market. Euro-equity issue is also the path being taken by some privatized firms, such as Tele-Danmark in 1994.

Cross-listings

Firms cross-list on foreign stock exchanges for a variety of reasons, whether or not they actually sell equity issues abroad (e.g. Modén and Oxelheim, 1997; Karolyi, 1998; and for an overview see Pagano et al., 2002). The main documented motives are as follows:

- Achieve a world pricing of its equity when the home market is segmented.
- Improve the international visibility of the firm's products and securities to its customers, suppliers, creditors and host governments.
- Make it easier for the firm's foreign stockholders to trade its shares in their home markets and currencies, thus increasing the stock's overall liquidity.
- Foreign underwriters insist on local listing in their markets to help market a new equity issue.
- Create a liquid secondary market for shares used to acquire foreign firms, or to distribute to employees of foreign subsidiaries.
- Comply with governmental requirements for financing foreign investments.

The extent to which a firm's stock price can be increased by merely cross-listing on a foreign stock exchange, without a simultaneous equity issue, depends on how severely the home market is segmented and what efforts the firm has made to attract international investors. Sundaram and Logue (1996) found a favorable effect on stock prices for foreign firms that cross-listed on the New York and American Stock Exchanges during 1982–92. However, Modén and Oxelheim (1997) report that a simultaneous equity issue and cross-listing on the New York and American Stock Exchanges by Swedish firms generates a higher shareholder value than a mere cross-listing because of the stronger commitment by the issuing firm it signals.

Foreign investors can acquire a firm's stock through transactions on foreign stock exchanges. By cross-listing on their home stock market, a firm can help those investors to trade shares and receive dividends in their home currency. The hope is to increase overall liquidity for trading the firm's shares and to encourage the foreign investors to hold the firm's shares rather than sell them back to the firm's home market.

Directed Stock Issue

A directed stock issue is defined as one targeted at investors in a single country and under-written in whole or in part by investment institutions from that country. The issue might or might not be listed on a stock exchange in the target market.

Directed stock issues were the investment of choice for Nordic firms in the 1980s and early 1990s. Segmentation of the home equity markets made it difficult to attract inter-national investors with a 'shotgun' approach. Indeed, the early Nordic equity issues abroad were focused and heavily promoted by Goldman Sachs and Company (Novo Industri A/S), and Morgan Stanley (L.M. Ericsson AB, Fortia AB/Pharmacia and Gambro).

Directed stock issues have been particularly useful to Nordic firms desiring to improve the liquidity of their shares, to achieve international pricing of their shares, and to become more visible to customers and suppliers. Even after the Nordic equity markets became less segmented, directed stock issues have been useful to fund acquisitions or new capital investments in the targeted foreign market. This was the motivation for Norwegian-based Hafslund Nycomed's directed share issues in London (1989) and the USA (1992), as well as its listing on the New York Stock Exchange (1992).

At the end of the 1990s the pattern of directed issues turned from having been more or less 100 percent cash issues into more or less 100 percent non-cash issues. All growth firms used their own shares to pay for acquisitions (Oxelheim, 2001). However, this pattern did nothing to reduce the burden on management of having a successful financial strategy.

Euro-equity Issues

Not only have Nordic equity markets become less segmented, but this trend is happening worldwide. This occurred simultaneously with a rapid increase in international portfolio investment over the last 25 years. As a result, a robust euro-equity market has evolved starting in the mid-1980s.

Firms are able to issue equity, which is underwritten and distributed in more than one foreign equity market, sometimes simultaneously with distribution in the home market. The same financial institutions that form the backbone of the eurobond market are the main players in the newer euro-equity market.

The euro-equity market has been the main vehicle for privatizing large public utilities from both industrialized and emerging markets. Nordic privatizations have in the recent past made use of the euro-equity market and are expected to do more of the same in the future. Notable examples are the privatization of Tele Danmark (1994), Telia of Sweden (2000) and Telenor of Norway (2000). It should be noted that this capital market only developed during the past decade, so earlier Nordic equity issues did not really have a choice to use it.

Simultaneous distribution in several equity markets implies a single worldwide price. This price is often somewhat different than the previous home market price but results from a compromise among the various national underwriters.

Strategic Alliances

Strategic alliances are usually created to take advantage of synergies in joint marketing, product development or other commercial activities. However, financial synergy may also arise if a financially strong firm helps a financially weak partner by injecting favorably priced equity or debt into it.

The equity-based strategic alliances have in most cases helped the receiving firm to boost its stock price. However, the alliance relationship has generally been a 'trial marriage'. After some years the strategic alliance typically ends with either a merger/ acquisition (as with Elektrisk Bureau). The strategic alliance between Huhtamaki and Procordia was finished after three years. However, Elektrisk Bureau A/S and ASEA AB ended as a merger after five years.

The key to financial synergy with respect to equity pricing is that portfolio investors price shares according to their expected risk-adjusted rate of return. This is necessarily somewhat biased by past performance, but in any case cannot usually anticipate the synergistic effects of a strategic alliance that does not yet exist. Thus the value of equity in Bang & Olufsen was higher from the perspective of Philips NV, which anticipated the operating and financial synergies, than Bang & Olufsen's value to the existing market of portfolio investors. Bang & Olufsen realized many of the anticipated synergies. Its operating performance improved dramatically. It also enjoyed a hefty share price increase compared to the Danish market as a whole. In 1997 it was able to repurchase its shares that were held by Philips NV but continued most other aspects of the strategic alliance.

Internationalization of Corporate Governance

The globalization of ownership creates an opportunity for foreign shareholders to buy large stakes in the firm. However, the investors must have confidence that the capital they provide will be properly monitored. For small shareholders the cost of getting involved may be prohibitive. But larger shareholders can afford active monitoring, for instance through foreign board membership (Shleifer and Vishny, 1986, 2007). Board representatives for large foreign shareholders are presumably 'outsiders' who will not use their influence as board members to obtain benefits that do not accrue to other shareholders (see e.g. Stulz, 1999). As they are more likely to perform the arm's-length monitoring, their entry as owners should increase the value of the firm.

Compliance with the stricter information and monitoring requirements of a more demanding corporate governance system can substantially increase a firm's costs. However, this also discourages managers from extracting private benefits, and it therefore strengthens the firm's commitment to protecting the interests of minority shareholders (Reese and Weisback, 2001). Foreign listing – or the undertaking of foreign equity issues – is a costly affair for the firm, both in terms of outright expenses and in terms of top management involvement (Oxelheim et al., 1998; Blass and Yafeh, 2001).

Many firms might *ex ante* consider a foreign listing too costly. For these firms, however, there is a way of achieving a global cost of capital at a lower outright cost. In exercising this option a firm signals its willingness to improve the monitoring opportunities by including foreign outsider members on the board. This alternative of 'importing' a more demanding corporate governance system by having one or more representatives of that system as board members signals a higher commitment to corporate monitoring and transparency. Oxelheim and Randøy (2003) suggest that the presence of at least one foreign outsider member representing a more demanding system, i.e. the Anglo-American system, will result in more active boards that are more independent of management. The key ingredient of this alternative is the bridging of the previously mentioned cross-border information gap, and an improvement in corporate governance – in which value can be created through access to new investors. New and/or improved access to a foreign investor clientele should entail a higher share price, and thus a lower cost of capital (Oxelheim et al., 1998; Bekaert and Harvey, 2000).

Most past corporate governance studies have presumed implicitly that a company is embedded in the corporate governance model of its home country (e.g. La Porta et al., 1998; La Porta et al., 1999) unless the firm is a subsidiary of a foreign company. An examination of the impact of outsider foreign board membership needs to consider three different board mandates. One alternative is that the board member has a mandate to represent an owner with a major commercial or long-lasting interest in the firm such as a foreign direct investment (FDI) or a subsidiary. A second alternative is that the board member represents a foreign owner with a big portfolio stake in the firm. Finally, the board member may be an independent outsider chosen by the company specifically to signal its willingness to comply with another corporate governance system. The choice is assumed here to be independent of ownership structure. By having at least one foreign board member in this third category and representing the Anglo-American system, the firm is signaling its willingness to be monitored by the rules of a more demanding corporate governance system.

The strongest consistent signal of commitment is assumed to emerge from a combination of a cross-listing on the Anglo-American markets and the inclusion of at least one independently chosen outsider foreign board member representing the Anglo-American corporate governance system. Both these features indicate an improvement in monitoring and an increase in transparency, which is valued by investors (Oxelheim and Randøy, 2003). Hence a fourth strategy and a low-cost alternative to foreign listing and equity issues is to add one or more independent directors from a prestigious capital market to the corporate board of directors (Oxelheim and Randøy, 2003). This might improve corporate governance of the firm, and help it to build confidence with foreign investors. Hence, given the substantial increases in costs related to foreign listings – particularly in the USA – a viable alternative to a foreign listing might be internationalization of the corporate boards and internationalization of the incentives system for top executives. The undertaking of an international cross-listing should not, on its own, be regarded as a completed mission.

Finance-specific Advantages and Foreign Investment

In efficient and internationally integrated financial markets, no firm has a financial advantage over another, since all firms have equal access to finance at equal (risk-adjusted) cost. Arguing for a finance-advantage effect thus requires an assumption of imperfect capital markets that are at least partially internationally segmented. While the theories underpinning Dunning's (e.g. 1993) eclectic ownership–location–internalization

(OLI) paradigm (especially internalization theory) largely build on imperfections in goods markets, the effects of financial market imperfections have received less attention.

In a conceptual paper, Oxelheim et al. (2001) argue that a firm's financial characteristics are not merely by-products of its competitive strength but constitute a distinct set of explanatory variables. By having a superior financial strategy a firm is able to minimize its cost and maximize its availability of capital relative to its competitors, both domestic and foreign. By lowering the discount factor of any investment, such a financial advantage increases the firm's likelihood of engaging in profitable FDI. Forssbæck and Oxelheim (2008) brings this argument to the data. As their point of departure, they focus on the OLI framework (Dunning, 1993) since, in its ambition of being all inclusive, it provides a list of 'standard' FDI determinants against which they test the added explanatory value from including financial factors. They thus construct a number of firm-level financial characteristics ranging from simple cost of capital and creditworthiness measures to outright financial strategies – such as listing the firm's equity on large and competitive foreign stock exchanges. The results, based on a sample of 1379 European non-financial firms' cross-border acquisitions in a total of 44 target markets, show a strongly significant explanatory power of a number of financial characteristics and of financial strategies undertaken in a period of up to 60 months prior to the investment. These results give a clear indication of the important role played by finance-specific factors and support the notion that firms can create ownership advantages by adopting strategies to improve their financial strength (in Forssbæck and Oxelheim, 2011, they find support for this also in a general model).

In the race for inward FDI, history reveals that governments are interested in attracting knowledge-intense firms by different means, altering at the last minute the OLI pattern to their own advantage. The high unemployment rate in most countries following from the financial crisis of 2008 and onwards made many governments inclined to use non-transparent measures such as subsidies, loan and equity on non-market conditions and warranties to convince firms to establish themselves in their country in order for governments to signal power by creating jobs. In this way they contribute artificially to lowering the cost of capital of the targeted firm (Oxelheim and Ghauri, 2008).

De-listing

International financial integration is a recurrent phenomenon in history. Financial integration was in the pre-World War I period close to perfect and allowed most firms access to global capital markets. In the Nordic region – as shown in Oxelheim (2001) – GN Store Nord from Denmark was listed in London as early as 1869. The Danish bank – Privatbanken (now Unibank) – listed in Amsterdam in 1899. Norsk Hydro was listed in Geneva and Paris in 1909. Even between the two world wars the financial markets were open to cross-border financial operations. The Swedish company Alfa Laval was listed at three exchanges in 1928 (London, Geneva and Amsterdam). Other Swedish companies cross-listing in that period were Electrolux (London, 1928), SKF (London, 1928; Paris, 1929 and Geneva, 1935) and Swedish Match (today famous for snuff). The last company stands out for its multi-market listing. It was listed at ten European markets between 1922 and 1930. The special feature is that the company was listed at as many as five markets in Switzerland (Basel, Bern, Geneva, Lausanne and Zürich). The pattern in the 2010s goes in the opposite direction. Once the firm has reached the top of the ladder in Figure.12.1

BOX 12.1   THE EFFECT OF A GLOBAL COST OF CAPITAL:
THE GLOBAL SHAREHOLDER REGIME

Effect on shareholders and governing structure

- Potentially higher stock price: increased shareholder returns
- More demanding shareholders and less 'loyal' if a company does not satisfy expectations.
- Top management and investor relations need to focus on international institutional investors
- Need to strengthen the corporate board and add more independent directors
- Need to redesign incentive packages for key personnel based on shareholder value

Effect on business strategy

- Need to focus business strategy on core competencies and disposal of non-core business lines
- Need to be able to attract large amount of funds: strategic flexibility
- The firm is more exposed to takeovers (taking down takeover defenses)
- Need to make the firm attractive as a partner for mergers

---

and received a global recognition and a global cost of capital, the firm starts cutting down its listing at multiple markets. The de-listing will reduce outright costs and further boost the de-listed firm's cost of capital – something that in the last two decades has been made possible by the development of information technologies.

Towards a Global Cost of Capital

Why is a lower cost of capital such an important issue for an aspiring global firm? We identify three major reasons why international managers should be concerned. First, in an increasingly integrated world of competitive and open product markets, producers have difficulties in passing on a potentially higher cost of capital to customers. Nokia of Finland – the number one cellular phone maker in the world (as of late 2010) – does not have a 'cozy' home market where it can enjoy premium prices. Second, the advent of the knowledge economy makes equity financing more important, as the knowledge-intensive firms do not make the kind of investments that produce collateral for debt financing. Third, the global wave of mergers and acquisitions makes it important for companies to boost stock prices in order to maintain influence after a potential merger and protect themselves from being taken over.

The globalization of ownership, and thus internationalizing the cost of capital, leads to the new global shareholder regime (Box 12.1). A successful internationalization of capital produces a very international ownership structure, as the firm becomes a necessary part of global investors' world portfolio. Just two years after Nokia of Finland was listed on the NYSE in 1994, as much as 61 percent of its shareholders were resident outside the home country. This increased further as Nokia succeeded and grew to about 86 percent in early 2010.

Lack of Transparency Means Higher Cost of Capital

While the meaning of 'transparency' can vary from one situation to another, the common denominator is that a lack of transparency creates some form of information asymmetry (Oxelheim, 2006). In the political context, this asymmetry often means a difficulty in understanding current policy and uncertainty as to what the next step may be. In relation to a specific business, greater transparency helps to bridge the information gap between the firm and its investors/potential investors. The price for this lack of transparency appears in the form of a risk premium for ambiguity and opaqueness at the firm level, and as higher cost of capital. Hence a good financial strategy encompasses the disclosure of relevant information in order to achieve 'optimal' transparency (Oxelheim, 2010).

The Link between Financial and Overall Corporate Strategies

As summarized in Box 12.1, shareholder value is the paramount measure of corporate success within the global shareholder regime. As stock ownership becomes increasingly international, the demands for accurate and timely information increase, and shareholders show less tolerance for meager performance. In order to build shareholder interest, this research suggests that companies need to have an active investor relations function. Building confidence with international institutional investors should be the main focus of this activity, and case histories such as Nokia show how this has been successful in the past (Oxelheim et al., 1998).

A company with global ambitions needs to focus on corporate governance in order to gain shareholder confidence. One possible firm response could be to strengthen the governing board by recruiting a larger number of outside directors. Oxelheim et al. (2011) highlight how it is mostly financial globalization that drives the internationalization of boards. Moreover, the NASDAQ Stock Exchange requires that a company that seeks listing have a majority of independent (outside) directors (NASDAQ, 2010). Furthermore, global investors expect top management compensation to be linked to the creation of shareholder value.

Furthermore, we argue that the financial strategy of gaining 'membership' of a global shareholder regime affects the business strategy of the firm. In the 'old world order', finance played a secondary role to business strategy; not so any more. Unless the company focuses on its core competence and disposes of non-core activities, it can be exposed to a hostile takeover attempt. Long-term confidence needs to be built with major institutional investors, such that a large amount of funds can be accessed if necessary (typically in relation to an acquisition). A company can strengthen its strategic flexibility and thus provide strategic real options by building trust with large investors. Within the global shareholder regime companies with an active defense against takeovers are penalized. For example, within the Nordic economies non-voting shares have become rather unattractive to investors. The cost of various takeover defenses can be measured in terms of lower stock price and thus a higher cost of capital. This provides closely controlled companies with a strong incentive for a more transparent shareholder policy. In fact, making the company an attractive partner of a potential merger becomes an important route to higher shareholder return.

CONCLUDING REMARKS

In this chapter we have shown ways for aspiring global companies to achieve an international cost of capital. We have illustrated our theoretical arguments by referring to some relevant case studies. These cases show how access to competitively priced capital accelerated the international growth prospects of companies from small and thin capital markets at the end of the twentieth century. In fact, without this funding the competitiveness of these firms would have been significantly hampered. We claim that the cases from the Nordic market provide an excellent 'laboratory' to understand successful execution of a global financial strategy and its implication for overall corporate strategy. At the beginning of the 2010s this is particularly appropriate for any small to medium-sized firm, as well as larger firms from more segmented capital markets in emerging economies.

We argue that the corporate motivation for internationalizing the cost of capital is the starting point for understanding a firm's globalization of ownership. Globalization of capital is particularly appropriate in conjunction with globalization on the product side. Second, we emphasize the need to link the business strategy with the financial strategy. Several avenues to internationalizing the cost of capital exist, such as international cross-listing, foreign stock issues, strategic equity alliances, internationalization of corporate governance and receiving support from governments. We argue that globalization of capital is more advantageous to companies with unique products/services and/or unique resources that serve high-growth markets.

The internationalization of ownership calls for a new shareholder regime. First of all the internationalization affects shareholders and governing of firms, as global capital tends to be less tolerant of meager performance. Second, this implies that executives need to focus on the core competencies of the firm, as investors do not approve of value-destroying diversification. Furthermore, global ownership also provides executives with greater opportunities to finance high-return/high-risk projects.

For the home country of aspiring global firms, internationalization of capital provides both opportunities and threats. On the positive side, internationalization of capital allows the small country to produce some impressive global companies, such as Novo of Denmark, Nokia of Finland and Ericsson of Sweden. On the other side, global firms are becoming more 'footloose' and without the right government policies (or other factors beyond the control of governments) companies will move abroad.

REFERENCES

Ahn, E. and F. Kudo (2011), 'Transmission of returns between the U.S. stock market and four other major international stock market indexes', *Journal of Economics and International Finance*, **3**(7): 468–74.

Bansal, R., D. Hsieh and R. Viswanathan (1993), 'A new approach to international arbitrage pricing', *Journal of Finance*, **48**: 1231–62.

Bekaert, G. and C.R. Harvey (2000) 'Foreign speculators and emerging equity markets', *Journal of Finance*, **55**: 565–613.

Blass, A. and Y. Yafeh (2001), 'Vagabond shoes longing to stay: why foreign firms list in the United States', *Journal of Banking and Finance*, **25**: 555–72.

Coffee, J.C. Jr (2002), 'Racing towards the top? The impact of cross-listings and stock market competition on international corporate governance', *Columbia Law Review*, **102**: 1757–831.

Cooper, I. and E. Kaplanis (1994), 'Home bias in equity portfolios, inflation hedging and international capital market equilibrium', *Review of Financial Studies*, **7**: 45–60.

Dahlquist, M. and G. Robertsson (2001), 'Direct foreign ownership, institutional investors, and firm characteristics', *Journal of Financial Economics*, **59**: 413–40.

Doidge, C., G. Karolyi and R. Stulz (2004), 'Why are foreign firms listed in the U.S. worth more?', *Journal of Financial Economics*, **71**: 205–38.

Dumas, B. (1994), 'Partial equilibrium versus general equilibrium models of the international capital market', in F. van der Ploeg (ed.), *The Handbook of International Macroeconomics*, Cambridge, MA: Blackwell, pp. 301–47.

Dunning, J.H. (1993), *Multinational Enterprises in the Global Economy*, Wokingham: Addison-Wesley.

Erb, C.B., C.R. Harvey and T.E. Viskanta (1994), 'Forecasting international equity correlations', *Financial Analysts Journal*, **50**: 32–45.

Forssbæck, J. and L. Oxelheim (2008), 'Finance-specific factors as drivers of cross-border investment – an empirical investigation', *International Business Review*, **17**(6): 630–41.

Forssbæck, J. and L. Oxelheim (2011), 'Corporate financial determinants of foreign direct investment', *Quarterly Review of Economics and Finance*, **51**: 269–82.

French, K. and J. Poterba (1991), 'Investor diversification and international equity markets', *American Economic Review*, **81**(2): 222–6.

Glen, J. and P. Jorion (1993), 'Currency hedging for international portfolios', *Journal of Finance*, **48**: 1865–86.

Graham, M. and J. Nikkinen (2012), 'Co-movement of the Finnish and international stock markets: a wavelet analysis', *European Journal of Finance*, forthcoming DOI: 10.1080/1351847X.2010.543839.

Harvey, C. (1991), 'The world price of covariance risk', *Journal of Finance*, **46**: 111–57.

Hearn, B., J. Piesse and R.Strange (2010), 'Market liquidity and stock size premia in emerging financial markets: the implications for foreign investment', *International Business Review*, **19**(5): 489–501.

Hietala, P.T. (1989), 'Asset pricing in partially segmented markets: evidence from the Finnish market', *Journal of Finance*, **44**: 697–718.

Ibbotson, R., L. Siegel and K. Love (1985), 'World wealth: market values and returns', *Journal of Portfolio Management*, **11**: 4–23.

Ibrahimi, F., L. Oxelheim and C. Wihlborg (1995), 'Macroeconomic fluctuations and international stock markets', in R. Aggarwal and D. Schirm (eds), *Global Portfolio Diversification*, New York: Academic Press, pp. 43–67.

Jorion, P. (1985), 'International portfolio diversification with estimation risk', *Journal of Business*, **58**: 259–78.

Karolyi, A.C. (1998), 'Why do companies list shares abroad? A survey of the evidence and its managerial implications', *Financial Markets, Institutions & Instruments*, **7**: 1–59.

King, M., E. Santana and S. Whadwani (1994), 'Volatility and links between national stock markets', *Econometrica*, **62**: 901–33.

Lang, M.H. and R.J. Lundholm (1996), 'Corporate disclosure policy and analyst behavior', *Accounting Review*, **71**: 467–92.

La Porta, R., F. Lopez-de-Silanes and A. Shleifer (1999), 'Corporate ownership around the world', *Journal of Finance*, **54**: 471–517.

La Porta, R., F. Lopez-de-Silanes, A. Shleifer and R. Vishny (1998), 'Law and finance', *Journal of Political Economy*, **106**: 1113–55.

Lau, S.T. and J.D. Diltz (1994), 'Stock returns and the transfer of information between the New York and Tokyo Stock Exchanges', *Journal of International Money and Finance*, **13**: 211–22.

Lin, W.L., R.F. Engle and T. Ito (1994), 'Do bulls and bears move across borders? International transmission of stock returns and volatility', *Review of Financial Studies*, **7**: 507–38.

Longin, F. and B. Solnik (1995), 'Is the international correlation of equity returns constant: 1960–1990?', *Journal of International Money and Finance*, **14**: 3–26.

Mittoo, U. and Z. Zhang (2008), 'The capital structure of multinational corporations: Canadian versus U.S. evidence', *Journal of Corporate Finance*, **14**(5): 706–20.

Modén, K.-M. and L. Oxelheim (1997), 'Why issue equity abroad? Corporate efforts and stock market responses', *Management International Review*, **37**: 223–41.

Mun, M. and R. Brooks (2012), 'The roles of news and volatility in stock market correlations during the global financial crisis', *Emerging Markets Review*, **13**(1): 1–7.

Naranjo, A. and A. Protopapadakis (1997), 'Financial market integration tests: an investigation using US equity markets', *Journal of International Financial Markets, Institutions & Money*, **7**: 93–135.

NASDAQ (2010), *Listing Requirements & Fees*, http://www.nasdaq.com/about/nasdaq_listing_req_fees.pdf.

O'Connor, T. (2011), 'Financial development, internationalisation and firm value', *Journal of Emerging Market Finance*, **10**: 21–71.

Odier, P. and B. Solnik (1993), 'Lessons for international asset allocation', *Financial Analysts Journal*, **49**: 63–77.

Oxelheim, L. (1990), *International Financial Integration*, Berlin: Springer Verlag.

Oxelheim, L. (1996), *Financial Markets in Transition – Globalization, Investment and Economic Growth*, London and New York: Routledge.

Oxelheim, L. (2001), 'Routes to equity market integration – the interplay between politicians, investors and managers', *Journal of Multinational Financial Management*, **11**: 183–211.

Oxelheim, L. (2006), *Corporate and Institutional Transparency for Economic Growth in Europe*, Oxford: Elsevier.

Oxelheim, L. (2010), 'Globalization, transparency and economic growth: the vulnerability of Chinese firms to macroeconomic shocks', *Journal of Asian Economics*, **21**(1): 66–75.

Oxelheim, L. and P. Ghauri (2008), 'EU–China and the non-transparent race for inward FDI', *Journal of Asian Economics*, **19**(4): 358–70.

Oxelheim, L. and T. Randøy (2003), 'The impact of foreign membership on firm valuation', *Journal of Banking and Finance*, **27**: 2369–92.

Oxelheim, L. and T. Randøy (2005), 'The Anglo-American financial influence on CEO compensation in non-Anglo-American firms', *Journal of International Business Studies*, **36**: 1–14.

Oxelheim, L., A. Gregoric, T. Randøy and S. Thomsen (2011), 'From global firms to global boards', Conference paper, Academy of International Business Annual Conference, Nagoya, June.

Oxelheim, L., T. Randøy and A. Stonehill (2001), 'On the treatment of finance-specific factors within the OLI paradigm', *International Business Review*, **10**: 381–98.

Oxelheim, L., A. Stonehill, T. Randøy, K. Vikkula, K.B. Dullum and K.-M. Modén (1998), *Corporate Strategies to Internationalize the Cost of Capital*, Copenhagen: Handelshøjskolens Forlag.

Oxelheim, L., C. Wihlborg and M. Thorsheim (2012), 'The CFO's information challenge in managing macroeconomic risk', in Ulrich Hommel, Michael Fabich, Ervin Schellenberg and Lutz Firnkom (eds), *The strategic CFO: Creating Value in a Dynamic Market Environment*, Berlin and Heidelberg: Springer-Verlag, pp. 189–208.

Pagano, M., A. Röell and J. Zechner (2002), 'The geography of equity listing: why do companies list abroad?', *Journal of Finance*, **57**: 2651–94.

Reese, W. Jr and M. Weisback (2001), 'Protection of minority shareholder interests, cross-listings in the United States, and subsequent equity offerings', Working Paper No. 8164, NBER.

Shleifer, A. and R. Vishny (1986), 'Large shareholders and corporate control', *Journal of Political Economy*, **94**: 461–88.

Shleifer, A. and R. Vishny (1997), 'A survey of corporate governance', *Journal of Finance*, **52**: 737–83.

Solnik, B. (1996), *International Investments*, Reading, MA: Addison Wesley.

Stulz, R.M. (1999), 'Globalization, corporate finance and the cost of capital', *Journal of Applied Corporate Finance*, **12**: 8–25.

Sundaram, A.K. and D.E. Logue (1996), 'Valuation effects of foreign company listings on U.S. exchanges', *Journal of International Business*, **27**: 67–88.

Susmel, R. and R.F. Engle (1994), 'Hourly volatility spillovers between international equity markets', *Journal of International Money and Finance*, **13**: 3–25.

Tesar, L. and I. Werner (1995), 'Home bias and high turnover', *Journal of International Money and Finance*, **14**: 467–92.

Useem, M. (1998), 'Corporate leadership in a globalizing equity market', *Academy of Management Executive*, **12**: 43–59.

Wheatley, S. (1988), 'Some tests on international equity integration', *Journal of Financial Economics*, **21**: 177–212.

Yeyati, E., S. Schmukler and N. Van Horen (2009), 'International financial integration through the law of one price: the role of liquidity and capital controls', *Journal of Financial Intermediation*, **18**(3): 432–63.

PART III

THE IMPLICATIONS OF DISTANCE FOR INTERNATIONAL STRATEGY

13 A new perspective on the regional and global strategies of multinational services firms
Alan M. Rugman and Alain Verbeke

INTRODUCTION

Conventional Approaches to the Globalization of Services

Rugman and Verbeke (2004, 2007a) have demonstrated that most of the world's largest 500 companies pursue regional, rather than global, strategies. They show that few firms actually have balanced sales across the broad triad regions of Europe, North America and Asia. They define a global firm as a company with less than 50 percent of sales in its home triad region and at least 20 percent in each of the two other triad regions. The typical *Fortune* Global 500 company averages over 70 percent of its overall sales in its home region of the broad triad, and substantially less than 20 percent of its overall sales in each of the two other regions. Such discrepancy in sales performance is then mostly reflected in regionally adapted strategies and structures (Rugman and Verbeke, 2007b). The home-region orientation of most multinational enterprises (MNEs) implies that the reality of globalization has been vastly exaggerated. Here, we extend Rugman and Verbeke's (2004, 2007a) regional strategy analysis in two ways, namely by adding the parameter of asset dispersion, and by focusing on the differences, if any, between manufacturing and services industries.

First, Rugman and Verbeke's (2004, 2007a) original data did not address the geographic dispersion of production activities. Yet low sales dispersion could be accompanied by high asset dispersion, for example if MNEs engage in substantial offshoring. MNEs may want to tap into attractive (sometimes low-cost) input markets in host regions, and subsequently import components or finished products for sale in their home region. A similar phenomenon occurs in services provision, as with offshored software development or call centers.

For MNEs pursuing a strategy of sourcing in host regions to support sales in the home region, one might observe a higher interregional dispersion of assets than sales. However, the normative implications of sales dispersion versus asset dispersion are different. High sales dispersion (assuming this occurs profitably) can be interpreted as effective performance in providing value to customers irrespective of geographic boundaries. High sales dispersion also reflects successful risk diversification at the downstream end of the value chain (even in the special case whereby foreign markets are penetrated to compensate for declining success at home). In contrast, high asset dispersion, covering both the upstream and downstream segments of the value chain, reflects the capability to manage a network of assets across borders. High asset dispersion is only an intermediate variable, not necessarily instrumental to improved performance (as compared with a situation of low asset dispersion) in terms of providing value to customers internationally or reducing risks. In fact, high asset dispersion, though often heralded as a managerial instrument to achieve flexibility, may lead to internal coordination challenges, and the loss of scale economies if a single value chain activity is performed in several locations. Nevertheless, the analysis of asset dispersion is useful as it provides information on the global reach (or lack thereof) of the MNE's production activities.

Second, Rugman and Verbeke (2004, 2007a) did not address explicitly the industry effect, especially the distinction between manufacturing and services. In terms of the latter issue, i.e. the difference between international expansion of services firms *vis-à-vis* manufacturing firms, two alternative hypotheses could be formulated based on conventional thinking.

Hypothesis 1   Services MNEs are likely to have a higher degree of globalization (in terms of sales and asset dispersion across the triad) than manufacturing MNEs because of lower required capital investments, more easily transferable intangible firm-specific advantages (FSAs), and more compelling first-mover advantages.

Here, host-region penetration may occur easily in cases of low levels of minimum scale efficient investments and a strong reliance upon the international transfer of intangible services provision routines (absent protectionist government regulation). Low capital investments and easy FSA transferability not only signal low entry barriers, but may also imply low exit barriers and a strong potential of alternative resource deployment. This means that the risks associated with international expansion in services may also be low. In addition, there may be first-mover advantages associated with international entry. Buyer uncertainty associated with purchasing intangible outputs is overcome, and customer loyalty is built early, thereby preempting imitation.

Hypothesis 2   Services MNEs are likely to be less global (in terms of sales and asset dispersion across the triad) than manufacturing MNEs because of problems related to higher human asset specificity, synchronization difficulties of supply and demand for non-storable services across geographic space, and market creation benefits accruing to late movers.

Pure services are indeed difficult for potential purchasers to evaluate because they are intangible by definition, i.e. they have no physical substance. Pure services therefore cannot be seen, touched, lifted or 'experienced' before actual purchase, in contrast to pure goods, and this constitutes an entry barrier by itself. Pure goods, in contrast to pure services, can usually also be made homogeneous in terms of quality, because quality control routines can be deployed during production, but before actual purchasing. In contrast, pure services provision may be associated with a higher degree of heterogeneity, to the extent that the human element, not captured fully in routines, remains important. Here, the service quality can differ from service provider to service provider, from consumer to consumer, and it can vary across time (Zeithaml et al., 1985). Service quality can therefore also be expected to vary across geographic space. The problem with expanding to high-distance host environments (including cultural, economic and institutional distance) is that it becomes more difficult to guarantee service quality and to correct quality deficiencies. To express this point differently: if the MNE does not want to compromise on service quality, then international entry barriers unrelated to capital investments, but linked to human asset specificity (meaning here the specific, cost-increasing or service-provision-delaying requirements to satisfy potential purchasers in terms of desired features of the individuals providing the service), may actually be higher than those in manufacturing.

Most services are perishable, in the sense that they cannot be stored. For example, a hotel room that is vacant is the equivalent of a loss, as 'storage' is impossible. Because services cannot be stored, there are difficulties in synchronizing supply and demand (Zeithaml et al., 1985). The international business context may amplify this challenge further, as a disconnect may occur between supply and demand, without the option to 'ship' the excess supply of services in one location to high demand occurring elsewhere.

Finally, the concept of first-mover advantages as a driver of services expansion abroad might be considered a non-starter in many cases. If buyer uncertainty is high, the first mover may actually be supporting late entrants by creating a new market for particular services. Whereas customer loyalty and customer switching costs may indeed be higher in the case of buyer uncertainty, the benefits of the initial market creation accruing to late movers may outweigh the difficulties faced by these same firms to attract early purchasers of the services, loyal to the first entrant(s).

It could of course be argued that in practice the likelihood of one of the above hypotheses gaining empirical support at the expense of the other one will largely depend on the specific type of services considered. In fact, intra-services industry differences might be as important as the differences between manufacturing and services. Zeithaml et al. (1985) attempted to capture the differences within services along four broad categories, the second of these actually reflecting international expansion (rather than viewing international expansion itself as an outcome of other variables) by: primary customer group, geographic spread, duration of benefits to the customer, and need for the customer's presence during service production.

According to Thomas (1978), services industries can be classified as equipment based or people based. Equipment-based services can be either largely automated, as is the case with vending machines, or monitored by relatively unskilled operators, as with dry cleaning services, or operated by highly skilled personnel, as with airline services, excavating services etc. People-based services can be provided either by relatively unskilled labor, as is the case with the provision of private security guards, or by more highly skilled labor, as with plumbing and appliance repair, or by highly qualified professionals, as with management consulting, legal services etc.

However, in the context of easy versus difficult international expansion and the resulting degree of multinationality, the knowledge intensity versus capital intensity of the services involved is considered by some scholars as the more important discriminating factor. Contractor et al. (2003) classified services subsectors as a function of their knowledge intensity versus capital intensity. Subsectors such as advertising, marketing research, publishing, securities and diversified financial services were classified as knowledge-based services, whereas air transportation, construction, hotels, restaurants, shipping and trucking services were classified as capital-intensive services. Contractor et al.'s (2003) empirical results suggest that knowledge-based services MNEs were more likely to succeed than capital-intensive services MNEs in the initial stage of internationalization. The importance of capital intensity in international services expansion has also been advocated by other authors, such as Erramilli and Rao (1993), who observed that when capital intensity is high, firms have a lower propensity to share control of their foreign operations.

We accept the above point that services firms can be very different in terms of key attributes affecting international expansion patterns and multinationality. The question then still arises, however, whether any general predictions can be made such as those embedded in Hypotheses 1 and 2, but which are based on conventional thinking, as to the international expansion and globalization of services firms versus manufacturing ones.

The Need for a New Perspective on the Globalization of Services Firms

Taking into account the above analysis, we adopt a new perspective on the globalization of services, and propose a third hypothesis, which we view as relevant for the services industry in general. This hypothesis suggests a major similarity and also a major difference with manufacturing.

Hypothesis 3　Goods manufacturing and services provision will, overall, show similar tendencies in terms of being largely home-region oriented rather than global, but the magnitude of globalization (in terms of sales and asset dispersion across the triad) will be significantly lower in services.

Our starting point is that MNEs, whether in manufacturing or in services, arise primarily to overcome market imperfections, especially in the context of the public-good nature of knowledge: transaction costs are reduced and value is created. All MNEs rely on proprietary, knowledge-based FSAs (Rugman, 1987). This has led to the statement that 'all MNEs are service MNEs' (Boddewyn et al., 1986, p. 51).

In addition, it is important to recognize that many goods are increasingly accompanied by services, as is the case with the simultaneous purchase of computers and after-sales services provision through electronic means. As another example, the brand names associated with many successful international products, and critical to these products' success, are intangible assets. Similarly, many services can only be provided when linked to tangible assets, as is the case with retail banking services relying increasingly on sophisticated, automated banking machines. Another example is telecommunications services designed for delivery through multi-purpose, handheld communication devices.

The above observations suggest that manufacturing and services MNEs are not intrinsically different in terms of rationale for their existence, nor in terms of prevailing transaction cost reduction and value creation challenges, in contrast to what was suggested by the contradictory substance embedded in Hypotheses 1 and 2. The actual transfer of intangible FSAs, featuring indeed more prominently in services, may actually occur more easily or with greater difficulty than in manufacturing, depending upon the situation. The parameters that matter include: knowledge tacitness (or non-codification); knowledge embeddedness; and absorptive capacity of the knowledge recipient in the host environment.

Entry and exit barriers (save government regulation) may also be higher or lower, depending upon the adaptation investments required in the host environment and the potential for redeployability of the resources invested. Finally, the costs and benefits of first-mover strategies depend upon the resulting increase in customer switching costs and the spillover effects of market creation benefiting late entrants. Thus we expect that services will, overall, across subsectors, encounter a liability of interregional foreignness similar to the liability faced by manufacturing MNEs, in accordance with the theory of regional strategy (Rugman and Verbeke 2004, 2007a).

However, the overall empirical reality can be expected to differentiate between both types of firms at a secondary level, more particularly in terms of the nature of the adaptation efforts required and the resulting complexity/magnitude of investments to overcome distance, whether cultural, economic or institutional/regulatory (Ghemawat, 2001).

In the remainder of the chapter, we first discuss at a conceptual level two key specificities of the services sector related to the challenge of adapting to distance, with implications for the expected level of services globalization. We then examine data that show that most of the world's largest MNEs, whether in manufacturing or in services, are indeed home-region oriented, whether measured by asset dispersion or sales dispersion. However, in terms of magnitude, we also show that services MNEs are even more home-region oriented than manufacturing MNEs. The chapter concludes with an integrated theory section, which explores the implications of the home-region orientation of services industries.

SPECIFICITIES OF SERVICES GLOBALIZATION

The issue of globalization of services firms versus manufacturing companies is not new. Li and Guisinger (1992) analyzed the international expansion of services MNEs with a home base in the core triad of Western Europe, the USA and Japan, and covering the period between 1976 and 1986. In general terms, their analysis showed that services foreign direct investment (FDI), as a partial measure of international expansion, was negatively affected by distance, especially cultural distance, from the home country. Such distance requires adaptation investments to reduce buyer uncertainty. Services were influenced positively by the openness of the host market to inward FDI in services and the presence of an oligopolistic market structure of the services sub-industry considered. Li and Guisinger's (1992) analysis raised two critical points.

First, as regards institutional/regulatory distance, they observed comparatively strong government restrictions in a variety of services sectors, reducing foreign entry. Assuming that the relative difference in restriction levels on foreign-owned operations between services industries and manufacturing has not changed much in recent decades, the expectation is a lower foreign sales to total sales ratio (F/T) achieved by services firms as compared to manufacturing. This is confirmed by strong remaining regulations of foreign firms' entry and operation in most countries in a myriad of services industries, including insurance, retailing, professional services, airlines etc. This discrepancy with goods manufacturing holds especially across regions, since much progress has been made in intraregional reduction of entry barriers, including most services industries, especially in the EU and the NAFTA environment, so that the challenges of successful host region entry versus home region FDI are comparatively higher.

Second, in terms of strategic purpose, Li and Guisinger (1992) observed that most FDI in services industries is market driven, in contrast to manufacturing, where other entry motivations than market seeking may prevail. In manufacturing the option usually exists to separate upstream and downstream segments of the value chain, but this is more difficult in services. Such inseparability is obviously not characteristic of all services provision (Erramilli and Rao, 1990; Blomstermo et al., 2006). In practice, however, total separability of services production and delivery can mostly not be achieved, in contrast with what is the case in manufacturing. This places an additional burden on services firms to tailor not only their downstream operations, but also their upstream ones to host environments, so as to overcome the liability of foreignness, whether at the level of a host country or host region (Rugman and Verbeke, 2007b).

Here, it is not FSA transferability *per se* that is necessarily relevant, but rather the limited exploitation potential of extant FSA bundles, before adaptation investments covering the entire value chain are made in the host environment. The strong linkages between upstream and downstream activities may also affect the flexibility in redeploying resources across borders: newly created downstream FSAs may not be redeployable by themselves, and selling services operations to third parties that cover inseparable upstream and downstream FSAs may be fraught with difficulties. In other words, overall redeployability of resources committed to production activities in a host environment may be low as compared to goods.

International services production must thus often include resource bundles, both tangible and intangible ones, covering simultaneously the upstream and downstream sides of the value chain, with the latter comparatively less separable from actual consumption than with goods manufacturing. In the presence of distance, the comparatively stronger requirements in services for (a) coupling upstream and downstream production activities, which systematically involve substantial bundles of intangible resources (Cloninger, 2004), and (b) linking those coupled activities directly with consumption, lead to higher risk of failure.

Given the comparatively weaker separability in services sectors between production and consumption, it is less clear what adaptation investments are required in these sectors, or the sequence in which they should be made to overcome the various distance components, thereby increasing the challenges of foreign expansion. This point is valid especially at the interregional level, given the liability of interregional foreignness (Rugman and Verbeke, 2007a). The potential to learn what constitutes appropriate adaptation through initial, lower-commitment entry modes such as exports is often limited. So is the feasibility to build up services production slowly (Carman and Langeard, 1980), even when faced with high levels of cultural, economic and institutional/regulatory distance in the host region. In manufacturing, production plants can take on increasingly complex tasks as they become more experienced and embedded in the host environment (Ferdows, 1997), whereas in services the 'producer–consumer intimacy is immediate' (Carman and Langeard, 1980, p. 18).

Related to this last point, services firms are – again as compared to goods manufacturers – often restrained in choosing an optimal location. Services MNEs can often not select the most efficient location from a supply-side perspective to produce services. The locus of consumption dictates the locus of production, even though some services subsectors have recently been able to offshore some value chain activities to low-cost locations such as India, geographically divorced from the places of consumption. This holds especially for ICT-supported services such as call centers, back-office technical consulting etc.

Li and Guisinger's (1992) analysis thus suggests a comparatively lower international market penetration in services as the result of three factors: first, more stringent government regulation of foreign services firms, which is largely an exogenous factor; second, fewer options to divorce production from consumption, thereby requiring more complex and wide-ranging resource bundles to be adapted to host environments. This factor is thus related to the nature of the services firms' FSAs; and third, more limited possibilities to engage in location choice optimization from a supply-side perspective. This factor is related to the services MNEs access to location advantages in host environments.

The main weakness of Li and Guisinger's (1992) work is their sole reliance, as a scope measure of international expansion, on growth in the number of affiliates abroad, thereby neglecting the actual size of the investments considered. This point is important when considering the statistical significance of the oligopolistic reaction variable, intended to measure the 'follow-the-leader' phenomenon. What Li and Guisinger (1992) actually measure are attempts at international expansion (i.e. a number of entries), possibly driven by the presence of other industry players, rather than success at such expansion (i.e. sales volumes achieved and the role thereof in overall company sales). Li and Guisinger do not actually test if services MNEs (with market-seeking entries in multiple countries) are able to translate such entries into significant market penetration, expressed as a percentage of company sales.

As noted above, services MNEs must adapt simultaneously – in a context of high distance – a comparatively more complex and more wide-ranging set of resource bundles to host environment requirements. In addition, these companies face comparatively stronger constraints in their location choices, which occur primarily as a function of demand considerations rather than joint demand and supply requirements. Hence international services expansion is likely to face more difficulties than foreign expansion in goods manufacturing.

The above analysis contradicts Lovelock and Yip's (1996) manifesto advocating the globalization of services. A careful reading of their study suggests, however, that the normative and predictive elements in their analysis are not always clearly separated. For example, they suggest that services mostly consist of core service products (such as key routines) and supplementary elements (related, *inter alia*, to order-taking, billing, payment etc.), with the latter being easily and inexpensively adaptable to relevant host environments. They do acknowledge that, in practice, the most important sources of successful globalization at the micro-level, namely FSAs, are difficult to deploy in host environments precisely because of the human/tacit element involved. They then go on to argue that 'globally standardized products' are 'perhaps the one feature most commonly identified with global strategy' (Lovelock and Yip, 1996, p. 77). Yet they follow the above observations that suggest great challenges of services globalization with the suggestion that services firms mostly have to adapt only their 'supplementary services' to local environments, arguing that this is easy to achieve, but without reflecting seriously on the actual cost implications and additional complexities created: which supplementary services should be adapted? To what extent should the firm engage on this path? How affordable is the creation of new FSAs, especially when expressed in percentage points of the core services' cost? How likely is it that the adaptation of the supplementary services will be successful *vis-à-vis* the services provided by insiders in the host environment?

Finally, they advocate standardized global branding, global advertising and 'globally-consistent corporate design' as a tool to overcome buyer uncertainty (Lovelock and Yip, 1996, p. 84). However, whereas attempts at successful global standardization may be a worthwhile endeavor, the likelihood of success for services companies engaged on this path is unclear. Is this strategy not the equivalent of ethnocentric attempts to create scale economies in manufacturing at the expense of being nationally/regionally responsive, an approach that has proven ineffective in most cases?

To conclude, Lovelock and Yip (1996) did a good job at creating awareness about the potential of some services firms to globalize, but they largely neglected the costs and challenges of such an expansion path. They ignore the comparatively more complex and wide-ranging FSA adaptation investments needed to cover simultaneously upstream and downstream activities, and the comparatively stronger restrictions on location optimization from a supply-side perspective. In the next section, we provide some empirical evidence suggesting that the case for services globalization has indeed been overstated. In the final section we link these data to the conceptual points made here as we develop a general theory of multinational services firms.

THE GEOGRAPHY OF REGIONAL SERVICES FIRMS

In earlier work, Rugman and Verbeke (2004, 2007a) and Rugman (2005) have explored the regional dimension of the world's largest 500 firms (based on the *Fortune* Global 500). Both of these studies used data for 2001. At that time, there were 280 services firms in the top 500, and only 220 in manufacturing. Data were available for only 380 firms on their geographic dispersion of sales. We found that 320 of these 380 firms (across both manufacturing and services) averaged 80 percent of their sales in their home region. There were only nine truly global firms with 20 percent or more of sales in each region of the triad and under 50 percent of sales in their home region. There were also some 36 bi-regional firms with over 20 percent of sales in two regions of the triad and less than 50 percent in their home region.

In Table 13.1 we provide new data across two dimensions. First, we have updated the sales data from 2000, up to and including 2006. This now provides data for a seven-year period for a large number of the world's largest 500 firms. Second, we have provided data on assets as well as on sales. This is done in order to include information about the nature of the production activities of these firms. The geographical dispersion of international sales and international production need not be identical. The asset data should therefore provide more details about the production aspect of globalization than the sales data, previously reported in Rugman and Verbeke (2004) and Rugman (2005). Yet, as will be seen, the addition of information on assets leads to essentially the same conclusion as for sales: most large firms are home-region based.

In Table 13.1, for each year we classify the data into two categories: manufacturing and services. The number of firms in the population over the seven-year period varies by year, due to mergers and acquisitions. There are entry and exits to the top 500 according to changes in total revenues. In Table 13.1 we include every firm that appears in the top 500 list in any of the seven years, 2000–06. This is a total of 697 firms.

In Table 13.1 (Panel A) there are 437 firms in 2000 and 503 in 2006. These numbers

Table 13.1   Intraregional sales of the largest firms in the services and manufacturing sectors

Panel A   Intraregional sales

Year	Number of firms	Intraregional sales (%)		
		All industries	Manufacturing	Services
2000	437	77.2	67.3	84.2
2001	511	76.7	66.0	84.3
2002	514	76.5	65.9	84.1
2003	513	76.5	65.6	84.3
2004	526	76.1	65.3	84.1
2005	529	75.5	65.1	83.3
2006	503	74.8	64.6	82.6
Weighted average		76.2	65.6	83.9

Panel B   Intraregional assets

Year	Number of firms	Intraregional assets (%)		
		All industries	Manufacturing	Services
2000	358	78.4	70.9	84.5
2001	413	77.4	70.4	83.3
2002	427	77.7	70.5	83.8
2003	431	78.0	70.9	83.9
2004	452	78.3	71.0	84.3
2005	461	78.3	71.2	84.1
2006	435	78.0	71.1	83.8
Weighted average		78.0	70.8	84.0

Source: Annual reports for 2000–06. Sample firms are included if they appear on the list for any year of the *Fortune* Global 500 during 2000–06.

reflect the firms reporting geographic segment information on sales across all seven years. In Table 13.1 (Panel B) there are fewer firms providing data on their geographic segments for assets.

Table 13.1 (Panel A) shows that the average intraregional sales figure for all firms is 76.2 percent with a plus or minus variation by year of under 2 percent. Further, services average 83.9 percent home-region sales as against 65.6 percent for manufacturing. This is a statistically significant difference. In Panel B of Table 13.1 there is a similar statistically significant difference in the average intraregional assets of services and manufacturing. The interpretation from both panels of Table 13.1 is that services are more home-region oriented than manufacturing across both sales activities and production activities.

THE THEORY OF REGIONAL STRATEGY FOR SERVICES INDUSTRIES

We have outlined the foundations of a theory of regional strategy elsewhere (Rugman and Verbeke 2004, 2005, 2007a, 2007b). In the context of market-seeking expansion, MNEs can penetrate foreign markets only if they can build upon non-location-bound FSAs, transferable and deployable in a profitable fashion in host environments. However, as the distance from the home country increases, with its regulatory/institutional, cultural and economic components, the non-location-bound FSAs become subject to decay, and the need increases to complement these FSAs with new, location-bound FSAs so as to overcome the liability of foreignness. In our past work, we have suggested that overall distance usually increases sharply when a firm expands outside of its home triad region (e.g. the EU environment) into a host triad region (e.g. Asia): there is a liability of inter-regional foreignness. For each of the three main distance components, there are often enormous additional costs of doing business in a host region (though acknowledging that these may be moderated in some cases by historical ties, e.g. former colonial linkages). These additional costs are reflected in the decay of extant, non-location-bound FSA bundles, and the challenge of complementing with new FSAs whatever remaining part of the extant FSA bundles is actually valued positively by potential buyers in the host region.

If the exploitation potential of the MNE's non-location-bound FSAs indeed declines dramatically in host regions because of distance, and the firm is unable to either (1) develop a new complementary set of location-bound FSAs internally as an adaptive response to host location requirements, or (2) acquire the equivalent knowledge in the external market, MNE managers have two options.

First, as suggested by Rugman and Verbeke (2004), they may focus on exploiting their existing FSA bundles in locations where customers confer a high value to these FSAs. For most companies these locations are likely to include countries in the home triad region. In fact, if the home region is characterized by efforts at regulatory/institutional and economic integration (as in the EU, the NAFTA environment and ASEAN), this may facilitate further the international but intraregional expansion of MNEs. Here the decay of non-location-bound FSAs is minimized by fine-tuning them for deployment throughout the region, and location-bound FSAs, previously exploitable in the home country only, can be upgraded for deployment throughout the region.

Second, MNEs may choose to cooperate with host region insider companies to benefit from their location-bound FSAs, that is to make use of their relevant knowledge about and skills for dealing with the local government and other local stakeholders, thereby achieving reciprocal resource synergies (Verbeke and Van den Bussche, 2005). However, the typically higher cultural distance in host regions may make cooperative strategies difficult (Brown et al., 1989).

Importantly, in the context of the above analysis of services firms, we also suggested that the level of decay of non-location-bound FSAs and the need for new, complementary FSAs, depend largely upon the value chain activity considered. Here, the main difficulty with services as compared to goods is the higher magnitude of inseparability of upstream and downstream activity adaptation, so that the complexity of addressing both FSA

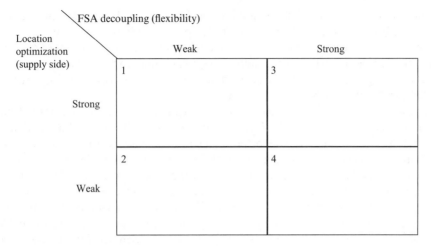

Figure 13.1 MNE interregional expansion potential

decay and new FSA requirements is also higher. In addition, if the MNE faces stronger challenges of FSA decay and new FSA development in host regions, but is constrained in selecting an optimal location to address these challenges, with demand-side require-ments prevailing over supply-side optimization, interregional expansion is again likely to be hampered.

The impossibility of decoupling the adaptation of upstream and downstream value chain activities, or engaging in the supply-side optimization of location advantages, is not necessarily characteristic of all services, but the magnitude of occurrence is higher in services than in goods manufacturing. In fact, the value chain of any MNE – and its individual business units – whether in services or in manufacturing, can be described in a stylized fashion, according to Figure 13.1 on the MNE's internal optimization capability in interregional market expansion. In Figure 13.1, the horizontal axis describes the MNE's FSA challenge: FSA decoupling (upstream versus downstream) flexibility. This can be weak or strong. Strong decoupling flexibility means that upstream and down-stream activities can easily be adapted separately. The vertical axis represents the MNE's location advantage challenge. It assesses the extent to which the MNE has a supply-side autonomy in location choices (weak or strong).

In quadrant 3 of Figure 13.1, we can position brand-named goods and services, whereby upstream production can be fully decoupled from marketing and sales, and the locus of operations in host environments can be chosen freely by the MNE without con-straints imposed by potential purchasers. Here, the goods or services can in principle be sold anywhere in the world, based upon their cost/quality features, without need for fundamental adaptation of the upstream end of the value chain. Some services provided through IT means may fit into this quadrant, e.g. software development by Indian com-panies, as well as some subsectors of the entertainment industry, but these are rather rare cases. The implications of this position in quadrant 3 of large parts of the goods manu-facturing sector have often been overstated, however, as even achieving national or regional responsiveness at the downstream end in high-distance host environments may be a challenging proposition.

In quadrant 2 of Figure 13.1, we find localized services with the opposite characteristics, namely little potential for decoupling fully upstream and downstream activities, and location choices largely determined by demand considerations: many services fit here, often in the context of stringent regulation, such as retail banking services, legal services, property management, utilities, transport and other professional services with high knowledge-related entry barriers.

Quadrants 1 and 3 are intermediate cases: in quadrant 1, the MNE has substantial internal autonomy in its location choices within a host environment, but upstream and downstream activities must largely be performed simultaneously (e.g. management consulting and engineering services). In contrast, in quadrant 4, only downstream activities must be performed in the host environment, but the location thereof is fully determined by demand-side considerations. Many services in the hospitality industry (hotels and resorts) fit in this quadrant, as does retail. Here, many back-office activities can be performed separately from operational management, but the actual location of downstream operations in the host environment is usually determined fully by demand-side preferences.

The point is that, as compared to goods, very few services would fit into quadrant 3 of Figure 13.1, which means that higher interregional distance will impose a significant additional burden of adaptation on services firms. This occurs because upstream and downstream activities must both be adapted simultaneously, rather than downstream activities alone, and/or because demand influences location choices in a way that is not conducive to optimal production from a supply-side perspective.

CONCLUSION

In this chapter we have focused on the differences between MNEs classified as services companies versus manufacturing firms. Both types of firms share an important characteristic: they operate mainly within their home region of the triad of the EU, North America and the Asia Pacific. However, the services MNEs are significantly more home-region based, averaging 83.9 percent of sales in their home region, in contrast to manufacturing firms with only 65.6 percent. Clearly, these summary data indicate that there are very few global firms, whether in services or manufacturing. Therefore both sets of firms can benefit from the analysis of regional strategy and structure, rather than from an analysis focusing primarily on alleged global strategy and structure. In this chapter we have attempted to advance the regional strategy agenda, building upon the observation of the regional nature of the sales and assets of most services MNEs.

In our analytical work we take as a central building block the concept of the value chain. In general, manufacturing MNEs are able to decouple upstream and downstream activities, and to adapt those two activity types separately to host environment requirements. These firms can also make location choices subject to supply-side optimization criteria. In contrast, many services MNEs exhibit a relative lack of such flexibility in adapting upstream and downstream activities separately, or in selecting activity locations as a function of supply-side considerations. Services MNEs are required to deliver their activities close to their consumers. Their FSAs are marketing and brand-name based. Upstream activities of services MNEs are intimately coupled with their downstream marketing and sales delivery, thereby making effective adaptation to high-distance host environments much more complex. This further limits the number of services MNEs that can be regarded as truly global in terms of sales and asset dispersion.

It is likely that only MNEs in narrow services subsectors such as IT and media can operate across geographic space similar to manufacturing MNEs, in the sense of exploiting flexibility in their value chains. The great majority of services MNEs lack such flexibility, as is the case with retail banking, legal services, utilities and the transportation sector. There may be a few special cases as regards the flexibility parameter. Consulting firms can usually locate their offices in a variety of places inside a host environment, but must still adapt their upstream and downstream activities simultaneously to this environment. In contrast, luxury hotel chains are often internationally successful because many back-office activities can be divorced from more downstream activities. However, the actual location of the hotels themselves in host locations is usually totally determined by demand-side location preferences (except for the rare cases where the hotel chain decides to develop a hotel in a unique/exclusive location, irrespective of present demand, but hoping that demand will follow).

Overall, we have found little evidence that services MNEs operate globally. There is little homogenization in the services sectors on a worldwide basis. In the future it is highly unlikely that more than a handful of the world's largest 500 firms, of which nearly 300 are in services, will be able to develop a truly global presence and operate global strategies. Instead, most of the services MNEs will need to wrestle with a regional approach to strategy for the reasons explored in this chapter.

REFERENCES

Blomstermo, A., Sharma, D.D. and Sallis, J. (2006), 'Choice of foreign market entry mode in service firms', *International Marketing Review*, **23**(2), 211–29.

Boddewyn, J., Halbrich, M.B. and Perry, A.C. (1986), 'Service multinationals: conceptualization, measurement and theory', *Journal of International Business Studies*, **1**, 41–57.

Brown, L.T., Rugman, A.M. and Verbeke, A. (1989), 'Japanese joint ventures with Western multinationals: synthesising the economic and cultural explanations of failure', *Asia Pacific Journal of Management*, **6**(2), 225–65.

Carman, J.M. and Langeard, E. (1980), 'Growth strategies of service firms', *Strategic Management Journal*, **1**(1), 7–22.

Cloninger, P.A. (2004), 'The effect of service intangibility on revenue from foreign markets', *Journal of International Management*, **10**(1), 125–46.

Contractor, F.J., Kundu, S.K. and Hsu, C.(2003), 'A three-stage theory of international expansion: the link between multinationality and performance in the service sector', *Journal of International Business Studies*, **34**(1), 5–18.

Erramilli, K.M. and Rao, C.P. (1990), 'Choice of foreign market entry modes by service firms: role of market knowledge', *Management International Review*, **30**(2), 135–50.

Erramilli, K.M. and Rao, C.P. (1993), 'Service firms' international entry-mode choice: a modified transaction-cost analysis approach', *Journal of Marketing*, **57**(3), 19–38.

Ferdows, K. (1997), 'Making the most of foreign factories', *Harvard Business Review*, **75**(2), 77–88.

Ghemawat, P. (2001), 'Distance still matters: the hard reality of global expansion', *Harvard Business Review*, **79**(8), 137–47.

Li, J.T. and Guisinger, S. (1992), 'The globalization of service multinationals in the Triad region: Japan, Western Europe, and North America', *Journal of International Business Studies*, **23**, 675–96.

Lovelock, C.H. and Yip, G.S. (1996), 'Developing global strategies for service businesses', *California Management Review*, **38**, 64–86.

Rugman, A.M. (1987), 'Multinationals and trade in services: a transaction cost approach', *Weltwirtschaftliches Archiv*, **123**(4), 651–67.
Rugman, A.M. (2005), *The Regional Multinationals: MNEs and 'Global' Strategic Management*, Cambridge: Cambridge University Press.
Rugman, A.M. and Verbeke, A. (2004), 'A perspective on regional and global strategies of multinational enterprises', *Journal of International Business Studies*, **35**(1), 3–18.
Rugman, A.M. and Verbeke, A. (2005), 'Towards a theory of regional multinationals: a transaction cost economics approach', *Management International Review*, **45** (Special Issue/1), 5–17.
Rugman, A.M. and Verbeke, A. (2007a), 'Liabilities of regional foreignness and the use of firm-level versus country-level data: a response to Dunning et al.', *Journal of International Business Studies*, **38**(1), 200–205.
Rugman, A.M. and Verbeke, A. (2007b), 'A regional solution to the strategy and structure of multinationals', mimeo.
Thomas, D.R.E. (1978), 'Strategy is different in service businesses', *Harvard Business Review*, **56**, 158–65.
Verbeke, A. and Van den Bussche, S. (2005), 'Regional and global strategies in the intercontinental passenger airline industry: the rise of alliance specific advantages', in A. Verbeke (ed.), *Internalization, International Diversification and the Multinational Enterprise* (Research in Global Strategic Management, 11), Oxford: Elsevier, pp. 119–46.
Zeithaml, V.A., Parasuraman, A. and Berry, L.L. (1985), 'Problems and strategies in services marketing', *Journal of Marketing*, **49**, 33–46.

14 Foundations of regional versus global strategies of MNEs

Christian Geisler Asmussen

INTRODUCTION

The geographic scope of the firm is a key strategic variable for multinational enterprises (MNEs). Over time, managers shape the geographic scope of their firm through their cumulative choices of which foreign markets to enter, in which order, and to what extent. We know by now that these are choices that have pervasive impact on the performance of the MNE, as they potentially affect its scale, risk exposure, cost structure and value-generating assets. In recognition of this development, the concept of geographic scope – broadly defined as the number and locations of geographic markets in which the firm does business – has received much attention from international business (IB) scholars. A large number of studies have looked into topics such as which factors guide MNEs' location decisions (e.g. Dunning, 1996; Rugman and Verbeke, 1993), the order and timing of foreign market entry (e.g. Kogut and Singh, 1988; Benito and Gripsrud, 1992), and the performance implications of international expansion (e.g. Morck and Yeung, 1991; Hitt et al., 1997).

Yet, despite all these studies, the best way(s) in which to conceptualize and dimensionalize the central variable – the geographic scope of the MNE – remains curiously elusive. Traditionally, the preoccupation with internationalization as a concept has led researchers to ask a series of 'how much' questions, e.g. 'How global are MNEs really?', and 'How much internationalization should a MNE pursue?' Recent research, in contrast, indicates that the 'how' question is as important as, and perhaps more important than, the 'how much' question (Vermeulen and Barkema, 2002; Goerzen and Beamish, 2003). These studies show that it is not only the level of internationalization *per se*, but also and perhaps even more so the pattern of internationalization that matters. Yet, translating the notion of internationalization patterns into theoretical constructs and operational measures remains a challenge in the absence of suitable candidates for the most relevant dimensions of this notion. Hence, given that unconstrained globalization has been replaced by 'semi-globalization' as the new dominant paradigm for international business (Ghemawat, 2003), the need for intermediate levels of aggregation between the local and global levels has become pertinent.

It is in this perspective that this chapter reviews the regional approach as a candidate for a simple and powerful way to slice geographic space. I first present a review of the evidence that has recently begun to accumulate as to the importance of the regional dimension in MNE strategy. The rest of the chapter is dedicated to an exploration of the theoretical foundations of this phenomenon, discussing how it may provide a new context in which to reapply the 'workhorses' of IB theory: liabilities of foreignness, transaction cost economics and the resource-based view. Finally, I collect these arguments in a formal model and present some results of a simulation of MNE performance and geographic scope.

Regional MNEs: The Evidence

The debate about the relative prevalence and attractiveness of regional versus global strategies – i.e. internationalization strategies that target the MNE's home region or the worldwide market, respectively – can be traced back to the study by Rugman and Verbeke (2004). Using a sample of *Fortune* Global 500 firms – the largest firms in the world by total sales – they found that 84 percent of these firms were largely regional in the sense that they derived more than half of their sales from their home region (North America, Europe or the Asia Pacific), and that only 2 percent of them could be considered truly global in the sense that they had a relatively even distribution of sales across these three regions. An eye-opening and perhaps provocative piece, this paper rapidly became highly influential in IB research, not least because it provided a timely and much-needed challenge to the notion that we live in a 'global world' where firms may target customers around the globe in an unconstrained way.

Rugman and Verbeke (2004, p. 5) acknowledged that their examination of MNE sales distributions 'should be considered a starting point for introducing systematically a regional component in international business research', and a large stream of subsequent regional studies has responded to that call by challenging, refining and extending their pioneering work. Collinson and Rugman (2008), for example, found that similar home region biases exist for MNE assets, responding to criticisms of sales as the original metric to operationalize geographic scope. Also, since Rugman and Verbeke (2004) included home country activity in the MNEs' home region figures, it was not initially possible to see whether the low degree of globalization in their sample reflected a strong degree of home region orientation in the firms' foreign operations. Again, however, subsequent refinement of their results has suggested that this is indeed so: Dunning et al. (2007) looked at the macro-data of FDI, which by definition excludes home country operations, and found some support for the home region orientation of this FDI. Their 'adjusted globalization index' – controlling for the size of the target economies – demonstrated that foreign markets in the home region absorbed about 52 percent of outward European FDI and 61 percent of American FDI.[1]

Another subject of debate has been Rugman and Verbeke's (2004) use of cut-off points to classify firms into categories such as regional and global. Osegowitsch and Sammartino (2008) provided a sensitivity analysis demonstrating how the results of this classification could change when the cut-off points are altered. In response, Rugman and Verbeke (2008) argued that the broad conclusions from their study remained intact, and with them the need to incorporate a regional dimension into IB theory. Asmussen (2009) addressed both the home country bias and cut-off point issues by making a modification of Rugman and Verbeke's (2004) original data set so as to control for home country biases, and estimated the degree of foreign sales penetration in the regional and global dimensions. Adding a confirmatory approach to the previous largely exploratory studies, he found that the firms were on average 30 percent internationalized in their home region but only 10 percent outside it, and that this difference in intra- and interregional barriers to MNE expansion was significant at the $p < 0.01$ level.

Another part of the regional versus global debate has pertained to the stability of the home region bias over time. Both Dunning et al. (2007) and Osegowitsch and Sammartino (2008) provided evidence that suggested a trend towards globalization, whereas Rugman and Verbeke (2008) presented data (based on Oh and Rugman, 2007) exhibiting no such trend, leaving this question somewhat unresolved.[2] On balance, the evidence suggests that regional borders matter; that this effect is significant even while it does not render national borders irrelevant; and that, if it is changing slowly over time, it is not likely to completely disappear, at least not in the short run. Meanwhile the debate continues, and with it an increasing interest among IB scholars in the region as a new and promising object of analysis.

THEORETICAL UNDERPINNINGS OF REGIONAL MNES

The observation that MNEs are regionally oriented is clearly an empirical phenomenon and as such does not add to or change the portfolio of theories – such as the liability of foreignness, the resource-based view, or transaction cost economics – that we usually apply in order to understand the behavior and performance of MNEs. However, it does change fundamentally the way in which we can and should apply these theories, by providing a new context in which to test them and, importantly, by altering the level at which key variables are conceptualized as well as the sources of variation presumed to be most important. It may therefore be fruitful to revisit these theories with a regional lens in order to provide, if not a 'theory of the regional MNE', then at least a theoretical explanation of their existence. A first step towards such an explanation can be taken by examining the regional component of the additional costs that MNEs experience in foreign markets.

The Liability of Foreignness in a Regional World

IB scholars have long recognized that MNEs incur costs related to internationalization. Hymer (1976) is often credited with the insight that firms face certain costs as they do business abroad, and that these costs place them at a competitive disadvantage *vis-à-vis* domestic incumbents in a local host market. This phenomenon was later termed 'the liability of foreignness' (LOF) and demonstrated empirically in a number of studies (e.g. Zaheer, 1995; Mezias, 2002). Several sources of the LOF have been identified, including local stakeholder discrimination against foreign firms, the MNE's uncertainty about host market conditions, and the complexity of doing business over a geographic distance (Zaheer, 1995).

Some components of the LOF are more or less temporary; for example, the initial uncertainty about local customer preferences, which may lead the MNE to sell a less-than-perfectly locally adapted product. This type of LOF can largely be overcome by learning (Petersen and Pedersen, 2002; Zaheer and Mosakowski, 1997) or potentially even avoided through prior market research. Other components, on the other hand, are more permanent in the sense that the foreignness of the entrant firm leads it to incur costs that can never be completely eliminated. For example, even if the subsidiary over time is able to overcome uncertainty completely through local learning, a degree of local maladaptation may remain because the MNE strives for consistency in its international product lineup. More generally, foreign firms are challenged with dual isomorphism pressures from their parent firms and the local environment (Rosenzweig and Singh, 1991), making it difficult for them to attain the same legitimacy as local firms in the host market (Kostova and Zaheer, 1999). Both temporary and permanent components of the LOF matter in practice, however, and indeed the distinction between these types of LOF may be less important than often presumed since there is a direct correspondence between firm value and profits (Denrell et al., 2003). Everything else being equal, the LOF has the effect of lowering the net present value of the profits stream to the MNE, irrespective of its timing.

LOF and the impact of distance
The LOF is traditionally seen as a consequence of internationalization – a cost incurred as soon as the MNE ventures outside its domestic market. However, it may vary significantly between different international markets depending on the diversity and distance between home and host markets (Zaheer, 1995). Eden and Miller (2004) discuss how the different components of the LOF respond to geographic, cultural and institutional distances. Empirical research also indicates that international diversity may be the most important determinant of the LOF (Vermeulen and Barkema, 2002; Goerzen and Beamish, 2003), leading regional scholars to suggest that the LOF occurs not primarily as the MNE crosses national boundaries, but mainly as it crosses regional boundaries (Rugman and Brain, 2003; Rugman and Verbeke, 2007). Because of the increased geographic distances and the variations in culture and political and economic institutions, interregional expansion involves additional sources of uncertainty and discrimination and leads the MNE's competitive advantage to become less applicable and require more adaptation. Case studies have illustrated some of these interregional adaptation problems: for example, when Wal-Mart entered Germany, the US retailer attempted replicating the Wal-Mart morning 'chant' and the point-of-entry 'greeter' – practices that were naturally accepted in North America but perceived as offensive to European employees and customers (Neissa and Trumbull, 2004). EuroDisney had similar problems in trying to enforce dress code and service personnel routines that were considered essential to the Disney image but did not appeal to employees in France (Black and Spyridakis, 1999).

Despite these studies and anecdotal evidence, however, we still have little quantitative knowledge about the extent to which the LOF varies with distance. Most of the attempts to operationalize the LOF have split firms into a dichotomy of foreign versus local and inferred the LOF as a performance differential between those two categories (e.g. Zaheer, 1995; Mezias, 2002; Zaheer and Mosakowski, 1997). While this approach has been sufficient to test the phenomenon of LOF itself and to explore the efficacy of firms' coping strategies, it does not tell us much about the variance in LOF that results from diversity or regional boundaries. Nachum (2003) tested the moderating effect on cultural distance on LOF but found only weak support for such an effect (or for the existence of the LOF, for that matter). So far, only indirect evidence points towards the existence of an interregional LOF. Based on three microeconomic models of the MNE, for example, Asmussen (2009) demonstrated that his findings were consistent with the existence of a significant interregional LOF: compared to their home country, the firms became 70 percent less effective in their home region and 90 percent less effective in foreign regions.

Theoretical foundations of the LOF

Arguably, the LOF is not a theory in itself but rather a phenomenon that has several more general theoretical explanations. In particular, most studies of it draw on mechanisms from transaction cost economics (TCE) and the resource-based view (RBV) in order to derive implications of foreignness and different types of distances on MNE performance. It is therefore important to bring forth those two perspectives as the two main pillars on which to base a theory of the regional MNE.

Transaction Costs and the Impact of Distance

Internationalization exposes the MNE to contractual hazards in its relations with foreign subsidiaries and partners, resulting in transaction costs (TC).[3] As a firm begins to address foreign markets, it may use a mix of market transactions (e.g. exporting or franchising) and hierarchical extensions (wholly owned subsidiaries) as well as hybrid forms such as joint ventures and alliances. However, common to these diverse foreign entry modes is the fact that they imply escalating transaction costs (Hitt et al., 1997; Jones and Hill, 1988) and that these costs are likely to be higher in an interregional context due to the impact of distance on internal and external transaction costs (Rugman and Verbeke, 2005).

Internationalization by market transactions

Market-based transactions generally – and external modes of foreign entry specifically – bring with them a number of organizing costs (Williamson, 1975). Dyer (1997) distinguishes between search costs, contracting costs, monitoring costs and enforcement costs. Hennart (1993) described the costs of using the price mechanism as including the costs of measuring outputs and the costs of residual cheating behavior by the parties to the transaction. All of these market-based transaction costs would be expected to increase with the geographic and cultural distance between the MNE and its foreign agents, because such distances inhibit trust by inhibiting personal relationship-building (Luo, 2001) and more generally 'magnify the problems of uncertainty, asymmetric information, and monitoring' (Bergen et al., 1992, p. 18). For example, if the MNE enters a foreign market via franchising, there is a risk that franchisees 'free-ride' on the MNE brand by investing too little in quality and service (Brickley and Dark, 1987). The MNE may try to reduce these risks by costly efforts to monitor the foreign agents and to contractually specify their inputs and processes (Klein and Saft, 1985), but also these 'policing costs' would be higher when the MNE is operating across high distances (Fladmoe-Lindquist and Jacque, 1995). Similar interest conflicts also exist in other types of market-based entry modes such as exports (Bello and Lohtia, 1995), and in hybrid forms such as joint ventures (Barkema et al., 1996).

Internationalization by FDI

As noted by Coase (1937), the costs of organizing within the firm also increase with the dissimilarity and spatial distance of the transactions. Once an MNE has established a wholly owned subsidiary in a foreign country, it needs to establish collaboration with, and control over, this subsidiary. Multinational collaborators are subject to moral hazard (as are, for that matter, national collaborators) because they bear the full private costs of their own effort but reap only part of the benefit (Holmstrom, 1982), leading the MNE to suffer a combination of monitoring costs and residual shirking behavior (Hennart, 1993). A process that has been found to alleviate moral hazard problems is team identification, i.e. when individual team members identify with the team and hence internalize the team's goals, as opposed to only their private costs and benefits, in their utility functions (Tyler and Blader, 2000). However, Shapiro et al. (2002) proposed that national and cultural diversity would lead to lower team identification and therefore, by implication, to larger shirking problems. Furthermore, distance tends to correlate with environmental and behavioral uncertainties (Brouthers and Brouthers, 2003), which make it more difficult to monitor country managers, and more costly to fail to do so (Bergen et al., 1992).

Implications for regional MNEs

Transaction cost economics (TCE) has had as its main goal the delineation of firm boundaries, based on comparative assessment of whether a certain transaction will be organized with markets or hierarchies. However, an important corollary to such an assessment is the prediction of firms' (geographic) scope, because it may tell us which (foreign) markets MNEs are likely to enter and how they will perform in these markets. As noted by Hennart, 'if [internal and external] organizing costs in firms are so high that they absorb all of the gains from exchange and coordination, then no economic interaction will take place, *either within firms or in markets*' (1993, p. 530, emphasis added). Combined with the impact of distance on transaction costs, this implies that firms will have lower propensities to enter global markets than regional markets, because it is more likely that the costs of organizing, within firms as well as in markets, are prohibitively high outside their home region. For the same reason, when they do enter interregional markets, they will incur higher TC and therefore be less successful than they are in their home region.

Resource Fungibility and the Impact of Distance

RBV scholars have long viewed firm-specific assets (FSAs) such as technologies, marketing knowledge or tacit managerial capabilities as being key determinants of firm performance and diversification (Peteraf, 1993). Firms possessing resources that are valuable, rare, difficult to imitate and non-substitutable (VRIN) will be able to earn economic rents from these resources (Barney, 1991). By expanding their scope, for example through international expansion, such firms will be able to leverage their rent-generating resources in other markets (Montgomery and Wernerfelt, 1988). Seen from this perspective, there are economies of scale in resource exploitation: once acquired, these resources can be redeployed at low marginal cost, especially if (like knowledge) they have public-good properties (Buckley and Casson, 1976; Rugman, 1981; Hennart, 1982). Compounding this imperative in an international context, as argued above, is the existence of the additional TC that MNEs face when they operate abroad, implying that internationalizing firms must have a resource-based advantage if they are to be competitive against local incumbents in foreign markets (Hymer, 1976). Hence FSAs underpin the internationalization of the MNE by giving it the incentive as well as the ability to expand abroad.

In itself, this argument does not tell us much about the optimal geographic scope of the firm: as long as the MNE's FSAs are VRIN enough to compensate for the additional TC, the MNE might become international in a way that is regional, global, or something in between. However, economists have recognized that the marginal rent from a given resource configuration is likely to decline as the firm moves into more distant markets (Montgomery and Wernerfelt, 1988). Teece (1982) was among the first to identify this phenomenon, and he defined the 'fungibility' of a resource as its ability to retain its value as it is applied in increasingly distant markets.

Fungibility in IB

In an international context, it has been suggested that downstream assets such as competence in sales and marketing tend to be less geographically fungible than technological assets (Anand and Delios, 2002). Rugman and Verbeke (1992) distinguished between location-bound and non-location-bound FSAs, the latter being fungible in the sense that they can be applied in international markets, and the former being completely specialized to their originating country. More recently, they extended the terminology to include region-bound FSAs (Rugman and Verbeke, 2004), which are fungible within the MNE's home region but lose some or all of their value when deployed outside it.

One may conceptualize the effect of low fungibility, or location-boundedness, on MNE performance in different ways. At the most basic level, low fungibility pertains primarily to the value of the resource (in the VRIN framework) embodied by its otherwise favorable impact on the firm's costs or on consumers' willingness to pay. If a resource is location-bound, this value will be lower or absent as soon as it is extended to foreign markets. For example, Wal-Mart's lack of understanding of German labor market laws and practices undermined its cost advantage, and German consumer perceptions of the US business models undermined its reputation for superior customer service (Neissa and Trumbull, 2004) – two FSAs that were driving its success in the North American market. In practice, however, the value of the firm's resources in foreign markets may be endogenous to the strategies of the firm, since the MNE can adapt its resources so that they become more valuable in foreign markets. Rugman and Verbeke (2005) talk about 'linking investments' that link the FSAs of the firm with location-specific advantages such as market access or local knowledge. In a market-seeking context, an MNE's investment in local host country knowledge can be considered a 'linking investment' in the sense that it links the MNE's home-based technological assets with the host country market. Or, in a resource-seeking context, it links the host country's labor market resources with the global markets already served by the MNE (FSA). With this understanding of (endogenous) resource value, fungibility may be conceptualized as the inverse of the costliness of such linking investments.

Regional scholars have argued that at least some linking investments are regional in scope (Rugman and Verbeke, 2005). This implies that, once undertaken, they may confer real options for future expansion on a regional level. Once the MNE has invested in adapting its FSAs to the unique characteristics of the host region, or in learning about these characteristics in order to reduce its LOF, it should be able to reap the returns on this investment in multiple countries in the region. Supporting these arguments with empirical evidence, Arregle et al. (2008) show that prior regional investments (up to a certain limit[4]) lead to a higher likelihood of subsequent FDI in a given country. This

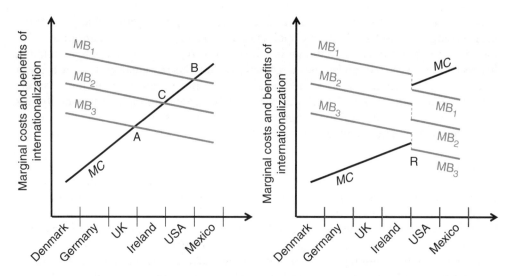

Figure 14.1   Discontinuities of distance at the regional boundary

seems to support the idea that international experience is fungible at the regional level, reducing the costs and thereby increasing the attractiveness of further investment in a region where sunk investments have already been incurred.

Regionalization and Discontinuities of Distance

As argued here, both TCE and the RBV are consistent with the idea that distance, broadly defined, has an inhibiting effect on international business activity by inflating transaction costs and constraining the fungibility of the firm's FSAs. Since countries within a region (everything else being equal, and with notable exceptions) are character-ized by lower mutual distance than are countries in different regions, this in itself suggests that firms should be more regionally than globally oriented. However, the regional effect may be reinforced by discontinuities of distance that occur at the regional boundary, and that are not fully captured by the above arguments. To fully understand what this means, it may be helpful to contrast a continuous with a discontinuous view of distance, as demonstrated in Figure 14.1.

Figure 14.1 shows a hypothetical firm's marginal costs (*MC*) and benefits (*MB*) of internationalizing into one additional country. 'Benefits' are defined broadly as the revenues that would be reaped in this country minus associated production costs, whereas 'Costs' are defined more narrowly as TC, as defined above.[5] Consider an inter-nationalizing Swedish firm that, for the sake of argument, exists in a highly simplified world where it ranks all foreign markets so that Denmark is closer than Germany, fol-lowed by the UK, Ireland, the USA and Mexico in order of increasing distance. The figure shows this ordering of host country distance and the marginal costs and benefits (the latter with three possible curves) of increasingly distant internationalization. *MB* decrease with the distance from the home market since the FSA of the firm is somewhat location-bound, and *MC* increase due to the escalation of the transaction costs. The rational firm stops internationalizing as soon as the marginal costs outweigh the marginal benefits.

With a more or less continuous view of distance, as captured by the curves in the left panel of Figure 14.1, a European geographic scope is a rather arbitrary outcome. As seen with the three possible marginal benefit curves, it is equally likely that the firm would stop internationalizing between the UK and Ireland (point A in the figure) or between the USA and Mexico (point B), as at the regional boundary between Ireland and the USA (point C). However, there are at least two major reasons, a geographic and a political one, why a discontinuity in distance as shown in the right panel of the figure may occur at the regional boundary.

Natural barriers and time zones

An important, but underemphasized, justification of the triad operationalization of regions is the presence of natural geological barriers that separate these areas. Europe, North America and the Asia Pacific are somewhat isolated from one another by a combination of oceans and vast landmasses, a fact that creates significant barriers to coordination in global firms, for two reasons. First, simply because of the additional distance, it makes business travel between these regions costly, inconvenient and physically taxing for managers and employees. Second, and perhaps more importantly, coinciding with these discontinuities in geographic distance are discontinuities in time separation, which have significant implications for IB activity by increasing coordination costs (Espinosa and Carmel, 2003).

To see this graphically we need only plot a proxy for IB activity across time zones. Such a proxy has been developed by Beaverstock et al. (1999, p. 445), who argue that a number of 'global cities' are capturing a disproportionately high share of the world's economic activity and are therefore 'integral to contemporary globalization processes'. Extending the traditional London–New York–Tokyo axis, they identify 55 global cities based on a rigorous methodology measuring the availability of advanced producer services used by MNEs. While the authors are largely silent about the geographic and regional implications of this exercise, Figure 14.2 demonstrates these implications clearly, by mapping the distribution of global cities in an East–West continuum.[6]

Figure 14.2 captures the discontinuity that occurs at the regional boundaries and that make the triad operationalization of regions an attractive and powerful one. Economic activity, proxied by the number and significance of global cities, is evidently concentrated in the three clusters, which in turn are separated by discontinuities (gaps) consisting of two, three, and six time zones, respectively.[7]

Why is such an interregional distance discontinuity important? One reason is the effect it presumably has on the localization of knowledge flows. It is well known that geographic distance inhibits incidental knowledge flows, demonstrated most famously in the seminal study by Jaffe et al. (1993). Keller (2001) estimated the 'geographic half-life' of knowledge – i.e. the distance at which R&D spillovers are reduced to half of their local impact – to be 1200 kilometers, and found that knowledge spillovers between adjacent countries tended to be 37 percent larger than between non-adjacent countries. Hussler (2004) demonstrated that national cultural distance did not significantly inhibit knowledge spillovers, whereas geographic distance did. Combining these results with the aforementioned geographic gap between regions suggests that knowledge will flow much more easily within regions than across them. Most studies have focused on technological knowledge (which is measurable with patent data) but, arguably, similar mechanisms can be expected for other types of knowledge such as knowledge about local markets, laws and values. For example, it is likely that German managers will know more about French culture than Japanese managers do, simply because a German is more exposed to it through travel, immigration, exports and so forth. On a more general level, in addition to reducing the LOF faced by German firms in France, this would lead to larger intraregional similarities in knowledge environments[8] so that international experience from one country becomes more fungible to other countries in the same region.

A more important implication of these interregional distance discontinuities, however, stems from the fact that they occur across longitudes rather than latitudes. Stein and Daude (2007) posit that 'longitude matters' to FDI because large distances in this dimension inhibit information-intensive, real-time coordination such as that between headquarters and subsidiaries, in two ways. First, time separation reduces and potentially eliminates overlaps in office and daytime hours between geographically dispersed collaborators, making it difficult to exploit telephone, email, videoconferencing and other technological advances that substitute for face-to-face interaction. This may impede coordination depending on the nature of task interdependencies (Thompson, 1967): sequential tasks may merely be slowed down, while reciprocal tasks may grind to a virtual halt if a whole workday has to pass for each email reply (Espinosa and Carmel, 2003). Second, even the use of travel as a coordination mechanism becomes less effective because of jet lag, which reduces managerial effectiveness or, at least, extends the time required for time difference adjustments. Both of these effects are absent in the case of North–South distance, suggesting that geographic distance is a particularly pertinent barrier to coordination when it occurs along the East–West dimension.

With MNEs depending on increasingly complex knowledge and pursuing ever more thinly sliced and geographically dispersed value chains, it is likely that these costs will increase rather than decrease over time. Empirical evidence support these arguments. Stein and Daude (2007) estimated a gravity model in which longitudinal distance was twice as strong an inhibitor of FDI as latitudinal distance, and that the addition of time zone differences to their model could account for this difference. From a finance perspective, Portes and Rey (2005) found that overlaps in stock market trading hours (the inverse of time separation) were a significant positive predictor of bilateral equity flows.

Regional integration processes
In addition to, and partly as a consequence of, the geographic proximity of countries within a region and the time separation between regions, political integration efforts tend to take place at the regional level, organized by institutions such as the EU, NAFTA and ASEAN. As noted by Rugman and Verbeke (2005, p. 7), 'a regional integration process (with only a limited number of participants that are geographically close, and with a comparatively low economic and institutional distance among them) is easier than a multilateral integration process that could involve all the members of the World Trade Organization'. Hence, while the distances between countries may vary in a semi-continuous way (e.g. Spain is further away from Denmark than Sweden is, but closer than the USA), integration processes have to take place at a certain level and, as a result, we

also get a politically driven discontinuity of distance at the regional boundary (e.g. Denmark, Sweden and Spain are subject to the same EU policies while the USA is not).

Being 'inherently discriminatory arrangements' (Crawford and Laird, 2001), these integration processes tend to increase the costs and diminish the benefits of international expansion, for example by giving EU firms preferential treatment to other foreign firms when they operate in European countries. Furthermore, they often coincide with harmonization efforts deliberately aimed at reducing intraregional differences in, for example, income laws, leading once more to higher regional fungibility of FSAs and international experience. Regional trade agreements also have an indirect effect on FDI, since tariffs inhibit much vertical FDI such as offshoring- or sales-related investments (Neary, 2009). Hence Cuevas et al. (2005) estimated that trade agreements could in fact enhance FDI flows by up to 60 percent.

Regional boundaries as inflection points

As a consequence of the discontinuities discussed above, the costs and benefits of internationalization may not behave as smoothly as suggested by the left panel of Figure 14.1 after all. The right panel shows how MC jump as soon as we cross the regional boundary, due to increased TC, and MB drop as a consequence of low interregional fungibility of the firm's FSAs. As a result, all three MB curves now lead to the same outcome as the firm stops internationalizing at point R: the regional MNE. Potentially, of course, the regional firm is still not the only possible outcome: one may get firms that are less than fully intraregionalized (if the benefits-to-costs ratio is sufficiently low) or partly globalized (if it is sufficiently high). But it is a much more likely outcome than other types of geographic scope, because it is consistent with a larger set of possible MB and MC curves, and less sensitive to changes in these curves. Also, even firms that deviate from the regional strategy should now deviate less, all else being equal, and observations of firms' geographic scope would therefore tend to cluster around that of regional MNE.

All in all, these arguments seem to support the use of the broad triad as the basis for operationalizing regions. Still, IB scholars have presented counterarguments, suggesting in particular that economic progress in emerging markets is making this operationalization less relevant to MNEs and that different country groupings should therefore be considered (Flores and Aguilera, 2007). Aguilera et al. (2007) identify no fewer than 12 such country clustering schemes grounded in different disciplines. In support of these arguments, Beaverstock et al. (2000) find a number of cities that are not global cities, but have 'global city potential', in the area between Europe and Asia – longitudes where half of the BRIC (Brazil, Russia, India and China) countries are located (see Figure 14.2). These developments make the triad definition of regions somewhat problematic: for example, how do we calculate intra- and interregional expansion of Indian or Russian firms? Adding a fourth region to the triad regions raises questions of definition and delineation, and has significant implications for the way in which we view symmetries in interregional distance, since such a region would in fact be geographically closer to Europe and Asia than to North America (as measured, for example, by the overlap in office hours). Generally, such asymmetries in interregional distances constitute an area that is relatively unexplored in IB research (Osegowitsch and Sammartino, 2008).

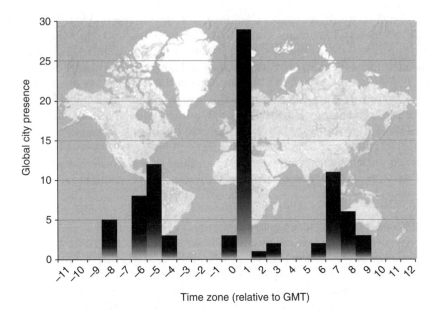

Figure 14.2   *Triad regions and the clustering of time zones*

IMPLICATIONS OF REGIONAL MNE THEORY: A SIMPLE MODEL

The theories laid out so far – the RBV, TCE, the intersection of these theories with distance, and the regional boundary as a discontinuity of distance – may serve as theoretical pillars for a framework explaining the data on regional MNEs. The rest of this chapter concentrates on the implications of this exercise for MNE performance and geographic scope, raising questions such as: should regional MNEs be more or less profitable than global MNEs? Do strong firms internationalize differently from weak firms? How may we estimate the effects of regions empirically in order to corroborate the theoretical propositions above?

To answer these questions, it is possible to extend the simple cost–benefit model from Figure 14.1. First, consider the performance of a population of firms operating in a given host country. Some of these can be called 'local' firms denoted L (domestic firms or MNEs with home base in the focal country), others can be called 'regional' firms, denoted R (MNEs with home bases in other countries within the region), and still others, denoted G, may be called 'global' firms (in the sense that they originate from outside the region in which the focal country lies). The host country performance – i.e. the host country's marginal contribution to the firm's profits – of firm i of type h (where $h \in [L, R, G]$) can then be described by the equation:

$$\pi_{ih} = B(i, h) - C(h) + \varepsilon_i = \pi_0 + \alpha f_h FSA_i - TC_h + \varepsilon_i \qquad (14.1)$$

The MNE's foreign performance consists of a number of factors, as indicated by the literature reviewed in this chapter, as well as luck, as captured by the random factor

ε_i.[9] The benefits of being in the host market are determined by the 'base profitability' of that market (captured by the intercept π_0), the FSAs of the MNE (FSA_i), and the extent to which these FSAs are fungible to the host country (f_h). The costs are defined as transaction costs (TC) in line with earlier definitions. Furthermore, we can see that the two core variables in the model – FSA fungibility and TC – depend on the type of the firm h (defined by its origin and home base). Local firms would tend to incur lower TC than foreign firms do because, by definition, they do not suffer an LOF, while global firms are subject to even higher TC than the regional 'insiders' due to the additional distances over which the former must operate. This may be expressed by $TC_L < TC_R < TC_G$. Similarly, $f_L = 1$ and $1 > f_R > f_G$, based on the idea that FSAs tend to be somewhat location and region bound. The differences $TC_G - TC_R$ and $f_R - f_G$ constitute what we can call the interregional LOF (Asmussen, 2009, Rugman and Verbeke, 2007).[10]

By defining two dummy variables for regional (R) and global (G) firms, we can transform this equation into a regression model

$$\pi_i = \pi_0 + \alpha \underbrace{(1 - (1 - f_R)R_i - (1 - f_G)G_i)FSA_i}_{\text{Fungibility of FSAs}}$$

$$\underbrace{- ((1 - R_i - G_i)TC_L + R_iTC_R + G_iTC_G)}_{\text{Incurred TC}} + \varepsilon_i$$

$$= \pi_0 - TC_L + \alpha FSA_i - \alpha(1 - f_R)R_iFSA_i - \alpha(1 - f_G)G_iFSA_i \qquad (14.2)$$

$$- (TC_R - TC_L)R_i - (TC_G - TC_L)G_i + \varepsilon_i$$

$$\equiv b_0 + b_1 FSA_i + b_2 R_iFSA_i + b_3 G_iFSA_i + b_4 R_i + b_5 G_i + \varepsilon_i$$

It can be seen from this equation that the interregional LOF can be evaluated by comparing the estimated coefficients on the direct effect of the regional/global dummy variables as well as on their interactions with the FSA term. In such a regression, the hypotheses of country- and region-bound FSAs would be operationalized by $b_3 < b_2 < 0 \Leftrightarrow f_G < f_G < 1$ and variation of transaction costs across national and regional boundaries by $b_5 < b_4 < 0 \Leftrightarrow TC_L < TC_R < TC_G$. These hypotheses could in principle be estimated, building on methodologies similar to those used by Zaheer (1995), Nachum (2003) and others.

While the results of such a study would be of strong interest to IB scholars, however, there would probably be an endogeneity problem related to the self-selection of firms into the sample (Hamilton and Nickerson, 2003): in particular, in anticipation of the LOF and the interregional LOF, regional and global firms with low FSAs would have lower entry rates. This would not be a problem if these FSAs were completely observable and hence could be controlled for, but complete observability is presumably an exception (Shaver, 1998). Suppose, for example, that the error term in Equation (14.2) partly reflects unobserved FSAs. Since foreign firms with low unobserved FSAs (low ε_i) would tend to stay out of the market, those foreign firms that do enter the sample would have higher unobserved FSAs than the domestic firms, biasing the results.[11]

Hence, looking at performance of firms is a useful, but ultimately insufficient, approach: even if it tells us something about the firms that entered foreign markets and experienced an LOF, it does not tell us about the firms that stayed out in anticipation of these problems. The same phenomenon could tempt us to make erroneous inferences from casual observation: we may observe highly successful global firms with significant interregional presence, not realizing that these firms may come from the extreme right tail of the FSA distribution. Therefore we must also look at the geographic scope of firms, since this is an outcome of managerial choices in the face of regional effects, and therefore presumably mirrors those effects.

Endogenous Geographic Scope: Results from a Simulation

Suppose now that instead of the entrants into one focal host country we are studying a population of firms that may choose to enter a number of different countries. The potential markets are assumed to be of equal size and include the home country of the firm, ten countries in the firm's home region, and ten countries outside its home region, for a total of 22 national markets. In each of these markets, the contribution to performance is as given in Equation (14.1) given that the firm enters the market by establishing a local subsidiary. The firms' FSAs are drawn from a random distribution, and based on this value they make rational choices about their entry strategies,[12] entering only those foreign markets in which they earn a positive marginal profit.[13]

Figure 14.3 shows the relationship between the strength of the firm's FSAs and its geographic scope and performance. In the top panel, internationalization is measured as the ratio of foreign-to-total subsidiaries (F/T), and globalization is measured as the ratio of global (interregional) subsidiaries to foreign subsidiaries (G/F). Profits are defined as the sum of all profits earned by the firm's portfolio of subsidiaries (as evidenced for example by earnings before interest and taxes or firm value) and profitability as the average profit of the firm's subsidiaries (e.g. ROA (return on assets) or Tobin's q).

Note how the firm's geographic scope changes as the FSA of the firm increases. After a certain threshold is reached, the firm becomes strong enough to overcome the LOF and internationalize within its home region, and we observe an increase in F/T. After this potential for regional expansion has been exhausted, the firm has to reach a new FSA threshold at which it becomes strong enough to be competitive also in the global market, and where G/F starts to increase. After this point, the firm is fully global and both curves flatten out.

The effect of FSAs on performance depends on which dimension of performance we are interested in. First, the firm's profits (in an absolute sense) are steadily increasing with the strength of its FSAs, because these FSAs lead the firm to add new countries to its scope and it is rational enough to add only profitable countries. Surprisingly, however, the firm's profitability in a relative sense declines temporarily as the FSAs increase and the firms begin to change from domestic to regional. At this point, highly profitable domestic firms begin to enter difficult foreign markets that only provide a small positive contribution to their income, and therefore their average return on investment will decline even though the total goes up – an international version of the 'importance of focus' argument (Wernerfelt and Montgomery, 1988). Hence these firms are actually

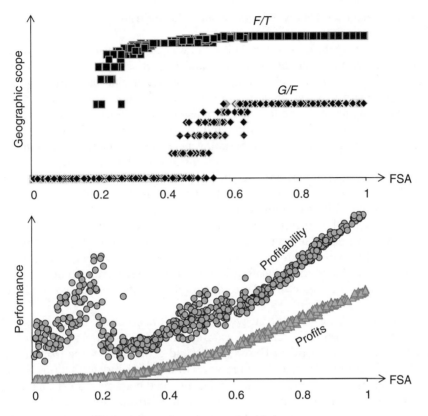

Figure 14.3   FSA strength, geographic scope and performance

pursuing profit-maximizing strategies and adding to shareholder value by doing so, even though this shows up as a dip in profitability. A similar, although less pronounced, effect occurs when the firms change from regional to global.

Nevertheless, it is clear from Figure 14.3 that, once we follow the received wisdom and eliminate domestic firms from our sample, we are likely to observe positive correlations both between internationalization and performance and between interregional orientation (globalization) and performance. It is also clear that both of these correlations are entirely spurious: each firm has chosen its optimal geographic scope by being present only in the markets that make a positive contribution to performance, and it is therefore effectively at the top of its own individual, FSA-determined inverted U-curve. Hence we observe correlations between geographic scope and performance only because all of these variables are driven by the FSA strength of the MNE. The model may thereby explain the findings of Delios and Beamish (2005), who observe a positive bivariate correlation between global orientation and performance. It is also consistent with those of Asmussen and Goerzen (2007), who demonstrated that, once FSAs such as technological and marketing assets are controlled for, the relationship between global orientation and performance disappears.

Towards a Contingency Theory of Regional and Global Strategy

These results support the more general idea that we might be mistaken if we aim to make universal predictions about the prevalence and attractiveness of regional and global strategies. In fact, a number of contingencies may determine the optimal geographic scope for a given firm, at a given point in time, and the identification of these contingencies and the mapping of their effects is a promising avenue for future regional research. The FSAs of the internationalizing firm, and the geographic fungibility of these FSAs, are clearly among the more important contingencies. In fact, in addition to the market-seeking explanation inherent in the above discussion simulation, strategic asset-seeking motives may further complicate the relationship between FSA strength and geographic scope. Scholars have argued that it is becoming increasingly difficult for firms to remain competitive through internal knowledge development (D'Aveni, 1994), and that external knowledge sourcing has therefore become a necessary extension of firms' knowledge management strategies (Almeida et al., 2003). Given that knowledge diversity is larger across regions than within them, and that knowledge diversity is conducive to innovation and value creation (Scott and Garofoli, 2007), this may create an incentive for firms to go beyond their home region in order to avoid 'blind spots' on their competitive radar screens (Ohmae, 1985).

In addition to making global strategy somewhat more attractive than suggested by the other arguments in this chapter, these external knowledge-sourcing imperatives may change the relationship between FSA strength and geographic scope from the pattern proposed in Figure 14.3 in an ambiguous way. On the one hand, weak firms would have a stronger incentive to acquire new knowledge in global markets than strong firms, suggesting a negative relationship. On the other hand, strong firms would have higher absorptive capacity to reap the benefits of such a global knowledge acquisition strategy, suggesting a positive relationship. The results of Asmussen and Goerzen (2007) suggest that the positive effect of FSAs on the global orientation of the firm outweigh the negative ones.

CONCLUSIONS

This chapter has examined the empirical evidence and theoretical foundations of regional and global strategies. It has been argued that regions are characterized by relatively low internal geographic, cultural and institutional distances, and that natural and political discontinuities at the regional boundary reinforce this effect. Implications for MNEs' geographic scope and performance have been discussed. Meanwhile, IB scholars are likely to continue the healthy debate about MNE geographic scope and the quest for a deeper understanding of regional effects in MNE strategy.

One of the questions that will continue to be central to IB researchers is what the right level of analysis is, and how different levels may be combined in a complementary way. As a top–down slicing of geographic space, the regional approach is clearly still on a high level of aggregation, and scholars have advocated more fine-grained approaches (Osegowitch and Sammartino, 2008; Aguilera et al., 2007). At the end of the day, however, choosing the right level (or combinations of levels) to analyze MNE strategy is not easy. Increasing geographic disaggregation will always tend to enhance explanatory power, but this comes at the expense of increased complexity and fewer degrees of freedom – in the extreme taking us back to the country level where we originally came from. Hence, which level is most useful and powerful is probably an empirical question, and perhaps also a somewhat judgmental one, and will depend much on the research question wielded by the researcher. More studies of MNE behavior, and future political and economic developments in the global economy, may reveal new directions for regional research.

NOTES

1. As they broke up the Asia-Pacific region (categorizing Australia and New Zealand as the 'rest of the world'), a direct comparison with Rugman and Verbeke (2004) is not possible for this region.
2. Difference in methodology may explain these divergent findings. Osegowitsch and Sammartino (2008) sampled the same firms in 1991 and 2001, whereas Rugman and Verbeke (2008) took out a new sample (the largest 500 firms in the world) in every year from 2001 to 2005. In addition to estimating trends towards globalization, the former approach may also capture learning and expansion trajectories of the individual MNEs; the latter reduces this effect while capturing instead the effects of the shifting composition of the *Fortune* 500.
3. This section defines transaction costs broadly as the costs of organizing either within the firm (internal TC) or using markets (external TC), consistent with earlier studies (Riordan and Williamson, 1985). It also subsumes under the TC heading agency costs, which are important parts of the costs of organizing in both markets and hierarchies. While some scholars make a distinction between transaction costs and agency costs, the line between the two types of costs is becoming increasingly blurred (Bergen et al., 1992).
4. They estimate an inverted U-shaped relationship, which is positively sloped until about 30 subsidiaries in the host region, reflecting saturation of the MNE's presence in the region. After that, more regional subsidiaries lead to a marginally lower propensity for country investment.
5. Hence costs of adapting the firm's FSAs to the host market is treated as a negative benefit (because it is a result of low fungibility and is interchangeable with the lower benefits that would be incurred instead by deploying the FSAs unadapted in the host market) and these costs are therefore included in the downward-sloping *MB* curve. Nevertheless, moving these costs to the *MC* curve instead would have no effect on the outcome of the analysis.
6. Figure 14.2 computes a weighted count of the global city activity within each time zone, where an 'alpha' city in the time zone has a weight of three, a 'beta' city has a weight of two, and a 'gamma' city has a weight of one. Greenwich mean time (GMT) is the benchmark (0) time zone and zones with half-hour deviations from GMT are rounded to the nearest integer.
7. Interestingly, Figure 14.2 also shows a small economic discontinuity (a gap of one time zone) between the North American east and west coasts. While this could be significant, however, it is likely to be alleviated by common institutions (e.g. the Canadian, US and Mexican federal governments) spanning this gap. Note also that developments since 1999 may have changed this picture somewhat due in particular to increased economic activity in emerging markets. These developments, and their implications for the regional framework, will be discussed below.
8. Interestingly, this may also have an effect on MNE strategy that is opposite to the other effects described here: if knowledge diversity is conducive to innovation (Page, 2007), and knowledge diversity is larger across interregional boundaries, this will make a global strategy more attractive from an external knowledge sourcing standpoint (Ghoshal, 1987; Doz et al., 2001). This and other advantages of global strategy will be discussed in more detail below.
9. I ignore a range of factors, such as industry profitability, in this equation in order to focus on the variables of theoretical interest. In practice, other influences can be either added as control variables or subsumed in the error term.
10. For simplicity, I assume away intraregional variation in the costs and benefits enjoyed by foreign firms.
11. In particular, it can be shown that this would lead to an underestimation of the incremental transaction costs incurred by regional and, in particular, global firms.
12. The assumption of rationality is more innocuous than it seems. It is easy to allow for bounded rationality, for example by adding a noise parameter to the MNEs' perceptions of host market profitability. This

would lower the statistical significance of most tests but not change the qualitative conclusions of the simulation.

13. The results presented here emerge from the following parameters: $\pi_0 = 0.1$, $\alpha = 1$, $f_R = 0.8$, $f_G = 0.6$, $TC_L = 0.025$, $TC_R = 0.325$, $TC_G = 0.425$. FSAs are drawn from $U[0,1]$, and each firm i has an error term in each market j, with $\varepsilon_{ij} \sim U[-0.075, 0.075]$.

REFERENCES

Aguilera, R.V., Flores, R.G. and Vaaler, P. (2007), 'Is it all a matter of grouping? Examining the regional effect in global strategy research', in S. Tallman (ed.), *International Strategic Management: A New Generation*, Cheltenham, UK and Northampton, MA, USA: Edward Elgar, pp. 209–28.

Almeida, P., Phene, A. and Grant, R. (2003), 'Innovation and knowledge management: scanning, sourcing, and integration', in M. Easterby-Smith and M.A. Lyles (eds), *The Blackwell Handbook of Organizational Learning and Knowledge Management*, Malden, MA: Blackwell, pp. 356–71.

Anand, J. and Delios, A. (2002), 'Absolute and relative resources as determinants of international acquisitions', *Strategic Management Journal*, 23(2): 119–34.

Arregle, J.L., Beamish, P.W. and Hébert, L. (2008), 'The regional dimension of MNEs' foreign subsidiary localization', *Journal of International Business Studies*, 40(1): 86–107.

Asmussen, C.G. (2009), 'Local, regional, or global? Quantifying MNE geographic scope', *Journal of International Business Studies*, 40(7): 1192–205.

Asmussen, C.G. and Goerzen, A. (2007), 'Geographic orientation and performance of global versus regional MNEs', *Academy of Management Best Paper Proceedings*, 1–6.

Barkema, H.G., Bell, J.H.J. and Pennings, J.M. (1996), 'Foreign entry, cultural barriers, and learning', *Strategic Management Journal*, 17(2): 151–66.

Barney, J.B. (1991), 'Firm resources and sustainable competitive advantage', *Journal of Management*, 17: 99–120.

Beaverstock, J.V., Smith, R.G. and Taylor, P.J. (1999), 'A roster of world cities', *Cities*, 16(6): 445–58.

Bello, D.C. and Lohtia, R. (1995), 'Export channel design: the use of foreign distributors and agents', *Journal of the Academy of Marketing Science*, 23(2): 83–93.

Benito, G.R.G. and Gripsrud, G. (1992), 'The expansion of foreign direct investments: discrete rational location choices or a cultural learning process?', *Journal of International Business Studies*, 23(3): 461–76.

Bergen, M., Dutta, S. and Walker Jr, O.C. (1992), 'Agency relationships in marketing: a review of the implications and applications of agency and related theories', *The Journal of Marketing*, 56(3): 1–24.

Black, J.S. and Spyridakis, T. (1999), 'EuroDisneyland', Thunderbird case A07-99-0007.

Brickley, J.A. and Dark, F.H. (1987), 'The choice of organizational form: the case of franchising', *Journal of Financial Economics*, 18(2): 401–20.

Brouthers, K.D. and Brouthers, L.E. (2003), 'Why service and manufacturing entry mode choices differ: the influence of transaction cost factors, risk and trust', *Journal of Management Studies*, 40(5): 1179–204.

Buckley, P.J. and Casson, M. (1976), *The Future of the Multinational Enterprise*, London: Macmillan.

Coase, R.H. (1937), 'The nature of the firm', *Economica*, n.s. 4(16): 386–405.

Collinson, S. and Rugman, A.M. (2008), 'The regional nature of Japanese multinational business', *Journal of International Business Studies*, 39(2): 215–30.

Crawford, J. and Laird, S. (2001), 'Regional trade agreements and the WTO', *The North American Journal of Economics and Finance*, 12(2): 193–211.

Cuevas, A., Messmacher, M. and Werner, A. (2005), 'Foreign direct investment in Mexico since the approval of NAFTA', *World Bank Economic Review*, 19(3): 473–88.

D'Aveni, R.A. (1994), *Hypercompetition*, New York: Free Press.

Delios, A. and Beamish, P.W. (2005), 'Regional and global strategies of Japanese firms', *Management International Review*, 45(Special Issue): 19–36.

Denrell, J., Fang, C. and Winter, S.G. (2003), 'The economics of strategic opportunity', *Strategic Management Journal*, 24(10, Special Issue): 977–90.

Doz, Y.L., Santos, J. and Williamson, P. (2001), *From Global to Metanational: How Companies Win in the Knowledge Economy*, Boston, MA: Harvard Business School Press.

Dunning, J.H. (1996), 'The geographical sources of the competitiveness of firms: some results of a new survey', *Transnational Corporations*, 5(3): 1–29.

Dunning, J.H., Fujita, M. and Yakova, N. (2007), 'Some macro-data on the regionalisation/globalisation debate: a comment on the Rugman/Verbeke analysis', *Journal of International Business Studies*, 38(1): 177–99.

Dyer, J.H. (1997), 'Effective interfirm collaboration: how firms minimize transaction costs and maximize transaction value', *Strategic Management Journal*, **18**(7): 535–56.

Eden, L. and Miller, S.R. (2004), 'Distance matters: liability of foreignness, institutional distance and ownership strategy', *Advances in International Management*, **16**: 187–221.

Espinosa, J.A. and Carmel, E. (2003), 'The impact of time separation on coordination in global software teams: a conceptual foundation', *Software Process: Improvement and Practice*, **8**(4): 249–66.

Fladmoe-Lindquist, K. and Jacque, L.L. (1995), 'Control modes in international service operations: the propensity to franchise', *Management Science*, **41**(7): 1238–49.

Flores, R.G. and Aguilera, R.V. (2007), 'Globalization and location choice: an analysis of US multinational firms in 1980 and 2000', *Journal of International Business Studies*, **38**(7): 1187–210.

Ghemawat, P. (2003), 'Semiglobalization and international business strategy', *Journal of International Business Studies*, **34**(2): 138–52.

Ghoshal, S. (1987), 'Global strategy: an organizing framework', *Strategic Management Journal*, **8**(5): 425–40.

Goerzen, A. and Beamish, P.W. (2003), 'Geographic scope and multinational enterprise performance', *Strategic Management Journal*, **24**(13): 1289–306.

Hamilton, B.H. and Nickerson, J.A. (2003), 'Correcting for endogeneity in strategic management research', *Strategic Organization*, **1**: 51–78.

Hennart, J.-F. (1982), *A Theory of Multinational Enterprise*, Ann Arbor, MI: University of Michigan Press.

Hennart, J.-F. (1993), 'Explaining the swollen middle: why most transactions are a mix of "market" and "hierarchy"', *Organization Science*, **4**(4): 529–47.

Hitt, M.A., Hoskisson, R.E. and Kim, H. (1997), 'International diversification: effects on innovation and firm performance in product-diversified firms', *The Academy of Management Journal*, **40**(4): 767–98.

Holmstrom, B. (1982), 'Moral Hazard in Teams', *The Bell Journal of Economics*, **13**(2): 324–40.

Hussler, C. (2004), 'Culture and knowledge spillovers in Europe: new perspectives for innovation and convergence policies?', *Economics of Innovation and New Technology*, **13**(6): 523–41.

Hymer, S.H. (1976), *The International Operations of National Firms: A Study of Direct Foreign Investment*, Cambridge, MA: MIT Press.

Jaffe, A.B., Trajtenberg, M. and Henderson, R. (1993), 'Geographic Localization of knowledge spillovers as evidenced by patent citations', *The Quarterly Journal of Economics*, **108**(3): 577–98.

Jones, G.R. and Hill, C.W.L. (1988), 'Transaction cost analysis of strategy–structure choice', *Strategic Management Journal*, **9**(2): 159–72.

Keller, W. (2001), 'Knowledge spillovers at the world's technology frontier', CEPR Working Paper 2815.

Klein, B. and Saft, L.F. (1985), 'The law and economics of franchise tying contracts', *Journal of Law and Economics*, **28**(2): 345–61.

Kogut, B. and Singh, H. (1988), 'The effect of national culture on the choice of entry mode', *Journal of International Business Studies*, **19**(3): 411–32.

Kostova, T. and Zaheer, S. (1999), 'Organizational legitimacy under conditions of complexity: the case of the multinational enterprise', *Academy of Management Review*, **24**(1): 64–81.

Luo, Y. (2001), 'Antecedents and consequences of personal attachment in cross-cultural cooperative ventures', *Administrative Science Quarterly*, **46**(2): 177–201.

Mezias, J.M. (2002), 'Identifying liabilities of foreignness and strategies to minimize their effects: the case of labor lawsuit judgments in the United States', *Strategic Management Journal*, **23**(3): 229–44.

Montgomery, C.A. and Wernerfelt, B. (1988), 'Diversification, Ricardian rents, and Tobin's q', *The Rand Journal of Economics*, **19**(4): 623–32.

Morck, R. and Yeung, B. (1991), 'Why investors value multinationality', *The Journal of Business*, **64**(2): 165–87.

Nachum, L. (2003), 'Liability of foreignness in global competition? Financial service affiliates in the City of London', *Strategic Management Journal*, **24**(12): 1187–208.

Neary, J.P. (2009), 'Trade costs and foreign direct investment', *International Review of Economics and Finance*, **18**(2): 207–18.

Neissa, L. and Trumbull, G. (2004), 'Wal-Mart in Europe', Harvard Business School Cases, 1.

Oh, C.H. and Rugman, A.M. (2007), 'Regional multinationals and the Korean cosmetics industry', *Asia Pacific Journal of Management*, **24**(1): 27–42.

Ohmae, K. (1985), *Triad Power: The Coming Shape of Global Competition*, New York: Free Press.

Osegowitsch, T. and Sammartino, A. (2008), 'Reassessing (home-) regionalisation', *Journal of International Business Studies*, **39**(2): 184–96.

Page, S.E. (2007), 'Making the difference: applying a logic of diversity', *Academy of Management Perspectives*, **21**(4): 6–20.

Peteraf, M.A. (1993), 'The cornerstones of competitive advantage: a resource-based view', *Strategic Management Journal*, **14**(3): 179–91.

Petersen, B. and Pedersen, T. (2002), 'Coping with liability of foreignness: different learning engagements of entrant firms', *Journal of International Management*, **8**(3): 339–50.

Portes, R. and Rey, H. (2005), 'The determinants of cross-border equity flows', *Journal of International Economics*, **65**(2): 269–96.

Riordan, M.H. and Williamson, O.E. (1985), 'Asset specificity and economic organization', *International Journal of Industrial Organization*, **3**(4): 365–78.

Rosenzweig, P.M. and Singh, J.V. (1991), 'Organizational environments and the multinational enterprise', *Academy of Management Review*, **16**(2): 340–61.

Rugman, A.M. (1981), *Inside the Multinationals: The Economics of Internal Markets*, London: Croom Helm.

Rugman, A. and Brain, C. (2003), 'Multinational enterprises are global, not regional', *Multinational Business Review*, **11**(1): 3–12.

Rugman, A.M. and Verbeke, A. (1992), 'A note on the transnational solution and the transaction cost theory of multinational strategic management', *Journal of International Business Studies*, **23**(4): 761–71.

Rugman, A.M. and Verbeke, A. (1993), 'Foreign subsidiaries and multinational strategic management: an extension and correction of Porter's single diamond framework', *Management International Review*, (Special Issue): 71–84.

Rugman, A.M. and Verbeke, A. (2004), 'A perspective on regional and global strategies of multinational enterprises', *Journal of International Business Studies*, **35**(1): 3–18.

Rugman, A.M. and Verbeke, A. (2005). 'Towards a theory of regional multinationals: a transaction cost economics approach', *Management International Review*, **45**(Special Issue 1): 5–17.

Rugman, A.M. and Verbeke, A. (2007), 'Liabilities of regional foreignness and the use of firm-level versus country-level data: a response to Dunning et al. (2006)', *Journal of International Business Studies*, **38**(1): 200–205.

Rugman, A.M. and Verbeke, A. (2008), 'A new perspective on the regional and global strategies of multinational services firms', *Management International Review*, **48**(4): 397–411.

Scott, A.J. and Garofoli, G. (eds) (2007), *Development on the Ground: Clusters, Networks and Regions in Emerging Economies*, Routledge Advances in Management and Business Studies, London and New York: Routledge/Taylor & Francis.

Shapiro, D.L., Furst, S.A., Spreitzer, G.M. and Von Glinow, M.A. (2002), 'Transnational teams in the electronic age: are team identity and high performance at risk?', *Journal of Organizational Behavior*, **23**(4): 455–67.

Shaver, M. (1998), 'Accounting for endogeneity when assessing strategy performance', *Management Science*, **44**(4): 571–85.

Stein, E. and Daude, C. (2007), 'Longitude matters: time zones and the location of foreign direct investment', *Journal of International Economics*, **71**(1): 96–112.

Teece, D.J. (1982), 'Towards an economic theory of the multiproduct firm', *Journal of Economic Behavior & Organization*, **3**(1): 39–63.

Thompson, J.D. (1967), *Organizations in Action*, New York: McGraw-Hill.

Tyler, T.R. and Blader, S.L. (2000), *Cooperation in Groups: Procedural Justice, Social Identity, and Behavioral Engagement*, Florence, KY: Psychology Press.

Vermeulen, F. and Barkema, H. (2002), 'Pace, rhythm, and scope: process dependence in building a profitable multinational corporation', *Strategic Management Journal*, **23**(7): 637–53.

Wernerfelt, B. and Montgomery, C.A. (1988), 'Tobin's q and the importance of focus in firm performance', *The American Economic Review*, **78**(1): 246–50.

Williamson, O.E. (1975), *Markets and Hierarchies*, New York: Free Press.

Zaheer, S. (1995), 'Overcoming the liability of foreignness', *Academy of Management Journal*, **38**(2): 341–63.

Zaheer, S. and Mosakowski, E. (1997), 'The dynamics of the liability of foreignness: a global study of survival in financial services', *Strategic Management Journal*, **18**(6): 439–63.

15 New insights on the role of location advantages in international innovation
Rajneesh Narula and Grazia D. Santangelo

INTRODUCTION

Understanding the reasons why economic activity prefers to locate in certain physical spaces (and not in others) forms the basis of much enquiry since at least the Enlightenment, and continues to do so. Although the jargon in such enquiry has evolved through the centuries, the concern with national competitiveness has driven many of these efforts and, connected to this, the propensity to trade, and the ensuing issues of balance of payments and national debt. Nonetheless, location and agglomeration of economic activity – until about 50 years ago – worked on the assumption that both capital and labour were location-bound, because firms and individuals showed little propensity to mobility. Thus competitiveness was primarily shaped by the attributes of the location, and as locations evolved in the nature of their inherent strengths and weaknesses, the kind of economic activity based there also fluctuated. This had obvious ramifications for the nature and extent of trade, and the conditions that permitted one region or country to be more successful than others.

The evolution of the modern multinational enterprise (MNE)[1] changed this with the growing level and intensity of foreign direct investment (FDI), intrafirm trade and complex sets of linkages among and between spatially dispersed economic actors. Mostly, this has gradually decoupled – but only to an extent – the severely linear relationship between the competitiveness of firms in a given location and the competitiveness of the location itself. That is, where capital and firms were physically static, the competitiveness of countries explained the competitiveness of firms located there, but rarely ever vice versa (Vernon, 1966). The firm as understood in this context was 'generic' in that it was neither multinational nor multi-plant, and was by itself organizationally and geographically a singularity, no different from other firms (Beugelsdijk et al., 2010).

However, the MNE has become a complex organism, with an ability to spatially reorganize its activities (and across borders) – and with growing ease – to take advantage of differences in the quality, availability and price of location-bound assets, both within countries and across countries, and these multiple engagements are dynamic in the sense that they are continuously evolving (Dunning, 1977, 1980). The more complex the MNE spatially and organizationally, the greater the need to interpret its interdependence with multiple locations and multiple contexts, each with differing degrees of embeddedness (Meyer et al., 2011). In short, locational characteristics (location (L) advantages) and the operations of the MNE (ownership (O) advantages) are concatenated, implying that they are inextricably linked, yet are not the same object. The MNE has the potential to shape the characteristics of the location, as much as it is shaped by its milieu (Cantwell, 1995).

This multilevel complexity means that the study of location is no mere academic exploration, with the aim to explain the success and failure of nations and its industries with the hindsight afforded to us by history. Firms must make locational choices, and 'wrong' choices can be costly because they also imply other opportunities forgone. Firms are resource-constrained and have cognitive boundaries that shape what they can and cannot do, and this makes location decisions strategic in nature, and insinuates a micro-aspect to the study and understanding of location. Similarly, governments are able to shape their policies to determine their locational attractiveness, as firms and individuals have a growing degree of flexibility in selecting where (and where not) to locate, and perhaps more importantly what aspects of their value-adding activities to concentrate in which particular locations. This brings out the macro-level significance of the study of location.

Engaging in high-value-adding activities implies higher competence levels (or in other words, greater O advantages) of MNE subsidiaries, which require L advantages that are non-generic in nature and are often associated with agglomeration effects, clusters and the presence of highly specialized skills (Lall and Pietrobelli, 2002). Firms are constrained in their choice of location for high competence subsidiaries by the L advantages of the host location. For instance, R&D activities tend to be concentrated in few locations, because the appropriate specialized resources are associated with only few locations. The embeddedness of firms is often a function of the duration of the MNEs' presence, since firms tend to build incrementally (Håkanson and Nobel, 2001; Rabbiosi and Santangelo, 2009). MNEs most often rely on L advantages that already exist in the host economy, and deepening of embeddedness occurs generally in response to improvements of the domestic technological capacity. However, while the scope of activities undertaken by a subsidiary can be modified more or less instantly, developing competence levels takes time (Cantwell and Mudambi, 2005; Nobel and Birkinshaw, 1998). MNE investments in high-value-added activities (often associated with high competence levels) have the tendency to be 'sticky'. Firms demonstrate greater inertia when it comes to relocating R&D activities. This reflects the high costs and considerable time required to develop linkages with the host country actors and institutions (Narula, 2002).

The complex interdependence of O and L advantages presents the MNE with a number of trade-offs when taking strategic decisions regarding the location of R&D. First, MNEs need to decide whether to centralize or decentralize. Second, MNEs need to decide whether to spatially separate from or co-locate with their rivals. Neither of these trade-offs is an either/or decision, nor are they diametrically opposed to each other. However, as is often the case in the nature of trade-offs, the choice is shaped by constraints most often associated with cognitive limits to resources, the bounded rationality of firms and the uncertainty inherent in innovation.

This chapter addresses this topic in five sections. The next section discusses L and O advantages, providing a classification of and some novel insights into their interaction. The third section focuses on innovation and location, and explains the relevance of the concept of and relationships between L and O advantages for R&D activity. The last two sections are concerned with the trade-off between centralization and decentralization, and spatial separation and co-location of R&D activity, respectively.

LOCATION AND OWNERSHIP ADVANTAGES – AN UPDATED SET OF DEFINITIONS

The essence of locational behaviour of MNEs (as well as other economic actors) reflects the interaction between O and L advantages (Cantwell, 1995; Dunning, 2008).

Ownership advantages are firm-specific in nature, and the competitiveness of firms is associated with the strength (or weakness) of their O advantages. In this instance, we use O advantages to refer to firm-specific assets that are essential in the generation of economic rent and/or market share retention/creation (Narula, 2010). There are two primary types of O advantages (Dunning and Lundan, 2008). The first refer to assets in the sense of the ownership of physical equipment, intellectual property, or privileged access to tangible and intangible resources (which also include knowledge possessed by employees). Such assets include knowledge of how and where resources may be accessed in any given location, the costs of acquiring such assets in one location relative to alternative locations, the knowledge to organize multi-location operations etc. These are asset-type O advantages (Oa). A second class of O advantages are transaction-type O advantages (Ot). These derive from (1) the knowledge to create efficient internal hierarchies (or internal markets) within the boundaries of the firm; and (2) being able to efficiently utilize external markets. Ot assets form a necessary and (sometimes) sufficient basis for a firm to remain competitive (Narula, 2003). Ot advantages also include the knowledge of institutions, because familiarity of institutions plays an important part in reducing the coordination costs, shirking costs and other transaction costs (Narula, 2010; Santangelo and Meyer, 2011). However, they are rarely in themselves a source of rent generation. It is important to distinguish between the O advantages of the MNE at large, and those associated with individual establishments or subsidiaries (Rugman and Verbeke, 2001). Much of the early literature on O advantages took a macro-perspective, and, given the nature of the typical MNE and its centralized management structure, at that time it was a reasonable assumption that the O advantages of the MNE were in principle available to and accessible by all subsidiaries. This, however, is increasingly hard to justify. The O advantages of the parent are not necessarily available to all its subsidiaries and to each individual operating unit, and vice versa.

L advantages are about the characteristics of specific locations, and are location-bound. Although it is increasingly popular to use country-specific assets as a synonym for L advantages (Rugman and Verbeke, 1992), the term 'L advantages' allows us to clearly distinguish between the various units of analysis, such as the country, national sub-regional and supranational regions.[2] It is well known that even within countries, regions compete for FDI by offering more attractive institutional frameworks (Hogenbirk, 2002; Meyer and Nguyen, 2005; Narula and Dunning, 2010). Supranational regions also exist – such as the European Union (EU) – which provide an additional layer of policies, regulations and laws. An MNE may engage with all three levels of L advantage. For instance, consider an MNE with a production site in Maastricht, in the Netherlands. The MNE will need to consider the L advantages of the Netherlands at large, the Limburg province, as well as that of the EU, in addition to the special status of Maastricht as part of the Meuse–Rhine Euregio, which addresses aspects peculiar to the contiguous multi-country border region of Germany, Belgium and the Netherlands.

L advantages are a set of characteristics associated with a location, and are in principle accessible and applicable to all firms equally that are physically or legally established in that location. We say 'in principle' for three reasons. First, full information about L advantages associated with a specific location may not be readily available. Second, even where information is available, there may be costs associated with accessing this knowledge. This knowledge may be available to incumbents (whether domestic or foreign), by virtue of their existing activities on that location, and acquired through experience. Third, these L advantages may be made available differentially by the actions of governments that seek to restrict (or encourage) the activities of a particular group of actors by introducing barriers to their use of certain L advantages. These may be for commercial reasons, or for strategic reasons such as national defence, or reflect the influence of interest groups who are able to influence government policy. These represent a subset of the 'liability of foreignness', when L advantages are available to local and foreign firms at differential costs (Zaheer, 1995).

Note that when location-bound assets are in the private domain (i.e. they are internalized by others), they are no longer L advantages but constitute O advantages, since they assist rent generation/market share retention by specific actors to the exclusion of other economic actors. Location advantages can be said to be 'public' because they are not private goods, but not always in the sense of being 'public goods' because they may not always be used without (some) detriment to their value to subsequent users. This aspect of L advantages will be discussed at length later.

A Classification of L and O Advantages

L advantages come in all shapes and sizes, and it is hard to make general statements and lists of all possible L advantages (although we try in Table 15.1!). This is because the L advantages relevant to a particular circumstance vary by a variety of MNE and affiliate-specific factors, such as the motive of the investment; the spatial, logistical and strategic relationships with other operations, both within the same MNE and outside the MNEs with other independent firms. It is important to understand that L advantages are about relevant complementary assets outside the boundaries of the MNE (or other firm actors) that are location-bound. We discuss this later, when we introduce the concept of co-location L advantages.

Table 15.1 classifies L advantages into three broad categories – at the country, industry and firm level. For each category, we identify specific type of L advantages and related sources, and provide examples. As we discuss below, these categories have a certain degree of overlap.

Country-level L advantages are 'contextual' in nature, in the sense that they provide the broad background of a location. They reflect the socioeconomic and political environment that is relevant to any location. They remain macro and 'generic' because they are public or quasi-public goods, and are relevant to all firms regardless of size, nationality, industry or geographical unit of analysis. Some are exogenous, in the sense that they are independent of economic stage of development, and are the natural assets of the location, such as population, climate, accessibility etc. Others are created assets but remain generic in the sense that they are expected to exist in all nation states although there are countries where the government is unable to provide these – basic infrastructure, legal and financial

Table 15.1   A classification of L advantages

	Type of L advantages	Sources of L advantages	Example of L advantages
Macro-region/country-level L advantages	Exogenous L advantages	These derive from natural assets (independent of development stage)	Sociological/anthropological ● Culture, norms, religion, political stability ● Land availability, rainfall, climate, extractive resources, basic population ● Proximity and accessibility to other markets
	Fundamental L advantages	Basic infrastructure	● Primary schools ● Health care ● Transport (roads, railways) ● Utilities (electricity, water) ● Telecoms ● Ports ● Efficient bureaucracy ● Public transport
		Legal infrastructure	● Legal system ● Security and police ● Tariff system ● Property rights ● Tax and excise
		Regulation and policy	● Incentives ● Subsidies ● Tax holidays ● Regulatory agencies ● Industrial policy ● Competition policy ● Capacity to enforce regulation
		Financial infrastructure	● Banking, insurance, stock exchange
	Knowledge asset L advantages	Knowledge infrastructure	● Tertiary education, universities ● Public research institutes
Industry-level L advantages	Structural L advantages	Market and demand structure	● Income distribution ● Size of potential market ● Wage rates ● Skilled employee mobility/scarcity
Firm-associated L advantages	Co-location L advantages	L advantages that derive from the presence of other actors in the same location	● Agglomeration economies ● Networks of suppliers ● Networks of customers ● Level of intra-industry competition ● Concentration ratio ● Market size and potential ● Presence of support industries (inter-industry)
		Industrial policy	● Specific policies associated with given industry
		L advantages that derive from location-bound O advantages of other actors	● Presence of significant customer ● Presence of significant supplier

infrastructure, and regulation and policy frameworks. The last category represents knowledge infrastructure L advantages. 'Knowledge infrastructure' as used here is 'generic, multi-user and indivisible', consisting of public research institutes, universities, organizations for standards, intellectual property protection etc. that enable and promote science and technology development (Smith, 1997). For obvious reasons, this can also be categorized as an industry-level L advantage, since such assets may be specifically geared to a particular set of industries.

In making an investment decision, MNEs seek specific, industry and market-related complementary assets (industry-associated L advantages). It is not enough, for instance, for an IT firm that is seeking to establish software design facilities that there is a large supply of low-wage university graduates, but that there is a large supply of IT graduates. Neither demand conditions nor market structure can be analysed using country-level L advantages. For a market-seeking investor, income distribution and the size of the specific market cannot be gauged from generic L advantages such as population. A luxury-watch manufacturer will be interested in knowing the market for other luxury goods, and opportunities for distributing her goods through channels specific to luxury goods, and the competition within that specific sector. Industry policy may also be seen to be industry-specific, by definition. A location that is home to a cluster of firms in a similar industry is likely to have access to a number of suppliers in support and related sectors. Governments may also provide specific incentives and policies to promote a specific sector, which may make a location more attractive for a specific industry, and not for others.

In this chapter we define an important sub-category of L advantages: 'co-location L advantages'. Where important competitors in the same industry are co-located, there is an opportunity to hire appropriately skilled and experienced potential workers, and the possibility of knowledge spillovers through mobile employees. In short, these are L advantages that derive from the presence of other actors in the same industry that are co-located (see Table 15.1 for more details). These include the essence of other co-located firms' O advantages, which contribute to the competitiveness of the location.

Although O advantages *per se* do not generate L advantages, the presence or absence of specific firms in a milieu can act as important inducements to co-locate (firm-associated L advantages). The physical location of a lead firm within a global production network acts as a powerful L advantage to its key suppliers. Others may seek specific L advantages to improve knowledge spillovers by being proximate to a market or industry leader. In this sense, L advantages overlap with O advantages, and differ from industry-associated L advantages.

Informal institutions deserve special mention as an L advantage. Informal institutions (which may or may not be linked to current formal institutions) are routines, habits and procedures that are in common use and that shape the manner in which economic actors in a given location interact in practice. Formal institutions may prescribe one set of actions, but economic actors may utilize other institutions that are *de facto*, and not *de jure*. Knowledge of such institutions is also in principle available to all firms that seek to acquire this, but because informal institutions are largely tacit, physical proximity is crucial in their acquisition. In other words, they require some degree of embeddedness to acquire. Embeddedness in a location provides membership to a 'club' of complex relationships with suppliers, customers and knowledge infrastructure through formal and informal institutions that have taken years to evolve a stock of knowledge that is only available to members by virtue of their constant interaction (Forsgren et al., 2005). There are 'goods' associated with these networks that are only available to those that are co-located, because they have evolved under the same informal institutions. Thus they are quasi-public goods, for which firms located there have invested in to acquire knowledge of these institutions (Narula and Santangelo, 2009). Knowledge of institutions can indeed represent O advantages, but only where markets are closed. This is why some authors (e.g. Dunning and Lundan, 2008) have classified them as O advantages, while others regard them to be L advantages (Narula, 2010).

It is worth highlighting the difference between location-bound O advantages and those that are non-location-bound (Rugman and Verbeke, 2001). Location-bound O advantages allow the firm to generate profits from these assets, but only in a specific location. This may be due to government-induced incentives, such as privileged access to specific natural resources, to capital, or specific infrastructure. In other cases, market entry may be restricted, providing the firm with a monopoly or a pseudo-monopoly, and consequent opportunities to generate rent (e.g. telecoms licences, petroleum-drilling rights). Location-bound O advantages may also derive from specific (non-government) L advantages that the firm is able to access only in the given location, the use of which requires physical presence in that specific location. Many MNEs are among the largest in their home markets, and are themselves part of large industrial groups (sometimes with cross-holdings and common ownership) with interests in several industries, and also derive location-bound O advantages from privileged access to intragroup transactions and intermediate goods within the same family of firms, but these advantages are not necessarily available when they move abroad (Narula and Nguyen, 2011). These may also derive from knowledge of institutions, and by being an 'insider'. By virtue of their size and importance in the home economy, they may have close relationships with state-owned organizations, ministries and policy-makers, and are able to influence domestic policy, as well as the associated knowledge infrastructure for their own needs, and, in many cases, these have evolved around and with their own domestic activities, often over a long period of time. Such linkages confer the basis to generate economic rent for incumbents, and are a cost to new entrants or those less entrenched in the domestic milieu (Cantwell and Mudambi, 2011). These advantages are not transferable to foreign markets, and establishing 'membership' in business and innovation networks in new locations is not costless (Narula, 2002).

Non-location-bound O advantages derive from skills, technology or other knowledge that the firm possesses to the exclusion of other economic actors operating in the same location. Such O advantages also tend to be a function of the home country. Firms typically build their original resource endowments in their home country and this original resource endowment drives their international growth (Narula and Nguyen, 2011; Tan and Meyer, 2010).

Interaction of L and O Advantages

There are circumstances where the differentiation between O and L advantages can be challenging, partly because of the interaction and concatenation of O and L advantages. Initial O advantages of any MNE derive from the L advantages of the home country, and as the work pioneered by Rugman and Verbeke (2003) has shown, many MNEs continue

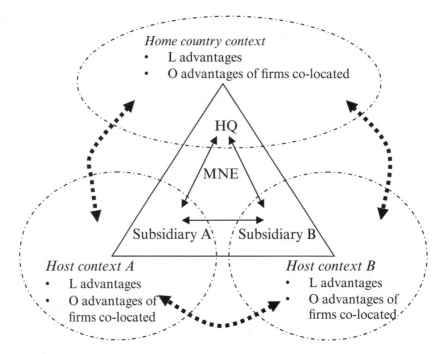

Source: Meyer et al. (2011).

Figure 15.1   Multinational enterprises and local context

to show a strong bias towards their home regions. For firms that are beginning to internationalize, the dependence on the home country is especially strong (Narula, 1996; Narula and Nguyen, 2011). However, there is a certain degree of obfuscation that derives from taking an MNE-level perspective on L and O advantages, which requires the aggregation of individual operations. The O advantages of MNEs – once they become embedded in new locations abroad – are influenced by multiple sets of L advantages, and create the challenge of multiple embeddedness (Meyer et al., 2011).

The MNE in any given location has to interact frequently with other actors in each host country, and additionally when it has multiple establishments, with multiple locations within the host country. Each interaction has the potential to change the knowledge base of all the participants and, by extension, the O advantages of the various participants. Where the domestic actors are locationally bound, this implies changes in the L advantages of the host country as well. Such interactions vary in intensity, depending upon a variety of factors. In general, the greater the scope and competence of an MNE subsidiary in a given location, the greater the degree of embeddedness in the host location, and the greater the interaction with other actors in that location (Holm and Pedersen, 2000). This implies managing a portfolio of subsidiary-level activities in multiple, heterogeneous, local contexts and plays an important role in defining its O advantages (Figueiredo, 2011). Figure 15.1 illustrates the complexities of this concept.

In particular, the O advantages of any given subsidiary ('subsidiary A' in Figure 15.1) are shaped by:

1. the parent firm. Since the O advantages of the parent firm are a function of the home country L advantages, by extension the O advantages of subsidiary A are also greatly influenced by these L advantages;
2. the extent to which the parent and the particular subsidiary are integrated. At the one extreme, a free-standing MNE may function as a completely autonomous set of subsidiaries with little or no intra-MNE interaction, and the O advantages of the subsidiary and the parent are independent sets. At the other extreme, the MNE may be completely integrated such that the O advantages of subsidiary A are a complete subset of the parent MNE;
3. the extent to which subsidiary A is embedded in the host country. This reflects a variety of factors. The quality of the linkages is associated with the scope and competence level of the subsidiary (Narula and Santangelo, 2009), and these in turn are co-determined by a variety of factors (for an extensive discussion see Narula and Bellak, 2009). These include MNE internal factors such as their internationalization strategy, the role of the location in their global portfolio of subsidiaries, and the motivation of the investment, in addition to the available location-specific resources that can be used for that purpose (Benito et al., 2003);
4. the relative strength of the association with other subsidiaries. Specific subsidiaries may function within a regional structure, along functional lines, or within a specific integrated product or supply chain. In such instances, the relationship with subsidiary B may be much more intensive than within the parent firm. As such, the O advantages of subsidiary A may be influenced to a greater extent by the O advantages of subsidiary B, and the L advantages associated with location B.

The subsidiary has to balance the forces that require local responsiveness to its host milieu with those that emanate from the parent MNE, which may require the subsidiaries' integration within the MNE's overall structure. Given that many larger MNEs are a complex aggregation of a large number of constituent subsidiaries, such multiple embeddedness generates trade-offs between external and internal embeddedness, since each subsidiary must reconcile the interests of its parent with those of its local business interests.

This implies – from the perspective of the interaction of the more global MNE – that its portfolio of O advantages is a complex blend of those derived from multiple contexts (Meyer et al., 2011), and therefore a complex set of L advantages of different locations. In each location, it absorbs and adapts its O advantages in response both to the L advantages available, and through linkages with co-located firms also adapts to the O advantages of these unaffiliated firms. Note that, by joining an agglomeration, the MNE itself become part of an agglomeration, and therefore enhances the L advantages of the host location for other firms.

INNOVATION AND LOCATION

The literature on motivation of R&D activities is reasonably well developed, and we shall not seek to revisit it, focusing instead on the broad dichotomy of asset-augmenting and asset-exploiting R&D motivations (Dunning and Narula, 1995;

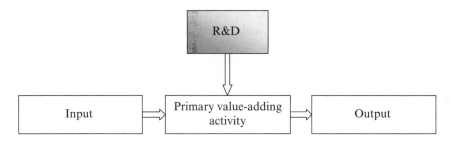

Figure 15.2a   A value chain where R&D is subordinate to the primary value-adding function

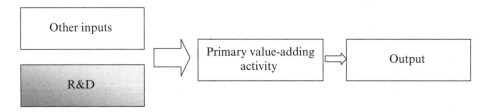

Figure 15.2b   A value chain where R&D is central to the primary value-adding function

Kuemmerle, 1999), and its relationship with motivation of more general FDI activities of MNEs (Dunning, 1993). It is important in this context to note that in certain industries and sectors, R&D performs a subordinate and supportive role to 'mainstream' activities such as production and sales, while in others, R&D is a primary input to these activities (Figure 15.2a,b). For instance, in sectors such as software and pharmaceuticals, R&D is a primary input to the firm's primary function, while in sectors such as paper products, R&D is a supportive input. In addition, firms are increasingly engaged in rationalizing their activities globally, so as to maximize the link with specific value-adding activities and locations that have specific competitive and comparative advantages. This has led to a tendency among MNEs to 'break up' their value chains and locate specific aspects in particular locations for purposes of maximum efficiency (Mudambi, 2008). As such, few locations host all parts of the value chain of one product for any given MNE, leading to an agglomeration of specific types of activities in particular locations. Prior to economic liberalization, MNEs responded to investment opportunities primarily by establishing truncated miniature replicas of their facilities at home, although the extent to which they are truncated varied considerably between countries (Papanastassiou and Pearce, 1999). The extent of truncation was determined by a number of factors, but by far the most important determinant of truncation – and thereby the scope of activities and competence level of the subsidiary – was associated with market size, and capacity and capability of domestic industry (Dunning and Narula, 2004).

MNEs may seek to engage in R&D in response to specific L advantages because R&D is more demand-oriented. This may reflect, for instance, large markets or scarce natural resources that are location-bound. These promote the outward spread of production, sales and other value-adding activities where MNEs attempt to exploit their existing assets and competences in conjunction with these L advantages. In such cases, innovation is undertaken in order to adapt existing products and services to local stimuli. Such R&D facilities tend to be relatively low in knowledge intensity, and remain somewhat footloose, requiring greater integration with the parent firm as well as the market, rather than a focus on the knowledge asset L advantages of the host country (Table 15.1). Such asset-exploiting activities are subordinate to the MNE's market-seeking FDI activities, in that R&D follows (perhaps reluctantly) the location of other aspects of the value chain. In such instances, the MNE's R&D activities are primarily determined by the same L advantages that shape their other activities, although not at the same intensity or timing.

An important set of L advantages for R&D activity is associated with the interaction of the knowledge infrastructure-related L advantages of locations and the L advantages that derive from the O advantages of firms already based in these locations (e.g. co-location L advantages). These in turn are strongly associated with L advantages that derive from knowledge of institutions. Note that the institutions themselves are L advantages, while the knowledge of these institutions is an O advantage. These particular L advantages play a pre-eminent role in shaping the location of innovation in three sets of circumstances: first, where MNE R&D is asset-augmenting in motivation and essentially represents supply-driven R&D; second, in market-seeking MNE activity where R&D is central (rather than subordinate) to the primary value-adding activities of firms; and third, where the MNE's activities are tightly linked and interdependent with other co-located firms' activities, as in the case with supply chains, production networks and *keiretsu*. All three have another common feature – the importance of the role of institutions, and the knowledge of these institutions.

The systems of innovation literature can be useful to explain this dynamic (Lundvall, 1992). In particular, this stream of research builds on the principle that innovation is a collective process that involves firms as well as other actors such as policy makers, universities, public research centres, investment banks etc.[3] These actors are bound together through rules, routines, habits and procedures that may be formally or informally defined, but that shape the nature and extent of interaction of the various parties. This ties into the idea propagated by Marshall (1920) about successful agglomerations – something that is 'in the air', a stock of knowledge that is available only to members with a particular location-specific absorptive capacity by virtue of their constant interaction.

Whatever the geographical unit of analysis, a systems view builds on the important principle that knowledge diffusion between actors in geographical proximity fosters innovation. Where knowledge is being exchanged, and this knowledge has a strong tacit nature, 'physical' or geographical proximity eases knowledge transmission (e.g. Blanc and Sierra, 1999). Knowledge spillovers tend indeed to be more intense between parties that are located close to each other in space (e.g. Jaffe and Trajtenberg, 1996, 1998; Jaffe et al., 1993; Maurseth and Verspagen, 2002). Thus MNEs are typically based in a particular location because of such L advantages, which often include quasi-public goods provided though universities and public research institutes (Asheim and Gertler, 2005). The point here is that proximity, linkages and institutions are inextricably tied together, and that especially where innovation (which has a tacit aspect) is concerned, firms share an inertia in seeking alternative locations.

MNES AND THE TRADE-OFF BETWEEN CENTRALIZATION AND DECENTRALIZATION

The innovation activities of MNEs follow the same general logic as other value-adding activities, in that they require access to specific L advantages. However, the nature of innovation and its strategic significance to the long-term well-being of the MNE means that MNEs have been more reluctant to internationalize R&D than other aspects of the value chain (Narula and Zanfei, 2005). Nonetheless, there is compelling evidence that this is changing as well, albeit much more cautiously, and with a time lag relative to other aspects of the value chain.

The issue of location in the innovatory activities of MNEs is complex. At the most elementary level, MNEs face the dual and (sometimes) opposing challenges of centralization and decentralization (Sanna-Randaccio and Veugelers, 2007), although the contradictions between the two are not necessarily always as stark – firms seek to do both simultaneously, depending upon the motivation of the R&D, and the centrality of R&D to the primary value-adding activities of the MNE. The willingness or reluctance to internationalize is due to a number of factors. First, the strategic importance of R&D means that firms may wish to exert as much control over the process as possible by keeping R&D close to headquarters, which can ensure an optimal level of monitoring and control over its activities. Second, there is a minimum efficient scale associated with R&D activities. Given the relatively high costs of R&D, MNEs prefer to maintain as few R&D facilities as possible, to reduce costs. Small firms are constrained by their limited resources – the expansion of R&D activities both at home and in overseas locations requires considerable resources in terms of both capital investment and managerial resources, which these firms simply do not have. *Ceteris paribus*, large firms have more money and resources to use on overseas activity. Third, a dispersion of R&D activities across the globe also requires extensive coordination – and particularly with headquarters – if they are to function in an efficient manner with regard to the collection and dissemination of information. Internal proximity between R&D and the rest of the MNE is an important issue (Blanc and Sierra, 1999). Spatially distributed R&D requires the establishment and management of networks internal to the firm, in addition to those between external networks and internal networks, and require complex coordination if they are to provide optimal benefits (Narula and Zanfei, 2005). Such networks are not only difficult to manage, but also require considerable resources (both managerial and financial). Managing spatially dispersed R&D – even within the same organization – is suboptimal, due to knowledge internal stickiness (Szulanski, 1996). Thus firms' default option is to maintain R&D in as few locations as possible, and to maintain strategic control by concentrating it close to headquarters.

Fourth, there are industry-specific reasons that may encourage or discourage centralization. The maturity of the core technology and its characteristics determines the extent to which the innovation process can be internalized (Narula, 2003; Teece, 1986) and geographically dispersed (Cantwell and Santangelo, 1999, 2000). Most mature technologies evolve slowly and demonstrate minor but consistent innovations over time. The technology is to a great extent codifiable, widely disseminated, and the property rights well defined. Intra-industry competition emphasizes price and therefore economies of scale. In the extreme – as in many resource-extractive industries – downstream activities add most value, with the natural resource being priced as a commodity. These sectors do not require outputs to be tailored to customers to the same extent, or as quickly. This means that constant and close interaction between customers is not an important determinant of R&D. Profits of firms are highly dependent on the costs of inputs, and proximity to the source of these inputs is often more significant than that of customers. At the other extreme, rapidity of technological change in 'newer' technologies requires a closer interaction between production and R&D. Technologies have a higher tacit, uncodifiable element, and this requires a closer coordination between users and producers of innovation.

In addition, though, supply-side considerations are especially important in asset-augmenting innovation. To engage in more intensive activities such as research (as opposed to development), complementary assets are necessary. These assets can be best described as non-generic, knowledge-intensive L advantages, which the firm cannot access (or as cheaply) in its home base (or other locations). Thus MNEs need to access 'unique' or scarce L advantages to do with the knowledge infrastructure and specialized sources of knowledge that may be either firm-specific and location-bound, or location-specific and available to all. In the case of asset-augmenting activity, MNEs may situate (or seek to establish) themselves in particular locations to (and in some cases only to) undertake innovation because of specific location-bound assets provided through the innovation system. Such innovation activities are more of the nature of stand-alone R&D facilities that are considerably knowledge intensive, and imply a considerably greater dependence on domestic knowledge sources and infrastructure.

MNES AND THE TRADE-OFF BETWEEN SPATIAL SEPARATION AND CO-LOCATION

Most theoretical perspectives (such as the innovation systems literature) provide arguments in favour of firms locating in close spatial proximity, particularly for R&D. However, recent research has provided a number of arguments challenging this view.

First, while all firms in principle seek to have positive inflows of knowledge, few firms wish to be the source of (unintended) knowledge outflows (Alcácer, 2006; Santangelo, 2012). Although in the case of R&D (compared to sales or manufacturing) there is a greater active interest in seeking spillovers, this tendency reflects the capabilities of the firm. R&D tends to be more concentrated relative to manufacturing and sales, but more capable firms co-locate less than less capable firms, regardless of the activity (Alcácer, 2006). In other words, firms may seek to avoid co-location of R&D to minimize leakages of value assets. Even where spillovers are the objective, being co-located is not always necessary. Of course, this varies considerably by industry, particularly in sectors where the tacit aspect is significant. Tacit knowledge is much more difficult to exchange or trade, and, as a result, tends to be sticky and geographically less mobile. In industries where the tacit aspect is significant, *ceteris paribus*, the propensity to geographically concentrate is higher (Iammarino and McCann, 2006) than in sectors where the knowledge being exchanged is codifiable. This is especially so in oligopolistic industries (as opposed to industries with a competitive market structure) where loss to rivals is perceived as costly, and the private-good aspect of knowledge is more important than the public-good aspect

(Iammarino and McCann, 2006; McCann and Mudambi, 2005). Empirical evidence has shown that the involvement of firms in clusters is extremely sensitive to the nature of the industry structure in which the firm operates (Cantwell and Kosmopoulou, 2002). That is, firms operating in the same R&D-intensive oligopolistic industry tend to spatially separate their core innovative activity (Cantwell and Santangelo, 2002). Unintended knowledge outflows from a firm can be quite valuable to its direct competitors and it is therefore important not to locate close to rivals (Cantwell and Santangelo, 2002), or the result may be an adverse selection of co-located firms (Shaver and Flyer, 2000). Thus, for oligopolistic industries, although the choice of R&D location is important in determining the capabilities of firms and their access to 'members-only' public goods, co-locating with rivals is not always the preferred option. Technically advanced firms prefer being proximate to universities, and are not interested in locating close to other firms in the same industry, whereas less competitive firms prefer to locate close to rivals (Alcácer and Chung, 2007).

Second, firms do not always co-locate because they wish to benefit from knowledge transfers (intended or unintended), but simply to have access to the same location-specific assets (such as skilled labour), which may be achieved by staying broadly in the same regional vicinity (Cantwell and Iammarino, 2003). When, however, the local system provides a combination of factors that contributes to innovation (such as skills, finance, production, user–producer linkages), the fear of knowledge spillovers to competitors may be counterbalanced by location-bound (i.e. associated with firm-specific advantages) or location-specific factors, and intra-industry spatial concentration then takes place. Firms – whether they are technological leaders or followers – often have little choice in their location, and may in fact be co-located in a cluster by virtue of their history, or because of the presence of an important university or public research establishment. In particular, firms often locate their R&D to take advantage of a specific scientific specialization of a university or public research establishment. The number of specialized universities and institutes in a given scientific field is finite, so even where a technological leader would prefer to avoid spatial proximity with its less able rivals, it cannot prevent these firms from co-locating in order to establish embedded relationships with these institutions. Thus, once competitors co-locate, the decision to embed locally in order to access local complementary knowledge depends on entry motivations and firms capabilities since such a decision may bring about risks of unintended knowledge spillovers (Perri et al., 2010; Santangelo, 2012). In particular, when domestic actors are valuable in terms of knowledge, rivals entering the market with a competence-creating motivation (as opposed to a non-competence-creating motivation) embed in the host economy as their expected payoffs of embeddedness exceed those of isolation (Santangelo, 2012). Moreover, empirical evidence documents that highly capable firms invest more in the relationships with local partners under conditions of low competition, but they also reduce their commitment more to such relationships when the perceived pressure from the competitive environment exceeds a certain threshold as a result of potential loss from outward spillovers (Perri et al., 2010).

Third, few technological leaders have superior capabilities in all subsectors, and may require complementary resources from their rivals. Alliances allow firms to effectively engage in knowledge exchange without the hazard of unintended knowledge spillovers (Narula and Santangelo, 2009). Firms are unable to properly protect their technological assets that they intentionally or unintentionally share with their neighbours, even though formal property rights have been obtained. This is particularly the case when they are geographically close since, while the marginal cost of transmitting codified knowledge across geographic space does not depend on distance, the marginal cost of transmitting tacit knowledge increases with distance (Criscuolo and Verspagen, 2008). The co-location of innovation activities therefore implies potential threat to competitive advantage of co-located rivals. This argument applies especially to alliances between firms operating in the same industry and core technological fields. In such cases, the need for closely monitoring knowledge transmission is greater, the higher the degree of competition, since co-located rival firms with technologically similar profiles compete both in the output market and the technological realm (Narula and Santangelo, 2009). Therefore, in these cases partnerships enable firms to directly monitor their co-located market and technological rivals as well as to access possible complementary capabilities.

IMPLICATIONS AND AVENUES FOR FUTURE RESEARCH

We have sought here to examine certain current issues in the role of location advantages in the spatial distribution of MNE R&D activity. In doing so, we have returned to first principles by revisiting our understanding of L and O advantages and their interaction. This interaction lies at the heart of innovation studies, economic geography and the economics of innovation (which takes a policy view of the competitiveness of locations), as well as innovation and strategic management (which take a firm-level perspective on the competitiveness of firms).

Returning to key insights from these related disciplines, we have revisited the meaning of L and O advantages, as opposed to their definitions. This has required us to return to the oft-cited (but under-utilized) differentiation between country-, industry- and firm-level issues, and offer a succinct differentiation of L advantages. Taking a systems view has allowed us to emphasize the importance of institutions, and flesh out the concept of co-location L advantages, which play an important role at the industry and firm levels of analysis. Just because a country possesses certain L advantages when viewed at a macro-level does not imply that these are available to all industries or all firms in that country without differential cost. When these are linked to the distinction between location-bound and non-location-bound O advantages, and when we distinguish between the portfolio of assets available to MNEs and their individual subsidiaries and establishments, it allows for a clearer understanding of the challenges the modern MNE faces in managing its spatially distributed activities.

These have been discussed in the context of R&D, which – in addition to the usual uncertainties faced by firms – must deal with the uncertainties associated with innovation. These have to do with the nature of knowledge, and how these inherent characteristics determine effective knowledge flows within the MNE, as well as with other actors that make up the host location. Although prior literature has sometimes framed the centralization/decentralization, spatial separation/co-location debates as a paradox facing firms, we feel that when viewed within the context of the cognitive limits to resources, the complexities of institutions and the glacial pace of the evolving specialization of locations, these are in actuality trade-offs firms must make.

It has not been our intention to provide a complete synopsis of the literature in this area, nor is it possible to raise all aspects of the conceptual and empirical lacunae that arise, but we shall offer a few suggestions.

First, neither the IB nor the innovation studies literature has as yet come to terms with the growing use of non-equity modes in cooperative R&D, and the role of location. Social network theory remains on the fringes of this research, and relatively little effort has been made to marry the seeming contradictions between the global nature of R&D cooperation and the stickiness of locations (Narula and Santangelo, 2009). The overlapping of complex supply chains, production networks and MNEs within and across locations presents a tapestry of establishments that is not as yet fully understood. Where are the boundaries of the firm where non-equity suggests legal separation and separate ownership, but where control suggests a *de facto* single organization?

This raises an interesting second line of future enquiry. This fuzziness of boundaries of the firm has implications for the fuzziness of boundaries of countries. Policy-makers have fewer tools at their disposal in building up the competitive advantage of individual nations where MNEs operate with alacrity across borders. Regulation, industrial policy and investment promotion no longer function as effectively (Narula, 2003; Narula and Dunning, 2010).

Third, the study of motives for MNE activity – while useful in providing texture to the discussion – is poorly understood conceptually, and the broad motivational arguments from Dunning (1993) are in need of revision. To cite a simple example, asset-exploiting and asset-augmenting activity are rarely done exclusively, and this is increasingly the case.

Fourth, the last two decades have seen a vigorous discussion of the benefits of clustering. In what way does spatial separation matter to firms in other aspects of the value chain? Does the propensity to co-locate vary by size of firm, and industry? Under what circumstances is co-location more important, and when does spatial separation represent a superior option?

NOTES

1. In this chapter we intentionally exclude the free-standing international company.
2. The use of the term 'advantage' is also troublesome, and reflects the path dependency of the eclectic paradigm and its provenance as an extension of trade theory (Dunning, 1977). It implies – in the same sense as comparative and absolute advantage – the relative strength or weakness of economic activity within a specific industry within a specific location (rather than between or relative to other locations). The term advantage also implies a subjective assessment, and as such we think it preferable to use the term 'characteristics'. In this chapter we shall use location advantage and locational characteristics as synonyms.
3. Although the concept of cluster *à la* Porter takes a broadly similar view (Porter, 1980, 1986, 1990), it has been criticized for being too general. The concept of clusters in innovation has been fleshed out by Iammarino and McCann (2006), who classify three types of clusters depending on the nature of innovation processes and structural conditions under which technical change occurs across space.

REFERENCES

Alcácer, J. (2006), 'Location choices across the value chain: how activity and capability influence collocation', *Management Science*, **52**(10), 1457–71.

Alcácer, J. and W. Chung (2007), 'Location strategies and knowledge spillovers', *Management Science*, **53**(5), 760–76.

Asheim, B. and M. Gertler (2005) 'The geography of innovation', in J. Fagerberg, D. Mowery and R. Nelson (eds), *The Oxford Handbook of Innovation*, Oxford: Oxford University Press, pp. 291–317.

Benito, G., G. Birgitte and R. Narula (2003), 'Environmental influences on MNE subsidiary roles: economic integration and the Nordic countries', *Journal of International Business Studies*, **34**, 443–56.

Beugelsdijk, S., P. McCann and R. Mudambi (2010), 'Introduction: place, space and organization, economic geography and the multinational enterprise', *Journal of Economic Geography*, **10**, 485–93.

Blanc, H. and C. Sierra (1999), 'The internationalisation of R&D by multinationals: a trade-off between external and internal proximity', *Cambridge Journal of Economics*, **23**(2), 187–206.

Cantwell, J. (1995), 'The globalisation of technology: what remains of the product cycle model?', *Cambridge Journal of Economics*, **19**(1), 155–74.

Cantwell, J. and S. Iammarino (2003), *Multinational Corporations and European Regional Systems of Innovation*, London: Routledge.

Cantwell, J. and E. Kosmopoulou (2002), 'What determines the internationalization of corporate technology?', in M. Forsgren, H. Håkanson and V. Havila (eds), *Critical Perspectives on Internationalisation*, London: Pergamon, pp. 305–34.

Cantwell, J. and R. Mudambi (2011), 'Physical attraction and the geography of knowledge sourcing in multinational enterprises', *Global Strategy Journal*, **1**(3–4), 206–32.

Cantwell, J. and G.D. Santangelo (1999), 'The frontier of international technology networks: sourcing abroad the most highly tacit capabilities', *Information Economics and Policy*, **11**(1), 101–23.

Cantwell, J. and G.D. Santangelo (2000), 'Capitalism, profits and innovation in the new techno-economic paradigm', *Journal of Evolutionary Economics*, **10**(1), 131–57.

Cantwell, J. and G.D. Santangelo (2002), 'The new geography of corporate research in information and communications technology (ICT)', *Journal of Evolutionary Economics*, **12**(1–2), 163–97.

Cantwell, J.A. and R. Mudambi (2005), 'MNE competence-creating subsidiary mandates', *Strategic Management Journal*, **26**(12), 1109–28.

Criscuolo, P. and B. Verspagen (2008), 'Does it matter where patent citations come from? Inventor versus examiner citations in European patents', *Research Policy*, **37**(10), 1892–908.

Dunning, J.H. (1977), 'Trade, location of economic activity and the MNE: a search for an eclectic approach', in B. Ohlin, P.-O. Hesselborn and P.-M. Wijkman (eds), *The International Allocation of Economic Activity*, London: Macmillan, pp. 395–431.

Dunning, J.H. (1980), 'Toward an eclectic theory of international production: some empirical tests', *Journal of International Business Studies*, **11**(1), 9–31.

Dunning, J.H. (1993), *Multinational Enterprises and the Global Economy*, New York: Addison-Wesley.

Dunning, J.H. (2008), 'Location and the multinational enterprise: a neglected factor?', *Journal of International Business Studies*, **40**(1), 5–19.

Dunning, J.H. and S. Lundan (2008), *Multinational Enterprises and the Global Economy*, 2nd edn, Cheltenham, UK and Northampton, MA, USA: Edward Elgar.

Dunning, J.H. and R. Narula (1995), 'The R&D activities of foreign firms in the United States', *International Studies of Management & Organization*, **25**(1/2), 39–74.

Dunning, J.H. and R. Narula (2004), *Multinational and Industrial Competitiveness: A New Agenda*, Cheltenham, UK and Northampton, MA, USA: Edward Elgar.

Figueiredo, P. (2011), 'The role of dual embeddedness in the innovative performance of MNE subsidiaries: evidence from Brazil', *Journal of Management Studies*, **48**(2), 417–40.

Forsgren, M., U. Holm and J. Johanson (2005), *Managing the Embedded Multinational – A Business Network View*, Cheltenham, UK and Northampton, MA, USA: Edward Elgar.

Håkanson, L. and R. Nobel (2001), 'Organization characteristics and reverse technology transfer', *Management International Review*, **41**(Special Issue 4), 392–420.

Hogenbirk, A.E. (2002), 'Determinants of inward foreign direct investment: the case of the Netherlands', Maastricht University.

Holm, U. and T. Pedersen (2000), *The Emergence and Impact of MNE Centres of Excellence: A Subsidiary Perspective*, London: Macmillan.

Iammarino, S. and P. McCann (2006), 'The structure and evolution of industrial clusters: transactions, technology and knowledge spillovers', *Research Policy*, **35**(7), 1018–36.

Jaffe, A. and M. Trajtenberg (1996), 'Flows of knowledge from universities and federal labs: modelling the flow of patent citations over time and across institutional and geographic boundaries', NBER Working Paper 5712.

Jaffe, A. and M. Trajtenberg (1998), 'International knowledge flows: Evidence from patent citations', NBER Working Paper 6507.

Jaffe, A., M. Trajtenberg and R. Henderson (1993), 'Geographical localisation of knowledge spillovers, as evidenced by patent citations', *Quarterly Journal of Economics*, **58**(3), 577–98.

Kuemmerle, W. (1999), 'Foreign direct investment in industrial research in the pharmaceutical and electronics industries – results from a survey of multinational firms', *Research Policy*, **28**(2–3), 179–93.
Lall, S. and C. Pietrobelli (2002), *Failing to Compete. Technology Development and Technology Systems in Africa*, Cheltenham, UK and Northampton, MA, USA: Edward Elgar.
Lundvall, B.-Å. (1992), *National Systems of Innovation: Towards a Theory of Innovation and Interactive Learning*, London: Pinter.
Marshall, A. (1920), *Principles of Economics*, London: Macmillan.
Maurseth, P. and B. Verspagen (2002), 'Knowledge spillovers in Europe: a patent citations analysis', *Scandinavian Journal of Economics*, **104**, 531–45.
McCann, P. and R. Mudambi (2005), 'Analytical differences in the economics of geography: the case of the multinational firm', *Environment and Planning A*, **37**(10), 1857–76.
Meyer, K., M. Ram and R. Narula (2011), 'Multinationals and local contexts', *Journal of Management Studies*, **48**(2), 235–53.
Meyer, K.E. and H.V. Nguyen (2005), 'Foreign investment strategies and sub-national institutions in emerging markets: evidence from Vietnam', *Journal of Management Studies*, **42**(1), 63–93.
Mudambi, R. (2008), 'Location, control and innovation in knowledge-intensive industries', *Journal of Economic Geography*, **8**(5), 699–725.
Narula, R. (1996), *Multinational Investment and Economic Structure*, London: Routledge.
Narula, R. (2002), 'Innovation systems and "inertia" in R&D location: Norwegian firms and the role of systemic lock-in', *Research Policy*, **31**, 795–816.
Narula, R. (2003), *Globalization and Technology. Interdependence, Innovation Systems and Industrial Policy*, Cambridge: Polity Press.
Narula, R. (2010), 'Keeping the eclectic paradigm simple', *Multinational Business Review*, **18**(2), 35–50.
Narula, R. and C. Bellak (2009), 'EU enlargement and consequences for FDI assisted industrial development', *Transnational Corporations*, **18**(2), 69–90.
Narula, R. and J.H. Dunning (2010), 'Multinational enterprises, development and globalisation: some clarifications and a research agenda', *Oxford Development Studies*, **38**, 263–87.
Narula, R. and Q. Nguyen (2011), 'Emerging country MNEs and the role of home countries: separating fact from irrational expectations', University of Reading Discussion Paper Series.
Narula, R. and G.D. Santangelo (2009), 'Location, collocation and R&D alliances in the European ICT industry', *Research Policy*, **38**(2), 393–403.
Narula, R. and A. Zanfei (2005), 'Globalization of innovation: the role of multinational enterprises', in J. Fagerberg, D. Mowery and R. Nelson (eds), *The Oxford Handbook of Innovation*, Oxford: Oxford University Press, pp. 318–45.
Nobel, R. and J. Birkinshaw (1998), 'Innovation in multinational corporations: control and communication patterns in international R&D operations', *Strategic Management Journal*, **19**, 479–96.
Papanastassiou, M. and R. Pearce (1999), *Multinationals, Technology and National Competitiveness*, Cheltenham, UK and Northampton, MA, USA: Edward Elgar.
Perri, A., U. Andersson, P. Nell and G.D. Santangelo (2010), 'Balancing the trade-off between learning prospects and spillover risks: MNC subsidiaries' vertical linkages patterns in developed countries', European International Business Academy annual conference, Porto, 9–11 December.
Porter, M.E. (1980), *Competitive Strategy*, New York: Free Press.
Porter, M.E. (1986), 'Competition in global industries. A conceptual framework', in M.E. Porter (ed.), *Competition in Global Industries*, Boston, MA: Harvard Business School Press, pp. 15–60.
Porter, M.E. (1990), *The Competitive Advantage of Nations*, New York: Free Press.
Rabbiosi, L. and G.D. Santangelo (2009), 'Parent company benefits from reverse knowledge transfer: the role of the liability of newness in MNEs', European International Business Academy annual conference, Valencia, 13–15 December.
Rugman, A.M. and A. Verbeke (1992), 'A note on the transnational solution and the transaction cost theory of multinational strategic management', *Journal of International Business Studies*, **23**(4), 761–72.
Rugman, A.M. and A. Verbeke (2001), 'Subsidiary-specific advantages in multinational enterprises', *Strategic Management Journal*, **22**(3), 237–50.
Rugman, A.M. and A. Verbeke (2003), 'Extending the theory of the multinational enterprise: internalization and strategic management perspectives', *Journal of International Business Studies*, **34**(2), 125–37.
Sanna-Randaccio, F. and R. Veugelers (2007), 'Multinational knowledge spillovers with centralized versus decentralized R&D: a game theoretic approach', *Journal of International Business Studies*, **38**(1), 47–63.
Santangelo, G.D. (2012), 'The tension of information sharing: effects on subsidiary embeddedness', *International Business Review*, **21**(2), 180–95.
Santangelo, G.D. and K.E. Meyer (2011), 'Extending the internationalization process model: increases and decreases of MNE commitment in emerging economies', *Journal of International Business Studies*, **42**(7), 894–909.

Shaver, J. and F. Flyer (2000), 'Agglomeration economies, firm heterogeneity and foreign direct investment in the United States', *Strategic Management Journal*, **21**(12), 1175–93.

Smith, K. (1997), 'Economic infrastructures and innovation systems', in C. Edquist (ed.), *Systems of Innovation: Technologies, Institutions and Organisations*, London and Washington, DC: Pinter, pp. 86–106.

Szulanski, G. (1996), 'Exploring internal stickiness: impediments to the transfer of best practice within the firm', *Strategic Management Journal*, **17**, 27–43.

Tan, D. and K.E. Meyer (2010), 'Business group's outward FDI: a managerial resources perspective', *Journal of International Management*, **16**(2), 154–64.

Teece, D.J. (1986), 'Profiting from technological innovation: implications for integration, collaboration, licensing and public policy', *Research Policy*, **15**, 285–305.

Vernon, R. (1966), 'International investment and international trade in the product cycle', *The Quarterly Journal of Economics*, **LXXX**(May), 190–207.

Zaheer, A. (1995), 'Overcoming the liability of foreignness', *Academy of Management Journal*, **38**(2), 341–63.

16 The tenuous link between cultural distance and international strategy: navigating the assumptions of cross-cultural research[1]

Hemant Merchant, Rosalie L. Tung and Alain Verbeke

International strategy researchers have often considered 'national culture' to be important for explaining firm performance. Much of the credit for this inclusion can be attributed to Hofstede's seminal 1980 book, *Culture's Consequences: International Differences in Work-related Values*, which – importantly – provided researchers with numerical scores on various dimensions of national cultures for several countries/regions worldwide. The inclusion of culture in empirical research received a further boost a few years later when Kogut and Singh (1988) published their now famous cultural distance index (henceforth K&S index), which is based on Hofstede's data. Indeed, despite several criticisms of Hofstede's work (e.g. see McSweeney, 2002; Oyserman et al., 2002), as well as ample recognition that national culture is but one element in the institutional profile of a country (Kostova, 1997), international strategy researchers continue to include this important construct in their empirical work.

Implicit in such use is the notion of a link between culture and firm performance, broadly defined. In other words, without explicit attention to culture, intercultural 'problems' arise that jeopardize performance or, at minimum, severely dilute it (Ricks, 2006). Conversely, attention to cross-cultural issues helps to better navigate these challenges and thus improves performance. Indeed, applied research about how to globalize managerial mindsets (e.g. see Earley and Mosakowski, 2004; Javidan et al., 2010) underscores just that very point. It seems that the influence of culture not only is not expected to diminish in an increasingly globalizing world (Ghemawat, 2001); the concept of national culture is expected to increase its impact on internationally oriented scholarly research (Leung et al., 2005) in far-reaching ways. To illustrate, culture plays an important role *vis-à-vis* the governance of international mergers and acquisitions (M&As) (Kang and Kim, 2010). Thus we should anticipate more studies that strive to better understand the role of cultural distance (CD) – the concept itself, as well as its dimensions and measures – in relation to strategic managerial decisions and firm performance. In other words, there is a need not only to highlight common assumptions made by empirical researchers (who have engaged CD in their work), but also to recommend some ways to circumvent the hazards thereof. This chapter attempts to fulfill these objectives. We begin by revisiting Shenkar's (2001) classic work on cultural distance.

In his frame-breaking study, Shenkar (2001) presented a critical review of the CD construct and outlined several hidden assumptions underlying its use. Moreover, he challenged the construct's theoretical and methodological properties (see Box 16.1). While Shenkar's work focused explicitly on K&S index, the implicit assumptions are also relevant to strategy-oriented studies that frequently investigate cross-national

---

BOX 16.1   CULTURAL DISTANCE IN EMPIRICAL RESEARCH: SOME COMMON LIMITATIONS

Type 1: Generic limitations of cultural distance measures

(1)   Assumption of symmetry: economic actors in two countries will each view their counterparts in exactly the same 'different' way.
(2)   Assumption of temporal stability: cultural distance dimensions and scores are invariant to time considerations.

Type 2: Limitations *vis-à-vis* empirical research design

(3)   Assumption of linearity: the effects of cultural distance on a given dependent variable are uniform at all points on the cultural distance continuum.
(4)   Assumption of omnipotence: there is a unambiguous dominant link between national culture and managerial choice or economic performance.
(5)   Assumption of surrogacy: the (incorrect) interchangeable treatment of cultural distance and psychic distance.

Type 3: Limitations requiring rethinking the empirical role of cultural distance

(6)   Assumption of spatial homogeneity: a country is presumed to be culturally homogeneous, regardless of the cultural diversity of various regions within it.
(7)   Assumption of negativity: greater cultural distance systematically engenders negative outcomes.
(8)   Assumption of corporate homogeneity: cultural distance has a uniform impact on managerial choices or economic performance regardless of the unique characteristics of firms.
(9)   Assumption of aggregate indices: it is appropriate to combine individual measures of various cultural distance dimensions into aggregate indices.

---

phenomena, such as performance effects of international joint venture formation (e.g. Merchant and Schendel, 2000). Clearly, our failure to consciously recognize, and circumvent, these assumptions could negatively affect the quality as well as the value added of managerial prescriptions. Thus we strongly encourage all scholars, especially those in strategy and international business (IB), to push the theoretical and methodological boundaries of the CD construct. This chapter offers a few starting points in that regard, especially for strategy scholars who might not be fully aware of the limitations of CD dimensions and measures.

GENERIC LIMITATIONS OF CULTURAL DISTANCE MEASURES

Limitation 1   Assumption of Symmetry

All strategy researchers who engage the CD construct should be attentive to two general assumptions noted in Box 16.1. Moreover, researchers should be cognizant that these assumptions do not usually hold in today's increasingly technologically interconnected world, which exposes various distinct cultures to one another. The assumption of symmetry, namely that economic actors in country A will view their counterparts in country B in exactly the same way that country B actors will view those in country A, is usually unwarranted (O'Grady and Lane, 1996). To illustrate, consider the economic relationship between Canada and the USA. Although both countries share the world's longest open border and trade principally with each other, Canadian perceptions about economic ties with the USA are not identical to those held by the USA (e.g. Alexandroff and Guy, 2003) – even though the absolute value of CD difference score(s) between the two countries is identical. Consequently, any strategic decision based on an assumption of symmetry would be suboptimal, at best. A similar argument can be made at the firm level, for, say, interactions between an American firm and its Mexican subsidiary. Even though the CD difference scores (on, say, Hofstede's power distance dimension) between the USA and Mexico are identical, the role and expectations held by an average Mexican employee working for the American firm's Mexican subsidiary will probably be incongruent with those held by an average American employee working for the same firm's Mexican subsidiary. The hinted 'distance' disconnect experienced by the two countries' actors is similar to Selmer et al.'s (2007) finding that it was much easier for German expatriates to adjust well in the USA than for American expatriates in Germany.

Limitation 2   Assumption of Temporal Stability

The assumption of temporal stability refers to the idea that CD dimensions and scores are invariant to time considerations, i.e. they are 'anchored' in time. This assumption is also unwarranted (Fang, 2005–06; Leung et al., 2005; Ralston et al., 1999). Here, the important issue is twofold: (i) does a particular dimension of CD 'move' over time – even if other dimensions of national cultures do not?; and (ii) does this movement induce a substantive strategic miscalculation that manifests itself in flawed managerial thinking and, therefore, ultimately in suboptimal firm performance? Clearly, strategic choices based on an assumption of temporal stability would backfire for firms if the industries in which they operate are, in fact, cultural migrants, even if only slow-moving ones!

To illustrate, it would be difficult to convincingly argue that consumers in any country – including a feminine country – would willingly 'accept' slow-performing computers that rely on older (and slower) technologies, even if they may have accepted them in the past. Indeed, the belief held by many Western firms that the foreignness of their products will always be in vogue elsewhere must be carefully re-examined in light of the subtle, but unmistakable, rise in nationalistic sentiments worldwide. Consider the change in Chinese consumers' demand for the latest, high-quality Western goods. Firms that offer relatively older technology-based goods at reduced prices – believing in the stability of Chinese long-term orientation (i.e. frugality) – seem to be at a clear disadvantage. This is because such consumption makes for a relatively larger proportion of discretionary spending. Why should Chinese consumers who are both able and willing to spend hard-earned money settle for anything less than the current world standard? Cultures can and do oscillate because their building blocks – people – oscillate, even if such oscillation is barely perceptible. Clearly, strategy researchers need to recognize this limitation, particularly if they intend to be prescriptively relevant.

To illustrate the relevance of recognizing intertemporal changes in CD, Heuer et al. (1999) surveyed Indonesian managers about Hofstede's individualism–collectivism and power distance dimensions. These authors reported smaller differences (over time) between Indonesian and American managers *vis-à-vis* the above dimensions, thus supporting Ralston's (2008) notion of cultural 'crossvergence'. Similarly, Fang (2005–06, p. 77) used the ocean metaphor to explain the '(1) paradoxical nature of culture, (2) the "moment" of culture, and (3) the new identity of national cultures in the era of globalization'. The ocean metaphor refers to the view that, at any given time, some country-specific cultural values may remain inactive until they are reignited by exogenous events (e.g. FDI growth). To illustrate, although entrepreneurial spirit and risk-taking were weakened in China at the peak of communism, these forces were unleashed quickly when China opened up to international trade. Indeed, Tung et al.'s (2008) study of Sino-Western business negotiations found that the ocean metaphor could capture the current dynamism and complexities in Chinese society better than numerical scores that supposedly measured China's salient cultural dimensions.

Addressing the Generic Limitations

It is reasonable to argue that the above-mentioned assumptions do not always directly affect the quality of strategic analysis, whether conceptual or empirical, but caution is still needed when cultural symmetry and stability are simply assumed. This is because the impact of these assumptions depends upon the particular configuration of firms' economic activity. To illustrate, the similarity assumption would be relatively less punitive for unimodal strategic investments (e.g. greenfield entry) in the extractive industries as opposed to bimodal strategic investments (e.g. international joint ventures) in consumer-goods industries. However, it is still important for researchers to specify the exact nature of the phenomenon they investigate and also to discuss why the intrinsic limitations of their assumptions do not negate the validity of offered conclusions. Likewise, any suggestion that a particular relationship would also be valid in the reverse direction ought to be avoided, especially in the absence of robustness checks. Including multiple countries in empirical studies (Franke and Richey, 2010) and conducting research programs studying the same phenomenon from several angles (e.g. varying choices of home and host countries in studies of international market entry decisions) can alleviate these generic challenges.

Researchers can also minimize the impositions of the stability assumption in simple ways. For example, in longitudinal studies covering extended periods of time, researchers can carefully reflect on the issue, especially if traditional variables are used for measuring CD dimensions. This would be imperative in empirical studies where distance proxy variables are employed as focal explanatory variables rather than as control, moderating or mediating variables. Despite the convenience, researchers must also refrain from merely asserting that a particular conventional measure of cultural dimension is still appropriate because previous researchers have used that measure, or assuming that the measure changes only gradually over time, without any valid grounds (see discussion of stability assumption above). Although it might be beyond the scope of single studies to measure the evolution of cultural dimensions, it is nevertheless useful to explicitly identify – as good scholars must – the parameters of one's research endeavors.

LIMITATIONS *VIS-À-VIS* EMPIRICAL RESEARCH DESIGN

Limitation 3   Assumption of Linearity

Strategy scholars need to be alert to three more assumptions pertaining to the use of 'national culture' in their research. Fortunately, these assumptions can often be circumvented through appropriate empirical modeling, as demonstrated in contemporary work. The linearity assumption refers to the presumed uniform effects of CD on a given dependent variable (e.g. firm performance) at all levels of the CD continuum; the slope of this relationship is a constant. Thus, if x units of cultural distance produce a y unit impact on the dependent variable, a $2x$ units' distance would produce a $2y$ unit impact, and so on. A corollary of this assumption would be that the marginal effect of a k unit increase in cultural distance at a point near the 'small' end of the CD continuum would be identical to the marginal effect of the same k unit increase in cultural distance near the 'large' end of the CD continuum. Clearly, this is a very strong assumption. A person might eat one more slice of pizza if s/he has eaten only two slices previously; however, it would be naïve to believe that the same person could eat the same additional slice if s/he has already eaten 15 slices. The marginal utility (or disutility) of moving farther along the CD continuum should be expected to follow the same laws of economics! The implication that it does not is, therefore, difficult to accept.

In the context of strategy research, the linearity assumption has two implications – neither of which has empirical support. One, the influence of culture is homogeneous across the life cycle of the firm engaged in a cross-border activity. Two, national culture is so 'dominant' as to be treated as a variable in and of itself; there is no need to combine it with other influences on the response variable. Indeed, several studies have long dispelled these myths. For example, Parkhe (1991) suggested that national cultural diversity may have a positive effect during the early stages of an international alliance and a negative effect during the alliance's implementation phase. Likewise, using the cluster analysis technique, Merchant (2008) found that culture's interaction with other firm-specific and contextual variables differentially impacted American firms' joint venture strategies into emerging markets. Cultural distance played a fundamentally different role for 'firm-dominant' configurations than for 'location-dominant' configurations – even though the average performance of firms in the former cluster was positive and statistically indistinguishable from that of firms in the other cluster. Many other recent studies have also adopted empirical approaches that consider a wide array of moderators to better understand the possible relationship between CD and managerial choices and performance (Tihanyi et al., 2005).

Limitation 4   Assumption of Omnipotence

This assumption refers to the alleged, unambiguous dominant link between culture and managerial choice or economic performance. There are at least two big leaps here. One, it is almost impossible to unequivocally demonstrate a direct relationship between culture and, say, firm performance. This is because of the large number of intervening factors, both context- as well as firm-specific factors; although culture is an important contextual variable, it is not the only salient contextual variable (Merchant, 2008). Moreover, other variables (e.g. a firm's foreign market experience) may moderate and/ or mediate the effect of culture on a strategic outcome variable. In turn, culture itself may moderate and/or mediate the relationship between a specific variable and perform-ance. Corporate strategic activity does not occur in a vacuum. It is driven by the inter-play among firm- and location-specific factors (Merchant, 2008). Such activity occurs because firms possess advantages that can be better leveraged by combining them with resources found elsewhere (Hennart, 2009; Merchant, 2008; Rugman, 1981; Verbeke, 2009). Stated differently, independent of a specific context, one should not expect a direct, generalizable link between CD and performance or managerial choice (Tihanyi et al., 2005).

Two, given the above, unless a researcher also explicitly specifies other salient contex-tual variables, any effect attributed to the role of culture must necessarily be made very cautiously. Model misspecification can seriously jeopardize the validity of offered conclu-sions. For example, what is the point of evaluating the effect of CD on firms' international sales if other constraints on firms' are entirely ignored? Indeed, it could be that a more accurate explanation for firms' high (low) sales may have more to do with, say, an exist-ing regulatory framework (e.g. NAFTA). Given such a scenario, little, if anything, can (or should) be concluded about the strategic relationship between cultural distance and sales (Tung and Verbeke, 2010). In fact, in the context of NAFTA, one would reach dia-metrically opposite conclusions about the role of cultural distance and American firms' sales to Canada, which is in greater cultural proximity to the USA, and those to Mexico, a country whose cultural proximity to the USA is considerably less! Moreover, given the strong tendency of strategy scholars to mostly use only the regression analysis tech-nique, we would caution that statistical significance of culture merely underscores an association – not a causal link – between it and a response variable.

Recommendations

To draw stronger inferences about the strategic role of culture, and also to validate the robustness of regression-based findings, researchers must necessarily employ other statis-tical techniques (e.g. cluster analysis; causal modeling); however, most published strategy studies do not do this. There is also the issue of what is the relevant dimension of culture *vis-à-vis* a given research question (see discussion of the assumption-of aggregate indices below). Is an aggregate index more appropriate or is it more useful to focus on specific dimension(s) of the CD construct? Another issue revolves around aggregating obviously heterogeneous samples – even if all other above-mentioned concerns were to be ignored, albeit only briefly. Such heterogeneity can lie within an industry (e.g. technology), across economic sectors (manufacturing; non-manufacturing), or even across countries (advanced economies; emerging economies; developing countries). While perhaps convenient, combining disparate samples severely compounds the hazards of drawing wrong inferences based on the omnipotence assumption (see discussion of the assumption of corporate homogeneity below).

To illustrate, Merchant (2006) found that cultural distance between American firms and their non-American joint venture partners had a negative performance effect for ventures located in Brazil, Russia, India and China (BRICs) and newly industrializing countries (NICs), a positive performance effect for ventures located in developed countries, and no effect for ventures located in less-developed countries. Similarly, Merchant and Gaur (2008) found that researchers not only blatantly disregarded sector-specific differences and combined manufacturing as well as non-manufacturing subsamples (without conducting *a priori* tests), but also simply reported aggregate results without recognizing fundamental differences between these economic sectors (Merchant, 1997). Additionally, many empirical studies that use secondary data and assess the impact of culture on economic performance and managerial choice hardly ever bother to verify the agreement (or lack thereof) of their statistical results with managerial reality (Barkema et al., 1996). Fortunately, such verification is manageable through proper research design and a truthful interpretation of empirical findings.

Limitation 5 Assumption of Surrogacy

This assumption refers to the (incorrect) interchangeable treatment of cultural distance and psychic distance. The latter construct refers to the 'subjectively perceived distance to a foreign country' (Håkanson and Ambos, 2010, p. 2) and can be traced to Beckerman's (1956) work on trade patterns. Psychic distance is often mistakenly equated with CD, even though the former is a much broader construct that includes sources of distance besides culture-related ones (e.g. see Johanson and Vahlne, 1977). In fact, psychic distance – not cultural distance – holds the key to strategic internationalization choices made by managers (Tung and Verbeke, 2010). Yet these choices are also influenced by the broader institutional context in which firms operate (Merchant, 2008). The credit for translating Beckerman's insight (that factors other than 'objective' economic parameters appeared to influence trade patterns) to micro-level decision-making goes to Uppsala studies (Johanson and Vahlne, 2009) that have long put forward the idea that 'soft' factors influence strategic internationalization decisions. Yet most strategy studies continue to ignore the point that, while convenient, the CD construct captures a very small slice of managerial reality.

To illustrate, Håkanson and Ambos (2010) analyzed 148 empirical studies that used the K&S index. In 40 percent of these studies, this index proxied psychic distance in an *ex ante* decision-making context (e.g. choices about investment location). The remaining 60 percent of studies employed the index in an *ex post* setting, supposedly reflecting the ease (or difficulty) of conducting business in a foreign country (Håkanson and Ambos, 2010). Thus the problem is that an index that is merely associated with expected challenges of doing business in a culturally distant context is frequently – and incorrectly – equated with the psychic distance construct (Dow, 2000; Dow and Karunaratna, 2006), which Johanson and Vahlne (1977) construe in terms of the 'sum of factors' affecting information to the market (Shenkar, 2001, p. 54).

Recommendations

As one example of the need to explicitly distinguish between the cultural and psychic distance constructs, Dow and Larimo (2008) suggest that the K&S index loses 75 percent of psychic distance's predictive power *vis-à-vis* entry mode selection; the index ignores other key psychic distance components such as economic development and sociodemographic differences between countries. Fortunately, strategy and IB researchers can take comfort in knowing that the above-mentioned deficiency can be overcome by employing scales that allow measuring differences across countries (e.g. see Dow and Karunaratna, 2006). In addition, many databases (other than Hofstede and GLOBE) also facilitate consideration of cross-cultural variations. These databases include Schwartz's Value Survey (Schwartz, 1994), the Trompenaars and Hampden-Turner ecological (cross-cultural) database (www.thtconsulting.com), and Inglehart and Associates' World Values Survey (www.worldvaluessurvey.org).

LIMITATIONS REQUIRING RETHINKING THE EMPIRICAL ROLE OF CULTURAL DISTANCE

The following four limitations represent more serious challenges to international strategy research because they create a distorted view of the role of national culture *vis-à-vis* the strategic activity of firms and, ultimately, firm performance. In other words, if scholars model influences on firm performance imperfectly, they jeopardize the explanatory power of these influences and render them irrelevant. This would give rise to prescriptively invalid – but statistically valid – managerial inferences. Hence it is imperative to substantively rethink the essence, meaning and value added of including the CD construct in international strategy research. Such efforts would have sustainable long-term payoffs.

Limitation 6   Assumption of Spatial Homogeneity

This assumption refers to the presumed cultural singularity of a nation. In other words, a country is presumed to be culturally homogeneous, regardless of the cultural diversity of various regions within it. Or, more leniently, cultural heterogeneity across-country dominates within-country cultural heterogeneity. Clearly, this is a strong assumption because several subcultures (co)exist even within a single country. Countries can – and do – have subcultures. Even the 272 square mile city-state of Singapore has three distinct cultural identities (Chinese, Indian and Malay), although these subgroups also view themselves as Singaporeans. Yet, viewing Singaporeans simply as Singaporeans ignores the rich cultural diversity within the country. Several other examples of intranational cultural subgroups abound (e.g. North and South Indians, Mainland and Hong Kong Chinese etc.). The significance of this observation is that a firm intending to sell its product/service to 'Singapore' will probably make managerial decisions that differ from those made by its direct competitor who wants to sell the same product to, say, Singapore's Malay populace. Thus intranational differences should be taken into full consideration. In fact, Tung (2008, p. 45) has warned that the 'fallacious assumption' of cultural uniformity could 'risk the generation of results that mask or confound the phenomena under investigation'. Her study has emphasized maintaining a balance between intranational and cross-national diversity in cross-cultural studies.

Growing diversity within many countries has highlighted conceptual and methodological problems associated with the assumption of cultural homogeneity inside a country. There is growing evidence to demonstrate that intranational diversity can be at least as salient as international diversity (Tung and Baumann, 2009). Such observations could have significant implications for firms. For example, businesses with owners or managers from a foreign ethnicity may identify individuals or firms having the same ethnic profile as their target market. Thus ethnicity might represent a firm-specific advantage, especially for emerging market firms (Miller et al., 2008) such as Reliance Communications, whose primary target market in the USA is ethnic Indians. This finding supports Fletcher and Fang's (2006, p. 435) position that a source of 'weakness in cross-cultural comparisons is the tendency in the literature to make comparisons between countries rather than ethnic groups . . . [when] globalization and the borderless economy are making nation states increasingly irrelevant'.

Understanding intranational diversity can be somehow more challenging than unpacking cultural distance because several variables (e.g. gender, ethnicity, religion etc.) affect the mindsets and practices of individuals within a given country. Arguably, it is more difficult to model the collective (interaction) impact of these concomitant demographic variables than to use scores reported by Hofstede or the GLOBE project. In contrast, there is no algorithm to quickly gauge numerous country-specific variations that can result from the diversity of people within a country. Hence it is crucial to realize that a score for a cultural dimension(s) is, at best, a snapshot of the characteristics of a specific segment in a given country. Thus it would be a mistake to interpret the values and beliefs of any country behavior based on a singular generic index. While such indices may still be useful in macro-level studies, they ought not to be mindlessly adopted in micro-studies. It is hoped that the growing acknowledgment of existence of intranational diversity will hasten the move toward 'accepting' culture as a multi-level, multilayered concept with considerable intranational variation (Gelfand et al., 2006; Leung et al., 2005; Miller et al., 2008). It should also be mentioned that the degree of intranational diversity can significantly differ across countries. In other words, two neighboring countries need not have the same level of 'cultural tightness–looseness' (Gelfand et al., 2006, pp. 1226–7), which is intended to measure 'how clear and pervasive norms are within societies, . . . and how much tolerance there is for deviance from norms'. An example of this concept is the intranational cultural diversity between China and India. Although these countries are similar along several cultural (and economic) dimensions, cultural diversity within India is, arguably, greater than that within China. Such varying levels of cultural tightness–looseness can also be found between Canada and the USA, and also between several European as well as African countries. Thus cultural tightness–looseness can complement existing measures of cultural dimensions.

Limitation 7 Assumption of Negativity

This assumption refers to the common view that greater cultural distance systematically engenders negative outcomes. The assumption needs to be carefully deconstructed for macro- as well as micro-level studies because it implies a subtle bias about the role of cultural diversity *vis-à-vis* strategic product and process innovations. Most empirical relationships are non-monotonic by nature, and many have a curvilinear form. Beyond a certain point, the form of relationship changes. This is especially true in the social sciences. Thus, if adopted by researchers (and conveyed to practitioners), the assumption of negativity can engender fundamentally wrong managerial prescriptions or negatively affect the performance of the firm as a self-fulfilling prophecy (Brown et al., 1988).

Consider the development of General Electric's (GE) handheld electrocardiogram (ECG), which Woolridge (2010, p. 6) hailed as 'a masterpiece of simplification [that] has reduced the cost of an ECG test to just $1 per patient'. This product was developed by various American and Indian specialists – with noticeably different cultural priors – to serve a market, India, where affordability generally is a binding constraint. Were predictions to be made about the 'success' of this product development, cultural difference would probably be seen as a negative influence. Arguably, too much 'surface' divergence between American and Indian cultures would lead to a wide range of process-based challenges in developing the product, ultimately compromising its creation. In reality, the opposite result emerged. Clearly, the different starting points engendered by cultural diversity led to a positive, not negative, outcome. Too 'many' cooks may spoil the broth, but a 'few' just might enhance its taste. Thus the interesting empirical issue is to identify an optimal level of cultural difference that can enhance firm performance: at what point does a presumed liability (here, cultural difference) become a certified asset (here, a proven frugal innovation), and vice versa?

To date, most strategy and IB studies on cross-national interactions have been directed by the concepts of psychic distance and homophily. In essence, homophily means that individuals prefer to associate and bond with those who are similar to themselves (Ibarra, 1993; Lazarsfeld and Merton, 1954). This explains, for example, why expatriates from the USA are generally more comfortable with assignments to UK and Canada contrasted with China, Japan and Korea (Tung, 1998), and why expatriates' superiors should account for the level of cultural difference between the home and host countries when assessing their performance (Selmer et al., 2007).

The psychic distance construct is similar to the homophily construct and is a main concept of the Johanson and Vahlne (1977, 2009) and Uppsala theories of incremental foreign market entry. These theories posit that firms prefer to expand to markets that are psychically closer to their home country before venturing into psychically distant markets. The view that psychic distance facilitates a firm's internationalization trajectory compares favorably with the homophily principle, which posits a greater propensity for clustering among people from similar cultural priors (i.e. that are psychically closer).

While the homophily and psychic distance principles may hold in the West, micro-level studies set in sub-Saharan Africa and Tanzania underscore the opposite result. For example, Mamman (1995) and Carr et al. (2001) found that host country residents were more likely to have negative stereotypes of expatriates from other developing, particularly neighboring, nations. Carr et al. (2001) explain the more favorable reception of individuals from culturally distant countries via the principle of inverse resonance. In physics, resonance refers to the tendency of a system to oscillate at a greater amplitude at some frequencies than at others.

The inverse resonance view is at odds with the homophily view in the mainstream IB and strategy literature. Even though inverse resonance studies have been done only in

African settings, we suspect that the former view holds in Asia as well. For instance, it would be a mistake to presume the merits of sending a Hong Kong Chinese or a Taiwanese Chinese to manage firms' operations in China. The point is not to discover a statistical relationship that best describes the link between cultural (or psychic) distance and managerial choice or performance. Instead, the real challenge is to understand – on the basis of direct observation – (i) what CD means in practice, (ii) why and under what contingencies 'high-distance' choices dominate 'low-distance' choices, and (iii) why and how the former types of choices could augment performance. Here, one should also recognize that other forms of distance (e.g. economic development levels) can explain the desirability of a high-distance solution (e.g. when related to a higher likelihood of knowledge transfers, as the GE example illustrated above). The convenience of wearing the homophily mask disguises cross-cultural complexity, which usually remains unaccounted for.

Limitation 8   Assumption of Corporate Homogeneity

This assumption refers to the uniform impact of CD regardless of the unique characteristics of firms making strategic cross-national decisions or undertaking cross-national activity. The assumption too is very limiting, for it ignores a dominant strategic management perspective, the resource-based view, which holds that every firm is a collection of idiosyncratic resources (see Penrose, 1959). Put differently, even if the CD between two countries is held constant, a previously rejected assumption (e.g. its interaction with heterogeneous resource bundles – i.e. firms) must, logically, produce heterogeneous effects. That is, culture cannot simply be seen as a stand-alone variable that is 'completely separate' from firms' strategic intent (Shenkar, 2012). Conversely, by ignoring the uniqueness of firms, due to their asymmetric resources, strategy researchers may unintentionally (and wrongly) ascribe a generic prescriptive role to culture. Such prescriptions ignore findings that demonstrate otherwise (Merchant, 2008). Consequently, it makes sense to assess how CD affects firms' (unique) strategic decisions such as location choices and sequences, entry mode choices and their timing, local and global managerial practices and ultimately firm performance.

At least five contingencies negate, or at least severely dent, any argument to neglect firm-level characteristics when evaluating the impact of CD in international strategy studies. First, a firm may command resources that alleviate problems that could arise in an allegedly high-distance context. For example, a US-based company contemplating expansion to Taiwan might not (or minimally) encounter distance-related difficulties if, for example, the firm employs Taiwanese born/raised individuals with active local networks, even if these individuals have resided outside Taiwan for an extended period. However, another US-based firm (operating in the same industry as the above firm) would face higher costs of doing business in Taiwan if it does not command appropriate resources (e.g. a Taiwanese manager).

Second, a firm's international experience can lower challenges arising from cultural distance (Hutzschenreuter and Voll, 2008; Hutzschenreuter et al., 2010). This experience effect needs to include the insights based on sequential market entry. Cultural distance need not be, as traditionally conceptualized, just between the home and host countries, but also – importantly – between the 'new' host country and a country of which the firm already has experience. Ideally, one should also be aware of the importance of intra-country differences (see discussion of assumption of spatial homogeneity) in the context of added cultural distance.

The issue of CD's positive effect is important given the rise of network firms (e.g. joint ventures and multinational corporations) because host country units can be strategic leaders and even marshal subsidiary-specific advantages (Rugman and Verbeke, 2001). In this context, it is important to examine the diversity in educational, functional and geographic experience of the senior management team. Indeed, as Tung and Chung (2010) found, Australian firms with immigrant owners from China, Taiwan and Hong Kong were more likely to expand to the respective prior domicile via joint or wholly owned ventures, whereas Australian firms without such connections entered markets via exporting and licensing.

Third, the impact of CD on managerial choices or performance probably differs significantly with the nature of value chain activity. It is conceivable that upstream activities (e.g. R&D) are more resistant to the effect of cultural differences than downstream activities (e.g. marketing) because of the differential basis of task-related knowledge. Interaction of scientists and engineers, for example, may well be confined to the language of science whereas interaction between a firm and its target audience in a 'foreign' country must necessarily invoke a culturally sensitive communication medium. On that point, Rugman and Verbeke (2004, 2005, 2008) suggest that the 'costs' of distance are lower for input versus output markets, because firms' output-side resource commitments generally are more singular than those on the input side.

Fourth, in accordance with our discussion of the assumption of negativity, viewing CD as a barrier/cost might be sensible for firms solely interested in exploiting their firm-specific advantages in new contexts with low adaptation requirements. However, such distance could actually bestow benefits on firms primarily interested in developing new firm-specific advantages in host environments (see the earlier discussion of GE's frugal innovation in India). Yet the merits of seeking out high CD contexts should neither be overestimated nor taken for granted (Verbeke and Kenworthy, 2008).

Fifth, previous micro-level research has described the impact of CD on strategic choices (e.g. make-or-buy decision). However, it is important to be aware that internalization essentially replaces external distance (e.g. dealing with differences in administrative regimes) with internal distance (e.g. working with local employees with distinct cultural priors). Thus unique bundles of (heterogeneous) resources will guide the optimal choice based on net benefits accruing to the firm (Hennart, 2009). While the assumption of corporate homogeneity (in terms of the likely impact of CD) can yield significant results, the managerial implications of these results may be muddled in terms of their relevance.

Limitation 9   Assumption of Aggregate Indices

This assumption refers to the appropriateness of combining individual cultural distance measures into aggregate indices that can easily be applied in empirical micro- or macro-level studies. Such indices are convenient from a expediency standpoint because of their ease of use and legitimacy, particularly if previous work has also adopted these indices. Unfortunately, these gains are offset by the validity and reliability of research outcomes, as shown in Håkanson and Ambos's (2010) empirical assessment of psychic distance among 25 countries. These authors found that the K&S index had particularly weak explanatory power. In contrast, the fifth Hofstede dimension, long-term orientation, added substantial explanatory power. Likewise, the individualism–collectivism dimension appeared to be important, but among other things, the masculinity–femininity dimension did not. Other empirical studies (e.g. Barkema and Vermeulen, 1997; Merchant, 2000) have identified Hofstede dimensions – notably uncertainty avoidance and individualism–collectivism – to be more critical to explaining managerial phenomena than other dimensions (Shenkar, 2001). These studies essentially question the wisdom of aggregating individual dimensions into a singular index.

Recommendations

Despite awareness of the importance of singular cultural distance dimensions, a growing stream of research now emphasizes institutional distance dimensions in addition to cultural distance dimensions. This is because of the complementary nature of cultural and institutional variables in international settings (Xu and Shenkar, 2002). For example, studies have analyzed the impact on firms' foreign entry mode decisions of cognitive, normative and regulative institutional factors (Yiu and Makino, 2002), sub-national institutional variables (Meyer and Nguyen, 2005), political systems (Dow and Karunaratna, 2006), corruption (Cuervo-Cazurra, 2006; Habib and Zurawicki, 2002), political risk (Brouthers and Brouthers, 2001), and intellectual property rights protection (Delios and Beamish, 1999; Oxley, 1999). Among the earliest studies of its kind, Meyer (2001) demonstrated the effect of macro-level governance distance on entry mode choice. Likewise, building on Scott (1995), Gaur and Lu (2007) distinguished between normative distance and regulative distance, and highlighted their effect on subsidiary survival. Estrin et al. (2007) found significant effects of institutional distance dimensions on entry mode choice.

This last approach proposes the nearly natural complementarity between cultural and institutional distance constructs, although much of the literature on institutional distance is further removed from the homophily assumption in the sense that institutional quality is considered to be more important than institutional proximity (Globerman and Shapiro, 2003; Kaufmann et al., 2003). Indeed, recent international strategy literature suggests that foreign regulatory contexts have a greater influence on multinational firms' behavior than previously recognized (Coeurderoy and Murray, 2008; Henisz, 2000; Kostova and Zaheer, 1999). In this sense, many scholars have argued that the degree of regional integration between countries significantly influences the costs of operating abroad (Benito et al., 2003; Berry et al., 2010; Hejazi, 2007; Rugman and Verbeke, 2004).

The bundling of individual dimensions of cultural distance into indices is intuitively appealing, but it is likely to mask or ignore the singular parameters that actually matter more to the phenomenon under investigation (Barkema and Vermeulen, 1997). This is not just an issue of research design. Rather, the issue goes to the heart of cross-cultural studies: what do empirical researchers really want to achieve and communicate – and to whom? Is their goal to posit a significant relationship or is it to generate a superior grasp of managerial choices and firm performance in a cross-cultural, cross-institutional context?

CONCLUSIONS

We have discussed nine common assumptions in research on CD dimensions and measures. Although there have been considerable advances in the field since Hofstede's (1980) influential work, our conclusion is not very encouraging in terms of the current state of the art. This is because a number of 'clubs' – each with very specific views on cultural distance – now populate the cross-cultural field. We believe that many journal reviewers and authors still consider it appropriate to use K&S type indices whereas many others reject this approach outright.

We see at least four challenges for researchers contemplating the use of K&S type indices: (i) addressing possible quality problems with raw data that constitute an aggregated index; (ii) determining the relevance of these inputs, which reflect coarse-grained values instead of managerial perceptions; (iii) reflecting on the usefulness of an equally weighted index that is independent of the research question under scrutiny; and (iv) explicitly highlighting assumptions about the utility of an index.

The Hofstede–GLOBE debate (see *Journal of International Business Studies*, 2010) sparked a vibrant dialog but has not responded to the question about potential complementarities between the two camps – although Venaik and Brewer's (2010) study briefly touched upon this issue. Moreover, these *JIBS* studies did not closely investigate linkages with other approaches (e.g. Schwartz paradigm; World Values Survey). Thus researchers may be tempted to incorporate both Hofstede-based and GLOBE-based measures along with alternative indices in their empirical work in order to evade the reviewers' ire. We do not think this is the right direction – and therefore advocate a three-pronged approach to facilitate a more refined understanding of the role and effect of cultural distance.

Towards a More Sophisticated Grasp of Cultural Distance

First, scholars must include a wide conceptual view of the distance construct to include cultural, institutional, economic and spatial components (e.g. Ghemawat, 2001), and dimensions that are most relevant to *ex ante* managerial choices and/or *ex post* economic performance. However, the goal is not simply to include all possible 'distance' dimensions and control variables. The goal should be to set up research designs that can explain the phenomena under investigation. An empirically driven 'shotgun' approach to research often finds its target; unfortunately, it also causes significant collateral damage. In contrast, a theoretically driven 'rifle' approach would also find its target – perhaps with relatively greater effort – but without causing significant collateral damage. Second, scholars should re-examine and challenge their research frames in relation to the impact of common assumptions on the scholarship and managerial relevance of empirical work. At a minimum, researchers should be explicit about why they accepted (or were forced to accept) some of these assumptions.

Third, the last four limitations, and within these the assumption of aggregate indices, seem to be the most critical. Arguably, some CD dimensions and scores for measures of distance might: (i) be minimally affected by intranational spatial idiosyncrasies; (ii) be invariant *vis-à-vis* the direction of their impact on a dependent variable; (iii) have a large, direct influence on discrete managerial choices or firm performance; and (iv) dominate the effect of other distance dimensions. In contrast, we know that some CD dimensions and scores for distance measures: (i) are affected by intranational locational characteristics; (ii) have a differential impact across contexts; (iii) may only be indirectly relevant to managerial choice and economic performance; and (iv) exert an influence in the presence of other dimensions. Under these and similar conditions, blending individual CD dimensions into aggregate indices would render a disservice to students (broadly defined) interested in discerning the role and impact of the cross-cultural phenomenon.

One way to augment the quality of management studies is for researchers to have an impeccable command of the complete arsenal of tools for measuring cultural distance. Such command should guide and inform the judicious – not expedient – selection of the relevant unbundled distance dimensions and their measures, while avoiding the endogeneity issue that haunts much previous research (see assumption of omnipotence). Cross-cultural analysis in management research should also systematically consider rival hypotheses and alternative explanations of the observed impact of distance dimensions, and not simply limit itself to adopting readily available indices to ascertain whether national culture truly matters.

Finally, there is an exciting opportunity for scholars engaged in conceptual research to investigate how cultural values morph across space and time, and in what way this evolution could be operationalized and measured meaningfully. It is time for scholars of all stripes to comprehensively revisit the existing toolkit in relation to cross-cultural research. We believe that the frontier of scholarship in this area will revolve around two themes: (i) which – if any – of the accessible tools truly maintain (in terms of validity and reliability) the standards of contemporary scholarly endeavors; and (ii) which – if any – cultural distance measures are appropriate in relation to the focal research questions and context.

NOTE

1. This chapter is based on a study by Tung and Verbeke (2010).

REFERENCES

Alexandroff, A.S. and Guy, D. (2003), 'What Canadians have to say about relations with United States', C.D. Howe Institute, Commentary no. 73.
Barkema, H.G. and Vermeulen, G.A.M. (1997), 'What differences in the cultural backgrounds of partners are detrimental for international joint ventures?', *Journal of International Business Studies*, **28**(4): 845–64.
Barkema, H.G., Bell, J.H.J. and Pennings, J.M. (1996), 'Foreign entry, cultural barriers and learning', *Strategic Management Journal*, **17**: 151–66.
Beckerman, W. (1956), 'Distance and the pattern of intra-European trade', *The Review of Economics and Statistics*, **38**(1): 31–40.
Benito, G.R.G., Grøgaard, B. and Narula, R. (2003), 'Environmental influences on MNE subsidiary roles: economic integration and the Nordic countries', *Journal of International Business Studies*, **34**(5): 443–56.
Berry, H., Guillén, M.F. and Zhou, N. (2010), 'An institutional approach to cross-national distance', *Journal of International Business Studies*, **41**(9): 1460–80.
Brouthers, K.D. and Brouthers, L.E. (2001), 'Explaining the national cultural distance paradox', *Journal of International Business Studies*, **32**(1): 177–89.
Brown, L., Rugman, A. and Verbeke, A. (1988), 'Japanese joint ventures with Western multinationals: synthesizing the economic and cultural explanations of failure', *Journal of Pacific Asian Management*, **6**(2): 225–42.
Carr, S.C., Rugimbana, R.O., Walkom, E. and Bolitho, F.H. (2001), 'Selecting expatriates in developing areas: "country-of-origin" effects in Tanzania?', *International Journal of Intercultural Relations*, **25**: 441–57.

Coeurderoy, R. and Murray, G. (2008), 'Regulatory environments and the location decision: evidence from the early foreign market entries of new-technology-based firms', *Journal of International Business Studies*, **39**(4): 670–87.

Cuervo-Cazurra, A. (2006), 'Who cares about corruption?', *Journal of International Business Studies*, **37**(6): 807–22.

Delios, A. and Beamish, P.W. (1999), 'Ownership strategy of Japanese firms: transactional, institutional, and experience influences', *Strategic Management Journal*, **20**(10): 915–33.

Dow, D. (2000), 'A note on psychological distance and export market selection', *Journal of International Marketing*, **8**(1): 51–64.

Dow, D. and Karunaratna, A. (2006), 'Developing a multidimensional instrument to measure psychic distance stimuli', *Journal of International Business Studies*, **37**(5): 578–602.

Dow, D. and Larimo, J. (2008), 'Psychic distance, international experience and establishment mode', paper presented at the Academy of International Business Annual Meeting, Milan, July, http://works.bepress.com/douglas_dow/14.

Earley, P.C. and Mosakowski, E. (2004), 'Cultural intelligence', *Harvard Business Review*, October: 139–46.

Estrin, S., Ionascu, D. and Meyer, K.E. (2007), 'Formal and informal administrative distance, and international entry strategies', William Davidson Working Paper no. 728.

Fang, T. (2005–06), 'From "onion" to "ocean": paradox and change in national cultures', *International Studies of Management and Organization*, **35**(4): 71–90.

Fletcher, R. and Fang, T. (2006), 'Assessing the impact of culture on relationship creation and network formation in emerging Asian markets', *European Journal of Marketing*, **40**(3/4): 430–46.

Franke, G.R. and Richey Jr R.G. (2010), 'Improving generalizations from multi-country comparisons in international business research', *Journal of International Business Studies*, **41**(8): 1275–93.

Gaur, A.S. and Lu, J.W. (2007), 'Ownership strategies and survival of foreign subsidiaries: impacts of administrative distance and experience', *Journal of Management*, **33**(1): 84–110.

Gelfand, M., Nishii, L. and Raver, J. (2006), 'On the nature and importance of cultural tightness–looseness', *Journal of Applied Psychology*, **91**: 1225–44.

Ghemawat, P. (2001), 'Distance still matters: the hard reality of global expansion', *Harvard Business Review*, September: 137–47.

Globerman, S. and Shapiro, D. (2003), 'Governance infrastructure and US foreign direct investment', *Journal of International Business Studies*, **34**: 19–39.

Habib, M. and Zurawicki, L. (2002), 'Corruption and foreign direct investment', *Journal of International Business Studies*, **33**(2): 291–307.

Håkanson, L. and Ambos, B. (2010), 'The antecedents of psychic distance', *Journal of International Management*, **16**(3): 195–210.

Hejazi, W. (2007), 'Reconsidering the concentration of US MNE activity: is it global, regional or national?', *Management International Review*, **47**(1): 5–27.

Henisz, W. (2000), 'The institutional environment for multinational investment', *Journal of Law, Economics and Organization*, **16**(2): 334–64.

Hennart, J.-F. (2009), 'Down with MNE-centric theories! Market entry and expansion as the bundling of MNE and local assets', *Journal of International Business Studies*, **40**(9): 1432–52.

Heuer, M., Cummings, J.L. and Hutabarat, W. (1999), 'Cultural stability or change among managers in Indonesia?', *Journal of International Business Studies*, **30**(3): 599–610.

Hofstede, G. (1980), *Culture's Consequences: International Differences in Work-related Values*, Beverly Hills, CA: Sage.

Hutzschenreuter, T. and Voll, J. (2008), 'Performance effects of "added cultural distance" in the path of international expansion: the case of German multinational enterprises', *Journal of International Business Studies*, **39**(1): 53–70.

Hutzschenreuter, T., Voll, J. and Verbeke, A. (2010), 'The impact of added cultural distance and cultural diversity on international expansion patterns: a Penrosean perspective', *Journal of Management Studies*, doi: 10.1111/j.1467-6486.2010.00966.x.

Ibarra, H. (1993), 'Personal networks of women and minorities in management: a conceptual framework', *Academy of Management Review*, **18**(1): 56–87.

Inglehart, R. and Associates (n.d.). World Values Survey, http://www.worldvaluessurvey.org/.

Javidan, M., Teagarden, M. and Bowen, D. (2010), 'Making it overseas', *Harvard Business Review*, April: 109–13.

Johanson, J. and Vahlne, J.-E. (1977), 'The internationalization process of the firm – a model of knowledge development and increasing foreign market commitments', *Journal of International Business Studies*, **8**(1): 23–32.

Johanson, J. and Vahlne, J.-E. (2009), 'The Uppsala internationalization process model revisited – from liability of foreignness to liability of outsidership', *Journal of International Business Studies*, **40**(9): 1411–31.

Kang, J.-K. and Kim, J.-M. (2010), 'Do foreign investors exhibit a corporate governance disadvantage? An information asymmetry perspective', *Journal of International Business Studies*, **41**(8): 1415–38.

Kaufmann, D., Kraay, A. and Mastruzzi, M. (2003), 'Governance matters III: governance indicators for 1996–2002', Working Paper, World Bank Policy Research Department.

Kogut, B. and Singh, H. (1988), 'The effect of national culture on the choice of entry mode', *Journal of International Business Studies*, **19**(3): 411–32.

Kostova, T. (1997), 'Country institutional profiles: concept and measurement', *Academy of Management Best Paper Proceedings*, **24**: 304–8.

Kostova, T. and Zaheer, S. (1999), 'Organizational legitimacy under conditions of complexity: the case of the multinational enterprise', *Academy of Management Review*, **24**(1): 64–81.

Lazarsfeld, P. and Merton, R. (1954), 'Friendship as a social process: a substantive and methodological analysis', in M. Berger (ed.), *Freedom and Control in Modern Society*, New York: Van Nostrand, pp. 18–66.

Leung, K., Bhagat, R.S., Buchan, N.R., Erez, M. and Gibson, C.B. (2005), 'Culture and international business: recent advances and their implications for future research', *Journal of International Business Studies*, **36**(4): 357–78.

Mamman, A. (1995), 'Expatriate adjustment: dealing with hosts attitudes in a foreign assignment', *Journal of Transnational Management Development*, **1**: 49–70.

McSweeney, B. (2002), 'Hofstede's model of national cultural differences and their consequences: a triumph of faith – a failure of analysis', *Human Relations*, **55**: 89–118.

Merchant, H. (1997), 'The international joint venture performance of firms in the non-manufacturing sector', in P.W. Beamish and J.P. Killing (eds), *Cooperative Strategies: North American Perspectives*, San Francisco, CA: New Lexington Press, pp. 428–56.

Merchant, H. (2000), 'Configurations of international joint ventures', *Management International Review*, **40**(2): 107–40.

Merchant, H. (2006), 'The international joint venture performance of American firms: a comparative analysis of emerging markets and non-emerging markets', in S. Jain (ed.), *Emerging Economies and the Transformation of International Business: Brazil, Russia, India, and China (BRICs)*, Cheltenham, UK and Northampton, MA, USA: Edward Elgar, pp. 294–312.

Merchant, H. (2008), 'International joint venture configurations in big emerging markets', *Multinational Business Review*, **16**(3): 93–119.

Merchant, H. and Gaur, A. (2008), 'Opening the "non-manufacturing" envelope: the next big enterprise for international business research', *Management International Review*, **48**(4): 380–96.

Merchant, H. and Schendel, D. (2000), 'How do international joint ventures create shareholder value?', *Strategic Management Journal*, **21**(7): 723–37.

Meyer, K.E. (2001), 'Institutions, transaction costs, and entry mode choice in Eastern Europe', *Journal of International Business Studies*, **32**(2): 357–67.

Meyer, K.E. and Nguyen, H.V. (2005), 'Foreign investment strategies and sub-national institutions in emerging markets: evidence from Vietnam', *Journal of Management Studies*, **42**(1): 63–92.

Miller, S., Thomas, D., Eden, L. and Hitt, M. (2008), 'Knee deep in the big muddy: the survival of emerging market firms in developed markets', *Management International Review*, **48**(6): 645–66.

O'Grady, S. and Lane, H.W. (1996), 'The psychic distance paradox', *Journal of International Business Studies*, **27**(2): 309–33.

Oxley, J. (1999), 'Institutional environment and the mechanisms of governance: the impact of intellectual property protection on the structure of inter-firm alliances', *Journal of Economic Behavior and Organization*, **38**(3): 283–309.

Oyserman, D., Coon, H.M. and Kemmelmeier, M. (2002), 'Rethinking individualism and collectivism: evaluation of theoretical assumptions and meta-analyses', *Psychological Bulletin*, **128**: 3–72.

Parkhe, A. (1991), 'Interfirm diversity, organizational learning, and longevity in global strategic alliances', *Journal of International Business Studies*, **22**(4): 579–601.

Penrose, E.T. (1959), *The Theory of the Growth of the Firm*, New York: John Wiley.

Ralston, D.A. (2008), 'The crossvergence perspective: reflections and projections', *Journal of International Business Studies*, **39**(1): 27–40.

Ralston, D.A., Egri, C.P., Stewart, S., Terpstra, R.H. and Yu, K.C. (1999), 'Doing business in the 21st century with the new generation of Chinese managers: a study of generational shifts in work values in China', *Journal of International Business Studies*, **30**(2): 415–28.

Ricks, D. (2006), *Blunders in International Business*, Malden, MA: Blackwell Publishing.

Rugman, A. (1981), *Inside the Multinationals: The Economics of Internal Markets*, New York: Columbia University Press.

Rugman, A. and Verbeke, A. (2001), 'Subsidiary-specific advantages in multinational enterprises', *Strategic Management Journal*, **22**: 237–50.

Rugman, A. and Verbeke, A. (2004), 'A perspective on regional and global strategies of multinational enterprises', *Journal of International Business Studies*, **35**: 3–18.

Rugman, A. and Verbeke, A. (2005), 'Towards a theory of regional multinationals: a transaction cost economics approach', *Management International Review*, **45**(Special Issue): 5–17.

Rugman, A. and Verbeke, A. (2008), 'The theory and practice of regional strategy: a response to Osegowitsch and Sammartino', *Journal of International Business Studies*, **39**(2): 326–32.

Schwartz, S.H. (1994), *Beyond Individualism/Collectivism: New Cultural Dimensions of Values*, Thousand Oaks, CA: Sage.

Scott, W.R. (1995), *Institutions and Organizations*, Thousand Oaks, CA: Sage.

Selmer, J., Chiu, R.K. and Shenkar, O. (2007), 'Cultural distance asymmetry in expatriate adjustment', *Cross Cultural Management: An International Journal*, **14**: 150–60.

Shenkar, O. (2001), 'Cultural distance revisited: towards a more rigorous conceptualization and measurement of cultural differences', *Journal of International Business Studies*, **32**(3): 519–35.

Shenkar, O. (2012), 'Beyond cultural distance: switching to a friction lens in the study of cultural differences', *Journal of International Business Studies*, **43**(1): 12–17.

Tihanyi, L., Griffith, D.A. and Russell, C.J. (2005), 'The effect of cultural distance on entry mode choice, international diversification, and MNE performance: a meta-analysis', *Journal of International Business Studies*, **36**(3): 270–83.

Trompenaars, F. and Hampden-Turner, C. (1997), *Riding the Waves of Culture: Understanding Cultural Diversity in Business*, 2nd edn, London: Nicholas Brealey.

Tung, R.L. (1998), 'American expatriates abroad: from neophytes to cosmopolitans', *Journal of World Business*, **33**(2): 125–44.

Tung, R.L. (2008), 'The cross-cultural research imperative: the need to balance cross-national and intra-national diversity', *Journal of International Business Studies*, **39**(1): 41–6.

Tung, R.L. and Baumann, C. (2009), 'Comparing the attitudes toward money, material possessions and savings of overseas Chinese vis-à-vis Chinese in China: convergence, divergence or cross-vergence, vis-à-vis "one size fits all" human resource management policies and practices', *International Journal of Human Resource Management*, **20**(11): 2382–401.

Tung, R.L. and Chung, H.F.L. (2010), 'Diaspora and trade facilitation: the case of ethnic Chinese in Australia', *Asia Pacific Journal of Management*, **27**(3): 371–92.

Tung, R.L. and Verbeke, A. (2010), 'Beyond Hofstede and GLOBE: improving the quality of cross-cultural research', *Journal of International Business Studies*, **41**(8): 1259–74.

Tung, R.L., Worm, V. and Fang, T. (2008), 'Sino-Western business negotiations revisited – 30 years after China's open door policy', *Organizational Dynamics*, **37**(1): 60–74.

Venaik, S. and Brewer, P. (2010), 'Avoiding uncertainty in Hofstede and GLOBE', *Journal of International Business Studies*, **41**(8): 1294–315.

Verbeke, A. (2009), *International Business Strategy*, Cambridge: Cambridge University Press.

Verbeke, A. and Kenworthy, T. (2008), 'Multidivisional versus metanational governance of the multinational enterprise', *Journal of International Business Studies*, **39**(2): 940–56.

Woolridge, A. (2010), 'The world turned upside down: a special report on innovation in emerging markets', *The Economist*, 17 April, 1–14.

Xu, D. and Shenkar, O. (2002), 'Institutional distance and the multinational enterprise', *Academy of Management Review*, **27**: 608–18.

Yiu, D. and Makino, S. (2002), 'The choice between joint venture and wholly owned subsidiary: an institutional perspective', *Organization Science*, **13**(6): 667–83.

17 Institutional distance and international strategy
Deeksha Singh and Ajai S. Gaur

Firms operating in international markets have to contend with a multitude of institutional environments. The institutional environment in a host market is often different from that in the home market of a firm. Understanding the differences between the home and the host country institutional environments and developing strategies to effectively manage the challenges arising due to these differences is the key to success in international business (IB) operations.

Cross-national differences, in some form or the other, have been at the core of international business research. Hymer (1960/1976), in his early work on multinational corporations (MNCs), argued that firms face additional costs when operating in foreign countries. These costs of doing business abroad, which were later termed liability of foreignness (Miller and Parkhe, 2002; Zaheer, 1995; Zaheer and Mosakowski, 1997), depend on the extent of similarity/dissimilarity between the home country and the host country. The stages model of internationalization (Johanson and Vahlne, 1977) also suggests that firms gradually internationalize from low-distance countries to high-distance countries. Johanson and Vahlne (1977) suggested that distance arises due to differences in language, educational system, culture, business practices and economic development of countries. More recently, the eclectic framework of firm internationalization (Dunning, 1993) also argues for the importance of distance between the home and the host countries. Dunning (1993) takes a more holistic perspective on distance, arguing that countries differ not only in geographic distance, but also in social, cultural and political institutions.

Scholars have advanced multiple constructs to understand and measure the differences in national institutional environments. Prominent among these are the constructs of cultural distance (Hofstede, 1980; Kogut and Singh, 1988), and institutional distance (ID) (Gaur and Lu, 2007; Kostova, 1999; North, 1990). A number of empirical studies examining the location choice, mode of entry, sequence of foreign entry, extent of internationalization and performance consequences of internationalization have utilized the construct of country differences in some form or another. However, we lack a comprehensive understanding of what different constructs refer to and in what ways they affect international strategy decisions.

In this chapter, we discuss one such construct, ID. We review prominent studies on cross-national differences as measured by the construct of ID and the effect of these differences on international strategy decisions. We focus on the conceptual definition and empirical operationalization of ID and theoretical and empirical developments in the IB field around this construct. It is important to note here that this review is not exhaustive of the literature on ID. Rather, the objective is to identify important trends and developments in this research stream and to propose directions for future research.

WHAT IS INSTITUTIONAL DISTANCE?

ID refers to the 'differences between the institutional environments of two countries' (Gaur and Lu, 2007, p. 87). It is based on Scott's (1995) conceptualization of national institutional environments as comprising three pillars – regulatory, normative and cognitive. The regulative pillar refers to the formal rules and regulations as sanctioned and enforced by a state (North, 1990). These include various regulatory bodies responsible for making and enforcing laws, the judicial system and the government. The normative pillar refers to norms and values held by the collective in a nation. According to Scott (1995, p. 37), norms introduce 'a prescriptive, evaluative and obligatory dimension into social life'. The cognitive pillar refers to 'the nature of reality and the frames through which meaning is made' (Scott, 1995, p. 40). Kostova (1999) suggests that cognitive elements affect the way people interpret the stimuli coming from the external environment and are widely shared by people in a given country.

Based on the three pillars of national institutional environment, Kostova (1999) and Kostova and Zaheer (1999) first conceptualized the construct of ID as comprising regulatory, normative and cognitive dimensions. Kostova (1999) linked ID to the effectiveness with which strategic organizational practices are transferred across different units of an MNC. Kostova (1999) argued that the success of transfer of a strategic organizational practice depends on the ID between the countries of the parent firm and its subsidiaries. Even though Kostova (1999) suggested that ID is a multidimensional construct, she did not develop more nuanced arguments linking different dimensions of ID to the dependent variable in her study. Kostova and Zaheer (1999) further theorized on ID, linking it to the challenges of establishing and maintaining legitimacy by foreign subsidiaries. They argued that the regulative, normative and cognitive aspects of institutional environments were different in their degree of formalization and tacitness. They also argued that because of these differences, the effect of different dimensions of ID on subsidiary legitimacy should also be different. This was one of the early works theorizing about the differential effect of ID dimensions on an important IB issue. Xu and Shenkar (2002) further built on Kostova (1999) and Kostova and Zaheer's (1999) conceptualization of ID to propose a set of relationships between ID and different aspects of IB strategy.

It is important to note here that there is a rich tradition of using country-level differences to predict different aspects of international strategy decisions. Empirical research on the effect of country-level differences picked up after the publication of Hofstede's (1980) work on national cultural differences and the operationalization of the construct of cultural distance by Kogut and Singh (1988). Since then, a number of studies examined the direct as well as moderating effect of cultural distance on different international strategy decisions such as entry mode (Brouthers and Brouthers, 2001; Contractor and Kundu, 1998; Kogut and Singh, 1988), ownership strategies (Hennart and Larimo, 1998), and survival and performance of foreign subsidiaries (Barkema and Vermeulen, 1997; Delios and Beamish, 2004; Li and Guisinger, 1991). Cultural distance, as a measure of national differences, was however criticized on the ground that it offers only partial conceptualization and measurement of national differences and environmental complexity (Gaur et al., 2007; Shenkar, 2001). In addition, the cultural distance score is time invariant, leading to heightened potential for Type 1 errors in large sample studies with longitudinal data (Gaur et al., 2007). With the theoretical developments in the construct of ID, it emerged as a more robust measure of national differences.

The theoretical developments in ID were followed by a few attempts to operationalize ID. Table 17.1 lists some of the important studies that have done this. There are important similarities in the measures of ID adopted by the studies reported in Table 17.1. First, a majority of the studies view ID as a multidimensional construct. This is important given that much of the prior research utilized cultural distance as a single indicator to measure national-level differences. Often, cultural distance did not accurately represent the theoretical arguments through which scholars linked cultural distance with different dimensions of international business strategy. National institutional environments include many complex dimensions and culture is just one of them. Thus the use of ID is an important advance in the IB domain.

The second notable aspect about ID operationalization is the similarity in the theoretical arguments proposed to conceptualize ID. Most studies rely on Scott's (1995) three pillars and Kostova's (1999) discussion. There are also notable similarities across different studies about the data sources used. Four out of the six studies listed in Table 17.1 use indices provided by the Global Competitive Reports, while one uses those by the Heritage Foundation. One study uses cultural distance as an indicator of institutional differences. In the next section, I discuss how different studies have used ID to explain different aspect of MNC strategies.

EFFECT OF ID ON MNCS

ID has been used to explain MNC strategies in both theoretical as well as empirical papers. In most studies, scholars have identified two intervening variables through which ID affects different international strategy decisions. First, ID affects the legitimacy challenges, which in turn affect the liability of foreignness that MNCs face in the host markets. In her original conceptualization of ID, Kostova (1999) suggested that ID reflects the extent of social legitimacy pressures that MNCs face when they transfer the strategic organizational practices from the parent firm to the subsidiary. Kostova and Zaheer (1999) further extended this idea, suggesting that ID poses two challenges to MNCs. First, a greater ID makes it more difficult for the MNC to understand the host environment and what the firms need to do to gain legitimacy in that environment. Second, a greater ID also makes it important that firms adapt their organizational practices to suit the local legitimacy requirements.

Eden and Miller (2004) built on Kostova and Zaheer's (1999) work to further link ID and local legitimacy challenges with the liability of foreignness (LOF). Eden and Miller argued that LOF is a subset of different costs of doing business abroad, and includes only social costs. These social costs arise due to unfamiliarity, relational and discriminatory hazards, which in turn arise due to uncertainty about a host country. Different components of ID affect the social costs and thereby the LOF that foreign firms face in a host market.

Second, scholars have argued that ID affects the uncertainty that firms face in host markets. While these uncertainties may contribute to LOF, they also enhance the public and private expropriation hazards for the foreign firms (Delios and Henisz, 2000; Gaur

Table 17.1 Operationalization of institutional distance

Study	Context	ID definition	ID operationalization
Estrin et al. (2009)	Entry mode choice in six emerging markets from 55 countries	ID as differences in formal and informal institutions	Difference in formal institutions measured from the regulatory factor of the Heritage Foundation Economic Freedom Index; differences in informal institutions measured using cultural distance
Gaur and Lu (2007)	Ownership strategies and survival of Japanese subsidiaries	ID as regulative and normative distance; the normative component includes cognitive distance	Based on 12 country-level characteristics from Global Competitiveness Report and Euromoney with annual variation
Gaur et al. (2007)	Expatriate staffing and survival of Japanese subsidiaries	Included cognitive distance as a separate component to Gaur and Lu's (2007) conceptualization	Regulative and normative distance similar to Gaur and Lu (2007). Cultural distance as an indicator of cognitive dimension
Jensen and Szulanski (2004)	Cross-border knowledge transfer, survey of 19 countries	Theorized institutional distance	Used cultural distance to capture the normative and cognitive aspects; did not include the regulative aspect
Yiu and Makino (2002)	Entry mode choice by Japanese MNCs	ID as regulative, normative and cognitive dimension	Single-item measures for regulative (state influence) and normative (ethnocentricity) distances from Global Competitiveness Report and past behavior of firms for cognitive dimension
Xu et al. (2004)	Ownership and staffing strategies in Japanese subsidiaries	ID as regulative and normative distance	Based on 14 country-level characteristics from Global Competitiveness Report.

and Lu, 2007). For example, in institutionally distant countries, firms may not understand the rules, regulations and norms for protecting intellectual property and may be discouraged from forming a joint venture in the fear of misappropriation by the joint venture partner. This conceptualization of ID extends prior work on the role of intangible assets in international strategy decisions by suggesting that firms not only need to be concerned with what they have, but also with where they are going to invest what they have.

Both LOF and host market uncertainty are used as the intervening mechanisms through which ID affects international strategy decisions. There are three important international strategy decisions and outcomes – location selection, entry mode/ownership strategies and performance/survival of foreign subsidiaries – which are dependent on LOF and host market uncertainty, and therefore ID. Table 17.2 presents a summary of a few important studies in these three domains, which we discuss below.

ID and Location Choice

The linkage between ID and location choice is the least researched one. Early research on location selection suggests that the choice of a foreign market is shaped by the parent firm characteristics such as the resource advantage, strategy and the structure of the parent firm (Dunning, 1980; Ghoshal and Nohria, 1989). However, the parent firm characteristics must be matched with the host country characteristics when making location selection decisions. Xu and Shenkar (2002) argued that parent firm characteristics must be matched with the ID as the latter represents the difficulties in transferring the resources and capabilities from the parent to the subsidiary and the legitimacy challenges the subsidiaries face in a host market. Xu and Shenkar (2002) developed propositions linking ID with the sources of competitive advantage of an MNC, its global strategy and the level of organizational diversity in affecting the location selection decisions.

With respect to the sources of competitive advantage, Xu and Shenkar (2002) argued that firms with routine-based competitive advantages will choose normatively similar markets while those with host-country-based competitive advantages will choose normatively distant markets to easily exploit the given competitive advantage. Further, they expected firms pursuing global strategy to choose institutionally closer markets (in terms of normative and cognitive distances), while those pursuing multidomestic strategy would choose institutionally distant markets. Finally, firms with low diversity are expected to enter institutionally closer markets as compared to firms with high diversity.

These theoretical propositions have not been extensively tested in empirical work. However, some scholars have examined the effect of cultural distance on location choice decision. Benito and Gripsrud (1992) examined the foreign expansion of 93 Norwegian firms in terms of cultural learning process, but did not find any effect of cultural distance on location decisions. Treviño and Mixon (2004) examined the effect of political risk and level of privatization on MNCs' investment decisions in seven Latin American markets, and found that markets with higher political risk and low level of privatization receive less investment. Bevan et al. (2004) linked the institutional development in 14 transition economies to location selection decisions of MNCs from five source country groups. Utilizing European Bank of Reconstruction and Development (EBRD)

Table 17.2 Key studies on cross national differences and international strategy decisions and outcomes

Study	Topic	Context	Distance measure	Key findings
Location choice				
Benito and Gripsrud (1992)	Location	201 cases of FDI from 93 Norwegian firms	CD	CD does not affect the sequence of entry in FDI decisions
Xu and Shenkar (2002)	Location/entry mode	Theoretical	Kostova's (1999) conceptualization of ID	Different dimensions of ID affect the location selection based on parent firms characteristics and entry mode choice
Treviño and Mixon (2004)	Location	FDI inflows to 7 Latin American markets	Political risk (from institutional investor) and level of privatization	Countries with higher political risk and low level of privatization receive less FDI
Bevan et al. (2004)	Location	5 source country groups and 14 destinations, country-level FDI flows	Institutional development (EBRD transition indices)	Quality of formal institutions is positively associated with the FDI inflows
Entry mode/ownership strategies				
Kogut and Singh (1988)	Entry mode	228 entries into USA	CD	Increasing CD leads to higher likelihood of shared control
Delios and Beamish (1999)	Ownership strategies	Japanese MNCs	Political risk (Euromoney), host govt restrictions (Global Competitiveness Report) and intellectual property protection (Global Competitiveness Report)	With greater risks and restrictions, firms prefer to take lower equity ownership
Meyer (2001)	Entry mode	269 German and UK firms into 5 countries	Institutional strength/development (EBRD transition indices)	Host country institutions affect entry mode decisions
Yiu and Makino (2002)	Entry mode	Japanese MNCs	Regulative – state influences (Global Competitiveness Report), normative – ethnocentricity (Global Competitiveness Report) and cognitive-past behavior (mimetic)	Absolute values of WCR indices used. The more restrictive the regulatory and normative domain, higher the chances of JV
Eden and Miller (2004)	Ownership strategies	Theoretical	Kostova's (1999) conceptualization of ID	ID (regulative, normative and cognitive) is the key driver of liability of foreignness, which in turn affects ownership strategies

Table 17.2 (continued)

Study	Topic	Context	Distance measure	Key findings
Entry mode/ownership strategies (cont.)				
Xu et al. (2004)	Ownership strategies	Japanese MNCs	Regulative and normative distances based on Global Competitiveness Report	The larger are the regulative and normative distances, the lower is the equity of the parent firms
Estrin et al. (2009)	Entry mode	FDI in 6 emerging markets	Formal distance (Heritage Foundation), informal distance (CD) and human resource distance	A linear relationship between formal distance and human resource distance and the choice between greenfield investments versus joint ventures, and a nonlinear relationship for informal distance
Performance and other outcomes				
Gomez-Mejia and Palich (1997)	MNC performance	228 large US firms	Cultural diversity based on nine different measures of CD	Cultural diversity does not affect MNC performance
Morosini et al. (1998)	Cross-border acquisition performance	52 acquisitions of Italian firms	CD	Increasing CD increases performance
Merchant (2002)	Shareholder returns in IJVs	350 JVs between a US and foreign firm	CD	CD has no significant effect
Evans and Mavondo (2002)	Performance of international retailing operations	102 retailers from USA, UK, Western Europe, Asia Pacific	Psychic, cultural and business distance (survey)	Proximity positively affects performance

Study	Focus	Sample	ID measure	Key finding
Kostova and Roth (2002)	Adoption of an organizational practice	Survey of employees of 104 subsidiaries in 10 countries	Regulative, normative and cognitive distances	The more favorable the country institutional profile, the easier the adoption
Jensen and Szulanski (2004)	Adaptation of organizational practices	19 countries (8 firms, survey)	Cultural distance as a measure of ID	ID affects stickiness positively and recipient's motivation negatively
Lu and Hebert (2005)	Foreign subsidiary survival	Japanese firms' foreign subsidiaries	External uncertainty – cultural distance and country risk (Euromoney)	External uncertainty negatively moderates the relationship between foreign equity and IJV survival
Dhanraj and Beamish (2005)	Foreign subsidiary survival	Japanese firms' foreign subsidiaries	Absolute scores of political openness (regulative), social openness (normative) (from Global Competitiveness Report) and density (cognitive)	Political and social openness increase the survival chances; density has a U-shaped effect
Gaur and Lu (2007)	Foreign subsidiary survival	Japanese firms' foreign subsidiaries	Regulative and normative distance (Global Competitiveness Report and Euromoney)	Regulative and normative distance increases the chances of subsidiary survival
Gaur et al. 2007	Foreign subsidiary productivity	Japanese firms' foreign subsidiaries	Regulative and normative distance (Global Competitiveness Report and Euromoney)	ID moderates the positive relationship between expatriate staffing and subsidiary productivity

335

transition market indices to measure institutional development, they found a positive link between institutional development and location selection for FDI.

ID and Foreign Market Entry Strategies

Foreign market entry is one of the most widely researched topics in the IB field. There are two aspects of foreign entry decision – entry mode choice and ownership strategies. Studies on entry mode decision mostly examine the choice between greenfield entry and acquisition. Studies on ownership strategies examine the choice between a joint venture and a wholly owned subsidiary and equity share in a joint venture as an indicator of desired control and commitment. Early work in this domain used cultural distance as an indicator of difficulties that a firm faces when it enters a foreign market. For example, Kogut and Singh (1988) argued that MNCs choose shared control in countries with greater cultural distance as it is difficult to manage the complexities arising due to cultural distance without the help of a local player.

Similar arguments have been advanced with respect to ID and entry mode choice. Xu and Shenkar (2002) in a theoretical piece argued that MNCs will prefer greenfield investments over acquisitions in countries that are at a greater distance from the home country on normative and cognitive dimensions. Using institutional theory, they argue that legitimacy concerns are the deciding factor in the choice between greenfield investment and acquisitions. Large normative and cognitive distances increase the local legitimacy concerns while at the same time making it more difficult to transfer strategic organizational practices from the parent to the subsidiary if the subsidiary is acquired (Kostova, 1999; Xu and Shenkar, 2002). Xu and Shenkar (2002) further theorize that MNCs prefer to enter through high control modes (a wholly owned subsidiary or a majority joint venture) if the foreign country is closer to the home country on the regulative dimension. This was one of the first attempts to theorize a complex relationship between different dimensions of ID and foreign entry strategies.

In another theoretical piece, Eden and Miller (2004) argue that liability of foreignness (LOF) is the core strategic issue for MNC managers and ID is the key driver behind LOF. MNC managers consider ID and LOF in making ownership decisions in their foreign subsidiaries. They propose that MNCs choose a low ownership strategy as the ID between the home country and the host country increases. They further break down the ID construct into regulative, normative and cognitive distances and develop propositions linking each of these components individually as well as jointly to ownership strategies.

While scholars were theorizing the construct of ID, simultaneous efforts were being made to examine how host country institutional environment affects MNCs' market entry strategies. Four studies are notable in this domain. Delios and Beamish (1999) examined the relationship between transactional and institutional factors and ownership strategies of Japanese MNCs. In this study, they examined three institutional factors – political risk, legal restriction in the host country, and intellectual property protection. They argued that MNCs will opt for lower equity positions in countries that have more restrictions on foreign equity participation or where political risk and threat to intellectual property is high. Delios and Henisz (2000) further examined the effect of public and private expropriation hazards on the choice of Japanese firms' equity ownership in their subsidiaries in emerging markets. The public expropriation hazard was measured using the political hazard index (Henisz, 2000), while the private expropriation hazard was measured using the technological intensity of the parent firm.

In another study, Yiu and Makino (2002) examined the relationship between institutional pressures and the choice between joint ventures and wholly owned subsidiaries in the case of Japanese firms' foreign entry decision. They argued that MNCs prefer joint ventures with local partners over wholly owned subsidiaries in countries where MNCs face greater regulative and normative pressures. Meyer (2001) also examined the effect of institutional development of the host country to explain the entry mode choice of German and UK firms entering Eastern Europe. While all these studies considered absolute level of institutional scores for the host countries, the idea of institutional differences beyond the cultural differences was inherent in these studies. The indicators these studies used to measure host country institutional pressures provided useful pointers to operationalize the ID construct in later studies.

Building on the above mentioned works, Xu et al. (2004) examined the effect of regulative and normative distances on the ownership strategies of Japanese MNCs. Xu et al. (2004) argued that ID represents the external legitimacy pressures that MNCs face in their foreign operations. In order to attend to external legitimacy concerns, MNCs will choose to give up some strategic control by assuming lower ownership stakes in countries with higher regulative and normative distances. Xu et al. (2004) calculated regulative and normative distances scores using the information provided in the Global Competitiveness Report.

Estrin et al. (2009) added another dimension to ID. They argued that ID comprises distance in formal institutions, informal institutions and human resources. The conceptualization of formal and informal distances was similar to that proposed by earlier studies (Gaur et al., 2007; Gaur and Lu, 2007; Kostova, 1999; Xu et al., 2004). Human resource distance was conceptualized as differences in human resource policies between the home and host countries. Estrin et al. (2009) used the Heritage Foundation data to measure the distance in formal institutions, cultural distance data to measure the distance in informal institutions and different indicators of technological and educational achievements to measure human resource distance. Estrin et al. (2009) proposed linear relationships between formal distance and human resource distance and the choice between greenfield investments versus joint ventures, and a nonlinear relationship between informal distance and the entry mode choice. These relationships further varied for first-time investors versus more experienced investors.

ID and Foreign Subsidiary Performance

As compared to foreign entry strategies, there is relatively less work directly linking ID to foreign subsidiary performance. Early work in this stream linked cultural distance as an explanatory variable or as a moderator to subsidiary survival and performance. Gomez-Mejia and Palich (1997) used nine different distance variables to measure cultural diversity of an MNC and its consequence for the performance of the MNC. Morosini et al. (1998) used cultural distance to assess the performance of cross-border acquisitions. Merchant (2002) used cultural distance and host country political risk to explain shareholder value creation in international joint ventures.

With the developments in the ID-related literature, and critique of cultural distance, scholars started shifting their attention from cultural distance to more comprehensive measures of national differences. Evans and Mavondo (2002) used a survey to measure cultural, psychic and business distances and linked these to the performance of international retailing operations of retailers from the USA, the UK, Western Europe and the Asia Pacific region. Kostova and Roth (2002) conducted a survey on employees of 104 subsidiaries in ten countries to develop measures of regulative normative and cognitive distance. Rather than linking the distance variables to performance, they examined how distance affected the adoption of an organizational practice by the subsidiaries of an MNC with the implicit assumption that more successful adoption will lead to superior subsidiary and MNC performance. Jensen and Szulanski (2004) theoretically linked ID to successful adaptation of organizational practices in cross-border knowledge transfer. However, in the empirical models Jensen and Szulanski (2004) used the cultural distance scores, arguing that cultural distance captures the normative and cognitive aspects of ID.

Following the trend of moving away from culture to institutions, Lu and Hebert (2005) theorized the effect of external uncertainty on survival of Japanese international joint ventures. They measured external uncertainty using cultural distance and country risk rating. Dhanraj and Beamish (2005) linked the host country institutional environment to the survival of foreign subsidiaries. They conceptualized institutional environment as comprising regulative, normative and cognitive dimensions and used political openness for regulative, social openness for normative and density of subsidiaries of the same parent for cognitive dimensions.

The studies by Gaur and Lu (2007) and Gaur et al. (2007) are notable exceptions in this domain of research as they directly linked the ID scores to subsidiary survival and performance. Following Kostova's (1999) and Kostova and Zaheer's (1999) conceptualization of ID, Gaur and Lu (2007) developed longitudinal scores on regulative and normative distance indicators. They utilized scores on 13 items related to regulative and normative domains as defined by Scott (1995) from different editions of the Global Competitiveness Reports and annual scores on country risk rating from different editions of Euromoney. They performed a factor analysis on these items and identified two distinct dimensions that they used as indicators of regulative and normative strengths of a country. They used the formula proposed by Kogut and Singh (1988) to calculate the distance scores between different countries. They argued for an inverted U-shaped relationship between regulative and normative distances and survival of foreign subsidiaries. Further, they suggested that in institutionally distant countries, foreign subsidiaries had enhanced survival chances if the parent firm assumed greater ownership than if the parent firm assumed lower ownership in the foreign subsidiaries. Gaur et al. (2007) used the same operationalization of regulative and normative distance but added the cognitive distance dimension as measured by Hofstede's (1980) cultural distance scores. They argued that ID determines the boundary conditions in the relationship between subsidiary staffing and productivity of foreign subsidiaries.

CONCLUSION AND FUTURE DIRECTIONS

ID as a new construct to measure differences in national institutional environments has gained significant attention in scholarly research in a short time. Much of the IB research utilized and continues to utilize cultural distance as an indicator of cross-national differences. There are several notable features of ID that make it more suitable than cultural distance to measure cross-national differences. First, culture is just one aspect of institutions. ID covers a broader spectrum of factors that may have an impact on international strategy decisions (Gaur et al., 2007). For example, the difference in intellectual protection enforcement is more of a regulative issue than a cultural one.

Second, culture and consequently the cultural distance scores remain relatively static over time. It is a difficult argument to suggest that an MNC that has operated in a foreign country for a number of years will still face cultural barriers when making future investments in that country. Even if culture changes, the procedure to obtain culture scores every few years is very resource and time intensive. This is partly why we continue to keep using the culture scores obtained by Hofstede (1980) about 30 years back. Institutions change. There are several reputable agencies that conduct surveys every year to obtain scores on different dimensions of institutions. As a result, it is possible to compute annual scores for different dimensions of ID. This aspect of ID is very appealing to IB scholars who use longitudinal data and are interested in assessing the effect of changes in the external environment on strategic adaptation.

Third, with ID, it is possible to modify the measure by including specific components of interest to suit a given situation. It has been argued that only certain types of institutional differences may affect a given international strategy decision (Xu and Shenkar, 2002). Consequently, depending on the particular decision being investigated, scholars may modify the ID dimension of interest. For example, in the high-technology industry, managers may be more concerned with protecting their intellectual property while making the entry mode decision. In such studies, variables such as intellectual property protection, rule of law, judicial system efficiency etc. may constitute the institutional dimension to explain the entry mode decision. At the same time, studies dealing with subsidiary staffing may be more concerned with differences in human resource practices and utilize human resource distance (Estrin et al., 2009) as an explanatory variable.

The last issue points to an important dimension for future research on ID. Theoretically, we need more clarity about the construct of ID. While the broad definition of the ID construct is consistent with Scott's (1995) conceptualization of institutions, there is not enough clarity on the underlying dimensions. Some scholars conceptualize ID as comprising regulative, normative and cognitive dimensions, in line with Scott (1995) and Kostova (1999). At the same time, others have conceptualized ID as comprising distance in formal and informal institutions, which is more in line with North (1990). We need to acknowledge that ID may have a different meaning for different international strategy decisions and its operationalization needs to be accordingly modified.

Only a handful of studies have directly linked ID with some aspects of international strategy decisions. As our review suggests, maximum research in this domain has been done in linking ID to entry mode decision. While the research in this domain is picking up, there is plenty of scope to theoretically and empirically link ID with international strategy decisions. More specifically, the domain of location choice and MNC and subsidiary performance opens areas for scholars to conduct studies.

Finally, we have relied too much and too long on cultural distance to measure cross-national differences. We rely on evidence that comes from studies that have used cultural distance. We need to conduct some comparative studies to assess the explanatory power of cultural distance *vis-à-vis* ID to better inform IB scholars and practioners.

REFERENCES

Barkema, H.G. and Vermeulen, G.A.M. (1997), 'What differences in the cultural backgrounds of partners are detrimental for international joint ventures?', *Journal of International Business Studies*, **28**(4): 845–64.

Benito, G.R.G. and Gripsrud, G. (1992), 'The expansion of foreign direct investments: discrete rational location choices or a cultural learning process?', *Journal of International Business Studies*, **23**(3): 461–76.

Bevan, A.A., Estrin, S. and Meyer, K.E. (2004), 'Institution building and integration of Eastern Europe in international production', *International Business Review*, **13**: 43–64.

Brouthers, K.D. and Brouthers, L.E. (2001), 'Explaining the national cultural distance paradox', *Journal of International Business Studies*, **32**: 177–89.

Contractor, F.J. and Kundu, S.K. (1998), 'Modal choice in the world of alliances: analyzing organizational forms in the international hotel sector', *Journal of International Business Studies*, **29**: 325–57.

Delios, A. and Beamish, P.W. (1999), 'Ownership strategies of Japanese firms: transactional, institutional and experience influences', *Strategic Management Journal*, **20**: 915–33.

Delios, A. and Beamish, P.W. (2004), 'Joint venture performance revisited: Japanese foreign subsidiaries worldwide', *Management International Review*, **44**: 69–91.

Delios, A. and Henisz, W.J. (2000), 'Japanese firms' investment strategies in emerging economies', *Academy of Management Journal*, **43**(3): 305–23.

Dhanraj, C. and Beamish, P.W. (2004), 'Effect of equity ownership on survival of international joint ventures', *Strategic Management Journal*, **25**: 295–305.

Dunning, J.H. (1980), 'Toward an eclectic theory of international production: some empirical tests', *Journal of International Business Studies*, **11**(1): 9–31.

Dunning, J.H. (1993), *Multinational Enterprises and the Global Economy*, Reading, MA: Addison-Wesley.

Eden, L. and Miller, S.R. (2004), 'Distance matters: liability of foreignness, institutional distance and ownership strategy', in Michael A. Hitt and Joseph L.C. Cheng (eds), *Theories of the Multinational Enterprise: Diversity, Complexity and Relevance* (Advances in International Management, Volume 16), Bingley, UK: Emerald Group Publishing Limited, pp. 187–221.

Estrin, S., Baghdasaryan, D. and Meyer, K.E. (2009), 'The impact of institutional and human resource distance on international entry strategies', *Journal of Management Studies*, **46**: 1171–96.

Evans, J. and Mavondo, F.T. (2002), 'Psychic distance and organisational performance: an empirical examination of international retailing', *Journal of International Business Studies*, **33**: 515–32.

Gaur, A.S. and Lu, J. (2007), 'Ownership strategies and subsidiary performance: impacts of institutions and experience', *Journal of Management*, **33**(1): 84–110.

Gaur, A.S., Delios, A. and Singh, K. (2007), 'Institutional environments, staffing strategies and subsidiary performance', *Journal of Management*, **33**(4): 611–36.

Ghoshal, S. and Nohria, N. (1989), 'Internal differentiation within multinational corporations', *Strategic Management Journal*, **10**: 323–37.

Gomez-Mejia, L.R. and Palich L.E. (1997), 'Cultural diversity and the performance of multinational firms', *Journal of International Business Studies*, **28**: 309–35.

Henisz, W.J. (2000), 'The institutional environment for economic growth', *Economics and Politics*, **12**(1): 1–31.

Hennart J.-F. and Larimo J. (1998), 'The impact of culture on the strategy of multinational enterprises: does national origin affect ownership decisions?', *Journal of International Business Studies*, **29**(3): 515–38.

Hofstede, G. (1980), *Culture's Consequences: International Differences in Work-related Values*, Beverley Hills, CA: Sage.

Hymer, S. (1960/1976), *The International Operations of National Firms: A Study of Direct Foreign Investment*, Cambridge, MA: MIT Press.

Jensen, R. and Szulanski, G. (2004), 'Stickiness and the adaptation of organizational practices in cross-border knowledge transfers', *Journal of International Business Studies*, **35**: 508–23.

Johanson, J. and Vahlne, J.E. (1977), 'The internationalization process of the firm: a model of knowledge development and increasing foreign market commitment', *Journal of International Business Studies*, **8**: 23–32.

Kogut B. and Singh, H. (1988), 'The effect of national culture on the choice of entry mode', *Journal of International Business Studies*, **19**: 411–32.

Kostova, T. (1999), 'Transnational transfer of strategic organizational practices: a contextual perspective', *Academy of Management Review*, **24**: 308–24.

Kostova, T. and Roth, K. (2002), 'Adoption of an organizational practice by the subsidiaries of the MNC: institutional and relational effects', *Academy of Management Journal*, **45**: 215–33.

Kostova, T. and Zaheer, S. (1999), 'Organizational legitimacy under conditions of complexity: the case of the multinational enterprise', *Academy of Management Review*, **24**: 64–81.

Li, J. and Guisinger, S. (1991), 'Comparative business failures of foreign-controlled firms in the United States', *Journal of International Business Studies*, **22**(2): 209–24.

Lu, J.W. and Hebert, L. (2005), 'Equity control and the survival of international joint ventures: a contingency approach', *Journal of Business Research*, **58**: 736–45.

Merchant, H. (2002), 'Shareholder value creation via international joint ventures: some additional explanations', *Management International Review*, **42**: 49–69.

Meyer, K.E. (2001), 'Institutions, transaction costs and entry mode choice in Eastern Europe', *Journal of International Business Studies*, **31**: 357–67.

Miller, S.R. and A. Parkhe (2002), 'Is there a liability of foreignness in global banking? An empirical test of banks' efficiency', *Strategic Management Journal*, **23**(1): 55–75.

Morosini, P., Shane, S. and Singh, H. (1998), 'National cultural distance and cross-border acquisition performance', *Journal of International Business Studies*, **29**: 137–58.

North, D. (1990), *Institutions, Institutional Change, and Economic Performance*, Cambridge: Cambridge University Press.

Scott, W.R. (1995), *Institutions and Organizations*, Thousand Oaks, CA: Sage.

Shenkar, O. (2001), 'Cultural distance revisited: towards a more rigorous conceptualization and measurement of cultural differences', *Journal of International Business Studies*, **32**: 1–17.

Treviño, L.J. and Mixon F. (2004), 'Strategic factors affecting foreign direct investment decisions by multinational enterprises in Latin America', *Journal of World Business*, **39**: 233–43.

Xu, D., Pan, Y. and Beamish, P.W. (2004), 'The effect of regulative and normative distances on MNE ownership and expatriate strategies', *Management International Review*, **44**: 285–308.

Xu, D. and Shenkar, O. (2002), 'Institutional distance and the multinational enterprise', *Academy of Management Review*, **27**: 608–18.

Yiu, D. and Makino, S. (2002), 'The choice between joint venture and wholly owned subsidiary: an institutional perspective', *Organization Science*, **13**: 667–83.

Zaheer, S. (1995), 'Overcoming the liability of foreignness', *Academy of Management Journal*, **38**: 341–63.

Zaheer, S. and Mosakowski, E. (1997), 'The dynamics of the liability of foreignness: a global study of survival in financial services', *Strategic Management Journal*, **18**: 439–64.

18 Real options theory and international investment strategy: past, present and future
Jing Li, Yong Li and Alan M. Rugman

INTRODUCTION

Uncertainty has been a persistent feature in international business, and multinational enterprises (MNEs) are required to deal with uncertainty (e.g. market, political, technological) in various strategic decisions concerning foreign market entry mode, scale and timing (Buckley and Casson, 1998). The conventional wisdom in international business (IB) is to view uncertainty as an unfavorable condition that complicates the decision-making process and exposes firms to downside risks and losses; as a result, much effort has been put into designing strategies to minimize potential negative outcomes in an uncertain environment (Buckley and Casson, 1976; Rugman, 1981). In contrast with the conventional wisdom, real options theory offers a fresh perspective to tackle uncertainty in international investment: uncertainty in the host market does not necessarily pose a threat to MNEs' profitability; it may also present valuable opportunities for MNEs to exploit (Dixit and Pindyck, 1994; Trigeorgis, 1996). From this perspective, MNEs should design strategies such that they have the flexibility to benefit from upside potentials while containing downside losses in future (Buckley and Casson, 1998; Chi and Seth, 2009). The unique contribution of real options theory is that it provides a general theoretical foundation on which IB scholars can conceptualize how MNEs make investment decisions in an uncertain environment as well as adjust their investment strategies in response to new information in the environment (Belderbos and Zou, 2007, 2009; Li and Li, 2010; Tong et al., 2008).

This chapter proceeds as follows. We start by providing an overview of real options theory. We then review the major applications of real options theory to international investment strategy. Our analysis shows that real options theory sheds light on important international investment issues such as when to invest in a foreign market, what entry mode to choose, and how to evaluate multinational networks. In the second part of the chapter, we discuss future research directions in four areas that we consider important to advance real options research on international investment strategies: (1) addressing the joint effects of institutional and market uncertainties on international strategy; (2) analyzing the antecedents and consequences of the internationalization strategy of emerging market MNEs; (3) developing a dynamic theory on international strategy; and (4) exploring the impact of the global financial crisis on international investment strategy and performance.

REAL OPTIONS AND REAL OPTIONS THEORY

Companies make capital investments in order to create and take advantage of profitable opportunities. These opportunities are real options – rights but not obligations to take some action in the future (Dixit and Pindyck, 1994; Trigeorgis, 1996). In this sense, real options are akin to financial options (Myers, 1977). A simple financial option gives its holder the right, but not the obligation, to buy or sell a specified quantity of an underlying asset at a specified price (i.e. the strike or exercise price) at or before a specified date (i.e. the maturity or expiration date). By analogy, a real option confers on the firm the right, but not the obligation, to take some action in the future. The option is 'real' because the underlying assets are usually physical and human assets rather than financial securities. Real options create economic value by generating future decision rights (McGrath et al., 2004), or more specifically, by offering management the flexibility to act upon new information such that the upside economic potential is retained while the downside losses are contained (Trigeorgis, 1996). International joint ventures (IJVs) are often viewed as real options; by establishing joint ventures with local partners, MNEs obtain the flexibility to act on new information in the environment: they can exploit upside potentials by acquiring additional equity stakes from local partners or limit downside losses by selling their equity to local partners or dissolving the venture (Chi and McGuire, 1996; Cuypers and Martin, 2010; Li and Li, 2010; Tong et al., 2008).

Since the seminal works of nearly three decades ago (Kester, 1984; Myers, 1977; Myers, 1984), real options theory has generated an increasing impact in the fields of management and international business (see Li et al., 2007 for a review in strategy and Li, 2007 for a review in IB). In the last two decades, real options theory has emerged as a major theoretical tool (Mahoney, 2005) to analyze (1) investment and divestment decisions, (2) investment mode choices, and (3) the organizational performance implications of creating and exercising real options.

Real options theory is a theory of investment under uncertainty (Dixit and Pindyck, 1994). It suggests that in a world of uncertainty, when investments are typically irreversible (i.e. the investments, once made, cannot be fully recovered or costlessly redeployed to other uses), the option to defer investing can be more economically valuable than immediate investment or delayed commitment because this option allows management the flexibility to invest when market conditions turn favorable but to back out if market conditions are adverse. Existing theoretical research and empirical analysis have shown that firms are better off delaying initial or subsequent investments under conditions of uncertainty and irreversibility (Dixit and Pindyck, 1994, 2000; Folta et al., 2006; Folta and Miller, 2002; Guiso and Parigi, 1999; Li, 2008), but competition and growth opportunities will probably reduce the value of holding the option to defer investing (Folta and O'Brien, 2004; Grenadier, 2000; Kulatilaka and Perotti, 1998; Li and Mahoney, 2011; Smit and Trigeorgis, 2004). The level of uncertainty and investment irreversibility increase the value of managerial flexibility embedded in an investment and thus the option value of the investment. When the market becomes competitive, or the option exercising right is not proprietary (i.e. many MNEs possess similar options), however, the option value of an investment is reduced (Rivoli and Salorio, 1996).

Real investments are often made not only for cash flows from the project but (perhaps primarily) for the economic benefits derived from subsequent investment opportunities.

Such future discretionary investment opportunities are growth options (Kester, 1984; Pindyck, 1988; Trigeorgis, 1988). For example, firms usually make foothold investments in a new foreign market for the possibility of expansion in the future (Chang, 1995; Kogut, 1983). Such growth-oriented investment may appear uneconomical when viewed in isolation but may enable firms to capture potential growth opportunities in the future (McGrath, 1997; McGrath et al., 2004).

In addition to the deferral and growth options, firms can abandon an investment project or switch inputs or outputs if market conditions turn out to be worse than expected. For example, when MNEs establish operations in multiple countries and build a multinational network, MNEs have the flexibility to defer investing in another country, expand or contract existing businesses, or switch production and distribution within the network (Kogut, 1983; Kogut and Kulatilaka, 1994). These decisions are contingent on how uncertainty is resolved in the institutional and economic environment of different countries comprising the network. Real options theory suggests that while availability and recognition of these abandonment and switch options will increase firms' propensity to invest (Dixit and Pindyck, 1995), particularly in the case of multistage projects (Chi and Nystrom, 1995), high uncertainty and irreversibility will discourage firms from abandoning or switching immediately (Kogut and Kulatilaka, 2001; Vassolo et al., 2004).

Real options theory has also offered insights into how investment activities should be organized or governed. Common investment modes and governance structures include collaboration (e.g. alliances and joint ventures), internalization (e.g. via acquisition), and market (spot) transaction, among others. Real options analysis emphasizes the strategic flexibility and learning advantages of collaborative ventures *vis-à-vis* acquisition or internal development under conditions of uncertainty (Chi and McGuire, 1996; Folta, 1998). Furthermore, real options theory has strategic implications for the governance choice between integration and market contracting. Under uncertainty, market mechanisms may incur greater short-term marginal production costs than integration, but may provide greater strategic flexibility whose value increases with uncertainty (Leiblein, 2003).

Real options theory is fundamentally a theory of economic valuation. It recognizes the strategic value of managerial flexibility to take alternative courses of action over time, including delaying investment, investing sequentially for growth options and abandoning/switching. The value of these discretionary opportunities or options can be substantial as compared with the value of assets in place (Kester, 1984; Myers, 1977; Pindyck, 1988). Trigeorgis (1996) proposed an expanded net present value (NPV) framework in which the economic value of an investment consists of not only direct static NPV and strategic commitment value, but also flexibility/options value. Most studies in this stream of research have focused on whether and how organizations can benefit from creation and exercise of real options embedded in projects, businesses and firms, and of corporate growth options in particular (Bowman and Hurry, 1993; Kumar, 2005; Tong et al., 2008).

Creating, managing and exercising real options can be a challenging task for firms (Adner and Levinthal, 2004; Bowman and Moskowitz, 2001). Option exercise cost can significantly reduce the option value of an investment. Furthermore, real options are often not included as a clause in formal contracts (Reuer and Tong, 2005), and thus option holders may not realize potential benefits from exercising the options due to the high exercise costs. For example, bargaining costs and the negotiation of an acquisition price between IJV partners *ex post* might diminish any value from exercising the growth option in the IJV (Chi and McGuire, 1996).

REAL OPTIONS THEORY AND INTERNATIONAL STRATEGY

Real options theory contributes to international strategy research due to its unique views of uncertainty and the means it suggests to deal with uncertainty in international business. Traditional theories in international business, such as internalization theory (Buckley and Casson, 1976; Rugman, 1981) and the OLI (ownership–location–internalization) model (Dunning, 1980), have not fully addressed the effect of uncertainty on decision-making by MNEs. For example, internalization theory, based on transaction cost economics, suggests that the imperfections of intermediate product markets motivate MNEs to internalize the knowledge market by building wholly owned subsidiaries (WOSs) in foreign markets. However, by committing large, irreversible investments to WOSs, MNEs lose flexibility to adjust their decisions and may suffer substantial losses when the future turns out to be unfavorable. Therefore the conditions of uncertainty and irreversibility should be carefully considered in market entry decisions by MNEs. Applications of transaction cost economics to international investments typically view uncertainty as a source of transaction costs and propose to use control mechanisms to minimize transaction costs (e.g. Anderson and Gatignon, 1986). These applications have yet to consider how MNEs can actually benefit from uncertainty. Real options theory contributes to IB by introducing a new way of thinking; that is, uncertainty implies risks as well as opportunities, and MNEs can benefit from uncertainty by creating real options and obtaining flexibility to adjust decisions when new information arrives (Buckley and Casson, 1998; Rivoli and Salorio, 1996).

Real options theory has offered insights into three research areas fundamental to IB research and practice: when to invest; what entry mode to use; and why and how to build a multinational network (Buckley and Casson, 1998; Kogut, 1983). Table 18.1 summarizes the existing applications of real options theory to international strategy. We briefly review each topic in turn.

The first stream of studies examines the optimal entry timing of MNEs, that is, the timing of initiating or increasing an investment in a foreign market (Rivoli and Salorio, 1996; Dixit, 1989; Campa, 1993). This set of studies conceptualizes that an MNE has the option to wait for more relevant information before deciding when to enter a market and how much to invest. The MNE will be better off holding open the option to defer under several conditions: the host country market is uncertain; the investment is irreversible, and the MNE is likely to maintain its ownership advantages over a long period of time. For example, Campa (1993) found that exchange rate volatility negatively influences the number of foreign entries in the US market, and that higher sunk costs indicating higher level of irreversibility strengthens the exchange rate volatility–foreign entry relationship. On the other hand, when the market becomes competitive and the option-exercising right is not proprietary (e.g. many MNEs have similar options to enter the market), competitors may act first and the MNE is inclined to exercise the option rather than delay it, in order to gain first-mover advantages and valuable growth options.

Table 18.1 Literature review on applications of real options theory to international strategy

Research subjects	Articles	Method	Main arguments/findings
Market entry timing/rate	Rivoli and Salorio (1996)	Conceptual	Investment deferment provides an MNE with an opportunity to wait for more relevant information to make wise investment decisions. This delay option is more valuable if the MNE tends to maintain its ownership advantages over a long period, and if the investment is difficult to reverse
	Dixit (1989)	Modeling	A risk-neutral firm will delay entering the market and keep the delay option for one more period as long as the expected change in the value of the option is higher than the expected return from entering the market for one period
	Gulamhussen (2009)	Modeling	Switching from deferring FDI to partial FDI is faster when banks can gather information only through a presence in the foreign market. Switching to partial FDI does not occur when full FDI enables more efficient production
	Campa (1993)	Empirical	Exchange rate volatility in the host country is negatively correlated with the number of foreign investments. This negative effect is most pronounced for industries where investment is highly irreversible
	Fisch (2008)	Empirical	Through constant learning after entry, MNEs perceive diminishing levels of uncertainty and shift their reason for investment from option values towards net present values
Market entry modes	Buckley and Casson (1998)	Conceptual	An IJV provides a better combination of characteristics than other entry modes when both the option to grow and the option to abandon are important
	Chi and McGuire (1996)	Modeling	The real options value of a joint venture depends on how partners forecast the expected value of the IJV; the option value is higher when partners have divergent expectations of the value of the joint assets
	Chi and Seth (2009)	Modeling	Factors that affect choice of mode for an MNE and a local firm include the parties' absorptive capacities, frictions in knowledge and asset markets, cost of switching from one mode to another, and cost associated with power jockeying
	Li and Rugman (2007)	Modeling	Choice of entry mode depends on both the magnitude (high vs low) and the type (exogenous vs endogenous) of uncertainty. High-commitment entry modes are preferred when uncertainty is high and endogenous
	Cuypers and Martin (2010)	Empirical	There are two forms of uncertainty: endogenous and exogenous. Only exogenous uncertainty has the impact predicted by real options theory on a foreign investor's choice of the amount of equity share to take in an IJV

	Jiang et al. (2009)	Empirical	Shorter duration of a technology licensing agreement provides more flexibility for firms to decide the next move. Market uncertainty and competitive threats in the host market are related to shorter duration of the licensing agreements
	Kouvelis et al. (2001)	Empirical	A strongly depreciated home currency encourages the use of export, whereas a strongly appreciated home currency encourages the use of IJVs or WOSs. However, the high costs of switching between different strategies forces a period of inaction during which the MNE continues to use its current mode
	Li and Li (2010)	Empirical	Under high uncertainty, MNEs choose more flexible ownership strategies that allow adjustment of investment decisions in future. Using flexible strategies becomes less valuable for MNEs when the industry they enter in the host country enjoys strong sales growth potential or has intense competition
	Reuer and Tong (2005)	Empirical	MNEs are likely to use explicit call options in IJVs with core businesses because they otherwise risk losing proprietary knowledge during the course of the collaboration
	Tong et al. (2008)	Empirical	IJVs enhance firms' growth option values, but only under certain circumstances; minority IJVs provide a higher growth option value than majority IJVs, and non-core IJVs provide a higher option value than IJVs in core businesses
	Xu et al. (2010)	Empirical	Sequential acquisitions are a real-option-based strategy, whereby the acquirer gathers information and resolves uncertainty through making toehold investments
Multinationality/ operational flexibility	Buckley and Casson (1998)	Conceptual	Choice of location in a multinational network should be strategic in order to enhance an MNE's operational flexibility (e.g. MNEs can choose a regional production and distribution hub, serving several neighboring countries)
	Kogut (1983)	Conceptual	The evaluation of a multinational network should include the value of holding the options to switch production, distribution and profits within the network
	Dasu and Li (1997)	Modeling	An MNE alters production quantities in different locations, taking advantage of the relative costs of production among the plants that result from differences in exchange rates and tariffs
	de Meza and van der Ploeg (1987)	Modeling	Producing in various locations benefits MNEs by generating opportunities for them to manufacture in places with lowest costs
	Huchzermeier and Cohen (1996)	Modeling	An MNE can alter product design and supply chain network design so as to mitigate the risks related to exchange rate volatility

Table 18.1 (continued)

Research subjects	Articles	Method	Main arguments/findings
Multinationality/ operational flexibility (cont.)	Kogut and Kulatilaka (1994)	Modeling	The value of a multinational network lies in the opportunity to benefit from uncertainty through coordination of geographically dispersed subsidiaries. Having the option to move production to a location with lower input prices helps the MNE to ensure against detrimental movements of the exchange rate
	Allen and Pantzalis (1996)	Empirical	Returns to multinationality increase when firms have greater breadth and less depth in their multinational networks
	Belderbos and Zou (2007)	Empirical	MNEs adjust affiliate employment in response to labor cost changes in other countries where they have subsidiaries. IJVs are less flexible than WOSs in response to changing environmental conditions in the focal country
	Belderbos and Zou (2009)	Empirical	MNEs are less likely to divest affiliates under conditions of unfavorable environmental changes if those affiliates provide valuable growth or switching options in response to economic uncertainty. An affiliate is less valuable if it shares with other affiliates the manufacturing platform role in the host country, or if economic conditions of the host country are highly correlated with those of other countries in which the MNE has affiliates
	Campa (1994)	Empirical	Exchange rate uncertainty has negative effects on capacity expansions of domestic firms, whereas the uncertainty has no effect on the probability of entry investments by MNEs. MNEs are better able to manage exchange rate uncertainty by shifting their production among different countries
	Chung et al. (2010)	Empirical	Two real options (within-country growth and across-country operational flexibility) can affect subsidiary performance during times of economic crises. Subsidiaries with cross-country orientations benefit from economic crises whereas those with within-country orientations suffer from the crises
	Lee and Makhija (2009a)	Empirical	FDI and export-related international investments provide valuable flexibility for firms during economic crisis. Such flexibility allows firms to adjust their operations in response to unforeseen negative environmental changes

Source	Type	Findings
Lee and Makhija (2009b)	Empirical	A multinational network characterized by greater breadth and less depth is associated with higher firm value under domestic economic uncertainty. A multinational network provides valuable real options that allow firms to better deal with domestic economic uncertainty
Miller and Reuer (1998a)	Empirical	FDI reduces MNEs' economic exposure to foreign exchange rate risks, whereas export has no such impact
Miller and Reuer (1998b)	Empirical	The economic exposure is asymmetric between the periods of currency appreciation and depreciation, suggesting that firms do possess real options for managing foreign exchange exposures
Pantzalis (2001)	Empirical	The average market value of MNEs whose network of subsidiaries does not include operations in developing regions is substantially lower than that of MNEs with operations in developing areas
Rangan (1998)	Empirical	MNEs systematically exploit currency shifts by selecting inputs from countries with favorable exchange rates for the production process
Reuer and Leiblein (2000)	Empirical	Inconsistent with the predictions by real options theory, firms' investments in dispersed FDI and IJVs do not have a negative impact on organizational downside risk
Tang and Tikoo (1999)	Empirical	The securities markets respond more to earnings changes of MNEs that have greater depth and less depth in their multinational networks
Tong and Reuer (2007)	Empirical	A curvilinear relationship exists between multinationality and downside risks of MNEs, suggesting that MNEs benefit from the switching options among dispersed subsidiaries while suffering from coordination costs needed to realize the options.

Notes: FDI: foreign direct investment; MNE: multinational enterprise; IJV: international joint venture; WOS: wholly owned subsidiary.

The second stream of studies analyzes different market entry modes and IJVs in particular. From a real options perspective, an IJV provides a firm with the option to exploit upside potential by acquiring the partner's equity in favorable conditions, and the option to avoid downside losses by selling the equity to its partner or dissolving the IJV in unfavorable conditions (Buckley and Casson, 1998; Cuypers and Martin, 2010; Kouvelis et al., 2001; Li and Li, 2010). Kogut (1991) found that while unexpected growth in the product market increases the likelihood of exercising the option to acquire joint ventures, unexpected shortfalls in product shipments have no effect on the likelihood of dissolution. This asymmetry in the results strongly supports the interpretation of joint ventures as real options to expand. Li and Li (2010) observed that, under high market uncertainty, MNEs tend to choose IJVs over WOSs in their investments in China during 2000–06. Furthermore, Chi and McGuire (1996) built a real options model to suggest that the options value of an IJV depends on how partners forecast the future value of the IJV – the option value is higher when partners have divergent expectations. Intuitively, the partner with a higher expected valuation is willing to pay a higher price than the other partner to acquire the IJV, which will result in a mutually beneficial trade in their stakes. These research studies on IJVs suggest that valuation of a market entry mode should include not only the net present value of future profits this entry mode can bring about, but also its option value – the value of switching to other entry modes in response to new information.

Real options theory has contributed substantially to the literature on market entry mode choice. The transaction cost economics perspective suggests that entry mode choice is determined by the need for control to minimize transaction costs arising from asset specificity and potential partner opportunism (Anderson and Gatignon, 1986). The institutional perspective, on the other hand, emphasizes that choice of entry mode is shaped by the institutional environment and proposes that MNEs may exchange ownership for legitimacy in the host country (Chan and Makino, 2007). Complementing the two perspectives, real options theory suggests that in addition to control and legitimacy, the entry mode decision is also fundamentally concerned with the trade-off between flexibility and commitment; under highly volatile market conditions in a host country, MNEs may prefer a flexible strategy such as IJVs over a committed strategy such as WOSs (Buckley and Casson, 1998; Li and Li, 2010).

The third stream of studies explores the relationship among multinationality, operational flexibility and performance. Real options theory suggests that a multinational network of subsidiaries can enhance an MNE's operational flexibility to respond to environmental changes (Kogut, 1983; Buckley and Casson, 1998; Kogut and Kulatilaka, 1994). Specifically, a multinational network provides an MNE with the option to switch sourcing, production or distribution within the network when the environment changes (Kogut and Kulatilaka, 1994). With such operational flexibility, the MNE can presumably better exploit upside economic potential while containing downside economic losses. Empirical studies found that MNEs indeed exercise the option to switch in response to environmental changes (Belderbos and Zou, 2007, 2009; Campa, 1994; Rangan, 1998). For instance, using the employment growth information of Japanese electronics manufacturing affiliates, Belderbos and Zou (2007) found that affiliate employment in one country grows faster if labor cost increases in other countries where the parent firm has operations, indicating that MNEs shift activities across countries in response to international cost changes.

Real options studies have also examined the performance implications of multinationality. In particular, the structure of a multinational network has been found to affect the benefits that MNEs can derive from multinationality (e.g. Lee and Makhija, 2009a, 2009b; Allen and Pantzalis, 1996). Lee and Makhija (2009b) examined the influence of domestic economic uncertainty on the real option value of international investments by Korean firms over 16 years of uncertainty and found that a firm has higher value when its international network is characterized by greater breadth (i.e. having subsidiaries in more countries) and less depth (i.e. having few subsidiaries in a particular country relative to total subsidiaries). This result is consistent with the findings in Allen and Pantzalis (1996). These results suggest that returns to multinationality increase as firms expand their holdings of real options by widening the breadth of their transnational network but decrease with the acquisition of redundant real options by increasing the subsidiaries in each country because of increased agency costs.

FUTURE RESEARCH DIRECTIONS

Real options theory offers a compelling framework to analyze irreversible international investments under uncertainty and their economic performance implications. In this section, we discuss four areas that are important to further advance real options research on international investment strategies.

Market Uncertainty, Institutional Uncertainty and International Strategy

Real options research has so far focused on how MNEs tackle market uncertainty, which can usually be attributed to unstable industry structures, unpredictable consumer tastes and evolving technological standards. Given such market uncertainty, MNEs can create real options (e.g. IJVs) and later decide whether to exercise or abandon these options according to the resolution of uncertainty. This real options logic has found some supportive evidence in the business world. For example, Coca-Cola built bottling IJVs when it first entered China, and as the local market grew and uncertainty was resolved favorably, it acquired these IJVs and achieved full ownership (www.coca-cola.com.cn). In contrast, Whirlpool exited its IJV in China when market competition in China's home appliance industry became too intense to maintain profitability (Tong and Li, 2008).

Institutional uncertainty is another important feature of international investments, in addition to market uncertainty (Henisz, 2000). Institutions are the rules of the game, and different nations tend to have different institutional environments (North, 1990). Institutional uncertainty arises when MNEs invest in a host country that has different and changing political systems, laws and regulatory policies. MNEs need to behold such institutional differences and adapt their investment strategies accordingly.

Future real options research can have an integrated analysis of the effects of market and institutional uncertainties on MNE investment strategy and performance. It is reasonable to expect that MNEs will be even more eager to create real options and obtain flexibility when the host country has both high market and institutional uncertainties. A case in point is FDI in the financial industry in China. Despite the enormous growth potential, the Chinese financial market entails substantial market uncertainty.

Furthermore, there is significant policy uncertainty; for example, the Chinese government has ownership restrictions on foreign banks operating in China, and such restrictions may change unpredictably over time. In response to the dual uncertainties, Western banks such as Bank of America, Goldman Sachs and HSBC all decided to take strategic stakes (up to 20 percent) in China's domestic banks through partial acquisition (Economist Intelligence Unit, 2007). Such strategic actions enable the banks to take advantage of future growth opportunities and to contain downside losses contingent on new information regarding market and/or institutional uncertainty. We expect that the more types of uncertainties surrounding an investment that provides future flexibility, the higher the option value of the investment. We also expect that when institutional uncertainty decreases, MNEs may adopt more committed strategies despite high market uncertainty. For example, since China lifted foreign ownership restrictions in many industries after joining the World Trade Organization in 2001, MNEs have been active in exercising their growth options in IJVs or partial acquisitions by buying out their partners' stakes (Tong and Li, 2008). We believe that the interaction of market and institutional uncertainties warrants more theoretical analysis. Further, large-sample empirical analysis, as well as field and case studies, can also advance real options research on international investment strategy by incorporating both market and institutional uncertainties.

Growth Options and Emerging Market MNEs

One critical new development in IB is the rapid internationalization of emerging market firms over the last decade. Traditional IB theories are developed largely based on the experience of MNEs in developed markets. As a result, some investment behaviors of emerging market MNEs seem puzzling and inexplicable to traditional IB theories. First, despite their limited international experiences and weak ownership advantages, emerging market MNEs are aggressively investing in developed markets (Luo and Tung, 2007). Second, emerging market MNEs, especially those from China, are actively investing in high political risk countries such as those in Middle East and Africa (Buckley et al., 2007).

Real options theory can shed some light on emerging market MNEs' entry into developed markets. As latecomers to the world economic stage, MNEs from emerging markets typically lag behind Western MNEs in technological and innovative capabilities and brand equity. Entry into developed markets can be viewed as creating valuable growth options for emerging market MNEs. For example, by acquiring targets in developed markets, emerging market MNEs obtain the options to build their brand equity, upgrade their technological capabilities and explore developed markets. Essentially, emerging market MNEs use entry into developed markets as a way to compensate for their weak ownership advantages and to compete with Western MNEs. From a real options perspective, whether emerging market MNEs can succeed in this endeavor depends, among other things, on whether option exercise costs exceed the expected benefits. In particular, the value of growth options will be significantly discounted if emerging market MNEs lack the capability to combine their knowledge with the knowledge in the acquired companies so as to generate synergy (Bowman and Hurry, 1993).

Real options theory also has useful implications for a puzzle such as the propensity of Chinese MNEs to invest in high political risk countries. Chinese MNEs are attracted to such destinations for underexplored growth opportunities. Whether Chinese MNEs can gain from such growth options depends on both the exclusiveness of the options and the MNEs' capabilities. First of all, the value of growth options in a host country is amplified when competition from developed country MNEs is limited. Real options theory suggests that the more exclusive an owner's right to exercise a growth option, the more valuable the option is to the owner. Competition can considerably reduce the exclusiveness of a firm's right to exercise a growth option and thus reduce the value of the growth option to the firm (Kester, 1984; Rivoli and Salorio, 1996; Trigeorgis, 1988). In countries already with intense competition from developed country FDI, growth options become less attractive for emerging market MNEs because such options are shared and collective opportunities. Moreover, when environmental uncertainty resolves favorably, Chinese MNEs, due to weak ownership advantages, are less capable of pursuing growth opportunities than developed country MNEs, which further reduces the value of growth options in destinations with many developed country MNEs. We therefore expect that when entering high political risk countries with a lower level of competition, the growth options become more valuable for emerging market MNEs than when they enter low political risk countries with a higher level of competition.

Future studies can conduct empirical analysis to test these real options predictions and advance IB research on emerging market MNEs. First, future studies can evaluate the growth option value provided by acquisition of firms in developed markets. Such acquisitions provide valuable growth opportunities but also present formidable challenges in post-acquisition integration. Whether such acquisitions actually enhance firm value requires more systematic investigation. Second, one can examine the respective and joint effect of competition and political risk on the location choice of emerging market MNEs. A place with high political risk but low competition may be more attractive to emerging market MNEs than a place with low political risk but high competition. Competition from developed country FDI may even have a stronger effect on the location choice of emerging market MNEs than the level of political risk.

Sequential Market Entry Strategies

MNEs adjust their investment strategies over time. One of the few IB theories to take a dynamic approach towards international investment strategy is the stages model of internationalization. This Uppsala model proposes that firms need to learn about foreign environments, so they gradually increase commitments to foreign markets; firms often begin by exporting to a foreign market, then set up a selling or distribution subsidiary, and finally form a production subsidiary such as an IJV or a WOS (Johanson and Vahlne, 1977; Sullivan and Bauerschmidt, 1990). However, exceptions to the predicted staged path of expansion are abundant, thereby reducing the stages model's empirical validity and generality (Benito and Gripsrud, 1992; Fina and Rugman, 1996).

Real options theory makes unique contributions concerning the dynamics of international investment strategy since the theory is inherently concerned with how firms adjust their investment decisions based on updated information over time (Bowman and Hurry, 1993; Trigeorgis, 1996). Specifically, real options theory (1) specifies the conditions under which firms incrementally increase their commitment to a foreign market, as suggested by the stages model, and (2) predicts when firms will deviate from the incremental internationalization process, thus prescribing the boundary conditions for the stages model.

Real options theory offers a sound economic explanation for incremental internation-alization. A sequential investment process provides MNEs with a series of options: upon the initial investment, MNEs have the option to invest subsequently (i.e. the option to grow) in good times and the option to abandon or defer the subsequent investment in bad times. By starting with low-commitment market entries through toehold investments, MNEs obtain learning opportunities to accumulate experience and reduce uncertainty about culture, market demand and the local business environment. Learning facilitates a more reliable prediction of the efficacy of MNEs' firm-specific advantages in local markets (Buckley et al., 2002) and helps MNEs to recognize market opportunities.

Real options theory further contributes to a dynamic theory of international invest-ment by suggesting when MNEs will switch from low-commitment to high-commitment entry strategies. MNEs can evaluate two options in determining sequential market entry strategies: the option to defer, and the option to grow. Real options theory predicts that MNEs will likely switch to high-commitment entry strategies when the growth option is more valuable than the deferral option, but will not switch otherwise. The value of the deferral and growth options depends, among other things, on uncertainty, investment irreversibility and competition.

When uncertainty is resolved favorably, the growth option becomes more valuable, and MNEs will probably increase resource commitment to local markets. On the other hand, when uncertainty remains high or unfolds unfavorably, the option to defer is more valuable, and MNEs will not increase market commitment.

Furthermore, when facing both high uncertainty and high investment irreversibility, MNEs will hesitate even more before switching to high-commitment entry strategies. In industries that require highly irreversible investments, high commitment will substan-tially limit managerial flexibility in dealing with uncertainty and may expose MNEs to significant losses if they decide to contract the investment project or withdraw from the market in the future.

Finally, competition can also impact international investment strategy under uncer-tainty. In industries with significant strategic advantages, MNEs may switch rapidly to high-commitment entry strategies despite a high level of uncertainty, because in such industries MNEs may obtain valuable growth opportunities ahead of competitors. Based on a game-theoretic model, Kulatilaka and Perotti (1998) found that by investing aggres-sively under high uncertainty, a firm may be able to pre-empt potential entries or force existing competitors to 'make room' for its entry. If this strategic effect is substantial, the growth option embedded in the investment will probably become more valuable than the deferral option, even when uncertainty is high. A case in point is Volkswagen's entry into China in the early 1980s despite high policy and economic uncertainty in China. Volkswagen's decision can be partially justified by its desire to obtain valuable growth options ahead of competitors. The fact that Volkswagen has enjoyed lucrative profits for a long time in the Chinese market indicates the significant value of strategic growth options.

In summary, the timing and pattern of internationalization depends on the trade-off between the option to defer and the option to grow. By switching the market entry mode or scale from low commitment to high commitment, firms lose the option to defer but gain the option to grow. When uncertainty remains highly unresolved and investment is highly irreversible, the option to defer becomes relatively more valuable, and MNEs may take an incremental approach towards internationalization; when uncertainty resolves favorably or when pre-emption benefits are high, MNEs may speed up the internationalization process despite high uncertainty. Such a dynamic internationalization process remains the most fertile ground for future real options research.

Global Financial Crisis, International Investment Strategy and Performance

The global financial crisis in the late 2000s provides an opportunity to research how unexpected, disruptive events affect international investment strategy and performance. A financial crisis in a market usually causes unpredictable shifts in the level of demand and in the relative costs of inputs, pushing firms to adjust or reconfigure their value chains in response to threats to profitability (Kogut, 1991). During economic crisis, firms that have international investments or export-related businesses tend to perform better than firms that focus on domestic markets only (Lee and Makhija, 2009a). Future studies can extend this line of research in several respects. First, future research can examine how the structure of a multinational network affects MNEs' performance during the global financial crisis. We expect that firms that have international investments in countries with low correlations in economic conditions tend to perform better than those that focus on international investments in countries with high economic correlations (Rugman, 2011). MNEs in the former case have greater flexibility in responding to the financial crisis because they can move production or sales from more deeply affected countries to less affected ones. In addition, we can examine how the organizational structure of an MNE affects its operational flexibility in dealing with environmental uncertainty. An MNE with a transnational structure (rather than a structure that has polycentric strategic orientation) is more capable of coordinating production or sales activities across countries and can thus better take advantage of a multinational network to deal with the financial crisis.

Future studies can further analyze how firms respond to a financial crisis by adjusting their international investment portfolios. Firms are likely to divest subsidiaries in countries that are deeply affected by a financial crisis, especially when these subsidiaries are redundant and have low option values (e.g. there are a few similar subsidiaries in the same host country) (Belderbos and Zou, 2009). On the other hand, firms will probably expand businesses in countries that are less affected by the financial crisis in order to take advantage of the growth opportunities. However, one would also expect a period of inaction during which MNEs continue to use their current strategies if there are high costs of switching between different strategies (Kouvelis et al., 2001). We also expect that the speed of divestiture is greater for subsidiaries in the form of IJVs than those in the form of WOSs because IJV partners provide a ready market for divestiture, whereas the speed of expansion is probably greater for WOSs than for IJVs because of faster decision-making in WOSs.

CONCLUSIONS

An emerging area of research in international strategic management is the application of real options theory to analyze international investment under uncertainty by MNEs. In this chapter, we reviewed recent developments in real options research on international investment strategy. Our review shows that, like extant IB theories such as internalization theory, the OLI model and the stages model, real options theory has offered substantial insights into topics of central concern to IB research and practice such as investment timing, market entry mode and multinationality. We also identified several promising areas for future research regarding application of real options in analysis of the joint effects of institutional and market uncertainty and international strategies in response to the global financial crisis. In particular, we believe that real options theory can make substantial and unique contributions to understanding international strategies by emerging market MNEs and in building a dynamic theory of international strategy. We call for future research that we hope can enhance the impact of real options as a dominant conceptual lens in international business.

REFERENCES

Adner, R. and D.A. Levinthal (2004), 'What is not a real option: considering boundaries for the application of real options to business strategy', *Academy of Management Review*, **29**(1), 74–85.

Allen, L. and C. Pantzalis (1996), 'Valuation of the operating flexibility of multinational operations', *Journal of International Business Studies*, **27**(4), 633–53.

Anderson, E. and H. Gatignon (1986), 'Models of foreign entry: a transaction cost analysis and propositions', *Journal of International Business Studies*, **17**(3), 1–26.

Belderbos, R. and J. Zou (2007), 'On the growth of foreign affiliates: multinational plant networks, joint ventures, and flexibility', *Journal of International Business Studies*, **38**(7), 1095–112.

Belderbos, R. and J. Zou (2009), 'Real options and foreign affiliate divestments: a portfolio perspective', *Journal of International Business Studies*, **40**(4), 600–620.

Benito, G.R.G. and G. Gripsrud (1992), 'The expansion of foreign direct investment: discrete rational location choices or a cultural learning process', *Journal of International Business Studies*, **23**(2), 461–76.

Bowman, E.H. and D. Hurry (1993), 'Strategy through the option lens: an integrated view of resource investments and the incremental-choice process', *Academy of Management Review*, **18**(4), 760–82.

Bowman, E.H. and G.T. Moskowitz (2001), 'Real options analysis and strategic decision making', *Organization Science*, **12**(6), 772–7.

Buckley, J.P. and M. Casson (1976), *The Future of the Multinational Enterprise*, New York: Holmes & Meier.

Buckley, J.P. and M. Casson (1998), 'Models of multinational enterprise', *Journal of International Business Studies*, **29**(1), 21–44.

Buckley, J.P., M. Casson and M.A. Gulamhussen (2002), 'Internationalisation: real options, knowledge management and the Uppsala approach', in V. Havila, M. Forsgren and H. Håkansson (eds), *Critical Perspectives on Internationalisation*, Amsterdam, Netherlands: Elsevier Science, pp. 229–61.

Buckley, P.J., L.J. Clegg, A.R. Cross, X. Liu, H. Voss and P. Zheng (2007), 'The determinants of Chinese outward foreign direct investment', *Journal of International Business Studies*, **38**(4), 499–518.

Campa, J.M. (1993), 'Entry by foreign firms in the United States under exchange rate uncertainty', *Review of Economics & Statistics*, **75**(4), 614–22.

Campa, J.M. (1994), 'Multinational investment under uncertainty in the chemical processing industries', *Journal of International Business Studies*, **25**(3), 557–78.

Chan, C.M. and S. Makino (2007), 'Legitimacy and multi-level institutional environments: implications for foreign subsidiary ownership structure', *Journal of International Business Studies*, **38**(4), 621–38.

Chang, S.J. (1995), 'International expansion strategy of Japanese firms: capability building through sequential entry', *Academy of Management Journal*, **38**(2), 383–407.

Chi, T. and D.J. McGuire (1996), 'Collaborative ventures and value of learning: integrating the transaction cost and strategic option perspectives on the choice of market entry modes', *Journal of International Business Studies*, **27**(2), 285–307.

Chi, T. and P.C. Nystrom (1995), 'Decision dilemmas facing managers – recognizing the value of learning while making sequential decisions', *Omega International Journal of Management Science*, **23**(3), 303–12.

Chi, T. and A. Seth (2009), 'A dynamic model of the choice of mode for exploiting complementary capabilities', *Journal of International Business Studies*, **40**(3), 365–87.

Chung, C.C., S.-H. Lee, P.W. Beamish and T. Isobe (2010), 'Subsidiary expansion/contraction during times of economic crisis', *Journal of International Business Studies*, **41**(3), 500–516.

Cuypers, I.R.P. and X. Martin (2010), 'What makes and what does not make a real option? A study of equity shares in international joint ventures', *Journal of International Business Studies*, **41**(1), 47–69.

Dasu, S. and L. Li (1997), 'Optimal operating policies in the presence of exchange rate variability', *Management Science*, **43**(5), 705–22.

de Meza, D. and F. van der Ploeg (1987), 'Production flexibility as a motive for multinationality', *Journal of Industrial Economics*, **35**(3), 343–51.

Dixit, A.K. (1989), 'Entry and exit decisions under uncertainty', *Journal of Political Economy*, **97**(3), 620–38.

Dixit, A.K. and R.S. Pindyck (1994), *Investment Under Uncertainty*, Princeton, NJ: Princeton University Press.

Dixit, A.K. and R.S. Pindyck (1995), 'The options approach to capital investment', *Harvard Business Review*, **73**(3), 105–15.

Dixit, A.K. and R.S. Pindyck (2000), 'Expandability, reversibility, and optimal capacity choice', in M.J. Brennan and L.G. Trigeorgis (eds), *Project Flexibility, Agency, and Competition: New Developments in the Theory and Application of Real Options*, New York: Oxford University Press, pp. 50–70.

Dunning, J.H. (1980), 'Toward an eclectic theory of international production: some empirical tests', *Journal of International Business Studies*, **11**(1), 9–31.

Economist Intelligence Unit (2007), *EIU Country Profile 2007*, London: EIU.

Fina, E. and A.M. Rugman (1996), 'A test of internalization theory and internationalization theory: the Upjohn company', *Management International Review*, **36**(3), 199–213.

Fisch, J.H. (2008), 'Investment in new foreign subsidiaries under receding perception of uncertainty', *Journal of International Business Studies*, **39**(3), 370–86.

Folta, T.B. (1998), 'Governance and uncertainty: the trade-off between administrative control and commitment', *Strategic Management Journal*, **19**(11), 1007–28.

Folta, T.B. and K.D. Miller (2002), 'Real options in equity partnerships', *Strategic Management Journal*, **23**(1), 77–88.

Folta, T.B. and J.P. O'Brien (2004), 'Entry in the presence of dueling options', *Strategic Management Journal*, **25**(2), 121–38.

Folta, T.B., D.R. Johnson and J. O'Brien (2006), 'Uncertainty, irreversibility, and the likelihood of entry: an empirical assessment of the option to defer', *Journal of Economic Behavior & Organization*, **61**(3), 432–52.

Grenadier, S.R. (2000), *Game Choices: The Interaction of Real Options and Game Theory*, London: Risk Books.

Guiso, L. and G. Parigi (1999), 'Investment and demand uncertainty', *Quarterly Journal of Economics*, **114**(1), 185–227.

Gulamhussen, M.A. (2009), 'A theoretical perspective on the location of banking FDI', *Management International Review*, **49**(2), 163–78.

Henisz, W.J. (2000), 'The institutional environment for multinational investment', *Journal of Law, Economics, and Organization*, **16**(2), 334–64.

Huchzermeier, A. and M.A. Cohen (1996), 'Valuing operational flexibility under exchange rate risk', *Operations Research*, **44**(1), 100–113.

Jiang, M.S., P.S. Aulakh and Y. Pan (2009), 'Licensing duration in foreign markets: a real options perspective', *Journal of International Business Studies*, **40**(4), 559–77.

Johanson, J. and J. Vahlne (1977), 'The internationalization process of the firm: a model of knowledge development and increasing foreign commitments', *Journal of International Business Studies*, **8**(1), 23–32.

Kester, W.C. (1984), 'Today's options for tomorrow's growth', *Harvard Business Review*, **62**(2), 153–60.

Kogut, B. (1983), 'Foreign direct investment as a sequential process', in C.P. Kindleberger and D. Audretsch (eds), *The Multinational Corporations in the 1980s*, Cambridge, MA: MIT Press, pp. 38–56.

Kogut, B. (1991), 'Joint ventures and the option to expand and acquire', *Management Science*, **37**(1), 19–33.

Kogut, B. and N. Kulatilaka (1994), 'Operating flexibility, global manufacturing and the option value of a multinational network', *Management Science*, **40**(1), 123–39.

Kogut, B. and N. Kulatilaka (2001), 'Capabilities as real options', *Organization Science*, **12**(6), 744–58.

Kouvelis, P., K. Axarloglou and V. Sinha (2001), 'Exchange rates and the choice of ownership structure of production facilities', *Management Science*, **47**(8), 1063–80.

Kulatilaka, N. and E.C. Perotti (1998), 'Strategic growth options', *Management Science*, **44**(8), 1021–31.

Kumar, M.V.S. (2005), 'The value from acquiring and divesting a joint venture: a real options approach', *Strategic Management Journal*, **26**, 321–31.

Lee, S.-H. and M. Makhija (2009a), 'Flexibility in internationalization: is it valuable during an economic crisis?', *Strategic Management Journal*, **30**(5), 537–55.

Lee, S.-H. and M. Makhija (2009b), 'The effect of domestic uncertainty on the real options value of international investments', *Journal of International Business Studies*, **40**(3), 405–20.

Leiblein, M.J. (2003), 'The choice of organizational governance form and performance: predictions from trans-action cost, resource-based, and real options theories', *Journal of Management*, **29**(6), 937–61.

Li, J. (2007), 'Real options theory and international strategy: a critical review', *Advances in Strategic Management*, **24**, 67–101.

Li, J. and Y. Li (2010), 'Flexibility versus commitment: MNEs' ownership strategy in China', *Journal of International Business Studies*, **41**(9), 1550–71.

Li, J. and A.M. Rugman (2007), 'Real options and the theory of foreign direct investment', *International Business Review*, **16**(6), 687–712.

Li, Y. (2008), 'Duration analysis of venture capital staging: a real options perspective', *Journal of Business Venturing*, **23**(5), 497–512.

Li, Y. and J.T. Mahoney (2011), 'When are venture capital projects initiated?', *Journal of Business Venturing*, **26**, 239–54.

Li, Y., B. James, R. Madhavan and J.T. Mahoney (2007), 'Real options: taking stock and looking forward', in J. Reuer and T. Tong (eds), *Advances in Strategic Management*, vol. 24, Oxford: JAI Press, pp. 31–66.

Luo, Y. and R.L. Tung (2007), 'International expansion of emerging market enterprises: a springboard perspective', *Journal of International Business Studies*, **38**(4), 481–98.

Mahoney, J.T. (2005), *Economic Foundations of Strategy*, Thousand Oaks, CA: Sage Publications.

McGrath, R.G. (1997), 'A real options logic for initiating technology positioning investments', *Academy of Management Review*, **22**(4), 974–96.

McGrath, R.G., W.J. Ferrier and A.L. Mendelow (2004), 'Real options as engines of choice and heterogeneity', *Academy of Management Review*, **29**(1), 86–101.

Miller, K. and J.J. Reuer (1998a), 'Firm strategy and economic exposures to foreign exchange rate movements', *Journal of International Business Studies*, **29**(3), 493–513.

Miller, K. and J.J. Reuer (1998b), 'Asymmetric corporate exposures to foreign exchange rate changes', *Strategic Management Journal*, **19**, 1183–91.

Myers, S.C. (1977), 'Determinants of corporate borrowing', *Journal of Financial Economics*, **5**(2), 147–75.

Myers, S.C. (1984), 'Finance theory and financial strategy', *Interfaces*, **14**(1), 126–37.

North, D.C. (1990), *Institutions, Institutional Change and Economic Performance*, Cambridge, New York and Melbourne: Cambridge University Press.

Pantzalis, C. (2001), 'Does location matter? An empirical analysis of geographic scope and MNC market valuation', *Journal of International Business Studies*, **32**(1), 133–55.

Pindyck, R.S. (1988), 'Irreversible investment, capacity choice, and the value of the firm', *American Economic Review*, **78**(5), 969–85.

Rangan, S. (1998), 'Do multinationals operate flexibly? Theory and evidence', *Journal of International Business Studies*, **29**(2), 217–37.

Reuer, J.J. and M.J. Leiblein (2000), 'Downside risk implications of multinationality and international joint ventures', *Academy of Management Journal*, **43**(2), 203–14.

Reuer, J.J. and T.W. Tong (2005), 'Real options in international joint ventures', *Journal of Management*, **31**(3), 403–23.

Rivoli, P. and E. Salorio (1996), 'Direct investment and investment under uncertainty', *Journal of International Business Studies*, **27**(2), 335–54.

Rugman, A.M. (1981), *Inside the Multinationals: The Economics of Internal Markets*, New York: Columbia University Press.

Rugman, A.M. (2011), 'The international financial crisis and multinational enterprise strategy', *Transnational Corporations*, **20**(1), 103–16.

Smit, H.T.J. and L.G. Trigeorgis (2004), *Strategic Investment: Real Options and Games*, Princeton, NJ: Princeton University Press.

Sullivan, D. and A. Bauerschmidt (1990), 'Incremental internationalization: a test of Johanson and Vahlne's thesis', *Management International Review*, **30**(1), 19–30.

Tang, C.Y. and S. Tikoo (1999), 'Operational flexibility and market valuation of earnings', *Strategic Management Journal*, **20**(8), 749–61.

Tong, T. and J.J. Reuer (2007), 'Real options in multinational corporations: organizational challenges and risk implications', *Journal of International Business Studies*, **38**(2), 215–30.

Tong, T.W. and J. Li (2008), 'Real options and MNE strategies in Asia Pacific', *Asia Pacific Journal of Management*, **25**(1), 153–69.

Tong, T.W., J.J. Reuer and M.W. Peng (2008), 'International joint ventures and the value of growth options', *Academy of Management Journal*, **51**(5), 1014–29.

Trigeorgis, L. (1988), 'A conceptual options framework for capital budgeting', *Advances in Futures and Options Research*, **3**, 145–67.

Trigeorgis, L. (1996), *Real Options: Managerial Flexibility and Strategy in Resource Allocation*, Cambridge, MA: MIT Press.

Vassolo, R.S., J. Anand and T.B. Folta (2004), 'Non-additivity in portfolios of exploration activities: a real options-based analysis of equity alliances in biotechnology', *Strategic Management Journal*, **25**(11), 1045–61.

Xu, D., C. Zhou and P.H. Phan (2010), 'A real options perspective on sequential acquisitions in China', *Journal of International Business Studies*, **41**(1), 166–74.

PART IV

NEW TOPICS IN
INTERNATIONAL STRATEGIC
MANAGEMENT

19 Management research on emerging markets: existing trends and future opportunities

Hemant Merchant and Lori Allen-Ford

The rise of emerging markets (EMs) worldwide over the past decade has now been widely documented in the popular business press. For example, in 1990, EMs represented less than 15 percent of the global economic output while the developed nations represented 77 percent. By 2010, EMs represented almost 30 percent of the global GDP (World Bank, 2010) and 37 percent of the inbound direct investment. Indeed, some experts predict that EMs will account for almost 80 percent of the global economy by 2050 (Rincon Hill Capital, 2010) with BRIC countries (Brazil, Russia, India and China) denoting a larger share of the global economy than their G-7 counterparts (Goldman Sachs, 2010; MSCI, 2010). Others believe that EMs are 'expected to prevail, at least for the foreseeable future' (Merchant, 2008a, p. ix). Thus it is not surprising that academic interest in EMs has also risen considerably over the past decade – urged on by the seminal work of Hoskisson et al. (2000).

A casual review of academic literature on EMs points to a vast spectrum of scholarly interest in the EM phenomenon, at least in the management discipline. Researchers have embraced the study of EMs and examined a wide array of topics within, relying on an equally diverse range of theoretical and empirical perspectives. Apparently, management scholars have been motivated in their endeavors by a nearly non-existent body of previous work on EMs. Indeed, we believe that virtually every conceivable EMs topic has offered, and continues to offer, limitless opportunity for academic inquiry – a boon for intellectual discovery. However, this opportunity is not without its attendant challenges. Perhaps the most pressing of these is the need to take stock of the intellectual progress we have made as a community of management scholars trying to understand an important phenomenon. The merits of such an assessment are non-trivial: it permits us to see how far we have come and, importantly, how much further still we can – and must – push the discipline's theoretical and empirical frontiers.

This study is a small step in that direction and, at least to us, the first known study of its kind to analyze the discipline's current intellectual history *vis-à-vis* EMs. Our objectives are threefold: (i) to systematically map the study of EMs across five leading management journals; (ii) to highlight strengths and weaknesses in the current literature; and (iii) to assist researchers, particularly doctoral students, discern where they can contribute to the future of management scholarship. To set our study's tone, we identify several common – but often non-overlapping – definitions of EMs. Next, we describe the protocol for selecting articles (published during the last 11 years) included in our assessment of the EM literature. Consistent with similar previous studies, we evaluate this work along several theoretical and empirical dimensions. Our intent is to generate a multidimensional 'density map' of current scholarly literature on EMs. This map should provide a useful starting point for future research. Finally, we conclude with a few proposals, some of them eclectic, about potentially interesting areas for scholarly work on EMs.

SCOPE OF THE STUDY

Some caveats are necessary before we begin. First, we relied on individual authors' definitions of EMs to include a study in our sample. Thus we included every study that portrayed itself as an EM study. Such inclusiveness was necessary given our objectives, but also because leading institutions/scholars currently offer definitionally fluid and partially overlapping lists of EMs. We attempt to tackle this diversity in the next section. Moreover, we included studies that did not view themselves as EM studies but nevertheless focused on EMs as a setting (either singularly or in conjunction with non-EM countries). We identified these 'EM setting' studies concurrently with self-identified EM studies.

Second, given resource constraints, we limited ourselves to studies published between 2000 and 2010 (both years inclusive) in five leading management journals: (i) *Academy of Management Journal* (*AMJ*); (ii) *Academy of Management Review* (*AMR*); (iii) *Journal of Management* (*JM*); (iv) *Journal of Management Studies* (*JMS*); and (v) *Strategic Management Journal* (*SMJ*). We selected these journals for a variety of reasons. First, all these journals focus on a broad variety of management-related issues and cover conceptual and empirical domains (Bruton and Lau, 2008). Second, there is general consensus that these journals are of high quality; hence they significantly impact the academic profession (Judge et al., 2007). Third, previous work with a similar 'mapping' focus has also included these journals (e.g. see Bruton and Lau, 2008; Lockett et al., 2006). Finally, these journals probably receive submissions from around the world and so presumably are comprehensive in terms of EM topics investigated by researchers worldwide. Moreover, the journals' editorial boards comprise scholars worldwide, suggesting a greater tolerance for the diversity of submitted manuscripts (Merchant and Gaur, 2008). Nonetheless, we should note that many studies published in the above-mentioned journals are authored by researchers based in 'developed' countries.

Third, we specifically excluded solely 'international' journals (e.g. *Journal of International Business Studies*; *JIBS*) as well as niche journals devoted singularly to publication of EM studies (e.g. *International Journal of Emerging Markets*). We did so mostly to conserve limited resources at our disposal but also because some of these journals did not meet at least one of our selection criteria. To illustrate, including *JIBS* alone would have nearly doubled our current sample. Moreover, we believe there is some conceptual merit in separating mostly 'management' issues from mostly 'international' issues. However, we realize that this dichotomy has fuzzy boundaries. Importantly, we do not expect our study to suffer from fatal weaknesses given the precedent for studies to consider only five leading management journals (e.g. see Trieschmann et al., 2000).

Fourth, we did not include studies presented at annual conferences associated with any of the five journals we considered because we believed it would be difficult to track and receive all work-in-progress EM studies. However, it is likely that such studies will eventually be published in the spectrum of journals we consider. In other words, these work-in-progress studies perhaps could be treated as those falling outside a truncated sample. Thus we would argue that 55 journal-years (5 journals times 11 years per journal) adequately capture the recent scholarly interest in EMs across leading management journals.

WHAT IS AN EMERGING MARKET REALLY?

Despite widespread interest in EMs, there still is considerable disagreement as to what constitutes an 'emerging' market. Indeed, as Wilson and Ushakov (2011) lament: 'Even though the word "emerging market" is an often used phrase . . . most authors do *not* give a formal definition. Today, there is simply no commonly accepted definition of what constitutes an emerging market' (p. 6; emphasis added). Ironically, even these authors do not provide a definition of the term.

Table 19.1 lists EM definitions coined by some individuals (academics as well as practitioners) and institutions. Moreover, it illustrates how EM definitions have evolved – even for the same institution. A review of the table reveals just how large a variance there is across definitions. Several trends are noteworthy. First, there often is no explicit definition of EMs and a clear admission to that effect (e.g. Arnold and Quelch, 1998; Garten, 1997). Second, when the definition exists, its foundations seem to depend upon who is defining the term. As expected, academic definitions generally are qualitative, theoretically oriented, holistic in their foundations, and difficult to operationalize (e.g. Khanna et al., 2006; Kvint, 2008) because of trade-offs involving the definition's multidimensionality. In contrast, institutional definitions (e.g. by the International Finance Corporation) generally are quantifiable, based on a narrow set of criteria, often based on salient macroeconomic indicators, and relatively easy to operationalize. In other words, at least for these economic institutions, the criteria indirectly hint at a definition that *per se* does not exist.

Third, the essence of what is 'emerging' about emerging markets varies dramatically, despite some overlap across definitions. To illustrate, Khanna et al. (2006) view EMs through a structural lens, in terms of 'institutional voids' (p. 2), whereas the International Finance Corporation views EMs through the lens of a country's capital markets, and the FTSE Group, an independent company owned by the *Financial Times* and the London Stock Exchange, views EMs in terms of their market infrastructure. Fourth, some institutional definitions add, over time, new criteria for a country to qualify as an EM (e.g. Standard & Poor's). At least theoretically, this evolving definition, while understandable from a relevance standpoint, creates a situation where a country (previously labeled as an EM) might not requalify as an EM even across definitions a few years apart. Moreover, although the definition's basis is quantifiable (e.g. GNI per capita), the statistic's threshold itself is susceptible to change over time. Finally, very few definitions explicitly recognize trade-offs and intertemporal consistency as being essential ingredients of a multidimensional definition of EMs (e.g. Khanna, et al., 2006; MSCI, 2010).

Emerging Markets: A Working Definition

Table 19.2 is a recent list of EMs as viewed by leading institutions and Hoskisson et al. (2000). Several observations are noteworthy. Above all, a review of Table 19.2 indicates just how much inconsistency exists across the five lists. Of the 71 countries mentioned in the table, only 18 (or about 25 percent) appear consistently across all lists and 35 (or about 50 percent) appear only on a single list. Only three countries appear on any four lists, another three countries appear on any three lists, and 12 countries appear on any two lists. Stated differently, approximately 75 percent of all countries mentioned in

Table 19.1   Emerging markets: some definitions and selection criteria

Author/institution	Definition/criteria
Garten (1997)	No explicit definition. 'In identifying the [big emerging markets], here are some of the key considerations used in selecting which countries qualify: (a) They have large populations, large resource bases, large markets, and are powerhouses in their respective regions, (b) They are bursting onto the world scene, shattering the status quo, (c) They are critical participants in the major political, economic, and social dramas taking place on the world scene, (d) They are the world's fastest expanding markets, and responsible for a good deal of the world's explosive growth of trade, and (e) They are all trying to open their economies, balance their budgets, and sell off their state companies. All but two [big emerging markets] have instituted substantial political liberalization' (pp. 13–15).
Arnold and Quelch (1998)	'There is no commonly accepted definition of "emerging market," but there are three aspects of a country's economy that often underlie various definitions. *First* is the absolute level of economic development, usually indicated by the average GDP per capita, or the relative balance of agrarian and industrial/commercial activity. This overlaps with other categorizations such as "less developed countries" (LDCs) or "Third World countries." *Second* is the relative pace of economic development, usually indicated by the GDP growth rate. *Third* is the system of market governance and, in particular, the extent and stability of a free-market system; if a country is in the process of economic liberalization from a command economy, it is sometimes defined as a "transitional" economy' (p. 9; italics in original).
Hoskisson et al. (2000)	'A country that satisfies two criteria: a rapid pace of economic development, and government policies favoring economic liberalization and the adoption of a free-market system (Arnold & Quelch [1998])' (p. 249).
Khanna et al. (2006)	'We define emerging markets by the absence, or poor functioning, of specialized intermediaries [who provide the requisite information and contract enforcement needed to consummate transactions between buyers and sellers]. That is, emerging markets are, literally, emerging, as they struggle to find ways to bring buyers and sellers of all sorts together for productive exchange' (p. 2).
Kvint (2008)	'A society transitioning from a dictatorship to a free market-oriented economy, with increasing economic freedom, gradual integration within the marketplace, an expanding middle class, improving standards of living and social stability and tolerance, as well as an increase in cooperation with multilateral institutions'.
Dow Jones (2010)	No explicit definition. 'Countries are categorized as either "developed" or "emerging" for the purpose of stock selection based on the stocks' International Monetary Fund (IMF) classifications.'

Table 19.1   (continued)

Author/institution	Definition/criteria
The Economist (2009)	No explicit definition. To determine whether a country qualifies as an EM, *The Economist* performs an annual analysis using eight criteria that it has employed consistently over the past decade. These criteria are: (i) market size; (ii) market growth rate; (iii) market intensity; (iv) market consumption capacity; (v) commercial infrastructure; (vi) economic freedom; (vii) market receptivity; and (viii) country risk.
FTSE (2010)	No explicit definition. 'The generic term "emerging markets" is used to describe a nation's social or business activity in the process of rapid industrialization. The term "rapidly growing economy" is now being used to denote emerging markets. The FTSE Group classified [EMs] according to a transparent, rules-based process that monitors markets status against fifteen defined Quality of Markets criteria. The FTSE Group has divided the emerging markets into advanced emerging and secondary emerging countries based on the development of their market infrastructure for greater granularity. These segments generally exhibit the following characteristics:
	Advanced Emerging: Upper middle-income GNI countries with advanced market infrastructures, and high-income GNI countries with lesser developed market infrastructures;
	Secondary Emerging: Lower middle- and low-income GNI countries with reasonable market infrastructures and significant size, and Upper middle-income GNI countries with lesser developed market infrastructures.'
International Finance Corporation (1981)	No explicit definition. 'What we did not have was an elevator pitch that liberated these developing economies from the stigma of being labeled as "Third World" basket cases . . . I at last came up with a term that sounded more positive and invigorating: *Emerging Markets*. "Third World" suggested stagnation; "Emerging Markets" suggested progress, uplift, and dynamism . . . I sat down at my desk at IFC and dashed off a memo that made my message explicit . . . Thus, a phrase was coined' (van Agtmael, 2007, p. 5; italics in original). Alternatively, middle- to high-income economies among developing countries with stock markets in which foreigners could buy securities.
IFC (2010)	All developing countries with a Gross National Income per capita of US$9265 or less.
International Monetary Fund (2004)	'Developing countries' financial markets that are less than fully developed, but are nonetheless broadly accessible to foreign investors.'
IMF (2010)	'The capital markets of developing countries that have liberalized their financial systems to promote capital flows with non-residents and are broadly accessible to foreign investors.'

Table 19.1   (continued)

Author/institution	Definition/criteria
Morgan Stanley Capital Index (2010)	'In general, emerging markets are considered to be fast-growing economies which tend to offer an opportunity for higher return, but also may carry more risk relative to developed markets. What drives the categorization of any country as developed or emerging in the MSCI index is the size, depth, breadth and transparency of the country's equity capital market as well as the availability of stocks for purchase by foreigners.'
Standard & Poor's (1995)	'The term "emerging market" implies a stock market that is in transition – increasing in size, activity, or level of sophistication. Most often the term is defined by a number of parameters that attempt to assess a stock market's relative level of development and/or an economy's level of development.
	'In general, Standard & Poor's classifies a stock market as "emerging" if it meets at least one of several general criteria: (i) it is located in a low or middle-income economy as defined by The World Bank, (ii) it does not exhibit financial depth; the ratio of the country's market capitalization to its GDP is low, (iii) there exist broad based discriminatory controls for non-domiciled investors, or (iv) it is characterized by a lack of transparency, depth, market regulation, and operational efficiency. Emerging markets generally fall short of the ideal standards for many of the [15 specific] criteria listed . . .'
	'Until 1995, the index definition of an emerging stock was based entirely on The World Bank's classification of low and middle-income economies. If a country's Gross National Income (GNI) per capita did not meet The World Bank's threshold for a high-income country, the stock market in that country was said to be "emerging." More recently, this definition has proven to be less than satisfactory . . .'
	'Accordingly, [S&P's] adopted new and more far-reaching criteria to classify markets as "developed" or "emerging." To graduate from emerging status, GNI per capita for an economy should exceed The World Bank's upper income threshold for at least three consecutive years . . .'
	'For a market to graduate from the emerging market series, it should have an investable-market-capitalization-to-GDP ratio near the average of markets commonly accepted as developed, for three consecutive years . . .'
	'There are also numerous qualitative features to consider when analyzing specific stock markets.'
S&P (2010)	'A stock market is 'emerging' if it meets one of the following criteria: i) it has a regulatory authority with a strong [USA's] *Securities and Exchange Commission*-like structure, ii) it is in transition (increasing in size, activity or level of sophistication), iii) it is located in a low- or middle-income economy, as defined by the World Bank, and iv) has a low market capitalization-to-GDP ratio.'

Table 19.2   Lists of emerging markets

Dow Jones (2010)	*Economist* (2009)	FTSE (2010)	MSCI (2010)	Hoskisson et al. (2000)
No. of EMs = 35	No. of EMs = 26	No. of EMs = 24	No. of EMs = 21	No. of EMs = 64
				Albania
Argentina	Argentina	Argentina		Argentina
				Armenia
				Azerbaijan
Bahrain				
				Bangladesh
				Belarus
				Bosnia
				Botswana
Brazil	Brazil	Brazil	Brazil	Brazil
Bulgaria				Bulgaria
Chile	Chile	Chile	Chile	Chile
China	China	China	China	China
Colombia	Colombia	Colombia	Colombia	Colombia
				Côte d'Ivoire
				Croatia
Czech Republic	Czech Republic	Czech Republic	Czech Republic	Czech Republic
				Ecuador
Egypt	Egypt	Egypt	Egypt	Egypt
Estonia				Estonia
				Georgia
				Ghana
				Greece
	Hong Kong			
Hungary	Hungary	Hungary	Hungary	Hungary
India	India	India	India	India
Indonesia	Indonesia	Indonesia	Indonesia	Indonesia
	Israel			Israel
				Jamaica
Jordan				Jordan
				Kazakhstan
				Kenya
	Korea, South		Korea	Korea
Kuwait				
				Kyrgyzstan
Latvia				Latvia
Lithuania				Lithuania
				Macedonia
Malaysia	Malaysia	Malaysia	Malaysia	Malaysia
Mauritius				Mauritius
Mexico	Mexico	Mexico	Mexico	Mexico
				Moldova
Morocco		Morocco	Morocco	Morocco
				Nigeria

Table 19.2   (continued)

Dow Jones (2010)	*Economist* (2009)	FTSE (2010)	MSCI (2010)	Hoskisson et al. (2000)
Oman				
Pakistan	Pakistan	Pakistan		Pakistan
Peru	Peru	Peru	Peru	Peru
Philippines	Philippines	Philippines	Philippines	Philippines
Poland	Poland	Poland	Poland	Poland
				Portugal
Qatar				
Romania		Romania		Romania
Russia	Russia	Russia	Russia	Russia
	Saudi Arabia			Saudi Arabia
Slovakia				Slovakia
				Slovenia
	Singapore			
South Africa	South Africa	South Africa	South Africa	South Africa
Sri Lanka				Sri Lanka
		Taiwan	Taiwan	Taiwan
				Tajikistan
Thailand	Thailand	Thailand	Thailand	Thailand
				Trinidad & Tobago
				Tunisia
Turkey	Turkey	Turkey	Turkey	Turkey
				Turkmenistan
				Ukraine
United Arab Emirates		United Arab Emirates		
				Uzbekistan
	Venezuela			Venezuela
				Zimbabwe

Table 19.2 are not consistently viewed as EMs across the lists considered here. Of course, some of these discrepancies can be traced to geopolitical changes (e.g. while Hong Kong now is a part of China, it still appears as a stand-alone 'country'), whereas others arise from Hoskisson et al.'s (2000) inclusive list of EMs that relied on 1999 data from the International Finance Corporation as well as 1998 data from the European Bank for Reconstruction and Development. These authors' lists of EMs includes all but seven countries shown on any of the more recent lists. Conversely, only the FTSE and MSCI lists have no outlier countries, although even these two lists do not overlap completely.

The 18 countries that appear on all five lists in Table 19.2 collectively represent seven regions worldwide: (i) Africa (South Africa); (ii) North America (Mexico); (iii) South America (Brazil; Chile; Columbia; Peru); (iv) Asia (China; India; Indonesia; Malaysia; Philippines; Thailand); (v) Europe (Czech Republic; Hungary; Poland; Turkey); (vi) Middle East (Egypt); and (vii) the former USSR (Russia). Importantly, the 18 countries include all leading EMs (Brazil, Russia, India, China and South Africa, the BRICS). While there is some skewness in terms of the number of countries within each region, there is no region in which an EM exists that is not represented above. To illustrate, although Central America and Oceania are not represented, no country in these two regions is considered to be an EM by any of the five lists. Consequently, we would submit that researchers treat the above-mentioned 18 countries as 'consensus' emerging markets, at least as of 2010. Doing so would introduce much-needed operational consistency to an important area of academic study. The merits of such consistency would be highly desirable. Operational homogeneity would aid theory development by eliminating confusion of the 'Blind Men and the Elephant' (a parable) variety wherein micro-sense to individual researchers might result in macro-nonsense to the discipline. Indeed, relying on the identified (within-region) subgroups of these 18 countries could aid the development of region-specific theories and perspectives and, some day, coalesce into a quasi-general 'theory' of EMs. Without such convergence, it is likely that different lists of core EMs will (mis)lead researchers into believing they all are studying the same phenomenon when, in fact, they may not be doing so (Hoskisson et al., 2000). This is because, as a recent study cautioned, 'all [EMs] are not the same or even similar, at least in a locational sense' (Merchant, 2008b, p. 111).

SAMPLE SELECTION

To systematically map EM studies in the management discipline, we reviewed all 3590 articles published in the five leading journals mentioned previously. We examined every article published between January 2000 and the latest 2010 issue (available at the time of data coding) in these journals, and reviewed the title, abstract and keywords of each to determine whether it focused on an EM phenomenon. This protocol has empirical precedent (e.g. see Kaplan, 2011; Morrison, 2010). We included an article in our sample if: (i) its authors considered it to be an EM study; (ii) it explicitly addressed some defining feature of EMs, for example privatization or deregulation (Eden, 2008); (iii) its research setting focused on any of the 71 emerging markets listed in Table 19.2; (iv) it compared and/or contrasted emerging and non-emerging market issues within the same research; or (v) we were unsure about its relevance to our study. If we could not clearly identify a study's emphasis, we downloaded the entire article and reviewed it. We erred on the conservative side and included an article in our sample even when we had the slightest doubt as to whether it fit our purpose. This inclusiveness was required to be consistent with our study's preference for comprehensiveness. Our sampling protocol is consistent with those employed in previous research (e.g. see Bruton and Lau, 2008; Merchant and Gaur, 2008).

The above-mentioned criteria resulted in a final sample of 188 theoretical and empirical articles published over 55 journal-years (5 journals times 11 years per journal). Due to space considerations, we do not list these 188 articles but will make the list available upon request. We downloaded these studies and coded them along several dimensions relevant to our study. Most of these dimensions were of an objective nature (e.g. Name of the EM country, Theoretical or empirical study) and therefore were not a source of disagreement. We independently coded an article's subjective dimensions (e.g. Topical theme, and Theoretical lens applied), relying on a pre-agreed set of decision rules. For example, we coded an article's central theme (phenomenon) by examining the authors' intent as suggested in the study's motivation, research question and/or keywords (e.g. Kaplan, 2011). Like Bruton and Lau (2008), we assigned only a single topic to a given article. Similarly, we relied on authors' self-reported phrases to classify an article's theoretical foundations – even when these authors coined peculiar labels for the frameworks they applied. Thus we did not impose our theoretical footprint on an article for which the authors provided a label. In 15 studies where such labels were not evident, we coded an article as having a 'Not specified' theoretical basis. These protocols agree with those of previous research with similar objectives (e.g. see Bruton and Lau, 2008; Merchant and Gaur, 2008).

MAJOR FINDINGS

Article Focus: EMs versus Non-EMs

The results in Table 19.3 indicate the extent and nature of EM studies by management scholars. Above all, the results demonstrate just how sparse the scholarly landscape presently is *vis-à-vis* research on EMs: only 188 out of a total of 3590 published articles have an EM focus (Panel A, Row C). Thus – despite growing interest over the past decade – merely 5 percent of all published management research focuses on EM-related topics (Row D). This is a minuscule number – particularly since we included articles that even remotely focused on EMs. Applying a more stringent sampling protocol surely would produce an even smaller number. Interestingly, as shown in Row E, more than two-thirds of EM-related management research appears in two journals, *Journal of Management Studies* and *Strategic Management Journal* (35 percent and 34 percent respectively). These statistics do not change even if we combine the two Academy journals, *AMJ* and *AMR*, each with its distinct orientation in publishing empirical and theoretical work respectively. However, even in *JMS* and *SMJ*, EM-related articles comprise less than 9 percent of all published articles (Row D): only 66 of 779 *JMS* studies focus on EMs whereas only 64 out of 758 *SMJ* studies pertain to EMs (Row C).

Panel B of the table disaggregates the above statistics by the type of published studies. Of the 188 published EM studies, 18 are theoretical studies (Row F) and the remaining 170 are empirical (Row G). Thus less than 10 percent of all published EM studies are theoretical studies. Among the journals, *Journal of Management Studies* has published the highest proportion of theoretical articles, 17 percent (Row H). Although it would appear that *AMR* deserves that honor, *AMR* publishes only theoretical studies, while its counterpart, *AMJ*, publishes only empirical studies. Hence we treat these two Academy journals as one outlet to aid comparability with their peers, who do not differentiate between theoretical and empirical studies. The proportion of theoretical studies in the Academy journals is about 11 percent. Nonetheless, *JMS* and *AMR* clearly lead the genre of EM theoretical studies, generating almost 90 percent of EM-oriented theory development (Row I).

Turning to genre of EM empirical publications, the journals we consider in our study are skewed towards empirical articles – between 83 percent and 98 percent of EM studies

Table 19.3   Distribution across journals

Panel A: EM articles vs non-EM articles

Row	Description	AMJ	AMR	AMJ+AMR	JM	JMS	SMJ	Total
[A]	Total published articles	790	737	1527	526	779	758	3590
[B]	Total non-EM articles published	749	732	1481	514	713	694	3402
[C]	Total EM articles published [Row C = Row A – Row B]	41	5	46	12	66	64	188
[D]	Journal's own rate (%) of EM articles publications [Row D = Row C ÷ Row A]:	5.19	0.68	3.01	2.28	8.48	8.44	5.24
[E]	Journal's share (%) of total EM articles published [Row E = Row C ÷ 188 studies]:	21.81	2.66	24.47	6.38	35.11	34.04	–

Panel B: Type of EM articles

Row	Description	AMJ	AMR	AMJ+AMR	JM	JMS	SMJ	Total
[C]	Total EM articles published	41	5	46	12	66	64	188
[F]	EM theoretical articles	0	5	5	1	11	1	18
[G]	EM empirical articles [Row G = Row C – Row F]	41	0	41	11	55	63	170
[H]	Journal's own rate (%) of EM theoretical publications [Row H = Row F ÷ Row C]:	0.00	100.00	10.87	8.33	16.67	1.56	–
[I]	Journal's share (%) of total EM theoretical articles [Row I = Row F ÷ 18 studies]:	0.00	27.78	27.78	5.56	61.11	5.56	–
[J]	Journal's own rate (%) of EM empirical publications [Row J = Row G ÷ Row C]:	100.00	0.00	89.13	91.67	83.33	98.44	–
[K]	Journal's share (%) of total EM empirical articles [Row K = Row G ÷ 170 studies]:	24.12	0.00	24.12	6.47	32.35	37.06	–

Table 19.4   Distribution by year and journal

	AMJ	AMR	AMJ+AMR	JM	JMS	SMJ	Total
2000	16	4	20	1	3	0	24
2001	1	0	1	4	7	4	16
2002	3	0	3	2	5	8	18
2003	1	0	1	0	6	5	12
2004	2	0	2	1	5	8	16
2005	1	0	1	1	12	5	19
2006	0	0	0	1	8	3	12
2007	4	0	4	0	3	7	14
2008	5	1	6	2	4	9	21
2009	6	0	6	0	5	10	21
2010	2	0	2	0	8	5	15
Total	41	5	46	12	66	64	188
Mean	3.73	0.45	4.18	1.09	6.00	5.82	17.09
Std dev.	4.47	1.21	5.62	1.22	2.65	2.93	3.88
Median	2	0	2	1	5	5	16

they have published, assuming *AMJ* and *AMR* are combined as discussed above (Row J). Only *Journal of Management Studies* seems to have achieved some balance between theoretical and empirical genres (17 percent and 83 percent respectively), although this ratio is also quite lop-sided. As shown in Row K, *Strategic Management Journal* and *Journal of Management Studies* lead in terms of publishing empirical EM studies (37 percent and 32 percent of 170 studies in this genre; 63 and 55 empirical studies respectively, as noted in Row G).

Temporal Distribution

The results in Table 19.4 highlight the temporal distribution of published EM articles. The results indicate an average annual publication rate of 17 articles across the five journals, with a median of 16 articles. While these could be viewed as respectable statistics, they are largely driven by two journals – *Journal of Management Studies* and *Strategic Management Journal*, the former journal slightly outperforming the latter. Over the 11-year period, *JMS* has the highest average publication rate among all journals: 6 articles per year with a standard deviation of 2.65 articles. Moreover, *Journal of Management Studies* displays an upward trajectory of EM-related publications over the last four years. In comparison, *SMJ* has a slightly lower average of 5.82 studies and a slightly higher deviation of 2.93. The median publication count in *JMS* as well as *SMJ* is 5 articles. While the Academy journals seem to approach these numbers, those statistics are driven by a single cluster of articles published in an *Academy of Management Journal* special issue on emerging markets (Hoskisson et al., 2000). Indeed, the median value for Academy journals is just 2 articles. Thus, at least from a historical perspective, *Journal of Management Studies* and *Strategic Management Journal* appear to consistently publish EM-related articles.

Table 19.5   Distribution by year and industry sectors

Type of study	Theo.	Empirical				
Type of sample	–	Manuf.	Non-mfg	Mixed	Unspec.	Total
Number of articles	18	78	15	47	30	188
% of total (n = 188)	10			90		100
% of empirical (n = 170)	–	46	9	28	18	–
2000	5	7	1	7	4	24
2001	1	8	1	4	2	16
2002	1	9	2	5	1	18
2003	1	4	0	5	2	12
2004	1	6	1	6	2	16
2005	4	9	3	1	2	19
2006	1	3	1	3	4	12
2007	0	8	1	5	0	14
2008	2	9	1	5	4	21
2009	0	7	3	3	8	21
2010	2	8	1	3	1	15

SECTORAL DISTRIBUTION

Table 19.5 contains the distribution of empirical EM articles in terms of 'manufacturing' and 'non-manufacturing' (including services) sectors. We coded industry sectors based on author-provided information, such as SIC codes or sample descriptions. Next, we consulted the SIC manual to establish whether a given study had a manufacturing (SIC codes 2000 through 3999) or non-manufacturing (all other SIC codes) focus. If a sample contained manufacturing as well as non-manufacturing data, we treated the study as a 'Mixed' sample study. We created an 'Unspecified' category for articles that did not furnish information about their sample's sectoral composition.

To reiterate, approximately 10 percent of all EM articles were theoretical studies, and the other 90 percent were empirical articles. As reported in Table 19.5, almost 46 percent of all empirical articles (78 out of 170 studies) were based on manufacturing data. In stark contrast, merely 9 percent of all empirical articles (n = 15 studies) focused purely on non-manufacturing data. This is a miniscule number – particularly over a period of 55 journal-years. Although 28 percent of all empirical articles analyzed a mixed sample, a general neglect to report results separately across the two broad industry sectors limits any insights that can be gleaned from across the subsamples. Indeed, recent surveys suggest that most 'mixed' samples are dominated by manufacturing sector firms (Merchant and Gaur, 2008). Nearly 18 percent of all empirical EM articles (n = 30 studies) did not provide any information about the composition of their samples.

Disciplines and Topical Themes

Table 19.6 highlights the distribution of 188 EM articles in terms of management sub-disciplines and themes within each. Depending upon how an article defined itself, we first

Table 19.6   Distribution by study type and sub-disciplinary themes

	Theo.	Emp.	AMJ	AMR	JM	JMS	SMJ	Total
Human resources	3	42	12	0	4	21	8	45
% of all theoretical ($n = 18$)	17	–	–	–	–	–	–	–
% of all empirical ($n = 170$)	–	25	–	–	–	–	–	–
% of all HR articles ($n = 45$)	7	93	27	0	9	47	18	–
Human resources themes								
Compensation	0	2	2	0	0	0	0	2
Culture and diversity	0	8	1	0	0	4	3	8
Employment and labor issues	0	12	5	0	1	5	1	12
Orgl citizenship behavior	0	1	0	0	0	1	0	1
Leadership	0	12	4	0	2	6	0	12
Training and development	3	7	0	0	1	5	4	10
Strategic mgmt	6	103	22	2	7	31	47	109
% of all theoretical ($n = 18$)	33	–	–	–	–	–	–	–
% of all empirical ($n = 170$)	–	61	–	–	–	–	–	–
% of all SM articles ($n = 109$)	6	94	20	2	6	28	43	–
Strategic management themes								
Alliances/M&As	0	24	6	0	1	5	12	24
Business groups	1	8	1	0	1	5	2	9
Capability development	0	9	1	0	1	2	5	9
Contracts/opportunism	0	2	0	0	0	1	1	2
Corporate turnaround	0	4	0	0	1	1	2	4
Dynamic capabilities	0	1	0	0	0	1	0	1
Governance and control	2	15	2	2	1	5	7	17
Market entry	1	12	4	0	0	5	4	13
Performance (econ./soc.)	1	9	2	0	1	1	6	10
Product-market diversif.	1	10	2	0	0	5	4	11
Product development	0	4	2	0	0	0	2	5
Risk and uncertainty	0	3	2	0	1	0	0	3
Social dimen. of strategy	0	2	0	0	0	0	2	2
Other	9	25	7	3	1	14	9	34
% of all theoretical ($n = 18$)	50	–	–	–	–	–	–	–
% of all empirical ($n = 170$)	–	15	–	–	–	–	–	–
% of all other articles ($n = 34$)	26	74	21	9	3	41	26	–
Other themes								
Economic reforms	5	17	2	3	1	9	7	22
Institutionalization	2	6	4	0	0	2	2	8
Organizational practices	2	1	1	0	0	2	0	3
Miscellaneous	0	1	0	0	0	1	0	1

coded its central theme (one per study) and then grouped related themes under 'Human resources' or 'Strategic management' categories. A third category ('Other') contained themes that did not neatly fall into the above two headings. Almost 60 percent of all EM articles had a Strategic management focus (109 out of 188 studies) and nearly 25 percent had a Human resources focus (45 out of 188 studies). The remaining studies mostly focused on macro-level, context-specific issues (34 out of 188 studies); these studies belonged to the 'Other' category.

Regardless of their sub-disciplinary focus, a vast majority of EM articles were empirical: 93 percent in Human resources, 94 percent in Strategic management, and 74 percent in the Other category. Thus there is a much greater imperative for theoretical work on EM issues across the entire management spectrum. This need is greatest for Human resources (17 percent of all 18 theoretical EM articles), closely followed by Strategic management (33 percent of all 18 theoretical EM articles). Surprisingly, 50 percent of all theoretical EM studies belonged to the 'Other' category (9 out of 18 articles). A closer scrutiny of the 'Other' category revealed that some management scholars seem to be in a theory-building stage and motivated to better understand the macro-level context specificity of EMs in general.

A similar commitment is also evident in the remaining two categories, although the focus there is relatively more on lower levels of analysis, closer to the firm. In the Human resources category (45 articles), there are six topical clusters led by 'Employment and labor issues' and 'Leadership' studies (12 articles each or 27 percent each of all Human resources articles). These two clusters are closely followed by 'Training and development' and 'Culture and diversity' studies (10 articles and 8 articles respectively). The intuitive proximity of these four clusters to one another demonstrates a scholarly commitment to 'people' issues in the EM context.

In comparison, the Strategic management category (109 articles) consists of a relatively broader array of themes (13 versus 6 in the Human resources category) with 'Alliance/ M&A' studies (24 articles or 22 percent of all Strategic management studies) receiving the most scholarly attention. This cluster is followed by 'Governance and control' studies (17 articles or 16 percent of all Strategic management studies). Strategy scholars have also coalesced around five other topical clusters: (i) Market entry (13 articles); (ii) Product-market diversification (11 articles); (iii) Performance (10 articles); (iv) Business groups (9 articles); and (v) Capability development (9 articles). At least to us, the intuitive closeness of these clusters suggests a scholarly commitment to the 'resource-linkage, resource-optimization' nexus.

Recasting the above-mentioned statistics in terms of publication outlets, *Journal of Management Studies* leads in two out of three categories ('Human resources' as well as the 'Other' category) in terms of the number of articles as well as percentages. Indeed, *JMS* has published a respectable 47 percent of all EM articles with a micro-level 'people' focus and over 40 percent of all EM articles with a macro-level 'context' focus. In the Strategic management category, *JMS* lags only behind *Strategic Management Journal*, which – not surprisingly – leads in publishing strategy articles (43 percent for *SMJ* versus 28 percent for *JMS*, or 47 versus 31 articles respectively). In comparison, the Academy journals have published relatively fewer percentage of articles in each of the three subdisciplines: 27 percent in Human resources, 22 percent in Strategic management, and 30 percent in the Other category.

Geographical Focus

The results in Table 19.7 highlight the distribution of EM studies across geographies. Panel A of this table lists the regional focus of these studies whereas Panel B identifies

Table 19.7   Distribution by geography

Panel A: Distribution across regions

	AMJ	AMR	JM	JMS	SMJ	Total	% of n = 188
Asia	22	0	8	44	47	121	64
Africa	0	0	0	3	0	3	2
America, North	0	0	1	1	1	3	2
America, South	5	0	0	0	3	8	4
Central and Eastern Europe	6	2	2	9	6	25	13
EMs in general	7	3	1	4	3	18	10
Middle East	0	0	0	2	1	3	2
Multiple regions	1	0	0	3	3	7	4
TOTAL	41	5	12	66	64	188	100
No. of regions covered	5	2	4	7	7	8	–

Panel B: Distribution by countries within a region

Asia (n = 121)	AMJ	AMR	JM	JMS	SMJ	Total	% of n = 188
China	16	0	7	30	33	86	46
India	0	0	0	1	4	5	3
Indonesia	0	0	0	1	0	1	1
Korea, South	2	0	0	3	3	8	4
Malaysia	0	0	0	2	0	2	1
Singapore	1	0	0	2	3	6	3
Vietnam	0	0	0	1	0	1	1
Multi-country	1	0	1	2	2	6	3
Unspecified	2	0	0	2	2	6	3
Africa (n = 3)							
South Africa	0	0	0	3	0	3	2
America, North (n = 3)							
Mexico	0	0	1	1	1	3	2
America, South (n = 8)							
Argentina	2	0	0	0	1	3	2
Brazil	0	0	0	0	1	1	1
Chile	1	0	0	0	1	2	1
Multi-country	1	0	0	0	0	1	1
Unspecified	1	0	0	0	0	1	1
Central and Eastern Europe (n = 25)							
Czech Republic	0	0	0	0	2	2	1
Greece	0	0	0	1	1	2	1
Hungary	1	0	1	1	0	3	2
Lithuania	0	0	0	0	1	1	1
Russia	3	1	0	1	1	6	3
Multi-country	1	0	0	2	0	3	2
Unspecified	1	1	1	4	1	8	4

Table 19.7 (continued)

Panel B: Distribution by countries within a region							
Asia (*n* = 121)	*AMJ*	*AMR*	*JM*	*JMS*	*SMJ*	Total	% of *n* = 188
EMs in general (*n* = 18)							
EMs worldwide	7	3	1	4	3	18	10
Middle East (*n* = 3)							
Egypt	0	0	0	1	1	2	1
Israel	0	0	0	1	0	1	1
Multi-region EMs (*n* = 7)							
Multi-country	1	0	0	3	3	7	4

countries within each region. Several points are noteworthy in Panel A. First, scholars have focused on every region in which EMs exist; no EM region has been overlooked. Second, almost 65 percent of all EM studies (i.e. 121 out of 188 articles) are set in Asia. While scholars have also considered other regions, the latter are dwarfed in comparison with the focus on Asia. To illustrate, the next largest cluster of EM studies includes only 25 articles: the Central and Eastern European EMs denote merely 13 percent of all EM articles. Clearly, such a lop-sided focus needs remediation if we are to better understand the EM phenomenon from a more generalizable perspective. Third, only 7 studies (or 4 percent of all EM articles) focus on multiple regions – and even then only on very few countries within each region (details available upon request). Fourth, 18 studies consider EMs in general. These articles often are theoretical studies whose focus is not on a single EM but, instead, on institutional-level differences between EMs and markets not considered to be so. However, this grouping also includes a few empirical studies that simply do not identify specific EMs emphasized in their work. Finally, examining the journal-specific focus on individual EM regions, *Journal of Management Studies* and *Strategic Management Journal* have the most dominant distributions of published EM articles. Studies published in these outlets have examined seven out of eight identified EM regions – a remarkable accomplishment that advances the generalization agenda mentioned previously.

Panel B of Table 19.7 presents the distribution of studies by specific EM regions. Several findings merit a mention. First, 101 out of 188 articles in our sample (i.e. over 50 percent of the total) focus on leading EMs (i.e. Brazil, Russia, India, China, and South Africa – the BRICS). Second, despite the appearance of all leading EMs on this list, it is remarkable that 46 percent of all published studies have focused on China (86 out of 188 articles). Third, the attention paid to EMs other than China is highly fragmented in that comparable statistics are very meager for the remaining countries. To illustrate, the next-largest single-country cluster after China is South Korea (eight studies). Fourth, it is also notable that only four studies (3 percent of the total) focus on India – the second-largest emerging market in terms of salient economic parameters (e.g. population and GDP growth rate). Fifth, despite persuasion that Africa is 'bursting [with] business and investment opportunities' (Babarinde, 2009, p. 319; Raman, 2009), South Africa is the only African nation considered by EM scholars. Finally, just seven studies (4 percent of all EM articles) demonstrate a multi-country, multi-region focus. Of these, only one study focuses on 14 countries across various regions.

Theoretical Foundations

To generate Table 19.8, we coded all EM articles in terms of theories that the authors self-identified in their work. If an article applied two distinct theories, we counted the study twice – once for each theory. As noted previously, we could not code the theoretical basis for 15 EM articles because these articles did not explicitly identify a theory. We had difficulty coding eight more articles because these were either descriptive or used esoteric labels (e.g. 'New' theory) which we could not comprehend. Hence we treated these 23 articles as having unspecified or unclear theoretical foundations and excluded them from further calculations. Consequently, Table 19.8 is based on 165 articles ($188 - 15 - 8 = 165$ articles).

Panel A of Table 19.8 identifies 26 theories that management scholars have applied to study various EMs phenomenon. Among all theories, the resource-based view and institutional theory clearly dominate the scholarly radar. Scholars have applied the former theory 69 times and the latter 47 times *vis-à-vis* a total of 294 applications of the noted 26 theories (i.e. 23 percent and 16 percent respectively). Other frequently used theories include transaction costs, agency theory and organization theory (29, 22 and 20 times respectively). These five theories account for nearly two-thirds of all theoretical usage in our sample (i.e. 187 out of 294 applications). However, Panel A also highlights several other theories as being significant to the study of EMs.

Despite the simplicity of the available data, Panel B of the table attempts to generate a deeper picture of EM studies' theoretical foundations. Row A of this panel identifies how many of the 26 distinct theories a journal's EM studies have applied. Again, *Journal of Management Studies* leads along this dimension in absolute as well as relative terms (see Row B), albeit only slightly. As suggested in Row C, management scholars have applied 26 theories 294 times across the 165 EM studies in which we could clearly identify a theoretical foundation (see Rows D, E and F).

Perhaps the most interesting statistics appear in rows G, H and I of Table 19.8's Panel B. Row G depicts a theory's 'density factor', which we define as the average number of applications of a single theory. Operationally, this is the ratio of 'Number of times all theories are applied' to 'Number of distinct theories applied' (i.e. Row C ÷ Row A). The figures in Row G indicate an overall density factor of 11.31 applications. This number suggests that, on average, articles in our sample apply a distinct theory over 11 times. Across journals, the most 'favorable' density factors exist for *Journal of Management Studies* and *Strategic Management Journal* (5.63 applications and 5.50 applications respectively).

Row H extends the above analysis to a theory's 'turnover rate', which we define as the average rate (in terms of the number of articles) at which a theory is churned before scholars apply another theory. Operationally, this is the ratio of 'Number of articles specifying a theory' to 'Number of distinct theories applied' (i.e. Row F ÷ Row A). The figures in Row H indicate an overall turnover factor of 6.35 articles. Thus, on average, every seventh study in our sample seeks out a new theoretical lens to investigate some EM phenomenon. The most 'favorable' turnover rates are for *Journal of Management*

Table 19.8   Distribution by theories applied

Panel A: Theories and frequency of their use

	AMJ	AMR	AMJ+AMR	JM	JMS	SMJ	Total
Agency/contracts	4	3	7	0	7	8	22
Behavioral decision	2	0	2	1	0	2	5
Contingency	0	0	0	1	0	6	7
Culture	1	0	1	1	4	2	8
Finance	6	0	6	0	3	3	12
Identity/legitimacy	4	0	4	2	0	0	6
Industrial organization	0	0	0	0	2	3	5
Information	1	0	1	1	3	5	10
Institutional	12	2	14	2	21	10	47
Internationalization	4	0	4	1	1	3	9
Leadership	2	0	2	1	2	0	5
Network/exchange	1	0	1	0	9	1	11
Organization	1	0	1	2	8	9	20
Procedural/social justice	3	0	3	1	1	0	5
Resource-based view	13	0	13	3	25	28	69
Resource-dependence	2	0	2	1	2	3	8
Social capital	0	0	0	0	1	2	3
Stakeholder	0	1	1	1	1	2	5
Transaction costs	5	0	5	1	13	10	29
Miscellaneous							
Attribution	0	0	0	0	2	0	2
Classic measurement	0	0	0	0	1	0	1
Deviance model	1	0	1	0	0	0	1
Environmental scanning	1	0	1	0	0	0	1
Goal	0	0	0	0	0	1	1
Retrenchment	0	0	0	0	0	1	1
Sabotage	0	0	0	0	1	0	1

Number of times all theories are applied (across 165 articles):

	AMJ	AMR	AMJ+AMR	JM	JMS	SMJ	Total
	63	6	69	19	107	99	294

Panel B: Statistics

	AMJ	AMR	AMJ+AMR	JM	JMS	SMJ	Total
[A] Number of distinct theories applied:							
	17	3	18	14	19	18	26
[B] Percentage of all theories [Row B = Row A ÷ 26 theories]							
	65	12	69	54	73	69	–
[C] Number of times all theories are applied:							
	63	6	69	19	107	99	294
[D] Number of published articles:							
	41	5	46	12	66	64	188
[E] Number of articles excluded from Table 19.8 calculations:							
	4	0	4	1	8	10	23

Table 19.8 (continued)

	AMJ	AMR	AMJ+AMR	JM	JMS	SMJ	Total
Panel B: Statistics (cont.)							
[F] Number of articles with an identifiable theory [Row F = Row D − Row E]:							
	37	5	42	11	58	54	165
[G] A theory's density factor [Row C ÷ Row A]:							
	3.71	2.00	3.83	1.36	5.63	5.50	11.31
[H] A theory's turnover rate [Row F ÷ Row A]:							
	2.18	1.67	2.33	0.79	3.05	3.00	6.35
[I] Journals' theoretical pluralism score [Row C ÷ Row F]							
	1.70	1.20	1.64	1.73	1.84	1.83	1.78
[J] Dispersion of theoretical perspectives applied (see Panel A):							
	3.67	1.00	3.99	0.63	7.00	6.42	15.71

Studies, followed closely by *Strategic Management Journal* (3.05 articles and 3.00 articles respectively).

Row I provides a journal's 'theoretical pluralism' score, which we define as the average number of theories applied per EM article. Operationally, this score is the ratio of 'Number of times all theories are applied' to 'Number of articles specifying a theory' (i.e. Row C ÷ Row F). The statistics in Row I highlight that, on average, an EM study applies 1.78 theories. Here again, *Journal of Management Studies* and *Strategic Management Journal* have the most favorable scores (1.84 and 1.83 respectively). Importantly, even the lowest score is greater than 1 – suggesting that an 'average' EM article is grounded in more than one theory – a heartening finding!

Likewise, Row J reports the dispersion rate of theories applied. This statistic is the standard deviation of individual columns in Panel A of the table, and is influenced by the (journal-specific) clustering of theories reported in Panel A. The figures in Row J indicate that articles published in *Journal of Management Studies* exhibit the greatest dispersion across the 26 theories used (s.d. = 7.00), suggesting that the journal is relatively 'most accepting' of diverse theories. *Strategic Management Journal* follows closely in second place (s.d. = 6.42). Importantly, we must also underscore that the overall acceptance of theoretical diversity in EM management studies is quite astonishing: our sample's dispersion rate is more than twice the highest journal-specific dispersion rate (15.71 versus 7.00 for *JMS*). Indeed, this is remarkable evidence that the journals' editors and editorial boards are strongly committed to a plurality of perspectives, at least insofar as published EM studies are concerned.

CONCLUSIONS

The findings reported above have several implications for management scholars. Above all, we believe it is crucial that scholars explicitly define what they mean by 'emerging markets'. Very few studies presently do so, perhaps because of the popular perception that we all 'know' what EMs are. Perhaps we do – but do we? To return to our 'Blind

Men and the Elephant' parable, what defines a elephant? Anything 'big, black, heavy, and living in Africa'? Or is there more? What *really* separates elephants from rhinos or hippos? Without identifying the essence of EMs, our well-intended endeavors are likely to drift in intellectual space. Preventing such atrophy is crucial, given the time-dependent nature of organizational phenomenon (Suddaby, 2010) – particularly given the rapid evolution of EMs – and, therefore, the scholarly expression of core research constructs (Avital, 2000; Zaheer et al., 1999). Importantly, such efforts would mitigate a 'black box' treatment of EMs that can hinder theory development especially since EMs are characterized by rapid change (Bruton and Lau, 2008).

However, imposing rigorous academic definitions has its drawbacks too, due to the difficulty of operationalizing the multidimensionality of EM definitions. Thus we advocate a mid-range approach in which a definition not only demonstrates cognizance of fundamental qualities of EM but also agrees with authors' research intent. Table 19.1 highlights these qualities. Our recommendation aligns with Suddaby's point that a definition 'should focus on the meaning of the term as narrowly as possible [but not] so narrow it lacks relevance and cannot be generalized' (2010, p. 347). We anticipate that such conscious efforts will – at least from a theory development perspective – better anchor the EM phenomenon, although the methodological merits of similar endeavors ought not be ruled out.

Despite strong and growing academic interest, the study of EMs has had quite a weak following: less than 5 percent of all studies published during the last 55 journal-years pertain to EMs. We see this deficiency as a golden prospect, and expect the statistic to improve for three reasons: (i) EMs continue to gain prominence in the economic and competitive domains of firms as well as nations; (ii) the nascency of all topical themes investigated (and not investigated) so far; and (iii) our conviction that in every void there lies an opportunity for theoretical and empirical advances. At least to us, the relative newness of EMs is a blessing for management scholars of all persuasions. Indeed, there is plentiful evidence to suggest that EMs will remain a fertile ground for intellectual inquiry (e.g. see Cappelli et al., 2010; *Economist*, 2010; Ghemawat and Hout, 2008; Raman, 2009; Woolridge, 2010). We elaborate on this point in the next section. Our findings revealed that most of this inquiry was, to date, of an empirical nature (90 percent of all EM articles). We were even more surprised that it was heavily skewed towards Asia, particularly China, and extremely sparse *vis-à-vis* other geographies. Surely we can do more to redress this lopsidedness. The rise of EMs is a worldwide occurrence; it is not restricted to Asia, even though the two largest EMs, China and India, are found there. Consequently, it is useful to quickly start thinking about designing studies with generalizability as a goal. Sadly, very few studies in our sample demonstrated this urgency. Needless to say, enlarging the academic footprint of our EM discourse now is desirable and promising, as well as overdue – even if the observed lacunae simply reflect the early stage of our academic inquiry and, possibly, challenges of data availability. Yet empirical extensions – such as theoretical extensions – will also require a careful blend of academic discipline and creativity. This is particularly important given the slim emerging markets' context-specific theoretical foundations upon which the literature currently rests.

Indeed, the 18 EM-oriented theoretical articles comprised just 10 percent of all EM articles published during 55 journal-years. These articles were grounded in theories that are also applied to study phenomena in developed economies (Meyer and Peng, 2005). Obviously, this anchoring is a useful starting point, but there may be considerable payoffs in developing a general theory of EMs (Bruton and Lau, 2008) that can augment our current thinking about management practice (Chen and Miller, 2010). Yet this development is easier said than done because forays into unconventional domains – while rewarding – require us to move out of our own comfort zones. Where and how, then, do we start? Fortunately, our study provides a clue. As we reported, the articles in our sample frequently relied upon several established theories – especially resource-based and institutional theories, but also transaction costs, agency and organizational theories. We recommend starting with this theoretical array and blending several perspectives in novel and interesting ways, relying upon several useful insights into developing new scholarship (e.g. see Bartunek et al., 2006; Corley and Gioia, 2011; Davis, 1971; Suddaby et al., 2011 and studies in their special issue on theory development). Such endeavors have important merits, including, for example, exposing significant topics of research inquiry (Okhuysen and Bonardi, 2011) and offering reality checks on the relevance of our work (Bamberger and Pratt, 2010). However, our recommendation also raises an issue. As reported in Table 19.8, although an average EM article used more than one theory, authors applied a single theoretical perspective merely 11 times and every seventh article invoked a different theory. We believe that the latter statistics are somewhat disconcerting given our study's time frame, and therefore ask: how many theories are 'too many'? Are there optimal ranges of theoretical churning? How much does theoretical diversity help or hinder our cause? And so on. We do not address these questions as they clearly are beyond our study's scope. Instead, we refer interested readers to positions offered elsewhere (e.g. see Kuhn, 1962; Lakatos, 1970; Morrison, 2010; Pfeffer, 1993; Van Mannen, 1995; Tsai and Wu, 2010).

LIMITATIONS

As with all studies, our work has its limitations. First, our survey is confined to a small number of leading management journals; it does not include 'international' or niche journals. This restriction may not be too limiting given empirical precedent and our preference – arising from resource constraints – to focus on one discipline. Our intent was to better understand the nature and scope of existing work, and we believe we accomplished this with a survey of 55 journal-years. Second, our survey is biased towards West-centric perspectives. The five journals we surveyed are all based in developed economies, the published articles usually have Western-based/trained authors and rely on theories that are also frequently used to understand phenomena in mature economies. Thus the themes reflected in our survey are likely to indicate 'Western' research priorities. It is highly conceivable that such priorities differ for authors/journals based in EMs. Yet one might take some comfort from knowing that although the journals we considered have a Western affiliation, their editors, editorial boards and reviewers are not all based in the West. Finally, our survey does not cover the entire methodological domain of studies. For example, it paid little formal attention to sampling time frames, sample sizes or statistical techniques. Including these elements would have enriched our intended contributions but had to be traded off against resource constraints and incremental value added (especially due to the diversity of topical themes and specific research questions asked). This neglect too may not be limiting to the extent that most studies like ours do not explicitly consider methodological aspects of the articles they survey.

FINAL THOUGHTS

Researchers will find it reassuring that all five leading management journals are receptive to theoretical and empirical EM studies. Yet we cannot ignore the fact that *Journal of Management Studies* and *Strategic Management Journal* stand out among these journals as dominant outlets for publishing EM work. Hence our particular thanks to the past and current editors, editorial boards and reviewers of these journals for creating and nurturing a forum for dialogue on a phenomenon of undeniable global significance. Indeed, editorial involvement is crucial to the construction of our discipline's future (Coombs, 2010; Walsh, 2011). Hence we implore all to proactively guide research in this general area. It may be difficult to step outside our academic comfort zones, but it can be – and has been – done. Perhaps we ought to continue to be relatively more concerned with novelty and relevance of research issues than the elegance and scientific rigor of methodological issues. Our suggestion must not be interpreted as 'going easy' on methods, but merely a caution that 'raising the bar' needs to be gradual: a decade of work on EMs can, mistakenly and easily, create the perception that it is time to impose normal scientific standards on a adolescent body of inquiry. One must also be grateful to Hoskisson et al.'s (2000) pioneering work – and to the work of many other scholars whom we do not name – for blazing an intellectually stimulating path for the management discipline. Of course, none of these platforms will matter unless researchers themselves consciously accept the challenges of studying a 'new' phenomenon at multiple levels of inquiry. Thus we hope that our work has identified some areas for a research program, which, we aver, will add momentum to the career progression of many scholars, especially doctoral students in whom the future of scholarship resides.

REFERENCES

Arnold, D.J. and Quelch, J.A. (1998), 'New strategies in emerging markets', *Sloan Management Review*, **40**, 7–20.

Avital, M. (2000), 'Dealing with time in social inquiry: a tension between method and lived experience', *Organization Science*, **3**, 665–73.

Babarinde, O.A. (2009), 'Africa is open for business: a continent on the move', *Thunderbird International Business Review*, **51**, 319–26.

Bamberger, P.A. and Pratt, M.G. (2010), 'Moving forward by looking back: reclaiming unconventional research contexts and samples in organizational scholarship', *Academy of Management Journal*, **53**, 665–71.

Bartunek, J.M., Rynes, S.L. and Ireland, R.D. (2006), 'What makes management research interesting, and why does it matter?', *Academy of Management Journal*, **49**, 9–15.

Bruton, G.D. and Lau, C.-M. (2008), 'Asian management research: status today and future outlook', *Journal of Management Studies*, **45**, 636–59.

Cappelli, P., Singh, H., Singh, J.V. and Useem, M. (2010), 'Leadership lessons from India', *Harvard Business Review*, **88**, 90–97.

Chen, M.-J. and Miller, D. (2010), 'West meets east: towards an ambicultural approach to management', *Academy of Management Perspectives*, **24**, 17–24.

Coombs, J.G. (2010), 'Big samples and small effects: let's not trade relevance and rigor for power', *Academy of Management Journal*, **53**, 9–15.

Corley, K.G. and Gioia, D.A. (2011), 'Building theory about theory building: what constitutes a theoretical contribution?', *Academy of Management Review*, **36**, 12–32.

Davis, M.S. (1971), 'That's interesting!: towards a phenomenology of sociology and a sociology of phenomenology', *Philosophy of the Social Sciences*, **1**, 309–44.

Dow Jones (2010), 'Dow Jones indexes: country classification systems', retrieved from www.djindexes.com.

Economist (2010), 'The new masters of management', 17 April, 11.

Eden, L. (2008), 'The rise of TNCs from emerging markets: threats or opportunities?', in K.P. Sauvant (ed.), *The Rise of Transnational Corporations from Emerging Markets*, Cheltenham, UK and Northampton, MA, USA: Edward Elgar, pp. 333–8.

FTSE (2010), 'Emerging markets', http://www.ftse.com/Research_and_Publications/FTSE_Glossary.jsp (accessed 3 April 2011).

Garten, J.E. (1997), 'Who are the big emerging markets, and why are they important?', in J.E. Garten, *The Big Ten: The Big Emerging Markets and How They Will Change Our Lives*, New York: HarperCollins, pp. 3–23.

Ghemawat, P. and Hout, T. (2008), 'Tomorrow's global giants: not the usual suspects', *Harvard Business Review*, **86**, 80–88.

Goldman Sachs (2010), 'Global investment research', http://www2.goldmansachs.com/services/research/gir/research-and-analysis.html (accessed 3 April 2011).

Hoskisson, R.E., Eden, L., Lau, C.-M. and Wright, M. (2000), 'Strategy in emerging economies', *Academy of Management Journal*, **43**, 249–67.

IFC (2010), 'Developing value', http://www.ifc.org/ifcext/enviro.nsf/AttachmentsByTitle/p_DevelopingValue_Ch1/$FILE/Developing_Value_Chapter1.pdf (accessed 3 April 2011).

IMF (2010), 'Global financial stability report', www.imf.org/external/pubs/ft/gfsr/2009/01/pdf/glossary.pdf (accessed 3 April 2011).

Judge, T.A., Cable, D.M., Colber, A.E. and Rynes, S.L. (2007), 'What causes a management article to be cited – article, author, or journal?', *Academy of Management Journal*, **50**, 491–506.

Kaplan, S. (2011), 'Research in cognition and strategy: reflections on two decades of progress and a look to the future', *Journal of Management Studies*, **48**, 665–95.

Khanna, T., Palepu, K. and Carlsson, K. (2006), 'Why study emerging markets?', Harvard Business School note 9-706-422.

Kuhn, T.S. (1962), *The Structure of Scientific Revolutions*, Chicago, IL: University of Chicago Press.

Kvint, V. (2008), 'Define emerging markets now', http://www.forbes.com/2008/01/28/kvint-developing-countries-oped-cx_kv_0129kvint.html (accessed 3 April 2011).

Lakatos, I. (1970), *Falsification and the Methodology of Scientific Research Programmes*, Cambridge, UK: Cambridge University Press.

Lockett, A., Moon, J. and Visser, W. (2006), 'Corporate social responsibility in management research: focus, nature, salience, and sources of influence', *Journal of Management Studies*, **43**, 115–36.

Merchant, H. (2008a), *Competing in Emerging Markets: Cases and Readings*, New York and London: Routledge.

Merchant, H. (2008b), 'International joint venture configurations in big emerging markets', *Multinational Business Review*, **16**, 93–119.

Merchant, H. and Gaur, A. (2008), 'Opening the non-manufacturing envelope: the next big enterprise for international business research', *Management International Review*, **48**, 379–96.

Meyer, K.E. and Peng, M. W. (2005), 'Probing theoretically into Central and Eastern Europe: transactions, resources, and institutions', *Journal of International Business Studies*, **36**, 600–621.

Morrison, E. (2010), 'OB in AMJ: what is hot and what is not?', *Academy of Management Journal*, **53**, 932–6.

MSCI (2010), 'What is an emerging market equity?', http://www.jpmorgan.com/cm/BlobServer/Emerging_Market_Equities_as_a_DC_Plan_Option.pdf?blobcol=urldata&blobtable=MungoBlobs&blobkey=id&blobwhere=1158609902476&blobheader=application%2Fpd (accessed 3 April 2011).

Okhuysen, G. and Bonardi, J.-P. (2011), 'The challenges of building theory by combining lenses', *Academy of Management Review*, **36**, 6–11.

Pfeffer, J. (1993), 'Barriers to advances of organizational science: paradigm development as a dependent variable', *Academy of Management Review*, **18**, 599–620.

Raman, A.P. (2009), 'The new frontiers: how the global slowdown is reshaping competition from emerging markets', *Harvard Business Review*, **87**, 130–37.

Rincon Hill Capital (2010), 'What are the emerging markets?', http://www.rinconhillcapital.com/index.php/emerging-markets (accessed 3 April 2011).

S&P (2010), 'S&P emerging markets index: index methodology', http://www2.standardandpoors.com/spf/pdf/index/SP_Emerging_Markets_Indices_Methodology_Web.pdf (accessed 3 April 2011).

Suddaby, R. (2010), 'Construct clarity in theories of management and organization', *Academy of Management Review*, **35**, 346–57.

Suddaby, R., Hardy, C. and Huy, Q.N. (2011), 'Where are the new theories of organization?', *Academy of Management Review*, **36**, 236–46.

Trieschmann, J.S., Dennis, A.R., Northcraft, G.B. and Nieme Jr, A.W. (2000), 'Serving constituencies in business schools: M.B.A. program versus research performance', *Academy of Management Journal*, **43**, 1130–41.

Tsai, W. and Wu, C.-H. (2010), 'Knowledge combination: a cocitation analysis', *Academy of Management Journal*, **53**, 441–50.

Van Agtmael, A.W. (2007), *The Emerging Markets Century*, New York: Simon and Schuster.

Van Mannen, J. (1995), 'Style as theory', *Organization Science*, **6**, 132–3.

Walsh, J. (2011), 'Embracing the sacred in our secular scholarly world', *Academy of Management Review*, **36**, 215–34.

Wilson, W.T. and Ushakov, N. (2011), 'Brave new world: categorizing the emerging market economies', SIEMS issue report, 1–48.

Woolridge, A. (2010), 'The world turned upside down: a special report on innovation in emerging markets', *The Economist*, 17 April, 1–14.

World Bank (2010), 'World development indicators database', http://data.worldbank.org/data-catalog/world-development-indicators (accessed 3 April 2011).

Zaheer, S., Albert, S. and Zaheer, A. (1999), 'Time scales and organizational theory', *Academy of Management Review*, **24**, 725–41.

20 Institutions and international entrepreneurship
Dara Szyliowicz and Tiffany Galvin

INTRODUCTION

Even in the current 'hard' economic times, governments and individuals hold up entre-preneurship as the way in which economies can recover and grow. Global entrepreneur-ship, however, is a topic that is much discussed but difficult to track. Scholars estimate that more than 500 million people per year are involved in establishing new firms (Moya, 2008) and that early-stage entrepreneurial activity makes up a significant portion of GDP (GEMS, 2010). The importance of the phenomenon has been paralleled by an increased amount of research on international entrepreneurship (IE).

The research in this area parallels the broad range of activity that is occurring in this arena, from rates of founding of new firms across countries to the role that traits of indi-vidual entrepreneurs play in choice to become an entrepreneur (see Acs et al., 2003; Autio, 2005; Oviatt and McDougall, 2005a, 2005b; Zahra, 2005; Dimitratos and Jones, 2005). Even though this research has produced a lot of empirical findings, there is agreement that there is an 'absence of a strong theoretical foundation' (Thomas and Mueller, 2000) and, as a result, there is uncertainty and debate (Oviatt and McDougall, 2005a). There is also concern that the absence of a theoretical foundation means that the creation of a field based on strong conceptual models is lacking. This is critical for the creation of a cumulative research stream (Rialp et al., 2005).

In this chapter, we propose that work in the area of international entrepreneurship can be considerably advanced with a broader application of institutional frameworks (stem-ming from the ideas of DiMaggio and Powell, 1991; Meyer and Rowan, 1977; Scott, 1995). This approach gives specific attention to the wider environmental context, societal and cultural institutions, and various aspects of social construction in which new ven-tures can emerge. As such, institutional theories are particularly suited to explaining the forces that influence international entrepreneurial phenomena as multiple social, his-torical, cultural and economic, to name a few, factors can impact theoretical understand-ings of global entrepreneurship. Unfortunately, current work has not 'lived up' to the promise that this work can offer as many scholars have over-relied on explaining struc-tures and outcomes, focusing on institutions as structures (e.g. rules, regulations, customs and traditions) and neglecting a focus on institutional processes and mecha-nisms (Bruton et al., 2010; Kostova et al., 2008; Veciana and Urbano, 2008). This chapter seeks to show how and why institutional theory can make a stronger contribution to future international entrepreneurship research by considering the breadth of topics as well as perspectives in both arenas and how more promising avenues for research agendas can be extended. Fundamentally we believe that the growth of international entrepre-neurship research will continue to be hindered by the 'way' in which we apply our theo-retical explanations; thus broader application of useful theoretical frameworks, like institutional theories, can offer promising avenues of research.

We begin by reviewing the current research in international entrepreneurship and institutional theory. By doing so, we lay a foundation for understanding the work that has been done and the questions that have been asked. This then allows us to examine the factors that have yet to be fully explored. By adding a different application of institutional theory we can then begin to look at the processes and mechanisms that allow for a different explanation of the international entrepreneurship phenomena. Applying this framework permits us to illuminate how issues are causally linked and the likely outcomes. These theoretical insights will have significant implications for entrepreneurs, practitioners and policy-makers, among others.

A BRIEF HISTORY OF INTERNATIONAL ENTREPRENEURSHIP

International entrepreneurship has been a setting for academic study for over 30 years. Early work focused on the international creation of new firms or new firms international activities (McDougall, 1989; Morrow, 1988; Oviatt and McDougall, 1994). As this field became more established, the work on international entrepreneurs expanded. By the mid-1990s, it was defined as new firm activity that crossed national borders with a focus on the areas in which they operate. However, scholars continue to expand the boundaries of international entrepreneurship, as evidenced by this recent definition:

> a combination of innovative, proactive, and risk-seeking behavior that crosses national borders and is intended to create value in organizations. The study of international entrepreneurship includes research on such behavior and research comparing domestic entrepreneurial behavior in multiple countries. Firm size and age are not defining characteristics here. Thus, international entrepreneurial behavior in large, established companies, often referred to as 'corporate entrepreneurship,' is included. Further, international entrepreneurial behavior may occur at the individual, group, or organizational levels. (McDougall and Oviatt, 2000, p. 903)

Today international entrepreneurship research deals with a wide variety of topics that include almost all aspects of new firms, strategy and organizations (Oviatt and McDougall, 2005a, 2005b). Specific research has been carried out on national entrepreneurial cultures (McGrath and MacMillan, 1992; Mueller and Thomas, 2001; Thomas and Mueller, 2000), alliances and cooperative strategies (Li and Atuahene-Gima, 2001; Steensma et al., 2000), small and medium-sized company internationalization (Lu and Beamish, 2001; Liu et al., 2008), top management teams (Reuber and Fischer, 1997), entry modes (Zacharakis, 1997), cognition (Mitchell et al., 2000; Zahra et al., 2005), country profiles (Busenitz et al., 2000), corporate entrepreneurship (Birkinshaw, 1997), exporting (Bilkey and Tesar, 1977), knowledge management (Kuemmerle, 2002), venture financing (Roure et al., 1992), and technological learning (Zahra et al., 2000). Moreover, some promising work has focused on a new phenomenon, that of entrepreneurial firms that internationalize at their founding, the 'born globals' (Gabrielsson et al., 2008; Hashai and Almor, 2004).

INSTITUTIONAL THEORY – A PROMISING AVENUE FOR INTERNATIONAL ENTREPRENEURSHIP

Not surprisingly, the stream of current literature in international entrepreneurship utilizes a variety of theoretical approaches for researching the phenomenon of interest. However, it is less obvious, but important, to realize that all the research areas in this domain share a concern with the cultural, political and social contexts surrounding the growth of new firms globally. It is this need to understand the context within which these entrepreneurs are acting and how they influence their behavior that makes institutional theory particularly well suited to explaining this phenomenon. We first give a review of institutional arguments before expanding the discussion to its applications in the stream of international entrepreneurship.

Institutional Arguments – From its Beginnings to Recent Application

Part of the potential of institutional theory in this context comes from the wide variety of disciplines upon which institutional arguments are based (i.e. sociology, political science and economics). As a result of these varying traditions, institutional theory has a broad appeal to deal with phenomena across different levels of analysis. Research has examined a wide spectrum of institutional phenomena from the microprocesses behind the creation of systems of meaning and culture to the construction of broad legal and regulatory systems. Currently, there is a diversity of perspectives within the domain of 'institutional theories'. Through the years, there has been a wide variety of conceptual and theoretical applications of the term 'institutions', applied in fields such as economics, political science, sociology and anthropology – all of which have been substantially reviewed in notable pieces such as Scott (2001) and Scott and Davis (2007). Due to the multidisciplinary nature of institutional arguments, there is a multitude of options for applying institutional approaches to the study of international entrepreneurship. This review will focus on institutional arguments as present in organizational research.

Institutional theory has been present in organizational studies since the late 1970s, emerging primarily from the work of Meyer and Rowan (1977), in which the symbolic properties of organizational forms were discussed. The core of these arguments was the emphasis on cultural and symbolic frameworks (i.e. myths and ceremony) and how these impact certain organizational characteristics – from processes to outcomes. From this work, DiMaggio and Powell (1983) developed more nuanced institutional arguments to explain how new institutions develop. In this work, several propositions were offered in which the nature of an organizational set, or field of activity, was discussed, with primacy given to symbolic and isomorphic actions. This work was the foundation of work that began to examine how institutional contexts, particularly at the level of an organizational field of activity, can influence the kind of organizational forms and activities that will often resonate with the values and interests of those institutional environments (DiMaggio, 1988; Westwood and Clegg, 2003). In the late 1980s, a 'new institutionalism' (e.g. DiMaggio and Powell, 1991; Hirsch and Lounsbury, 1997) emerged in response to criticism that the role of agency and power relations was being neglected (DiMaggio, 1988) in institutional arguments – with too much emphasis purportedly on mimicry and legitimating actions. In addition, critics felt that there was an overemphasis on research that explained the static or stable characteristics of organizations, or how institutions exist and persist, rather than processes of change, or how institutions develop or evolve (Powell, 1990). As a result, the more current applications of institutional arguments in organizational theorizing give primacy to processes of institutionalization (as opposed to outcomes) and emphasis on power and agency.

Current applications of institutional approaches direct more attention to the complex interactions among institutional processes at multiple levels. As such, there is a movement away from an emphasis on isomorphism and totalistic arguments (DiMaggio and Powell, 1988) towards more detailed attention to the specifics of institutional variety at the organization sector or societal levels (Scott, 2008a). When applied to understandings about globalization processes, such as economic development and entrepreneurship, institutional arguments now focus on areas in which structure and activities converge, and how institutional processes can promote diversity and innovation. There is now more recognition that isomorphic processes can result in diverse outcomes due to the complexity and interplay between regulative, normative and cultural–cognitive mechanisms that can occur across national contexts. Institutionalism occurs in many forms.

This change in how institutional arguments are being applied is not new; it has just required a re-evaluation of how institutions have been defined and conceived in the past. Scott's conception of institutions (1995, 2001) gives important emphasis to shared beliefs, assumptions, organizing templates and schema (cultural–cognitive phenomena) in explaining activity both within and among organizations. Institutions have a multifaceted nature in that they consist of ideas, as well as interests and actors, and symbolic elements that connect and reflect social activities, social relations and material resources (Scott, 2008a; Scott and Davis, 2007).

Scott (2001)'s definition of the three main 'pillars' or components of institutions – regulative, normative and cultural–cognitive – recognizes that each component is highly interdependent while remaining distinct. This is important because, in the past, some research streams have given an overemphasis to one component at a time, or have merged the three components in such a way as to lose both the interdependence and distinctiveness. Without attention to the differences, subtle nuances that explain important institutional processes, not just outcomes, have been overlooked. For instance, each pillar has differences in its basis for explaining compliance within a field of activity – regulative is based on experience; normative, on social obligation, and cultural–cognitive on shared understandings or taken-for-grantedness. As another example, each institutional component would explain order and stability on different grounds – regulative is based on regulative rules; normative on binding expectations; and cultural–cognitive on constitutive schema. The mechanisms of influence and influence processes within a field differ by component as well – regulative relies on coercion; normative on norms; and cultural–cognitive on mimetic forces. Related to these influence processes is also a difference in the type of social logics that influence, as the regulative component of institutions would be associated with instrumentality, normative with appropriateness, and cultural–cognitive with orthodoxy. Each of the three pillars can be identified differently, which has implications for what research methodologies are employed and what indicators are measured and observed – regulative components are identified by rules, laws and sanctions; normative by certifications and accreditations, and cultural–cognitive by common beliefs and shared logics of action. Finally, it is important to recognize that each of the institutional components has a distinct basis for understanding legitimating processes – regulative conjures up legal sanctions for legitimacy; normative focuses on what is morally governed, and cultural–cognitive is based on comprehension, recognizability and culturally supported activities.

Thus, as stated before, institutionalism can take many forms as each of the conceptualized components of institutions has multifaceted dimensions that can explain different processes, structures, activities, and even forms and actors. Yet, through the years, and not just in the realm of international entrepreneurship research, theorists have varied in the extent to which they focus analytical attention on one or another of these pillars. There has been a tendency to give primacy to regulative elements that are more easily identifiable (and measurable or tractable) as they are more formalized, more explicit, more easily planned and strategically crafted (Scott, 2008b; Scott and Davis, 2007). However, institutional accounts or applications need to give attention to combinations of the three elements or pillars of institutions in order to be a more complete or thorough application of the richness of institutional arguments. Although analytically distinct, the three pillars or components of institutions are nested and interdependent, and should be applied as such. Roland (2004) provides an example of the importance of making these distinctions in conceptualizing institutional change processes – rules, laws and sanctions can be readily identifiable, but a lack of attention to deeper cultural–cognitive elements in which the categories and distinctions that are expressed in such regulations can lead to a superficial understanding of institutional processes since regulative components can change more quickly than cultural–cognitive or normative components. The activities and structures present at any given time in any organizational field may not be accurately explained by existing regulative elements of institutions, so more primacy needs to incorporate normative and cultural–cognitive elements within institutional explanations for a richer understanding of the variance in prominence or salience in certain elements' influence over time (see Hoffman, 1999). The various 'pillars' of institutions operate simultaneously to channel and constrain some structure and behaviors, and also to support or empower others (Scott, 2008a; Scott and Davis, 2007) – over-reliance on one element leads to incomplete understandings of institutional phenomena.

Recent 'neo-institutional' approaches (DiMaggio and Powell, 1991; Hirsch and Lounsbury, 1997) give attention to the generative role that institutions can play, recognizing that institutions can formulate 'particular configurations and forms of actors, and particular opportunities of action' (Dacin et al., 1999; Droege and Brown-Johnson, 2007). Normative and cultural–cognitive elements, such as ideas, norms and schema, about goals, means–end relations, appropriate forms, processes or actors, routines for example, are essential factors that can interact with and give meaning and value to the material resources that organizational actors (such as entrepreneurs) have to draw from in any environment (Campbell, 2004; Sewell, 1992). Greater attention needs to be given to the role that all institutional components, or pillars, can play in the emergence of new organizations or even populations and broader economies. For example, recent research streams in sociology and organizational theory that focus on the embedded nature of new organizational forms or populations might be a fruitful avenue for building on arguments about the embedded nature of all entrepreneurial activity across international contexts. As such, the embeddedness of entrepreneurial activity becomes the application of institutional lenses, not just the role of institutional actors, policies or regulations.

Extending Current Institutional Arguments

The field of organizational studies currently acknowledges that institutional arguments, as a primary research avenue, is a fruitful avenue that is 'ripe' for advancing all areas within management and organization studies (Davis and Marquis, 2005; Scott, 2004, 2008a; Scott and Davis, 2007; Suddaby, 2010). Considerable advances have been made in 'taking stock' of what institutional theory has accomplished as a body of work, its limitations as well as the underexplored avenues that could advance our understanding of multiple phenomena (see Greenwood et al., 2008b; Suddaby, 2010). Institutional theory continues to thrive within and across the discipline of organization studies (Greenwood et al., 2000a; Scott, 2008b) and several future directions exist that can aid in the advancement of research activity across management and organization disciplines, such as international entrepreneurship. The basic tenets within institutional research have been redirected from an emphasis on arguments based on examining the influences of context and legislative actions, social values and cognitive understandings (i.e. the institutional environment encompassing all three pillars – Scott and Davis, 2007), *on* organizations to research that now recognizes the continual interplay *of* organizations and their environment. As such, the field is moving towards the exploration of questions and arguments related to the following objectives (as adapted from arguments in Greenwood et al., 2008a and Szyliowicz and Galvin, 2010):

1. The continued application of institutional theory to multiple levels, topics and settings, with 'institutions' defined as a broad construct encompassing cognitive, normative, and regulative structures and processes.
2. An appreciation of the different manifestations of institutionalization, such that we can trace the source, persistence and diffusion to varied organizational phenomena. Hence a move away from 'institutions are X' to 'institutions can be Y' or 'what is institutional about Z'.
3. Movement towards contextualizing the phenomena we study, whether that context encompasses regulatory, historical, political, cognitively tacit, or socially embedded values or norms.

Overall, the objective for researchers should be to move beyond a rather rudimentary application of institutional theory, using the theory as a 'catch-all' for the cultural–cognitive, social, normative and regulative factors that other theories cannot monitor, capture or measure in the empirical sense, to instead 'stimulate contextualization' (Szyliowicz and Galvin, 2010). This means that exploring institutional context requires attention to richer and more comprehensive complexities. For example, Greater attention is being given to issues of institutional isomorphism as a complex phenomenon of intra- and inter-organizational-based responses to institutional pressures (e.g. Boxenbaum and Jonsson, 2008; Davis and Greve, 1997; Greenwood and Hinings, 1993, 2006; Hasse and Krücken, 2008; Kraatz and Block, 2008; Westphal and Zajac, 2001), as well as identity-based responses (e.g. Elsbach and Kramer, 1996; Fox-Wolfgramm et al., 1998; Glynn, 2008; Kostova and Roth, 2002) or translation/interpretation-based responses (e.g. Czarniawska, 2008; Czarniawska and Sevon, 1996; Sahlin-Andersson, 1996; Sahlin and Wedlin, 2008). In addition, there is now more questioning of the concept of legitimacy with attention to its acquisition, management and use, such that legitimacy is conceptualized as 'agency', not just something to be acquired or a static characteristic of an organization or action (e.g. Deephouse and Suchman, 2008; Elsbach and Sutton, 1992; Elsbach, 1994; Arndt and Bigelow, 2000; Westphal and Zajac, 2001). Now institutional arguments can be more precisely applied to explain what organizations and organizational actors do to succeed and survive in environments – particularly new organizations and actors across a variety of global environments. Current work also gives greater attention to institutional change and institutional entrepreneurship that acknowledges the conflicting, contested or legally constrained terrain of organizational fields (e.g. Battilana et al., 2009; Beckert, 2010; Dacin et al., 2002; Droege and Brown-Johnson, 2007; Leca et al., 2006; Lawrence and Suddaby, 2006; Hwang and Powell, 2005; Schneiberg and Lounsbury, 2008). As such, the complexity of environments needs to be continually recognized as both constraining and enabling change if research streams are to be expanded for greater understanding of new forms, structures, practices and relationships.

Lastly, there is a growing body of work in organization studies that places emphasis on institutional logics, or overarching cognitive belief systems or schema and ideologies, which exist within all organizational fields, societal or national contexts, and broader world polities. These cultural–cognitive components can impact the range of activities that exist as well as the potential for change, as logics intersect, exist in multiplicity and 'contest' over time (e.g. Friedland and Alford, 1991; Thornton, 2004; Thornton and Ocasio, 2008). This work focuses on both the processes and outcomes of 'meaning' and 'meaning-making' that make certain actions possible, endorse certain actors and forms, and provide opportunities for the deinstitutionalization of old actors, forms, and fields, and the development of new domains of activity. As such, this is an avenue ripe for exploring the connection between institutional logics, cultural–cognitive schemas and entrepreneurial activity. Such a focus would also require an expansion in the kinds of questions posed and the kinds of methodologies employed.

Overall, organization studies recognizes that the complexity of arguments within an institutional perspective needs to be elaborated on, moving away from overly broad, or narrow, applications of its arguments (Greenwood et al., 2008b; Scott, 2004; Lawrence and Suddaby, 2006). Institutional perspectives hold much promise for greater and richer explanatory power as more work concentrates on institutional mechanisms as opposed to outcomes, and processes as opposed to structures (Davis, 2006; Davis and Marquis, 2005). This requires increased attention to the complexities of embeddedness and social factors, understanding the nature of organizational or individual actor responses. This focus on institutions as a process, and something that has to be enacted to be maintained as well as changed (Lawrence and Suddaby, 2006), can lead to different questions that are essential for advancing institutional entrepreneurship research (Szyliowicz and Galvin, 2010) – questions such as 'what explains new organizations?' or 'what explains the type of new organizing that we are seeing?' or even 'how can we better understand the variety of contexts in which new organizations emerge?' In the following section, we further explore research avenues for IE research that can more aptly employ current institutional frameworks and theorizing emphasizing processes, mechanisms and change.

GAPS IN THE CURRENT WORK IN INTERNATIONAL ENTREPRENEURSHIP USING INSTITUTIONAL THEORY

One of the main strengths of institutional theory is its understanding of the complexities of how societies have developed over time in a variety of conditions and at different rates. These changes/progressions may be the result of distinctive institutional arrangements, path-depending processes as well as the competitiveness of nations (Murmann and Tushman, 2001; Nelson, 1993). However, the current studies have failed to consider the interaction of regulative, normative and cultural–cognitive components in explaining change, whether it be patterns of entrepreneurial activity, growth of industries or shifts in emerging economies. Instead these studies in international entrepreneurship often reduce this variation to international or national – historical, legal, technological or structural – differences. With this assumption, no cross-cultural study can yield powerful analytical results.

Moreover, this work utilizes 'classic' institutional theory, basing many of its arguments on Scott's 'three-pillar' conception of institutions with its emphasis on cognitive, normative and regulatory processes. Although it is an important framework, advances in neo-institutional theory should also be considered. In particular, current work in international entrepreneurship often focuses on the 'visible' or 'overt' aspects of institutions and cultures such as regulations, policies, ceremonies, artifacts and technologies rather than the dynamics and processes stressed by neo-institutional theory. This theory is utilized in a variety of disciplines – economics, political science, anthropology and sociology. Notable examples include Bourdieu and Wacquant (1992), Campbell (2004), Hall and Soskice (2001), Nee (2005), North (1990, 2005), Ostrom (1999), Pierson (2004) and Williamson (1983, 1979). Unfortunately the insights from these related fields have not been adequately applied to the questions asked by international entrepreneurship researchers.

The focus on the dynamics and processes that promote different regulatory, cultural and cognitive environments by this research is precisely the theoretical diversity that would facilitate the intellectual progress of the field of international entrepreneurship. This theoretical foundation can contribute to the development of cross-national as well as single-country studies and the findings would be of interest to scholars, policy-makers and practitioners. In the sections that follow, we demonstrate how the application of neo-institutional concepts can contribute towards a better understanding of historical trajectories, sociocultural complexity and the role of informal and formal institutions.

As international entrepreneurship has become a more important topic of study, the research has looked at a wide variety of topics. Several scholars have sought to classify the work that has used institutional frameworks with international entrepreneurship literature. Cox (1997) has classified the literature along four dimensions: (1) individual entrepreneurs; (2) the entrepreneurial process; (3) environmental factors; and (4) smaller entrepreneurial ventures. Not surprisingly, the environmental factor dimension has the largest number of studies that use an institutional theory framework. The process and types of actors are critical (as represented by the other categories), but scholars utilize the environmental factors to understand causal relationships leading to entrepreneurial outcomes. It is the different aspects of the environment that are critical for understanding international entrepreneurship.

However, what constitutes the environment is the subject of some debate (Szyliowicz and Galvin, 2010; Welter and Smallbone, 2011). Although it is usually thought of in terms of regulatory issues, Gnyawali and Fogel (1994) consider this one element along with socioeconomic conditions, entrepreneurial and business skills, financial opportunities and other support. Cox built on these for his classifications; however, one of the most interesting aspects of these studies is that they do not include national culture as part of the environment even though it is considered of critical importance to understanding international activity (Hofstede, 1983; Trompenaars, 1994). One way in which scholars have tried to introduce culture is through the understanding of 'entrepreneurial' traits and discussing what role culture plays in influencing behavior. Instead the research focus is on the effects of the wider 'context' on entrepreneurship that the work often labels 'institutional environment'. Although this is a good first step, these studies fail to recognize the multiple dynamics that impact these processes. It is these broader insights of institutional theory that need to be applied if significant advances in the field are to be achieved in the future.

To answer the question of how institutional theory can be effectively integrated with international entrepreneurship, we first must look at the state of current research. To do so we searched the top two business databases for papers on international entrepreneurship and institutional theory. These papers were then classified in terms of how they applied institutional theory to the entrepreneurial process. We created two tables (see Tables 20.1 and 20.2) that divide and review the literature to demonstrate how institutional theory has been utilized to date. By doing so, we can see whether the full range of institutional theory is being applied.

Overall, research at the intersection of institutional theory and international entrepreneurship needs to more fully integrate the insights of institutional theory. These range from the critical role that social construction plays, how rules of interaction are influenced by power, and the role of resource distributions in both constraining and enabling actors. Moreover the study of the role of social power and how actors are able to effectively harness wider resources is a promising avenue that deserves exploration. Current studies, however, tend to focus on the regulatory or cultural aspects (the most 'visible' aspects of institutions) and contrast them with more traditional economic frameworks. It is this variation in legal, cultural and regulatory issues that most studies identify as drivers for international entrepreneurship.

The role of the wider environment is one major factor that most of these studies share. Several focus on the emergence of entrepreneurial activity in a specific country, such as Yu's (2000) study of entrepreneurship in Hong Kong or Scheela and Van Hoa's (2004) study of Vietnamese women entrepreneurs. One notable exception that looks at multiple countries is the study by Welter et al. (2004), which compared entrepreneurial behavior across Estonia, Russia and Germany.

In addition to the focus on entrepreneurship, most of these studies utilize W.R. Scott's seminal theoretical framework on the institutional environment, especially the cognitive, regulatory and normative, known as the three 'pillars'. This line of research examines one pillar's effect on entrepreneurial behavior – such as looking at the role of culture (cognitive pillar). Ahlstrom and Bruton's (2002) study demonstrates the role that cultural patterns play in Chinese foreign joint ventures management of an 'often hostile institutional environment'. Although only some of these joint ventures are entrepreneurial, this study directly examines the role of the environment on firm activity. Other studies look at

Table 20.1   International entrepreneurship and institutional theory – explaining context

Topic	Sources	Example of type of work
Environment – 'country effects'	Spencer and Gómez (2004) Eid (2006) Ahlstrom et al. (2007) Bruton et al. (2002) Bruton et al. (2005) Mueller and Thomas (2001) Thomas and Mueller (2000) Zacharakis et al. (2007) Ravasi and Marchiso (2003) Szyliowicz et al. (2004) Yeung (2002) Busenitz et al. (2000) Manolova et al. (2008) Dimitratos et al. (2004)	Impact of Regulatory, and Cultural systems on entrepreneurship The role of national culture, regulatory regimes and domestic policies on entrepreneurship
Environment – single country and comparative country analysis	Welter et al. (2004) Yu (2000) Scheela and Van Hoa (2004)	Entrepreneurial activity in a specific country Entrepreneurs across countries
Environment – effect of shift in the external environment	Manolova and Yan (2002) Ahlstrom and Bruton (2002) Newman (2000) Wright et al. (2005) Lado and Vozikis (1996) Chen and Lin (2006) Karra et al. (2008) Lim et al. (2010) Welter and Smallbone (2011)	Changes in institutional environments

multiple effects of the institutional environment on entrepreneurial behavior. Bulgaria's institutional environment, as evidenced by lawmakers, tax collection agencies and regional authorities responsible for issuing business permits and licenses, reduced growth of entrepreneurial firms (Manolova and Yan, 2002) due to a high level of corruption, hostility and unpredictability. Lim et al. (2010) carried out a comparative analysis of the role of various institutional dimensions on the decision to create a new firm in eight countries. The question of how uncertainty influences international entrepreneurial performance was also examined by Dimitratos et al. (2004) and, more recently, by Welter and Smallbone (2011).

Some studies examine the institutional environment more narrowly, looking at the effect that the environment within a sector or industry might have on entrepreneurial behavior. Yeung (2002) demonstrates not only how the behavior of transnational entrepreneurs is affected by the institutional environment, but also how their awareness and understanding of this environment allow them to be successful. Karra et al. (2008) trace the experience of one entrepreneur in creating a successful international business and how he is both affected by and manages the institutional environment.

Table 20.2   Using institutional theory to explain international entrepreneurship

Topic	Sources	Examples of types of work
Linking entrepreneurship and international business approaches	Birkinshaw (1999, 2000) Birkinshaw and Hood (2001) Jones and Coviello (2005) Drori et al. (2006) Kostova et al. (2008) Mathews and Zander (2007) Mudambi and Zahra (2007) Di Gregorio (2005)	Role institutional theory can play in better understanding international business
Institutional entrepreneurs	Beckert (1999) Delemarle (2007) Chatterjee et al. (2002) Demil and Besédrine (2005) Spencer et al. (2005)	Role of specific individuals in shaping and guiding change in a firm or industry
Institutional theory – concepts and approaches	Alvarez (1992) Honig and Karlsson (2004) Lewin et al. (1999) Yeung (2002)	Understanding the diffusion of the concept of entrepreneurship worldwide

However, separating industry or sector conditions from the wider environment is virtually impossible, and many of these studies utilize culture or country effects to explain how industries and sectors differ. Given the importance of access to capital for entrepreneurial firms, the critical aspect to be explained is variation in financing and the role that the institutional environment plays in creating and mobilizing capital. This issue lies at the intersection of the entrepreneur and their knowledge of the local environment to access financing. To understand this relationship, several studies focus on different parts of the financial sector in specific countries, whether it be venture capital, stock markets or access to private equity. The role of venture capital has been extensively studied. Ahlstrom and Bruton, along with a variety of co-authors, have examined the way in which different institutional environments influence venture capital in several countries. In their studies on venture capital in Asia, they demonstrate that differences in the environment influence not only the industry and firms, but also the behavior of individuals (Ahlstrom et al., 2007; Bruton et al., 2002; Bruton et al., 2005). In a similar vein, Zacharakis et al. (2007) also show how the institutional environment affects the decision-making of venture capitalists. Often these studies focus on the lack of the necessary institutions to allow entrepreneurs to be successful. Eid (2006) argues that widespread reform is necessary for private equity in the Middle East and North Africa to thrive. Lee et al. (2011) in their 29-country study demonstrate that rigid bankruptcy laws inhibit entrepreneurial behavior. Furthermore, institutional environments shape the nature and amount of initial public offerings (Ravasi and Marchisio, 2003; Szyliowicz et al., 2004).

Many other studies have focused on the ways in which changes in the institutional environment affect entrepreneurs (Newman, 2000). Much of this research has dealt with how the transition from planned to market economies has affected entrepreneurial behavior (Wright et al., 2005). One issue that is a focus of this research is identifying factors that further the growth of entrepreneurship in various geographic regions or nations (Lado and Vozikis, 1996; Chen and Lin, 2006). Additionally, there is a large body of work on economic development and entrepreneurship. One approach has been to compare and contrast entrepreneurship across countries by developing measures of institutional profiles (Busenitz et al., 2000). Some scholars have used this approach to better understand the situation in emerging economies (Manolova et al., 2008).

Another major area of research involves the intersection of international business and entrepreneurship. Drori et al. (2006) build on institutional theory and create an analytic framework to examine international entrepreneurship and Di Gregorio (2005) has applied widely accepted entrepreneurship concepts in an effort to expand the study of international management. Other scholars have suggested that in order to analyze this relationship, it is essential to examine the ways and degree to which the cross-border activities embody innovative and risk-seeking dimensions (McDougall and Oviatt, 2000). And, since practically any kind of international business activity can be considered 'entrepreneurial', this area incorporates a very wide range of studies. These range from the role of MNC subsidiaries (Birkinshaw, 1999, 2000; Birkinshaw and Hood, 2001) to firm internationalization strategies (Jones and Coviello, 2005), especially how firms take advantage of the resources offered by different institutional environments (Kostova et al., 2008; Mathews and Zander, 2007; Mudambi and Zahra, 2007). These studies encompass both existing firms entering new markets and the 'born globals'.

Many scholars have also examined the activities and impacts of specific 'institutional entrepreneurs'. These studies have considered both the ways in which the environment shapes their activities and the ways in which these entrepreneurs shape the context in which they operate (Beckert, 1999). Their influence is especially profound in the development and strengthening of those institutional and legal arrangements that will permit them and their technologies to succeed (Chatterjee et al., 2002; Delemarle, 2007). Perhaps not surprisingly, many studies have demonstrated that these efforts are designed to advance the interests of a specific company, industry or sector (Demil and Bensédrine, 2005; Spencer et al., 2005). Nasra and Dacin (2010) examine the role of the state as an institutional entrepreneur and the ways in which its policies promoted the transformation of Dubai into a modern economy. However, the role of individual entrepreneurs in bringing about change has recently been questioned on the grounds that only through collective action does institutional change take place (Aldrich, 2011).

This large literature does not, however, include many works that apply the theoretical and conceptual approaches that are to be found in the institutional theory field in a way that is consonant with the latest scholarship. For example, discussions of the 'environment' are seldom rigorously developed. Most fail to engage with the many dimensions that are involved or the factors that shape those dimensions over time. Notable exceptions deal with the dissemination of practices and ideas. This includes Alvarez (1992), who has studied the diffusion of managerial ideology (including the concept of entrepreneurship) cross-nationally and how it becomes institutionalized; Honig and Karlsson (2004), who discussed how institutional forces influenced Swedish entrepreneurs' business plans; and Lewin et al. (1999), who analyzed the relationship between institutional environmental change and organizational forms.

SUGGESTIONS FOR FUTURE RESEARCH – INSIGHTS FROM THEORY

As shown above, international entrepreneurship research has yet to fully utilize the insights afforded by institutional theory. Although many scholars agree that institutional theory can enhance, in many ways, our understanding of international entrepreneurship, its potential remains unfulfilled. To date, it has been applied in a limited way, mostly in an attempt to better understand the role of the wider environment. These studies have examined a wide range of entrepreneurial activity across different national contexts, but most have focused on the visible aspects of institutions – the laws, regulations and cultural artifacts. We argue that institutional theory can make a much larger contribution if the current streams from neo-institutional theory dealing with change and agency are applied.

Such an effort requires the appropriate conceptualization and application of institutional arguments. To begin, such studies should be sensitive to issue of scope and magnitude such as units and levels of analysis. Effective research requires an understanding of how to differentiate between the various levels that impact and provide a context for entrepreneurial activity. Similarly, the focus should be explicitly placed upon the appropriate unit, whether it be a firm, a regulatory agency or a policy-making body. Especially critical for future research is the use of current theorizing that focuses on change and agency. If this is done, scholars can better understand transnational and single-country phenomena. As demonstrated in the above literature review, most current research seeking to apply institutional theory to international entrepreneurship is restricted to a consideration of limited aspects of the environment. Often these studies are limited to single countries so that, unless carefully constructed, they may have limited generalizability and contribute little to the refinement of theory. Second, this approach disregards the embedded nature of institutional relations. Thus the context becomes divorced from the relationships that are being studied and a critical variable is omitted from the analysis.

These problems can be solved through the use of a coherent, unified theoretical approach that not only looks at the environment in which entrepreneurship occurs, but encompasses the full range of mechanisms that drive behavior. Moreover, the focus on a particular national setting must be structured in an analytic manner that permits the findings to be compared with the results of other studies. Unless this is done, scholars cannot effectively build upon other research to refine existing theories. Engaging in more sophisticated single case studies as well as more numerous cross-national analyses with multiple observations would facilitate our understanding of the phenomenon of international entrepreneurship.

Such an approach requires scholarly agreement on a specific paradigm, and one scholar has proposed a framework to accomplish that end (Etemad, 2004). He proposes that any understanding of international entrepreneurship requires recognition of the interplay of four levels – the entrepreneur, the firm, the market and the international environment. Although this is a useful start, it requires modification so as to harmonize it with the accepted levels of analysis used by institutional theorists. Therefore we suggest that scholars consider the following levels when dealing with international entrepreneurship issues – the entrepreneur, the firm, the country and the world system.

Although these levels are analytically distinct, it is necessary to recognize that they are interconnected. Understanding that the characteristics and relationships at each level influence behavior, but also that these firms are embedded across levels, is crucial. This is an important insight that institutional theory offers. Below we suggest how each level can provide promising research possibilities.

Level 1 – The Entrepreneur

In recent years the critical role of cultural–cognitive processes in influencing firm behavior has gained increasing recognition. These include the mechanisms of social construction and systems of meaning (Philips and Malhotra, 2008; Zilber, 2008). Much of this research considers the 'microfoundations' of institutions, how the behavior of individual actors leads to sustaining or changing wider institutional processes (Powell and Colyvas, 2008). Critical to this effort would be work that explicitly engages with the role of culture and cognitive processes and how they influence individual decisions to become an entrepreneur, and how entrepreneurial opportunities are viewed within a society. Entrepreneurs, as embedded actors (Dana, 1995; Jones and Conway, 2004; Keeble et al., 1998), emerge and function as the result of their own backgrounds, educational and other experiences, and the nature of the environment in which they operate.

Accordingly, a greater emphasis on the role of socio- and cognitive cultural elements on the emergence, role and functioning of individual entrepreneurs is necessary (Dodd, 2002). The role of mechanisms of institutional processes that are usually studied at the industry, field or global level (Powell and Colyvas, 2008) also needs to be considered at the individual level. Specific areas that deserve greater attention, therefore, include understanding how individuals enact, interpret, translate and give meaning to behavior. The sociocultural influences on individual entrepreneurs can best be understood within the broader context of all of the 'arenas' of an entrepreneur's identity that can impose meaning or give rise to action (or constrain actions as well) (Glynn, 2008). By examining metaphors and meanings used by entrepreneurs in the USA, Dodd (2002) created a cultural framework of entrepreneurship that could be compared with the understandings of Northern Europeans (Koriranen, 1995). Doing so represents an initial move towards identifying and explicating the harmonies and discordances across cultures. It is also necessary to recognize that entrepreneurial experiences and orientations are likely to change more rapidly owing to the ever-escalating interactions with other cultures (Andersson et al., 2004; Kedia and Mukherji, 1999; Knight, 2001; Kuivalainen et al., 2004).

Comparative research utilizing qualitative and quantitative methods along these lines will enhance our knowledge of the role and functioning of critical institutions. In this way, it is likely that new insights into the nature of entrepreneurial practices and processes will be generated, especially since this processual and constructivist approach will facilitate the emergence of new perspectives on entrepreneurship. This view will allow understanding of an entrepreneurial experience that is highly dynamic while also taking into account evolving transnational differences that are often described in more macro and static terms (Steyart, 1998). The result can be a better understanding of entrepreneurial motivations (Schumpter, 1934/1993) both within and across transnational contexts (Djelic and Quack, 2008).

Level 2 – The Firm

Firms are critical actors in entrepreneurship research, but for institutional theorists, understanding the role played by firms requires viewing the organization as embedded in a wider field of activity. The role the 'field plays' is essential for understanding both individual and firm behavior, as is the feedback that exists in this relationship. Entrepreneurial firms shape and are shaped by the field in which they operate. Thus the drivers of performance can only be understood in terms of the field in which the firm is embedded. One of the most crucial ideas for understanding this relationship is that of 'institutional logics' or shared systems of meaning. Institutional logics reflect aggregate preferences as well as specific values and motivations for action (Thornton and Ocasio, 2008; Scott and Davis, 2007). By incorporating the cultural, structural, normative and symbolic influences in a specific field, logics help explain actions and practices within it. Logics are critical for understanding international entrepreneurship because they provide the bridge between broader macro-forces such as culture, societal norms and industry-specific activity. As a result, the function and effects of the external environment can be more fully understood.

Unlike classic entrepreneurial arguments that focus on individual traits, decision-making procedures, search processes or behavior, institutional arguments place a priority on the influence of the wider environment. Entrepreneurship can be seen as activities that advance change (emergence of new organizational forms, fields and industries). Shifting institutional environments embodying complexity and multiple systems of meaning and rules permits entrepreneurs to have more 'choice' and 'creativity' (Scott, 2007). By understanding the intricacy of logics, schemas, routines and scripts, one can better predict the actions of entrepreneurial actors. Thus the application of institutional arguments, including changes in norms, values, beliefs and logics, makes a richer understanding of entrepreneurship.

Suchman et al. (2001) posit that entrepreneurial activity can be better explained through the cultural process of diffusion, combination and sense-making. As they state,

> Diffusion introduces preexisting models into new fields . . . entrepreneurship may simply involve imitating the organizational forms of one field when launching new endeavors in another. Recombination goes one step further, constructing novel organizations, but from preexisting standardized components . . . sensemaking, the most radical form of instructional entrepreneurship, involves the construction of genuinely novel cultural accounts to address unexpected and anomalous events. (2001, p. 355)

The issue of how organizations form and diffuse is the subject of current work by Suchman. He utilizes a biological metaphor and suggests that models or templates create 'organizational genetics'. Organizations diffuse and reproduce through a process of 'filiation', when a new organization copies an existing organization, versus 'compilation', which occurs when an external actor observes differences in forms and practices and organizes them into models that can be copied. The final process is 'bricolage', the combination and recombinations of organizations creating new, hybrid forms (Campbell, 1997, 2004; Douglas, 1986). These 'models of organizing' carry within them institutional understandings about practices and structure as well as the role of actors and standards of behavior (normative and cultural–cognitive elements). These processes of diffusion and adoption involve interpretation as well as enactment. All of these are important macro-processes critical to further our understandings of international entrepreneurship.

The role of institutional logics in international entrepreneurial behavior is a fertile area for research given the fact that research has shown the strong influence that they have on firm- and individual-level action (e.g. Cooper et al., 1996; Czarniawska and Gendell, 2002; Green et al., 2008; Kitchener, 2002; Reay and Hinings, 2005; Suddaby and Greenwood, 2005; Thornton, 2002; Townley, 2002 – cf. Thornton and Ocasio, 2008). The multiple methodologies used to measure institutional logics can also be applied to investigating how logics influence entrepreneurial activity, especially across national contexts. Prior scholarship suggests that logics affect both opportunity identification and the manner in which the business is implemented, an argument that warrants empirical testing over time across different cultural contexts.

Level 3 – The Country

Nation-states are recognized by scholars as the critical actor in international entrepreneurship. Accordingly, they have been the subject of numerous studies, most of which deal with regulation, laws and culture at a general level. However, insights into how and why these dimensions influence entrepreneurial activity seldom emerge from this literature. However, a rich body of literature known as 'societal institutionalism' incorporates a broad range of theoretical and empirical work that investigates political and sociocultural country-level differences and their role on firm activity (Djelic and Quack, 2008). Institutions such as the state, stock markets and banking systems, schools and universities, and labor markets, as well as particular cultural norms and values, have all been analyzed by institutional theorists (Hall and Soskice, 2001; Maurice and Sorge, 2000; Whitley, 1999). They have paid attention to the role these mechanisms play for individual managers and groups, as well as firm structure and strategy (Djelic and Quack, 2008).

Societal institutionalism is considered critical by many authors because, unlike factors such as culture that do not change quickly or easily, they can be dramatically transformed in a relatively short time by political decisions. The role of regulatory frameworks and the power of the state has long been understood to be critical for the success of entrepreneurs. In particular, the crucial role that property rights have on entrepreneurship is the subject of much work by economists (Baumol, 1968). When property rights are not established and enforced appropriately by the state, scholars have empirically demonstrated that entrepreneurship is inhibited. It is not just access to property that is the issue, but the ability to leverage these assets to start and build a business (De Soto, 2000).

As important as regulatory and legal systems are, they cannot be understood in isolation from the sociocultural, political and normative environment in which they are embedded. International entrepreneurship research can be aided by institutional work carried out by Edelman and colleagues (see Edelman, 1992; Edelman et al., 1992; Edelman et al., 1993; Edelman and Suchman, 1997; Edelman et al., 1999) and Dobbin and colleagues (Dobbin, 1994; Dobbin and Dowd, 1997, 2000; Dobbin et al., 1993), who have studied the factors that shape regulatory frameworks and the role individual actors as well as culture, values and norms play in creating various legislative structures. How institutions are defined and how they interact with the state is not agreed upon (Greenwood et al., 2008b). In particular, laws and regulations become instantiated and reflect wider interests (Dobbin, 1994; Edelman, 1992). The significant insight of these scholars is not just that regulations either promote or inhibit opportunities, but that they are reflective of cognitive schema that are historically dependent (Edelman and Suchman, 1997). The implicit and explicit political and social mechanisms are reflected in a country's regulatory framework, expanding narrow traditional notions that focus on regulations as a purely coercive influence enlarging our understanding of entrepreneurial behavior within and between countries.

These mechanisms interact at all levels of analysis by influencing perceptions of appropriateness regarding structures and activities. Much institutional theory research has dealt with national differences regarding how firms are organized, and various forms ranging from *keiretsus* to multidivisional forms have been identified. Orru et al. (1991, p. 363) effectively summarize these relationships as 'represent[ing] qualitatively distinct conceptualizations of what constitutes appropriate economic activity'. Any realistic effort to analyze entrepreneurship, therefore, must incorporate a country's norms and values into the study.

Furthermore, the state itself is an important actor directly and indirectly. Many governments (e.g. the USSR) have attempted to influence the sociocultural system directly, but more commonly their policies in other sectors have consequences for values and norms. Moreover, the state has a wide range of policy options regarding business structures and operations. Jepperson and Meyer (1991) identify two basic dimensions that differentiate state–business relations. The first is the degree to which individual actors are free to operate within the economy, and the second is the degree to which the state controls economic institutions. By considering these two variables, it is possible to predict variations in entrepreneurial structures and behavior. However, work in international entrepreneurship has not, to date, taken advantage of such conceptual distinctions even though entrepreneurial activity is always shaped by such environments.

Research on international entrepreneurship along these lines could consist of empirical studies on the relationship between the level of state involvement and the behavior of individual actors. More ambitious work could be comparative and cross-national. The findings of such research could lead to a better understanding of the kinds of environment that permit entrepreneurship to flourish.

Level 4 – The World System

In recent years, many social scientists have examined the ways in which the world system is structured and how it functions. They have studied the ways in which it has changed over time and agree that the contemporary world system is characterized by ever-growing interdependencies. As a result, states and other international actors are adopting ever more similar policies in regard to trade and business. Furthermore, such research has also identified the specific factors that influence state behavior such as converging ideologies, international governance mechanisms and social action. Of particular interest has been the role of such powerful international organizations as the World Bank, the IMF and the WTO, as well as bilateral agreements and social interactions. This increasing interdependence and the functioning of these organizations has inexorably led to the widespread acceptance of various practices, policies and structures. This is not to argue that actors and policies at the world level determine the structure and functioning of domestic institutions, but rather that existing institutions are subject to new influences so that they increasingly reflect internationally accepted cultural and value systems.

As Meyer et al. (1997, pp. 144–5) have pointed out, 'many features of the contemporary nation-state derive from models constructed and propagated through global cultural and associational processes'. In short, in order to apply institutional arguments effectively, it is necessary, as stated earlier, to consider these four levels of analysis. Doing so provides a useful framework that not only permits but facilitates the exploration of the relevance and applicability of institutional arguments that have provided more important insights into institutional processes than those that have been applied heretofore in the study of international entrepreneurship.

Since these levels are interconnected, this framework can enrich and facilitate the development of understanding within IE research. To cite but one example, research has shown that activities and interactions at the world level lead to shared conceptions about a given problem or issue that affects country-level outcomes. Because of their embeddedness in global networks, nations tend to adopt similar policies and perspectives in such areas as patent legislation (Hironaka, 2002), views of science (Shofer, 2003) and educational systems (Drori et al., 2003). These findings highlight the significance of the need to expand our studies of international entrepreneurship because schools, patent offices and science are critical institutions that not only determine some of the key characteristics of entrepreneurship but also determine what is seen, counted and identified. Moreover, international organizations gather and disseminate vast amounts of empirical data in numerous areas that are critical for any analysis of the rates and growth of entrepreneurship. Indeed, their statistical activities reflect their frameworks and conceptions and thus greatly influence how we define 'entrepreneurship'. To what extent they have done so in different countries, and with what consequences, represents an important area of research. Additionally, research utilizing this type of institutional framework could examine the diffusion of a particular activity cross-nationally, paying special attention to its impact on entrepreneurial behavior. Given the contemporary concern with microfinance as a powerful tool for stimulating entrepreneurship at local levels, a study that examined the rise of microfinance, the role that international institutions and states have played in its diffusion and its impact on entrepreneurial activity within countries would be especially valuable.

REFERENCES

Acs, Z., Dana, L.-P. and Jones, M. (2003), 'Toward new horizons: the internationalization of entrepreneurship', *Journal of International Entrepreneurship*, **1**: 5–12.

Ahlstrom, D. and Bruton, G.D. (2002), 'An institutional perspective on the role of culture in shaping strategic actions by technology-focused entrepreneurial firms in China', *Entrepreneurship: Theory and Practice*, **26**(4): 53–69.

Ahlstrom, D., Bruton, G.D. and Yeh, K.S. (2007), 'Venture capital in China: past, present, and future', *Asia Pacific Journal of Management*, **24**(3): 247–68.

Aldrich, H. (2011), 'Heroes, villains, and fools: institutional entrepreneurship, not institutional entrepreneurs', *Entrepreneurship Research Journal*, **1**(2): 1–4.

Alvarez, J.L. (1992), 'The international diffusion and industrialization of the new entrepreneurship movement: a study in the sociology of organizational knowledge', *Journal of International Business Studies*, **23**(3): 583–94.

Andersson, S., Gabrielsson, J. and Wictor, I. (2004), 'International activities in small firms – examining factors influencing the internationalisation and export growth of small firms', *Canadian Journal of Administrative Science*, **21**(1): 22–34.

Arndt, M. and Bigelow, B. (2000), 'Presenting structural innovation in an institutional environment: hospitals' use of impression management', *Administrative Science Quarterly*, **45**(3): 494–522.

Autio, E. (2005), 'Creative tension: the significance of Ben Oviatt's and Patricia McDougall's article "Toward a theory of international new ventures"', *Journal of International Business Studies*, **36**(1): 9–19.

Battilana, J., B. Leca and E. Boxenbaum (2009), 'How actors change institutions: towards a theory of institutional entrepreneurship', *Academy of Management Annals*, **3**(1): 65–107.

Baumol, W. (1968), 'Entrepreneurship in economic theory', *The American Economic Review*, **58**(2): 64–71.

Beckert, J. (1999), 'Agency, entrepreneurs, and institutional change: the role of strategic choice and institutionalized practices in organizations', *Organization Studies*, **20**(5): 777–99.

Beckert, J. (2010), 'How do fields change? The interrelations of institutions, networks, and cognition in the dynamics of markets', *Organization Studies*, **31**(5): 605–27.

Bilkey, W.J. and Tesar, G. (1977), 'The export behavior of smaller-sized Wisconsin manufacturing firms', *Journal of International Business Studies*, **8**: 93–8.

Birkinshaw, J. (1997), 'Entrepreneurship in multinational corporations: the characteristics of subsidiary initiatives', *Strategic Management Journal*, **18**: 207–29.

Birkinshaw, J. (1999), 'The determinants and consequences of subsidiary initiative in multinational corporations', *Entrepreneurship: Theory and Practice*, **24**(1): 9–36.

Birkinshaw, J. (2000), *Entrepreneurship in the Global Firm*, London and Thousand Oaks, CA: Sage.

Birkinshaw, J. and Hood, N. (2001), 'Unleash innovation in foreign subsidiaries', *Harvard Business Review*, **79**(3): 131–7.

Bourdieu, P. and Wacquant, L. (1992), *An Invitation to Reflexive Sociology*, Chicago, IL: University of Chicago Press.

Boxenbaum, E. and Jonsson, S. (2008), 'Isomorphism, diffusion, and decoupling', in R. Greenwood, C. Oliver, R. Suddaby and K. Sahlin (eds), *The Sage Handbook of Organizational Institutionalism*, Thousand Oaks, CA: Sage, pp. 78–98.

Bruton, G.D., Ahlstrom, D. and Li, H. (2010), 'Institutional theory and entrepreneurship: where are we now and where do we need to move in the future?', *Entrepreneurship: Theory and Practice*, **34**(3): 421–40.

Bruton, G.D., Ahlstrom, D. and Singh, K. (2002), 'The impact of the institutional environment on the venture capital industry in Singapore', *Venture Capital*, **4**(3): 197–218.

Bruton, G.D., Fried, V.H. and Manigart, S. (2005), 'Institutional influences on the worldwide expansion of venture capital', *Entrepreneurship: Theory and Practice*, **29**(6): 737–60.

Busenitz, L.W., Gomez, C. and Spencer, J.W. (2000), 'Country institutional profiles: unlocking entrepreneurial phenomena', *Academy of Management Journal*, **43**(5): 994–1003.

Campbell, J. (1997), 'Mechanisms of evolutionary change in economic governance: interaction, interpretation, and bricolage', in L. Magnusson and J. Ottosson (eds), *Evolutionary Economics and Path Dependence*, Cheltenham, UK and Lyme, NH, USA: Edward Elgar, pp. 10–31.

Campbell, J. (2004), *Institutional Change and Globalization*, Princeton, NJ: Princeton University Press.

Chatterjee, D., Grewal, R. and Sambamurthy, V. (2002), 'Shaping up for e-commerce: institutional enablers of the organizational assimilation of web technologies', *MIS Quarterly*, **26**(2): 65–89.

Chen, I. and Lin, F. (2006), 'Regional development and sources of superior performance across textile and IT sectors in Taiwan', *Entrepreneurship and Regional Development*, **18**(3): 227–48.

Cooper, D., Hinings, C.R. and Greenwood, R. (1996), 'Sedimentation and transformation in organizational change: the case of Canadian law firms', *Organization Studies*, **17**(4): 623–47.

Cox, L. (1997), 'International entrepreneurship: a literature review', Working Paper, Florida International University.

Czarniawska, B. (2008), 'How to misuse institutions and get away with it: some reflections on institutional theory', in R. Greenwood, C. Oliver, R. Suddaby and K. Sahlin (eds), *The Sage Handbook of Organizational Institutionalism*, Thousand Oaks, CA: Sage, pp. 769–82.

Czarniawska, B. and Gendell, K. (2002), 'Gone shopping? Universities on their way to the market', *Scandinavian Journal of Management Studies*, **18**(4): 455–74.

Czarniawska, B. and Sevon, G. (1996), *Translating Organizational Change*, Berlin: Walter de Gruyter.

Dacin, M.T., Goodstein, J. and Scott, W.R. (2002), 'Institutional theory and institutional change: introduction to the special research forum', *Academy of Management Journal*, **45**(1): 45–7.

Dacin, M.T., Ventresca, M. and Beale, B. (1999), 'The embeddedness of organizations', *Journal of Management*, **25**: 317–56.

Dana, L. (1995), 'Entrepreneurship in a remote sub-arctic community', *Entrepreneurship: Theory and Practice*, **20**(1): 57–72.

Davis, G. (2006), 'Mechanisms and the theory of organizations', *Journal of Management Inquiry*, **15**(2): 114–18.

Davis, G. and Greve, H.R. (1997), 'Corporate elite networks and governance changes in the 1980s', *American Journal of Sociology*, **103**: 1–37.

Davis, G. and Marquis, C. (2005), 'Prospects for organization theory in the early twenty-first century: institutional fields and mechanisms', *Organization Science*, **16**(4): 332–43.

De Soto, H. (2000), *The Mystery of Capital: Why Capitalism Triumphs in the West and Fails Everywhere Else*, New York: Basic Books.

Deephouse, D. and Suchman, M. (2008), 'Legitimacy in organizational institutionalism', in R. Greenwood, C. Oliver, R. Suddaby and K. Sahlin (eds), *The Sage Handbook of Organizational Institutionalism*, Thousand Oaks, CA: Sage, pp. 49–77.

Delemarle, A. (2007), 'Temporality of the mobilisation process encountered by the institutional entrepreneur', *Academy of Management Proceedings*, 1–7.

Demil, B. and Bensédrine, J. (2005), 'Processes of legitimization and pressure toward regulation', *International Studies of Management and Organization*, **35**(2): 56–77.

Di Gregorio, D. (2005), 'Rethinking country risk: insights from entrepreneurship theory', *International Business Review*, **14**: 209–26.

DiMaggio, P.J. (1988), 'Interest and agency in institutional theory', in L.G. Zucker (ed.), *Institutional Patterns and Organizations: Culture and Environment*, Cambridge, MA: Ballinger, pp. 3–21.

DiMaggio, P. and Powell, W.W. (1983), 'The iron cage revisited: institutional isomorphism and collective rationality in organizational fields', *American Sociological Review*, **48**: 147–60.

DiMaggio, P. and Powell, W. (1991), 'Introduction', in W.W. Powell and P. DiMaggio (eds), *The New Institutionalism in Organizational Analysis*, Chicago, IL: University of Chicago Press, pp. 1–38.

Dimitratos, P. and Jones, M. (2005), 'Future directions for international entrepreneurship research', *International Business Review*, **14**(2): 119–28.

Dimitratos, P., Lioukas, S. and Carter, S. (2004), 'The relationship between entrepreneurship and international performance: the importance of domestic environment', *International Business Review*, **13**: 19–41.

Djelic, M.L. and Quack, S. (2008), 'Institutions and transnationalization', in R. Greenwood, C. Oliver, R. Suddaby and K. Sahlin (eds), *The Sage Handbook of Organizational Institutionalism*, Thousand Oaks, CA: Sage, pp. 299–324.

Dobbin, F. (1994), *Forging Industrial Policy: The United States, Britain, and France in the Railway Age*, New York: Cambridge University Press.

Dobbin, F. and Dowd, T. (1997), 'How policy shapes competition: early railroad foundings in Massachusetts', *Administrative Science Quarterly*, **42**: 501–29.

Dobbin, F. and Dowd, T. (2000), 'The market that antitrust built: public policy, private coercion, and railroad acquisition, 1825 to 1922', *American Sociological Review*, **65**: 631–57.

Dobbin, F., Sutton, J., Meyer, J. and Scott, W.R. (1993), 'Equal opportunity law and the construction of internal labor markets', *American Journal of Sociology*, **99**: 396–427.

Dodd, S. (2002), 'Metaphors and meaning: a grounded cultural model of US entrepreneurship', *Journal of Business Venturing*, **17**: 519–35.

Douglas, M. (1986), *How Institutions Think*, New York: Syracuse University Press.

Droege, S.B. and N. Brown-Johnson (2007), 'Broken rules and constrained confusion: toward a theory of meso-institutions', *Management and Organization Review*, **3**(1): 81–104.

Drori, I., Honig, B. and Ginsberg, A. (2006), 'Transnational entrepreneurship: toward a unifying theoretical framework', *Academy of Management Proceedings*, Q1–Q6.

Drori, G., Meyer, J., Ramirez, F. and Schofer, E. (2003), *Science in the Modern World Polity: Institutionalization and Globalization*, Stanford, CA: Stanford University Press.

Edelman, L. (1992), 'Legal ambiguity and symbolic structures: organizational mediation of civil rights law', *American Journal of Sociology*, **97**: 1531–76.

Edelman, L. and Suchman, M. (1997), 'The legal environment of organizations', *Annual Review of Sociology*, **23**: 479–515.

Edelman, L., Abraham, S. and Erlanger, H. (1992), 'Professional construction of law: the inflated threat of wrongful discharge', *Law and Society Review*, **26**(1): 47–83.

Edelman, L., Erlanger, H. and Lande, J. (1993), 'Internal dispute resolution: the transformation of civil rights in the workplace', *Law and Society*, **27**(3): 497–534.

Edelman, L., Uggen, C. and Erlanger, H. (1999), 'The endogeneity of legal regulation: grievance procedures as rational myth', *American Journal of Sociology*, **105**(2): 406–54.

Eid, F. (2006), 'Private equity finance as a growth engine: what it means for emerging markets', *Business Economics*, **41**(3): 7–22.

Elsbach, K. (1994), 'Managing organizational legitimacy in the California cattle industry: the construction and effectiveness of verbal accounts', *Administrative Science Quarterly*, **39**(1): 57–88.

Elsbach, K. and Kramer, R. (1996), 'Members' responses to organizational identity threats: encountering and countering the *Business Week* ratings', *Administrative Science Quarterly*, **41**(3): 442–76.

Elsbach, K. and Sutton, R. (1992), 'Acquiring organizational legitimacy through illegitimate actions: a marriage of institutional and impression management theories', *Academy of Management Journal*, **35**(4): 699–738.

Etemad, H. (2004), 'International entrepreneurship as a dynamic adaptive system: towards a grounded theory', *Journal of International Entrepreneurship*, **2**(1): 5–59.

Fox-Wolfgramm, S., Boal, K. and Hunt, J. (1998), 'Organizational adaptation to institutional change: a comparative study of first-order change in prospector and defender banks', *Administrative Science Quarterly*, **43**(1): 87–126.

Friedland, R. and Alford, R. (1991), 'Bringing society back in: symbols, practices, and institutional contradictions', in W. Powell and P. DiMaggio (eds), *The New Institutionalism in Organizational Analysis*, Chicago, IL: University of Chicago Press, pp. 311–36

Gabrielsson, M., Manek Kirpalani, V.H., Dimitratos, P., Solberg, C.A. and Zucchella, A. (2008), 'Born globals: propositions to help advance the theory', *International Business Review*, **17**(4): 385–401.

Global Entrepreneurship Monitor (GEM) (2010), *GEM 2010 Results*, Babson, MA: GEM.

Glynn, M.A. (2008), 'Beyond constraint: how institutions enable identities', in R. Greenwood, C. Oliver, R. Suddaby and K. Sahlin (eds), *The Sage Handbook of Organizational Institutionalism*, Thousand Oaks, CA: Sage, pp. 413–30.

Gnyawali, D. and Fogel, D. (1994), 'Environments for entrepreneurship development: key dimensions and research implications', *Entrepreneurship: Theory and Practice*, **18**(4), 43–62.

Green, S.E., Babb, M. and Alpaslan, C.M. (2008), 'Institutional field dynamics and the competition between institutional logics: the role of rhetoric in the evolving control of the modern corporation', *Management Communication Quarterly*, **22**(1): 40–73.

Greenwood, R. and Hinings, C.R. (1993), 'Understanding strategic change: the contribution of archetypes', *Academy of Management Journal*, **36**(5): 1052–82.

Greenwood, R. and Hinings, C.R. (2006), 'Radical organizational change', in S. Clegg, C. Hardy, W.W. Nord and T. Lawrence (eds), *Handbook of Organization Studies*, 2nd edn, Thousand Oaks, CA: Sage, pp. 814–42.

Greenwood, R., Oliver, C., Suddaby, R. and Sahlin, K. (eds) (2008a), *The Sage Handbook of Organizational Institutionalism*, Thousand Oaks, CA: Sage.

Greenwood, R., Oliver, C., Suddaby, R. and Sahlin, K. (eds) (2008b), 'Introduction', in R. Greenwood, C. Oliver, R. Suddaby and K. Sahlin (eds), *The Sage Handbook of Organizational Institutionalism*, Thousand Oaks, CA: Sage, pp. 1–46.

Hall, P. and Soskice, D. (eds) (2001), *Varieties of Capitalism*, Oxford: Oxford University Press.

Hashai, N. and Almor, T. (2004), 'Gradually internationalizing "born global" firms: an oxymoron?', *International Business Review*, **13**(4): 465–83.

Hasse, R. and Krücken, G. (2008), 'Systems theory, societal contexts, and organizational heterogeneity', in R. Greenwood, C. Oliver, R. Suddaby and K. Sahlin (eds), *The Sage Handbook of Organizational Institutionalism*, Thousand Oaks, CA: Sage, pp. 539–59.

Hironaka, Ann (2002), 'The globalization of environmental protection: the case of environmental impact assessment', *International Journal of Comparative Sociology*, **43**(1): 65–78.

Hirsch, P.M. and Lounsbury, M. (1997), 'Ending the family quarrel: toward a reconciliation of "old" and "new" institutionalism', *American Behavioral Scientist*, **40**(4): 406–18.

Hoffman, A.J. (1999), 'Institutional evolution and change: environmentalism and the US chemical industry', *Academy of Management Journal*, **42**(4): 351–71.

Hofstede, G. (1983), 'The cultural relativity of organizational practices and theories', *Journal of International Business Studies*, Fall: 75–89.

Honig, B. and Karlsson, T. (2004), 'Institutional forces and the written business plan', *Journal of Management*, **30**(1): 395–419.

Hwang, H. and Powell, W. (2005), 'Institutions and entrepreneurship', in *Handbook of Entrepreneurship Research*, Amsterdam: Kluwer, pp. 179–210.

Jepperson, R. and Meyer, J. (1991), 'The public order and the construction of formal organizations', in W. Powell and P. DiMaggio (eds), *The New Institutionalism in Organizational Analysis*, Chicago, IL: University of Chicago Press, pp. 204–31.

Jones, M., and Coviello, N. (2005), 'Internationalization: conceptualizing an entrepreneurial process of behaviour', *Journal of International Business Studies*, **36**(3): 284–303.

Jones, O. and Conway, S. (2004), 'Social-embeddedness and geographical reach in entrepreneurial networks: the case of James Dyson', in H. Etemad (ed.), *International Entrepreneurship in Small and Medium-Sized Enterprises: Orientation, Environment and Strategy*, Cheltenham, UK and Northampton, MA, USA: Edward Elgar, pp. 87–106.

Karra, N., Phillips, N. and Tracey, P. (2008), 'Building the born global firm: developing entrepreneurial capabilities', *Long Range Planning*, **41**(4): 440–58.

Kedia, B.L. and Mukherji, A. (1999), 'Global managers: developing a mindset for global competitiveness', *Journal of World Business*, **34**(3): 230–51.

Keeble, D., Lawson, C., Smith, H., Moore, B. and Wilkison, F. (1998), 'Internationalisation processes, networking and local embeddedness in technology-intensive small firms', *Small Business Economics*, **11**(4): 327–42.

Kitchener, M. (2002), 'Mobilizing the logic of managerialism in professional fields: the case of academic health centre mergers', *Organization Studies*, **23**(3): 391–420.

Knight, G. (2001), 'Entrepreneurship and strategy in the international SME', *Journal of International Management*, **7**(3): 155–72.

Koriranen, M. (1995), 'North European metaphors of "entrepreneurship" and "an entrepreneur"', in W.D. Bygrave et al. (eds), *Frontiers in Entrepreneurship Research 1995*, Waltham, MA: P&R Publications, pp. 203–16.

Kostova, T. and Roth, K. (2002), 'Adoption of organizational practices by subsidiaries of multinational corporations: institutional and relational effects', *Academy of Management Review*, **45**(1): 215–33.

Kostova, T., Roth, K. and Dacin, T. (2008), 'Institutional theory in the study of MNCs: a critique and new directions', *Academy of Management Review*, **33**(4): 994–1006.

Kraatz, M. and Block, E. (2008), 'Organizational implications of institutional pluralism', in R. Greenwood, C. Oliver, R. Suddaby and K. Sahlin (eds), *The Sage Handbook of Organizational Institutionalism*, Thousand Oaks, CA: Sage, pp. 243–75.

Kuemmerle, W. (2002), 'Home base and knowledge management in international ventures', *Journal of Business Venturing*, **17**(2): 99–122.

Kuivalainen, O., Sundqvist, S., Puumalainen, K. and Cadogan, J. (2004), 'The effect of environmental turbulence and leader characteristics on international performance: are knowledge-based firms different?', *Canadian Journal of Administrative Science*, **21**(1): 35–50.

Lado, A.A. and Vozikis, G.S. (1996), 'Transfer of technology to promote entrepreneurship in developing countries: an integration and proposed framework', *Entrepreneurship: Theory and Practice*, **21**(2): 55–72.

Lawrence, T. and Suddaby, R. (2006), 'Institutions and institutional work', in S. Clegg, C. Hardy, T. Lawrence and W. Nord (eds), *Handbook of Organization Studies*, 2nd edn, Thousand Oaks, CA: Sage, pp. 215–54.

Leca, B., Battilana, J. and Boxembaum, E. (2006), 'Taking stock of institutional entrepreneurship', paper presented at Academy of Management Meetings, Atlanta, GA, August.

Lee, S.-H., Y. Yamakawa, M.W. Peng and J.B. Barney (2011), 'How do bankruptcy laws affect entrepreneurship development around the world?', *Journal of Business Venturing*, **26**(5): 505–20

Lewin, A.Y., Long, C.P. and Carroll, T.N. (1999), 'The coevolution of new organizational forms', *Organization Science*, **10**(5): 535–50.

Li, H. and Atuahene-Gima, K. (2001), 'Product innovation strategy and the performance of new technology ventures in China', *Academy of Management Journal*, **44**(6): 1123–34.

Lim, D., Morse, E., Mitchell, R. and Seawright, K. (2010), 'Institutional environment and entrepreneurial cognitions: a comparative business systems perspective', *Entrepreneurship: Theory and Practice*, **34**(3): 491–516.

Liu, X., Wen, X. and Huang, X. (2008), 'Bounded entrepreneurship and internationalisation of indigenous Chinese private-owned firms', *International Business Review*, **17**(4): 488–508.

Lu, J.W. and Beamish, P.W. (2001), 'The internationalization and performance of SMEs', *Strategic Management Journal*, **22**(6): 565–86

Manolova, T.S. and Yan, A. (2002), 'Institutional constraints and entrepreneurial responses in a transforming economy: the case of Bulgaria', *International Small Business Journal*, **20**(2): 163–84.

Manolova, T.S., Rangamohan, V., Eunni, R.V. and Gyoshev, B.S. (2008), 'Institutional environments for entrepreneurship: evidence from emerging economies in Eastern Europe', *Entrepreneurship: Theory and Practice*, **32**(1): 203–18.

Mathews, J.A. and Zander, I. (2007), 'The international entrepreneurial dynamics of accelerated internationalisation', *Journal of International Business Studies*, **38**(3): 387–403.

Maurice, M. and Sorge, A. (2000), *Embedding Organizations*, Amsterdam and Philadelphia, PA: Benjamins.

McDougall, P.P. (1989), 'International versus domestic entrepreneurship: new venture strategic behavior and industry structure', *Journal of Business Venturing*, **4**: 387–99.

McDougall, P. and Oviatt, B. (2000), 'International entrepreneurship: the intersection of the two research paths', *Academy of Management Journal*, **43**(5): 902–6.

McGrath, R.G. and MacMillan, I.C. (1992), 'More like each other than anyone else? A cross-cultural study of entrepreneurial perceptions', *Journal of Business Venturing*, **7**(5): 419–29.

Meyer, J., Boli, J., Thomas, G. and Ramirez, F. (1997), 'World society and the nation-state', *American Journal of Sociology*, **103**(1): 144–81.

Meyer, J. and Rowan, B. (1977), 'Institutionalized organizations: formal structure as myth and ceremony', *American Journal of Sociology*, **83**(2): 440–63.

Mitchell, R.K., Smith, B., Seawright, K. and Morse, E.A. (2000), 'Cross-cultural cognitions and venture creation decision', *Academy of Management Journal*, **43**(5): 974–93.
Morrow, J.F. (1988), 'International entrepreneurship: a new growth opportunity', *New Management*, **3**: 59–61.
Moya, M. (2008), Worldwide Business Startups, http://www.moyak.com/researcher/resume/papers/business_startups.html (accessed 23 April 2008).
Mudambi, R. and Zahra, S.A. (2007), 'The survival of international new ventures', *Journal of International Business Studies*, **38**(2): 333–52.
Mueller, S. and Thomas, A. (2001), 'Culture and entrepreneurial potential: a nine country study of locus of control and innovativeness', *Journal of Business Venturing*, **16**(1): 51–75.
Murmann, J. and Tushman, M. (2001), 'From the technology cycle to the entrepeneurship dynamic: placing dominant designs in social context', in C. Schoonhoven and E. Romanelli (eds), *The Entrepreneurship Dynamic: The Origins of Entrepreneurship and Its Role in Industry Evolution*, Palo Alto, CA: Stanford University Press, pp. 178–206.
Nasra, R. and Dacin, T. (2010), 'Institutional arrangements and international entrepreneurship: the state as institutional entrepreneur', *Entrepreneurship: Theory and Practice*, **34**(3): 421–40.
Nee, V. (2005), 'The new institutionalisms in economics and sociology', in N. Smelser and R. Swedberg (eds), *The Handbook of Economic Sociology*, 2nd edn, Princeton, NJ and New York: Princeton University Press and Russell Sage Foundation, pp. 49–74.
Nelson, Richard, R. (1993), *National Innovation Systems: A Comparative Approach*, Oxford: Oxford University Press.
Newman, Karen, L. (2000), 'Organizational transformation during institutional upheaval', *Academy of Management Review*, **25**(3): 602–61.
North, D. (1990), *Institutions, Institutional Change, and Economic Performance*, Cambridge: Cambridge University Press.
North, D. (2005), *Understanding the Process of Economic Change*, Princeton, NJ: Princeton University Press.
Orru, M., Biggart, N. and Hamilton, G. (1991), 'Organizational isomorphism in East Asia', in W. Powell and P. DiMaggio (eds), *The New Institutionalism in Organizational Analysis*, Chicago, IL: University of Chicago Press, pp. 361–89.
Ostrom, E. (1999), 'Coping with tragedies of the commons', *Annual Review of Political Science*, **2**: 493–535.
Oviatt, B.M. and McDougall, P.P. (1994), 'Toward a theory of international new ventures', *Journal of International Business Studies*, **25**(1): 45–64.
Oviatt, B.M. and McDougall, P.P. (2005a), 'Defining international entrepreneurship and modeling the speed of internationalization', *Entrepreneurship: Theory and Practice*, **29**(5): 537–53.
Oviatt, B.M. and McDougall, P.P. (2005b), 'The internationalization of entrepreneurship', *Journal of International Business Studies*, **36**(1): 2–8.
Philips, N. and Malhotra, N. (2008), 'Taking social construction seriously: extending the discursive approach in institutional theory', in R. Greenwood, C. Oliver, R. Suddaby and K. Sahlin (eds), *The Sage Handbook of Organizational Institutionalism*, Thousand Oaks, CA: Sage, pp. 702–20.
Pierson, P. (2004), *Politics in Time: History, Institutions and Social Analysis*, Princeton, NJ: Princeton University Press.
Powell, W.W. (1990), 'Neither market nor hierarchy: network forms of organization', *Research in Organizational Behavior*, **12**: 295–336.
Powell, W.W. and Colyvas, J.A. (2008), 'Microfoundations of institutional theory', in R. Greenwood, C. Oliver, R. Suddaby and K. Sahlin (eds), *The Sage Handbook of Organizational Institutionalism*, Thousand Oaks, CA: Sage, pp. 276–98.
Ravasi, D. and Marchisio, G. (2003), 'Going public and the enrichment of a supportive network', *Small Business Economics*, **21**(4): 381–95.
Reay, T. and Hinings, C.R. (2005), 'The recomposition of an organizational field: health care in Alberta', *Organization Studies*, **26**(3): 351–84.
Reuber, A.R. and Fischer, E. (1997), 'The influence of the management team's international experience on the internationalization behavior of SMEs', *Journal of International Business Studies*, **28**(4): 807–25.
Rialp, A., Rialp, J. and Knight, G. (2005), 'The phenomenon of early internationalizing firms: what do we know after a decade (1993–2003) of scientific inquiry?', *International Business Review*, **14**(2): 147–66.
Roland, G. (2004), 'Understanding institutional change: fast-moving and slow-moving institutions', *Studies in Comparative International Development*, **38**(4): 109–31.
Roure, J.B., Keeley, R. and Keller, T. (1992), 'Venture capital strategies in Europe and the U.S. Adapting to the 1990's', in N.C. Churchill et al. (eds), *Frontiers of Entrepreneurship Research*, Babson Park, MA: Babson College, pp. 345–59.
Sahlin, K. and Wedlin, K. (2008), 'Circulating ideas: imitation, translation, and editing', in R. Greenwood, C. Oliver, R. Suddaby and K. Sahlin (eds), *The Sage Handbook of Organizational Institutionalism*, Thousand Oaks, CA: Sage, pp. 218–42.

Sahlin-Andersson, K. (1996), 'Imitating by editing success: the construction of organizational fields', in B. Czarniawska and G. Sevon (eds), *Translating Organizational Change*, Berlin: de Gryuter, pp. 69–92.

Scheela, W. and Van Hoa, T.T. (2004), 'Women entrepreneurs in a transition economy: the case of Vietnam', *International Journal of Management and Decision Making*, **5**(1): 1–20.

Schneiberg, M. and Lounsbury, M. (2008), 'Social movements and institutional analysis', in R. Greenwood, C. Oliver, R. Suddaby and K. Sahlin (eds), *The Sage Handbook of Organizational Institutionalism*, Thousand Oaks, CA: Sage, pp. 650–72.

Schumpeter, J. (1934/1993), *The Theory of Economic Development*, New Brunswick, NJ: Transaction Books.

Scott, W.R. (1995), *Institutions & Organizations*, Thousand Oaks, CA: Sage.

Scott, W.R. (2001), *Institutions & Organizations*, 2nd edn, Thousand Oaks, CA: Sage.

Scott, W.R. (2004), 'Institutional theory: contributing to a theoretical research program', in Ken G. Smith and Michael A. Hitt (eds), *Great Minds in Management: The Process of Theory Development*, Oxford: Oxford University Press, pp. 460–84.

Scott, W.R. (2007), 'Prefatory chapter: institutions and social innovation', in T. Hamalainen and R. Heiskala (eds), *Social Innovations, Institutional Change and Economic Performance*, Cheltenham, UK and Northampton, MA, USA: Edward Elgar, pp. vii–xx.

Scott, W.R. (2008a), *Institutions & Organizations*, 3rd edn, Thousand Oaks, CA: Sage.

Scott, W.R. (2008b), 'Approaching adulthood: the maturing of institutional theory', *Theory and Society*, **37**(5): 427–42.

Scott, W.R. and Davis, G.F. (2007), *Organizations: Rational, Natural, and Open Systems*, Thousand Oaks, CA: Sage.

Seung-Hyun, L., Yamakawa, Y., Peng, M. and Barney, J. (2011), 'How do bankruptcy laws affect entrepreneurship development around the world?', *Journal of Business Venturing*, **26**(5), 505–20.

Sewell, W. (1992), 'A theory of structure: duality, agency, and transformation', *American Journal of Sociology*, **98**(1): 1–29.

Shofer, E. (2003), 'The global institutionalization of geological science', *American Sociological Review*, **68**(5): 730–59.

Spencer, J.W. and Gómez, C. (2004), 'The relationship among national institutional structures, economic factors, and domestic entrepreneurial activity: a multi-country study', *Journal of Business Research*, **57**(10): 1098–107.

Spencer, J.W., Murtha, T.P. and Lenway, S.A. (2005), 'How governments matter to new industry creation', *Academy of Management Review*, **30**(2): 321–37.

Steensma, K., Marino, L., Weaver, M. and Dickson, P. (2000), 'The influence of national culture in the formation of technology alliances by entrepreneurial firms', *Academy of Management Journal*, **43**(5): 951–73.

Steyart, C. (1998), 'A qualitative methodology for process studies of entrepreneurship', *International Studies of Management and Organization*, **27**(3): 13–33.

Suchman, M., Steward, D. and Westfall, C. (2001), 'The legal environment of entrepreneurship: observations on the legitimation of venture finance in Silicon Valley', in C.B. Schoonhoven and E. Romanelli (eds), *The Entrepreneurship Dynamic: Origins of Entrepreneurship and the Evolution of Industries*, Stanford, CA: Stanford University Press, pp. 349–82.

Suddaby, R. (2010), 'Challenges for institutional theory', *Journal of Management Inquiry*, **19**(1): 14–20.

Suddaby, R. and Greenwood, R. (2005), 'Rhetorical strategies of legitimacy', *Administrative Science Quarterly*, **50**(1): 35–67.

Szyliowicz, D. and Galvin, T. (2010), 'Applying broader strokes: extending institutional perspectives and agendas for international entrepreneurship research', *International Business Review*, **19**(4): 317–33.

Szyliowicz, D., Kennedy, K.H. and Nelson, T. (2004), 'Shaping of strategic behavior: how macro-environmental effects pattern the country-level participation of non-US firms in US equity markets', *Technology Analysis and Strategic Management*, **16**(2): 223–40.

Thomas, A.S. and Mueller, S.L. (2000), 'A case for comparative entrepreneurship: assessing the relevance of culture', *Journal of International Business Studies*, **31**(2): 287–301.

Thornton, P.H. (2002), 'The rise of the corporation in a craft industry: conflict and conformity in institutional logics', *Academy of Management Journal*, **45**(1): 81–101.

Thornton, P.H. (2004), *Markets from Culture*, Stanford, CA: Stanford University Press.

Thornton, P.H. and Ocasio, W. (2008), 'Institutional logics', in R. Greenwood, C. Oliver, R. Suddaby and K. Sahlin (eds), *The Sage Handbook of Organizational Institutionalism*, Thousand Oaks, CA: Sage, pp. 99–129.

Townley, B. (2002), 'The role of competing rationalities in institutional change', *Academy of Management Journal*, **45**(1): 163–79.

Trompenaars, F. (1994), *Riding the Waves of Culture: Understanding Diversity in Global Business*, New York: Irwin.

Veciana, J. and Urbano, D. (2008), 'The institutional approach to entrepreneurship research', *International Entrepreneurship and Management Journal*, **4**(4): 365–79.

Welter, F. and Smallbone, D. (2011), 'Institutional perspectives on entrepreneurial behavior in challenging environments', *Journal of Small Business Management*, **49**(1): 107–25.

Welter, F., Kauonen, T., Chepurenko, A., Malieva, E. and Venesaar, U. (2004), 'Trust environments and entrepreneurial behavior – exploratory evidence from Estonia, Germany, and Russia', *Journal of Enterprising Culture*, **12**(4): 327–49.

Westphal, J. and Zajac, E. (2001), 'Decoupling policy from practice: the case of stock repurchase programs', *Administrative Science Quarterly*, **46**(2): 202–28.

Westwood, R. and Clegg, S. (eds) (2003), *Debating Organization: Point–Counterpoint in Organization Studies*, Malden, MA: Blackwell.

Whitley, R. (1999), *Divergent Capitalisms*, Oxford: Oxford University Press.

Williamson, O. (1979), 'Transaction cost economics: the governance of contractual relations', *Journal of Law and Economics*, **22**(2): 233–61.

Williamson, O. (1983), 'Credible commitments: using hostages to support exchange', *American Economic Review*, **73**(4): 519–40.

Wright, M., Filatotchev, I., Peng, M. and Hoskisson, R. (2005), Strategy research in emerging economies: challenging conventional wisdom', *Journal of Management Studies*, **42**(1): 1–33.

Wright, M., Pruthi, S. and Lockett, A. (2005), 'International venture capital research: from cross-country comparisons to crossing borders', *International Journal of Management Reviews*, **7**(3): 135–65.

Wright, R.W. and Ricks, D.A. (1994), 'Trends in international business research: twenty-five years later', *Journal of International Business Studies*, **25**(4): 687–701.

Yeung, H. (2002), 'Entrepreneurship in international business: an institutional perspective', *Asia Pacific Journal of Management*, **19**(1): 29–61.

Yu, T. (2000), 'Hong Kong's entrepreneurship: behaviors and determinants', *Entrepreneurship and Regional Development*, **12**(3): 179–94.

Zacharakis, A.L. (1997), 'Entrepreneurial entry into foreign markets: a transaction cost perspective', *Entrepreneurship Theory and Practice*, **21**(3): 23–39.

Zacharakis, A.L., McMullen, J.S. and Shepherd, D.A. (2007), 'Venture capitalists' decision policies across three countries: an institutional theory perspective', *Journal of International Business Studies*, **38**(5): 691–708.

Zahra, S. (2005), 'A theory of international new ventures: a decade of research', *Journal of International Business Studies*, **36**(1): 20–28.

Zahra, S.A., Ireland, R.D. and Hitt, M.A. (2000), 'International expansion by new venture firms: international diversity, mode of market entry, technological learning and performance', *Academy of Management Journal*, **43**: 925–50.

Zahra, S.A., Juha, S.K and Yu, J. (2005), 'Cognition and international entrepreneurship: implications for research on international opportunity recognition and exploitation', *International Business Review*, **14**: 129–46.

Zilber, T. (2008), 'The work of meanings in institutional processes and thinking', in R. Greenwood, C. Oliver, R. Suddaby and K. Sahlin (eds), *The Sage Handbook of Organizational Institutionalism*, Thousand Oaks, CA: Sage, pp. 151–69.

21 Offshoring and MNC strategy
Debmalya Mukherjee and Ben L. Kedia

Scholars and practitioners widely acknowledge that the ability to develop and implement innovation is a key strategic component of capturing and maintaining competitive advantage in today's highly competitive, global business environment (Mudambi, 2008; Mudambi and Tallman, 2010). Such activities are driven by trends toward the growing modularization of businesses across industries, as managers pursue disintegration strategies and shed non-core business functions so that they can concentrate on value-generating core functions (Demirbag and Glaister, 2010; Doh et al., 2009). The process of unbundling value chain activities, which results in the relocation of business functions to independent foreign vendors and offshore subsidiaries, has left many firms and organizations dependent on external knowledge sources to complement, augment or even replace their own innovation-producing business activities (Lahiri et al., 2012; Mudambi and Tallman, 2007).

With offshoring, firms relocate their value chain activities to another country. The term encompasses different governance modes, including offshore outsourcing, captive offshoring and hybrid models (e.g. joint ventures, alliances, other loosely coupled interorganizational designs) that link the client and the foreign firm. The past decade has observed a dramatic rise in the number and importance of offshoring activities by firms of all sizes and spheres. One estimate suggests that the global business process offshoring market may reach US$975 billion in 2012 (Lahiri et al., 2012), spanning both routine and high-value-added core activities. For example, R&D traditionally has remained one of the least internationalized and most centralized value chain activities of multinational corporations (MNCs) (Huggins et al., 2007; UNCTAD, 2005). Yet more recently, MNCs have started to offshore R&D activities to exploit the market and technological heterogeneity that exists in different locations, giving rise to R&D innovation centers worldwide (Kenney et al., 2009; Lehrer and Asakawa, 2002).

Extant research in turn has examined the phenomenon of offshoring from different slants. One stream has focused on location-specific intangible resources and knowledge attributes that attract firms to relocate their value chain activities in foreign locations (Bunyaratavej et al., 2007; Graf and Mudambi, 2005), while also considering the performance implications of such types of offshoring (e.g. Bhalla et al., 2008). A second stream has investigated the antecedents of offshoring decisions with regard to low-value-added peripheral activities compared with high-value-added functions such as R&D (Demirbag and Glaister, 2010). A third stream addresses the factors that drive offshore vendor performance and related issues (e.g. Lahiri et al., 2012).

Despite a recent surge in offshoring literature across these three streams, a distinct paucity of research on how firms approach offshoring remains, including the factors that influence their choice of an appropriate offshore governance mode, and how offshoring as a viable strategic device creates value. Many recent studies thus have emphasized the need for a closer examination of the offshoring process, especially with regard to the global dispersion of high-value-added activities (Bunyaratavej et al., 2011; Kumar et al., 2009) and in an attempt to better understand the changing nature of the phenomenon (Mudambi and Venzin, 2010; Kotabe and Mudambi, 2009). Recent attempts to fill this void (Kedia and Mukherjee, 2009) have introduced the DLE framework, based on Dunning's classic OLI framework (Dunning, 1977, 1979, 1993). It proposes that organizations embark on offshoring when they perceive three sets of interrelated advantages: first, organizations disintegrate (D) their value chain activities when they perceive benefits of such a choice in the form of increased modularity and flexibility. Second, firms make location (L) choices regarding who will perform dispersed activities, according to their perceptions of location-specific human capital advantages. Third, the activities get externalized (E), using independent business partners, assuming that the externalization advantages, such as mutual organizational learning and relationship capital, are sufficient; they remain internal (captive center model) if the perceived risks of knowledge misappropriation are too high. By integrating this DLE framework of offshoring with the co-evolutionary theory of offshoring (Lahiri and Kedia, 2011; Manning et al., 2008), this chapter argues that the decisions to disintegrate, relocate and externalize/internalize value chain activities are interdependent and intricately intertwined with a broader set of environmental conditions, such as advancements in Internet and communication technologies, the emergence of a global human capital pool, the emergence of specialized suppliers in emerging economies and so forth (Contractor and Mudambi, 2008; Manning et al., 2008). These environmental conditions reinforce the DLE advantages, and such offshoring decisions in turn may affect the environmental factors.

Thus the objective of this chapter is to examine the DLE framework in conjunction with the co-evolutionary framework, which explores relationships between firm-level offshoring choices and population-level selection forces. Such an integration implies that the dynamics of offshoring are not an outcome of strategic decisions or of environmental selection but rather the combined outcomes of firm-level choices and macro-environmental factors (Lewin and Volberda, 1999; Manning et al., 2008; Volberda and Lewin, 2003). The chapter thus revolves around the following research themes:

1. How do offshoring choices made by a firm (i.e. strategic choices with regard to the disintegration of value chain activities, location and ownership [externalization or internalization]) co-evolve with external factors?
2. How do DLE factors influence sourcing mode choices?
3. What are the theoretical and practical implications of this analysis, and, therefore, where do we go from here?

Several contributions emerge from answering these questions. First, this chapter enriches offshoring literature and research into the internationalization of R&D by extending understanding of the R&D offshoring process, through the careful integration of the theoretical underpinnings of the DLE framework and the co-evolutionary framework of offshoring. This integration of the DLE perspective with the co-evolutionary framework provides a means to study the changing nature of the offshoring phenomenon over time and enrich extant literature by addressing the interaction of a sourcing firm with its dynamic global environment. Second, this research focuses on the dynamics of the sourcing process, which capture the evolution of organizational configuration and subsequent value creation. Third, this research contributes to a better understanding of firms' offshoring process and related factors with regard to location and ownership decisions. Specifically, it aims to show how locational advantages vary from one location to another and how ownership decisions may be contingent on such advantages. To this end, it offers a matrix of offshoring activities and governance choices, based on disintegration–location–externalization advantages.

Here is the roadmap for the chapter: we begin with a brief discussion on the growing trend of high-value-added activity offshoring and the rise of innovation centers around the globe. In the next section, we discuss the conceptual foundations of this study by integrating the DLE framework and co-evolutionary perspective, and elucidating how environmental drivers of offshoring and DLE advantages might co-evolve. Next, we detail a 2 × 2 matrix of different offshore models, based on the DLE framework. We conclude the chapter with theoretical and managerial implications, as well as further research directions.

OFFSHORING OF HIGH-VALUE-ADDED ACTIVITIES AND GLOBAL CENTERS OF INNOVATION

Over the years, offshoring has emerged as a growing business practice, pursued by firms in a wide array of industries. Offshoring manufacturing services from high-cost countries to low-cost destinations started in the 1960s (Jensen and Pedersen, 2011); offshoring of service activities has been more recent. It gained impetus in the early 1990s when companies, driven by increasing cost pressures, started to offshore routine IT activities such as testing, simple coding and data entry to countries such as India, China and the Philippines. The next wave of offshoring started with the relocation of business processes to lower-cost countries. By nature, business processes are more knowledge intensive than low-complexity IT activities. As offshoring service providers scaled up their operations and attained specialized status, increasing number of MNCs began to offshore more knowledge-intensive IT and business process functions. This wave of offshoring has been called 'knowledge process offshoring', or KPO. It can be performed internally, by captive centers, or externally, by specialized third-party providers located offshore. These shifts have sparked a great deal of interest and debate about how offshoring affects society, the companies involved, and the employees in the offshore and the home countries.

On the question of competitiveness at the firm level, there is virtual unanimity among researchers and practitioners that firms cannot prosper and sustain a competitive edge unless they manage their knowledge-based resources properly. One way to do so is to focus on core competencies and create new ones by engaging in interorganizational designs with external collaborators or perform this process internally by setting up offshore R&D centers around the world. That is, the geographical dispersion of value creation is a relatively recent trend that plays an increasingly important role in analyses of offshoring (Iammarino and McCann, 2008; Mudambi, 2008). Innovation systems scattered around the world provide a location-specific supply base of technological and knowledge resources that firms draw on to enhance their competitiveness (Mudambi, 2008). Firms can enhance their competitive advantage by dispersing their creative endeavors and tapping into multiple innovation centers that coordinate knowledge across geographic space (Lorenzen, 2004; Mudambi, 2008). A research hub or innovation center refers to a subsidiary that has been selected by headquarters to pursue and remain in possession of distinct knowledge in a certain field (Forsgren et al., 2000; Manning et al., 2008; Pearce, 1997). The knowledge centers can be part of larger corporate networks that aim to source global human capital and establish linkages with specialized suppliers who have superior capabilities (Adenfelt and Lagerström, 2008). Offshore innovation centers often engage in extensive high-value-added research, scan technological developments in foreign markets, and enrich the technological capabilities of the focal firm by providing access to a foreign talent base (Bardhan, 2006). Researchers agree that this trend is likely to persist as firms worldwide continue producing goods and services in multiple locations (Cantwell and Mudambi, 2000; Contractor and Mudambi, 2008; Kumar et al., 2009); the human talent required to perform these complex tasks will need to be sourced globally (Kedia and Mukherjee, 2009; Kenney et al., 2009; Manning et al., 2008).

Three interrelated streams of research outline the process firms use to seek benefits from the international sourcing of activities. Hymer (1976) has argued that the internationalization process of the firm is determined by its leveraging of firm-specific advantages into a bigger market. In contrast, the internalization theory argues that MNCs bring in foreign-based activities by calculating the associated transaction costs (Buckley and Casson, 1976). Finally, the eclectic paradigm posits that firms internalize ownership-specific and location-specific advantages in foreign locations (Dunning, 1979, 1993). The phenomenon of offshoring innovation or R&D labs is often described as a variation on internationalization, by which firms disaggregate their value chain activities across several locations, potentially handing over in-house business processes and capabilities to third-party service providers (Lewin et al., 2009).

Firms often set up centers in a foreign country and hire local labor forces to run their operations. Such an arrangement allows the focal firm to maintain the advantages of internal communications and coordination, while also gaining labor and knowledge arbitrage benefits from its recruitment of local human capital. For example, Lampel and Bhalla (2008) cite the case of Goldman Sachs, which set up a back-office service center in Bangalore in 2004 with 250 people to provide technology and analytical research support to its global operations. Today, the center is the firm's third-largest office, employing more than 1200 people, including software designers and increasingly skilled analysts who produce modeling and other data that appear in Goldman research reports. Similarly, big MNCs such as Texas Instruments, Sony Ericsson and Cisco run their R&D centers in India. However, many managers remain somewhat reluctant to choose offshore outsourcing to an independent vendor and prefer a captive model that can turn particular locations into 'centers of excellence'. For example, the oil giant Shell operates five offshore captive centers located in Malaysia, the UK, Poland, the Philippines and Guatemala. The core competences of these centers may be grounded in specialized capabilities that get combined with unique local resources at different locations. Thus globalization of centers may locate revenue generation close to the markets, production centers at the lowest cost locations, logistics units in a transportation hub or R&D centers in a existing technology cluster (Meyer, 2006).

CONCEPTUAL UNDERPINNINGS

The DLE Framework of Offshoring

The DLE framework (Kedia and Mukherjee, 2009) builds on Dunning's OLI framework, one of the most extensively used perspectives in international business research. The OLI framework proposes three groups of variables to explain the internationalization of a firm's activities: ownership-specific advantages (O), location-specific advantages (L), and internalization-specific advantages (I). It further identifies two kinds of ownership advantages: asset and transaction cost-minimizing advantages. Asset advantages represent a form of firm-specific ownership advantages that arise from the control of particular intangible assets, such as multinational experience, experience with a specific technology, or the type of R&D project. This aspect of the OLI paradigm can be extended to explain the internationalization of R&D by MNCs, such that the domestically available, ownership-specific competencies of a firm get complemented or augmented by the assets created by R&D at foreign locations. However, in the context of offshore R&D captive centers, firms disintegrate R&D to exploit the labor and knowledge advantages of a foreign market. Such ownership advantages permit the MNC to augment its knowledge base and remain competitive in the global marketplace.

The internalization advantage of MNCs, in the context of offshoring R&D, instead refers to the capabilities to unbundle sections of R&D, combined with system integration capabilities that enable them to integrate R&D projects carried out in different countries (or regions) of the world, as well as information and communication network capabilities. Information and communication networks are significant components of R&D offshoring, and with such networks at their disposal, MNCs can deploy core and non-core R&D activities to different host countries while maintaining control over the whole process (Mudambi and Tallman, 2010).

The DLE framework instead contends that the juxtaposition of the three sets of interrelated advantages, as perceived by the firms, can explain why firms embark on offshoring (Kedia and Mukherjee, 2009). In simple terms, firms contemplate offshoring when they discover advantages associated with the disintegration of activities from their value chain. These disintegration advantages derive from an increase of modularity in their structure, as well as from an increased focus on the core capabilities of the focal firm. Another set of advantages stems from location-specific resourcing, such that firms attempt to harness superior external resources and move offshore if they perceive good infrastructure, low wage rates and high-quality intellectual capital that will enable them to carry out the disintegrated activities effectively in another location. Finally, boosted by the advantages associated with externalization, in the form of co-specialization and interorganizational learning, firms may externalize the first two sets of advantages to independent foreign service providers (offshore outsourcing) or internalize them if the disintegrated activities are sources of competitive advantage (captive offshoring). In summary, the DLE framework, to explain ownership issues (in-house or outsource), highlights the actual advantages gained from each stage and identifies sources of the value creation. However, the different stages in the DLE framework may or may not be sequential. Therefore the next section discusses the co-evolutionary framework of offshoring and creates a logical platform for exploring and tracing DLE advantages in light of such a co-evolutionary framework.

Co-evolutionary Framework of Offshoring

The co-evolutionary perspective contends that the 'co-evolution of organizations is an outcome of the interplay between forces internal and external to organizational environments' (Lewin et al., 1999, p. 539; Lewin and Volberda, 1999; Volberda and Lewin, 2003). This perspective attempts to reconcile seemingly disparate views of organizational survival, namely, population-level selection and firm-level adaptation (see Volberda and Lewin, 2003). Therefore, by considering organizations, their populations and their environments, this perspective suggests that organizational adaptation is an interdependent outcome of the influences of the external environment and managerial intentionality. In other words, the co-evolutionary approach suggests that adaptation and selection are fundamentally interrelated, not orthogonal forces impinging on organizations. The robustness of this co-evolutionary perspective lies in its ability to offer a new lens for research that combines two important academic fields: organization theory and strategy (Volberda and Lewin, 2003).

According to the co-evolutionary framework, organizations behave similarly to living organisms in adjusting or adapting to various external changes so that they may avoid being selected out by their environments and instead ensure their continued survival. In the case of organizations, the strategic choices made by firms aid their adjustments or 'fit' with the environment (Hrebiniak and Joyce, 1985). In the present context, this approach implies that offshoring firms are part of the broader global business landscape and function while residing in their respective external environments, which drive and shape the nature of the strategic choices. In other words, firm behavior is not only affected by various firm-level factors but also is contingent on the different attributes of the environment that lie outside the firm boundary. A more complete and meaningful analysis of this growing practice therefore should include the dynamic interaction between the changing external environment and internal strategic choices.

In this chapter, we synthesize the preceding two perspectives and contend that the disintegration, location and externalization (or internalization) choices made by firms co-evolve with broader external factors, such as globalization; increased global and domestic market competition; simultaneous cost pressure, liberalization and economic reforms in emerging markets; reduced communication costs; the emergence of a global talent pool; and local clustering of specialized partner firms. Accordingly, we next discuss the components of the DLE framework in light of external factors and delineate the advantages of this framework from a co-evolutionary perspective.

Environmental Factors and Disintegration Advantages

Globalization, technological advancements that have led to the increased digitization of work, hypercompetition, changing consumer preferences and economic reforms in emerging economies have all altered the way international business is conducted (Townsend et al., 2009). To face these challenges, firms worldwide are rethinking their existing business practices, as well as their ways of organizing and structuring their value chain activities (Manning et al., 2008). Multinational and global firms need to be more flexible and leaner to compete and respond to competition to the ever-changing environment (Achrol, 1997; Jacobides, 2005). One way to address the efficiency of an organization is to assess its structure on an ongoing basis and thereby confirm that it is consistently attuned with the design of its value chain (Prahalad and Ramaswamy, 2004). The reconfiguration of value chain activities by disintegrating non-core activities and shifting and increasing focus on core areas will generate value for firms and customers. The most important factor that drives the latest form of offshoring is the increase in the organizational and technological capabilities of firms that unbundle and coordinate a network of remotely located, in-house and external partners that perform complex activities (Mudambi, 2008). In other words, the disintegration of activities may help firms improve their business flexibility and result in increased market responsiveness (Achrol, 1997), especially as they embrace a more modular and leaner structure. Increased flexibility translates into faster responses to market changes and greater risk-sharing with providers, which in turn implies lower susceptibility to market uncertainties.

However, the process of disintegrating value chain activities is not totally free of risk (Lampel and Bhalla, 2008). The disintegration of core activities may result in a firm's inability to rebuild competencies in house or unbundle activities that have been strategically integrated into its knowledge-based resources. Such misdirected disintegration efforts may result in competence destruction or a 'hollowing out' of the firm (Chesbrough and Teece, 2002).

Emergence of a Global Talent Pool and Location-specific Resourcing Advantages

Some scholars support the notion that advanced countries such as the USA, the UK and other Western European countries already face a deficiency of skilled professionals in knowledge-intensive sectors (Lewin and Couto, 2007). In the face of skills shortages in various work domains, in particular science and engineering, Western firms are often left with little alternative than to search out alternative sources of talent (Deloitte, 2004). Simultaneously, the available human capital bases have expanded throughout emerging economies, such as India and China, which feature growing young populations, improving higher education systems and increasing domestic career opportunities. These countries have undertaken huge initiatives to transform their local universities, many of which model their programs on US and European universities and technological institutes. Thus India, China, the Philippines, Ireland and Singapore produce 2 100 000, 950 000, 380 000, 42 200 and 125 000 college graduates, respectively, each year (Budhwar et al., 2006). Furthermore, national tax incentives, growing personal networks and communities of home-based science and engineering graduates, together with related perceptions of attractive career prospects, are working to 'reverse the brain drain' by attracting human talent back to their home countries. The need to access skilled labor at lower costs than the level at which it is available in domestic contexts has propelled many firms in Western economies to establish innovation centers (internalization) or develop business relationships with independent offshore providers operating in low-wage countries (externalization). For example, almost 75 percent of the surveyed participants of a Duke CIBER & Booz Allen Hamilton study (Lewin and Couto, 2007) indicated that accessing pools of qualified personnel in low-wage countries such as India or China is the most important driver of their offshoring strategy. Such importance is understandable, given that countries like India and China produce a surplus of well-educated university graduates who possess most of the qualities required to function in rapid-growth, high-technology industries.

In summary, labor arbitrage, in the form of inexpensive human capital, and knowledge arbitrage, in the form of a high-quality talent pool, are driving technology-intensive firms to disperse their value chain activities in multiple locations. There may be some economic advantages to offshoring, but significant challenges also may arise, associated with the decision to move services offshore. For example, choosing the correct location is complex when every country offers a different mix of strengths and weaknesses (Vestring et al., 2005). Therefore firms may respond by spreading their foreign operations and offshoring relationships over a broader, widely balanced mix of regions and countries (Vestring et al., 2005).

Emergence of Specialized Partner Firms and Balanced Externalization Advantages

International business researchers have revealed that national institutional systems (e.g. education, industry) shape distinct trajectories of differential knowledge development (Bartholomew, 1997). Considering this variety, MNCs are inclined to enlarge the scope of their geographical diversity to expand their technological dimensions and increase the likelihood of new combinations that can generate innovation. Externalization usually implies handing over activities to independent service providers, and it may result in advantages that stem mainly from specialized partner capabilities and mutual learning. Furthermore, external learning from host countries contributes to the emergence of novel ideas (Almeida and Phene, 2004). Recent innovation research suggests that a multinational firm's presence in a local technology network can help it realize and appreciate the value of locally developed technology, which increases its innovative productivity (Ahuja and Katila, 2004; Kuemmerle, 1999). For example, firms that offshore to Bangalore may benefit from that region's unique human capital pool, presence of specialized companies and overall technological infrastructure. By broadening their international presence, firms can integrate diverse elements from offshore locations into promising new inventions and further enhance their innovative capabilities to attain a better position.

Offshoring partnerships are often important conduits of organizational learning for focal firms (Kedia and Lahiri, 2007). The combined experience of the partners and their learning scope is valued in offshoring relationships and can generate outcomes that are transformational in nature. The importance of such partnership-based learning in the context of strategic alliances, joint ventures and other types of interorganizational relationships has been effectively highlighted (Hatonen, 2009; Jensen, 2009). Moreover, when offshoring firms search for the best service providers, through negotiations with potential partners, the offshoring firms learn more about the industry-specific needs and the environment, which should help them compete more successfully. Thus externalization advantages accrue from partner-specific specialized expertise and learning. However, the externalization process also may entail potential risks pertaining to opportunistic behavior and 'hold-up' by external suppliers. In addition, *ex ante* and *ex post* transactions costs can increase if contracts with the suppliers are too complicated (Barthélemy and Quélin, 2006). The contract must be diligently prepared and should include all relevant clauses

Table 21.1   DLE advantages: boosting the growth of high-value-added offshoring activities

Co-evolving factors	Type of advantage	Nature of advantages
• Globalization • Increased competition • Technological advances leading to decreased telecommunication costs and increased digitization	Disintegration	• Increased focus on core competencies • Increased modularity
• Emergence of a global talent pool • Economic reforms in emerging economies	Location-specific	• Infrastructure • Government policy • Labor arbitrage in the form of cost reduction • Knowledge arbitrage in the form of high-quality talent and technology clusters
• Emergence of a collaborative mindset among firms	Externalization	• Advantages related to co-specialization and co-innovation • Advantages related to mutual organizational learning

Source: Adapted from Kedia and Mukherjee (2009).

that make it tightly applicable, including specified service levels, payment terms, deliverables and due diligence, while also flexible in defining the ways in which both sides interact to achieve mutual value enhancement (Brown and Wilson, 2005).

Overall, the offshoring of high-value-added activities and the globalization of R&D, which translates into the emergence of innovation centers or research hubs around the world, is a strategic response to the globalization of markets, increased competition, technological advancements and the emergence of human capital pools in different pockets around the world. That is, offshoring is induced by a combination of advantages related to the disintegration–location–externalization of activities. A recent example of a wind turbine producer from Denmark (Jensen and Pedersen, 2011, p. 2) highlights the intricacies and interconnectedness of these advantages. The authors put it succinctly:

> The firm had by 2008 established a global R&D network with R&D centers in Denmark, UK, Singapore, and Chennai in India, and in early 2009, a center was opened in the U.S. Each of these locations is favorable for different reasons, and they are hot-spots for various knowledge resources (software knowledge in India, energy knowledge in the U.S., system knowledge in Denmark, etc.). Organized in a new strategic business unit, Vestas Technology R&D, the globalization of R&D reflects the firm's strive to access technological hotspots around the world and foster a global search for talent. However, some research centers are also important assets in Vestas' marketing and market access strategy. The research center in Singapore created a gateway to the increasingly important Chinese market. In the same vein the most recent research center in Houston, Texas, is closely related to the firm's marketing strategy as it is expected to give Vestas a closer connection to one of the most prominent markets of the world for wind turbines.

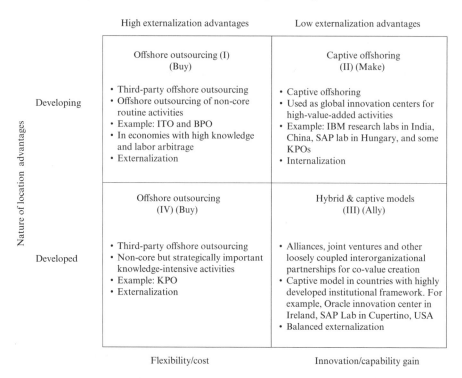

Source: Adapted from Kedia and Mukherjee (2009).

Figure 21.1   Typology of offshoring

Table 21.1 summarizes such intertwined factors.

Different Types of Offshoring Governance Models

Figure 21.1 summarizes four types of offshoring models that surface when we combine the perceived disintegration advantages and location-specific resourcing advantages. In the following paragraphs, we briefly describe each resulting quadrant.

Quadrant I includes firms that are facing stiff price competition and cost pressures in their industry. To serve their customers better and remain abreast of the competition, these firms often disintegrate their value chain activities and hand them over to vendors located abroad. In turn, the firms can focus on their core competencies and ensure good service to their domestic customers. The presence of abundant suppliers in low-wage foreign destinations (e.g. China, the Philippines, India) makes it easier for these firms to externalize their disintegrated activities to outside independent foreign suppliers. However, such cost advantages are short term in nature; competitors and other firms soon follow. Offshoring of most non-core IT activities, along with other low-value-added routine activities (e.g. billing, call centers), follows this model, referred to as offshore third-party outsourcing. In general, the relationship between the client firm and the vendor is transactional and contract-based in nature. Such arrangements are often short term, because the client firm constantly moves to the destination with the lowest wage rate.

Quadrant II contains firms that face pressure to be innovative and perceive high disintegration advantages if they hope to stay competitive and meet increasing customer demands. The complexity of the value chain activities involved (usually highly complex and core processes, such as R&D or product design), transaction cost-related concerns (mainly opportunism) and the risks associated with knowledge dissipation to outside suppliers prompt these firms to internalize the benefits related to the superior resources they have found abroad. Typically, they set up their own offshore centers and benefit from labor and knowledge arbitrage. This sourcing model can thus be termed the captive offshoring model. For example, in the automotive sector, most major manufacturers have relocated their R&D and certain elements of their product design to India. These tasks require human capital, including employees with master's degrees or, preferably, doctoral degrees in aerospace, computer science, industrial design, mechanical engineering, software engineering or materials science. The focal firm can thus augment its knowledge base and use the captive centers to expand into foreign markets.

Firms in Quadrant III are very similar to Quadrant II firms. Their main motive for offshoring is to gain external capability. The process is executed through a hybrid model, such as co-marketing initiatives with developed country foreign firms or R&D alliances between two developed country firms. Such arrangements are ubiquitous in the pharmaceutical industry. Gradually, with the development of their own institutional infrastructure, some emerging market companies, such as Ranbaxy and Dr Reddy's from India, are also engaging in interorganizational designs with firms from developed countries. The value chain activities involved in such arrangements tend to be highly complex, tacit and knowledge-intensive in nature. Thus the complete externalization of these activities is not common, and most companies prefer hybrid models.

Finally, Quadrant IV firms outsource their knowledge-intensive but non-core functions (KPO) to independent providers located in countries with developed institutional frameworks. The KPO involves the performance of high-end, value-added work by resources whose co-location with the focal client is not necessary. It demands an understanding of the client's industry segment, as well as how the client works, and a specialized educational background. A small section of the organizational pyramid performs high-end critical knowledge work; therefore KPO generally does not achieve great economies of scale in an offshored or outsourced environment. Many European companies outsource knowledge processes to other European countries with similar work cultures or similar contract enforcement policies, whereas KPO centers in emerging economies have often been internalized by the client firm. This approach mitigates the fear of knowledge loss, and the focal firm reaps the benefit of high-quality human capital located in these countries. For example, some proprietary databases, models and algorithms in equity research would be critical to the client firm. Similarly, the databases and research findings of a clinical trial from a pharmaceutical company would need to be protected from misappropriation (TPI, 2008). As mentioned at the outset, usually client firms outsource such activities only to developed country companies, but gradually, emerging economy multinationals are scaling up their service operations, thereby snatching KPO activities away from developed economy companies.

DISCUSSION

We are living in a globalized world, where economies are interconnected and the fates of MNCs are interdependent. This world is simultaneously flat, due to technological advancements and the emergence of global players, and filled with spikes, due to the existence of challenges and dilemmas – cross-cultural differences, institutional variation, religious disputes, political and economic disparities, to name just a few. Thus ownership advantages of firms erode quickly through imitation, competition and technological advancements (Doh, 2005; Kedia and Mukherjee, 2009). To create value, firms worldwide are revisiting the structure of their value chain activities to ensure no redundancies, as well as to exploit more effectively labor and knowledge arbitrage scattered around the globe. To this end, this analysis contributes to burgeoning literature on offshoring by focusing on the co-evolution of environmental, firm-specific and interorganizational factors in determining appropriate governance choice (externalization versus internalization) and value creation. The basic tenets of this analysis are in concert with a scholarly perspective that argues that offshoring of routine and advanced activities does not necessarily lead to the hollowing out of offshoring firms but instead presents a value-creating opportunity for strategic business development and organizational change, if executed appropriately. By delving deeper into the dynamics of offshoring, we have attempted to investigate a set of questions that would help offshoring literature undergo a more fine-grained analysis in the future (Doh, 2005; Farrell, 2005; Lahiri et al., 2012). Answering these questions is important, because they directly shed light on the viability of the global sourcing of human talent as a strategic device. We contend that, to create value, focal firms must attain a better understanding of the related variables and make appropriate resource uses in each stage. In simple terms, the DLE framework argues that firms start offshore outsourcing when they perceive disintegration and offshore location-specific resourcing advantages (Kedia and Mukherjee, 2009). Although the DLE framework discusses the actual advantages explicitly, it does not shed enough light on the sources of those advantages. This chapter develops further the DLE framework introduced by Kedia and Mukherjee (2009).

In doing so, we recognize that DLE advantages cannot be analyzed in isolation and must be understood within a broader set of environmental variables, intertwined with the strategic choices made by offshoring firms. Therefore we have employed a co-evolutionary framework to understand DLE advantages more clearly. We argue that these advantages grow in parallel with factors such as globalization, technological advances, increased competition in domestic and global markets leading to cost pressure, liberalization of emerging economies, declining science and engineering talents in Western economies, a growing talent pool in areas such as India and China, and the emergence of specialized firms – all of which reinforce offshoring decisions. On the one hand, we subscribe to the dominant strategic choice perspective and contend that value creation in global sourcing or offshoring and the choice of an appropriate sourcing type are largely firm-specific and internal in nature. On the other hand, we acknowledge that such choices made by a firm often are part of a larger co-evolutionary process.

The related decision of where to offshore knowledge-intensive activities is another important strategic issue that we have attempted to address. Extant literature argues that the decision is contingent on an array of factors that determine location attractiveness

(Contractor and Mudambi, 2008; Doh et al., 2009; Graf and Mudambi, 2005). As the nature of the offshored activities moves up the value chain and becomes more knowledge intensive, location-specific factors, such as the availability of a highly skilled and motivated talent pool, highly functional technology infrastructures and the availability of a local knowledge cluster, gain in significance.

Although this chapter discusses the actual advantages explicitly, for the sake of brevity and parsimony it does not shed light on the sources of those advantages. Further studies should continue to develop the DLE framework by identifying the sub-processes involved.

A final implication, derived from the conceptual development, is associated with the ongoing debate about firms' governance choices in a global environment. In line with the reasoning put forward by resource-based theorists (Mayer and Salomon, 2006), we contend that a firm's governance (internalization or externalization) choice is influenced partly by its internal resource/capability requirements and partly by the global context within which it operates. For example, R&D labs (innovation entities) in technology-focused firms had long been considered core activities that had to remain tightly controlled by the home country location and conducted within the boundaries of the firm. But we noticed that R&D centers today are helping MNCs grow further and stay competitive, in support of our contention that internalization or externalization decisions are often functions of a careful comparison of the potential costs of opportunism and the potential benefits of external partnerships (Maskell et al., 2007). In the presence of a suitable talent pool, specialized partners, and a technology cluster from which the focal firm can absorb knowledge, the threat of potential *ex ante* and *ex post* transaction costs is partly alleviated.

Our analysis also has several practical implications for managers who are directly or indirectly involved with offshore outsourcing. First, the framework outlined in this chapter provides solid guidance for managers and organizations regarding how to manage their resources while embarking on offshore outsourcing. Second, we identify specific uncertainties that could be associated with the offshore outsourcing decision-making processes. Third, we have stressed the internal facilitators that may help overcome potentially challenging uncertainties. For example, operating managers and employees should pursue a sophisticated understanding of the connection between their own employees and offshore vendors or offshore human capital, so that they can accrue long-term benefits for both partners. Thus organizations and individuals may develop collective trust, which is conceptually similar to other types of shared resources. Fourth, developing various organizational systems can help managers and employees overcome potential barriers to initiating trust. Focal firms may also provide training and educational opportunities to enable and enhance employee trustworthy behavior. Such can enhance managers' competencies, skills and capabilities, especially in the areas of shared leadership, contract management abilities, performance management capabilities, unambiguous communication and absorptive capacity. As managers increase the specific skills associated with relationship management capabilities through training and development opportunities, they are more likely to initiate and exercise them.

Finally, environmental and competitive pressures are pushing organizations toward flatter and nimbler core structures with multiple external partnerships. Understandably, organizational researchers have started to put greater emphasis on trust-based interorganizational processes. Some scholars have even argued that trust-based relational capital can be a source of competitive advantage. Such changes will come about, however, with increased trust between offshore human and focal firm management. Considering the limits of formal contracting (Gaur et al., 2011), high levels of mutual trust between managers and employees seem critical for the success of offshoring efforts. Organizations that attain high levels of managerial trustworthiness should enjoy a competitive advantage in the marketplace, compared with those that do not (Kedia and Lahiri, 2007). More importantly, companies that anticipate these changes, designing themselves and encouraging their boundary-spanning managers to initiate and establish trusting relationships, will be well positioned for the future, because they will have attained the competitive advantages associated with strategic and structural innovations that can be generated from offshoring.

CONCLUSION AND AGENDA FOR FUTURE RESEARCH

It is noteworthy that most prominent offshoring destinations (e.g. India, China, Russia, the Philippines) in academic and practitioner discourses are emerging economies, many of which suffer from weak institutional frameworks and poorly functioning legal systems that cannot protect intellectual property rights or enforce contracts. Therefore externalizing value chain activities and offshoring as a strategic choice requires an understanding of DLE factors. In today's knowledge-based economy, innovation and learning are vital for firm value creation. Myriad researchers have pointed out that firms not only develop strategies based on core knowledge and capabilities, but also work to restructure, rebundle and leverage their external partnerships to create value in dynamic environments. These processes – generally referred to as global resource management – are essential for enhancing the firm's core knowledge base and creating new value. By drawing logical connections that link the DLE perspective to co-evolutionary theory, we contribute to a framework that explicates how firms might strategically manage the process and make different mode choices. Our analysis thus should encourage further research along similar lines of inquiry.

We also attempt to pave avenues for further research. For example, large-scale longitudinal studies and in-depth case studies might identify cause–effect relationships between offshoring stages and DLE advantages, then extrapolate the findings to a population of firms. Other studies could concentrate on the development of constructs and measures that capture the sub-processes associated with each DLE stage, which requires an in-depth understanding of different delivery models, perhaps achieved through qualitative and quantitative inquiry. For example, research could concentrate on the disintegration stage and investigate the impact of increased modularity and flexibility (strategic and operational) on firm value creation and performance. Another issue that deserves further attention is customer value creation through offshoring. The potential of offshoring to deliver benefits to the focal firm and the offshore partner is being increasingly explored, although the focus on customer value creation seems limited. Ongoing research endeavors should investigate the link of offshoring and a broad range of aspects linked to customer value creation, such as decreased price and increased service quality.

Another potential avenue for research would be to investigate how DLE advantages affect offshoring service providers in emerging economies as they continue to expand their business scope and augment their product scope. Most providers seem focused on partnering with specific (mostly US) clients and providing services in specific domains that reflect their best capabilities. As global competition increases and industries mature, we might reasonably expect that providers also will increase the types of services (i.e. industry domains) they provide and attempt to reach newer clients in other parts of the world. We can already witness Indian companies, such as Tata Consultancy Services, offshoring their activities to countries such as Egypt, China and Uruguay. Do DLE advantages affect such emerging economy firms differently when they operate in different institutional frameworks?

In summary, we have delineated how the process of offshoring is often determined by co-evolving environmental and firm-specific advantages. We also have identified how DLE advantages might affect offshoring model choices. By noting several potential areas of research that could further fortify our understanding of this important domain, we sincerely hope that this chapter stimulates more such endeavors.

REFERENCES

Achrol, R.S. (1997), 'Changes in the theory of interorganizational relations in marketing paradigm', *Journal of the Academy of Marketing Science*, **25**: 56–71.

Adenfelt, M. and Lagerström, K. (2008), 'The development and sharing of knowledge by centers of excellence and transnational teams: a conceptual framework', *Management International Review*, **48**(3): 319–38.

Ahuja, G. and Katila, R. (2004), 'Where do resources come from? The role of idiosyncratic situations', *Strategic Management Journal*, **25**: 887–907.

Almeida, P. and Phene, A. (2004), 'Subsidiaries and knowledge creation: the influence of the MNC and host country on innovation', *Strategic Management Journal*, **25**: 847–64.

Bardhan, A.D. (2006), 'Managing globalization of R&D: organizing for offshoring innovation', *Human Systems Management*, **25**: 103–14.

Barthélemy, J. and Quélin, V.B. (2006), 'Complexity of outsourcing contracts and ex post transaction costs: an empirical investigation', *Journal of Management Studies*, **43**(8): 1775–97.

Bartholomew, S. (1997), 'National systems of biotechnology innovation: complex interdependence in the global system', *Journal of International Business Studies*, **28**(2): 241–66.

Bhalla, A., Sodhi, M. and Son, B. (2008), 'Is more IT offshoring better? An exploratory study of Western companies offshoring to South East Asia', *Journal of Operations Management*, **26**(2): 322–35.

Brown, D. and Wilson, S. (2005), *The Black Book of Outsourcing: How to Manage the Changes, Challenges, and Opportunities*, New York: John Wiley.

Buckley, P.J. and Casson, M. (1976), *The Future of the Multinational Enterprise*, London: Macmillan.

Budhwar, P., Luthar, H.K. and Bhatnagar, J. (2006), 'The dynamics of HRM systems in Indian BPO firms', *Journal of Labor Research*, **27**(3): 339–60.

Bunyaratavej, K., Doh, J.P., Hahn, E.D., Lewin, A.Y. and Massini, S. (2011), 'Conceptual issues in services offshoring research: a multidisciplinary review', *Group and Organization Management*, **36**, 70–102.

Bunyaratavej, K., Hahn, E.D. and Doh, J.P. (2007), 'International offshoring of services: a parity study', *Journal of International Management*, **13**(1): 7–21.

Cantwell, J.A. and Mudambi, R. (2000), 'The location of MNE R&D activity: the role of investment incentives', *Management International Review*, Special Issue, **40**(1): 127–48.

Chesbrough, H.W. and Teece, D.J. (2002), 'Organizing for innovation: when is virtual virtuous?', *Harvard Business Review*, **80**(3): 90–99.

Contractor, F. and Mudambi, S. (2008), 'The influence of human capital investment on the exports of services and goods: an analysis of the top 25 services outsourcing countries', *Management International Review*, **48**(4): 433–45.

Deloitte (2004), 'It's 2008: do you know where your talent is? Why acquisition and retention strategies don't work', Deloitte Research Study.

Demirbag, M. and Glaister, K.W. (2010), 'Factors determining offshore location choice for R&D projects: a comparative study of developed and emerging regions', *Journal of Management Studies*, **47**, 8,

Doh, J.P. (2005), 'Offshore outsourcing: implications for international business and strategic management theory and practice', *Journal of Management Studies*, **42**(3): 695–705.

Doh, J.P., Bunyaratavej, K. and Hahn, E.D. (2009), 'Offshoring administrative and technical work: implications for globalization, corporate strategies, and organizational designs', *Journal of International Business Studies*, **40**: 926–43.

Dunning, J.H. (1977), 'Trade, location of economic activity and the multinational enterprise: a search for an eclectic approach', in B. Ohlin, P. Hesselborn and P. Magnus (eds), *The International Allocation of Economic Activity*, New York: Holmes & Meier, pp. 395–418.

Dunning, J.H. (1979), 'Explaining changing patterns of international production: in defence of the eclectic theory', *Oxford Bulletin of Economics & Statistics*, **41**(4): 269–95.

Dunning, J.H. (1993), *Multinational Enterprise and the Global Economy*, Wokingham: Addison Wesley.

Farrell, D. (2005), 'Offshoring: value creation through economic change', *Journal of Management Studies*, **42**(3): 675–83.

Forsgren, M., Johanson, J. and Sharma, D.D. (2000), 'In search of MNC centres of excellence', in U. Holm and T. Pedersen (eds), *The Emergence and Impact of MNC Centres of Excellence*, London: Macmillan, pp. 45–67.

Gaur, A.S., Mukherjee, D., Gaur, S.S. and Schmid, F. (2011), 'Environmental and firm level influences on inter-organizational trust and SME performance', *Journal of Management Studies*, DOI: 10.1111/j.1467-6486.2011.01011.x.

Graf, M. and Mudambi, S. (2005), 'The outsourcing of IT-enabled business processes: a conceptual model of the location decision', *Journal of International Management*, **11**: 253–68.

Hatonen, J. (2009), 'Making the locational choice: a case approach to the development of a theory of offshore outsourcing and internationalization', *Journal of International Management*, **15**: 61–76.

Hrebiniak, L.G. and Joyce, W.F. (1985), 'Organizational adaptation: strategic choice and environmental determinism', *Administrative Science Quarterly*, **30**: 336–49.

Huggins, R., Demirbag, M. and Ratcheva, V.I. (2007), 'Global knowledge and R&D foreign direct investment flows: recent patterns in Asia Pacific, Europe, and North America', *International Review of Applied Economics*, **21**(3): 437–51.

Hymer, S. (1976), *The International Operations of National Firms*, Cambridge, MA: MIT Press.

Iammarino, S. and McCann, P. (2008), *Multinationals and Economic Geography: Location, Technology and Innovation*, Princeton, NJ: Princeton University Press.

Jacobides, M.G. (2005), 'Industry change through vertical disintegration: how and why markets emerged in mortgage banking', *Academy of Management Journal*, **48**: 465–98.

Jensen, P.D. (2009), 'A learning perspective on the offshoring of advanced services', *Journal of International Management*, **15**(2): 181–93.

Jensen, P. and Pedersen, T. (2011), 'Offshoring and international competitiveness: antecedents of offshoring advanced tasks', *Journal of the Academy of Marketing Science*, DOI 10.1007/s11747-011-0286-x.

Kedia, B.L. and Lahiri, S. (2007), 'International outsourcing of services: a partnership model', *Journal of International Management*, **13**: 22–37.

Kedia, B.L. and Mukherjee, D. (2009), 'Understanding offshoring: a research framework based on disintegration, location and externalization advantages', *Journal of World Business*, **44**(3): 250–61.

Kenney, M., Massini, S. and Murtha, T. (2009), 'Offshoring administrative and technical work: new fields for understanding the global enterprise', *Journal of International Business Studies*, **40**: 887–900.

Kotabe, M. and Mudambi, R. (2009), 'Global sourcing and value creation: opportunities and challenges', *Journal of International Management*, **15**(2): 121–5.

Kuemmerle, W. (1999), 'Foreign direct investment in industrial research in the pharmaceutical and electronics industries', *Research Policy*, **28**: 179–93.

Kumar, K., Van-Fenema, P. and Von Glinow, M.A. (2009), 'Offshoring and the global distribution of work: implications for task interdependence theory and practice', *Journal of International Business Studies*, **40**(4): 642–67.

Lahiri, S. and Kedia, B.L. (2011), 'Coevolution of institutional and organizational factors in explaining offshore outsourcing', *International Business Review*, **20**(3): 252–63.

Lahiri, S., Kedia, B.L. and Mukherjee, D. (2012), 'The impact of management capability on the resource–performance linkage: examining Indian outsourcing providers', *Journal of World Business*, doi:10.1016/j.jwb.2011.02.001.

Lampel, J. and Bhalla, A. (2008), 'Embracing realism and recognizing choice in IT offshoring initiatives', *Business Horizons*, **51**(5): 429–40.

Lehrer, M. and Asakawa, K. (2002), 'Offshore knowledge incubation: The "third path" for embedding R&D labs in foreign systems of innovation', *Journal of World Business*, **37**: 297–306.

Lewin, A.Y. and Couto, V. (2007), 'Next generation offshoring: the globalization of innovation', Durham, NC: Duke University CIBER & Booz Allen Hamilton Report.

Lewin, A.Y. and Volberda, H.W. (1999), 'Prolegomena on coevolution: a framework for research on strategy and new organizational forms', *Organization Science*, **10**(5): 519–34.

Lewin, A.Y., Long, C.P. and Carroll, T.N. (1999), 'The coevolution of new organizational forms', *Organization Science*, **10**(5): 535–50.

Lorenzen, M. (2004), 'Knowledge and geography', *Industry and Innovation*, **12**(4): 399–407.

Manning, S., Lewin, A. and Massini, S. (2008), 'A dynamic perspective on next-generation offshoring: the global sourcing of science and engineering skills', *Academy of Management Perspectives*, **22**: 35–54.

Maskell, P., Pedersen, T., Petersen, B. and Dick-Nielsen, J. (2007), 'Learning paths to offshore outsourcing: from cost reduction to knowledge seeking', *Industry & Innovation*, **14**: 239–57.

Mayer, K.J. and Salomon, M.R. (2006), 'Capabilities, contractual hazards, and governance: integrating resource-based and transaction cost perspectives', *Academy of Management Journal*, **49**: 942–59.

Meyer, K.E. (2006), 'Globalfocusing: from domestic conglomerates to global specialists', *Journal of Management Studies*, **43**: 1109–44.

Mudambi, R. (2008), 'Location, control and innovation in knowledge-intensive industries', *Journal of Economic Geography*, **8**: 699–725.

Mudambi, S.M. and Tallman, S. (2010), 'Make, buy or ally? Theoretical perspectives on knowledge process outsourcing through alliances', *Journal of Management Studies*, **47**(8): 1434–56.

Mudambi, R. and Venzin, M. (2010), 'The strategic nexus of offshoring and outsourcing decisions', *Journal of Management Studies*, **47**(8): 1510–33.

Pearce, R.D. (1997), 'Decentralized R&D and strategic competitiveness: globalized approaches to generation and use of technology in MNEs', *Research Policy*, **28**: 157–78.

Prahalad, C.K. and Ramaswamy, V. (2004), 'Co-creation experiences: the next practice in value creation', *Journal of Interactive Marketing*, **18**(3): 5–14.

Townsend, J.D., Yeniyurt, S. and Talay, M.B. (2009), 'Getting to global: an evolutionary perspective of brand expansion in international markets', *Journal of International Business Studies*, **40**(4): 539–58.

TPI (2008), 'Knowledge process offshoring: a balanced view of an emerging market', retrieved from http://www.tpi.net/pdf/researchreports/KPO_ResearchReport_july07.pdf.

UNCTAD (2005), 'Prospects for foreign direct investment and the strategies of transnational corporations 2005–2008', United Nations Report. New York and Geneva.

Vestring, T., Rouse, T. and Reinert, U. (2005), 'Hedge your offshoring bets', *MIT Sloan Management Review*, 27–9.

Volberda, H.W. and Lewin, A.Y. (2003), 'Co-evolutionary dynamics within and between firms: from evolution to co-evolution', *Journal of Management Studies*, **40**: 2111–36.

22 Bottom-of-the-pyramid strategies and networks
Miguel Rivera-Santos and Carlos Rufín

A large percentage of people on the planet live in poverty, meaning that they do not have sufficient income to cover basic needs, such as food, health, and shelter (World Bank, 2000). Although recent trends suggest that some parts of the world, especially Asia, are experiencing a rapid decrease in the number of people living under national poverty lines, other parts of the world, such as sub-Saharan Africa, are seeing both the number of poor stagnate or even increase (Chen and Ravaillon, 2008).

Complementing the traditional debate between aid and local market development as the best approach to eradicating poverty that is prevalent in the economic development literature (Collins et al., 2009), Prahalad (Prahalad and Hart, 1999) introduced, about a decade ago, the controversial bottom- (or base-) of-the-pyramid (BOP) approach, which has since then sparked considerable interest in the business community and among development agencies (Karnani, 2009; Rivera-Santos and Rufín, 2010). The basic premise of the BOP approach is that multinational enterprises (MNEs) have an important role to play in global poverty alleviation. By targeting the poor as a new market worldwide, MNEs can incorporate the poor into global markets from which they are currently isolated and give them new entrepreneurial opportunities, helping them escape poverty. Prahalad's counter-intuitive claim is thus that MNEs can pursue new revenue and profit opportunities in the context of quickly saturating developed markets and fast-growing markets in emerging countries, while helping eradicate poverty at the same time.

While this idea has sparked interest in the business community and among development agencies, the BOP literature has been significantly less successful in convincing the academic community that there is a strong case for research in this field. In spite of the rapidly growing number of papers published in the BOP literature, the percentage of papers published in top journals is still extremely low, maybe because of important definitional issues and of a sometimes tenuous connection with broader international business (IB) and strategic management frameworks in theories (Kolk et al., 2010). In turn, these issues have led to virulent criticism contesting both the profitability of BOP markets and the positive impact of MNEs on poverty (Karnani, 2007a) resulting in calls for a more rigorous and theory-grounded approach to the study of the BOP (Rivera-Santos and Rufín, 2010; Rivera-Santos et al., forthcoming).

The goal of this chapter is to answer the calls for a greater connection with existing theories and frameworks by systematically exploring the relationship between the characteristics of BOP environments and MNE strategies at the BOP. Grounding our reasoning in institutional theory and industrial organization, we analyze how the institutional and competitive environments prevalent in BOP markets shape business networks at the BOP and, in turn, influence the type of strategies that MNEs can pursue in these markets. In other terms, our goal is to conceptually explore one of the major claims of the BOP literature: that BOP markets are so different from other markets that MNEs need to develop different products and highly innovative business models to be successful at the

BOP (Hart and Christensen, 2002; Prahalad, 2005; Simanis and Hart, 2008). With this chapter, we contribute to a more systematic connection between existing theories and the study of the BOP, thus helping better understand the extent to which the characteristics of the BOP justify a different approach for MNEs.

In a first section, we analyze the specificities of BOP markets from an institutional and competitive perspective. Building on this section, we explore the implications of these specificities on the business networks prevailing in these markets, and, as a consequence, on the type of strategies that MNEs may pursue at the BOP. We conclude with a discussion of the implications of this chapter for future research on the BOP.

HOW DIFFERENT IS THE BOP? INSTITUTIONAL AND COMPETITIVE SPECIFICITIES

BOP (or subsistence) markets can be defined as markets in which poverty prevails, meaning that the majority of consumers barely have sufficient resources for day-to-day living (Viswanathan et al., 2010). Although a precise definition is elusive in the BOP literature (Kolk et al., 2010), most papers follow Prahalad's original articles (Prahalad and Hammond, 2002; Prahalad and Hart, 2002), and refer to income thresholds of either $1 or $2 per day on a purchasing power parity basis, widely used in both academic and practitioner discussions of poverty (Banerjee and Duflo, 2007) to define the boundaries of the BOP. More imprecise definitions abound, however, with references to the '4 billion' poorest people in the world (Hammond et al., 2007), for instance, or low-income populations in general, including people who can afford a small car (e.g. Rangnekar, 2010; Van den Waeyenberg and Hens, 2008). Although BOP markets are typically studied in developing and emerging countries, they can also exist in developed countries (Kolk et al., 2011).

Development economists have long established a link between weak institutional environments and poverty (Tebaldi and Mohan, 2010) and, more generally, between weak formal institutions and low levels of development (e.g. North, 1990). Institutional theory (De Soto, 2000; North, 1990) is thus a helpful lens to understand how BOP markets may differ from more developed markets. In turn, prevailing institutions have an important impact on the way business is conducted and on the type of firms that emerge in a given market (Khanna and Palepu, 1999). In this section, we start by exploring the specificities of institutions in BOP markets and derive from these specificities the competitive characteristics of firms prevailing at the BOP.

Institutions at the BOP

Institutional theorists distinguish between two important types of institutional environments. Formal institutions refer to legally valid and enforceable norms and correspond to the institutions typically discussed in the economic development literature (North, 1990). Informal institutions refer to norms with no legal validity, even though they may have customary validity (De Soto, 2000; Rivera-Santos and Rufín, 2010). BOP markets are characterized by a prevalence of informal institutions (De Soto, 2000; Rivera-Santos and Rufín, 2010; Rivera-Santos et al., forthcoming), thus contrasting with more developed markets, in which strong formal institutions prevail or coexist with strong informal institutions. In fact, research in anthropology and political science suggests that there is a continuum of institutional evolution (Cheater, 2003; Mair, 1962): from the informal institutions prevailing in BOP markets, embedded in non-specialized kinship, age-group, religious or other intragroup ties; to an institutional 'middle stage' characteristic of many developing countries, where informal institutions are linked to the formal institutions of the state and political organizations through clientelistic networks; and, finally, to the formal institutions prevailing in developed markets, which are characterized by specialization, the replacement of intragroup ties by impersonal and transactional relationships, and more generally by norms of 'bureaucratic rationality' (Weber, 1947). Indeed, a fundamental difference between informal and formal institutions is the less specialized nature of informal institutions, leading to important overlaps between business and non-business relationships.

This prevalence of informal institutions in BOP markets is a combination of particularly weak formal institutions and particularly strong informal institutions (Rivera-Santos et al., forthcoming). First, BOP markets are characterized by severe institutional gaps, defined as the lack of formal institutions to support economic activities (Khanna and Palepu, 1997, 1999). Low enforceability of formal laws and regulations (Ricart et al., 2004), accompanied by high levels of corruption (Aidt, 2003; Viswanathan et al., 2010), in turn lead to low levels of protection and to an overall voicelessness for subsistence market consumers (Karnani, 2007b; World Bank, 2000). By contrast, informal institutions are particularly strong and substitute for the weakness of formal institutions to a certain extent (De Soto, 2000), although they can contradict formal institutions (Arnould and Mohr, 2005; Johnson, 2007). Embedded in traditional ties developed within communities (De Soto, 2000; London and Hart, 2004), these informal institutions are significantly stronger within the community than between communities, leading to localized structures with few bridges across communities (Arnould and Mohr, 2005).

While the prevalence of informal institutions is a characteristic of all subsistence markets, there are important variations regarding the types of informal institutions that exist (Kolk et al., 2011). Research in anthropology and ethnology suggests that there are two main types of informal institutions (Cheater, 2003). In 'acephalous' communities, like the Nuer in Sudan, for instance, community norms are based on social capital embedded in networks, and there is no well-defined authority structure. Communal punishment of transgressors thus takes the form of exclusion from the community. By contrast, in 'monarchical' or centralized communities, like the Swazi, a single person, such as a king, a religious leader or even a gang leader, concentrates most attributes of power. Conflict resolution thus takes the form of the exercise of judicial power by a centralized authority.

This prevalence of informal institutions is associated with an important degree of isolation, which is another major characteristic of BOP markets (Arnould and Mohr, 2005; Rivera-Santos and Rufín, 2010). This isolation both explains and is a result of the weakness of formal institutions in BOP markets, and can be illustrated by the lack of police access to some *favelas* in Rio de Janeiro, Brazil, or by the lack of government control in the eastern parts of the Democratic Republic of Congo. In most cases, however, isolation is not as extreme, and a continuum exists between completely isolated BOP markets, as may be the case in remote communities with no connection whatsoever with the rest of the country, and BOP markets with some connection to the markets and the formal institutions that exist in the rest of the country. The majority BOP markets seem to be actually somewhat connected to outside markets and institutions, creating complex institutional environments in which local and mostly informal institutions coexist with (relatively) weak institutions originating from outside a given BOP market (Rivera-Santos et al., forthcoming).

Competitive Dynamics at the BOP

The prevalence of informal institutions, regardless of their type or of the extent to which they coexist with formal institutions originating outside the BOP market, has important implications for business transactions in BOP markets (Rivera-Santos and Rufín, 2010; Rivera-Santos et al., forthcoming). Contrasting with some early claims in the literature that BOP ventures essentially compete against 'non-consumption' (Hart and Christensen, 2002), research on poverty suggests that businesses not only exist at the BOP but are also the most important source of income for people living in poverty (Banerjee and Duflo, 2007; Collins et al., 2009). In other terms, the poor are customers and BOP markets exist with or without MNEs.

The main characteristic of BOP customers is, logically, poverty. While BOP scholars typically define poverty in terms of income (Kolk et al., 2011), the extensive scholarship on poverty in development economics suggests that poverty is best defined by five dimensions (World Bank, 2000): low and unpredictable levels of income, poor health, poor education, vulnerability and exclusion. These five dimensions are interrelated and create poverty traps, from which it is very difficult for the poor to emerge. As we mentioned above, isolation is another major characteristic of BOP customers, whether they are geographically dispersed, as is the case for the rural poor (e.g. Anderson and Markides, 2007) or whether they live in densely populated areas, as is the case for slum-dwellers in major conurbations (e.g. Johnson, 2007). This isolation typically leads to strong local cultures and less contact with national or international consumer habits, even though the expansion of radio, television, cell phones and other communication means somewhat reduces the cultural isolation of many BOP markets (Kolk et al., 2011), leading to the counterintuitive finding that the poor can sometimes be highly brand-sensitive in their purchasing habits (Subrahmanyan and Gomez-Arias, 2008; Viswanathan and Rosa, 2010).

In turn, BOP firms are shaped by the institutional environment and consumer characteristics. They are typically informal, few in number and small, and they offer low-quality products and services at prices that may be higher than prices for similar products and services in more developed markets (London and Hart, 2004; Prahalad and Hammond, 2002; Rivera-Santos and Rufín, 2010). They rely on informal rules embedded in the local institutions to govern their relationships, rather than formal contracts or equity (Rivera-Santos and Rufín, 2010; Rivera-Santos et al., forthcoming). In addition to informal firms, informal self-employment, including, for instance, at-home sewing services or meals sold in the streets, is common as a way to complement the family income (Banerjee and Duflo, 2007), even though these activities typically represent a tiny fraction of the total income (Collins et al., 2009). While both informal firms and informal self-employment represent the two prevailing types of businesses at the BOP, they have very distinct profiles. Both are typically weak in the competitive sense, providing limited value to their customers, but informal firms can be connected to the local informal powers, and thus be competitively weak but institutionally strong competitors. Overall, businesses and markets exist and may thrive at the BOP, but important gaps in the business ecosystems are also characteristic of BOP markets (Anderson and Markides, 2007; Wheeler et al., 2005). These gaps typically include gaps in the economic infrastructure, such as electricity or water supply, in support activities, such as financing or distribution, and in the information infrastructure. In turn, these gaps may lead local firms to incorporate activities left to the market in more developed markets (Khanna and Palepu, 1999) and non-governmental organizations (NGOs) to substitute for activities typically left to firms (Rivera-Santos and Rufín, 2010).

Our analysis of the specificities of BOP markets, grounded in institutional theory and industrial organization, suggests that BOP markets differ from other markets in both their institutional environment and their competitive dynamics. Institutions at the BOP are characterized by a coexistence of strong informal institutions, acephalous or monarchical, and weak formal institutions. The relative importance of both types of institutions is related to the extent to which the BOP market is isolated from other markets in the country. In turn, this has important implications for competitive dynamics at the BOP, which exist regardless of the presence of an MNE. Consumers are characterized by poverty in its five dimensions, and by their relative isolation from mainstream markets. Local firms are typically informal and competitively weak, even though they may be institutionally strong if they are connected to local powers. Finally, the business ecosystem is characterized by gaps, which can be filled by firms or by NGOs. In the next section, we explore how these characteristics impact the business networks that prevail at the BOP and the strategies that can be pursued by MNEs in BOP markets.

BUSINESS NETWORKS AT THE BOP

The specificities of the institutional and competitive environments at the BOP discussed above have important implications for the way business is run in BOP markets. In particular, they lead to business networks that can be significantly different from their counterparts in more developed markets (Rivera-Santos and Rufín, 2010). In this section, we build on recent research on BOP networks to explore the characteristics of networks at the BOP. A network can be defined as 'a group of three or more organizations connected in ways that facilitate achievement of a common goal' (Provan et al., 2007, p. 482). The broad literature on networks has extensively analyzed the different dimensions of business networks (Provan et al., 2007; Scott, 1991; Uzzi, 1997; Wasserman and Faust, 1994). We group these dimensions into four main categories in this discussion: membership, structural characteristics, boundaries and dynamics.

Network Membership

The relationship between the diversity of the members comprising a network and the benefits accruing to each of the members has long been established in the network literature (Baum et al., 2000; Goerzen and Beamish, 2005, among others), making network membership, and in particular the degree of diversity among the members of a network, one of the most important dimensions of networks. Compared to their counterparts in more developed markets, BOP networks are likely to be more diverse (Rivera-Santos and Rufín, 2010), due to the prevalence of institutional and of competitive gaps in BOP environments.

As mentioned above, BOP markets are characterized by severe institutional gaps and by the coexistence of strong informal institutions and weak formal institutions. Informal institutions act as substitutes for formal institutions, although their ability to provide a stable and reliable environment to sustain business activity is limited, as the established link between underdeveloped formal institutions and low levels of economic development suggests (e.g. North, 1990). As a consequence, non-market actors take on a role they do not typically have in more developed markets, as they substitute for gaps in the formal institutional environment (Anderson and Markides, 2007; Rivera-Santos and Rufín, 2010; Wheeler et al., 2005). The three sectors, i.e. profit, non-profit and public, compensate for different institutional gaps, however, meaning that no single actor and, most importantly, no single sector is able to provide the complete set of institutions needed to support economic activity (Rivera-Santos et al., forthcoming). As a result, business networks at the BOP will typically need to incorporate actors from the three sectors in order to fill the market's institutional gaps as much as possible. Firms, for instance, can contribute contacts with the central government or their knowledge of other regulative institutions, such as international agencies (Petersson, 2011). NGOs, which typically seek to compensate for institutional gaps in BOP markets as their core activity, including the supply of education and health care (Doh and Teegen, 2002), can contribute this activity to the network. Governments can provide protection against unpredictable changes in regulations (Rufín and Arboleda, 2007). Beyond the three sectors, the communities themselves take on a particularly important institutional role at the BOP, as they provide the backbone to many institutions, especially in the case of acephalous communities. Networks at the BOP will thus typically also incorporate the BOP community, either as a whole in the case of acephalous communities or represented by the central power holders in the case of monarchical communities. Of course, the extent to which networks will incorporate actors from the three sectors and community representatives will depend on the degree of isolation of BOP markets from mainstream markets, as less isolated markets will typically be characterized by fewer institutional gaps.

BOP markets are not only characterized by institutional gaps, though; networks also have to deal with gaps in the business ecosystem. Businesses at the BOP, whether they are large informal firms or informal self-employment, face a lack of economic infrastructure, support activities and information infrastructure. As a result, non-market actors, especially NGOs, fill these gaps, offering, for instance, business and personal financing through microfinance initiatives or information and communication technology (ICT) services. These gaps in the business ecosystem reinforce the need for diverse members in the network, thereby ensuring that the support activities needed to sustain business are present in the network. Firms can provide business resources such as capital, managerial expertise or technology; NGOs can provide access to potential customers, facilities and support capacity not directly accessible through other means; and governments can provide access to otherwise unavailable resources, such as financing, and help grant security (Kolk et al., 2008; Rivera-Santos et al., forthcoming; Seelos and Mair, 2007; Simanis and Hart, 2008).

This reasoning suggests that diversity of members will be wider and that the overall number of members will typically be greater in BOP business networks than in their counterparts in more developed markets. This membership diversity will be particularly important in acephalous communities and in very isolated BOP markets. Several examples of existing BOP ventures illustrate this idea. SC Johnson established a BOP venture in Kibera, the largest slum in Africa, located near Nairobi, through which it sells its house cleaning products to customers living in the slum (Johnson, 2007). Realizing that it could not access the slum on its own, the company partnered with an NGO, Carolina for Kibera, and with community-based organizations, which help lift local youth out of poverty. Together, they trained young members of the community to help them start entrepreneurial ventures offering house cleaning services to people living in the slum. SC Johnson thus created a cross-sector business network to be able to enter Kibera's market. Similarly, the electric utility AES Eletropaulo invested significant time to gain community approval, with more than 13 000 initial and follow-up visits over a one-year period, when it developed a program to regulate access to the electricity grid in the Paraisópolis *favela* (slum) in São Paulo, Brazil (Petersson, 2011). The more isolated the markets are, the more the need for diverse networks increases. When the cell phone company Celtel Nigeria decided to expand into rural markets, it had to partner not only with NGOs and local communities, but also with traditional kings to be allowed to recruit local entrepreneurs as distributors and ensure safe passage for its staff, thus reflecting the strongly monarchical nature of some rural regions of Nigeria (Anderson and Kupp, 2008).

Structural Characteristics of the Network

Beyond the type and number of network members, the specificities of BOP institutions also influence the structural characteristics of networks. The network literature suggests that several dimensions characterize network structures, including centralization, density and structural holes. Centralization refers to the fact that a few firms have direct connections to most other network members, while most network members only have a few direct connections within the network (Wasserman and Faust, 1994, p. 95). While variations exist, networks in developed markets tend to be organized around a few leading players (McGuire and Dow, 2003). Density refers to the extent to which ties are redundant within a network, meaning that members are connected both directly and indirectly through other members. Density is related to the degree to which networks are linear, meaning that they are composed of supplier–customer relationships along a value chain (Porter, 1980). Networks in developed markets tend to exhibit relatively high density of ties (Williams, 2005) and have been evolving from linear value chains to more complex value constellations (Normann and Ramirez, 1993). Finally, the number and location of structural holes, which are ties in the network that bridge two otherwise unconnected sections of the network, are an important dimension of network structure (Ahuja, 2000). Networks in developed markets tend to be built around a few structural holes (Ahuja, 2000; Sharma et al., 1994), although business ecosystems in developed markets typically include relatively few structural holes (Khanna and Palepu, 1997). All three structural dimensions of networks are influenced by the institutional and competitive characteristics of BOP environments.

BOP networks will typically be less centralized than networks in developed markets (Rivera-Santos and Rufín, 2010). The inclusion of market and non-market actors, such as NGOs or local communities, in BOP networks means that the members will bring significantly different connections to the network, as their core activities require the actors to be embedded in very different external networks. NGOs, for instance, may be connected to donors and international agencies, while firms may be connected to international suppliers and customers. As they become members of the BOP network, these different actors contribute very different connections with limited overlap, leading to networks that will be characterized by at least several centers and thus a lower degree of centralization. This will be particularly true in acephalous communities, the institutional environment of which is characterized by very low levels of centralization. When Celtel Nigeria expanded its operations to cover rural BOP markets, it included village chiefs and local community leaders in its network (Anderson and Kupp, 2008), reflecting the monarchical nature of many Nigerian communities, especially in Yorùbá areas, and leading to networks in which at least two centers coexist: the firm and the local authority. Similarly, both DuPont's subsidiary Solae and SC Johnson emphasized the need to 'co-create' BOP initiatives with local communities in India and Kenya respectively (Simanis and Hart, 2008), reflecting a less centralized institutional environment and leading to networks significantly less centralized than their typical counterparts in developed markets. Of course, the extent to which BOP networks will differ from networks in more developed markets in regard to their centralization will also depend on the degree of isolation from mainstream markets of the specific BOP community in which the BOP network is created.

The specificities of BOP environments will also significantly impact the density of networks at the BOP, although this impact will be different at the local and at the broader levels (Rivera-Santos and Rufín, 2010). As we mentioned above, the BOP is characterized by a prevalence of gaps in the competitive environment, especially in the physical and information infrastructures, and in the connection with mainstream markets, leading to various degrees of isolation. This isolation leads to very high levels of network density within BOP communities, especially in communities that are either particularly isolated or characterized by acephalous institutions, although high density is a characteristic of BOP networks overall. The embeddedness of business ties in broader social ties characteristic of informal institutions (De Soto, 2000; Wheeler et al., 2005) further reinforces the density of ties within the community and their informal nature, as both business and non-business relationships will be embedded within the same network, and leads to networks that are typically non-linear in nature. The proportion of direct ties is, as a consequence, also greater in BOP networks. In turn, the relative isolation characteristic of BOP communities means that ties between the community and mainstream markets are few (London and Hart, 2004; Tigges et al., 1998) and typically controlled by intermediaries bridging the gap between the community and the outside world (Arnould and Mohr, 2005). BOP networks will thus be characterized by a high density of direct and mostly informal ties within the community and low density of ties between the community and mainstream markets. This is likely to be particularly true in BOP markets with acephalous informal institutions, since the lack of a centralized authority will lead to more developed social networks within the community, and in BOP markets characterized by a high degree of isolation. The Egyptian agribusiness company Sekem, for instance, buys produce from low-income farmers and sells it globally, thus creating a tie between isolated farmers and global markets (Elkington and Hartigan, 2008). Locally, the company had to develop long-term relationships with the farmers and become embedded in local business and social networks, which included developing personal trust bonds and providing access to health care and education to the local community. Becoming part of the farming community's local network, Sekem thus ensures a supply of high-quality grain and produce, often at prices below market level.

Finally, the specificities of BOP environments will also lead to a prevalence of structural holes (Rivera-Santos and Rufín, 2010). The gaps in both the competitive and the institutional environments characteristic of BOP markets create as many structural holes in the business network, which are typically filled by market intermediaries or formal institutions in more developed markets. As a result, network members will need to fill these structural holes either themselves or by helping create entrepreneurial ventures to fill these gaps. Honey Care Africa, for instance, is a company that buys honey from poor farmers in Kenya, Tanzania and Uganda, and sells it internationally (Branzei and Valente, 2007). The lack of suppliers, of financing and of education, led Honey Care Africa to incorporate all these activities into its own business, selling beehives to the farmers, providing access to loans for farmers to buy the beehives, and training farmers in how to use the beehives themselves. In other terms, Honey Care Africa responded to the presence of structural holes in the market by modifying the boundaries of its business. SC Johnson, by contrast, responded to the lack of distribution networks in its BOP initiative in Kibera, Kenya, by spurring local entrepreneurship (Johnson, 2007). It partnered with the NGO Carolina for Kibera to recruit and train local youth, who then started small house-cleaning businesses that use SC Johnson's products and thus create a distribution network for SC Johnson.

The structure of BOP networks is thus characterized by less centralization, higher density within BOP communities, lower density between the BOP community and the outside world, and more structural holes than the structure of their counterparts in more developed markets. The extent to which BOP networks will differ in their structure is, however, dependent on the degree of isolation of a given BOP market and on the acephalous or monarchical nature of its local informal institutions.

Boundaries of the Network

A third important dimension of networks identified by the literature is their boundaries, which include their scope and the domains included in the ties that constitute the network. Scope refers to the range of activities carried out within a network and is typically relatively narrow in developed markets, due to inter-network competition, network specialization and the pursuit of efficiency through the integration of only essential players into the network (Koza and Lewin, 1998; Lorenzoni and Lipparini, 1999; Rothaermel and Deeds, 2004). Tie domains refer to the extent of the number of different dimensions, including business dimensions, social dimensions, political dimensions etc., that are included within network ties (Wasserman and Faust, 1994). Tie domains in developed markets tend to focus on business dimensions, although firms can also develop networks for non-market or political purposes (Hansen and Mitchell, 2000; Parmigiani and Rivera-Santos, 2011).

The prevalence of gaps in the competitive and institutional environments at the BOP leads to networks with a wider scope than their counterparts in more developed markets (Rivera-Santos and Rufín, 2011b). In response to these gaps, networks will need to incorporate activities that are typically accessed through specialized market interme-diaries or functioning institutions in more developed markets. Such activities typically include consumer financing, distribution, or supply (Hammond et al., 2007; Wheeler et al., 2005), although the additional activities included in a BOP network will depend on the specific gaps characteristic of a given BOP environment. Codensa, an electricity distribution subsidiary of Endesa, for instance, developed a consumer credit program for its customers in the poor neighborhoods of Bogotá, Colombia, when they realized that many of their customers were excluded from credit markets, in spite of good payment records for their electricity bills (Millán et al., 2007).

In addition to a broader scope, networks at the BOP are characterized by broader tie domains. As we mentioned above, the BOP is characterized by the coexistence of strong informal institutions with weak formal institutions. One of the major differences between the two types of institutions is the specialization of formal institutions, which contrasts sharply with the overlap between social, political and economic institutions at the BOP (Rivera-Santos et al., forthcoming), especially in acephalous communities. Network ties in BOP environments are thus likely to incorporate not only business aspects, but also social and political aspects, as they will be embedded within the broader social institutions that govern both business and social interactions at the BOP. Furthermore, the inclusion in BOP networks of non-market members, such as NGOs or community representatives, reinforces the breadth of network ties, as non-business members are likely to demand that the network include domains of activity connected to their missions or preoccupations in exchange for their participation in the network (London and Hart, 2004). DuPont subsidiary Solae, for instance, sent three employees to participate in a range of activities with local villagers, including harvesting rice, manning a small kiosk selling drinks, operating a village pay-phone, and preparing a mid-day meal for children at a government-run crèche, before launching its BOP initiative in two adjacent villages of Parvathagiri Mandal in Hyderabad, India (Simanis and Hart, 2008).

Here again, it is important to point out that BOP environments are extremely varied, and that this variation has important implications for the way networks are structured. In particular, the scope of the network and its tie domains will be particularly broad in acephalous communities highly isolated from mainstream markets, even though they will be broader at the BOP than in more developed markets regardless of the specificities of a given BOP environment.

Network Dynamics

Finally, networks are also characterized by their dynamics, especially their degree of stability, as members enter and others leave the network (Olk and Young, 1997). While the network literature has not devoted as much attention to network dynamics as to the other dimensions of networks discussed above, findings suggest that networks in developed markets balance the need for adaptability and the need for stability, resulting in evolving networks that can last for relatively long periods of time (Dhanaraj and Parkhe, 2006; Parmigiani and Rivera-Santos, 2011).

At the BOP, network dynamics are significantly different, due to their competitive and institutional specificities (Rivera-Santos and Rufín, 2010). Overall, BOP networks are likely to evolve at the same time rapidly and slowly, leading to very complex dynamics.

These complex dynamics are due to a unique combination of a greater instability and unpredictability of formal ties and of a greater resilience of informal ties at the BOP. As we mentioned above, BOP networks are characterized by mostly informal ties, but the weakness of formal institutions still has important implications for the stability of BOP networks. In particular, poor governance arising from weak formal institutions typically leads to greater economic and political instability (Acemoglu et al., 2003), with wide swings in political decisions and economic policies, and, in extreme cases, disruption and even violence (Gates et al., 2006). Economists focusing on poverty alleviation have long argued that poor institutions and the lack of proper infrastructure exacerbate the vulnerability of formal ties to diseases or natural disasters (World Bank, 2000). While it would of course be an exaggeration to claim that the BOP is systematically characterized by violence or natural disasters, findings suggest that the 'probability of being exposed to a number of . . . risks (violence, crime, natural disasters, being pulled out of school)' (World Bank, 2000, p. 19) is an important characteristic of BOP environments and of poverty in general.

At the same time, the informal institutions prevalent at the BOP are surprisingly resilient, as long as the social networks and authority structures that sustain these institutions survive. The lack of differentiation between business and non-business ties characteristic of BOP networks suggests that business ties are likely to survive external shocks as long as the underlying social structure itself is not disrupted. In fact, these informal ties typically become stronger as formal institutions become weaker. De Soto (2000) found, for instance, that slum communities in the metropolitan area of Lima in Peru developed strong informal networks and rules, when they realized that the state could not help in spite of severe economic disruptions. Similarly, Banerjee and Duflo (2007) found that informal networks in poverty-stricken communities replace, at least to a certain extent, unavailable formal insurance mechanisms against external shocks.

In its BOP initiative in Kibera, Kenya, SC Johnson witnessed both the instability and the resilience characteristic of BOP environments (Johnson, 2007). SC Johnson describes how its executives were surprised to see how, as their network suffered major disruptions from not only political unrest and gang violence, but also natural disasters such as flooding, the community showed resilience and helped sustain SC Johnson's network in Kibera. We should note that, while BOP communities are surprisingly resilient, locally based institutions can only provide limited assistance when the entire community faces a disaster. The global NGO Oxfam and the international re-insurance company Swiss Re, for instance, partnered to create a weather insurance program in Ethiopia, recognizing that local informal insurance tools were not sufficient when the entire community faces the same climate-change-related droughts (Satterthwaite and Way, 2011).

Our reasoning suggests that the specificities of the institutional and competitive environments at the BOP have important implications for all network dimensions at the BOP. Network members will include business and non-business actors, leading to more varied networks with a greater number of members than their counterparts in developed markets. The structural characteristics of BOP networks will include relatively low levels of centralization, high density of mostly informal and direct ties within the BOP community, low density of ties outside the BOP community, and a relatively high number of structural holes. The scope of the network and its domain ties will be relatively broad, and its evolution will be characterized by complex dynamics of vulnerability and resilience in the face of a typically unstable external environment. These network characteristics have important implications for the strategy of firms deciding to enter BOP markets. We discuss these implications in the following section.

BOP STRATEGIES

Business environments at the BOP are significantly different from their counterparts in more developed markets for both competitive and institutional reasons, even though, as we argued earlier, important variations exist across BOP markets, especially, but not only, with regard to their acephalous or monarchical institutional structure and the degree to which they are isolated from mainstream markets. These differences lead to business networks that exhibit unique characteristics and set them apart from equivalent networks in more developed markets. In turn, BOP scholars have long argued that strategies at the BOP need to be unique, rather than an adaptation of existing strategies, and that firms, especially multinationals, deciding to enter the BOP have to develop radically innovative business models (Hart and Christensen, 2002; Prahalad and Hammond, 2002). Yet the theoretical justification of why, or whether, such innovations are actually needed has not been thoroughly explored, leading to calls for a clearer grounding of BOP arguments in existing theories and literatures (Kolk et al., 2010). In this section, we discuss three major dimensions of BOP strategies and link them to our analysis of the specificities of BOP business environments and networks: the role of the poor in BOP strategies; innovation in BOP strategies; and the type of resources and capabilities that external firms may need to enter BOP markets.

The Poor in BOP Strategies

The main characteristic of any BOP strategy is, of course, the fact that it targets people who live in poverty (Prahalad and Hammond, 2002). Who the poor are, and what it means to target the poor, however, is more complex and still open to debate. As we mentioned above, BOP scholars tend to define the poor through their level of income. Different BOP studies take very different income thresholds to define the BOP and often do not explicitly state the threshold used in the study, leading to a lack of a precise definition regarding what the BOP actually is (Kolk et al., 2010). Some authors follow Prahalad's lead (Prahalad and Hammond, 2002; Prahalad and Hart, 2002) and use a per capita income threshold of $1500 or $2000 per annum expressed in internationally comparable 'purchasing power parity' basis. Other authors refer to the poverty threshold of $1 or $2 per day, widely used in both academic and practitioner discussions of poverty (Banerjee and Duflo, 2007). Others simply refer to the '4 billion' poorest people in the world (Hammond et al., 2007), to low-income populations in general including people in a position to afford a small (Nano) car (Rangnekar, 2010; Van den Waeyenberg and Hens, 2008), rural populations in general (e.g. Ahmad et al., 2004), slum dwellers (e.g. Whitney and Kelkar, 2004), or often more simply 'the poor' (e.g. Heeks, 2008). This lack of a universally accepted definition is a major issue in the literature (Kolk et al., 2010), even though recent attempts at segmenting the BOP (Rangan et al., 2011) are likely to help develop more nuanced definitions of the BOP, recognize the variations that exist across different BOP markets, and help firms develop strategies adapted to very different BOP contexts (Rivera-Santos and Rufín, 2011a).

What it means for a firm to 'target' the BOP is also a subject of discussion in the literature. A review of the literature suggests that three main types of involvement exist: the poor can be consumers, producers or co-creators (Kolk et al., 2010). Viewing the poor as an underserved market that could represent a fortune for firms, especially multinationals, corresponds to CK Prahalad's original call (e.g. Hammond and Prahalad, 2004), and has been virulently criticized by scholars considering that selling to the poor and making a profit is akin to the exploitation of an unprotected population (Karnani, 2007b, 2009). Interestingly, some multinationals have been successfully targeting the poor as consumers without referring to the BOP approach, suggesting that different industries and different BOP markets may lead to very different successful strategies. The South-Africa-based cell phone company MTN, for instance, has expanded throughout Africa and is successfully outcompeting both local and global competitors by adapting its offers to low-income customers (Rivera-Santos and Rufín, 2009). Populations living at the BOP have also been viewed as producers, rather than consumers, thus providing a slightly different take on the idea of targeting the poor, and responding to concerns expressed by critics of the BOP approach (Karnani, 2007b, 2009). Honey Care Africa, for instance, buys honey from poor farmers in Eastern Africa, and helps them achieve higher quality, but sells it internationally in developed markets rather than locally or in BOP markets (Branzei and Valente, 2007). Finally, the poor can be viewed as 'co-creators' of BOP strategies. Authors and companies promoting this approach argue that firms cannot find a fortune at the BOP, but, rather, should create a fortune 'with' the BOP through an emphasis on mutual value creation (Hart, 2011; London et al., 2010). Several high-profile global companies have thus entered partnerships with universities and NGOs to develop new strategies to co-create initiatives with BOP populations. In 2006, DuPont subsidiary Solae, which develops soy-based technologies and ingredients, for instance, launched a BOP initiative in Andhra Pradesh, India, in collaboration with the BOP Protocol center (Simanis and Hart, 2008). After repeated consultations with the community and in collaboration with a local NGO called Modern Architects for Rural India (MARI), Solae designed the 'Culinary Park', which uses green spaces on the slums' rooftops to grow high-quality produce. We should note that several companies following this approach have pointed to how difficult it is to be profitable through co-creation in BOP markets (e.g. Johnson, 2007).

Innovation in BOP Strategies

The difficulty of targeting the poor, as consumers, producers, or co-creators, has been noted repeatedly in the BOP literature, and many BOP scholars have argued that, because of the uniqueness of the BOP, firms need to be highly innovative if they want to enter a BOP market successfully (Hart and Christensen, 2002; Prahalad and Hammond, 2002). Our analysis of the characteristics of BOP environments and networks helps inform us to what extent BOP strategies need to be different from more mainstream strategies.

This need for innovation can come from the specific competitive environment characteristic of BOP markets. As we mentioned above, the business environment at the BOP is characterized, in addition to the poverty of its consumers, by local firms that are typically informal and competitively weak, but that can be institutionally strong if they are connected to local powers, and by gaps, which can be filled by firms or by NGOs. In other terms, the type of competitors that a firm is likely to encounter at the BOP is significantly different from what is customary in more developed markets. In turn, this may create the need for different competitive and marketing strategies, as a lower price or a better product may not be sufficient to ensure acceptance by BOP consumers, especially in markets characterized by isolation and strong local cultures. Local legitimacy, for instance, is likely to become a crucial key success factor, and will require that firms spend time building trust locally, thus leading to a relatively new approach to entering markets, even though legitimacy is arguably important in any market. This helps explain why firms like Sekem in Egypt, SC Johnson in Kenya, or Solae in India (Elkington and Hartigan, 2008; Johnson, 2007; Simanis and Hart, 2008) need to invest so much time and effort into becoming an accepted member of the local community. The prevalence of gaps in the business ecosystem also has important implications for BOP strategies, as firms will need to either fill these gaps themselves, as is the case of Honey Care Africa (Branzei and Valente, 2007), or to help local entrepreneurs fill the gaps, as is done by SC Johnson in Kenya to overcome the lack of distribution system in the Kibera slum (Johnson, 2007).

The need for innovation can also come from the institutional environment at the BOP. As we mentioned above, the BOP is characterized by the coexistence of weak formal institutions and strong informal institutions, leading to BOP networks in which both business and non-business members are needed to help fill the various institutional gaps that exist in a given BOP market. This has important implications for BOP strategies, as the traditional governance mechanisms that are available to firms to govern their business transactions in more developed environments will not be available in BOP markets, especially when they are characterized by a high degree of isolation. Firms will thus need to rely on partnerships with NGOs, governments or local community representatives to protect their investments and govern their transactions, leading to complex governance structures that bridge both local and external institutional environments (Rivera-Santos et al., forthcoming). AES Eletropaulo, for instance, sells electricity in the Paraisópolis *favela*, a slum of São Paulo, Brazil, from which the police has traditionally been absent (Petersson, 2011). In order to increase its reputation within the community and thus be able to ensure that its business would not be disrupted, since contracts could not be enforced in court, the company replaced 9588 incandescent bulbs by compact fluorescent bulbs, and 497 old refrigerators by new, energy-efficient ones, free of charge, as a gift to show commitment. It also rewired the internal electrical cables and fixtures of 496 homes, and placed 505 lights for street lighting, further signaling its commitment to the community beyond the simple distribution of electricity.

The analysis of the competitive and institutional environments at the BOP thus helps better understand the need for innovation, and identifies four major BOP-oriented adaptations of traditional strategies. First, because competition follows different and informal rules, traditional competitive advantages, such as low price or good quality, may not be sufficient, highlighting instead the need to develop local legitimacy as a competitive advantage. This need to become part of the local community is reinforced by the fact that formal institutions cannot protect the firm's investment in BOP settings and that firms will need to rely on local, informal institutions to govern their transactions. Second, the relative isolation of BOP markets also leads to high degrees of localization, not only because of strong local cultures, but also because informal institutions are highly local-ized, meaning that firms need to adapt both their product or service and their governance structure at the BOP (Rivera-Santos et al., forthcoming). SC Johnson, for instance, notes that its presence in Kibera, Kenya, cannot easily be leveraged outside the boundaries of the slum (Johnson, 2007). As such, the BOP provides an interesting, albeit extreme, case in the localization–standardization continuum. Third, a firm entering the BOP will need to adapt its boundaries as a result of the prevalence of gaps in the competitive environ-ment, leading to different levels of diversification, either by the firm itself or through its network. Finally, the prevalence of institutional gaps will not only require the develop-ment of local legitimacy, but will also require partnerships with non-business actors in order to overcome some of these gaps, leading to a prevalence of strategies involving multiple sectors and multiple stakeholders, which contrast with more traditional business-focused strategies. Of course, we reiterate the importance of recognizing the variation that exists across BOP settings. In particular, both the distinction between acephalous and monarchical communities, and the extent to which a given BOP market is isolated from mainstream markets, have important implications for competitive and institutional BOP strategies.

What Does it Take to be Successful at the BOP?

The specificities of BOP environments and the difficulties associated with conducting business in these environments have led a significant number of firms to abandon BOP markets after failed market entry attempts (Karamchandani et al., 2011). This raises the question of what it takes to be successful at the BOP. While it is too early to conclusively answer this question, our analysis of the institutional and competitive characteristics of BOP settings and networks points to a few characteristics that seem to be necessary to succeed in BOP markets.

First, a clear definition of what success at the BOP means seems particularly important. While this may seem obvious, many firms report the need for new metrics to correctly measure the success of BOP initiatives, arguing that traditional profitability measures may not be sufficient (e.g. Johnson, 2007). A recent review of the BOP literature shows that only roughly half of published papers report profitability measures, and the variety of measures used makes it very difficult to compare across cases (Kolk et al., 2010). Scholars critical of the BOP approach have emphasized the fact that only seeking profit-ability at the BOP, as opposed to seeking a return on investment similar to that of other ventures, essentially means not taking the opportunity cost of capital into account and thus not actually maximizing profitability at the firm level (Garrette and Karnani, 2010). By contrast, several BOP scholars have argued that using profitability as a measure of success may be insufficient, as a BOP initiative typically pursues both economic and social goals, leading to the recent development of broader measures of impact (London, 2009). Clearly defining measures of success adapted to BOP settings thus seems to be a relatively obvious, but actually relatively controversial, prerequisite for firms targeting the BOP.

Regardless of the measure of success, several firm characteristics needed to be success-ful at the BOP emerge from our analysis of BOP strategies. First, the ability to effectively manage cross-sector partnerships seems crucial. As we mentioned above, non-business actors play a significant role in BOP settings, and it seems difficult for a firm to successfully enter a BOP market without a partnership with an NGO, a government or community representatives. The literature on cross-sector partnerships has shown that these partnerships, while similar to traditional alliances in some ways, are actually significantly along many dimensions, including governance (Jamali and Keshishian, 2009; Rivera-Santos and Rufín, 2011b; Selsky and Parker, 2005), suggesting that firms can develop partnership capabilities similar to, but different from, traditional alliance capabilities (Kale and Singh, 2007). Second, the ability to adapt to highly localized environments seems very important. As we have discussed above, BOP settings require not only an important adaptation of products and services to fit the needs and tastes of relatively isolated populations, but also embeddedness in local institutions, thus providing an extreme case of localization strategies. The difficulty faced by companies like SC Johnson as they try to expand their BOP initiatives beyond a given BOP market, compared with the relative success that companies like MTN seem to have expanding into a variety of BOP markets, suggests that both industry structures and firm-specific capabilities help inform firms' localization strategies in BOP settings. Third, and maybe most obviously, the ability to deliver highly localized products and services at very low cost seems necessary, even though industry characteristics are likely to impact the balance between localization and cost, as Coca-Cola's success across BOP markets with relatively standardized products and price points suggests (McNeil, 2001). Contrasting with Prahalad's original call for multinationals to find their fortune at the BOP, this exploratory list of firm characteristics associated with success at the BOP raises the somewhat counterintuitive question of whether Western multinationals are actually better positioned to succeed at the BOP than local and smaller companies (Kolk et al., 2011).

CONCLUSIONS

In this chapter, we have sought to answer the call for a greater connection with existing theories and frameworks by systematically exploring the relationship between the characteristics of BOP environments and MNE strategies at the BOP. Grounding our reasoning in institutional theory and industrial organization, we have analyzed how the institutional and competitive environments prevalent in BOP markets shape business networks at the BOP and, in turn, influence the type of strategies that MNEs can pursue in these markets. Our conceptual analysis provides support to one of the major claims of the BOP literature: BOP markets are so different from other markets that MNEs need to develop different products and highly innovative business models to be successful at the BOP (Hart and Christensen, 2002; Prahalad, 2005; Simanis and Hart, 2008). By systematically analyzing the institutional and competitive differences between BOP and other markets, and the implications for MNE strategies at the BOP, we contribute to establishing a more systematic connection between existing theories and the study of the BOP.

To begin with, our analysis of the specificities of BOP markets, grounded in institutional theory and industrial organization, suggests that BOP markets differ from other markets in both their institutional environment and their competitive dynamics. Institutions at the BOP are characterized by the coexistence of strong informal institutions, acephalous or monarchical, and weak formal institutions. BOP consumers are

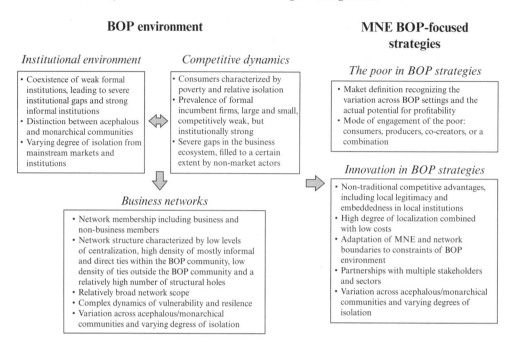

Figure 22.1   Characteristics of BOP environments and networks, and implications for MNE strategies

characterized by poverty in its five dimensions, and by their relative isolation from mainstream markets. Local firms are typically informal and competitively weak, even though they may be institutionally strong if they are connected to local powers. Finally, the business ecosystem is characterized by significant gaps.

These characteristics of BOP markets have major implications for MNE strategies targeting the BOP. First, the lack of a universally accepted definition of the BOP means that MNEs must recognize the variations that exist across different BOP markets and develop strategies adapted to very different BOP contexts. Second, MNEs must decide on the terms on which they plan to engage BOP populations: as consumers, producers, or co-creators, or a combination of any of these. Third, MNEs will need to develop innovative strategies along four dimensions: the development of local legitimacy as a competitive advantage; a high degree of localization to cope with strong local cultures and highly localized informal institutions; the adaptation of the MNE's boundaries to address gaps in the competitive environment; and the establishment of partnerships involving multiple stakeholders from multiple sectors.

The key elements of our analysis are summarized in Figure 22.1, which shows the characteristics of BOP environments at the competitive and institutional levels, the characteristics of BOP networks, and the implications for MNE strategies.

To be sure, we view the ideas presented in this chapter as a first step in providing a stronger theoretical foundation for the concept of the BOP, hoping that other scholars will find them interesting or provocative enough to build on them or offer alternative approaches and conclusions. Our analysis draws on institutional theory and industrial organization, as well as bringing in concepts from network theory; other theoretical lenses may bring additional or even contradictory perspectives on the BOP and MNE strategies. Perhaps even more importantly, our speculations must ultimately be corroborated empirically. Indeed, one of the serious limitations of the BOP literature thus far has been its extensive reliance on case studies. As more MNEs undertake BOP strategies, we hope that enough data will be made available to scholars to put our claims to rigorous tests.

REFERENCES

Acemoglu, Daron, Simon Johnson, James Robinson and Yunyong Thaicharoen (2003), 'Institutional causes, macroeconomic symptoms: volatility, crises and growth', *Journal of Monetary Economics*, **50**(1), 49–123.

Ahmad, Pia Sabharwal, Michael E. Gorman and Patricia H. Werhane (2004), 'Case study: Hindustan Lever Limited and marketing to the poorest of the poor', *International Journal of Entrepreneurship and Innovation Management*, **4**(5), 495–511.

Ahuja, Gautam (2000), 'Collaboration networks, structural holes, and innovation: a longitudinal study', *Administrative Science Quarterly*, **45**(3), 425–57.

Aidt, Toke S. (2003), 'Economic analysis of corruption: a survey', *The Economic Journal*, **113**(491), F632–F652.

Anderson, Jamie and Martin Kupp (2008), 'Celtel Nigeria: Serving the Rural Poor', TiasNimbas Case Study, Tilburg.

Anderson, Jamie and Costas Markides (2007), 'Strategic innovation at the base of the pyramid', *MIT Sloan Management Review*, **49**(1), 83–8.

Arnould, Eric J. and Jakki J. Mohr (2005), 'Dynamic transformations for base-of-the-pyramid market clusters', *Academy of Marketing Science Review*, **33**(3), 254–74.

Banerjee, Abhijit V. and Esther Duflo (2007), 'The economic lives of the poor', *Journal of Economic Perspectives*, **21**(1), 141–67.

Baum, Joel A.C., Tony Calabrese and Brian Silverman (2000), 'Don't go it alone: alliance network composition and startups' performance in Canadian biotechnology', *Strategic Management* Journal, **21**(3), 261–94.

Branzei, Oana and Mike Valente (2007), 'Honey Care Africa: a tripartite model for sustainable beekeeping', Richard Ivey School of Business Case Studies (907M60).

Cheater, Angela P. (2003), *Social Anthropology*, New York: Routledge/Taylor & Francis.

Chen, Shaohua and Martin Ravaillon (2008), 'The developing world is poorer than we thought, but no less successful in the fight against poverty', Policy Research Working Paper no. 4703, The World Bank, Washington, DC.

Collins, Daryl, Jonathan Morduch, Stuart Rutherford and Orlanda Ruthven (2009), *Portfolios of the Poor – How the World's Poor Live on $2 a Day*, Princeton, NJ: Princeton University Press.

De Soto, Hernando (2000), *The Mystery of Capital: Why Capitalism Triumphs in the West and Fails Everywhere Else*, New York: Basic Books.

Dhanaraj, Charles and Arvind Parkhe (2006), 'Orchestrating innovation networks', *Academy of Management Review*, **31**(3), 659–69.

Doh, Jonathan P. and Hildy Teegen (2002), 'Nongovernmental organizations as institutional actors in international business: theory and implications', *International Business Review*, **11**, 665–84.

Elkington, John and Pamela Hartigan (2008), *The Power of Unreasonable People*, Boston, MA: Harvard Business Review Press.

Garrette, Bernard and Aneel Karnani (2010), 'Challenges in marketing socially useful goods to the poor', *California Management Review*, **52**(4), 29–47.

Gates, Scott, Håvard Hegre, Mark P. Jones and Håvard Strand (2006), 'Institutional inconsistency and political instability: polity duration, 1800–2000', *American Journal of Political Science*, **50**(4), 893–908.

Goerzen, Anthony and Paul W. Beamish (2005), 'The effect of alliance network diversity on multinational enterprise performance', *Strategic Management Journal*, **26**(4), 333–54.

Hammond, Allen L., William J. Kramer, Robert S. Katz, Julia T. Tran and Courtland Walker (2007), *The Next 4 Billion: Market Size and Business Strategy at the Base of the Pyramid*, Washington, DC: World Resources Institute/International Finance Corporation.

Hammond, Allen L. and C.K. Prahalad (2004), 'Selling to the poor', *Foreign Policy*, **142**(May/June), 30–37.

Hansen, Wendy L. and Neil J. Mitchell (2000), 'Disaggregating and explaining corporate political activity:

domestic and foreign corporations in national politics', *The American Political Science Review*, **94**(4), 891–903.

Hart, Stuart (2011), 'Writing the unfinished symphony at the Base of the Pyramid', *Voice of the Planet*, www.stuartlhart.com/blog, 28 May.

Hart, Stuart L. and Clayton Christensen (2002), 'The great leap: driving innovation from the base of the pyramid', *Sloan Management Review*, **44**(1), 51–6.

Heeks, R. (2008), 'ICT4D 2.0: the next phase of applying ICT for international development', *Computer*, **41**(6), 26–33.

Jamali, Dima and Tamar Keshishian (2009), 'Uneasy alliances: lessons learned from partnerships between businesses and NGOs in the context of CSR', *Journal of Business Ethics*, **84**(2), 277–95.

Johnson, Scott (2007), 'SC Johnson builds business at the base of the pyramid', *Global Business and Organizational Excellence*, **26**(6), 6–17.

Kale, Prashant and Harbir Singh (2007), 'Building firm capabilities through learning: the role of the alliance learning process in alliance capability and firm-level alliance success', *Strategic Management Journal*, **28**(10), 981–1000.

Karamchandani, Ashish, Mike Kubzansky and Nishant Lalwani (2011), 'Is the bottom of the pyramid really for you?', *Harvard Business Review*, **89**(3), 107–11.

Karnani, Aneel (2007a), 'Doing well by doing good – case study: "Fair & Lovely" whitening cream', *Strategic Management Journal*, **28**(13), 1351–7.

Karnani, Aneel (2007b), 'The mirage of marketing to the bottom of the pyramid: how the private sector can alleviate poverty', *California Management Review*, **49**(4), 90–111.

Karnani, Aneel (2009), 'The bottom of the pyramid strategy for reducing poverty: a failed promise', Working Paper, United Nations, Department of Economics and Social Affairs.

Khanna, Tarun and Krishna Palepu (1997), 'Why focused strategies may be wrong for emerging markets', *Harvard Business Review*, **75**, 41–51.

Khanna, Tarun and Krishna Palepu (1999), 'The right way to structure conglomerates in emerging markets', *Harvard Business Review*, **77**, 125–34.

Kolk, Ans, Miguel Rivera-Santos and Carlos Rufín (2010), 'What do we really know about the base of the pyramid concept?', Academy of Management Meeting, Montréal, 6–10, August.

Kolk, Ans, Miguel Rivera-Santos and Carlos Rufín (2011), 'Multinationals and the bottom of the pyramid: quo vadis?', C.K. Prahalad Legacy Conference, San Diego, 15–17 September.

Kolk, Ans, Rob Van Tulder and Esther Kostwinder (2008), 'Business and partnerships for development', *European Management Journal*, **26**(4), 262–74.

Koza, Mitchell P. and Arie Y. Lewin (1998), 'The co-evolution of strategic alliances', *Organization Science*, **9**(3), 225–64.

London, Ted (2009), 'Making better investments at the base of the pyramid', *Harvard Business Review*, **87**(5), 106–13.

London, Ted and Stuart L. Hart (2004), 'Reinventing strategies for emerging markets: beyond the transnational model', *Journal of International Business Studies*, **35**(5), 350–70.

London, Ted, Ravi Anupindi and Sateen Sheth (2010), 'Creating mutual value: lessons learned from ventures serving base of the pyramid producers', *Journal of Business Research*, **63**(6), 582–94.

Lorenzoni, Gianni and Andrea Lipparini (1999), 'The leveraging of interfirm relationships as a distinctive organizational capability: a longitudinal study', *Strategic Management* Journal, **20**(4), 317–37.

Mair, Lucy (1962), *Primitive Government*, Harmondsworth, UK: Penguin.

McGuire, Jean and Sandra Dow (2003), 'The persistence and implications of Japanese keiretsu organization', *Journal of International Business Studies*, **34**(4), 374–89.

McNeil, Donald G. Jr (2001), 'Coca-Cola joins AIDS fight in Africa', *New York Times*, 21 June.

Millán, J., C. Caballero and N. Millán (2007), *CODENSA 10 años*, Bogotá: Fedesarrollo.

Normann, R. and R. Ramirez (1993), 'From value chain to value constellation: designing interactive strategy', *Harvard Business Review*, **71**(July/August), 65–77.

North, Douglass (1990), *Institutions, Institutional Change, and Economic Performance*, Cambridge: Cambridge University Press.

Olk, Paul and Candice Young (1997), 'Why members stay in or leave an R&D consortium: performance and conditions of membership as determinants of continuity', *Strategic Management Journal*, **18**(11), 855–77.

Parmigiani, Anne and Miguel Rivera-Santos (2011), 'Clearing a path through the forest: a meta-review of interorganizational relationships', *Journal of Management*, **37**(4), 1108–36.

Petersson, Ivar (2011), 'One step toward citizenship: the Slum Electrification and Loss Reduction Pilot Project in São Paulo, Brazil', in Patricia Márquez and Carlos Rufin (eds), *Private Utilities and Poverty Alleviation: Market Initiatives at the Base of the Pyramid*, Cheltenham, UK and Northampton, MA, USA: Edward Elgar, pp. 207–41.

Porter, Michael E. (1980), *Competitive Strategy*, New York: Free Press.

Prahalad, C.K. (2005), *The Fortune at the Bottom of the Pyramid*, Upper Saddle River, NJ: Wharton School Publishing/Pearson Education.

Prahalad, C.K. and Allen L. Hammond (2002), 'Serving the world's poor, profitably', *Harvard Business Review* (September), 48–57.

Prahalad, C.K. and Stuart Hart (1999), 'Strategies for the bottom of the pyramid: creating sustainable development', unpublished ms.

Prahalad, C.K. and Stuart L. Hart (2002), 'The fortune at the bottom of the pyramid', *Strategy+Business*, **20**, 1–13.

Provan, Keith G., Amy Fish and Joerg Sydow (2007), 'Interorganizational networks at the network level: empirical literature on whole networks', *Journal of Management*, **33**(3), 479–516.

Rangan, V.K., M. Chu and D. Petkoski (2011), 'Segmenting the base of the pyramid, *Harvard Business Review*, **89**(6), 113–17.

Rangnekar, Sharu S. (2010), 'Nano strategy: focusing on the bottom of the pyramid', *SIES Journal of Management*, **6**(2), 55–8.

Ricart, Joan Enric J.R., Michael J. Enright, Pankaj Ghemawat, Stuart L. Hart and Tarun Khanna (2004), 'New frontiers in international strategy', *Journal of International Business Studies*, **35**(3), 175–200.

Rivera-Santos, Miguel and Carlos Rufin (2009), 'MTN Cameroon, the competitive advantage of being African', Harvard Business Review Publishing, BAB135-PDF-ENG.

Rivera-Santos, Miguel and Carlos Rufin (2010), 'Global village vs. small town: understanding networks at the base of the pyramid', *International Business Review*, **19**, 126–39.

Rivera-Santos, Miguel and Carlos Rufin (2011a), 'How different are BOP markets really? International market selection at the base of the pyramid', Academy of Management Meeting, San Antonio, 12–16 August.

Rivera-Santos, Miguel and Carlos Rufin (2011b), 'Odd couples: understanding the governance of firm–NGO alliances', *Journal of Business Ethics*, **94**, 55–70.

Rivera-Santos, Miguel, Carlos Rufin and Ans Kolk (forthcoming), 'Bridging the institutional divide: partnerships in subsistence markets', *Journal of Business Research*, retrieved from www.scopus.com.

Rothaermel, Frank T. and David L. Deeds (2004), 'Exploration and exploitation alliances in biotechnology: a system of new product development', *Strategic Management Journal*, **25**(3), 201–22.

Rufin, Carlos and Luis Fernando Arboleda (2007), 'Utilities and the poor: a story from Colombia', in Kash Rangan, John Quelch, Gustavo Herrero and Brooke Barton (eds), *Business Solutions for the Global Poor: Creating Social and Economic Value*, San Francisco, CA: Jossey-Bass, pp. 107–16.

Satterthwaite, David and Mark Way (2011), 'Swiss Re and Oxfam's presentation on weather insurance in Ethiopia', Academy of Management 71st Annual Meeting, San Antonio, 12–16 August.

Scott, John T. (1991), *Social Network Analysis: A Handbook*, Newbury Park, CA: Sage.

Seelos, Christian and Johanna Mair (2007), 'Profitable business models and market creation in the context of deep poverty: a strategic view', *Academy of Management Perspectives*, **21**(4), 49–63.

Selsky, John W. and Barbara Parker (2005), 'Cross-sector partnerships to address social issues: challenges to theory and practice', *Journal of Management*, **31**(6), 1–25.

Sharma, Sanjay, Harrie Vredenburg and Frances Westley (1994), 'Strategic bridging: a role for the multinational corporation in Third World development', *Journal of Applied Behavioral Science*, **30**(4), 458–76.

Simanis, Erik and Stuart L. Hart (2008), '*The Base of the Pyramid Protocol: toward next generation BoP strategy (Version 2.0)*', Ithaca, NY: Center for Sustainable Global Enterprise.

Subrahmanyan, Saroja and J. Tomas Gomez-Arias (2008), 'Integrated approach to understanding consumer behavior at bottom of pyramid', *Journal of Consumer Marketing*, **25**(7), 402–12.

Tebaldi, Edinaldo and Ramesh Mohan (2010), 'Institutions and poverty', *The Journal of Development Studies*, **46**(6), 1047–66.

Tigges, Leann M., Irene Browne and Gary P. Green (1998), 'Social isolation of the urban poor: race, class, and neighborhood effects on social resources', *Sociological Quarterly*, **39**(1), 53–77.

Uzzi, Brian (1997), 'Social structure and competition in interfirm networks: the paradox of embeddedness', *Administrative Science Quarterly*, **42**(1), 35–67.

Van den Waeyenberg, Sofie and Luc Hens (2008), 'Crossing the bridge to poverty, with low-cost cars', *Journal of Consumer Marketing*, **25**(7), 439–45.

Viswanathan, Madhu and José Antonio Rosa (2010), 'Understanding subsistence marketplaces: toward sustainable consumption and commerce for a better world', *Journal of Business Research*, **63**(6), 535–7.

Viswanathan, Madhu, Srinivas Sridharan and Robin Ritchie (2010), 'Understanding consumption and entrepreneurship in subsistence marketplaces', *Journal of Business Research*, **63**(6), 570–81.

Wasserman, Stanley and Katherine Faust (1994), *Social Network Analysis: Methods and Applications*, Cambridge: Cambridge University Press.

Weber, Max (1947), *The Theory of Social and Economic Organization*, tr. A.M. Henderson and T. Parsons, New York: Oxford University Press.

Wheeler, David, Kevin McKague, Jane Thomson, Rachel Davies, Jacqueline Medalye and Marina Prada (2005), 'Creating sustainable local enterprise networks', *MIT Sloan Management Review*, **47**(1), 33–40.

Whitney, Patrick and Anjali Kelkar (2004), 'Designing for the base of the pyramid', *Design Management Review*, **15**(4), 41–7.

Williams, Trevor (2005), 'Cooperation by design: structure and cooperation in interorganizational networks', *Journal of Business Research*, **58**(2), 223–31.

World Bank (2000), *World Development Report 2000/2001: Attacking Poverty*, Oxford: Oxford University Press.

23 Reconceptualizing the MNE–development relationship: the role of complementary resources[1]

Jonathan P. Doh and Jennifer Oetzel

INTRODUCTION

There is substantial controversy regarding the impact of multinational enterprises (MNEs) on host country development, particularly in less developed countries (LDCs). This controversy has generated substantial debate, not only in academia but among those engaged in international development, finance and global governance. On the one hand, some researchers have a positive view about the impact of MNEs on developing countries. MNEs are important actors, they argue, for promoting economic growth since they transfer technology and management skills, increase competition, stimulate entrepreneurship and have access to capital (Caves, 1974; Lowe and Kenney, 1999; Teece, 1977; Rugman, 1981). On the other hand, another group of researchers is more pessimistic, suggesting that MNEs are more likely to crowd out local firms, use technology that is inappropriate for local circumstances, actively constrain potential technology spillovers and reduce (rather than complement) the domestic capital stock and tax basis due to transfer price manipulation and excessive profit repatriation (De Backer and Sleuwaegen, 2003; Görg and Greenaway, 2002; Haddad and Harrison, 1993).

Debate about the impact of MNEs on developing countries is not limited to economic effects alone. There has also been extensive research on the potentially damaging effects of MNE activity on host country society (Baran, 1957) and the natural environment (Daly, 1993; Clapp and Dauvergne, 2005). Scholars have argued that MNEs operating in developing countries may have inadequate safety standards, pollute the host country environment, employ child labor and create sweatshop conditions in their factories (Daly, 1993; Korten, 2001; Clapp and Dauvergne, 2005). In fact, it has been suggested that MNEs may seek out countries with low environmental, labor and safety standards to reduce operating costs and maximize output (Daly, 1993; Porter, 1999; Wheeler, 2001). Developing countries wishing to attract and retain MNEs and foreign direct investment (FDI) are thus pressured to participate in a global 'race to the bottom' where the country with the lowest standards receives a greater proportion of investment. Questioning this argument, other scholars have criticized the 'race to the bottom' perspective, suggesting that MNEs may actually raise the environmental, labor and safety standards in less developed countries (Christmann and Taylor, 2001; Dowell et al., 2000; Wheeler, 2001).

Controversy surrounding the role of MNEs in promoting development, and their impact on developing countries, leads to the two research questions we focus on in this conceptual chapter: (1) what do the prominent theories in the international business literature suggest about the role of MNEs in host country development? To the extent that they do not sufficiently address the role of MNEs in social and economic development, (2) can collaboration between MNEs and non-governmental organizations (NGOs) offer a more promising approach for promoting economic development in developing host countries? To answer the first question, we begin by briefly reviewing past research on MNEs and their impact on economic development, including the empirical evidence, where available. Then we focus our analysis more narrowly by critically examining two of the most prominent theories in international business that relate to MNE operations in developing countries and the potential for economic development: the 'spillovers' perspective on the impact of MNE investment on host countries (Aitken and Harrison, 1999; Blomström and Persson, 1983; Rodriguez-Clare, 1996) and the liabilities of foreignness (LOF) view that specifies the constraints MNEs must overcome to succeed in local, developing country markets (Zaheer, 1995, 2002; Zaheer and Mosakowski, 1997). In deconstructing these theories, we reveal their conceptual and practical limitations.

Expanding on our critique of the literature, we discuss the emergent role of NGOs. Then, building upon the literature on cross-sectoral alliances, we propose how the integration of global MNE and NGO capabilities can contribute to host country development and to MNE and NGO strategic goals. In doing so, we argue that MNEs and MNE capabilities can be harnessed by, and integrated with, locally based NGOs to advance development. We propose an alternative conceptualization of MNE–host country relations in which MNEs and NGOs pursue collaborative relationships that make positive, collective contributions to host country development in ways that neither sector is positioned to do alone. A reconceptualization of the relationship between MNEs and host country development, we argue, is necessary to go beyond the current perspectives that rely on the MNE to merely contribute residual resources or simply assimilate to the local environment.

MNES, DEVELOPMENT AND INTERNATIONAL BUSINESS (IB) THEORY

Assessing the impact of MNEs on host country development is fundamental to research in IB. Given the increasing interdependence between developed and developing countries, the interests of both types of countries must be fully considered and advanced for productive relationships to develop (Ghauri and Cao, 2006). For MNEs to be credible partners in host country development, scholars must acknowledge the range of economic and social impacts of modern global capitalism, including its negative side-effects (Dunning, 2003). Here, we briefly review some recent criticisms of IB research as it relates to MNEs and development before examining two specific IB literatures in detail.

MNEs, IB and Development: Critical Perspectives

In a critical assessment of international management (IM) research and its application to economic development, Cooke (2004) argues that despite the fact that management theories and practices now permeate social and economic development thought and policy, IM research has largely ignored the developing world. A review of the IM research over the last several decades reveals that scholars have focused on countries in the triad (the USA, Western Europe and Japan), rather than emerging market and developing country contexts. Cooke (2004) further questions whether economic efficiency goals espoused by the World Trade Organization (WTO), adopted in the developed world, and promoted for the developing countries, are actually mechanisms that advance first-world MNE expansion and profit motives rather than economic development. For example, he suggests that WTO and World Bank policies are aimed at diminishing the role of the state, expanding global markets and promoting labor market flexibility, goals that directly support MNE interests over third-world development concerns. In his critique of IMF and World Bank policies, Joseph Stiglitz, the Nobel prize-winning economist and former Senior Vice President and Chief Economist at the World Bank (1997–2000), made similar arguments. He asserted that these organizations advise clients (host country governments) to liberalize their industries without informing them about the consequences of such actions (Stiglitz, 2002; Dalgic, 2005). More ardent critics have even suggested that economic progress in the developing world is contrary to the interests of advanced capitalist countries (Baran, 1957). Palma (1978) asserts that MNEs and governments from the developed world may form alliances with developing country elites to pave the way for easy access to developing countries' raw materials and cheap resources.

In response to this debate, a number of IM researchers have recognized the need for a more critical approach to MNEs and their impact on host countries. MNEs, by definition, span national borders, but local firms and organizations in developing countries may be more geographically restricted (Eden and Lenway, 2001). Eden and Lenway (2001, p. 388) have argued that the resulting 'asymmetry in mobility means that the less mobile may pay more of the costs of globalization, incur greater instability in earnings, and see their relative bargaining power fall'. Despite his skepticism of the need for MNEs to engage in non-business activities, Rugman (1993, p. 87) has recognized that 'the single goal of efficient economic performance through a simplistic globalization strategy will be compromised by the need for the MNE to be more responsive to social needs and national interests'.

MNEs, Development and Spillovers

As the previous discussion demonstrates, debate surrounding the developmental impact of MNEs on the host countries in which they do business is extensive and unsettled (see Meyer, 2004 for a review; Wells, 1998). One stream of research that has sought to integrate insights from development with the study of MNEs has focused on spillovers – the residual benefits that MNEs contribute to host country economies (Aitken and Harrison, 1999; Blomstrom and Persson, 1983; Globerman, 1979; Kosova, 2004; Mansfield and Romeo, 1980; Teece, 1977). Researchers advocating the benefits of MNE spillovers to developing host countries suggest that foreign firms bring advanced technologies, knowledge and skills that spill over to local individuals, firms and industries. In turn, these spillovers can be used to enhance productivity and increase the knowledge and skills base in the host country (Caves, 1974; Lowe and Kenney, 1999; Teece, 1977). Indeed, as advocated by bargaining power theorists, MNEs should use the promise of technology spillovers to strengthen their position *vis-à-vis* host country governments (Fagre and Wells, 1982; Kindleberger, 1969). An assumption of the spillover perspective is that if local firms conduct their normal business activities, benefits will naturally spill over and be absorbed by them. The spillover view suggests that economic progress will be a by-product of its operations; therefore there is no need or necessity for the MNE to directly contribute to host country development.

Another assumption of the spillover view is that knowledge and technology will spill over in a similar fashion across countries. More recent work suggests that successful technology transfer cannot occur without certain conditions in place. For instance, the level of institutional development, advanced skills base and absorptive capacity in the industry may be crucial conditions for spillover success (Buckley et al., 2002; Caves, 1996; Rodrik, 1999; Spencer, 2008).

Empirical research on the existence and prevalence of positive spillover effects (e.g. technology transfer, skills transfer, knowledge transfer and backward and forward linkages with local suppliers and distributors between MNEs and the host country) is not encouraging. Reviewing the literature, Görg and Greenaway (2002) find an extensive body of empirical research on intra-industry spillovers, including work in developing, transition and developed economies. Across all three country types, the authors find that evidence of productivity spillovers is weak at best 'with only a small proportion of studies finding supportive evidence' (Görg and Greenaway, 2002, p. 4). The authors explain the lack of empirical support for spillovers by noting that MNEs may actively try to prevent or reduce the possibility of spillovers from occurring in the first place since spillovers indicate that the firm is not capturing the full benefits (or rents) from its investment (Görg and Greenaway, 2002). Other studies have found similar results. In a study of Hungary, researchers found that the presence of MNEs did little to generate technology spillovers (Gunther, 2002). Moreover, while MNEs operating in Hungary cooperated among themselves, they had little interaction with locally owned firms (Gunther, 2002).

In the area of spillover effects, scholarly attention is now focusing on the role of absorptive capacity – that is, the possibility for local firms to absorb and internalize the potential benefits of technology spillovers. However, limits to 'absorptive capacity' are potentially extensive, and could arise from both country- and firm-level conditions. For example, some research (e.g. Kokko, 1994) has found 'demand-side' (i.e. local firm) effects to be significant, while others (e.g. Haskel et al., 2002) have not found them to be as relevant. Another group of researchers has sought to examine variance on the 'supply side', specifically the MNE side of the equation, which may affect technology spillover to local firms. These MNE factors are argued to include characteristics of the industries in which MNEs operate (Narula and Dunning, 2000) and variance in MNE strategy (Wang and Blomström, 1992).

Although empirical studies have shown limited support for positive spillover effects, research has found evidence of negative economic, social and environmental spillovers from MNE activity (Aitken and Harrison, 1999; Görg and Greenaway, 2002; Gunther, 2002; Haddad and Harrison, 1993). Several studies have found that foreign firms tend to crowd out local firms and that, over the long term, knowledge sharing and technology and skills transfers does not tend to occur (Aitken and Harrison, 1999; Chang and Xu, 2006; De Backer and Sleuwaegen, 2003). Particularly troubling is the fact that serious negative social and environmental spillovers – also termed externalities – including human rights violations such as the use of child labor, exploitation of workers, unsafe working conditions, corruption, violent conflict, pollution and environmental degradation, have also been associated with MNEs' activity in developing countries (Clapp and Dauvergne, 2005; Dunning, 2006; Korten, 2001; Porter, 1999).

In summary, the spillover perspective reinforces an assumption that MNEs will capture the bulk of the financial benefits, leaving those in developing host countries only marginal or residual benefits. Furthermore, much of the empirical research suggests that these benefits may not even exist. Additionally, the spillover view does not assume an active role by MNEs in the generation of positive spillover benefits (or the minimization of negative spillovers). Rather, spillovers are considered a by-product of the MNE's operations. Next, we discuss the LOF perspective and how it relates MNEs to developing host countries.

MNEs, Development and Liabilities of Foreignness

The liabilities of foreignness view is another influential perspective in IM that relates the MNE to the host country environment. While the spillover perspective focuses on the residual effects of the MNE on host country development, the LOF view is more concerned with the competitive disadvantages that the MNE may have in foreign markets. The LOF perspective has important implications for business's impact on economic and social development in foreign markets because it determines how the MNE views its relationship with the host country, what its role is in foreign markets, and whether, how and why MNEs should consider host country organizations as partners.

The LOF view grew out of empirical research and practical observations demonstrating that MNEs continued to face challenges in foreign markets. Beginning with Hymer's (1976) seminal work, researchers identified the importance of the social, political and economic costs – termed liabilities of foreignness (LOF) – associated with identification and operation as a foreign firm within a particular host country context (Eden and Miller, 2004; Luo et al., 2002; Zaheer, 1995, 2002; Zaheer and Mosakowski, 1997). A core tenet of the LOF view is that because MNEs face added operating costs abroad – costs not incurred by locals – foreign firms may be less profitable *vis-à-vis* their local counterparts, all else being equal (Hymer, 1976; Zaheer, 1995; Sethi and Guisinger, 2002).

Despite its grounding in economic, normative and cognitive streams of institutional theory, LOF research has generally advocated tactical rather than strategic solutions for MNEs. For instance, foreign firms can work to mitigate liabilities by hiring local staff, putting a local face on the firm, and otherwise seeking to become isomorphic with the local society and culture (Hymer, 1976; Zaheer, 1995, 2002; Zaheer and Mosakowski, 1997). Although this perspective can be useful in some cases, in many developing countries foreign MNEs are rarely viewed as local. More importantly, defining their international character as a 'liability' to be overcome may constitute a misspecification of the relationship between multinational and local organizations. This is especially the case in emerging economies where there is a clear demarcation between indigenous and foreign firms.

For several reasons, the focus on liabilities is an insufficient perspective for understanding the role of MNEs in developing countries. One reason is that the majority of studies on LOF have focused on firms from triad countries entering other triad countries (Zaheer, 1995, Zaheer and Mosakowski, 1997). Another reason is that efforts to 'adapt' to the local environment via human resources, marketing or alliance relationships may be viewed by local institutions and communities as transparent strategies, potentially generating a political backlash. As an alternative, MNEs may be better served by recognizing and emphasizing their uniqueness and identifying how their resources can be used to directly contribute to the host country environment.

Although MNEs may rarely be viewed as local, defining their international character as a 'liability' to be overcome underspecifies the potential of MNEs to leverage their international connections and linkages and make significant contributions to development. For instance, in an external evaluation of the developmental impact of Unilever's operations in Indonesia, it appears that rather than displacing local goods, the company was providing useful products that would not otherwise be available (Clay, 2005). Indeed, Hymer (1976, p. 43) explicitly recognized that domestic firms operating in foreign countries that are not well integrated into the world economy – that lack liquid capital markets and have relatively few skilled workers – would be at a competitive disadvantage relative to foreign firms. He suggested that in such situations MNEs could bring valuable assets related to their foreignness. These assets, we argue, can be combined with those of locally based organizations to intentionally promote development.

MNEs can also serve as conduits to resolve information asymmetries that often plague local businesses as they may possess knowledge of specific trends in global markets. An example is in agricultural commodities. In this sector, large MNEs such as Starbucks and others have much greater insight into commodity pricing trends and projections than local farmers. By sharing this knowledge with local producers, MNEs can help farmers to better plan investments, crop rotation and specific marketing decisions.

Indeed, existing local businesses and organizations may actually be perceived as less legitimate than foreign firms. Under these conditions, foreignness may constitute an asset rather than a liability. Studies on country-of-origin effects support the notion that foreignness can be an advantage. Empirical analyses have shown that a brand's country of origin is an important signal of product quality (Han, 1989). Indeed, brands from highly developed Western nations are often preferred by developing country consumers (Batra et al., 2000; Han, 1989).

Although we have reviewed only two of the theories relating MNEs and developing host countries, they – and related perspectives[2] – are two of the more influential perspectives. Furthermore, they exemplify the wider limitations inherent throughout much of the IB literature. Specifically, these IB theories do not view MNEs as taking an active role in the economic, social and environmental development of the host countries in which they operate. In fact, bargaining power theorists have used the LOF and spillover views to gain an advantage over host country governments when negotiating new investments (Fagre and Wells, 1982; Kindleberger, 1969; Vernon, 1971). In addition, by leveraging firm- and investment-specific capabilities and assets, and the competitive advantages associated with being foreign (e.g. firm size, economies of scale, resource advantages etc.), MNEs can also gain an advantage over host country firms (Porter, 1990). Conceptualizing the MNE–host country relationship in this way encourages MNEs to view their relationship with developing host countries in a win–lose dynamic. Moreover, both perspectives have largely ignored the role of NGOs. To the extent that it has considered them, the LOF perspective would probably view them as mechanisms to assist the MNE in overcoming its disadvantages and not as partners for development.

Research on the base of the pyramid (BOP), it is argued, goes beyond these limitations by redirecting attention from an almost exclusive focus on market opportunities in the triad and wealthy consumers in developing country markets to the poorest people in the world as potential consumers (Prahalad, 2004; Prahalad and Hammond, 2002; Prahalad and Hart, 2002; Prahalad and Lieberthal, 1999). However, like the majority of research in IB, it emphasizes the financial benefits and incentives for the MNE (Prahalad, 2004; Prahalad and Hart, 2002). Indeed, the primary criticism of the BOP framework is that it is not appropriate for addressing development since development depends more on developing the poor as producers rather than as consumers (Karnani, 2006). By engaging with NGOs and other locally based actors, we argue that MNEs may be able to promote sustainable economic and social development, not just short-term economic growth, in the developing host countries where they operate.

In the next section, we discuss the role of civil society and how MNEs can begin to work with locally based organizations to promote development. More specifically, we argue that the limitations associated with the spillover, LOF and other mainstream IB perspectives suggest a reframing of the role of MNEs in developing countries that acknowledges the foreign character of the MNE and the need for more direct contributions to local economic development. The perspective we propose argues for a productive exchange of the respective resources and advantages of both the MNE and local institutions that can be leveraged through a collaborative relationship. These collaborations, which take advantage of the MNE's foreign character, can help embed the MNE in the social fabric of the developing country (but without replicating local contributions). At the same time, these collaborations can create a powerful long-term competitive advantage that will be difficult for competitors to imitate.

RECONCEPTUALIZING THE ROLE OF MNES IN DEVELOPMENT: A RESOURCE COMPLEMENTARITY PERSPECTIVE

In this section, we introduce our reconceptualization of the role of MNEs in development, a perspective we term resource complementarity. We begin with a discussion of the emerging role of NGOs in business and in society, and link that discussion to the potential for MNE–NGO engagement to generate positive contributions to development.

The Role of Non-Governmental Organizations (NGOs)

Echoing Shenkar's (2004) argument that contemporary interpretations of IB have overemphasized the strategic and financial benefits of internationalization for the MNE, neglecting broader and potentially much more important questions related to the very nature of IB and its utility in serving broader societal needs, we propose that scholars consider the role of NGOs in IB and development. Indeed the study of NGOs is a promising area of emerging research that is consistently identified as requiring further exploration for scholars of the MNE and IB (Buckley and Ghauri, 2004; Doh, 2005; Peng, 2004). Buckley and Ghauri (2004, p. 95) note that

> The external effects of MNEs (linkages, spillovers) need to be more closely related to the analysis of strategy so that IB researchers can contribute more to the literature on development and underdevelopment. Theoretical avenues include the full incorporation of spatial issues in

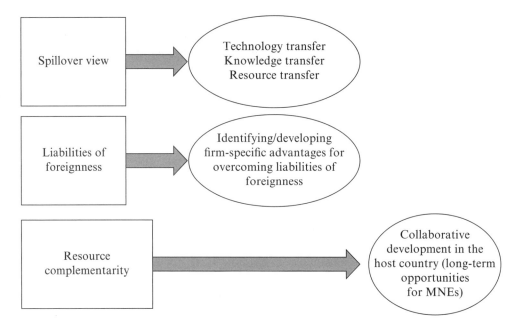

Figure 23.1   Dependent variables associated with spillover, liabilities of foreignness and resource complementarity perspectives

the strategy of MNEs, the integration of the role of new institutions such as NGOs and fuller attention to the political implications of the activities and changing organization of MNEs.

Given this confluence of developments, there is now an opportunity to move beyond the view that developing countries are either an easy source for cheap raw materials or a dumping ground for outmoded products and technologies and that MNEs' and NGOs' values are inherently incompatible.

While there are many definitions of NGOs (UNDP, 2002; Vakil, 1997), we follow a simple definition offered by Teegen et al. (2004, p. 466), who refer to social purpose NGOs as 'private, not-for-profit organizations that aim to serve societal interests by focusing on social, political, and economic goals, including, *inter alia*, equity, education, health, environmental protection, and human rights'. According to a 1995 World Bank report, 'since the mid-1970s, the NGO sector in both developed and developing countries has experienced exponential growth . . . It is now estimated that over 15 percent of total overseas development aid is channeled through NGOs' (World Bank, 1995, p. 16). Indeed, a report published by the United Nations and the NGO SustainAbility notes that the global non-profit sector, with its more than $1 trillion turnover, could rank as the world's eighth-largest economy (Hooper, 2003). Teegen et al. (2004) propose that the emergence of civil society in general, and the activism of civic NGOs in particular, have broad implications for the role, scope and definition of corporations in the global economy, and therefore for international management as a research field. They suggest that traditional research paradigms, such as the historically conceived MNE–host country government dyadic, must be relaxed to account for these new actors. In addition, the alliance literature, with its emphasis on resource exchange between private firms, must also be respecified when non-profit NGOs occupy one side of the equation. Next, we discuss how MNEs and NGOs can work together to further economic development along with the challenges these partnerships may face.

Leveraging MNE and NGO Capabilities for Development

In considering emerging relationships between MNEs and locally based stakeholders such as NGOs, we see a range of potentially complementary benefits. The MNE brings size, scale, experience and resources to the table and the NGO enables the MNE to access stakeholders that would be difficult to reach without the partnership. Together, these two organizational forms may be in a position to fill institutional voids (Khanna and Palepu, 1997) in a way that preserves the separation between local and foreign status. For the resource complementarity perspective to truly contribute to development, the MNE cannot simply bring new or advanced resources to the host country in hopes that the NGO or other actors will absorb the knowledge and that it will 'trickle down' to others in the economy. Instead, this model requires that MNEs actively work to build local capacity through partnerships with NGOs that generate more sustainable capabilities and skills. In this section, we elaborate on how this may be achieved.

NGOs may seek opportunities to bypass existing institutions and organizations in the host country (because of corruption, inefficiency, lack of competence in an area etc.) and may therefore prefer the MNE as a partner rather than working with a local private firm or going it alone. In many cases, governments in developing countries may simply lack the capacity and resources to assist NGOs in their efforts and to create the type of institutions that are able to promote development. In others, host country elites may consider the presence of NGOs, and perhaps even MNEs, as a threat to their political and business interests. In such situations, NGOs may prefer to work outside the local political and economic system in the host country and obtain the influence and support of powerful MNEs. For these reasons, MNEs may find that local organizations – such as churches, community groups and other stakeholders – are willing partners that not only provide access to valuable markets and resources, but may also confer legitimacy on firms. Through such collaborations, NGOs that are respected in the community can share and transfer some of their reputation advantages to partnering firms.

Firms may cooperate with locally based NGOs and other stakeholder organizations to learn more about the genuine needs of the host country, to contribute to social development efforts, and to gain legitimacy in the host country market. The firm-specific advantages of MNEs may in turn help NGOs and other stakeholder organizations to provide improved products and services to their constituent groups and to provide access to international markets.

Research on alliances and networks among firms in competitive commercial environments suggests that each partner benefits when the other brings resources, capabilities or other assets that it cannot easily attain on its own. These 'combinative capabilities' allow the firm to acquire and synthesize resources and build new applications from those resources, generating innovative responses to rapidly evolving environments (Kogut and Zander, 1992). We extend this notion to collaborative relationships among MNEs and NGOs in developing country environments, a conceptualization that challenges some of the established orthodoxies of both IB and development theory. Next, we elaborate on the proposed resource complementarity perspective by addressing the potential gains and challenges of MNE–NGO collaboration.

Potential Mutual Gains from MNE–NGO Collaboration

Although they may be inherently unstable, MNE–NGO collaborations benefit from the tensions and frictions that are intrinsic to the nature of these relationships. One fundamental element of these collaborations is the different organizational characteristics of MNEs and NGOs that include disparate organizational types, mandates, missions, goals, incentive structures and sponsors. As such, collaborative relationships among NGOs and MNEs are qualitatively different than those with private firms, yet these differences may be the source of mutual gains. For example, network relationships with NGOs may provide MNEs with access to different skills, competencies and capabilities than those that are otherwise available within their organization or that might result from alliances with for-profit organizations.

According to Rondinelli and London (2003), cross-sector alliances – collaborative relationships among non-profit organizations and private corporations – may provide opportunities for MNEs to achieve the legitimacy and develop the capabilities needed to respond to increasing pressure from stakeholders to address environmental and other social issues (Waddock, 1998; Westley and Vredenbrug, 1991), an increasingly important prerequisite for successful operation in developing countries. They note that firms seek to learn new skills or acquire tacit knowledge through alliances: 'Alliance, in fact, may be the only option for companies interested in accessing the knowledge held by [NGOs] since internal development of such expertise may be too costly, inefficient, and time-consuming for most companies, and merger with or acquisition of an [NGO] is highly unlikely' (Rondinelli and London, 2003, p. 62). Doh and Ramamurti (2003) report that in infrastructure sectors, legal guarantees and commitments by host governments are often illusory, and only through effective relationships with all stakeholders – including NGOs – are MNEs' investments likely to be sustainable over the longer term.

Host country populations and firms benefit from the international capabilities of MNEs when MNEs partner with local NGOs and other organizations to facilitate direct access to consumers in developed country markets. MNE–NGO collaborations provide producers with opportunities to compress the supply chain and circumvent price mark-ups by intermediaries. They can also facilitate establishment of premium brand recognition for products produced or harvested and otherwise promote greater awareness and support for developing country working conditions and income needs. Collaboration among MNEs and NGOs can also create emergent institutions at the micro-level to the benefit of both the MNE and the local system. For example, in developing countries, capital markets imperfections, lack of knowledge of credit assessment and risk, macro-economic risk and bureaucratic inefficiencies severely constrain access to credit in poor and rural areas. MNE experience and establishment of parallel – but highly functional – financial infrastructure can improve provision of these services.

Table 23.1 summarizes the spillovers, liabilities and resource complementarity perspectives on the role of MNEs in host country development.

Table 23.1   The resource complementarity perspective

	Resource complementarity
Principal perspective on role of MNEs in host country development	MNEs serve dual purposes: generate income for owners/investors and contribute to development process. These purposes are complementary. MNEs bring specific benefits to development process, including: • providing local firms access to global markets • providing greater access to capital at more competitive rates • transferring knowledge, managerial skill and financial leverage unavailable in the local context Attempts to mask foreign character not productive for long-term MNE interests or development In order to activate the above benefits, MNEs must: • Identify needs of local communities • Work with local NGOs in order to activate above benefits
Role of MNE	In addition to the role of MNEs in coordinating and arbitraging knowledge, capabilities and expertise, MNEs: • serve as vehicles to integrate foreign and local capabilities • help fill institutional voids • provide long-term economic, technological and managerial contributions
Role of civil society/ NGOs	NGOs: • provide knowledge and information on local social and economic context • confer legitimacy and credibility to the MNE • contribute expertise and services not available to the MNE
Assumptions about power relations, MNE strategy and the basis for MNE legitimacy	Although MNE economic power is strong, this power is subject to influence by other social actors such as NGOs. For this reason, MNEs do not maintain exclusive control over their perceived legitimacy and social license to operate in developing countries MNEs may therefore seek long-term sustainable positions in developing countries and are willing to sacrifice some short-term gain in order to attain those positions; long-term survival is facilitated by contributing to development through their foreign character and access and collaboration with local civil society organizations

Challenges to MNE–NGO Collaboration and Potential Mechanisms for Success

We do not mean to suggest here that MNE–NGO collaborations are a cure-all for the complex and deeply embedded challenges on how best to leverage MNE investment for development goals. For NGOs, participation in a cross-sector alliance, especially with foreign MNEs, is not without risk. Relations between large corporations and NGOs, especially in the emerging markets context, have often been characterized by hostility and mistrust. Cross-sector alliances face an additional challenge because organizational learning among alliance partners requires some level of common experience, a condition that is often weak or missing in alliances between profit-making and non-profit organizations (Rondinelli and London, 2003). This lack of common experience, trust and communication can sometimes result in conflict, even when partnerships have been established that appear to signal shared values and commitments. For MNEs, partnerships with NGOs may sometimes open a path to escalating (and unrealistic) demands for firms to upgrade their commitments to social development (Yaziji, 2004).

Although NGOs often have distinct advantages in reaching local stakeholders, they may lack assets or capabilities that MNEs bring to collaborative relationships. NGOs' altruistic motives and social consciousness, arguably two of their strengths, may result in less organizational focus on organizational performance or on acquiring financial expertise. To the extent that they are small and dispersed, NGOs may be more agile; however, they may also have a higher cost structure because they are not able to capitalize on economies of scale and scope. The NGO culture of social mission translates to operational practices that may not reflect the financial discipline of either the institution or the program recipient. NGOs also operate under different organizational models than for-profit entities and are often not prepared to manage the organization's financial accounting needs, maintain sufficient cash flow, engender client confidence, design and maintain information systems or address important human resource issues necessary to implement savings and credit programs.

Researchers have also raised concerns about the ultimate effect that some NGO networks may have on development. They argue that the conceptualization of social networks and social capital, defined by Woolcock and Narayan (2000) as the norms and networks that enable people to act collectively, is overly optimistic and neglects the possibility that some networks and social ties may actually perpetuate dysfunctional and exclusive network relationships (Dolfsma and Dannreuther, 2003; Dalgic, 2005). Research has shown, for instance, that organizations may inadvertently perpetuate discrimination and perhaps even fuel violent conflicts through their hiring and other management practices (Banfield et al., 2003). Thus, under these conditions, simply bringing market-based approaches to the developing world may exacerbate rather than alleviate sources of inequality in these societies. For this reason, NGOs should evaluate the wider networks in which they are involved to determine whether there is a systematic bias in membership.

Other challenges related to the idiosyncratic features of MNE–NGO collaboration include the ability of each partner to credibly commit to the other (Williamson, 1983) and the likelihood that the absence of credible commitment will breed distrust. Given that MNEs may possess greater economic power and influence in the relationship, NGOs must use their power to ensure that the MNE's objectives and interests will not dominate the relationship. Although the firm may have greater financial resources, the NGO may hold greater social power and influence because of its reputation and high perceived social legitimacy. As such, NGOs may effectively hold the MNE's reputation hostage as a means of ensuring commitment to the alliance. Further, since network ties and organizational legitimacy are often the valuable resources NGOs bring to a partnership, the NGO must be assured that the MNE will not devalue these assets by using contacts and networks for profit-seeking purposes and renege on their commitment to fulfill the social mission of the relationship.

MNEs also have legitimate concerns when selecting an appropriate NGO partner. Additional obstacles may be created by the structure of the partnership itself. Should the NGO and MNE develop a contractual relationship with shared resources? How will decisions be made within the alliance? As researchers have noted, when boundaries change between organizations, in this case between MNEs and NGOs joining an alliance, communication and other costs can also change significantly (Casson and Wadeson, 1998; Dolfsma and Dannreuther, 2003). Changing organizational boundaries and the roles of organizational members can also lead to changes in the power structures and systems of meaning within the partnering organizations (Llewellyn, 1994). Even in alliances between for-profit firms, where each firm seeks to maximize profits, meshing different organizational cultures and deciding how disagreements will be resolved can be extremely challenging (Gulati, 1995). In collaborations between MNEs and NGOs, resolving differences can be even more challenging. Generally, MNEs and NGOs face different types of costs and cost structures and the managers of these organizations frequently do not share the same educational backgrounds, mindsets or organizational mandates (Doh, 2006). For MNE–NGO collaboration to be successful, each organization must identify strategies for minimizing the costs of partnering and credibly committing to one another. For example, Pearce and Doh (2005) argue that collaborative social initiatives among corporations and non-profit NGOs is most effective when each draws on its core capabilities, thus lowering the adjustment and adaptation costs of partnering.

Organizational intent in entering an alliance is also important to the ultimate success of the relationship. The past policies, practices and beliefs of an organization can provide valuable information about the organization's possible intent in forming the alliance. Does the MNE have a history of attempting to hide inappropriate or unethical practices? Alternatively, does the NGO have a history of constructive relationships with partner organizations? How does each organization handle interactions with the media? Such issues should be thoroughly considered before entering into an alliance.

Vachani (2006) and Vachani and Smith (2004) detail some of the inherent challenges and difficulties associated with MNE–NGO interactions in the context of pressure by NGOs on governments and pharmaceutical companies to liberalize trade rules in order to permit the compulsory licensing and/or price reduction of AIDS drugs. They report that MNEs initially pushed back when NGOs urged them to respond to this health crisis, but that ultimately some collaborative relationships were developed among the pharmaceutical companies, generic producers from developing countries, foundations and NGOs.

In reviewing the theoretical framework and illustrations above, it is clear that interorganizational collaborations will have mixed success, depending on a range of environmental, institutional, organizational and individual variables. Specifically, country-, industry-, company-, NGO- and managerial-level factors will all influence the potential success of these collaborations. For example, the sector and orientation of NGOs will affect the potential compatibility of a given NGO with a given company, and this strategic fit will influence the likelihood, form and satisfaction of the collaboration. We also would highlight that prior experience with 'the other' sector will influence affective perceptions of managers from that sector and that these perceptions will shape managerial inclination to collaborate. Overall, we believe the degree of complementarity among the resources and capabilities of the MNE and NGO will be a principal variable affecting success. Table 23.2 compares MNE alliances with for-profit corporations and collaboration with NGOs.

CONCLUSIONS, LIMITATIONS AND IMPLICATIONS

The purpose of this chapter was to argue that two strands of IB theory have systematically compromised the ability of IB research to value the potential for MNEs to contribute to host country development while also fulfilling their strategic objectives. Our aim was to offer an alternate view that seeks to more fully capture the role and character of MNEs and locally based NGOs and stakeholder organizations. We do so by focusing on the distinctive competencies of both MNEs and NGOs to advance social and economic objectives in developing countries. We conclude with a summary of our key contributions, discuss the implications for managers and offer suggestions for future research.

MNEs, Economic and Social Development and the Rationale for Engagement

While the impact of MNEs is of obvious interest to policy-makers in developing countries and to development studies scholars in general, managers and some IM scholars may question why this impact should be of concern to MNEs. We suggest that the main reason MNE managers should pay increasing attention to host country development is that foreign firms operate at the will of the local communities. To be accepted and operate effectively, MNEs need to be more aware of the economic, social and environmental needs of the countries in which they locate (Jain and Vachani, 2006). Without a social license to operate and the legitimacy it confers, MNEs should prepare for greater operational risk and potential host government policy shifts towards MNEs (Doh and Ramamurti, 2003). Over the last two decades many developing countries have undertaken a dramatic shift by moving from isolationist, import substitution policies to open market policies aimed at increasing FDI. Nevertheless, these policies are not irreversible (Wells, 1998). Host country governments have opened their markets to generate greater domestic economic growth, not for the sole benefit of MNEs. If government officials and policy-makers believe that MNEs are not generating benefits, then their attitudes toward FDI could (and many already have) become decidedly pessimistic, leading to increased barriers to entry and greater host country regulation on FDI.

Table 23.2 Comparing MNE alliances with private corporations vs collaboration with NGOs

	Alliances with for-profit organizations	Collaboration with NGOs
Purposes of relationship from MNE perspective	Local knowledge of markets Local connections with government Market presence and penetration Legitimacy with customers	Expression of corporate social responsibility Legitimacy with civil society
Purposes of relationship from local partner perspective	Access to technology Access to managerial expertise Access to global markets	Access to technology Access to managerial expertise Access to MNE financial resources Access to global markets
Strategic mandate of local partner	Seek to maximize profits and shareholder returns and rely primarily on economic measures of performance	Seek to maximize operational reach and scope, providing services to as many clients as possible, particularly those most in need who also may be the least able to pay
Results measurement	Return on investment/sales/profits Market entry Market growth Greater market penetration Higher legitimacy	Social, environmental and economic impact
Key stakeholders	Shareholders	Clients/customers of the collaboration Donor/grant-making organizations
Governance and potential sustainability of the relationship	Generally have a shared understanding of financial, managerial, marketing and other professional business skills Must agree on decision-making and organizational control issues in alliance Potentially unstable due to differences in size, scale and objectives; if dissolved or restructured, may result in power shift in which one party acquires the assets of the other	MNEs and NGOs must agree on financial and managerial practices since these are likely to differ between organizations Potentially greater communication costs because of differences in backgrounds of personnel and organizational objectives and the *a priori* mistrust that each organization may have of the other Potentially unstable due to differences in culture, motivations and historic power relationships; if restructured, higher likelihood of dissolution as merger or acquisition is not possible due to different organizational forms described above

There is no doubt that MNEs from the triad have had an important historical geopolitical advantage over developing countries. Governments from the triad countries have largely controlled the WTO, global trade policies, the International Monetary Fund (IMF) and the World Bank (WB). As the economic and political power of Brazil, Russia, India and China (the BRICs) increases over the coming years, certain countries in the developing world have increasing influence over the terms of trade and demand a greater role in multinational organizations (e.g. WTO, IMF, WB etc.). At various times the Indian and Brazilian governments have chosen not to enforce multinational pharmaceutical firms' intellectual property rights over patented medicines. They have done so to meet the medical needs of their citizens and foster domestic development in the industry, among other reasons. These policies have led pharmaceutical firms from the USA and Western Europe to reconsider their strategies and plan for a new competitive environment characterized by downward pressure on prices.

A second reason MNEs should be concerned about economic development abroad is that they have a direct interest in the long-term growth and prosperity of developing countries. Publicly held MNEs are under pressure to continuously increase shareholder returns. To do this, they must not only identify new market opportunities, but also continually generate valuable firm-specific capabilities that are difficult for competitors to imitate. As large MNEs saturate their home markets and those of the triad countries, firms need access to developing countries in order to continue to grow. To succeed in these markets, MNEs cannot simply replicate their home country strategies. Firms must learn to compete in new ways in developing countries, particularly in the face of institutional and economic underdevelopment. By collaborating with NGOs, MNEs may gain access to geographic and demographic groups that would otherwise be out of their reach. In addition, they may be able to gain access to resources and products that would otherwise be reserved for locally based organizations. Firms involved in MNE–NGO collaborations may also gain intangible benefits such as the legitimacy that arises from the firm's status as a contributor to local development.

Limitations and Implications for Research and Practice

Our objective was to critique the LOF and spillover perspectives and propose an alternative framework in which to consider the relationship of MNEs to the developing countries in which they operate. In this chapter, we argued that MNEs are inextricably intertwined with local communities and have a positive stake in the development process. More importantly, MNEs are in a position to make a much greater impact on society than is generally recognized in the literature or in practice (Westney, 1993). Reasons that they have not done so or tried to do so may be that they have simply overlooked the opportunities for engaging in host country development and the possibilities of mutual benefit. In other cases, MNEs have disregarded or minimized their ethical or social obligations when operating abroad. Yet another reason may be that some MNEs have even intentionally taken advantage of the social and economic conditions in developing host countries to further their short-term financial interests.

Although others have also argued for new thinking regarding the role of MNEs in development (see Wells, 1998; Ramamurti, 2004), we have offered a specific critique of current theories – a critique that questions basic assumptions of the key literatures relating to MNEs and development. We argue that the ability of MNEs to contribute to development is inhibited by the dominant paradigms that constrain the role of MNEs in economic development. We also offer an alternative perspective for considering MNEs' involvement in host developing countries. This perspective emphasizes the fact that MNEs and NGOs may have overlapping interests and complementary resources and capabilities that make joint collaboration highly beneficial for both parties. We see this as a valuable contribution since existing theories have overlooked these opportunities for collaboration.

We do not intend to suggest that MNE–NGO collaborations are a panacea for development; nor is such collaboration right for every firm or NGO. There is no doubt that corporations and NGOs have fundamentally different structures and values (Rondinelli and London, 2003), and relations between corporations and NGOs, especially in emerging markets, have often been characterized by hostility and mistrust. Organizational learning generally requires some level of common experience, a factor that can make cross-sector alliances particularly challenging. Common experiences are often weak or missing in alliances between profit-making and non-profit organizations (Rondinelli and London, 2003). This can sometimes result in conflict, even when partnerships have been established that appear to signal shared values and commitments. Even more challenging than forming traditional alliances between foreign and local firms may be identifying appropriate partners with whom to collaborate (Hitt et al., 2000). For a variety of reasons, NGOs may prefer to work with local firms rather than MNEs. NGOs or other host country actors may be concerned that MNEs may crowd out local enterprises or lack a long-term commitment to the host country. Alliances with local organizations may also better fit the NGO's social mission. While recognizing the challenges associated with MNE–NGO collaborations, we argue that this alternative perspective for conceptualizing MNE involvement in developing countries offers new approaches for enhancing the performance of MNEs and furthering wider development objectives of their host developing countries.

The perspective we propose here has clear managerial implications. For one, MNE managers might invest less time and attention in masking the international character of the companies they represent and devote more to identifying and collaborating with local organizations and actors that can facilitate more direct contributions to local economic and social development. Successful and stable MNE–NGO collaborations may also enable foreign firms to consider long-term commitments to developing countries rather than short-term investments.

For policy-makers, MNE–NGO collaborations and the 'combinative capabilities' that they can generate may constitute innovative and alternative approaches to the development challenge in emerging markets. There is some evidence that donor agencies and other development policy-makers are beginning to embrace the joint role of private corporations and NGOs in supporting development. One indicator of this shift is the growing reliance on private capital and NGO initiatives in developing countries. In the 1970s, approximately 70 percent of resource flows from the USA to the developing world were from official development assistance. Only 30 percent of the resources were from private sources. By 2003 only 15 percent of the $102.5 billion in resource flows comprised direct government assistance. The remaining 85 percent of resources came from non-governmental sources.

CONCLUSION

As scholars are questioning the relevance of international management to contemporary global challenges, a redirection of the IB literature towards the issue of MNE impact on host country development is vital. To maintain its relevance, IB must address broader issues beyond the narrow questions of MNE performance (Buckley, 2002; Buckley and Ghauri, 2004; Shenkar, 2004). The IB field has arguably lagged other disciplines (e.g. economics and international relations) in its relatively limited attention to the relationship between MNE activities and social and economic development. In addition, it has omitted the important emerging role of NGOs in global economics and management. To fully capture the dynamics between MNEs and developing host countries, new actors such as non-governmental organizations (NGOs) must be incorporated into the study and practice of international management (Teegen et al., 2004).

Understanding how to promote development in underdeveloped countries, what the role of various actors should be, and how MNEs can facilitate the development process has posed major challenges for researchers, government officials, international development institutions, managers and societies. Given these challenges and their importance, our aim in this chapter was to redirect the discussion away from traditional perspectives (as they relate to MNEs), and offer a new conceptualization that we believe is more appropriate for current circumstances. Our intention is to stimulate future research regarding the potential contribution of MNEs to the social and economic progress of developing host countries. We also hope to heighten interest in the opportunities presented by MNE–NGO collaborations. We argue that this proposed research perspective is as important to MNEs as it is to developing countries. For MNEs seeking to manage investment risk and to understand how different institutional and political environments in developing countries affect firm strategy and performance, a large number of unanswered questions still remain. Nevertheless, we believe that MNE and host country objectives can be better reconciled. Indeed, there is great potential for mutual gain, generating the possibility for more sustainable development paths that have more lasting impact.

NOTES

1. This chapter is adapted from J. Oetzel and J.P. Doh (2009), 'Multinational enterprise and development: a review and reconceptualization', *Journal of World Business*, **44**(2), 108–20.
2. For example, the LOF view is an extension of Hymer's original views on the cost of doing business abroad, and the spillover perspective extends to other contemporary research on the global distribution of work, the location of economic activity etc.

REFERENCES

Aitken, B.J. and A.E. Harrison (1999), 'Do domestic firms benefit from direct foreign investment? Evidence from Venezuela', *The American Economic Review*, 605–18.
Banfield, J., V. Haufler and D. Lilly (2003), *The Political Economy of Armed Conflict: Beyond Greed and Grievance*, Boulder, CO and London: Lynne Rienner.
Baran, P.A. (1957), *The political Economy of Growth*, New York: Monthly Review Press.
Batra, R., V. Ramaswany, D. Alden, J.E.M. Steenkamp and S. Ramachander (2000), 'Effects of brand local

and nonlocal origin on consumer attitudes in developing countries', *Journal of Consumer Psychology*, **9**(2), 83–95.

Blomström, M. and H. Persson (1983), 'Foreign investment and spillover efficiency in an underdeveloped economy: evidence from the Mexican manufacturing industry', *World Development*, **11**(6), 493–501.

Buckley, P. (2002), 'Is the international business research agenda running out of steam?', *Journal of International Business Studies*, **33**(2), 365–73.

Buckley, P.J. and P.N. Ghauri (2004), 'Globalization, economic geography and the strategy of multinational enterprises', *Journal of International Business Studies*, **35**(2), 81–98.

Buckley, P., J. Clegg and C. Wang (2002), 'The impact of inward FDI on performance of Chinese manufacturing firms', *Journal of International Business Studies*, **33**(4), 637–55.

Casson, M. and N. Wadeson (1998), 'Communication costs and the boundaries of the firm', *International Journal of the Economics of Business*, **5**: 5–27.

Caves, R. (1974), 'Multinational firms, competition, and productivity in host countries', *Economica*, **38**, 176–93.

Caves, R. (1996), *Multinational Enterprise and Economic Analysis*, Cambridge: Cambridge University Press.

Chang, S.J. and D. Xu (2006), 'Competitive dynamics among foreign entrants and local firms in an emerging market', paper presented at the Academy of International Business Conference, Beijing, China.

Christmann, P. and G. Taylor (2001), 'Globalization and the environment: determinants of firm self-regulation in China', *Journal of International Business Studies*, **32**: 439–58.

Clapp, J. and P. Dauvergne (2005), *Paths to a Green World: The Political Economy of the Global Environment*, Cambridge, MA: MIT Press.

Clay, J. (2005), 'Exploring the links between international business and poverty reduction: a case study of Unilever in Indonesia', http://oxfam.intelli-direct.com/e/d.dll?m=234&url= http://www.oxfam.org.uk/what_ we_do/issues/livelihoods/downloads/unilever.pdf, accessed 24 February 2011.

Cooke, B. (2004), 'The managing of the (third) world', *Organization*, **11**(5), 603–29.

Dalgic, U. (2005), 'Social capital, gender, and microfinance: the World Bank in the 1990s', www.northwestern. edu/rc19/Dalgic.pdf, accessed 30 January 2006.

Daly, H.E. (1993), 'The perils of free trade', *Scientific American*, November, 51–5.

De Backer, K. and L. Sleuwaegen (2003), 'Does foreign direct investment crowd out domestic entrepreneurship?', *Review of Industrial Organization*, **22**(1), 67–102.

Doh, J.P. (2005), 'Review of Dunning, J. (Ed.) Making globalization good: The moral challenge of global capitalism', *Journal of International Business Studies*, **36**(1), 119–21.

Doh, J.P. (2006), 'Global governance, social responsibility, and corporate–NGO collaboration', in S. Vachani (ed.), *Transformations in Global Governance: Implications for Multinationals and Other Stakeholders*, Cheltenham, UK and Northampton, MA, USA: Edward Elgar, pp. 209–24.

Doh, J.P. and R. Ramamurti (2003), 'Reassessing risk in developing country infrastructure', *Long Range Planning*, **36**(4), 337–53.

Dolfsma, W. and C. Dannreuther (2003), 'Subjects and boundaries: contesting social capital-based policies', *Journal of Economic Issues*, **37**(2), 405–13.

Dowell, G., S. Hart and B. Yeung (2000), 'Do corporate global environmental standards create or destroy market value?', *Management Science*, **46**(8), 1059–74.

Dunning, J.H. (2003), *Making Globalization Good: The Moral Challenges of Global Capitalism*, Oxford: Oxford University Press.

Dunning, J.H. (2006), 'Upgrading the quality of global capitalism: the moral dimension', in S.C. Jain and S. Vachani (eds), *Multinational Corporations and Global Poverty Reduction*, Cheltenham, UK and Northampton, MA, USA: Edward Elgar, pp. 346–79.

Eden, L. and S. Lenway (2001), 'Introduction to the symposium multinationals: the Janus face of globalization', *Journal of International Business Studies*, **32**(3), 383–400.

Eden, L. and S.R. Miller (2004), 'Distance matters: liability of foreignness, institutional distance and ownership', *Advances in International Management*, **16**, 187–221.

Fagre, N. and L.T. Wells (1982), 'Bargaining power of multinationals and host governments', *Journal of International Business Studies*, **13**(2), 19–24.

Ghauri, P.N. and X. Cao (2006), 'Managing the interdependence between multinationals and developing countries', in S. Vachani (ed.), *Transformations in Global Governance: Implications for Multinationals and Other Stakeholders*, Cheltenham, UK and Northampton, MA, USA: Edward Elgar, pp. 168–88.

Globerman, S. (1979), 'Foreign direct investment and "spillover" efficiency benefits in Canadian manufacturing industries', *Canadian Journal of Economics*, **12**(1), 42–56.

Görg, H. and D. Greenaway (2002), 'Much ado about nothing? Do domestic firms really benefit from foreign investment?', CEPR Discussion Paper 3485.

Gulati, R. (1995), 'Does familiarity breed trust? The implications of repeated ties for contractual choice in alliances', *Academy of Management Journal*, **38**(1), 85–112.

Gunther, J. (2002), 'FDI as a multiplier of modern technology in Hungarian industry', *Intereconomics*, **37**(5), 263–9.

Haddad, M. and A. Harrison (1993), 'Are there positive spillovers from direct foreign investment? Evidence from panel data for Morocco', *Journal of Economic Development*, **42**, 51–74.

Han, C.M. (1989) 'Country image: halo or summary construct?', *Journal of Marketing Research*, **29**, 222–9.

Haskel, J., Pereira, S. and M. Slaughter (2002), 'Does inward foreign direct investment boost the productivity of domestic firms?', NBER Working Paper series, No. 8724.

Hitt, M.A., T. Dacin, E. Levitas, J.-L. Arregle Edhec and A. Borza (2000), 'Partner selection in emerging and developed market contexts: resource-based and organizational learning perspectives', *Academy of Management Journal*, **43**(3), 449–67.

Hooper, S. (2003), 'NGOs reach out to business, government', *Ethical Corporation*, 30 June.

Hymer, S.H. (1976), *The International Operations of National Firms: A Study of Direct Investment*, Cambridge, MA: MIT Press.

Jain, S.C. and S. Vachani (2006), *Multinational Corporations and Global Poverty Reduction*, Cheltenham, UK and Northampton, MA, USA: Edward Elgar.

Karnani, A. (2006), 'Fortune at the bottom of the pyramid: a mirage', Working Paper No. 1035, Ross School of Business Working Paper Series at the University of Michigan.

Khanna, T. and K. Palepu (1997), 'Why focused strategies may be wrong for emerging markets', *Harvard Business Review*, **75**(4), 41–9.

Khanna, T. and K. Palepu (2000a), 'Is group affiliation profitable in emerging markets? An analysis of diversified Indian business groups', *Journal of Finance*, **55**(2), 867–91.

Khanna, T. and K. Palepu (2000b), 'The future of business groups in emerging markets: long-run evidence from Chile', *Academy of Management Journal*, **43**(3), 268–85.

Kindleberger, C.P. (1969), *American Business Abroad: Six Lectures on Direct Investment*, New Haven, CT: Yale University Press.

Kogut, B. and U. Zander (1992), 'Knowledge of the firm, combinative capabilities, and the replication of technology', *Organization Science*, **3**(3), 383–97.

Kokko, A. (1994), 'Technology, markets characteristics, and spillovers', *Journal of Development Economics*, **43**, 279–93.

Korten, D.C. (2001), *When Corporations Rule the World*, San Francisco, CA: Berrett-Koehler.

Kosova, R. (2004), 'Do foreign firms crowd out domestic firms? Evidence from the Czech Republic', University of Michigan, unpublished dissertation.

Llewellyn, S. (1994), 'Managing the boundary. How accounting is implicated in maintaining the organization', *Accounting, Auditing and Accountability Journal*, **7**(4), 4–23.

Lowe, N. and M. Kenney (1999), 'Foreign investment and the global geography of production: why the Mexican consumer electronics industry failed', *World Development*, **27**(8), 1427–43.

Luo, Y., O. Shenkar and M. Nyaw (2002), 'Mitigating liabilities of foreignness: defensive versus offensive approaches', *Journal of International Management*, **8**(3), 283–300.

Mansfield, E. and A. Romeo (1980), 'Technology transfer to overseas subsidiaries by U.S.-based firms', *Quarterly Journal of Economics*, **95**(4), 737–50.

Meyer, K. (2004), 'Perspectives on multinational enterprises in emerging economies', *Journal of International Business Studies*, **35**(4), 259–76.

Narula, R. and J.H. Dunning (2000), 'Industrial development, globalisation and multinational enterprises: new realities for developing countries', *Oxford Development Studies*, **28**, 141–67.

Palma, G. (1978), 'Dependency: a formal theory of underdevelopment or a methodology for the analysis of concrete situations of underdevelopment?', *World Development*, **6**, 899–902.

Peng, M. (2004), 'Identifying the big question in international business research', *Journal of International Business Studies*, **35**, 99–108.

Pearce, J.A. II and J.P. Doh (2005), 'The high impact of collaborative social initiatives', *Sloan Management Review*, **46**(2), 30–39.

Porter, M.E. (1990), *The Competitive Advantage of Nations*, New York: Free Press.

Porter, G. (1999), 'Trade competition and pollution standards: "Race to the bottom" or "stuck at the bottom"?', *The Journal of Environment & Development*, **8**(2), 133–51.

Prahalad, C.K. (2004), *The Fortune at the Bottom of the Pyramid: Eradicating Poverty through Profits*, Philadelphia, PA: Wharton School Publishing.

Prahalad, C.K. and H. Hammond (2002), 'Serving the world's poor, profitably', *Harvard Business Review*, **80**(9), 48–57.

Prahalad, C.K. and S. Hart (2002), 'The fortune at the bottom of the pyramid', *Strategy + Business*, **26**, 1–14.

Prahalad, C.K. and K. Lieberthal (1999), 'The end of corporate imperialism', *Harvard Business Review*, July–August, 68–79.

Ramamurti, R. (2004), 'Developing countries and MNEs: extending and enriching the research agenda', *Journal of International Business Studies*, **35**(4), 277–83.

Rodriguez-Clare, A. (1996), 'Multinational linkages and economic development', *American Economic Review*, **86**(4), 852–73.

Rodrik, D. (1999), *The Global Economy and Developing Countries: Making Openness Work*, Washington, DC: Overseas Development Council.

Rondinelli, D. and T. London (2003), 'How corporations and environmental groups collaborate: assessing cross-sector collaborations and alliances', *Academy of Management Executive*, **17**(1), 61–76.

Rugman, A.M. (1981), *Inside the Multinationals: The Economics of Internal Markets*, New York: Columbia University Press.

Rugman, A. (1993), 'Drawing the border for a multinational enterprise and a nation state', in Lorraine Eden and Evan Potter (eds), *Multinationals in the Global Political Economy*, New York: St Martin's Press, pp. 84–100.

Sethi, D. and S. Guisinger (2002), 'Liability of foreignness to competitive advantage: how multinational enterprises cope with the international business environment', *Journal of International Management*, **8**(3), 223–40.

Shenkar, O. (2004), 'One more time: international business in a global economy', *Journal of International Business Studies*, **35**(2), 161–71.

Spencer, J.W. (2008), 'The impact of multinational enterprise strategy on indigenous enterprises: horizontal spillovers and crowding out in developing countries', *Academy of Management Review*, **33**(2), 341–61.

Stiglitz, J. (2002), *Globalization and its Discontents*, New York: Norton.

Teece, D.J. (1977), 'Technology transfer by multinational firms: the resource cost of transferring technological know-how', *The Economic Journal*, **87**(346), 242–61.

Teegen, H., J.P. Doh and S. Vachani (2004), 'The importance of nongovernmental organizations (NGOs) in global governance and value creation: an international business research agenda', *Journal of International Business Studies*, **25**(6), 463–83.

United Nations Development Program (UNDP) (2002), 'Millennium development goals', http://www.undp.org/mdg/abcs.html, accessed 1 February 2011.

Vachani, S. (2006), 'Introduction', in S. Vachani (ed.), *Transformations in Global Governance: Implications for Multinationals and other Stakeholders*, Cheltenham, UK and Northampton, MA, USA: Edward Elgar, pp. 1–21.

Vachani, S. and C.N. Smith (2004), 'Socially responsible pricing: lessons from the pricing of AIDS drugs in developing countries', *California Management Review*, **47**(1), 117–45.

Vakil, A.C. (1997), 'Confronting the classification problem: toward a taxonomy of NGOs', *World Development*, **25**(12), 2057–70.

Vernon, R. (1971), *Sovereignty at Bay: The Multinational Spread of U.S. Enterprise*, New York: Basic Books.

Waddock, S. (1998), 'Building successful social partnerships', *Sloan Management Review*, **29**(4), 17–23.

Wang, J.-Y. and M. Blomström (1992), 'Foreign investment and technology transfer: a simple model', *European Economic Review*, **36**, 137–55.

Wells, L.T. (1998), 'Multinationals and developing countries', *Journal of International Business Studies*, **29**(1), 101–14.

Westley, F. and H. Vredenburg (1991), 'Strategic bridging: the collaboration between environmentalists and business in the marketing of green products', *The Journal of Applied Behavioral Science*, **27**(1), 65–90.

Westney, D.E. (1993), 'Institutionalization theory and the multinational corporation', in S. Ghoshal and D.E. Westney (eds), *Organization Theory and the Multinational Corporation*, New York: St Martin's Press, pp. 53–76.

Wheeler, D. (2001), 'Racing to the bottom? Foreign investment and air pollution in developing countries', *Journal of Environment and Development*, **10**(3), 225–45.

Williamson, O.E. (1983), 'Credible commitments: using hostages to support exchange', *The American Economic Review*, **73**, 519–40.

Woolcock, M. and D. Narayan (2000), 'Social capital: implications for development theory, research, and policy', *World Bank Research Observer*, **15**(2), 225–50.

World Bank (1995), *Working with NGOs*, Washington, DC: The World Bank.

Yaziji, M. (2004), 'Turning gadflies into allies', *Harvard Business Review*, February, 110–15.

Zaheer, S. (1995), 'Overcoming the liability of foreignness', *Academy of Management Journal*, **38**, 341–63.

Zaheer, S. (2002), 'The liability of foreignness, redux: a commentary', *Journal of International Management*, **8**(3), 351–8.

Zaheer, S. and E. Mosakowski (1997), 'The dynamics of the liability of foreignness: a global study of survival in financial services', *Strategic Management Journal*, **18**, 439–64.

24 Multinational enterprises and climate change strategies
Ans Kolk and Jonatan Pinkse

Climate change is often perceived as the most pressing environmental problem of our time, as reflected in the large public, policy and corporate attention it has received, and the concerns expressed about the (potential) consequences. Particularly due to temperature increases, climate change affects physical and biological systems by changing ecosystems and causing extinction of species, and is expected to have a negative social impact and adversely affect human health (IPCC, 2007). Moreover, as a result of the economic costs and risks of extreme weather, climate change could have a severe impact on economic growth and development as well, if no action is taken to reduce emissions (Stern, 2006). This means that it can affect multinational enterprises (MNEs) active in a wide variety of sectors and countries. Climate change is not a 'purely' environmental issue because it is closely linked to concerns about energy security due to dependence on fossil fuels and oil in particular, and to energy efficiency and management more generally. Controversy about the climate change issue has led to a broadening of the agenda in some cases, with policy-makers targeting energy to avoid commotion about the science and politics of climate change, and firms likewise, also because addressing climate change in practice usually boils down to an adjustment in the energy base of business models.

Regardless of the precise motivation and focus, be it climate or also energy, the strategic impact of climate change has been surrounded with great uncertainty, for example, about the type, magnitude and timing of the physical impact; about the best technological options to address the issue; and about the materialization of public policies. It is now more than 20 years since the first deliberations on regulation of greenhouse gas emissions started, until sufficient ratification and thus entry into force of the Kyoto Protocol, in early 2005. The adoption of the Kyoto Protocol in 1997 set some things in motion, such as an emissions trading scheme in the EU (the EU-ETS, which started as of 1 January 2005). For firms, however, the overall policy context has been ambiguous with a range of national and international initiatives, some binding, others voluntary, and with a multitude of actors involved. Moreover, as the Kyoto Protocol expires in 2012, there is large uncertainty as to future emission reduction targets and policy arrangements at the various levels. This also affects emissions trading and the Clean Development Mechanism that were approved as integral parts of the Kyoto Protocol.

While recent international climate conferences were supposed to result in a successor to the Kyoto Protocol, this has not materialized so far. The EU and several countries, including the USA and emerging economies (including China and India), have committed individually to greenhouse gas reductions but an overall binding framework and a coherent international approach are still lacking. There are ongoing attempts to deal with the many unresolved issues on the table. These include the level of the emission reduction targets for both industrialized and emerging/developing economies; the future shape of emissions trading schemes and the relationship between them; the transfer of money and technology to less developed countries; and of course the accompanying timetable and encompassing legal frameworks. The difficulties also stem from the multiple trade-offs related to climate change, involving social equity, development, innovation and competitiveness, relevant to MNEs as well.

Increasing societal and regulatory attention to climate change has led MNEs to consider how climate change affects markets in which they operate and has engendered a variety of responses, both market and non-market (political) in nature (Kolk and Levy, 2004; Kolk and Pinkse, 2005, 2007, 2008; Levy and Kolk, 2002; Pinkse and Kolk, 2007, 2009). While MNEs clearly show awareness of the issue, they often tend to be cautious in taking steps in one particular direction. This is due to the fact that MNEs have been facing a complex international context of continuously changing climate policies, and partly related to this, doubt the flexibility of climate-induced investments and fear to make irreversible green mistakes (cf. Rugman and Verbeke, 1998). Moreover, tackling climate change might require firms to move away from existing technologies and build new, unrelated firm-specific advantages (FSAs) instead. For these reasons, the vast majority have only recently started to develop FSAs in response to climate change. Nevertheless, quite a few early movers, particularly in those sectors most confronted with it, hope to seize possible opportunities to gain a strategic advantage over their rivals. Climate change exemplifies an issue from which MNEs can learn how to anticipate future developments in a context of uncertainty and exercise leadership that combines societal and strategic concerns.

This chapter gives an overview of MNEs and climate change, to give insight into one of the 'new topics in international strategic management' included in this volume. In the framework of this contribution, it is not possible to deal extensively with all the dimensions of the issue; we refer to our earlier work for those interested in understanding more details, including empirical findings and the array of research avenues. The chapter will present the main factors relevant to MNEs and climate change, considering particularly those that play a role at the sector, firm and country levels. Table 24.1 summarizes the main elements that influence corporate positions on climate change and that have come to the fore in our research over the years. This chapter will not specifically examine issue-specific factors. We included them in Table 24.1 as they have been important in shaping the issue arena. Moreover, factors like these may also be relevant for those interested in exploring the implications of other environmental and social topics that emerge in international strategic management, such as water, poverty or health.

Below we shall discuss sector-specific, firm-specific and country-specific factors, consecutively, to arrive at a synopsis relevant to MNEs. Before addressing some of the elements of Table 24.1, particularly with an eye to their importance for MNE competitiveness, we first give a brief overview of the relevance of climate change for different categories of firms.

Table 24.1   Factors that influence corporate positions on climate change

Factors	Components
Issue-specific factors	• Impact of the issue on sectors, countries, locations
	• Institutional infrastructure for addressing the issue
	• Degree to which issue and regulation are global
	• Complexity and uncertainty associated with the issue
Sector-specific factors	• Nature and extent of threat posed by climate change
	• Availability and cost of alternatives
	• Degree of globalization and type of supply chain
	• Political power of the industry
	• Technological and competitive situation
	• Growth and concentration levels
Firm-specific factors	• Position within the supply chain; nature of value chain
	• Economic situation and market positioning
	• History of involvement with (technological) alternatives
	• Degrees of (de)centralization and internationalization
	• Availability and type of internal climate expertise
	• Nature of strategic planning process
	• Corporate culture and managerial perceptions
	• Ability to anticipate risks, spread vulnerabilities and manage stakeholders
Country-specific factors	• Societal concerns about climate change
	• National policies on climate change
	• National industrial promotion policies
	• Geography/natural capital (e.g. in relation to possibilities for renewables)
	• Societal views on the roles and responsibilities of firms
	• Regulatory culture (litigational or consensus-oriented)

Sources: Adapted from Kolk and Levy (2004); Pinkse and Kolk (2009).

DIFFERENT CATEGORIES OF FIRMS IN RELATION TO CLIMATE CHANGE

In the field of climate change, a distinction has been made between different categories of firms related to the degree to which they are affected by climate change and also, related to this, for which it can be a potential source of competitive advantage (Kolk and Pinkse, 2008) (see Table 24.2). Most confronted are firms in high-salience industries such as oil and gas, automobiles and utilities, as their core activities are at stake, with their fossil-fuel-based business models being threatened. At the same time, an early change to develop new key capabilities in a lower-carbon direction may transform climate change into a driver for future profitability and growth, particularly if firms are early movers.

Automotive and oil and gas MNEs will have to reorient strategically in response to climate change, given that the issue directly threatens their core activities but also offers new competitive opportunities (Kolk and Levy, 2004). Power generation is central to a

Table 24.2　Relevance of climate change for different categories of firms

Category of firms	Impact of climate change issue
Firms in high-salience sectors	Strongly affected in view of energy intensity and dependence Early change in business models might be source of competitive advantage
Firms specialized in climate-relevant goods and services	Can profit by helping firms mitigate climate change impacts or to anticipate, influence or respond to climate policy
Remaining firms with low-emission activities	No main source of profitability/growth, may gain legitimacy from acting visibly Address issue via external markets, possibility for internalization arbitrage

move to a lower-carbon economy as well, but utilities and electricity networks are more attached to location than the other sectors. Moreover, the introduction of renewables in electricity production means intermittent generation instead of the constant generation that characterizes conventional fossil-fuel-based power plants, which creates a barrier as transmission networks need to be changed. This gives incumbent utilities, which most often own these fossil-fuel-based plants, a clear argument to stick to their established business model and resist changing course as opportunities are not obvious. Thus, while they are crucial for climate change, utilities face a somewhat different situation than oil and automobiles, sectors where change is assumed although it is unclear which technology will prevail in the coming years. As a result, investments in transition technologies, and exploration of other options, have predominated so far.

Continuous reflection on the development of FSAs via internal investments (dynamic capabilities) seems also important for those firms that specialize in goods or services that can help to mitigate climate change impacts, or to anticipate, influence or respond to climate policy developments (Kolk and Pinkse, 2008). This includes, for example, emissions trading and offsetting firms, which in a sense profit from other firms' lack of knowledge on how to deal with the Kyoto-related mechanisms, and insurance firms. Firms in this category develop new products and services that help, *inter alia*, to facilitate emissions trading, develop offset projects, trade certified emissions rights themselves or act as an intermediary for other firms. In addition to specialized firms, banks, brokers, exchanges, consultants, auditors and legal services providers can also fall in this category if they focus on climate change. This also applies to diversified firms such as General Electric and Siemens, which supply energy-related technologies, including renewables.

For the remaining firms, climate change is not likely to be a main source of profitability and growth, but they may gain legitimacy if they act visibly on the issue (Kolk and Pinkse, 2008). For them, there is no compelling reason to develop FSAs internally in managing climate change. Their route for addressing the issue will go through external markets, for example, purchasing greener and productivity-enhancing technologies, adopting externally developed tools and routines (such as on mitigation, emissions trading, measurement instruments), and 'outsourcing' certain activities to outsiders (who can, for example, take care of lobbying and stakeholder management). This category includes those firms operating in low-emission sectors such as media and retail. In this situation, FSAs may arise from 'internalization arbitrage' (cf. Ghemawat, 2003; Rugman and Verbeke, 2004) in the sense that MNEs obtain an advantage from proximity and easy access to multiple external markets that offer such best available practices.

It is crucial to take differences between categories of firms into account when examining the relevance of climate change for MNEs. While the categorization overlaps to a considerable extent with sector boundaries, particularly in the case of those with high emissions, this is not necessarily the case as some firms may seek opportunities while others from the same sector do not (e.g. some banks engaged in emissions trading and in the development of offset projects; others did not). This means that we shall consider sectors separately, followed by firm-specific and country-specific factors, and then discuss implications for MNE competitiveness.

SECTOR-SPECIFIC FACTORS

Variance between sectors stems from several factors, as the overview in Table 24.1 shows, which shape the room for manoeuvre in developing a climate change strategy. One factor that determines how the impact of climate change differs between sectors is the technological change that its emergence brings about. A complete integration of climate change and a transition to a low-carbon economy ultimately asks for a competitive reconfiguration (or replacement) of several of the most powerful sectors, namely those that supply fossil fuels and/or have products that demand massive amounts of fossil fuels (Holdren, 2006). Firms in the carbon-intensive sectors have received much attention in the climate change debate because they are significant emitters. At the same time, they also hold the key to finding (technological) solutions, but this is not without its complexities as quick and easy solutions are not so often at hand. While it is widely recognized that a much greater deployment of low-carbon or carbon-free alternatives is needed, it is not at all clear what should replace the prevailing fossil-fuel-based technologies – there is no technological 'silver bullet' solution at the moment. Alternatives are being explored but problems usually come to the fore when they are scaled up. This leads to the broader question of whether the focus should be on addressing limitations for further deployment, thus trying to fully exploit existing know-how and technologies to scale them up, or on developing new possibilities that may imply a departure from the current energy infrastructure and technological trajectories. In most cases, there is not just one 'solution', however.

For example, there are various options for investing in renewables, ranging from more mature to much less well-developed technologies (Neuhoff, 2005). Most mature are hydropower, biomass combustion, solar boilers and geothermal technologies, which in specific, beneficial circumstances are already cost-competitive with conventional sources. Wind and solar are seen as emerging technologies that are not yet really cost-competitive under current market conditions and macroeconomic models. And there are renewable technologies that are still in the R&D phase – e.g. specific forms of solar power, ocean energy and advanced bio-energy – which completely lack market penetration, and largely depend on public R&D programmes for further development. It should be noted that the level of technological dynamism in a sector also shapes the room for manoeuvre, as illustrated by the difference in R&D patterns between the power generation and the automotive sectors (Margolis and Kammen, 1999). R&D intensity in power generation has been notoriously low, due to the fact that innovation involves massive capital investments combined with limited opportunities for product differentiation. In automobiles, the technological environment is much more dynamic and therefore there is greater pressure as well as opportunities to develop alternative drive-train technologies, such as hybrids, electric vehicles and fuel cells.

In addition to technology, the issue of how to develop new markets should be considered. There are various routes, with pros and cons, for a move to a non-fossil-fuel-based economy: via the development of niche markets that allow opportunity to experiment, or via incremental changes and transition technologies. Automobiles can serve to illustrate both. The fact that the fuel cell vehicle was long predestined as the ultimate solution was partly because it followed the route of niche development; this, however, meant that it has been difficult to move beyond the niche into mainstream markets, also because a sequence of market niches requires many resources (Raven, 2007). Transition technologies, on the other hand, may become dominant themselves and then stand in the way. A case in point is that the success of hybrid cars might have serious consequences for the further development of the fuel cell vehicle. The fuel cell's main advantage compared to the internal combustion engine – that it performs much better in terms of emissions – almost completely fades away compared to hybrids and may not weigh up to the much higher costs of bringing the fuel cell vehicle to the market. In other words, because resources for new technology development tend to be scarce, there is a trade-off between developing carbon-efficient transition technologies for mainstream markets and developing carbon-free end-points for niche markets.

In some cases more systemic, infrastructure-related change is required. For example, to be able to commercialize the fuel cell vehicle, the car industry needs the chemical and oil industries to supply the hydrogen necessary to attract prospective customers. This necessitates a major breakthrough in the production and distribution of hydrogen, which has not occurred yet because it is threatening to fossil-fuel suppliers as well. As the car industry will not be able to supply the hydrogen itself, it thus faces a major barrier in bringing the fuel cell vehicle to the market. It is basically a chicken-and-egg problem: oil firms will not scale up their hydrogen activities until automobile firms come up with more affordable fuel cell vehicles, and the latter will only launch such models if there is a hydrogen infrastructure (Romm, 2006). A somewhat comparable problem exists regarding plug-in hybrids or electric cars, which need electricity networks capable of meeting (peak) demands to charge the vehicles and thus depend on utilities. For a more widespread use, there must also be a sufficient number of charging points and/or places to exchange batteries, which often requires cooperation with local authorities and electricity grid operators, and substantial investments. A crucial issue regarding electric/plug-in solutions is whether the electricity originates from fossil fuels or from renewables, because if the former prevails, a 'solution' to the climate problem has not come any nearer.

Finally, whether there are opportunities to create a market for new technologies with a comprehensive approach also depends on growth and concentration levels and the structure of a specific sector. The sector dynamic in which firms are involved in the interaction with their competitors also affects their behaviour *vis-à-vis* climate change. Firms compete for external funding on the best conditions, and want to increase market share, attract new customers and talented staff, and maintain good relations with investors. This leads to continuous efforts to be more 'attractive' and agile than competitors. Firms closely watch the behaviour of competitors, with a tendency to 'follow the leader' (see Knickerbocker, 1973) or to jump on the bandwagon (see Abrahamson and Rosenkopf, 1993), regardless of or even despite the fact that this may imply inefficiencies or losses. This behaviour is particularly pervasive in highly concentrated markets, dominated by a few large multinationals (Kolk and Levy, 2004), but it may also be a simple lack of knowledge about what the 'winning' approach will be. At the same time, given the complexity of the climate change problem, cooperation is usually needed as one firm (or other actor) cannot deliver solutions single-handedly. This raises the question of how far firms are willing to go in taking responsibility for climate change when they need responses from others to achieve a positive outcome, and also how they deal with the competitive dimensions involved. This is where firm-specific factors start to become crucial.

FIRM-SPECIFIC FACTORS

The factors as shown in Table 24.1 are important in shaping corporate decision-making about climate change strategies. It should be noted that, in balancing the various factors – in the context of broader firm objectives such as profit, growth and market share – managerial perceptions play a large role.

If we focus on those firm-level factors that have not come to the fore already, the position of a firm in the supply chain stipulates the nature of the core products and services, and the responsiveness of customers to the climate change issue. Rethinking product design or developing new products or services is particularly valuable for firms that operate closer to markets for the end-consumer, where differentiation may pay off if consumers are environmentally conscious. Firms that are positioned higher up the supply chain generally produce commodities instead of consumer products and do not have the same opportunity to differentiate their products. Whether the customer is an individual or another business will also affect the decision to develop a climate strategy. Whereas business customers are less known for demanding environmentally friendly products, when they choose to do so, their demand will create more leverage, as they are more powerful than an individual consumer. In recent years, for example, firms such as Wal-Mart and McDonald's, which used to have rather bad track records on sustainability, have started to demand more sustainable products, thus creating large pressure on supplier firms. If a firm sells directly to end-consumers instead, this used to lead to a niche strategy, because the willingness to pay for climate products was often limited to a group of environmentally conscious consumers. However, increased consumer awareness of climate change in recent years may start to lead to a change in this respect, and create the opportunity to service mass markets with climate-friendly products as well (Bonini et al., 2008).

Many MNEs that are vertically integrated may also consider spillover effects throughout the value chain, and thus whether climate-induced changes affect the upstream (back-end) or downstream (customer-end) activities or both (Kolk and Pinkse, 2008). For example, one possibility is that climate change may help a firm to create an FSA from developing a climate-friendly technology through upstream R&D activities, which is then commercialized by way of existing downstream FSAs in market-related activities. However, it may also lead to a change in downstream activities for the customer-end of the value chain, including sales, marketing and distribution. By developing FSAs in downstream activities, such as green marketing, an MNE could not only commercialize existing technologies that have previously unexploited green attributes, but also create an FSA out of a purchased technology. In both instances, climate change can have a positive impact on MNEs, because they can leverage some of their existing upstream or downstream FSAs, which creates a buffer from competitors (Tripsas, 1997). A more challenging case, however, is when climate change disrupts FSAs throughout the whole value chain. If MNEs are able to adapt both upstream and downstream activities simultaneously, this will contribute more to a sustainable competitive advantage, because such investments will be more difficult to imitate, and lead to higher-order capabilities of combining technological (upstream) and non-technological (downstream) FSAs (Rothaermel and Hill, 2005). However, it will also be riskier for MNEs to accommodate the change because they cannot leverage existing FSAs and thus open the door to new entrants. Hence MNEs may also have an incentive to attempt at obstructing such a change (Tripsas, 1997).

There are other firm-specific factors that shape the specific approach taken. This includes, for example, top management commitment and the degree of internationalization of top management (Levy and Kolk, 2002). In addition, organizational structure plays a role, as this influences the strategic planning process and the extent to which decision-making about an issue such as climate change is centralized or decentralized. Moreover, organizational culture and a firm's specific history shape the perception of climate change. For example, one of the reasons that ExxonMobil was rather reluctant to invest in renewable energy sources was because it made huge losses on such investments in the 1980s when the Reagan Administration suddenly stopped granting large subsidies instigated by the preceding president, Carter. This, combined with the fact that decision authority had been highly centralized as well, left hardly any room for local initiatives that went against the reactive stance of top management (Kolk and Levy, 2004).

Whether or not climate change becomes a strategic issue depends in the end on how it is perceived to affect a firm's main value proposition (Porter and Reinhardt, 2007). Even though firms typically emphasize the business opportunities related to climate change rather than the risks, it is not always the case that climate change is necessarily an issue of strategic importance. Nevertheless, the corporate emphasis on the business opportunities in relation to climate change is not that surprising as it reflects the overall trend that 'win–win' views have started to prevail (Kolk, 2000; Rugman and Verbeke, 1998). Of course not all firms have adopted this win–win mentality in the same way. On the one hand, the approach may be that climate change is evaluated just as any other business issue, which means that it has to compete (at some stage) with other investment opportunities on the same financial criteria. On the other hand, the moral case for climate change may prevail, which means that climate-related activities are pursued, preferably but not necessarily to make a profit (Berger et al., 2007). It is here that stakeholder concerns and other country-specific factors come into play as well.

COUNTRY-SPECIFIC FACTORS

As already indicated in the introduction, climate change has aroused considerable stakeholder concerns and public debate – in some countries more than others and with variety over the years. Traditionally, stakeholder pressure for taking action on climate change has been highest in the developed countries, but concerns have been growing elsewhere as well, given increasing environmental, pollution and health problems in large cities in, for example, China. Among developed countries, which agreed to emissions reductions under the Kyoto Protocol, the USA has been notable for its heated domestic debate about the 'science' and relevance of the issue, and for its refusal to ratify the Kyoto Protocol. Countries' positions on climate change, as taken in international negotiations in the past decades, have been influenced by economic, geographical and political factors (as summarized in Table 24.3). These will not be further examined here, as we concentrate on current 'outcomes' in terms of national and international policies to assess the implications for MNEs.

Most important in the context of this chapter and the current international policy debate is an upcoming differentiation in three broad types of countries – developed, emerging and developing economies. Differences relate to emissions reduction requirements and related constraints likely to be imposed on MNEs based in these contexts, on the one hand, and the opportunities resulting from (clean development/green) funds transferred from developed to other countries, on the other. Under the Kyoto Protocol,

Table 24.3   Countries' positions on climate change: influencing factors

Factors	Components
Economic factors	• Domestic supply and demand, and costs of different sources of energy
	• Current and expected energy efficiency and emission levels
	• Economic importance of large energy producers and consumers
	• Economic importance of those that expect to profit from emission reductions
	• Competitive implications of emission reductions relative to other countries
Geographical factors	• Position of the country relative to the sea level
	• Vulnerability to more extreme weather conditions
	• Existing supplies of fossil fuels
	• Suitability for alternative sources of energy
Political factors	• Political importance of large energy producers and consumers
	• Political importance of opponents/proponents of emission reductions
	• Public awareness of environmental issues
	• Possibilities for arriving at political 'package deals' in which negotiations on climate are linked to one or more other topics
	• Degree to which other countries are seen as taking measures with comparable 'sacrifices'

Source: Kolk (2000), p. 63.

emissions reductions applied only to developed countries, but the policy debate is, albeit with much difficulty, moving towards the extension to emerging countries. This reflects economic growth patterns and industrial expansion of particularly China, but also India and Brazil. Funding for green technology, mitigation and adaptation to climate change initially applied to all non-developed countries, but as the Clean Development Mechanism turned out to fund projects mostly in emerging countries, especially China and India, a new green fund aims to help developing countries specifically.

While the trichotomy parallels the division made for sustainability and corporate responsibility more broadly in terms of risks and possibilities for the development of FSAs by MNEs (Kolk, 2010; Verbeke, 2009), climate change may be special in some respects. First, the deadlock in the discussions on an international climate treaty means that boundaries between the three categories are becoming more fluid: not so much in the negotiations themselves (where they are very vivid), but in the actual domestic policies implemented, as national priorities will and can prevail at that level. Second, compared to social and ethical issues, where cultural traditions play a larger role, climate-related technological gaps may be easier to bridge. It is here that entrepreneurship can be important, but also the enabling environment in terms of government incentives.

Industrial policies have come to the fore particularly in the aftermath of the financial crisis, when stimulus packages adopted in a range of countries included often substantial climate-related components (Robins et al., 2009). Relevant to MNEs have been concerns about (implicit) protectionism and the fact that measures appeared to favour incumbents that struggled rather than stimulating new (innovative) ventures. Much attention focused on incentive schemes to scrap old, energy-inefficient cars earlier and boost demand for more efficient ones. These induced a large debate about distortion of competition in a range of countries, including Germany, France, Japan and the USA (Kolk and Pinkse, 2010). This extended beyond cash-for-clunkers schemes; in the case of wind energy grants handed out by the US government in the autumn of 2009, more than 80 per cent went to foreign turbine manufacturing firms, suggesting that the majority of jobs were created abroad despite funding set up for domestic purposes (Luce, 2009).

This brings us to the importance of country-specific advantages (CSAs) for MNEs, considering both home and host locations. The final section of this chapter will discuss the implications for competitiveness (based on Kolk and Pinkse, 2008), with a specific focus on geographical factors related to climate change as these define the specificities of MNEs. The strategic complexity for MNEs is that they have to combine FSAs and CSAs, which usually means adapting FSAs, to attain optimal FSA–CSA configurations (see Rugman and Verbeke, 2003).

IMPLICATIONS FOR MNE COMPETITIVENESS

There may well be particular geographical factors that are conducive to the development of climate-related FSAs, which can also mean that benefits for the MNE arise at a specific location only. A clear location-specific factor has been national regulation, which has varied considerably, for example, between the USA and Europe (respectively rejection of the Kyoto Protocol versus the EU-ETS). Climate change policy in the home country may help MNEs to develop technologies that give them a competitive advantage over their rivals if that country is at the technological frontier. However, host country locations can also form a potential source of CSAs as MNE subsidiaries may tap into local external knowledge. The broader institutional framework also plays a role. The presence in the local context of a network of other firms or non-profit organizations that are in the process of developing climate-friendly technologies can be complementary to an MNE's own FSA development. Local consumer awareness of climate change may also form a CSA as it makes them responsive to green marketing campaigns and products with green(er) qualities. MNEs may benefit from climate-related CSAs either because they already have facilities in this particular location or because they move to these locations in an effort to seek strategic assets to complement their existing FSAs (Dunning, 1998). The locus (or loci) of origin of FSA development thus depends on the geographical spread of an MNE, as it is partly determined by the 'local' institutional context.

The impact of climate-related CSAs on the way in which MNEs transform existing or develop new FSAs depends to a large extent on the geographical origin of FSA development. If an MNE perceives climate change as a global issue, decision-making power on this issue will be at the level of its headquarters. In this case, an MNE believes that the consequences of climate change will have a significant impact on the organization globally, which is therefore dealt with at the highest management level. Headquarters' support considerably increases MNEs' potential for becoming global leaders in tackling climate change. However, since the worldwide institutionalization of climate change policies is still quite fragmented, many MNEs may also deal with the issue through their regional centres or national subsidiaries. It then becomes a matter of local responsiveness to climate-related institutional pressures from regulators, NGOs or the investment community. The more localized the decision, however, the less likely it is that climate change will have a significant strategic impact on the MNE as a whole, because it will be quite difficult for a local subsidiary to convince MNE headquarters that climate change requires a proactive response. Instead of a global leader, an MNE may then produce local heroes at best.

This is not to say that a local response is of no use at all, however. If, through their subsidiaries, MNEs are located in countries that have been frontrunners on climate change, they have been facing climate-related pressures for a longer period of time already. This could have enabled them to start learning from the issue from an early stage. Therefore, if a country initiates new regulations to curb emissions, this will probably be a much greater shock to domestic firms than to MNEs. Nonetheless, experience with climate change in a specific location will only create a cross-border advantage if MNEs are able to transfer FSAs from other locations. One of the main challenges for MNEs is whether they will develop different types of location-bound FSAs that fit with CSAs of individual countries, or non-location-bound FSAs that can be transferred and deployed globally (Rugman and Verbeke, 2004). The peculiarities of MNEs particularly arise from the potential to leverage non-location-bound FSAs. Similar or identical procedures for every subsidiary facilitate the exchange of experiences, breed internal consistency, allow benchmarking and is clear to outsiders. Some MNEs, therefore, strive to harmonize their environmental management system and standards at all locations. Yet the situation in specific countries, for example, as a result of stakeholder or government pressure, may create location-bound FSAs as well (related to local responsiveness). In some cases these can only be used in the country in question; in others they might help to increase MNEs' competitiveness elsewhere.

The transferability of an FSA typically depends on the attributes of the knowledge bundles that establish it: the higher the tacitness of the knowledge, the less transferable it becomes (Kogut and Zander, 1993; Singh, 2007). A higher level of tacitness may be due to the extent to which an FSA results from linkages with external parties (e.g. governmental bodies, universities or NGOs). These linkages are in general much better in an MNE's home country (or region), which explains findings that many MNEs are organized on a regional basis (Ghemawat, 2003; Rugman and Verbeke, 2004). Host country attributes also determine transferability of an FSA to a foreign location. Transfer of FSAs to relatively 'distant' countries (Ghemawat, 2001) in terms of dissimilarity of environmental policies usually results in higher adaptation costs of alignment with the CSAs of these particular host countries. In other words, transfer of environmental best practices is not always without problems (Tsai and Child, 1997). A global approach to environmental management usually relies on advanced technologies, but their successful implementation in developing countries can be very expensive due to a lack of adequate infrastructure there.

If climate-related CSAs stimulate specific R&D that translates into new technological FSAs, these would, on the face of it, be non-location-bound. It should be relatively easy to transfer a technology to other geographical locations, regardless of whether it originates from corporate headquarters, a regional centre or a national subsidiary. A public-policy-driven CSA such as a subsidy or tax break for the development of renewable energy technologies typically only has a function at the start of the life cycle of an FSA: once the technology is incorporated in products it can be redeployed to other locations (Helfat and Peteraf, 2003), thus becoming a non-location-bound CSA. Climate-friendly technologies, for example related to hydrogen or fuel cells, are no longer of a tacit nature or tied to external parties such as local governments, and sourcing and production of these technologies can take place anywhere in the world (Rugman and Verbeke, 2004).

However, if the CSA continues to be of value further along the life cycle, transferability becomes more difficult. For example, for some specific technologies related to renewable energy, the location of production depends on a country's natural capital. Such geographic-site specificity is crucial for hydroelectric and wind power, which require mountainous areas and sufficient wind speed respectively (Russo, 2003). Such an FSA cannot simply be redeployed, but needs to be combined with a similar CSA in another geographical location (Helfat and Peteraf, 2003). Nevertheless, most technologies for climate-related FSAs are more likely to strongly depend on CSAs when they have further advanced in the life cycle and have moved downstream and reached the sales stage. A lack of transferability of FSAs is thus not necessarily the result of the tacitness of the knowledge on which they are based and local geographical circumstances, but is also linked to the ability of MNEs to create market acceptance for new technologies to realize global sales (Rugman and Verbeke, 2004). In other words, although MNEs may have some influence on market acceptance through marketing campaigns, it largely depends on CSAs related to consumer responsiveness to climate-friendly products and services, and the availability of the necessary public infrastructure.

CONCLUDING REMARKS

The role that climate change plays in MNE strategy is determined by a broad conglomerate of factors involving governmental as well as societal and market forces, working at different levels, (sub)national, regional and global. Climate change creates a geographically disparate and moving target: while it may form a threat in one location, it can be an opportunity in another. Regardless of whether regional or local characteristics are seen as a potential advantage or disadvantage, liability or risk, geographical differences are something to be faced by MNEs and those firms that excel in doing this are the ones most likely to develop climate-related FSAs. Hence learning from climate change does not merely mean that MNEs need dynamic capabilities to cope with technological change; constantly rejuvenating FSAs by being responsive to a wide range of climate-relevant CSAs is what gives them an edge *vis-à-vis* competitors as well. MNEs that are most responsive to a wide range of relevant locational factors may develop FSAs with implications for their profitability, growth and survival.

At the same time, it should be noted that climate change may not be of a strategic nature for quite a few firms, given the nature of their activities and the inconclusiveness of policy-making at the international, and thus also the national, level. Systematic MNE responses to climate change are still emerging, also due to the uncertainties regarding proper institutional frameworks and future policies. This will continue to present challenges for both managers and policy-makers, and for researchers as well, as this emergent topic may be crucial for the future of the planet but rather difficult to study given its evolving nature and lack of systematic data. This does not diminish its relevance for international strategic management, though, also in the years to come.

REFERENCES

Abrahamson, E. and Rosenkopf, L. (1993), 'Institutional and competitive bandwagons: using mathematical modeling as a tool to explore innovation diffusion', *The Academy of Management Review*, **18**(3), 487–517.

Berger, I.E., Cunningham, P.H. and Drumwright, M.E. (2007), 'Mainstreaming corporate social responsibility: developing markets for virtue', *California Management Review*, **49**(4), 132–57.

Bonini, S.M.J., Hintz, G. and Mendonca, L.T. (2008), 'Addressing consumer concerns about climate change', *McKinsey Quarterly*, **2**, 52–61.

Dunning, J.H. (1998), 'Location and the multinational enterprise: a neglected factor?', *Journal of International Business Studies*, **29**(1), 45–66.

Ghemawat, P. (2001), 'Distance still matters: the hard reality of global expansion', *Harvard Business Review*, **79**(8), 137–47.

Ghemawat, P. (2003), 'Semiglobalization and international business strategy', *Journal of International Business Studies*, **34**, 138–52.

Helfat, C.E. and Peteraf, M.A. (2003), 'The dynamic resource-based view: capability lifecycles', *Strategic Management Journal*, **24**, 997–1010.

Holdren, J.P. (2006), 'The energy innovation imperative: addressing oil dependence, climate change, and other 21st century energy challenges', *Innovations: Technology, Governance, Globalization*, **1**(2), 3–23.

IPCC (2007), *Climate Change 2007: The Physical Science Basis – Contribution of Working Group I to the Fourth Assessment Report of the IPCC*, Cambridge: Cambridge University Press.

Knickerbocker, F.T. (1973), *Oligopolistic Reaction and the Multinational Enterprise*, Boston, MA: Harvard University Press.

Kogut, B. and Zander, U. (1993), 'Knowledge of the firm and the evolutionary theory of the multinational corporation', *Journal of International Business Studies*, **24**(4), 625–45.

Kolk, A. (2000), *Economics of Environmental Management*, Harlow: Financial Times Prentice Hall.

Kolk, A. (2010), 'Social and sustainability dimensions of regionalization and (semi)globalization', *Multinational Business Review*, **18**(1), 51–72.

Kolk, A. and Levy, D. (2004), 'Multinationals and global climate change: issue for the automotive and oil industries', in S.M. Lundan (ed.), *Multinationals, Environment and Global Competition*, Vol. 9, Amsterdam: Elsevier, pp. 171–93.

Kolk, A. and Pinkse, J. (2005), 'Business responses to climate change: identifying emergent strategies', *California Management Review*, **47**(3), 6–20.

Kolk, A. and Pinkse, J. (2007), 'Multinationals' political activities on climate change', *Business & Society*, **46**(2), 201–28.

Kolk, A. and Pinkse, J. (2008), 'A perspective on multinational enterprises and climate change: learning from "an inconvenient truth"?', *Journal of International Business Studies*, **39**(8), 1359–78.

Kolk, A. and Pinkse, J. (2010), 'Business and climate change: key strategic and policy challenges', *Amsterdam Law Forum*, **2**(2), 41–50.

Levy, D.L. and Kolk, A. (2002), 'Strategic responses to global climate change: conflicting pressures on multinationals in the oil industry', *Business & Politics*, **4**(3), 275–300.

Luce, E. (2009), 'Wind energy stimulus dollars spent overseas', *Financial Times*, 30 October.

Margolis, R.M. and Kammen, D.M. (1999), 'Evidence of under-investment in energy R&D in the United States and the impact of Federal policy', *Energy Policy*, **27**(10), 575–84.

Neuhoff, K. (2005), 'Large-scale deployment of renewables for electricity generation', *Oxford Review of Economic Policy*, **21**(1), 88–110.

Pinkse, J. and Kolk, A. (2007), 'Multinational corporations and emissions trading: strategic responses to new institutional constraints', *European Management Journal*, **25**(6), 441–52.

Pinkse, J. and Kolk, A. (2009), *International Business and Global Climate Change*, London: Routledge.

Porter, M.E. and Reinhardt, F.L. (2007), 'A strategic approach to climate', *Harvard Business Review*, **85**(10), 22–6.

Raven, R. (2007), 'Niche accumulation and hybridisation strategies in transition processes towards a sustainable energy system: an assessment of differences and pitfalls', *Energy Policy*, **35**, 2390–400.

Robins, N., Clover, R. and Singh, C. (2009), *Building a Green Recovery – Governments Allocate USD470bn – and Counting*, London: HSBC Global Research.

Romm, J. (2006), 'The car and fuel of the future', *Energy Policy*, **34**, 2609–14.

Rothaermel, F.T. and Hill, C.W.L. (2005), 'Technological discontinuities and complementary assets: a longitudinal study of industry and firm performance', *Organization Science*, **16**(1), 52–70.

Rugman, A.M. and Verbeke, A. (1998), 'Corporate strategies and environmental regulations: an organizing framework', *Strategic Management Journal*, **19**, 363–75.

Rugman, A.M. and Verbeke, A. (2003), 'Extending the theory of the multinational enterprise: internalization and strategic management perspectives', *Journal of International Business Studies*, **34**, 125–37.

Rugman, A.M. and Verbeke, A. (2004), 'A perspective on regional and global strategies of multinational enterprises', *Journal of International Business Studies*, **35**, 3–18.

Russo, M.V. (2003), 'The emergence of sustainable industries: building on natural capital', *Strategic Management Journal*, **24**, 317–31.

Singh, J. (2007), 'Asymmetry of knowledge spillovers between MNCs and host country firms', *Journal of International Business Studies*, **38**(5), 764–86.

Stern, N. (2006), *The Economics of Climate Change – The Stern Review*, Cambridge: Cambridge University Press.

Tripsas, M. (1997), 'Unraveling the process of creative destruction: complementary assets and incumbent survival in the typesetter industry', *Strategic Management Journal*, **18**(Summer Special Issue), 119–42.

Tsai, T. and Child, J. (1997), 'Strategic responses of multinational corporations to environmental demands', *Journal of General Management*, **23**(1), 1–22.

Verbeke, A. (2009). *International Business Strategy*, Cambridge: Cambridge University Press.

Index

Abbreviations used in the index:
BOP – bottom-of-the-pyramid
IB – international business
MP – multinationality–performance

Titles of publications are shown in *italics*.